Spontaneity (page 403)

Skill	Use	Procedure	Example
Being responsive to the ideas of your speech.	To ensure that your audience perceives your speech as a lively and fresh interaction even though it has been well practiced.	1. Learn the ideas of your speech. 2. In each practice, express the idea and its development in slightly different language.	As Connie was talking about day care, she allowed herself to report a personal experience that she had not planned on using in the speech.

Eye Contact (page 404)

Skill	Use	Procedure	Example
Looking directly at members of the audience while you are talking with them.	To strengthen the sense of interaction.	1. Consciously look at the faces of groups of people in your audience while you are talking. 2. If your eyes drift away, try to bring them back.	As Bill was talking about how people can sign up for tutoring other students, he was talking to people near the back of the room. When he looked down at his notes to make sure he had included all he wanted, he found himself continuing to look at his note card rather than at the audience. As he moved to the next point of his speech, he forced himself to look at people sitting in the front right of the room.

SKILL BUILDERS

 PULL OUT SECTION

Empathy (page 129)

Skill	Use	Procedure	Example
Intellectually identifying with or vicariously experiencing the feelings, thoughts, or attitudes of another.	To create or to promote a supportive climate.	1. Adopt an attitude of respect by actively attending to what the person says. 2. Concentrate on understanding both verbal and nonverbal messages. 3. Use the person's behavioral cues to ascertain his or her emotional state. 4. Try to feel with the person, or try to recall or imagine how you would feel in similar circumstances, or allow yourself to experience your own feelings of concern, compassion, or sorrow for the person. 5. Respond in a way that reflects those feelings.	When Jerry says, "I really feel embarrassed about wearing braces in college," Mary smiles ruefully and replies, "Yeah, it makes you feel like a little kid, doesn't it? I remember the things I had to put up with when I wore braces."

Paraphrasing (page 133)

Skill	Use	Procedure	Example
A response that conveys your understanding of another person's message.	To increase listening efficiency; to avoid message confusion; to discover the speaker's motivation.	1. Listen carefully to the message. 2. Notice what images and feelings you have experienced from this message. 3. Determine what the message means to you. 4. Create a message that conveys these images or feelings.	Grace says, "At two minutes to five, the boss gave me three letters that had to be in the mail that evening!" Bonita replies, "If I understand, you were really resentful that your boss dumped important work on you right before quitting time when she knows you have to pick up the baby at day care."

SKILL BUILDERS

Public Speaking

Writing Speech Goals (page 301)

Skill	Use	Procedure	Example
A single statement that specifies the exact response the speaker wants from the audience.	To give direction to the speech.	1. Write a first draft. 2. Revise the draft until you have a complete sentence that states the specific response or behavior you want from your audience. 3. Make sure the goal statement contains only one idea. 4. Revise the infinitive or infinitive phrase until it indicates the specific audience reaction desired. 5. Write at least three different versions of the goal statement.	Ken first writes, "I want my audience to know what to look for in buying a canine companion." As he revises, he arrives at the wording "I want my audience to understand four considerations in purchasing the perfect canine companion." Once Ken assures himself that the goal has a single focus and that the infinitive "to understand" indicates the preferred audience reaction desired, he then writes two differently worded goals to make sure his first one is the best.

Recording Data (page 328)

Skill	Use	Procedure	Example
Having a written record of information drawn from a source with complete documentation.	To provide information and its source in a speech or to report the documentation to anyone who might question the accuracy of the information.	1. Indicate the topic in the upper-left-hand corner. 2. Record each factual statement or expert opinion on a separate four-by-six-inch or larger index card. Any part of the information that is quoted directly should be enclosed with quotation marks. 3. For a book, write the name of the author, the title, the publisher, the date, and the page number from which the information was taken. 4. For a periodical or newspaper, write the name of the author, if one is given, the title of the article, the name of the periodical or newspaper, the date, and the page number from which the information was taken. 5. For online sources, include the URL for the Web site, the author and title if one is given, the heading under which you found the information, and the date that you accessed the site.	While gathering material for a speech on U.S. Postal Service monetary problems, Tamika found an article with relevant information. In the upper-left-hand corner of one four-by-six-inch card, she wrote U.S. Postal Service Debt. Then she wrote the data she had discovered: After five years of operating at a surplus, the U.S. Postal Service "has plunged as much as $3 billion in the red, its greatest deficit in modern history." Marianne Lavelle, "Why the Postman Can't Deliver Profits: Full Service Costs the Postal Service Dearly," *U.S. News & World Report,* April 9, 2001, p. 46.

Group Communication

Brainstorming (page 254)

Skill	Use	Procedure	Example
An uncritical, nonevaluative process of generating associated ideas.	To generate a list of potential solutions to a problem.	1. Verbalize ideas as they come to mind. 2. Refrain from evaluating the merits of ideas. 3. Encourage outrageous and unique ideas. 4. Build on or modify the ideas of others. 5. Use extended effort to generate more ideas. 6. Record the ideas.	Problem: "What should we do to raise money to help a child who needs a liver transplant?" Ideas: sell cookies, sell candy, sell wrapping paper, wrap packages at mall for donations, find corporate sponsors, have a corporate golf outing, a youth golf outing, a tennis tournament, a bowling tournament, a paint-ball tournament, auction donated paintings, do odd jobs for money.

Problem Solving: Fact/Value Questions (page 255)

Skill	Use	Procedure	Example
Arriving at a conclusion about a fact or value question.	A guide for groups to follow in arriving at conclusions to fact or value questions.	1. Clarify the specific fact or value question. 2. Analyze the problem by determining the criteria that must be met to establish the fact or value. 3. Examine the facts to determine whether the subject meets those criteria.	The question is whether Branson is an effective leader. The key criteria for determining effective leadership are having a vision and being able to motivate employees. Evidence shows that Branson is successful in meeting both criteria.

Problem Solving: Policy Questions (page 256)

Skill	Use	Procedure	Example
Arriving at a solution to a policy question by following six steps.	A guide for groups to follow in finding solutions to policy questions.	1. Clarify the specific policy problem question. 2. Analyze the problem. 3. Determine the solution criteria that must be met to find an acceptable solution. 4. Brainstorm potential solutions. 5. Evaluate the solutions to determine which best meet the criteria. 6. Decide which is best.	Question: "What should we do to increase alumni donations to the Department Scholarship Fund?" The group begins by discussing "Why are alumni not donating to the fund?" and asking "What criteria must be met to find an acceptable solution?" After brainstorming potential solutions, the group evaluates each and selects the one or ones that best meet the criteria.

Describing Feelings (page 167)

Skill	Use	Procedure	Example
Putting an emotional state into words.	For self-disclosure; to teach people how to treat you.	1. Indicate what has triggered the feeling. 2. Mentally identify what you are feeling. Think specifically. Am I feeling hate? Anger? Joy? 3. Verbally own the feeling. Begin your statement with "I feel. . . ." 4. Verbally state the specific feeling.	"As a result of not getting the job, I feel depressed and discouraged" or "Because of the way you stood up for me when I was being put down by Leah, I'm feeling very warm and loving toward you."

Assertiveness (page 177)

Skill	Use	Procedure	Example
Standing up for yourself and doing so in interpersonally effective ways that describe your feelings honestly and exercise your personal rights while respecting the rights of others.	To show clearly what you think or feel.	1. Identify what you are thinking or feeling. 2. Analyze the cause of these feelings. 3. Choose the appropriate skills necessary to communicate these feelings, as well as any outcome you desire, if any. 4. Communicate these feelings to the appropriate person. Remember to own your feelings.	When Gavin believes he is being unjustly charged, he says, "I have never been charged for a refill on iced tea before—has there been a change in policy?"

Describing Behavior, Consequences, and Feelings (page 210)

Skill	Use	Procedure	Example
Describing the basis of a conflict in terms of behavior, consequences, and feelings (b-c-f).	To help the other person understand the problem completely.	1. Own the message. 2. Describe the behavior that you see or hear. 3. Describe the consequences that result. 4. Describe your feelings.	Jason says, "I have a problem that I need your help with. When I tell you what I'm thinking and you don't respond (b), I start to think you don't care about me or what I think (c), and this causes me to get very angry with you (f)."

Thesis Statement (page 338)

Skill	Use	Procedure	Example
A sentence that outlines the specific elements of the speech supporting the goal statement.	To identify items of information that will become the subject of the main points of the speech.	1. List the elements of your speech goal that might become the main points of your speech. 2. After selecting the specific elements that best reflect your speech goal, combine them into a complete sentence that is your thesis statement.	For her speech goal, good novels are the product of several important qualities, Vanessa listed "creativity," "vividness," "plot," "character," "background," "setting," and "dialogue." As she weighed and evaluated her information, she elected to write the thesis statement, "Good writing is the product of creative plot, character, and setting."

Enthusiasm (page 401)

Skill	Use	Procedure	Example
Using your voice and bodily action to show the audience that you are excited about the topic and your opportunity to talk with the audience about it.	To ensure audience perception of the importance and relevance of the information to them.	1. Make sure you are truly excited about your topic. 2. As you speak, re-create your original feelings of excitement. 3. Focus on sharing that feeling of excitement with the audience.	As Trisha was practicing her speech on Alberta, Canada, she refocused on her feelings of awe as she first saw mountain peak after mountain peak. She also reminded herself of how much she wanted her audience to actually "see" what she had experienced.

Vocal Expressiveness (page 402)

Skill	Use	Procedure	Example
Using contrasts in pitch, volume, rate, and quality.	To express the meanings you want audiences to get from the sentences you present.	1. Identify the words you want to stress to best express your intended meaning. 2. Raise your pitch or increase your volume on key words.	As Marquez thought about what he wanted to emphasize, he said, "You need to put your *left hand* at the *bottom* of the bat."

Foundations of Communication

Perception Checking (page 46)

Skill	Use	Procedure	Example
Making a verbal statement that reflects your understanding of the meaning of another person's nonverbal cues.	To clarify the meaning of nonverbal behavior.	1. Watch the behavior of another. Describe the behavior to yourself or aloud. 2. Ask yourself: What does that behavior mean to me? 3. Put your interpretation of the nonverbal behavior into words to verify your perception.	Vera comes walking into the room with a completely blank expression and neither speaks to Ann nor acknowledges that she is in the room. Ann says, "Vera, I get the feeling that something has happened to put you in a state of shock. Am I right? Is there something I can do?"

Clarity—Specific, Concrete, Precise Words (page 60)

Skill	Use	Procedure	Example
Clarify meaning by narrowing what is understood from a general category to a particular group within that category, by appealing to the senses, or by choosing words that symbolize exact thoughts and feelings.	To help the listener picture thoughts analogous to the speaker's.	1. Assess whether the word or phrase used is less specific, concrete, or precise than it should be. 2. Pause to mentally brainstorm alternatives. 3. Select a more specific, concrete, or precise word.	Instead of saying, "Bring the stuff for the audit," say, "Bring the records and receipts from the last year for the audit." Or, instead of saying "I was really cold," say "I nearly froze."

Interpersonal Communication

Politeness (page 112)

Skill	Use	Procedure	Example
Relating to others in ways that meet their need to be appreciated and protected.	To determine the degree of politeness necessary to achieve your objective.	1. Recognize when what you are planning to say is likely to be recognized as a face-threatening act. 2. Consider how well you know each other, whether one person holds power over the other, and the risk of hurting the other person. 3. Construct the wording of a positive politeness or a negative politeness statement based on the issues of relationship, power, and risk.	Chris thinks her boss did not consider all that he should have in determining her year's bonus. She might construct the following negative politeness statement: "Mr. Seward, I know you put considerable time into your bonus decisions, but you have been willing to talk about your decisions in the past. I was hoping you'd be willing to take a few minutes to discuss your decision with me."

www.wadsworth.com

wadsworth.com is the World Wide Web site for Wadsworth and is your direct source to dozens of online resources.

At wadsworth.com you can find out about supplements, demonstration software, and student resources. You can also send email to many of our authors and preview new publications and exciting new technologies.

wadsworth.com
Changing the way the world learns®

FROM THE WADSWORTH SERIES IN SPEECH COMMUNICATION

Communicate!

TENTH EDITION

Rudolph F. Verderber
Distinguished Teaching
Professor of Communication,
University of Cincinnati

Kathleen S. Verderber
University of Northern Kentucky

WADSWORTH
™
THOMSON LEARNING

Australia ■ Canada ■ Mexico ■ Singapore ■ Spain
United Kingdom ■ United States

Executive Editor: Deirdre Cavanaugh
Publisher: Clark Baxter
Assistant Editor: Nicole George
Editorial Assistant: Mele Alusa
Executive Marketing Manager: Stacey Purviance
Marketing Assistant: Neena Chandra
Technology Project Manager: Jeanette Wiseman
Project Manager: Cathy Linberg
Print/Media Buyer: Mary Noel
Permissions Editor: Bob Kauser

Production Service: Cecile Joyner, The Cooper Company
Text Designer: Ross Carron Design
Photo Researcher: Terri Wright
Copyeditor: Kay Mikel
Cover Designer: Jeanne Calabrese Design
Cover Illustrator: Otto Steininger
Cover Printer: Phoenix Color Corporation
Compositor: New England Typographic Service
Printer: Quebecor/World, Taunton, MA

Printed in the United States of America
1 2 3 4 5 6 7 05 04 03 02 01

Library of Congress Cataloging-in-Publication Data
Verderber, Rudolph F.
    Communicate! / Rudolph F. Verderber, Kathleen S. Verderber.
    —10th ed.
        p. cm.
    Includes bibliographical references and index.
    ISBN 0-534-56116-0
        1. Communication. I. Verderber, Kathleen S. II. Title.

P90.V43 2001
302.2—dc21   2001026059

Wadsworth/Thomson Learning
10 Davis Drive
Belmont, CA 94002-3098
USA

For more information about our products, contact us:
Thomson Learning Academic Resource Center
1-800-423-0563
http://www.wadsworth.com

International Headquarters
Thomson Learning
International Division
290 Harbor Drive, 2nd Floor
Stamford, CT 06902-7477
USA

UK/Europe/Middle East/South Africa
Thomson Learning
Berkshire House
168-173 High Holborn
London WC1V 7AA
United Kingdom

Asia
Thomson Learning
60 Albert Street, #15-01
Albert Complex
Singapore 189969

Canada
Nelson Thomson Learning
1120 Birchmount Road
Toronto, Ontario M1K 5G4
Canada

Brief Contents

Contents

Part II Interpersonal Communication   94

Chapter 5 Conversations   96

Preface

In this landmark tenth edition of *Communicate!* we have tried not only to impart conceptual understanding of relevant theory and research but to provide the kind of guidance and features that help students translate what they have read into genuine communication competence.

With a combination of theory, skills practice, and competency evaluation, students (1) learn to understand the major concepts from communication theory and research, (2) become able to recognize how these concepts and theories provide a basis for communication skills, (3) have access to a range of communication skills, and (4) begin to apply what they learn in class to real-life situations, thus increasing communication competence in all settings.

Strengths of the Text

This edition continues to emphasize the elements of communication competence in a way that is appealing both to the student learning the skills and to the instructor who is guiding that learning. A major challenge is to be sensitive to the burgeoning research in communication while still providing a manageable, coherent introduction that makes a real difference to the development of students' skills.

Thus, this revision continues to feature what previous users have said is a reliable learning model. This model consists of six integrated steps:

1. **Theoretical understanding** of communication theories that provide the foundation for specific skills.

2. **Examples** enabling students to identify effective skill usage.

3. **Steps** involved in the performance of skills.

4. **Practice** in using skills.

5. **Self-assessment** through which students are encouraged to write goal statements to help them with their mastery of key skills.

6. **Review.**

We present this model through a clear, concise writing style and through the use of ample examples and numerous suggestions for practice integrated within chapters.

New to This Edition

We are excited to present you with a conceptually and technologically enhanced tenth edition, with the learning model as its strong foundation and guided by valuable feedback from faculty around the country.

For the convenience of those who are familiar with the previous editions of *Communicate!*, most of the chapters, their main headings, and key features such as Skill Builders remain the same. However, there are several content changes and technological resources, such as the Communicate! CD-ROM included in the back of this text, that distinguish this new edition. We outline the content and feature changes here:

Throughout the book, examples of the many ways in which technology is affecting and changing communication are emphasized, highlighting the fact that the Internet, the Web, and interactive technologies have shrunk the distance between people and cultures.

On a chapter-by-chapter basis, you will see these significant revisions:

Chapter 1 Communication Perspective includes a major section on electronic communication in *Communication Settings*, pages 12 to 15. In addition to a completely revised section on ethical implications, the section on *Communication Principles* also includes a new section titled "Communication Is Culturally Bound," pages 18 and 19. Material in these two sections gives a firmer foundation for both the inclusion of the *Diverse Voices* boxes and the chapter-ending features *A Question of Ethics*.

Chapter 5 Conversations (formerly Chapter 7) has been moved to the start of Part II, as it is the major vehicle for interpersonal communication. The chapter includes a new section *Skills of Effective Electronically Mediated Conversationalists* starting on page 112.

Chapter 8 Communicating in Relationships has a new section *Role of Electronic Communication in Building Relationships*, starting on page 195, with material on the development of electronically mediated relationships and the dark side of such relationships.

Chapter 9 Interviewing has a new section on online résumés starting on page 222.

Chapter 10 Participating in Group Communication has been completely rewritten and now includes sections on characteristics of effective work groups, stages of group development, and problem solving in groups.

Chapter 11 Member Roles and Leadership in Groups also has been completely rewritten and now includes sections on member roles, member responsibilities in group meetings, leadership, leading group meetings, and evaluating group effectiveness.

Chapter 13 Doing Research is an anchor chapter in our trademark *Public Speaking* section. This chapter includes the introductory section *Where to Look: Traditional and Electronic Sources of Information*, page 308. It has been completely revised to stress the need to know and utilize library and Internet electronic databases for speech research. Numerous examples, including a step-by-step subject search on InfoTrac College Edition, help bridge the gap between the conceptual and the practical.

Chapter 14 Organizing contains a major revision of the discussion of outlining the body of a speech.

Chapter 15 Adapting Verbally and Visually includes a revised section on Adapting to Audiences Visually, starting on page 375, including a detailed discussion of computer-generated visual aids.

Chapter 16 Practicing the Presentation of Your Speech has a revised section on preparing speech notes, and it includes a new sample speech.

Chapter 17 Informative Speaking and Chapter 18 Persuasive Speaking feature new sample speeches. You can watch, listen to, and critique these sample speeches under the Speech Interactive program on the Communicate! CD-ROM.

New Features

As previewed above, *Communicate!* Tenth Edition features a completely integrated multimedia program in the form of the Communicate! CD-ROM and the companion Communicate! Web site at the Human Communication Resource Center on the Wadsworth Communication Café.

The new, interactive Communicate! CD-ROM is packaged at the back of the text. This dynamic multimedia learning tool expands text content online through access to *InfoTrac® College Edition* and chapter-by-chapter resources at Wadsworth's Communication Café. The CD also features *Communicate! In Action* and *Speech Interactive.* These programs feature videos of the conversation scenarios in Chapters 5–8 and the sample student speeches included in Chapters 17 and 18. Finally, the CD offers a preview of *Thomson Learning WebTutor™* and the electronic version or "ebook" of this text available through metatext/NetLibrary. Icons located throughout the text prompt exploration with these engaging resources. In addition to the CD-ROM, the tenth edition includes the following new in-text features:

- Communicate! Using Technology margin features provide useful tips for making the most of online resources, as well as practical information and insights into technologies that impact communication ranging from computer software to cellular phones. Many segments include questions and exercises, leading students to various URLs on the Web and expanding the classroom into an online environment.

- A Margin Glossary and an end-of-chapter Key Terms list provide students with quick reference to the important terms of each chapter.

- Communicate! Online study resource centers follow the Chapter Summary and Key Terms. These new end-of-chapter sections overview the technological resources available to expand skills practice and learning online. Screen grabs from the Communicate! CD-ROM, the Communicate! Web site, and InfoTrac College Edition provide visual prompts for the specific online activities suggested. The end-of-part *Self-Review* feature is now included in this section.

Revised Features

■ *Spotlight on Scholars* boxes feature the work of nine eminent scholars. Based on interviews with the scholars, these features, 20% of which are new to this edition, describe the scholar's background, including a description of what motivated the scholar to study that topic. Then a brief summary of the findings and methods of research used by the scholars are presented. This feature is designed to help undergraduates understand the research and theory-building process and to provide a glimpse of some of the people who have been especially influential in developing interpersonal communication theories.

■ *Diverse Voices* features appear throughout the text to give voice to the experiences of people from a wide range of backgrounds and cultural experiences. These excerpts, 30% of which are new to this edition, highlight the personal thoughts and experiences of individuals on topics related to the contents of each chapter, helping students to understand how culture affects communication.

■ *Skill Builders* boxes visually reinforce learning of many specific skills that are described and exemplified in the text. Each box includes the definition of the skill, a brief description of its use, the steps for enacting the skill, and an example that illustrates the skill. A convenient tear-out chart at the beginning of the book provides a summary of all Skill Builders. The skills in the chart are grouped into categories for easy reference.

■ *Communicate! Using InfoTrac College Edition* features have been enhanced for this edition. This margin feature integrates InfoTrac College Edition questions and exercises throughout the text. We encourage you to use the subscription that accompanied a new copy of this text to explore chapter topics in detail and to complete speech research.

■ *Thinking About. . .* exercises ask students to reflect on their motivations, behaviors, and values in order to see how who they are relates to others.

■ *Observe and Analyze: Journal Activity* exercises require students to observe a specific event or series of events that are related to concepts they are learning. Then they are asked to analyze what happened, using the theories and concepts from the chapter. For convenience, journal space is provided in the new *Student Workbook*.

■ *Test Your Competence* exercises require students to put their understanding of skills into practice.

■ *Self-Review* exercises appear at the end of each part. In accord with the findings of noteworthy research, students are encouraged to set specific goals for skill improvement by writing skills-improvement plans. These are provided at the end of each part within the Communicate! Online study resource center.

■ *What Would You Do? A Question of Ethics* is a feature that outlines ethical challenges and requires students to think critically in sorting through a variety of ethical dilemmas faced by communicators. Material in Chapter 1 lays a groundwork for the criteria on which students may make their assessments. But in each case the dilemma posed focuses on issues raised in the specific chapter.

Supplementary Materials

In addition to the Communicate! CD-ROM and Web site, the tenth edition is accompanied by a suite of integrated resources for students and instructors.

Student Resources

■ **InfoTrac® College Edition**   A *free* four-month subscription to this extensive online library is enclosed with every new copy of Verderber and Verderber's book! This easy-to-use database of reliable, full-length articles (not abstracts) from hundreds of top academic journals and popular sources is ideal for selecting and researching speech topics and expanding text content. *InfoTrac College Edition Student Activities Workbooks* are available and feature extensive individual and group activities that utilize InfoTrac College Edition for human communication, public speaking, interpersonal communication, and intercultural communication. These workbooks can be bundled for free with the text.

■ **Student Workbook**   New to this edition and written by Leonard E. Assante of Volunteer State Community College, the student workbook offers chapter-by-chapter skill-building exercises, vocabulary lists, quizzes, and space to respond to the in-text *Observe and Analyze: Journal Activity* features. The workbook can be bundled with the text at a discount.

WebTUTOR Advantage

■ **Thomson Learning WebTutor™ Advantage, 2.0 for WebCT and Blackboard**   is a Web-based teaching and learning tool that takes a course beyond classroom boundaries to an anywhere, anytime environment. *WebTutor for Communicate!* corresponds chapter-by-chapter and topic-by-topic with the book, including flashcards (with audio), practice quizzes, and online tutorials. Instructors can use WebTutor to provide virtual office hours, post syllabi, set up threaded discussions, and track student progress on the practice quizzes.

■ **Speech Interactive: Student Speeches for Critique and Analysis**   This multimedia CD-ROM can be used in addition to the *Speech Interactive for Communicate!* program featured on your Communicate! CD-ROM. The original Speech Interactive CD-ROM features six sample speeches for interactive critique and analysis.

■ **eCommunicate! Tenth Edition**   An ebook version of *Communicate!* delivered entirely over the Internet includes exercises linked to the Web, easy note-taking and highlighting capability, linked key terms and glossaries, and links to other online tools such as Web Tutor and InfoTrac College Edition. You can preview eCommunicate! from the Communicate! Web site.

■ **Service Learning in Communication Studies: A Handbook** *by Rick Isaacson, Bruce Dorries, and Kevin Brown.*   This handbook can be bundled with the text and is an invaluable resource for students in the basic course that integrates or is planning to integrate a service learning component. The handbook provides guidelines for connecting service learning work with classroom concepts and advice for working effectively with agencies and organizations. The handbook also provides model forms and reports and a directory of online resources.

■ **A Guide to the Basic Course for ESL Students** *by Esther Yook, Mary Washington College.*   Available bundled with the text, this guide assists the non-native speaker. Features FAQs, helpful URLs, and strategies for accent management and overcoming speech apprehension.

Instructor Resources

■ **Instructor's Resource Manual with Test Bank** *by Nader Chaaban, Montgomery College, Rockville, Maryland.*   This indispensable manual features changes from the Ninth Edition to the Tenth Edition, sample syllabi, chapter-by-chapter outlines, summaries, vocabulary lists, suggested lecture and discussion topics, classroom exercises, and assignments, as well as a comprehensive *Test Bank* with answer key and rejoinders.

■ **ExamView®**   is a fully integrated collection of test creation, delivery, and classroom management tools that feature all of the test items found in the Instructor's Resource Manual.

ExamView®

■ **CommLink: A Microsoft® PowerPoint® Presentation Tool for Human Communication, v. 2.0**   This presentation tool, created by Martin H. Brodey of Montgomery College, Rockville, Maryland, contains a searchable database of PowerPoint slides tailored to the tenth edition, including text art and cued video clips—many from CNN. Instructors can import information from previously created lectures into the program.

■ **CNN Today Videos**   Organized by topics covered in a typical course, this multivolume video series is available to qualifying adopters. Videos are divided into short segments—perfect for introducing key concepts.

CNN

■ **Student Speeches for Critique and Analysis.** This four-volume video series offers both imperfect and award-winning sample student speeches. Several of the speeches presented in this text, including the informative speech in Chapter 17 and the persuasive speech in Chapter 18, are available in this series.

■ **Communication Scenarios for Critique and Analysis.** This video provides faculty and students with real-life contexts of interpersonal communication in action. A great tool for helping students learn to critique and analyze interpersonal communication skills, this video features a dozen scripted, videotaped scenarios including the conversations featured in Chapters 5–8 and on the Communicate! CD-ROM.

■ **Wadsworth Communication Video Library** is available to qualifying adopters. The Video Library includes a variety of instructional videos as well as the *Great Speeches®* video series.

■ **Media Guide for Interpersonal Communication** *by Charles G. Apple, University of Michigan–Flint.* This guide provides faculty with media resource listings focused on general interpersonal communication topics. Each listing provides compelling examples of how interpersonal communication concepts are illustrated in particular films, books, plays, Web sites, or journal articles. Discussion questions are provided.

■ **The Teaching Assistant's Guide to the Basic Course** *by Katherine G. Hendrix, University of Memphis.* Based on leading communication teacher training programs, the guide covers general teaching and course management topics as well as specific strategies for communication instruction, such as providing effective feedback on performance, managing sensitive class discussions, and conducting mock interviews.

Acknowledgments

The tenth edition could not have been completed without the help of many people. Most important are the reviewers, whose names are listed on the inside front cover of this book. Their insights, candor, and suggestions for refining the book were invaluable. Many of these reviewers have been faithful adopters of *Communicate!* We are grateful for their support.

We would like to express our gratitude to the Wadsworth/Thomson Learning Communication Team: Deirdre Cavanaugh, Executive Editor; Stacey Purviance, Executive Marketing Manager; Jeanette Wiseman, Technology Project Manager; Cathy Linberg, Senior Project Manager; Nicole George, Assistant Editor; Mele Alusa, Editorial Assistant; and Neena Chandra, Marketing Assistant. Others at Wadsworth, including Stephen Rapley, Creative Director; Linda Yip, Advertising Coordinator; and Clark Baxter, Publisher, have offered their support and expertise. Cecile Joyner of The Cooper Company oversaw the production of this book.

Communicate!

one

Although you communicate in specific

settings, principles and skills of perception,

verbal communication, and nonverbal

communication are common to all of them. This

four-chapter unit provides a solid foundation

on which to develop your skills in

interpersonal communication, group

communication, and public speaking.

I

FOUNDATIONS OF COMMUNICATION

Geoff Brightling/FPG International

OBJECTIVES

After you have read this chapter, you should be able to answer these questions:

■ What is the definition of communication?

■ Why is communication effectiveness so important to you?

■ How does the communication process work?

■ What functions does communication serve?

■ How do communication settings vary?

■ Why should a communicator be concerned about diversity?

■ What major ethical issues face communicators?

■ What are six basic principles of communication?

■ What is the measure of communication competence?

■ How can you improve your communication skills?

CHAPTER

1

Communication Perspective

As the selection committee deliberated, they felt they had four viable candidates for the position. "They all look good on paper," Carson said, "but I must admit I was especially impressed with the way Corrie Jackson presented herself to us. Not only did she have a clear vision for where we need to be five years from now, but she also explained that vision with precise, concrete statements. I was really convinced that she was on the right track. She gets my vote."

Your presence in this course may be far more important to you than you imagined when you chose (or were required) to take it, for communication effectiveness is vital to success in nearly every walk of life. For instance, studies done in the last several years conclude that for most any job two of the most highly sought-after skills in new hires are oral communication skills and interpersonal abilities (Goleman, 1998, pp. 12–13). So, whether you aspire to a career in business, industry, government, education, or almost any other field you can name, communication skills are likely to be a prerequisite to your success.

In this chapter we will explain the communication process, provide an overview of the role of communication in daily life, discuss major communication principles, and consider means for becoming a competent communicator.

The Communication Process

communication–*the process of creating or sharing meaning in informal conversation, group interaction, or public speaking.*

Communication is the process of creating or sharing meaning in informal conversation, group interaction, or public speaking. The process includes participants, context, messages, channels, presence or absence of noise, and feedback.

Participants

participants–*the people communicating, assuming the roles of senders and receivers during communication.*

The **participants** are the people who communicate, assuming the roles of senders and receivers during communication. As senders, participants form messages and attempt to communicate them to others through verbal symbols and nonverbal behavior. As receivers, they process the messages and behaviors that they receive and react to them.

Context

context–*the physical, social, historical, psychological, and cultural settings in which communication occurs.*

Context is the physical, social, historical, psychological, and cultural settings in which communication occurs.

physical context–*location, the environmental conditions (temperature, lighting, noise level), the physical distance between communicators, any seating arrangements, and time of day.*

Physical context The **physical context** of a communication event includes its location, the environmental conditions (temperature, lighting, noise level), the physical distance between communicators, any seating arrangements, and time of day. Each of these factors can affect the communication. For instance, the boss sitting behind her desk in her office talking with members of her staff creates a different context from her talking with those same people while sitting at a round table in the conference room.

social context–*the purpose of the event as well as the existent relationships between and among the participants.*

Social context The **social context** includes the purpose of the event as well as the existent relationships between and among the participants. Whether a communication event takes place at a family dinner, a formal wedding, or a business meeting, and whether it occurs among family members, friends,

Addison Geary/Stock, Boston

In what ways, if any, might the communication of these people differ from their conversation if they were at a table in a pizza parlor?

acquaintances, work associates, or strangers influences what and how messages are formed, shared, and understood. For instance, most people interact differently talking with their children across the dinner table than when talking with a customer at work.

Historical context   The **historical context** includes the background provided by previous communication episodes between the participants that influence understandings in the current encounter. For instance, suppose one morning Chad tells Shelby that he will get the draft of the report that they had left for their boss to read. As Shelby enters the office that afternoon, she sees Chad and says, "Did you get it?" Another person listening to the conversation would have no idea what the "it" is to which Shelby is referring. Yet Chad may well reply, "It's on my desk." Shelby and Chad understood one another because of the contents of the earlier exchange.

historical context–*the background provided by previous communication episodes between the participants that influence understandings in the current encounter.*

Psychological context   The **psychological context** includes the moods and feelings each person brings to the communication. Suppose Corinne is under a great deal of stress as she tries to finish a report due the next morning. If her husband jokingly suggests that she take a speed-typing course, Corinne, who is normally good natured, may explode with an angry tirade. Why? Because her stress level provides the psychological context within which she hears this message and it taints what she understands.

psychological context–*the moods and feelings each person brings to the communication.*

cultural context–*beliefs, values, attitudes, meanings, social hierarchies, religion, notions of time, and roles of a group of people.*

Cultural context The **cultural context** includes the beliefs, values, attitudes, meanings, social hierarchies, religion, notions of time, and roles of a group of people (Samovar & Porter, 2000, p. 7). In the United States the dominant ethnic culture is European American. Many "white" Americans may not think of themselves as "ethnic," but as Sonia Nieto (2000) points out, "we are all ethnic, whether we choose to identify ourselves in this way or not" (p. 27). Because our dominant ethnic cultural context is European American, a general assumption when interacting with others has been that they share the beliefs, values, and norms common to this American experience. But because the United States is a nation of immigrants, its citizens are quite culturally diverse. As a result, a wide variety of other cultural contexts also exist and influence communication.

Messages

message–*the elements of meaning, symbols, encoding and decoding, and form or organization.*

Communication takes place through sending and receiving **messages,** which include the elements of meaning, symbols, encoding and decoding, and form or organization.

meaning–*the ideas and feelings that exist in your mind.*

Meaning **Meanings** are the ideas and feelings that exist in your mind. You may have ideas about how to study for your next exam, what your career goal is, and whether taxes should be raised or lowered; you also may have feelings such as jealousy, anger, and love. The meanings you have within you, however, cannot be transferred magically into another's mind.

symbols–*words, sounds, and actions that represent specific content meaning.*

Symbols To share meanings, you form messages comprising verbal and nonverbal symbols. **Symbols** are words, sounds, and actions that represent specific content meaning. As you speak, you choose words to convey your meaning. At the same time facial expressions, eye contact, gestures, and tone of voice—all nonverbal cues—accompany your words and also affect the meaning your listener receives from the symbols you use. As you listen, you use both the verbal symbols and the nonverbal cues to make sense of what is being said.

encoding–*the process of transforming ideas and feelings into words, sounds, and actions.*

decoding–*the process of transforming messages back into ideas and feelings.*

Encoding and decoding The cognitive thinking process of transforming ideas and feelings into symbols and organizing them into a message is called **encoding** a message; the process of transforming messages from another back into one's own ideas and feelings is called **decoding.** Ordinarily you may not consciously think about either the encoding or the decoding process. But when you have difficulty communicating, you become more aware of them. For example, if during a speech you see puzzled frowns, you may go through another encoding process to select expressions that better convey your meaning. Likewise, you may become aware of the decoding process when you must figure out the meaning of an unfamiliar word based on its use in a particular sentence.

The encoding process is made more difficult when verbal and nonverbal cues conflict. For instance, if a coworker says, "Yes, I'm very interested in the way you arrived at that decision," the meaning you decode will be very different if the person leans forward and looks interested or yawns and looks away.

Form or organization When meaning is complex, we may need to organize it in sections or in a certain order. Message form is especially important when one person talks without interruption for a relatively long time, such as in a public speech or when reporting an event to a colleague at work.

Channels

A **channel** is both the route traveled by the message and the means of transportation. Messages are transmitted through sensory channels. Face-to-face communication has two basic channels: sound (verbal symbols) and light (nonverbal cues). People can and do communicate by any of the five sensory channels, however, and a fragrant scent or a firm handshake may contribute as much to meaning as what is seen or heard. In general, the more channels used to carry a message, the more likely the communication will succeed.

channel–*both the route traveled by the message and the means of transportation.*

Noise

Noise is any external, internal, or semantic stimulus that interferes with sharing meaning.

noise–*any stimulus that interferes with sharing meaning.*

   External noises are sights, sounds, and other stimuli in the environment that draw people's attention away from what is being said or done. For instance, while a person is giving directions on how to work the new food processor, your attention may be drawn away by the external noise of a radio playing an old favorite of yours.

external noises–*sights, sounds, and other stimuli that draw people's attention away from what is being said or done.*

   Internal noises are thoughts and feelings that interfere with the communication process. If you have ever tuned out the words of the person with whom you are communicating and tuned into a daydream or a past conversation, then you have experienced internal noise.

internal noises–*thoughts and feelings that interfere with the communication process.*

   Semantic noises are the unintended meanings aroused by certain symbols, inhibiting the accuracy of decoding. If a friend describes a forty-year-old secretary as "the girl in the office" and you think "girl" is an odd and condescending term for a forty-year-old woman, you might not even hear the rest of what your friend has to say. Use of ethnic slurs, profanity, and vulgar speech can have the same effect.

semantic noises–*unintended meanings aroused by certain symbols inhibiting the accuracy of decoding.*

Feedback

Feedback is the response to a message. Feedback indicates to the person sending a message whether and how that message was heard, seen, and understood. If the verbal or nonverbal response indicates to the sender that the intended meaning was not heard, the originator may try to find a different way of encoding the message to align the meaning that was understood with the initiator's original personal meaning. This reencoded message is also feedback because it gives meaning to the original receiver's response. In all of our communication, whether interpersonal, small-group, or public-speaking, we want to stimulate as much feedback as the situation will allow.

feedback–*the response to a message.*

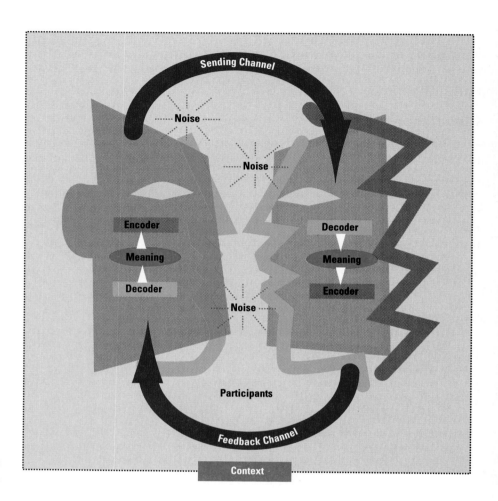

Figure 1.1
A model of communication
between two individuals.

A Model of the Process

Figure 1.1 illustrates the communication process between two people. In the minds of these people are meanings, thoughts, or feelings that they intend to share. The nature of those thoughts or feelings are created, shaped, and affected by their total field of experience, including such specific factors as values, culture, environment, experiences, occupation, sex, interests, knowledge, and attitudes. To turn meaning into messages, people encode a thought or feeling into words and actions and send it via sending channels—in this case, sound (speech) and light (nonverbal behavior).

Meanings that have been encoded into symbols are turned back into meaning by participants through the decoding process. This decoding process is affected by the participants' total field of experience—that is, by all the same factors that shape the encoding process.

The area around the people represents the physical, social, psychological, and cultural contexts in operation during the communication. During the entire

TEST YOUR COMPETENCE

Identifying Elements of the Communication Process

For the following interaction, identify the context, participants, channel, message, noise, and feedback.

Maria and Damien are meandering through the park drinking bottled water. As Damien finishes his bottle, he replaces the lid and tosses the bottle into the bushes at the side of the path. Maria comes to a stop, puts her hands on her hips, stares at Damien, and says angrily, "I can't believe what you just did!" Damien blushes, averts his gaze, and mumbles, "Sorry, I'll get it—I just wasn't thinking." As the tension drains from Maria's face, she gives her head a playful toss, smiles, and says, "Well, just see that it doesn't happen again."

transaction, external, internal, and semantic noise may be occurring at various points that affect the people's ability to share meanings.

In a conversation among several people, in a problem-solving group or in a public-speaking situation, for example, all these elements of communication operate simultaneously—and differently—for everyone present. As a result, communication among more than two people becomes more complex. Whereas some people focus on the speaker's message, others may be distracted by noise—whether external (the hum of the air conditioning), internal (preoccupation with personal matters), or semantic (a reaction to the speaker's choice of words). Furthermore, all the participants bring their unique perspectives to the communication transaction. Less skillful communicators are oblivious of such factors and plunge ahead regardless of whether they are being understood or even heard. Skillful communicators attend to verbal and nonverbal feedback and adapt their words and nonverbal behavior until they are confident that their listeners have received the meanings they intend to share.

OBSERVE & ANALYZE
Journal Activity

Conversations

Think of two recent conversations that you participated in, one that you thought went really well and one that you thought went poorly. Compare them. Using Journal Activity 1.1 in your Student Workbook, describe the context in which the conversations occurred, the participants, the rules that seemed to govern your behavior and that of the other participants, the messages that were used to create the meaning, the channels used, any noise that interfered with communication, the feedback that was shared, and the result.

Communication in Our Lives

Communication serves many functions, takes place in many settings, and is as likely to occur electronically as in person.

Communication Functions

Communication serves several important functions for us.

1. **We communicate to meet needs.** Because we are by nature social animals, we need other people just as we need food, water, and shelter. Two people may converse happily for hours gossiping and chatting about inconsequential matters that neither remembers afterward. When they part, they may have exchanged little real information, but their communication has served the purpose of meeting the important need simply to talk with another human being.

2. **We communicate to enhance and maintain our sense of self.** Through our communication, we learn who we are, what we are good at, and how people react to how we behave. We explore this important function of interpersonal communication in detail in Chapter 2, "Perception of Self and Others."

3. **We communicate to fulfill social obligations.** We use such statements as "How are you doing?" to a person we sat next to in class last quarter and "What's happening" or simply "Hi" when we pass people we know in order to meet social obligations. By saying, "Hi, Josh, how's it going?" we acknowledge a person we recognize. By not speaking we risk being perceived as arrogant or insensitive.

4. **We communicate to develop relationships.** Not only do we get to know others through our communication with them, but more important, we develop relationships with them—relationships that grow and deepen or stagnate and wither away. We discuss how relationships begin and develop in Chapter 8, "Communicating in Relationships."

5. **We communicate to exchange information.** Some information we get through observation, some through reading, some through television, and a great deal through direct communication with others. Whether we are trying to decide how warmly to dress or whom to vote for in the next presidential election, all of us have countless exchanges that involve sending and receiving information. We discuss communication as information exchange in Chapter 5, "Conversations," Chapter 10, "Participating in Group Communication," and in Chapter 17, "Informative Speaking."

6. **We communicate to influence others.** It is doubtful whether a day goes by in which you don't engage in behavior such as trying to convince your friends to go to a particular restaurant or to support a political candidate, to persuade your spouse to quit smoking, or (an old favorite) to convince an instructor to change your course grade. We discuss the role of influencing others in Chapter 11, "Member Roles and Leadership in Groups," and in Chapter 18, "Persuasive Speaking."

Communication Settings

In this book you will be introduced to skills that you can choose from to help you achieve communication competence in interpersonal settings, problem-solving groups, and public-speaking settings.

OBSERVE & ANALYZE
Journal Activity

Communication Functions

Keep a log of the various communication episodes you engage in today under Journal Activity 1.2 in your Student Workbook. Tonight, categorize each episode by one of the six functions it served. Each episode may serve more than one function. Were you surprised by the variety of communication you engaged in even in such a relatively short period?

Interpersonal communication settings Most of our communication takes place in **interpersonal communication settings** that are characterized by informal conversations between two or more people. Talking to a friend on campus, chatting on the phone with your mother, arguing the merits of a movie with friends, and comforting a friend who has been jilted by his girlfriend are all examples of interpersonal communication.

In our discussion of interpersonal communication, we will focus on holding effective conversations, listening and responding empathically, sharing personal information, self-disclosure and feedback, and developing, maintaining, or improving relationships.

Problem-solving group settings **Problem-solving group settings** are characterized by participants who come together for the specific purpose of solving a problem or arriving at a decision. For many of us, this kind of communication takes place in meetings.

In our discussion of problem-solving group settings we will focus on group interaction, problem solving and decision making, and leadership.

Public-speaking settings Some of our most important communication occurs in speeches. **Public-speaking settings** are characterized by a speaker delivering a prepared formal message to an audience in a public setting. All the variables of communication are present in this one-to-many situation, but their use in public speaking differs greatly from their use in other situations.

In our discussion of communication in public-speaking settings, we will focus on determining goals, gathering and evaluating material, organizing and developing material, adapting material to a specific audience, and presenting the speech, as well as variations in procedure for information exchange and persuasion.

If you are like most people, you already make conscious or unconscious use some of these skills, whereas others may not currently be part of your repertoire. Regardless of how accomplished you already are, careful study and practice can enhance your competence and empower you to better achieve your goals.

Electronically mediated communication settings Today we are increasingly likely to communicate with others in ways that are electronically mediated. **Electronically mediated communication settings** are characterized by participants who do not share a physical context but communicate through the use of technology. As a result, the meaning of a message that is normally transmitted nonverbally is unavailable to the receiver.

For a growing number of people a common way to keep in touch with distant family and friends is through **email**, electronic correspondence conducted between two or more users on a network. Today more than 25 percent of the U.S. population has access to email, and a great number of those use it as their primary way of communicating with others long distance.

Likewise, an increasing number of people are communicating with people they don't know but with whom they share a common interest through newsgroups

interpersonal communication settings–*characterized by informal conversations between two or more people.*

problem-solving group settings–*characterized by participants who come together for the specific purpose of solving a problem or arriving at a decision.*

public-speaking settings–*characterized by a speaker delivering a prepared formal message to an audience in a public setting.*

electronically mediated communication settings–*characterized by participants who do not share a physical context but communicate through the use of technology.*

email–*electronic correspondence conducted between two or more users on a network.*

Use of Email

Do you use email? Consider the mailing you have done over the last week. Under Journal Activity 1.3 in your Student Workbook, classify the kinds of messages you have written (use such headings as letters to friends, inquiries to Web sites, questions to professors, and so forth). How many messages do you receive each day? What percentage of those do you reply to? Compare your email use to regular mail. How many letters (not bills, advertisements, or solicitations) do you send or receive each day?

Email has taken the place of letter writing in most settings.

Steve Dunwell/The Image Bank

newsgroup–*an electronic gathering place for people with similar interests.*

Internet chat–*interactive message exchange between two or more people.*

and online chat. A **newsgroup** is "an electronic gathering place for people with similar interests" (Miller, 1999, p. 187). Think of a newsgroup as a collecting place for messages on a common topic. To communicate in a newsgroup, a user posts a message (called an *article*). These messages may be about a variety of topics that are appropriate for the site. Other users read these articles and, when so disposed, respond. The result is a kind of ongoing discussion in which many users (ten, fifty, or maybe even hundreds) may participate. On the Internet there are literally thousands of newsgroup opportunities (Sherman, 1999, p. 137).

Internet chat is an interactive message exchange between two or more people. Whereas in newsgroups you post articles and people post responses, in a chat room typed responses appear instantly on participants' computer screens. In a chat room as few as two people can hold a conversation; however, some are licensed for twenty-five, fifty, or hundreds or more participants. Chat approximates face-to-face conversation in that feedback is relatively instantaneous. Michael Miller (1999), author of numerous computer books, likens online chat to 900-number telephone chat lines—"except you use your keyboard instead of a telephone, and you don't run up bills at $1.99/minute or more" (p. 217).

If the written communication revolution is taking place online, the oral communication revolution is taking place on cellular and digital telephones. In the past, if a person was not home, he or she had to go to a place where a telephone was housed. But now large numbers of people have their own "telephone booths" with them. They can make and receive telephone calls from wherever they happen to be—in a car, on a bus, in a classroom, or on the street.

As we consider various communication skills, we will consider how they can be applied to electronic as well as in-person communication.

Communication Principles

Now that we have seen the elements that comprise the communication process and considered the nature of communication in our lives, we can turn to the principles that guide our communication: communication has purpose, communication is continuous, communication messages vary in conscious encoding, communication is relational, communication is culturally bound, communication has ethical implications, and communication is learned.

Communication Has Purpose

When people communicate with one another, they have a purpose for doing so. Or, as Kathy Kellerman (1992), a leading researcher on interpersonal contexts, puts it, "all communication is goal-directed" whether or not the purpose is conscious (p. 288). The purpose of a given transaction may be serious or trivial, but one way to evaluate the success of the communication is to ask whether it achieved its purpose. When Beth calls Leah to ask whether she'd like to join her for lunch to discuss a project they are working on, her purpose may be to resolve a misunderstanding, to encourage Leah to work more closely with her, or simply to establish a cordial atmosphere. When Kareem shares statistics he has found with other members of student government to show the extent of drug abuse on campus, his purpose may be to contribute information to a group discussion or to plead a case for confronting the problem of drug abuse. Depending on the speaker's purpose, even an apparently successful transaction may fail to achieve its goal. And, of course, different purposes call for different communication strategies.

Speakers may not always be aware of their purpose. For instance, when Jamal passes Tony on the street and says lightly, "Tony, what's happening?" Jamal probably doesn't consciously think, "Tony's an acquaintance and I want him to understand that I see him and consider him worth recognizing." In this case the social obligation to recognize Tony is met spontaneously with the first acceptable expression that comes to Jamal's mind. Regardless of whether Jamal consciously thinks about the purpose, it still motivates his behavior. In this case Jamal will have achieved his goal if Tony responds with an equally casual greeting.

Communication Is Continuous

Because communication is nonverbal as well as verbal, we are always sending behavioral messages from which others draw inferences or meaning. Even silence or absence are communication behaviors if another person infers meaning from them. Why? Because your nonverbal behavior represents reactions to your environment and to the people around you. If you are cold, you shiver; if you are hot or nervous, you perspire; if you are bored, happy, or confused, your face or body language probably will show it. As skilled communicators, we need to be aware of the messages, whether explicit or implicit, we are constantly sending to others.

Communication Messages Vary in Conscious Encoding

As we discussed earlier in this chapter, sharing meaning with another person involves encoding messages into verbal and nonverbal symbols. This encoding process may occur spontaneously, may be based on a "script" you have learned or rehearsed, or may be carefully considered based on your understanding of the situation in which you find yourself (Reardon, 1987, pp. 11–12).

spontaneous expression—
messages encoded without much conscious thought.

For each of us there are times when our communication reflects a **spontaneous expression** of emotion. When this happens, our messages are encoded without much conscious thought. For example, when you burn your finger, you may blurt out "Ouch." When something goes right, you may break out in a broad smile.

scripted messages—
conversational phrases we have learned from past experience to be appropriate for the situation.

At other times, however, our communication is **scripted**; that is, we use conversational phrases we have learned from our past encounters and judge to be appropriate to the present situation. To use scripted reactions effectively, we learn or practice them until they become automatic. Many of these scripts are learned in childhood. For example, when you want the sugar bowl but cannot reach it, you may say, "Please pass the sugar," followed by "Thank you" when someone complies. This conversational sequence comes from your "table manners script," which you may have had drilled into you at home. Scripts enable us to use messages that are appropriate to the situation and are likely to increase the effectiveness of our communication. One goal of this text is to acquaint you with general scripts (or skills) that can be adapted for use in your communication encounters across a variety of relationships, situations, and cultures.

constructed messages—
messages we encode at the moment to respond when our known scripts are thought to be inadequate.

Finally, messages also may be carefully constructed to meet the particular situation. **Constructed messages** are those that we encode at the moment to respond to the situation for which our known scripts are inadequate. These messages help us communicate both effectively and appropriately.

Creatively constructed responses are perhaps the ideal communication vehicle, especially in public-speaking settings. When you are able to both envision what you want to say and construct how to say it, you are likely to form messages where your intended meaning can be shared. Another goal of this text is to help you become so familiar with a variety of message forming skills that you can use them to construct effective and appropriate messages.

Communication Is Relational

Saying that communication is relational means that in any communication setting people not only share content meaning but also negotiate their relationship. For instance, in an interpersonal communication setting when Laura says
to Jennie "I've remembered to bring the map," she is not only reporting information, but through the way she says it, she may also be communicating "You
can always depend on me" or "Or I am superior to you—if it weren't for me,
we'd be missing an important document for our trip."

Two aspects of relationships can be negotiated during an interaction. One
aspect is the affect (love to hate) present in the relationship. For instance, when
José says, "Hal, good to see you," the nonverbal behavior that accompanies the
words may show Hal whether José is genuinely happy to see him (positive
affect) or not. For instance, if José smiles, has a sincere sound to his voice, looks
Hal in the eye, and perhaps pats him on the back or shakes hands firmly, then
Hal will recognize the signs of affection. If, however, José speaks quickly with
no vocal inflection and with a deadpan facial expression, Hal will perceive the
comment as solely meeting some social expectation.

Another aspect of the relational nature of communication seeks to define
who is in control (Watzlawick, Beavin, & Jackson, 1967, p. 51). Thus, when Tom
says to Sue, "I know you're concerned about the budget, but I'll see to it that we
have money to cover everything," he can, through his words and the sound of his
voice, be saying that he is "in charge" of finances, that he is in control. How Sue
responds to Tom determines the true nature of the relationship. The control
aspect of relationships can be viewed as complementary or symmetrical.

In a **complementary relationship** one person lets the other define who is to
have greater power. Thus, the communication messages of one person may
assert dominance while the communication messages of the other person
accepts the assertion. In some cases the relationship is clarified in part by the
nature of the context. For instance, in traditional American businesses most
boss–employee relationships are complementary, with the boss in the control
position. Likewise, most public-speaking relationships are complementary, for
people in the audience have come to hear what the person has to say and in so
doing often consider the speaker's information as authoritative.

In a **symmetrical relationship** people do not "agree" about who is in control. As one person shows a need to take control, the other challenges the person's right and asserts his or her own power. Or, as one person abdicates power,
the other refuses to assume it. For example, Tom may say, "I think we need to
cut back on credit card expenses for a couple of months," to which Sue may
respond, "No way! I need a new suit for work, the car needs new tires, and you
promised we could replace the couch." Here both people are asserting control.

Control is not negotiated in a single exchange. Relational control is determined through many message exchanges over time. The interaction of communication messages, as shown through both language and nonverbal behavior, defines

complementary relationship
*—one in which a person lets the
other define who is to have
greater power.*

symmetrical relationship
*—one in which people do not
"agree" about who is in control.*

Michael Keller/The Stock Market

What messages about affect and control do wedding couples send as they feed each other cake? Power in relationships is influenced by both verbal and nonverbal messages.

and clarifies the complementary or symmetrical nature of people's relationships. In complementary relationships open conflict is less prevalent than in symmetrical ones, but in symmetrical relationships power is more likely to be evenly shared.

Communication Is Culturally Bound

cultural diversity–*variations between and among people.*

What message is formed and how it is interpreted depends on the cultural background of the participants. **Cultural diversity,** variations between and among people, affects every aspect of communication. Even though we both speak English, our cultural differences will influence the meanings we share.

Because we are a nation of immigrants, we are likely to differ in some message formation and interpretation skills. We often miscommunicate with one another because we unknowingly violate a cultural "rule" or preference of the person or misinterpret a message based on our own cultural rules or preferences. For example, Madison and Lee are newly acquainted freshman roommates. Madison is fourth-generation Swedish American from a small town in Iowa. Lee is first-generation Chinese American from San Francisco. Both women are excited about the opportunity to live with and learn from someone who has a different background. Over lunch with several other students, Madison suggests to Lee that they save money on books by sharing the cost of the book that is required for the Introduction to Psychology class they are both taking. Lee doesn't want to do this. Because other people are present, Lee follows the Chinese cultural rule of avoiding embarrassing Madison in front of their friends. So she lowers her eyes and quietly says, "That might be nice." Based on this conversation, Madison stops by the bookstore and purchases the book. When she arrives back at the dorm room and presents the book to Lee, she is dumbfounded by Lee's refusal to pay half the cost. Lee is equally surprised that Madison misinterpreted her face-saving comment as actual agreement!

Because the people who live in the United States come from a variety of cultures, opportunities for misunderstanding abound. Cultural diversity in the United States continues to grow. At the end of the twentieth century 30 percent of the population of the United States was comprised of people with Hispanic, Asian, or African roots. Within the next twenty years this figure is predicted to rise to more than 40 percent (*Chronicle of Higher Education*, 1999, p. 7). Of course in your own corner of the country the ratios may differ.

Different regions of the United States vary in the proportion of residents with various cultural backgrounds. For instance, in 1996 of the 3.5 million residents of Los Angeles, more than 1 million (29 percent) reported that they were Hispanic, whereas in neighboring San Francisco, a city of 750,000, more than 250,000 (39 percent) reported being from Asian backgrounds. In some midwestern cities, such as Cincinnati and St. Louis, more than 40 percent of the population is African American (Carpenter, 1996). In contrast, the residents of some western states are more than 90 percent European in background (Horner, 1998).

The most widely discussed aspects of cultural diversity are ethnicity and race, but cultural diversity in communication is also occasioned by gender, age, sexual orientation, class, education, and religious differences among people. Just as people of different ethnicity may have different rules that guide message construction and interpretation, so too do people who differ in age or sex or who profess different religions. Many older people consider it rude to address someone by his or her first name unless invited by that person to do so. By contrast, many younger people refer to everyone by first name with no disrespect intended.

Within each chapter of this book we will discuss ways in which various cultural groups are different and similar to each other in their communication practices. In addition, the feature Diverse Voices, which is found in some of the chapters, will focus on the way cultural diversity in communication has affected one person. This will give you an opportunity to empathize with a variety of people who come from different cultural backgrounds.

Communication Has Ethical Implications

In any encounter we choose whether or not we will communicate ethically. **Ethics** is a set of moral principles that may be held by a society, a group, or an individual. Although what is considered ethical is a matter of personal judgment, various groups still expect members to uphold certain standards. These standards influence the personal decisions we make. When we choose to violate the standards that are expected, we are viewed to be unethical.

COMMUNICATE! Using InfoTrac College Edition

Cultural issues play an important role in global business. For example, in the airline industry gate agents, flight attendants, and other service providers must be able to communicate effectively with people who come from different cultures and speak different languages. Using InfoTrac College Edition, you can find an interesting article on this subject. After typing in "Intercultural Communication" as the Subject Guide, locate the article "Plane Talk," by John Freivalds. Read what the airline industry is doing to make language learning a priority among flight attendants and pilots. How is this training working to achieve industry goals?

ethics—*a set of moral principles that may be held by a society, a group, or an individual.*

When we communicate, we cannot avoid making ethical choices with ethical implications. To understand how our ethical standards influence our communication, we must recognize the ethical principles guiding our behavior. Five ethical standards influence our communication and guide our behavior.

truthfulness and **honesty**— *standards that compel us to refrain from lying, cheating, stealing, or deception.*

moral dilemma—*a choice involving an unsatisfactory alternative.*

1. **Truthfulness** and **honesty** are standards that compel us to refrain from lying, cheating, stealing, or deception. "An honest person is widely regarded as a moral person, and honesty is a central concept to ethics as the foundation for a moral life" (Terkel & Duval, 1999, p. 122). Although most people accept truthfulness and honesty as a standard, they still confess to lying on occasion. We are most likely to lie when we are caught in a **moral dilemma,** a choice involving an unsatisfactory alternative.

    The operating moral rule is to tell the truth if you possibly can. The fundamental requirement of this rule is that we should not intentionally deceive, or try to deceive, others or even ourselves. Only when we are confronted with a true moral dilemma involving making a choice that we deem justified by the circumstances (not warning an enemy about a planned attack in order to save lives) or selecting the lesser of two evils (protecting confidentiality over lying) should we even consider lying.

integrity—*maintaining a consistency of belief and action (keeping promises).*

2. **Integrity** means maintaining a consistency of belief and action (keeping promises). Terkel and Duval (1999) say, "A person who has integrity is someone who has strong moral principles and will successfully resist the temptation to compromise those principles" (p. 135). Integrity then is the opposite of hypocrisy. A person who had promised to take a friend to the doctor would live up to this promise even if he or she had an opportunity to go out with a friend.

fairness—*achieving the right balance of interests without regard to one's own feelings and without showing favor to any side in a conflict.*

3. **Fairness** means achieving the right balance of interests without regard to one's own feelings and without showing favor to any side in a conflict. Fairness implies impartiality or lack of bias. To be fair to someone is to gather all the relevant facts, consider only circumstances relevant to the decision at hand, and not be swayed by prejudice or irrelevancies. For example, if two of her children are fighting, a mom is exercising fairness if she allows both children to explain "their side" before she decides who is at fault.

respect—*showing regard or consideration for a person and for that person's rights.*

4. **Respect** means showing regard or consideration for a person and for that person's rights. Often we talk of respecting another as a fellow human being. For instance, someone's affluence, job status, or ethnic background should not influence how we communicate with the person. We demonstrate respect through listening to and understanding others' points of view, even when they are vastly different from our own.

responsibility—*being accountable for one's actions.*

5. **Responsibility** means being accountable for one's actions. A responsibility is something that one is bound to do either through promise or obligation or because of one's role in a group or community. A responsibility may indicate a

duty to a moral law or to another human being. Some would argue that we have a responsibility not to harm or interfere with others. Others would argue that we have a responsibility not only not to harm others but to help others.

At various places in this text we will confront situations where these issues come into play. We often face ethical dilemmas where we must sort out what is more or less right or wrong. In making these choices we usually reveal what values we hold most dear. So in this book, at the end of each remaining chapter, you will be asked to think about and discuss various ethical dilemmas that relate to the chapter content.

Communication Is Learned

Because communication appears to be a natural, inborn, unchangeable behavior, we seldom try to improve our skills however inadequate they may be. But communication is learned. Thus, throughout this text we will identify interpersonal, group, and public-speaking skills that will be valuable to you in all walks of life. In the next section we look at how to go about learning and improving your skills.

COMMUNICATE!
Using Technology

Interested in learning more about ethical dilemmas? Take a look at the Web site sponsored by the Markkula Center for Applied Ethics at Santa Clara University. This site, called Ethics Connection, is open to anyone but was designed with students in mind. It focuses on issues such as how to recognize ethical dilemmas and how to think through to resolutions. Issues covered include health care, social policy, business and technology, human rights, and everyday decision making. The Ethics Connection:
http://www.scu.edu/SCU/Centers/Ethics/

Increasing Our Communication Competence

Communication competence is the impression that communicative behavior is both appropriate and effective in a given situation (Spitzberg, 2000, p. 375). Communication is *effective* when it achieves its goals; it is *appropriate* when it conforms to what is expected in a situation. We create the perception that we are competent communicators through the verbal messages we send and the nonverbal behaviors that accompany them.

Because communication is at the heart of how we relate to one another, one of your goals in this course will be to learn those things that will increase the likelihood that others will view you as competent. In the Spotlight on Scholars we feature Brian Spitzberg on Interpersonal Communication Competence. Spitzberg believes perceptions of competence depend in part on personal motivation, knowledge, and skills (p. 377).

Motivation is important because we will only be able to improve our communication if we are *motivated*—that is, if we want to. People are likely to be more motivated if they are confident and if they see potential rewards.

Knowledge is important because we must know what is involved in increasing competence. The more *knowledge* people have about how to behave in a given situation, the more likely they are to be able to develop competence.

communication competence
–the impression that communicative behavior is both appropriate and effective in a given situation.

SPOTLIGHT ON SCHOLARS

Brian Spitzberg, Professor of Communication at San Diego State University, on Interpersonal Communication Competence

Although Brian Spitzberg has made many con- tributions to our understanding of interper- sonal communication, he is best known for his work in interpersonal communication competence. This interest in compe- tence began at the University of South- ern California. For an interpersonal com- munication seminar assignment he read the research that had been done on inter- personal competence and found that the research conclusions went in different directions. Spitzberg's final paper for the seminar was his first effort to synthesize these perspectives into a comprehensive theory of competence.

Today, the model of interpersonal communi- cation competence that Spitzberg formulated guides most thinking and research in this area. He views competence neither as a trait nor a set of behaviors. Rather Spitzberg says that interper- sonal communication competence is a perception that people have about themselves or another per- son. If competence is a perception, it follows that your perception of your interpersonal communi- cation competence or that of your relationship partner will affect how you feel about that relationship. So people are more likely to be satis- fied in a relationship when they perceive them- selves and the other person as competent. According to Spitzberg, we make these compe- tence judgments based on how each of us acts when we talk together. But what determines how we act in a particular conversation?

During the time when Spitzberg was organiz- ing his thinking about competence, he was taking another course that introduced him to the theories of dramatic acting. These theories held that an actor's performance depended on the actor's moti- vation, knowledge of the script, and acting skills. Spitzberg found that these same variables could be applied to communication competence, and he incorporated them into his theory. How we behave in a conversation depends first on how personally motivated we are to have the conversa- tion, second on how personally knowledgeable we are about what behavior is appropriate in situa- tions like this, and third on how personally skilled we are at actually using the appropriate behaviors during the conversation. In addition, Spitzberg suggests that context variables such as the ones discussed in this chapter also affect how we choose to act in a conversation and the percep- tions of competence that are created.

Although Spitzberg formed most of these ideas while he was still in graduate school, he and others have spent the last eighteen years refining the the- ory, conducting programs of research based on the theory, and measuring the effectiveness of the the- ory. Research has fleshed out parts of the theory and provided some evidence of the theory's accu- racy. Over the years Spitzberg has developed about a dozen specific instruments to measure parts of the theory. One of these measures, the Conversational Skills Rating Scale, has been adopted as the stan- dard measure of interpersonal communication skills by the National Communication Association (a leading national organization of communication scholars, teachers, and practitioners).

Spitzberg's continuing interest in communica- tion competency has led him to study abusive and dysfunctional relationships from a competence perspective. Recently he has studied obsessive relational intrusion (ORI) and stalking. In such situations, the intruder's motivation is at odds with the motivation of the victim; the intruder wants to begin, escalate, or to continue a relationship, and the victim does not agree with the intruder's definition of the relationship. Their interactions are actually "arguments" over the very definition of the relationship. The intruders may perceive themselves to be "competent" within their definitions of competency. As research into these "dark side" relationships continues, scholars using our understanding of communication competency may be able to determine if certain communication behaviors are more effective than others in discouraging ORI and stalking behaviors.

Lately, Spitzberg has expanded his ORI work to examine the new phenomenon of "cyberstalking." In addition to the numerous articles that Spitzberg has published based on the results of his work, he has coauthored two books on interpersonal communication competence with William Cupach. For a list of some of Spitzberg's major publications, see the references list at the end of the book.

Whether the situation is a first date or a job interview, a conflict with a roommate or an intimate discussion of your feelings, Spitzberg believes it is important that others perceive you to be competent.

For more information about Brian Spitzberg, log on to http://www-rohan.sdsu.edu/dept/schlcomm/Spitzbergbbio.html

Skill is important because we must know how to act in ways that are consistent with our communication knowledge. **Skills** are goal-oriented actions or action sequences that we can master and repeat in appropriate situations. The more skills you have, the more likely you are to be able to structure your messages effectively and appropriately.

skills–*goal-oriented actions we can master and repeat in appropriate situations.*

Tony Freeman/PhotoEdit, Inc.

As communication motivation, knowledge, and skill increase, communicator competence increases.

The combination of our motivation, knowledge, and skills lead us to perform confidently in our encounters with others. The rest of this book is aimed at helping you increase the likelihood that you will be perceived as competent. In the pages that follow you will learn about theories of interpersonal, group, and public speaking that can increase your knowledge and your motivation. You will also learn how to perform specific skills, and you will be provided with opportunities to practice them. Through this practice, you can increase the likelihood that you will be able to perform these skills when needed.

Writing Goal Statements

To get the most from this course, we suggest that you write personal goals to improve specific skills in your own interpersonal, group, and public-communication repertoire. Why written goal statements? A familiar saying goes, "The road to hell is paved with good intentions." Regardless of how serious you are about changing some aspect of your communication, bringing about changes in behavior takes time and effort. Writing specific goals makes it more likely that your good intentions to improve won't get lost in the busyness of your life.

Before you can write a goal statement, you must first analyze your current communication skills repertoire. After you read each chapter and practice the skills described, select one or two skills to work on. Then write down your goal statement in four parts.

1. **State the problem.** Start by stating a communication problem that you have. For example: "Problem: Even though my boss consistently gives all the interesting tasks to coworkers, I haven't spoken up because I'm not very good at describing my feelings."

2. **State the specific goal.** A goal is *specific* if it is measurable and you know when you have achieved it. For example, to deal with the problem stated above, you might write, "Goal: To describe my feelings about task assignments to my boss."

3. **Outline a specific procedure for reaching the goal.** To develop a plan for reaching your goal, first consult the chapter that covers the skill you wish to hone. Then translate the general steps recommended in the chapter to your specific situation. This step is critical because successful behavioral change requires that you state your objective in terms of specific behaviors you can adopt or modify. For example: "Procedure: I will practice the steps of describing feelings. (1) I will identify the specific feeling I am experiencing. (2) I will encode the emotion I am feeling accurately. (3) I will include what has triggered the feeling. (4) I will own the feeling as mine. (5) I will then put that procedure into operation when I am talking with my boss."

4. **Devise a method of determining when the goal has been reached.** A good goal is measurable, and the fourth part of your goal-setting effort is to

determine your minimum requirements for knowing when you have achieved a given goal. For example: "Test of Achieving Goal: This goal will be considered achieved when I have described my feelings to my boss on the next occasion when his behavior excludes me."

Once you have completed all four parts of this goal-setting process, you may want to have another person witness your commitment and serve as a consultant, coach, and support person. This gives you someone to talk to about your progress. A good choice would be someone from this class because he or she is in an excellent position to understand and help. (Also, perhaps you can reciprocate with your support for his or her goal statements in return.)

At the end of each section you will be challenged to develop a goal statement related to the material presented. Figure 1.2 provides another example of a communication improvement plan, this one relating to a public-speaking problem.

Summary

We have defined communication as the process of creating or sharing meaning, whether the context is informal conversation, group interaction, or public speaking.

The elements of the communication process are context, participants, messages, channels, noise, and feedback.

Communication plays a role in all aspects of our lives. First, communication serves many important functions. People communicate to meet needs, to enhance and maintain a sense of self, to develop relationships, to fulfill social obligations, to exchange information, and to influence others. Second, communication occurs in interpersonal, group, public-speaking, and electronically

Problem: When I speak in class or in the student senate, I often find myself burying my head in my notes or looking at the ceiling or walls.

Goal: To look at people more directly when I'm giving a speech.

Procedure: I will take the time to practice oral presentations aloud in my room. (1) I will stand up just as I do in class. (2) I will pretend various objects in the room are people, and I will consciously attempt to look at those objects as I am talking. (3) In giving a speech, I will try to be aware of when I am looking at my audience and when I am not.

Test of Achieving Goal: This goal will be considered achieved when I am maintaining eye contact with my audience most of the time.

Figure 1.2
Communication improvement plan.

mediated settings. In addition to communicating in person, we now communicate with each other in email, newsgroups, chat rooms, and nearly any place via cellular telephones and electronic pagers.

Our communication is guided by at least six principles. First, communication is purposeful. Second, interpersonal communication is continuous. Third, interpersonal communication messages vary in degree of conscious encoding. Messages may be spontaneous, scripted, or constructed. Fourth, interpersonal communication is relational, defining the power and affection between people. Relational definitions can be complementary or symmetrical. Fifth, communication is culturally bound. Sixth, communication has ethical implications. Ethical standards that influence our communication include truthfulness, integrity, fairness, respect, and responsibility. And seventh, interpersonal communication is learned.

A primary issue in this course is competence—we all strive to become better communicators. Competence is the perception by others that our communication behavior is appropriate as well as effective. It involves increasing our knowledge of communication and our understanding of the situations we face, identifying and attaining goals, and being able to use the various behavioral skills necessary to achieve our goals. Skills can be learned, developed, and improved, and you can enhance your learning this term by writing goal statements to systematically improve your own skill repertoire.

Communicate! Online

Use your Communicate! CD-ROM for quick access to the electronic study resources that accompany this text. Included on your CD-ROM is access to InfoTrac College Edition, the World Wide Web, a demo of WebTutor for Communicate!, and the Communicate! Web site at the Wadsworth Communication Café. The Communicate! Web site offers chapter by chapter activities, quizzes, and a digital glossary.

Review the following key terms and access the Web links included in this chapter online at
    http://communication.wadsworth.com/humancomm/verderber

Key Terms

channel (9)
communication (6)
communication competence (21)

complementary relationship (17)
constructed messages (16)
context (6)
cultural context (8)
cultural diversity (18)

decoding (8)
electronically mediated
    communication settings (13)
email (13)
encoding (8)
ethics (19)
external noises (9)
fairness (20)
feedback (9)
historical context (7)
integrity (20)
internal noises (9)
Internet chat (14)
interpersonal communication
    settings (13)
meaning (8)
message (8)
moral dilemma (20)

newsgroup (14)
noise (9)
participants (6)
physical context (6)
problem-solving group
    settings (13)
psychological context (7)
public-speaking settings (13)
respect (20)
responsibility (20)
scripted messages (16)
semantic noises (9)
skills (23)
social context (6)
spontaneous expression (16)
symbols (8)
symmetrical relationship (17)
truthfulness and honesty (20)

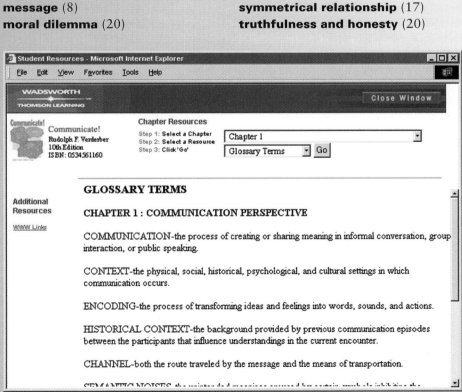

Sam Rappaport Photography

OBJECTIVES

After you have read this chapter, you should be able to answer these questions:

- What is perception?
- How does the mind select, organize, and interpret information?
- What is the self-concept, and how is it formed?
- What is self-esteem, and how is it developed?
- How do our self-concept and self-esteem affect our communication with others?
- What affects how accurately we perceive others?
- What are some methods for improving the accuracy of social perception?

2

Perception of Self and Others

"**A**llie, I really blew it. I can't believe it."

"What do you mean, Sal?"

"Well, I just forgot everything—I mean it was like I was standing there for five minutes saying nothing?"

"Sal, I saw you pause for a few seconds, really everything fit together well. You really had your speech well organized! It seemed to me that everyone in class thought you were in total control."

"Come on, Allie, you're just trying to make me feel good."

"Trust me, Sal, if you had 'blown it,' I'd let you know. I'd be commiserating with you—not telling you what a good job you did."

Whose view is correct? Sal's or Allie's? Of course, we don't know—we didn't hear the speech. But what we do know is that Sal and Allie perceived this event very differently. Our perception affects not only how we see things but how we talk about what we have seen.

In this chapter we consider some basic concepts of perception, how the perceptions we have about ourselves are formed and changed, how we perceive others, and how we can increase the accuracy of both our self-perception and our perceptions of others. As you will see, perception is a foundation piece in both our own communication and our evaluation of the communication of others.

The Perception Process

perception–*the process of selectively attending to information and assigning meaning to it.*

Perception is the process of selectively attending to information and assigning meaning to it. Your brain selects the information it receives from your sense organs, organizes the information selected, and interprets and evaluates it.

Attention and Selection

Although we are subject to a constant barrage of sensory stimuli, we focus attention on relatively little of it. How we choose depends in part on our needs, interests, and expectations.

Needs We are likely to pay attention to information that meets our biological and psychological needs. When you go to class, how well in tune you are to what is being discussed is likely to depend on whether you believe the information is important to you—that is, does it meet a personal need?

Interest We are likely to pay attention to information that pertains to our interests. For instance, you may not even recognize that music is playing in the background until you find yourself suddenly listening to some "old favorite." Similarly, when are really interested in a person, we are more likely to pay attention to what that person is saying.

Expectation Finally, we are likely to see what we expect to see and to ignore information that violates our expectations. Take a quick look at the phrases in the triangles in Figure 2.1.

Figure 2.1
A sensory test of expectation.

If you have never seen these triangles, you probably read "Paris in the spring-time," "Once in a lifetime," and "Bird in the hand." But if you reexamine the words, you will see that what you perceived was not exactly what is written. Do you now see the repeated words? It is easy to miss the repeated word because we don't *expect* to see the word repeated.

Organization of Stimuli

Even though our attention and selection process limits the stimuli our brain must process, the absolute number of discrete stimuli we attend to at any one moment is still substantial. Our brains use certain principles to arrange these stimuli to make sense out of them. Two of the most common principles we use are simplicity and pattern.

Simplicity If the stimuli we attend to are very complex, the brain simplifies the stimuli into some commonly recognized form. Based on a quick perusal of what someone is wearing, how she is standing, and the expression on her face, we may perceive her as "a successful businesswoman," "a flight attendant," or "a soccer mom." Similarly, we simplify the verbal messages we receive. So, for example, Tony might walk out of his hour-long performance review meeting with his boss in which the boss described four of Tony's strengths and three areas for improvement and say to Jerry, his coworker, "Well, I better shape up or I'm going to get fired!"

Pattern A second principle the brain uses when organizing information is to find patterns. A **pattern** is a set of characteristics that differentiates some things from others used to group those items having the same characteristic. A pattern makes it easy to interpret stimuli. For example, when you see a crowd of people, instead of perceiving each individual human being, you may focus on the characteristic of sex and "see" men and women, or you may focus on age and "see" children, teens, adults, and seniors.

> **pattern**–*a set of characteristics that differentiates some things from others used to group those items having the same characteristic.*

In our interactions with others we try to find patterns that will enable us to interpret and respond to their behavior. For example, each time Jason and Bill encounter Sara, she hurries over to them and begins an animated conversation. Yet when Jason is alone and runs into Sara, she barely says "Hi." After a while Jason may detect a pattern to Sara's behavior. She is warm and friendly when Bill is around and not so friendly when Bill is absent.

Interpretation of Stimuli

As the brain selects and organizes the information it receives from the senses, it also **interprets** the information by assigning meaning to it. Look at these three sets of numbers. What do you make of them?

> **interpret**–*assign meaning to the information that has been selected and organized.*

A. 631 7348

B. 285 37 5632

C. 4632 7364 2596 2174

In each of these sets, your mind looked for clues to give meaning to the numbers. Because you use similar patterns of numbers every day, you probably interpret A as a telephone number. How about B? A likely interpretation is a Social Security number. And C? People who use credit cards may interpret this set as a credit card number.

In the remainder of this chapter we will apply this basic information about perception to the study of perceptions of self and others in our communication.

Perceptions of Self: Self-Concept and Self-Esteem

self-concept–*one's self-identity.*

self-esteem–*one's overall evaluation of one's competence and personal worthiness.*

Self-concept and self-esteem are the two self-perceptions that have the greatest impact on how we communicate. **Self-concept** is one's self-identity (Baron & Byrne, 2000, p. 160). It is the idea or mental image that you have about your skills, your abilities, your knowledge, your competencies, and your personality. **Self-esteem** is your overall evaluation of your competence and personal worthiness (based on Mruk, 1999, p. 26). In this section we present how we come to understand who we are and how we determine whether what we are is good. Then we examine what determines how well these self-perceptions match others' perceptions of us and the role self-perceptions play when we communicate with others.

Forming and Maintaining a Self-Concept

How do we learn what our skills, abilities, knowledge, competencies, and personality are? Our self-concept comes from the unique interpretations about ourselves that we have made based on our experience and from others' reactions and responses to us.

Self-perception We form impressions about ourselves based on our own perceptions. Through our experiences, we develop our own sense of our skills, our abilities, our knowledge, our competencies, and our personality. For example, if you perceive that it is easy for you to strike up conversations with strangers and that you enjoy chatting with them, you may conclude that you are outgoing or friendly.

We place a great deal of emphasis on the first experience we have with a particular phenomenon. For instance, someone who is rejected in his first try at dating may perceive himself to be unattractive to the opposite sex. If additional experiences produce results similar to the first experience, the initial perception will be strengthened. Even if the first experience is not immediately repeated, it is likely to take more than one contradictory additional experience to change the original perception.

When we have positive experiences, we are likely to believe we possess the personal characteristics that we associate with that experience, and these characteristics become part of our picture of who we are. So if Sonya quickly debugs a computer program that Jackie has struggled with, she is more likely to incorporate "competent problem solver" into her self-concept. Her positive experience confirms that she has that skill, so it is reinforced as part of her self-concept.

Reactions and responses of others In addition to our self-perceptions, our self-concept is formed and maintained by how others react and respond to us. For example, if during a brainstorming session at work, one of your coworkers tells you "You're really a creative thinker," you may decide that this comment fits your image of who you are. Such comments are especially powerful in affecting your self-perception if you respect the person making the comment. And the power of such comments is increased when the praise is immediate rather than delayed (Hattie, 1992, p. 251). We use other people's comments as a check on our own self-descriptions. They serve to validate, reinforce, or alter our perception of who and what we are.

Some people have very rich self-concepts; they can describe numerous skills, abilities, knowledge, competencies, and personality characteristics that they possess. Others have weak self-concepts; they cannot describe the skills, abilities, knowledges, competencies, or the personality characteristics that they have. The richer our self-concept, the better we know and understand who we are and the better able we will be to cope with the challenges we will face as we interact with others.

Our self-concept begins to form early in life, and information we receive from our families shapes our self-concept (Demo, 1987). One of the major responsibilities that family members have is to talk and act in ways that will

OBSERVE & ANALYZE
Journal Activity

Self-Perceptions

How do you see yourself? Under Journal Activity 2.1 in your Student Workbook, list the skills, abilities, knowledge, competencies, and personality characteristics that describe how you see yourself. To generate this list, try completing the sentences: "I am skilled at. . . ," "I have the ability to. . . ," "I know things about . . . ," I am competent at doing. . . ," and "One part of my personality is that I am. . . " over and over again. List as many characteristics in each category as you can think of. What you have developed is an inventory of your self-concept. Review each item on your list. Recall how you learned that you had each talent or characteristic. How does this review help you to understand the material you are studying?

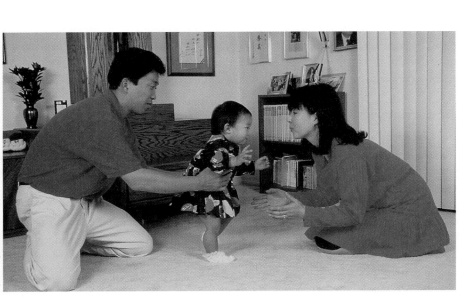

Myrleen Ferguson/PhotoEdit, Inc.

The feedback you get from your parents has an enormous influence on your self-concept and self-esteem.

OBSERVE & ANALYZE
Journal Activity

Others' Perceptions

How do others see you? Repeat the self-perception exercise from Journal Activity 2.1, but this time, for Journal Activity 2.2, use these statements: "Other people believe I am skilled at. . . ," "Other people believe I have the ability to. . . ," "Other people believe I know things about. . . ," "Other people believe I am competent at doing. . . ," and "One part of my personality is that other people believe I am. . . ." Again review the items on the list. Recall who told you about these talents and characteristics.

help develop accurate and strong self-concepts in other family members. For example, the mom who says, "Roberto, your room looks very neat. You are very organized." or the brother who comments, "Kisha, lending Tomika five dollars really helped her out. You are very generous." is helping Roberto or Kisha to recognize important parts of their personalities.

Unfortunately, in many families members damage each others' self-image and especially the developing self-concepts of children. Blaming, name-calling, and repeatedly pointing out another's shortcomings are particularly damaging. When dad shouts, "Terry, you are so stupid! If you had only stopped to think, this wouldn't have happened," he is damaging Terry's belief in his own intelligence. When big sister teases, "Hey, Dumbo, how many times do I have to tell you, you're too clumsy to be a ballet dancer," she is undermining her younger sister's perception of her gracefulness.

Developing and Maintaining Self-Esteem

You'll recall that *self-esteem* is our overall evaluation of our competence and personal worthiness—it is our positive or negative evaluation of our self-concept. Notice that self-esteem is not just feeling good about oneself but having reason to do so. Our evaluation of our personal worthiness is rooted in our values and develops over time as a result of our experiences. As Mruk (1999) points out, self-esteem is not just how well or poorly we do things (self-concept) but the importance or value we place on what we do well or poorly (pp. 26–27). For instance, as part of Fred's self-concept he believes he is physically strong. But if Fred doesn't believe physical strength or other characteristics he possesses are worthwhile characteristics to have, then he will not have high self-esteem. Mruk argues that it is both the perception of having a characteristic and personally believing that the characteristic is of positive value that produce high self-esteem.

When we successfully use our skills, abilities, knowledge, or personality traits in endeavors we believe to be worthwhile, we raise our self-esteem. When we are unsuccessful in using our skills, abilities, knowledge, competencies, or personality traits—or when we use them in unworthy endeavors—we lower our self-esteem.

Accuracy of Self-Concept and Self-Esteem

The accuracy of our self-concept and self-esteem depends on the accuracy of our own perceptions and how we process others' perceptions of us. All of us experience success and failure, and all of us hear praise and criticism. If we are overly attentive to successful experiences and positive responses, our self-concept may become overdeveloped and our self-esteem inflated. If, however, we perceive and dwell on failures and give little value to our successes, or if we only remember the criticism we receive, our self-image may be underformed and our self-esteem low. In neither case does our self-concept or self-esteem accurately reflect who we are.

incongruence—*the gap between our inaccurate self-perceptions and reality.*

Incongruence, the gap between our inaccurate self-perceptions and reality, is a problem because our perceptions of self are more likely to affect our behavior than are our true abilities (Weiten, 1998, p. 491). For example, Sean may actually possess all the skills, abilities, knowledge, competencies, and personality characteristics for effective leadership, but if he doesn't perceive that he has these characteristics, he won't step forward when leadership is needed. Unfortunately, individuals tend to reinforce their self-perceptions by adjusting their behavior to conform with perceived self-conceptions. That is, people with high self-esteem tend to behave in ways that lead to more affirmation, whereas people with low self-esteem tend to act in ways that confirm the low esteem in which they hold themselves. The inaccuracy of the distorted picture of oneself is magnified through self-fulfilling prophecies and by filtering messages.

Self-fulfilling prophecies Self-fulfilling prophecies—events that happen as the result of being foretold, expected, or talked about—are likely to be either self-created or other-imposed.

Self-created prophecies are those predictions you make about yourself. We often "talk ourselves into" success or failure. For example, Stefan sees himself as quite social and able to get to know people easily; he says, "I'm going to have fun at the party tonight." As a result of his positive self-concept, he looks forward to encountering strangers and, just as he predicted, makes several new acquaintanceships and enjoys himself. In contrast, Arthur sees himself as unskilled in establishing new relationships; he says, "I doubt I'll know hardly anyone—I'm going to have a miserable time!" Because he fears encountering strangers, he feels awkward about introducing himself and, just as he predicted, spends much of his time standing around alone thinking about when he can leave.

Self-esteem has an important effect on the prophesies people make. For instance, people with positive self-esteem view success positively and confidently prophesy that they can repeat successes; people with low self-esteem attribute their successes to luck and so prophesy that they will not repeat them (Hattie, 1992, p. 253).

The prophecies others make about you also affect your performance. For example, when teachers act as if their students are able, students "buy into" the expectation and succeed. Likewise, when teachers act as if students are not able, students may live "down" to these imposed prophecies. Thus, when we talk to ourselves or when we speak to others, we have the power to affect future behavior.

Filtering messages A second way that our self-perceptions can become increasingly distorted is through the way we filter what others say to us. Even though we may "hear" messages accurately (that is, our ears receive the messages and our brain records them), we do not perceive them equally. For example, suppose you prepare an agenda for your study group. Someone comments that you are a good organizer. You may not really hear it, ignore it, or reply, "Anyone could have done that—it was nothing special." If you do think you are a good organizer, however, you will pay attention to the compliment and may even reinforce it by responding with something like, "Thanks, I've worked hard to learn to do this, but it was worth it. It comes in handy."

self-fulfilling prophecies
—events that happen as the result of being foretold, expected, or talked about; likely to be either self-created or other-imposed.

OBSERVE & ANALYZE
Journal Activity

Who Am I?

Compare your self-perception and others' perception lists under Journal Activity 2.3 in your Student Workbook. How are the lists similar? Where are they different? Do you understand why they differ? Are your lists long or short? Why do you suppose that is? Reflect on how your own interpretations of your experiences and what others have told you about you have influenced your self-concept. Now organize the lists you created, perhaps finding a way to group characteristics. Use this information to write an essay titled "Who I am, and how I know this."

How do you see yourself? A distorted self-concept can become a self-fulfilling prophecy.

Charles Gupton/Stone

Changing self-concepts and self-esteem Self-concept and self-esteem are enduring characteristics, but they can be changed. In his analysis of numerous other research studies, Christopher Mruk (1999) found that self-esteem can be enhanced. He reports, "in the final analysis, then, self-esteem is increased through hard work and practice, practice, practice—there is simply no escaping this basic existential fact" (p. 112).

In this book we consider many specific communication behaviors that are designed to increase your communication competence. As you begin to practice and to perfect these skills, you may begin to receive positive responses to your behavior. If you continue to work on these skills, the positive responses you receive will help improve your self-concept and increase your self-esteem.

Presenting Ourselves

We also present our self-image and self-esteem to others through various roles we enact. A **role** is a pattern of learned behaviors people use to meet the perceived demands of a particular context. For instance, during the day you may enact the roles of "student," "brother or sister," and "sales clerk."

Roles that we enact may result from our own needs, relationships that we form, cultural expectations that are held for us, the groups we choose to be part of, and from our own conscious decisions. For instance, if you were the oldest

role—*a pattern of learned behaviors people use to meet the perceived demands of a particular context.*

child in a large family, your parents may have cast you in the role of oldest brother that involved such functions as disciplinarian, brothers' and sisters' keeper, or housekeeper, depending on how they see family relationships. Or, if your peers look on you as a "joker," you may go along by enacting your role, laughing and telling funny stories even though you really feel hurt or imposed on. Everyone enacts numerous roles each day, and we draw on different skills and attributes as we enact these roles. With each new situation we may test a role we know how to enact, or we may decide to try to enact a new role.

Self-Concept, Self-Esteem, and Communication

Just as our self-concept and self-esteem affect how accurately we perceive ourselves, so too do they influence our communication by moderating competing internal messages in our self-talk and influencing our personal communication style.

Self-perceptions moderate competing internal messages When we are faced with a decision, we may be especially conscious of the different and often competing "voices" in our head. Listen to the conversation Corey had upon returning from a job interview.

Corey: I think I made a pretty good impression on the Personnel Director—I mean, she talked with me for a long time. Well, she talked with me, but maybe she was just trying to be nice. After all, it was her job. No, she didn't have to spend that much time with me. And she really lit up when I talked about the internship I had at Federated. So, she said she was interested in my internship. Talking about that is not exactly telling me that it would make a difference in her view of me as a prospective employee.

If Corey feels good about himself, he will probably conclude that the interviewer was sincere, and he will feel good about the interview. But if he believes he is unworthy, that he does not have the relevant skills and abilities to do a good job, he is more likely to "listen" to the negative voices in his head and conclude that he doesn't have a chance for the job.

Self-perception influences how we talk about ourselves with others If we feel good about ourselves, we are likely to communicate positively. For instance, people with a strong self-concept and higher self-esteem usually take credit for their successes. Likewise, people with healthy self-perceptions are inclined to defend their views even in the face of opposing arguments. If we feel bad about ourselves, we are likely to communicate negatively by downplaying our accomplishments.

Why do some people put themselves down regardless of what they have done? People who have low self-esteem are likely to be unsure of the value of their contributions and expect others to view them negatively. As a result, perhaps, people with a poor self-concept or low self-esteem find it less painful to put themselves down than to hear the criticism of others. Thus, to preempt the likelihood that others will comment on their unworthiness, they do it first.

OBSERVE & ANALYZE
Journal Activity

Monitor Your Enacted Roles

For three days keep a record of your roles in various situations under Journal Activity 2.4 in your Student Workbook: for example, "Lunch with best friend" or "Meeting with manager about vacation schedule." Describe the roles and images you chose to project in each setting. At the end of the period, write an analysis of your self-monitoring. To what extent does your communication behavior differ and remain the same across situations? What factors in a situation seem to trigger certain behaviors in you? How satisfied are you with the images or "selves" you displayed in each situation? Where were you most pleased? Least pleased?

COMMUNICATE!
Using Technology

The Internet has numerous sites and pages devoted to material on self-concept and self-esteem. One particularly provocative opinion is that of Dr. Richard O'Connor in his statement entitled "Self-esteem: in a culture where winning is everything and losing is shameful." He asks whether self-esteem as a general construct is always helpful. What points does O'Connor make? How does his conclusion square with what you have observed? To open his statement, go to http://www.pioneerthinking.com/esteem.html

COMMUNICATE! Using InfoTrac College Edition

Some people believe "the greater the discrepancy between a person's own assessment of his or her interpersonal style and the perception of others, the greater will be that individual's reported psychological stress."

What does research show? Using InfoTrac College Edition, look under the subject "Self-evaluation: Periodicals." See Amy VanBuren (1997), "Awareness of interpersonal style and self-evaluation," *Journal of Social Psychology, 137,* p. 429.

Can you find any additional related studies?

Cultural and Gender Differences

Culture influences perception and affect participants' views of self. Most U.S. citizens share what is called the "Western view of self." This says that the individual is an independent entity with distinct abilities, traits, motives, and values and that these attributes cause behavior. Moreover, people with this Western view see the individual as the most basic social unit. In Western cultures a positive self-concept and self-esteem are built on the central values of independence from others and discovery and expression of individual uniqueness.

Yet people from other cultures use different values to build positive self-concepts and self-esteem. In many Eastern cultures the family, not the individual, is the smallest social unit. These cultures neither assume nor value independence; rather, *interdependence* among individuals is valued (Markus & Kitayama, 1991, p. 19). An individual who is a self-reliant individualist in a Western culture would see these characteristics as strengths and would develop positive self-esteem. An individual in an Eastern culture who possessed these same characteristics would view these as shortcomings and would develop negative self-esteem.

In Western cultures children will come to value those personal characteristics that are associated with independence, developing high self-esteem from them. In Eastern cultures, however, the child is seen as needing to be acculturated toward greater interdependency (Jordan, 1991, p. 137). These children will develop higher self-esteem when they perceive themselves to be cooperative, helpful, and self-effacing.

Similarly, men and women are socialized to view themselves differently and to value who they are based on whether their behavior corresponds to the behavior expected of their sex in their culture. If women are expected to be nurturing caregivers who attend to home and family life, then those women who perceive that they have the skills, abilities, knowledge, competencies, and personality characteristics needed for these jobs will have enriched self-concepts and high self-esteem. But women who do not have these attributes are likely to be less confident of who they are and are likely to have lower self-esteem.

Perception of Others

uncertainty reduction theory—*the process individuals use to monitor their social environment and come to know more about themselves and others.*

When two people meet, they form initial impressions of each other to guide their behavior. As Berger and Brada (1982) explain, people engage in uncertainty reduction. **Uncertainty reduction theory** describes the process individuals use to monitor their social environment and to come to know more about themselves and others (Littlejohn, 1999, p. 260). As people continue to interact, these perceptions will be reinforced, intensified, or changed. Just as with our self-perceptions, our social perceptions are not always accurate. The factors that are likely to influence our social perceptions of others include physical characteristics and social behaviors, stereotyping, and emotional states.

Physical Characteristics and Social Behaviors

Our first impressions are made on the basis of people's physical characteristics, in this order: race, gender, age, appearance, facial expressions, eye contact, movement, personal space, and touch. These characteristics help us to categorize people as friendly, courageous, intelligent, cool, or their opposite (Gardenswartz & Rowe, 1998, p. 29). Early impressions are also formed on the basis of a person's social behaviors. For instance, a person who is observed interrupting another may be perceived as "rude." A child who addresses adults as Mr. or Ms. may be perceived as well behaved.

Women and men differ in attributes they perceive in others. Scholar Leslie Zebrowitz (1990) says that men and boys are more likely to see and describe others in terms of their abilities ("She writes well"), whereas women and girls are more likely to see and describe others in terms of their self-concepts ("She thinks she's a good writer"). In addition, Zebrowitz has found that males' descriptions include more nonsocial activities ("She likes to fly model airplanes"), whereas females include more interpersonal interactions ("He likes to get together with his friends") (p. 24).

Some judgments of other people are based on what are called "implicit personality theories," which are assumptions people have developed about which physical characteristics and personality traits or behaviors are associated with one another (Michener & DeLamater, 1999, p. 106).

Because your own implicit personality theory says that certain traits go together, you are likely to perceive that a person has a whole set of characteristics when you have actually observed only one characteristic, trait, or behavior. When you do this, your perception is exhibiting what is known as the **halo effect**. For instance, Heather sees Martina personally greeting and welcoming every person who arrives at the meeting. Heather's implicit personality theory views this behavior as a sign of the characteristic of warmth. She further associates warmth with goodness, and goodness with honesty. As a result, she perceives that Martina is good and honest as well as warm.

In reality, Martina may be a con artist who uses her warmth to lure people like Heather into a false sense of trust. This example demonstrates a "positive halo" (Heather assigned Martina positive characteristics), but we also use implicit personality theory to inaccurately impute bad characteristics. In fact, Hollman (1972) found that negative information more strongly influences our impressions of others than does positive information. So we are more likely to negatively halo others than to positively halo them.

Halo effects seem to occur most frequently under one or more of three conditions: (1) when the perceiver is judging traits with which he or she has limited experience, (2) when the traits have strong moral overtones, and (3) when the perception is of a person that the perceiver knows well.

halo effect—*perception that a person has a whole set of characteristics when you have actually observed only one characteristic, trait, or behavior.*

THINKING ABOUT . . .

Halo Effects

What traits or personal characteristics do you group together? Suppose you discover that a new acquaintance is deeply religious. What attitudes and behavioral characteristics would you now assume this person has? The next time you draw a conclusion based on halo effect, make a mental note to think about it.

Given limited amounts of information, then, we fill in details. This tendency to fill in details leads to a second factor that explains social perception, stereotyping.

Stereotyping

Perhaps the most commonly known factor that influences our perception of others is stereotyping. **Stereotypes** are simplified and standardized conceptions about the characteristics or expected behavior of members of an identifiable group. These characteristics, taken as a whole, may be perceived as positive or negative and may be accurate or inaccurate (Jussim, McCauley, & Lee, 1995, p. 6). When we stereotype, we perceive a person as possessing certain characteristics because we identify that person as belonging to a certain group.

We are likely to develop generalized perceptions about any group we come in contact with. Subsequently, any number of perceptual cues—skin color, style of dress, a religious medal, gray hair, sex, and so on—can lead us to project our generalizations onto a specific individual.

Stereotyping contributes to perceptual inaccuracies by ignoring individual differences. For instance, if part of Dave's stereotype of personal injury lawyers is that they are unethical, then he will use this stereotype when he meets Denise, a highly principled woman, who happens to be a successful personal injury lawyer. You may be able to think of instances when you have been the victim of a stereotype based on your gender, age, ethnic heritage, social class, physical characteristics, or other qualities. If so, you know how hurtful the use of stereotypes can be.

If stereotypes lead to inaccurate perceptions and miscommunication, why do they persist? Stereotyping is a shortcut that enables us to confer order on the complex social world in which we interact (McCrae, Milne, & Bodenhausen, 1994, p. 45). In addition, stereotypes are helpful (Deaux, Dane, & Wrightsman, 1993, p. 94). Although people may learn to go beyond a stereotype in forming opinions of individuals, stereotypes provide a "working hypothesis." That is, when we encounter a new person who we determine is from a particular race or culture, we can reduce our uncertainty about that person by attributing the characteristics of our stereotype to the person. Then we relate to this person based on the stereotype until we receive sufficient information to enable us to perceive the person as an individual (Jones, 1990, p. 110).

As these examples suggest, stereotyping can lead to prejudice and discrimination. According to Terkel and Duval (1999), **prejudice** is a preconceived judgment—a belief or opinion that a person holds without sufficient grounds (p. 217). **Discrimination** is treating members of one group differently from members of another in a way that is unfair or harmful (p. 69). Thus, prejudice is evaluative and discrimination is behavioral (Weston, 1999, p. 790). For instance, when Laura discovers that Wasif, a man she has just met, is a Muslim, she may stereotype him as a chauvinist. If she is a feminist, she may use this stereotype to prejudge him and assume that he will expect women to be subservient. Thus she holds a prejudice against him. If she acts on her prejudice—that is, if she discriminates against Wasif—she may abruptly end her conversation with

stereotypes–*simplified and standardized conceptions about the characteristics or expected behavior of members of an identifiable group.*

THINKING ABOUT . . .

Stereotyping

Think of a recent encounter you have had with someone of a different race or ethnic background. Recall how you felt. To what extent were you comfortable with this person? How did the person's race or ethnic background influence how you acted or reacted? Did it affect the topics you discussed or the care with which you phrased your sentences? To what extent was this conversation effective and satisfying?

prejudice–*a preconceived judgment; a belief or opinion that a person holds without sufficient grounds.*

discrimination–*treating members of one group differently from members of another in a way that is unfair or harmful.*

Bob Daemmrich/Stock, Boston

What is the relationship between these women? How did stereotyping influence your perception?

him. So, without really having gotten to know Wasif, Laura may decide that she does not like him. In this case, Wasif may never get the chance to be known for who he really is, and Laura will have lost an opportunity to get to know someone from a different cultural background.

The Diverse Voices selection in this chapter turns the situation around. What if you are the subject of prejudice or discrimination because you are, in the words of Arturo Madrid, "the other"?

Stereotypes, prejudice, and discrimination, like self-concept and self-esteem, can be difficult to change. People are likely to maintain their stereotypes and prejudices and continue to discriminate against others even in the face of evidence that disproves their stereotypes.

Racism, ethnocentrism, sexism, ageism, able-ism, and other "-isms" occur when a powerful group believes its members are superior to those of another group and that this superiority gives the powerful group the right to dominate or discriminate against the "inferior" group. Because "isms" can be deeply ingrained and subtle, it is easy to overlook behaviors we engage in that are racist or sexist. The behavior appears to be inconsequential, such as directing an African American student to the financial aid line at registration. It may appear unconscious, such as leaving more space between you and a blind person on a bus. Telling jokes, laughing at jokes, or encouraging repetition of jokes that demean women is sexist behavior. So is planning a meeting or flex time only for women employees.

racism, ethnocentrism, sexism, ageism, able-ism *—beliefs that the behaviors or characteristics of one group are inherently superior to those of another group and that this gives the "superior" group the right to dominate or discriminate against the "inferior" group.*

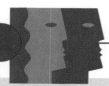

DIVERSE VOICES

Social Perception

by Arturo Madrid

Arturo Madrid served as the President of Tomas Rivera Center, a national institute for policy studies on Hispanic issues. In this selection Madrid describes the conflicting experiences of those who see themselves as different from what has stereotypically been described as "American." Experiencing oneself and being perceived as "other" and "invisible" are powerful determinants of one's self-concept and form a very special filter through which one communicates with others.

My name is Arturo Madrid. I am a citizen of the United States, as are my parents and as were my grandparents, and my great-grandparents. My ancestors' presence in what is now the United States antedates Plymouth Rock, even without taking into account any American Indian heritage I might have.

I do not, however, fit those mental sets that define America and Americans. My physical appearance, my speech patterns, my name, my profession (a professor of Spanish) create a text that confuses the reader.

I am very clearly the *other,* if only your everyday, garden-variety, domestic *other.* I've always known that I was the *other,* even before I knew the vocabulary or understood the significance of otherness.

Despite the operating myth of the day, school did not erase my *otherness.* The true test was not our speech, but rather our names and our appearance, for we would always have an accent, however perfect our pronunciation, however excellent our enunciation, however divine our diction. That accent would be heard in our pigmentation, our physiognomy, our names. We were, in short, the *other.*

Being the *other* involves a contradictory phenomenon. On the one hand, being the *other* frequently means being invisible. On the other hand, being the *other* sometimes involves sticking out like a sore thumb. What is she/he doing here?

If one is the *other,* one will inevitably be seen stereotypically; will be defined and limited by mental sets that may not bear much relation to existing realities.

There is sometimes a darker side to otherness as well. The *other* disturbs, disquiets, discomforts. It provokes distrust and suspicion. The *other* frightens, scares.

For some of us being the *other* is only annoying; for others it is debilitating; for still others it is damning. For the majority otherness is permanently sealed by physical appearance. For the rest otherness is betrayed by ways of being, speaking, or of doing.

The first half of my life I spent downplaying the significance and consequences of otherness. The second half has seen me wrestling to understand its complex and deeply ingrained realities; striving to fathom why otherness denies us a voice or visibility or validity in American society and its institutions; struggling to make otherness familiar, reasonable, even normal to my fellow Americans.

One of the principal strengths of our society is its ability to address on a continuing and substantive basis the real economic, political, and social problems that have faced and continue to face us. What makes the United States so attractive to immigrants are the protections and opportunities it offers; what keeps our society together is tolerance for cultural, religious, social, political, and even linguistic difference; what makes us a unique, dynamic, and extraordinary nation are the power and creativity of our diversity.

The true history of the United States is the one of struggle against intolerance, against oppression, against xenophobia, against those forces that have prohibited persons from participating in the larger life of the society on the basis of their race, their gender, their religion, their national origin, their linguistic and cultural background. These phenomena are not only consigned to the past. They remain with us and frequently take on virulent dimensions.

If you believe, as I do, that the well-being of a society is directly related to the degree and extent to which all of its citizens participate in its institutions, then you will have to agree that we have a challenge before us. In view of the extraordinary changes that are taking place in our society, we need to take up the struggle again, unpleasant as it is. As educated and educator members of this society, we have a special responsibility for assuring that all American institutions, not just our elementary and secondary schools, our juvenile halls, or jails, reflect the diversity of our society. Not to do so is to risk greater alienation on the part of a growing segment of our society; is to risk increased social tension in an already conflictive world; and, ultimately, is to risk the survival of a range of institutions that, for all their defects and deficiencies, provide us the opportunity and the freedom to improve our individual and collective lot.

Let me urge you, as you return to your professional responsibilities and to your personal spaces, to reflect on these two words—*quality* and *diversity*—and on the mental sets and behaviors that flow out of them. And let me urge you further to struggle against the notion that quality is finite in quantity, limited in its manifestations, or is restricted by considerations of class, gender, race, or national origin; or that quality manifests itself only in leaders and not in followers, in managers and not in workers; or that it has to be associated with verbal agility or elegance of personal style; or that it cannot be seeded, or nurtured, or developed.

Excerpted from Arturo Madrid, "Diversity and Its Discontents." From Intercultural Communication: A Reader, *7th ed., eds. Larry A. Samovar and Richard E. Porter (Belmont, CA: Wadsworth, 1994), pp. 127–131. Reprinted by permission of Black Issues in Higher Education.*

All people can be prejudiced and can discriminate. Nevertheless, "prejudices of groups with power are farther reaching in their consequences than others" (Sampson, 1999, p. 131).

Emotional States

A final factor that affects how accurately we perceive others is our emotional state at the time of the interaction. Based on the finding in his studies, Joseph Forgas (1991) has concluded that "there is a broad and pervasive tendency for people to perceive and interpret others in terms of their (own) feelings at the time" (p. 288). If, for example, you received the internship you had applied for, your good mood—brought on by your good fortune—is likely to spill over so that you perceive other things and other people more positively than you might under different circumstances. If, however, you receive a low grade on a paper you thought was well written, your perceptions of people around you are likely to be colored by your disappointment or anger due to this grade.

THINKING ABOUT . . .

Racist and Sexist Talk

Think of a recent situation in which you heard someone tell a racist or sexist joke or make a racist or sexist remark. How did you react? How did others present react? Are you pleased with your reaction? If not, think about how you might have reacted differently.

Our emotions also cause us to engage in selective perceptions, ignoring inconsistent information. For instance, if Donna sees Nick as a man with whom she would like to develop a strong relationship, she will focus on the positive side of Nick's personality and tend to overlook or ignore the negative side that is apparent to others.

Our emotions also may affect our attributions (Forgas, 2000, p. 397). **Attributions** are reasons we give for others' behavior. In addition to making judgments about people, we attempt to construct reasons about why people behave as they do. According to attribution theory, what we determine—rightly or wrongly—to be the causes of others' behavior has a direct impact on our perceptions of them. For instance, suppose a coworker with whom you had a noon luncheon appointment has not arrived by 12:20. If you like and respect your coworker, you are likely to attribute his lateness to something external: an important phone call at the last minute, the need to finish a job before lunch, or some accident that may have occurred. If you are not particularly fond of your coworker, you are likely to attribute his lateness to something internal: forgetfulness, inconsiderateness, or malicious intent. In either case, your causal attribution further affects your perception of the person.

Like prejudices, causal attributions may be so strong that they resist contrary evidence. If you do not particularly care for the person, when he does arrive and explains that he had an emergency long-distance phone call, you are likely to disbelieve the reason or discount the urgency of the call. Being aware of the human tendency toward such cognitive biases can help you correct your perceptions and improve your communication.

In the final part of this chapter we focus on procedures that will enable us to improve our social perceptions of people regardless of their culture or gender.

attributions–*reasons we give for others' behavior.*

TEST YOUR COMPETENCE

Factors Leading to Misperceptions of Others

For the following situation, use the concepts you have studied to identify the factors influencing Amanda's impression of the drycleaning clerk.

Amanda was depressed. Her daughter was having problems in school, she had just been informed that her work hours were being cut back, and her mother was facing possible surgery. On her way home from campus, she stopped at the dry cleaner to pick up her laundry. There was a new man working the counter. From looking at him, Amanda could tell he was quite old. She thought to herself that he could be a problem. When she requested her laundry, he asked to see her claim check. Because no one had ever asked her for this before, Amanda had started throwing these away so she responded that she had thrown the receipt away. "Well," the man firmly replied, "I'm not able to give you clothes without a claim check. It's store policy." After demanding to see the manager and being informed that she had left for the day, Amanda stormed out of the store. "I'll fix him," she fumed to herself. "It's just like an old man to act so rigidly!"

Improving Social Perception

The following guidelines can aid you in constructing a more realistic impression of others as well as in assessing the validity of your own perceptions.

1. **Question the accuracy of your perceptions.** Questioning accuracy begins by saying, "I know what I think I saw, heard, tasted, smelled, or felt, but I could be wrong. What else could help me sort this out?" By accepting the possibility of error, you may be motivated to seek further verification. In situations where the accuracy of perception is important, take a few seconds to double-check. It will be worth the effort.

2. **Seek more information to verify perceptions.** If your perception has been based on only one or two pieces of information, try to collect additional information before you allow yourself to form an impression so that you can increase the accuracy of your perceptions. At least note that your perception is tentative—that is, subject to change. You can then make a conscious effort to collect more data to determine whether the original perception is accurate.

   The best way to get information about people is to talk with them. Unfortunately we tend to avoid people we don't know much about. It's OK to be unsure about how to treat someone from another culture or someone who is disabled. But rather than letting this hold you back, ask the person for the information you need to be more comfortable.

3. **Realize that perceptions of people may need to be changed over time.** People often saddle themselves with perceptions that are based on old or incomplete information and find it easier to stick with a perception, even if it is wrong, than to change it. Willingness to change means making an effort to observe this person's behavior at other times without bias and being prepared to modify your perception if the person's behavior warrants it. It takes strength of character to say to yourself or others, "I was wrong." But communication based on outdated, inaccurate perceptions can be more costly than revising your perceptions.

4. **Use perception checking to verify conclusions you have drawn.** A perception check is a verbal statement that reflects your own understanding of the meaning of another person's *nonverbal* cues. Perception checking calls for you to (1) watch the behavior of the other person, (2) ask yourself, "What does that behavior mean to me?" and (3) put your interpretation of the behavior into words to verify whether your perception is accurate.

   In these two examples the final sentence in each is a perception check:

   Ted, the company messenger, delivers a memo to Erin. As Erin reads the note, her eyes brighten and she breaks into a smile. Ted says, "Hey, Erin, you seem really pleased. Am I right?"

   Cesar, speaking in short, precise sentences with a sharp tone of voice, gives Bill his day's assignment. Bill says, "From the sound of your voice, Cesar, I can't help but get the impression that you're upset with me. Are you?"

perception check–*a verbal statement that reflects your own understanding of the meaning of another person's nonverbal cues.*

Perception checking brings the meaning that was received through nonverbal cues into the verbal realm where it can be verified or corrected. For instance, when Bill says, "I can't help but get the impression that you're upset with me. Are you?" Cesar may say (1) "No, whatever gave you that impression?" in which case Bill can further describe the cues he received; (2) "Yes, I am," in which case Bill can get Cesar to specify what has caused the feelings; or (3) "No, it's not you; it's just that three of my team members didn't show up for this shift." If Cesar is not upset with him, Bill can deal with what caused him to misinterpret Cesar's feelings. If Cesar is upset with him, Bill has the opportunity of changing the behavior that caused Cesar to be upset. Even though you may be correct most of the time in identifying another person's feelings, if you do not verbally perception-check, you are still guessing what the other person is really feeling.

You will want to check your perceptions whenever the accuracy of your understanding is important (1) to your current communication, (2) to the relationship you have with the other person, or (3) to the conclusions you draw about that person. Most of us use this skill far too little, if at all.

Although perception checking may not always eliminate defensive behavior, it can reduce the likelihood of misinterpreting another's nonverbal cues and thus the likelihood of defensiveness. As with most skills, to become competent you must practice.

SKILL BUILDERS   Perception Checking

Skill	Use	Procedure	Example
Making a verbal statement that reflects your understanding of the meaning of another person's nonverbal cues.	To clarify the meaning of non-verbal behavior.	1. Watch the behavior of another. Describe the behavior to yourself or aloud.	Vera comes walking into the room with a completely blank expression and neither speaks to Ann nor acknowledges that she is in the room. Ann says, "Vera, I get the feeling that something has happened to put you in a state of shock. Am I right? Is there something I can do?"
		2. Ask yourself: What does that behavior mean to me?	
		3. Put your interpretation of the nonverbal behavior into words to verify your perception.	

Perception Checking

Write a well-phrased perception check for each of the following situations:

Franco comes home from the doctor's office with pale face and slumped shoulders. Glancing at you with a forlorn look, he shrugs his shoulders.

You say:

As you return the tennis racket you borrowed from Liam, you smile and say, "Here's your racket." Liam stiffens, grabs the racket, and starts to walk away.

You say:

Natalie comes dancing into her room with a huge grin on her face.

You say:

In the past, your adviser has told you that almost any time would be all right for working out your next term's schedule. When you tell her you'll be in Wednesday at 4 p.m., she pauses, frowns, sighs, and says "Uh" and nods.

You say:

Compare your written responses to the guidelines for effective perception checking discussed earlier. Edit your responses where necessary to improve them. Now say them aloud. Do they sound "natural"? If not, revise them until they do.

WHAT WOULD YOU DO?
A QUESTION OF ETHICS

Neikko, a large out-of-town corporation that had just bought out Rustown's major factory, decided to move its headquarters there and to expand the current plant, creating hundreds of new jobs.

Rustown inhabitants had mixed reactions to this takeover. They were excited by the increased business that was expected, but they knew that many of the new factory managers as well as some of the new employees were Japanese. Rustown had never had an Asian family in its community and some of the townspeople openly worried about the effect Japanese would have on their community.

At work on the first day, Sam Nuguki, one of the Neikko managers who had agreed to move to Rustown, noticed that the workers seemed very leery of him, but by the end of the first week the plant was running smoothly and Mr. Nuguki was feeling the first signs of acceptance. On Monday morning of the next week, Mr. Nuguki accidentally overheard a group of workers talking on their break, trading lies about Japanese and using vulgarities and racist slurs in discussing negative stereotypical views.

A bit shaken, Mr. Nuguki returned to his office. He had a problem. He recognized his workers' prejudices, but he did not know how to change them. Moreover, he wanted to establish good work relationships with his workers for the sake of the company, but he also wanted to create a good working atmosphere for other Japanese who would be coming to Rustown. What should Mr. Nuguki do?

Devise a plan for Mr. Nuguki. How could he use his social perceptions of Rustown to address the problem in a way that is within ethical interpersonal communication guidelines?

Summary

Perception is the process of gathering sensory information and assigning meaning to it. Our perceptions are a result of our selection, organization, and interpretation of sensory information. Inaccurate perceptions cause us to see the world not as it is but as we would like it to be.

Self-concept is the idea or mental image you have about your skills, your abilities, your knowledge, your competencies, and your personality. Self-esteem is the degree to which you have a favorable impression of yourself. The inaccuracy of a distorted picture of oneself becomes magnified through self-fulfilling prophecies and by filtering messages. Our self-concept and self-esteem moderate competing internal messages in our self-talk, influence our perception of others, influence our personal communication style, and influence how we present ourselves to others in the roles we play.

Perception also plays an important role in forming impressions of others. Factors that are likely to influence our social perceptions are physical characteristics and social behaviors, stereotyping, and emotional states. Because research shows that the accuracy of people's perceptions and judgments varies considerably, your communication will be most successful if you do not rely entirely on your impressions to determine how another person feels or what that person is really like. You will improve (or at least better understand) your perceptions of others if you take into account physical characteristics and social behaviors, stereotyping, and emotional states.

You can learn to improve perception if you actively question the accuracy of your perceptions, seek more information to verify perceptions, talk with the people about whom you are forming perceptions, realize that perceptions of people need to change over time, and check perceptions verbally before you react.

Communicate! Online

Use your Communicate! CD-ROM for quick access to the electronic study resources that accompany this text. Included on your CD-ROM is access to the Communicate! Web site at the Wadsworth Communication Café. The Communicate! Web site offers chapter-by-chapter activities, quizzes, and a digital glossary.

Review the following key terms and complete the Perception Checking Activity for Chapter 2 online at

http://communication.wadsworth.com/humancomm/verderber

Key Terms

able-ism (41)
ageism (41)
attributions (44)
discrimination (40)
ethnocentrism (41)
halo effect (39)
incongruence (34)
interpret (31)
pattern (31)

perception (30)
perception check (45)
prejudice (40)
racism (41)
role (36)
self-concept (32)
self-esteem (32)
self-fulfilling prophecies (35)
sexism (41)
stereotypes (40)
uncertainty reduction theory (38)

Student Resources - Microsoft Internet Explorer

File   Edit   View   Favorites   Tools   Help

WADSWORTH
THOMSON LEARNING

Close Window

Communicate!
Rudolph F. Verderber
10th Edition
ISBN: 0534561160

Chapter Resources
Step 1: Select a Chapter
Step 2: Select a Resource
Step 3: Click 'Go'

Chapter 2

Activity   Go

Additional
Resources

WWW Links

Perception Checking
Purpose: *to practice effective perception checking*
Process: Fill in a well-phrased perception check for each of the following situations:

Franco comes home from the doctor's office with a pale face and slumped shoulders. Glancing at you with a forlorn look, he shrugs his shoulders.

You say:

As you return the tennis racket you borrowed from Liam, you smile and say, "Here's your racket." Liam stiffens, grabs the racket, and starts to walk away.

You say:

OBJECTIVES

After you have read this chapter, you should be able to answer these questions:

■ What is the relationship between language and meaning?

■ What is the difference between the denotative and the connotative meaning of words?

■ How can you improve your language usage so that it is more precise, specific, and concrete?

■ How can you use the skills of dating and indexing generalizations to increase the accuracy of your messages?

■ What happens when people use language that is inappropriate for the situation?

■ How can you phrase messages so that they are perceived as appropriate for the situation?

Verbal Communication

"Kyle, why do you keep obfuscating the plan?"

"Now just a minute, Derek. There's no need for you to get obscene with me. I may not have looked at the job the same way you did, but I wouldn't, uh . . . I'm not going to lower myself to repeat your language!"

"Obfuscating" means confusing. What in the world did Derek mean when he accused Kyle of "obfuscating the plan"? And why did Kyle think Derek was talking obscenely? Many years ago I. A. Richards (1965) observed that communication is "the study of misunderstanding and its remedy" (p. 3). And in this instance, we have a classic example of misunderstanding. The remedy? Clearer and more appropriate language.

Whether you are trying to iron out a problem with a friend or explain your views on reducing domestic violence in a group discussion or a public speech, your effectiveness will depend on your verbal and nonverbal communication usage. In this chapter, we discuss verbal communication: how people use language, the relationship between language and meaning with emphasis on denotation, connotation, and cultural and gender differences, and the skills that help us speak clearly and appropriately.

The Nature of Language

language–*the body of words and the systems for their use that are common to the people of the same language community.*

Language is the body of words and the systems for their use that are common to the people of the same language community.

Uses of Language

Although language communities vary in the words that they use and in their grammar and syntax systems, all languages serve the same purposes.

1. **We use language to designate, label, define, and limit.** Thus, when we identify a house as a "Tudor," we are differentiating it from another that may be identified as an "A-frame."

2. **We use language to evaluate.** Through language we give positive or negative slants. For instance, if you see Hal taking more time than others to make a decision, you could describe Hal positively as "thoughtful" or negatively as "dawdling."

3. **We use language to discuss things outside our immediate experience.** Language enables us to speak hypothetically, to talk about past and future events, and to communicate about people and things that are not present. Thus, we can use language to discuss where we hope to be in five years, to analyze a conversation two acquaintances had last week, or to learn about the history that shapes the world we live in.

4. **We can use language to talk about language.** We can use language to discuss how someone phrased a statement and whether better phrasing would

---

THINKING ABOUT . . .

Labeling and Limiting

Imagine that you are going to a party with a friend where you are to meet Terrance, who was your friend's best friend in high school. Suppose that your friend has only told you either that Terrance is a Ph.D. student in anthropology at Harvard or that Terrance is a "Big Brother" and regularly volunteers with Habitat for Humanity. Would you have any different expectations of Terrance the Harvard Ph.D. student versus Terrance the Big Brother and volunteer? Suppose both descriptions of Terrance are accurate, how would your expectations change?

have resulted in a clearer meaning or a more positive response. For instance, if your friend said she would see you "this afternoon," but she didn't arrive until 5 o'clock, when you ask her where she's been, the two of you are likely to discuss the meaning of "this afternoon."

Language and Meaning

On the surface, the relationship between language and meaning seems perfectly clear: We select the correct word, and people will interpret our meaning correctly. In fact, the relationship between language and meaning is not nearly so simple for two reasons: Language must be learned, and the use of language is a creative act.

First, we are not born knowing a language. Rather, each generation within a language community learns the language anew. We learn much of our language early in life from our families; much more we learn in school. But we do not all learn to use the same words in the same way.

A second reason the relationship between language and meaning is complicated is that even though languages have systems of syntax and grammar each utterance is a creative act. When we speak, we use language to create new sentences that represent our meaning. Although on occasion we repeat other people's sentence constructions to represent what we are thinking or feeling, some of our talk is unique.

A third reason language and meaning is so complicated is that people interpret the meaning of words differently. Words have two kinds of meaning: denotative and connotative. Thus, when Melissa tells Trish that her dog died, what Trish understands Melissa to mean depends on both word denotation and connotation.

Denotation The direct, explicit meaning a language community formally gives a word is its **denotation**. Word denotation is the meaning found in a dictionary. So, denotatively, when Melissa said her dog died, she meant that her domesticated canine no longer demonstrates physical life. In some situations the denotative meaning of a word may not be clear. Why? First, dictionary definitions reflect current and past practice in the language community; and second, the dictionary uses words to define words. The end result is that words are defined differently in various dictionaries and often include multiple meanings that change over time.

Moreover, meaning may vary depending on the context in which the word is used. For example, the dictionary definition of *gay* includes both having or showing a merry, lively mood and homosexual. Thus, **context,** the position of a word in a sentence and the other words around it, has an important effect on correctly interpreting which denotation of a word is meant. Not only will the other words and the syntax and grammar of a verbal message help us to understand the denotative meaning of certain words, but so will the situation in which they are spoken. Whether the comment "He's really gay" is understood to be a comment on someone's sexual orientation or on his merry mood may depend on the circumstances in which it is said.

OBSERVE & ANALYZE
Journal Activity

Denotative Meanings

1. Under Journal Activity 3.1 in your Student Workbook, compile a list of ten slang or "in" words. Discuss how the meanings you assign to these words differ from the meanings your parents or grandparents assign to them (for example, "He's bad!").

2. Write your own definition of each of the following words; then go to a dictionary and see how closely your definition matches the dictionary's.

building	justice
love	ring
success	band
glass	peace
freedom	honor

denotation—*the direct, explicit meaning a language community formally gives a word.*

context—*the position of a word in a sentence and the other words around it.*

connotation–*the feelings or evaluations we associate with a word.*

Connotation   The feelings or evaluations we associate with a word represent the **connotation** and may be even more important to our understanding of meaning.

C. K. Ogden and I. A. Richards (1923) were among the first scholars to consider the misunderstandings resulting from the failure of communicators to realize that their subjective reactions to words are based on their life experiences. For instance, when Melissa tells Trisha that her dog died, Trisha's understanding of the message depends on the extent to which her feelings about pets and death—her connotations of the words—correspond to the feelings that Melissa has about pets and death. Melissa, who sees dogs as truly indispensable friends, may be trying to communicate a true sense of grief, but Trish, who has never had a pet and doesn't particularly care for dogs, may miss the sense of Melissa's statement.

Word denotation and connotation are important because the only message that counts is the message that is understood, regardless of whether it is the message you intended.

Meaning Varies across Subgroups in the Language Community

As we mentioned earlier, within a larger language community, subgroups with unique cultures are sometimes formed. These subgroups develop variations on the core language that enable them to share meanings unique to their subcultural experience. People from different subcultures approach the world from

DIVERSE VOICES

That's Greek to Me: Between a Rock and a Hard Place in Intercultural Encounters

by Wen-Shu Lee

In addition to word connotation, idiomatic language (an expression in the usage of a language that is peculiar to itself either grammatically or in having a meaning that cannot be derived from the conjoined meanings of its elements) also makes communication between and among cultures difficult. This excerpt both exemplifies the concept of an idiom and shows why its use is frustrating to people of different cultures.

There are four reasons why idioms should be an important subject in intercultural communication. First, idioms are figurative in nature.

Second, figurative meanings often cause comprehension problems for people from different cultures. Third, we do not explain idioms completely.

Finally, idioms open up an avenue to interpersonal closeness. Let me explain these related reasons in detail for you.

First, an idiom and its meaning often do not match because they have a *figurative* rather than a *literal* relationship. The meaning of an idiom is rarely predictable from its constituent components; consider, "bought the farm," "get your feet wet," "get your hands dirty," "a wild goose chase," "like a duck on a June bug." Like the "It's Greek to me" example, "bought the farm" has no literal relationship with "someone died," and "like a duck on a June bug" has no literal relationship with "I will confront you immediately with what you have done."

Second, communication breakdowns often occur when people use idioms in communicating with those who do not comprehend the idiomatic meaning. For people who use idioms "naturally," the figurative link between an idiom and its meaning often goes unnoticed. But this link becomes problematic for those who do not share the lifeworld with the idiom users. This problem is more easily solved by those who speak English as a first language (hereafter, L1 speakers) than those who speak English as a second language (hereafter, L2 speakers). For example, a young college student, Susan, living in San Jose uses "Check it out, there's a stud muffin" with her friend, Jenny, while shopping with her Mom. Her mother, an L1 speaker in her fifties who does not share the lifeworld of "college life" with Susan and Jenny, may ask "What do you mean by a 'stud muffin'?" knowing that it is an expression among young people that she is not familiar with. But if Susan and Jenny are shopping with an L2 speaker, Huei-Mei, the problem becomes more complex. She may not hear "stud muffin" clearly. Or, she may hear the idiom but remain quiet about it, suspecting that her English is not good enough. Even if she has the courage to ask for the meaning of "stud muffin," Huei-Mei may still have a hard time linking "a handsome guy" with "a male breeding horse" and "English breakfast food." Finally, even if she knows the linguistic meaning of "stud muffin," she may use

it in an inappropriate relational context. For example, she may want to compliment her handsome seminar professor: "Professor Spano, you are a stud muffin." Therefore, the study of idioms is important to intercultural communication competence.

Third, as is apparent in the stud muffin, a complete explanation of an idiom requires a linguistic discussion about the meaning of idiom words and a relational discussion about the association between the two people who use an idiom together. Most of us engage in a linguistic explanation but leave out the relational one. For example, Susan forgets to tell Huei-Mei that "stud muffin" is used between friends (usually females) to comment on a third person, a handsome male. We do not use it with someone who has a formal, professional relationship with us. Huei-Mei as a result, needs to know that one should not use "stud muffin" with a professor. For this reason, we need to study idiom explanations more carefully in intercultural encounters.

Finally, idioms hold one of the keys to interpersonal closeness. Idioms are commonly used in informal situations between casual acquaintances, friends, and pals. The ability to use idioms accepted by a group may not guarantee closeness, but it can increase the possibilities of shortening interpersonal distance if so desired. That is, if people from different cultural backgrounds can use each other's idioms, formal and awkward discomfort may be replaced by a sense of informality and even closeness. This may facilitate intercultural relationships in a variety of contexts—interpersonal relationships between classmates and friends, working relationships in a company, and teaching–learning relationships in the classroom.

Excerpted from Wen-Shu Lee, "That's Greek to Me: Between a Rock and a Hard Place in Intercultural Encounters." From Intercultural Communication: A Reader, *8th ed., eds. Larry A. Samovar and Richard E. Porter (Belmont, CA: Wadsworth, 1997), pp. 213–221. Reprinted by permission of the author.*

different perspectives, so they are likely to experience some difficulty sharing meaning when they talk with each other. As the Diverse Voices feature showed, one of the most confounding uses of language and its interpretation for people from different cultures is the use of idioms.

In addition to subgroups based on race, religion, and national origin, there are also subgroup cultures associated with generation, social class, and political interests. The need for awareness and sensitivity in applying our communication skills does not depend on someone's being an immigrant or from a different ethnic background. Rather, the need for being aware of potential language differences is important in every type of communication. Developing our language skills so that the messages we send are clear and sensitive will increase our communication effectiveness in every situation.

Speaking More Clearly

Regardless of whether we are conversing, communicating in groups, or giving speeches, we can speak more clearly by reducing the ambiguity and confusion. Compare these two descriptions of a close call in an automobile: "Some nut almost got me with his car a while ago" versus "An older man in a banged-up Honda Civic crashed the light at Calhoun and Clifton and came within inches of hitting me last week while I was waiting to turn left at the cross street." The differences are in clarity. In the second example, the message used language that was specific, concrete, and precise as well as statements that are dated and indexed.

Specificity, Concreteness, and Precision in Language Use

specific words—*words that clarify meaning by narrowing what is understood from a general category to a particular item or group within that category.*

Specific words clarify meaning by narrowing what is understood from a general category to a particular item or group within that category. Thus saying "It's a

Frank and Ernest

Frank & Ernest reprinted by permission of NEA, Inc.

Honda Civic" is more specific than saying "It's a car." **Concrete words** are sense-related. In effect we can see, hear, smell, taste, or touch concrete words. Thus we can picture that "banged up" Civic. Abstract ideas, such as justice, equality, or fairness, can be made concrete through examples or metaphors. **Precise words** are those that most accurately express meaning—they capture shades of difference. It is more precise to note that the Civic came "within inches of hitting me" than it is to say "some nut almost got me."

Often, as we try to express our thoughts, the first words that come to mind are general, abstract, and imprecise. The ambiguity of these words makes the listener choose from many possible images rather than picturing the single focused image we have in mind. The more listeners are called on to provide their own images, the more likely they are to see meanings different from what we intend.

For instance, if Nevah says that Ruben is a "blue-collar worker," you might picture any number of occupations that fall within this broad category. If, instead, she is more specific and says he's a "construction worker," the number of possible images you can picture is reduced. Now you select your image from the subcategory of construction worker, and your meaning is likely to be closer to the one she intended. If she is even more specific, she may say "Ruben is a bulldozer operator." Now you "see" Ruben driving the dozer, and you are clearer on Ruben's occupation.

In the preceding example, the continuum of specificity goes from blue-collar worker to construction worker to construction vehicle operator to bulldozer operator. Figure 3.1 provides another illustration of this continuum.

concrete words–*words that appeal to our senses; we can see them, hear them, smell them.*

precise words–*words that most accurately express meaning, capturing shades of difference.*

OBSERVE & ANALYZE
Journal Activity

Synonyms

One good way to increase specificity, concreteness, and precision is to play "synonyms." Think of a word, then list words that mean about the same thing. For example, synonyms for "happy" are *glad, joyful,* and *pleased.* When you have completed your list, refer to a book of synonyms, such as *Roget's Thesaurus,* to find other words. Then, under Journal Activity 3.2 in your Student Workbook, write what you think is the meaning of each word, focusing on the shades of difference in meaning among the words. When you are done, look up each word, even those of which you are sure of the meaning. The goal of this exercise is to select the most specific, concrete, or precise word to express your idea.

Art

Painting

Oil painting

Impressionist oil painting

Renoir's *La Promenade*

Figure 3.1
Levels of specificity.

COMMUNICATE!
Using Technology

How your ideas are worded can make a great deal of difference in whether people will understand or be influenced by what you say. You can use your word processing software to help you with your brainstorming. Nearly every word processing package has a thesaurus (a list of words and their synonyms) for the user to access. For instance, in the Microsoft Word package, the user can highlight a specific word, click on "Tools," drag down to "Thesaurus," and be presented with synonyms for that word. For practice, select any word that you would like to improve upon and look at the synonym choices available. Then select the choice you believe would be most meaningful. For instance, if you highlighted "difficult" when you clicked on the Thesaurus, you would be shown *hard, laborious, arduous,* and *strenuous*. If you wanted more choices, you could then highlight one of these words to see additional choices. If you are trying to make the point that studying can be difficult, you might decide to use *arduous* as the most precise word. Merriam-Webster's online Collegiate® Thesaurus is available at www.m-w.com/thesaurus.html

As we move from general to specific, we also move from abstract to concrete. Consider the word *speak*. This is a general, abstract term. To make it more concrete, we can use words such as *mumble, whisper, bluster, drone, jeer,* or *rant*. Say these words aloud. Notice the different sound of your voice when you say *whisper* as opposed to *bluster, jeer,* or *rant*.

Finally, we seek words that are precise—those that most accurately or correctly capture the sense of what we are saying. In seeking the most precise word to describe Phillip's speech, at first we might say, "Phillip blustered. Well, to be more precise, he ranted." Notice that we are not moving from general to specific; both words are on roughly the same level of abstraction. Nor are we talking about abstract versus concrete; both words are concrete. Rather, we are now concerned with precision in meaning. *Blustering* means talking in a way that is loudly boastful; *ranting* means talking in a way that is noisy or bombastic. So, what we are considering here is shades of meaning: Depending on how the person was talking, *blustering* or *ranting* would be the more precise word. Let's try another one. "Susan laughed at my story; well, to be more precise, she chuckled." What do you see as the difference between laughing and chuckling? A laugh is a loud show of mirth; a chuckle is a more gentle sound expressing suppressed mirth. Similar? Yes. But different—showing shades of meaning.

Although specific, concrete, and precise words enable us to reduce ambiguity and sharpen meaning through individual words, sometimes clarity is best achieved by adding a detail or an example. For instance, Linda says, "Rashad is very loyal." The meaning of "loyal" (faithful to an idea, person, company, and so on) is abstract, so to avoid ambiguity and confusion, Linda might add, "He never criticizes a friend behind her back." By following up her use of the abstract concept of loyalty with a concrete example, Linda makes it easier for her listeners to "ground" their idea of this personal quality in a concrete or "real" experience.

You will know that you have improved your message clarity when instead of saying "He lives in a *really big house,*" you say "He lives in a *fourteen-room Tudor mansion.*" Or instead of saying, "I think Prof. Morgan is a *fair grader,*" you say, "I think Prof. Morgan is a fair grader; she *uses the same standards for grading all students.*"

Developing the Ability to Speak More Clearly

Being able to speak more clearly requires us to build our working vocabulary and to brainstorm to generate word choices from our active vocabulary.

Vocabulary building   As a speaker, the larger your vocabulary, the more choices you have from which to select the word you want. As a listener, the larger your vocabulary, the more likely you are to understand the words used by others.

One way to increase your vocabulary is to study one of the many vocabulary building books on the shelves of most any bookstore, such as *Merriam*

Webster's Vocabulary Builder (Cornog, 1998). You might also study magazine features such as "Word Power" in the *Reader's Digest*. By completing this monthly quiz and learning the words with which you are not familiar, you could increase your vocabulary by as many as twenty words per month.

A second way to increase your vocabulary is to make note of words that you read or that people use in their conversations with you and look them up. For instance, suppose you read or hear, "I was inundated with phone calls today!" If you wrote inundated down and looked it up in a dictionary later, you would find that "inundated" means *overwhelmed* or *flooded*. If you then say to yourself, "She was inundated—overwhelmed or flooded—with phone calls today," you are likely to remember that meaning and apply it the next time you hear the word. If you follow this practice, you will soon notice the increase in your vocabulary.

Mental brainstorming Having a larger vocabulary won't help your speaking if you do not have a procedure for using it. One way to practice accessing choices from your memory is to brainstorm during practice sessions and later in conversation. **Brainstorming** is an uncritical, nonevaluative process of generating alternatives. Suppose someone asked you about how well preregistration was working. You might initially say, "Preregistration is awful." If you don't think that *awful* is the right word, you might be able to quickly brainstorm the words *frustrating, demeaning, cumbersome,* and *annoying.* Then you could say, "What I really meant to say is that preregistration is overly cumbersome."

brainstorming–*an uncritical, nonevaluative process of generating alternatives.*

Clearly stating our verbal messages is hard work, but as you build your vocabulary and learn to mentally brainstorm, you will find that you are able to make such adjustments even in the middle of sentences when you need to. For instance, to describe Mike's behavior you might say, "Mike was just a jerk yesterday—well, I guess I mean he was inconsiderate." Or when you are analyzing Pauline's talents you might say, "I agree that Pauline is a tough manager, but I think she's a good one because she is fair—she treats everyone exactly alike."

When we are relaxed and confident, our word choice flows smoothly and is likely to be most effective. When we are under pressure, however, our ability to select the best symbols to convey our thoughts is likely to deteriorate. People

TEST YOUR COMPETENCE

Brainstorming

Set up a tape recorder and talk about a course you are taking, a game, or a movie you saw. When you come to a key word or phrase as you talk, assess whether that word or phrase is specific, precise, or concrete enough for your message to be correctly understood. If you think not, pause momentarily to brainstorm alternative word choices, and then use the more specific, precise, or concrete word.

SKILL BUILDERS   Clarity—Specific, Concrete, Precise Words

Skill	Use	Procedure	Example
Clarify meaning by narrowing what is understood from a general category to a particular group within that category, by appealing to the senses, or by choosing words that symbolize exact thoughts and feelings.	To help the listener picture thoughts analogous to the speaker's.	1. Assess whether the word or phrase used is less specific, concrete, or precise than it should be. 2. Pause to mentally brainstorm alternatives. 3. Select a more specific, concrete, or precise word.	Instead of saying, "Bring the stuff for the audit," say, "Bring the records and receipts from the last year for the audit." Or, instead of saying "I was really cold," say "I nearly froze."

sometimes think one thing and say something entirely different. For example, a math professor might say, "We all remember that the numerator is on the bottom and the denominator is on the top of the fraction, so when we divide fractions. . . ." "Professor," a voice from the third row interrupts, "You said the numerator is on the bottom and. . . ." "Is that what I said?" the professor replies. "Well, you know what I meant!" Did everyone in the class know? Probably not.

You will really know that you have made strides in improving specificity, precision, and concreteness when you find that you can form clear messages even under pressure.

TEST YOUR COMPETENCE

Specific, Concrete, and Precise

1. For each word listed, find three words or phrases that are more specific or more concrete.

implements	building	nice	education
clothes	colors	chair	bad
happy	stuff	things	car

2. Make the following statements clearer by editing words that are not precise or not specific and concrete:

"You know I love basketball. Well, I'm practicing a lot because I want to get better."

"Paula, I'm really bummed out. Everything is going down the tubes. You know what I mean?"

"Well, she just does these things to tick me off. Like, just a whole lot of stuff—and she knows it!"

"I just bought a beautiful outfit—I mean, it is really in style. You'll love it."

"I've really got to remember to bring my things the next time I visit."

Dating Information

Because nearly everything changes with time, it is important that we **date** the information we communicate by telling when it was true. Not dating leads to inaccuracies that can be dangerous. For instance, Parker says, "I'm going to be transferred to Henderson City." Laura replies, "Good luck—they've had some real trouble with their schools." On the basis of Laura's statement, Parker may worry about the effect his move will have on his children. What he doesn't know is that Laura's information about this problem in Henderson City is five years old! Henderson City still may have problems, but then, it may not. Had Laura replied, "Five years ago, I know they had some real trouble with their schools. I'm not sure what the situation is now, but you may want to check," Parker would look at the information differently.

Let's consider two additional examples:

dating information—telling when the information was true.

Undated: Professor Powell brings great enthusiasm to her teaching.

Dated: Professor Powell brings great enthusiasm to her teaching—at least she did *last quarter* in communication theory.

Undated: You think Mary's depressed? I'm surprised. She seemed her regular high-spirited self when I talked with her.

Dated: You think Mary's depressed? I'm surprised. She seemed her regular high-spirited self when I talked with her *the day before yesterday.*

To date information, (1) consider or find out when the information was true and (2) verbally acknowledge it. We have no power to prevent change. Yet we can increase the effectiveness of our messages through verbally acknowledging the reality of change if we date the statements we make.

Indexing Generalizations

Generalizing—drawing a conclusion from particulars—enables people to use what they have learned from one experience and apply it to another. For instance, when Glenda learns that tomatoes and squash grow better if the ground is fertilized, she generalizes that fertilizing will help all of her vegetables grow better. Glenda has used what she learned from one experience and applied it to another.

Indexing generalizations is the mental and verbal practice of acknowledging that individual cases can differ from the general trend while still allowing us to draw on generalizations. For instance, we may have a generalized concept of "men." But we must recognize that although Fred, Darnell, and William are all men, they are likely to have individual differences. So, how do we index in ordinary speaking? Let's consider two examples:

generalizing—drawing a conclusion from particulars.

indexing—the mental and verbal practice of acknowledging individual differences while still allowing us to draw generalizations.

Generalization: Because men are stronger than women, Max is stronger than Barbara.

Indexed Statement: In general men are stronger than women, so *Max is probably stronger* than Barbara.

Generalization: Your Chevrolet should go 50,000 miles before you need a brake job; Jerry's did.

Indexed Statement: Your Chevrolet may well go 50,000 miles before you need a brake job; Jerry's did, *but of course, all Chevrolets aren't the same.*

To index, (1) consider whether what you want to say is about a specific object, person, or place, or whether it is a generalization about a class to which the object, person, or place belongs. (2) If what you want to say is a generalization about the class, qualify it appropriately so that your assertion does not go beyond the evidence that supports it. All people generalize at one time or another, but by indexing statements we can avoid the problems that hasty generalization sometimes creates.

Cultural Differences in Verbal Communication

Cultures vary in how much meaning is embedded in the language itself and how much meaning is interpreted from the context in which the communication occurs.

low-context cultures—
information is embedded mainly in messages transmitted and presented directly.

high-context cultures—
messages are presented indirectly, and individuals must infer meaning from the physical, social, and relational context.

In **low-context cultures,** such as in Northern Europe or the United States, meaning (1) is embedded mainly in the messages transmitted and (2) is presented directly. In low-context cultures, people say what they mean and get right to the point (Gudykunst & Matsumoto, 1996, pp. 29–30). So, in a low-context culture, "Yes" means "Affirmative, I agree with what you have said." In **high-context cultures,** such as Asian or Middle Eastern countries, meaning is interpreted based on the physical, social, and relational context. High-context culture people expect others to use context cues to interpret meaning. As a result, they present meanings indirectly. In a high-context culture, "Yes" may mean "Affirmative, I agree with what you have said," or it may mean "In this setting it would embarrass you if I said 'No,' so I will say 'Yes,' to be polite, but I really don't agree and you should know this, so in the future don't expect me to act as if I have just agreed with what you said." People from high-context cultures expect others to understand unarticulated feelings and subtle nonverbal gestures that people from low-context cultures don't even process. As a result, misunderstandings often occur.

The United States has a low-context national culture, as described previously. But the United States is a country of immigrants, and we know that individual Americans differ in whether they are high or low context in their approach to language. So, although knowing the characteristics of a national culture or culture of origin may be useful, we still need to be aware that people may or may not behave in line with their ethnic cultures (Adamopoulos, 1999, p. 75). Then why mention these differences at all? Because they give us a clue to

Suzanne Szasz/Photo Researchers, Inc.

Cultural traditions influence how we learn and interpret language.

how and why people and cultures may differ. An essential aspect of communication is being sensitive to needs and differences among us, so we must be aware of what the nature of those differences might be.

Gender Differences in Verbal Communication

Over the last two decades, stirred by such book titles as *Men Are from Mars, Women Are from Venus,* people have come to believe gender differences in verbal messages are genetic. Yet research strongly states that differences in gender behaviors are learned rather than biological and that the differences are not nearly as large as portrayed (Wood & Dindia, 1998, pp. 34–36).

There is no evidence to suggest that the differences that have been identified between women's message construction patterns and those of men cause "problems" for either group (Canary & Hause, 1993, p. 141). Nevertheless, a number of specific differences between women's and men's speech patterns have been found, and understanding what has led to them has intrigued scholars. Mulac (1998) notes two differences in language usage between men and women that seem to have the greatest support (pp. 133–134):

1. **Women tend to use both more intensifiers and more hedges than men.** Intensifiers are words that modify other words and serve to strengthen the idea represented by the original word. So, according to studies of the actual speech practices of men and women, women are more likely to use words such as *awfully, quite,* and *so* (as in "It was quite lovely" or "This is so

important"). Hedges are modifying words that soften or weaken the meaning of the idea represented by the original word. According to the research, women are likely to make greater use of such words as *somewhat, perhaps,* or *maybe* (as in "It was somewhat interesting that . . ." or "It may be significant that . . .").

2. **Women ask questions more frequently than men.** Women are much more likely to include questions like "Do you think so?" and "Are you sure?" In general, women tend to use questions to gain more information, get elaboration, and determine how others feel about the information.

But are these differences really important? Mulac goes on to report that "our research has shown that language used by U.S. women and men is remarkably similar. In fact, it is so indistinguishable that native speakers of American English cannot correctly identify which language examples were produced by women and which were produced by men" (p. 130). If this is so, then why even mention differences? Even though the differences are relatively small, they have judgmental consequences: "Observers perceive the female and male speakers differently based on their language use" (p. 147). Female speakers are rated higher on *socio-intellectual status* and *aesthetic quality.* Thus people perceive women as having high social status, being literate, and being pleasant as a result of perceived language differences. Men rated higher on *dynamism.* That is, people perceive men to be stronger and more aggressive as a result of their language differences. These judgments tend to be the same whether observers are male or female, middle-aged or young (p. 148).

Julia Wood (1997) explains these differences in language usage as resulting from differences in the basic psychological orientation each sex acquires in growing up. Women establish gender identity by seeing themselves as "like" or connected to mother. They learn to use communication as a primary way of establishing and maintaining relationships with others (p. 167). Men establish their gender identity by understanding how they are different or "separate" from mother. Thus they use talk as a way to "exert control, preserve independence, and enhance status" (p. 173).

Speaking Appropriately

During the last few years, we have had frequent discussions and disagreements in the United States about "political correctness." Colleges and universities have been on the forefront of this debate. Although several issues germane to the debate on political correctness go beyond the scope of this chapter, at the heart of this controversy is the question of what language behaviors are appropriate—and what language behaviors are inappropriate.

Speaking appropriately means choosing language and symbols that are adapted to the needs, interests, knowledge, and attitudes of listeners in order to avoid language that alienates them. Through appropriate language, we communicate our respect and acceptance of those who are different from us. In this section, we discuss specific strategies that will help you craft appropriate verbal messages.

speaking appropriately– *choosing language and symbols that are adapted to the needs, interests, knowledge, and attitudes of the listener.*

Formality of Language

Language should be appropriately formal for the situation. Thus, in interpersonal settings, we are likely to use more informal language when we are talking with our best friend and more formal language when we are talking with our parents. In a group setting, we are likely to use more informal language when we are talking with a group of our peers and more formal language when we are talking with a group of managers. In a public-speaking setting, we are likely to use more formal language than in either interpersonal or group settings.

One type of formality in language that we usually observe is the manner by which we address others. In formal settings, we address others by their titles followed by their surnames unless they invite us to do something else. So in business settings or at formal parties, it is appropriate to call people "Mr. X," "Ms. B," "Rabbi Z," "Dr. S," or "Professor P." In addition, we generally view it as appropriate to refer to those older than we are, those of higher status, or those whom we respect by title and surname unless otherwise directed.

Jargon and Slang

Appropriate language should be chosen so that **jargon** (technical terminology) and **slang** (informal, nonstandard vocabulary) do not interfere with understanding. We form language communities as a result of the work we do, our hobbies, and the subcultures with which we identify. But we can forget that people who are not in our same line of work or who do not have the same hobbies or are not from our group may not understand language that seems to be such a part of our daily communication. For instance, when Jenny, who is sophisticated in the use of cyberlanguage, starts talking with her computer-illiterate friend Sarah about "Social MUDs based on fictional universes," Sarah is likely to be totally lost. If, however, Jenny

jargon–*technical terminolgy or characteristic idiom of a special activity or group.*

slang–*informal nonstandard vocabulary.*

Shoe by Jeff MacNelly; reprinted by permission of Tribune Media Services.

recognizes Sarah's lack of sophistication in cyberlanguage, she can work to make her language appropriate by discussing the concepts in words that her friend understands. In short, when talking with people outside your language community, you need to carefully explain, if not abandon, the technical jargon or slang.

Profanity and Vulgar Expressions

Appropriate language does not include profanity or vulgar expressions. There was a time when uttering "hell" or "damn" would have resulted in severe punishment for children and social isolation for adults. Today we tend to tolerate commonplace profanities and vulgarities, and there are many subcultures where the use of profanity and vulgarity are commonplace. Under the influence of film and television writers who aim to scintillate and entertain, we have become inoculated to these expressions. In fact, it is common to hear elementary schoolchildren utter strings of "four letter" words in school hallways, lunchrooms, and on playgrounds.

Why do people swear and engage in coarse language? DeKlerk (1991, p. 165) suggests that swearing is one way of asserting independence by breaking adult taboos. In a society that prizes adulthood and independence, the movement to increase vulgar and profane use of language at younger and younger ages is not surprising. Despite this trend in our society, we believe profane and vulgar language continues to be inappropriate in most settings (especially public speaking). Even in informal conversation, it is offensive to many people, although our current social conventions would preclude them from stating this.

Unfortunately, profanity and vulgarity are habits that are easily acquired and hard to extinguish. In fact, an alarming number of people use such language as filler expressions, which add little or no meaning to the content of the message. These expressions are liberally peppered into the verbal message out of habit. Thus for some folks the ubiquitous "f--k" has come to serve the same purpose as "like" and "you know."

What does the use of profanity communicate? Well, when used infrequently, profanity and vulgar expressions communicate strong emotions for which there may be no other appropriate words. Profanity and vulgarity are meant to shock and to communicate one's deep disgust or contempt. When profanity and vulgarity are used frequently, others assume that the person using these expressions intends them to threaten or intimidate. Unfortunately, for far too many people, profanity and vulgarity have lost all meaning and have become nothing more than symbols that the individual is unable to express his or her thoughts or feelings at any but the basest and most ignorant level. Competent communicators avoid using profanity and vulgarity because their use is more likely to damage than to strengthen relationships.

Sensitivity

Language is appropriate when it is sensitive to usages that others perceive as offensive. Some of the mistakes in language that we make result from using expressions that are perceived to be sexist, racist, or otherwise biased—that is,

---

THINKING ABOUT ...

Profanity and Vulgarity

How much do you use profanity and vulgarity? Has your usage increased, decreased, or remained the same since you started college? Does your use of profanity and vulgarity change depending on whom you are speaking with? If so, articulate the decision rules that seem to guide your behavior. Overall, how comfortable are you with how frequently you use profanity and vulgarity in your verbal messages?

any language that is perceived as belittling any person or group of people by virtue of their sex, race, age, handicap, or other identifying characteristic. Two of the most prevalent linguistic uses that communicate an insensitivity are generic language and nonparallel language.

Generic language   Generic language uses words that may apply only to one sex, race, or gender as though they represent both sexes, races, or genders. Such use is a problem because it linguistically excludes part of the group of people it ostensibly includes. Let's consider some examples.

Traditionally, English grammar called for the use of the masculine pronoun *he* to stand for the entire class of humans regardless of sex. So, in the past, standard English called for such usage as, "When a person shops, *he* should have a clear idea of what *he* wants to buy." Even though these statements are grammatically correct, they are now considered sexist because they inherently exclude females. Despite traditional usage, it would be hard to maintain that we picture people of both sexes when we hear the masculine word *he*.

One way to avoid this problem is to recast the sentence using plurals. Instead of "Because a doctor has high status, his views may be believed regardless of topic," you could say "Because doctors have high status, their views may be believed regardless of topic." Alternatively, you can use both male and female pronouns: "Because a doctor has high status, his or her views may be believed regardless of topic." These changes may seem small, but they may mean the difference between alienating and not alienating the people with whom you are speaking. Stewart, Cooper, Stewart, and Friedley (1998) cite research to show that using "he and she," and to a lesser extent "they," gives rise to listeners' including women in their mental images, thus increasing gender balance in their perceptions (p. 63).

A second problem results from the traditional reliance on the use of the generic *man*. Many words have become a common part of our language that are inherently sexist because they seem to apply to only one gender. Consider the term *manmade*. What this really means is that a product was produced by human beings, but its underlying connotation is that a male human being made the item. Some people try to argue that just because a word has "man" within it does not really affect people's understanding of meaning. But research has demonstrated that people usually visualize men (not women) when they read or hear these words. Moreover, when job titles end in "man," their occupants are assumed to have stereotypically masculine personality traits (Gmelch, 1998, p. 51).

When considering such words as *policeman, postman,* and *chairman,* you can substitute *police officer, mail carrier,* and *chairperson.* When considering such words as *mankind* and *manmade,* substitute *humankind* and *made by hand.*

Nonparallel language   Nonparallel language occurs when terms are changed because of the sex, race, or other characteristic of the individual. Because it treats groups of people differently, nonparallel language is also belittling. Two common forms of nonparallelism are marking and unnecessary association.

COMMUNICATE! Using InfoTrac College Edition

Although it is easy to spot sexism in language when someone uses a negative slang term to describe a person of the opposite sex, there are other ways language can be considered "sexist."

Using the InfoTrac College Edition subject guide, enter the search term "sexism in language." Click on "Periodical references." See "Gender Issues in Advertising Language," Nancy Artz (1999). Focus on one of the issues discussed in the article. What is the significance of the examples presented? Why should people be concerned about this issue?

Marking means adding sex, race, age, or other designations unnecessarily to a general word. For instance, saying "female" doctor or "black" lawyer would be marking. Marking is offensive to some people because the speaker appears to be trivializing the person's role by emphasizing an irrelevant characteristic. For instance, this usage seems to imply that Jones is a good doctor for a woman or Smith is a good lawyer for a black person. Because you would be very unlikely to ever say "Jones is a good male doctor" and "Smith is a good white lawyer," leave sex, race, age, and other markers out of your labeling.

Another form of nonparallelism is to emphasize one person's association with another when you are not talking about the other person. Very often you will hear a speaker say something like this: "Gladys Thompson, whose husband is CEO of Acme Inc., is the chairperson for this year's United Way campaign." In response to this sentence, you might say that the association of Gladys Thompson with her husband gives further credentials to Gladys Thompson. But using the association may be seen to imply that Gladys Thompson is important not because of her own accomplishment but because of her husband's. If a person has done or said something noteworthy, you should recognize it without making unnecessary associations.

Very few people can escape all unfair language. By monitoring your usage, however, you can guard against frustrating your attempts to communicate by assuming that others will react to your language the same way you do, and you can guard against saying or doing things that offend others and perpetuate outdated sex roles, racial stereotypes, and other biased language.

How can you speak more appropriately? (1) Assess whether the word or phrase used is less appropriate than it should be; (2) pause to mentally brainstorm alternatives; and (3) select a more appropriate word.

Causes and Effects of Insensitive Language

You've heard children shout, "Sticks and stones may break my bones, but words will never hurt me." This rhyme may be popular among children because they know it is a lie, but it gives them a defense against cruel name-calling. Whether we admit it or not, words do hurt, sometimes permanently. Insensitive language is often a sign of prejudice that results in efforts to discriminate and as a result may be considered unethical as well. Think of the great personal damage done to individuals throughout history as a result of being called "hillbilly," "nigger," "fag," or "yid." Think of the fights started by one person calling another's sister or girlfriend a "whore." Of course, we all know that it is not the words alone that are so powerful; it is the context of the words—the situation, the feelings of the participants, the time, the place, or the tone of voice. You may recall circumstances in which a friend called you a name or used a four-letter word to describe you and you did not even flinch; you may also recall other circumstances in which someone else made you furious by calling you something far less offensive.

Where does offensive racist language come from? According to Molefi Asante (1998), an internationally known scholar, racist language has its roots in our personal beliefs and attitudes. To a great extent, these have been conditioned by the knowledge system to which we have been exposed. Until recently, this knowledge system has had a Eurocentric bias (1998, pp. 95–96). Thus the contributions to the development of humankind by cultures other than European have been ignored or minimized.

We should always be aware that our language has repercussions. When we do not understand or are not sensitive to our listeners' frame of reference, we may state our ideas in language that distorts the intended communication. Many times a single inappropriate sentence may be enough to ruin an entire interaction. For instance, if you say, "And we all know the problem originates downtown," you may be alluding to the city government. However, if the listeners associate downtown not with the seat of government but with the residential area of an ethnic or social group, the sentence will have an entirely different meaning to them. Being specific will help you avoid such problems; recognizing that some words communicate far more than their dictionary meanings will help even more.

OBSERVE & ANALYZE
Journal Activity

Monitoring Your Use of Language

Tape-record at least ten minutes of your conversation with a friend or a family member. Talk about a subject that you hold strong views about: affirmative action, welfare, school levies, candidates for office. Be sure to get permission from the other person before you tape. At first, you may feel self-conscious about having a recorder going. But as you get into discussion, it is quite likely that you will be able to converse normally.

Play back the tape and take notes of sections where your language might have been clearer. Using these notes, write better expressions of your ideas for each section you noted by using more precise, specific, and concrete language and by dating and indexing generalizations.

Replay the tape. This time take notes on any racist, sexist, or biased expression that you used. Using these notes, write more appropriate expressions for the ones you used.

Write a paragraph or two that describes what you have learned about your use of language from this experience under Journal Activity 3.3 in your Student Workbook.

Summary

Language is a system of symbols used for communicating. Through language, we designate, label, and define; evaluate; talk about things outside our immediate experience; and talk about language itself.

You will be a more effective communicator if you recognize that language symbols are arbitrary, that language is learned and is creative, and that language and perception are interrelated.

The denotation of a word is its dictionary meaning. Despite the ease with which we can check a dictionary meaning, word denotation can still present problems because most words have more than one dictionary meaning. Changes in meanings occur faster than dictionaries are revised, words take on

WHAT WOULD YOU DO?
A QUESTION OF ETHICS

One day after class, Heather, Terry, Paul, and Martha stopped at the Student Union Grill before their next class. After they had talked about class for a few minutes, the conversation shifted to students who were taking the class.

"By the way," Paul said, "do any of you know Porky?"

"Who?" the group responded in unison.

"The really fat guy who was sitting a couple of seats from me. We've been in a couple of classes together—he's a pretty nice guy."

"What's his name?" Heather asked.

"Carl—but he'll always be Porky to me."

"Do you call him that to his face?" Terry asked.

"Aw, I'd never say anything like that to him—Man, I wouldn't want to hurt his feelings."

"Well," Martha chimed in, "I'd sure hate to think that you'd call me 'skinny' or 'the bitch,' when I wasn't around."

"Come on—what's with you guys," Paul retorted. "You trying to tell me that you never talk about another person that way when they aren't around?"

"Well," said Terry, "maybe a couple of times—but I've never talked like that about someone I really like."

"Someone you like?" queried Heather. "Why does that make a difference? Do you mean it's OK to trash talk someone so long as you don't like the person?"

1. Sort out the ethical issues in this case. How ethical is it to call a person you supposedly like by an unflattering name that you would never use if that person were in your presence?

2. From an ethical standpoint, is whether you like a person or not what determines when such name-calling is OK?

different meanings as they are used in different contexts, and meanings can become obscured as words become more abstract.

The connotation of a word is the emotional and value significance the word has for the listener. Regardless of how a dictionary defines a word, we carry with us meanings that stem from our experience with the object, thought, or action the word represents.

You can improve your clarity of language by selecting the most specific, concrete, and precise word possible and by dating and indexing generalizations.

Cultural differences in language result from similarities and differences in behavior between low-context and high-context cultures. Gender differences in language are less than previously noted, although in usage, women tend to use more intensifiers and hedges than men do, and women tend to add tag questions to sentences more than men do.

Speaking appropriately means using language that adapts to the needs, interests, knowledge, and attitudes of the listener and avoiding language that alienates. Inappropriate language can be minimized by avoiding such exclusionary usages as generic *he* and generic *man* and by eliminating such nonparallel usages as marking and unnecessary association.

Communicate! Online

Use your Communicate! CD-ROM for quick access to the electronic study resources that accompany this text. Included on your CD-ROM is access to InfoTrac College Edition, the World Wide Web, a demo of WebTutor for Communicate!, and the Communicate! Web site at the Wadsworth Communication Café. The Communicate! Web site offers chapter by chapter activities, quizzes, and a digital glossary.

Review the following key terms and complete the activity on jargon and slang under Chapter 3 online at

http://communication.wadsworth.com/humancomm/verderber

Key Terms

brainstorming (59)
concrete words (57)
connotation (54)
context (53)
dating information (61)
denotation (53)
generalizing (61)

high-context cultures (62)
indexing (61)
jargon (65)
language (52)
low-context cultures (62)
precise words (57)
slang (65)
speaking appropriately (65)
specific words (56)

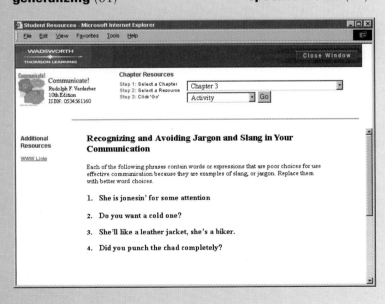

OBJECTIVES

After you have read this chapter, you should be able to answer these questions:

- What types of body motions have communication functions?

- What is paralanguage?

- What are the elements of paralanguage, and how does each affect message meaning?

- How do clothing, touching behavior, and use of time affect self-presentation?

- How is communication affected by the use of physical space?

- How do temperature, lighting, and color affect communication?

- What are three ways to improve the messages you communicate through your nonverbal behavior?

Nonverbal Communication

Marsha Collins steps into Houston's office and says, "I'm not going to be able to meet with you to talk about the report you wrote because I'm swamped with work."

In a speech to her constituents, Stephanie Morris, a candidate for Congress, says, "I want you to know I am committed to the needs of the people of this district."

How will Houston take Marsha Collins's excuse? Likewise, how much faith will Stephanie Morris's constituents have in her commitment? In both cases, the answer will rest largely on how Houston and Morris's constituents interpret Marsha's and Stephanie's vocal inflections, facial expressions, and gestures as much as their words. In reality, the meaning of any communication is based on both the content of the verbal message and the interpretation of the nonverbal behavior that accompanies and surrounds the verbal message.

In this chapter, we provide a framework for analyzing and improving non-verbal communication behavior in all contexts. We begin by studying the nature of nonverbal behavior and the way verbal and nonverbal communication messages interrelate. We then look at the major types of nonverbal communication: body motions, paralanguage, self-presentation, and management of the environment. We conclude our discussion by suggesting methods for increasing the accuracy with which nonverbal behavior is understood.

The Nature of Nonverbal Communication Behavior

Nonverbal communication behaviors are those bodily actions and vocal qualities that typically accompany a verbal message, that are usually interpreted as intentional, and that have agreed-upon interpretations within a culture or speech community (Burgoon, 1994, p. 231).

When we say that nonverbals are interpreted as intentional, we mean that people act as if they are intended even if they are performed unconsciously or unintentionally (p. 231). So, when Anita says "I've had it" as she slams a book down on the table, we interpret the loudness of her voice and the act of slamming the book down as intentionally emphasizing the meaning of the words.

Likewise, when we refer to agreed-upon interpretations in a culture or speech community, we recognize that although people from around the world use many of the same nonverbal cues they may interpret them differently. For instance, a smile may mean a positive experience, or it may mean enjoyment with contact, or it may simply be a means of saving face in an uncomfortable situation.

In addition to bodily actions and vocal qualities that accompany verbal messages, nonverbal communication also includes the messages sent by our use of physical space and our choices of clothing, furniture, lighting, temperature, and color.

Because much of what is considered appropriate nonverbal behavior depends on culture, we begin by discussing each type of behavior from a U.S. cultural perspective. Then we describe some of the most important ways nonverbal communication behavior is interpreted differently in other cultures and communities.

nonverbal communication behaviors–*actions and vocal qualities that typically accompany a verbal message.*

Body Motions

Of all nonverbal behavior, you are probably most familiar with **kinesics,** or **body motions,** which include the use of eye contact, facial expression, gesture, and posture to communicate.

kinesics or **body motions**–*the study of body motions used in communication.*

Eye Contact

Eye contact, also referred to as **gaze,** is how and how much we look at people with whom we are communicating. Eye contact serves many functions in our communication. Its *presence* shows that we are paying attention. *How* we look at a person also reveals a range of emotions such as affection, anger, or fear. Moreover, intensity of eye contact may also be used to exercise dominance

eye contact or **gaze**–*looking directly at the person or people with whom we are communicating.*

(Pearson, West, & Turner, 1995, p. 121). For instance, we describe people in love as looking "doe eyed"; we comment on "looks that could kill," and we talk of someone "staring another person down."

Moreover, through our eye contact we monitor the effect of our communication. By maintaining your eye contact, you can tell when or whether people are paying attention to you, when people are involved in what you are saying, and whether what you are saying is eliciting feelings.

The amount of eye contact differs from person to person and from situation to situation. Although people look at each other as they talk, studies show that talkers hold eye contact about 40 percent of the time and listeners nearly 70 percent of the time (Knapp & Hall, 1992, p. 298).

We generally maintain better eye contact when we are discussing topics with which we are comfortable, when we are genuinely interested in a person's comments or reactions, or when we are trying to influence the other person. Conversely, we tend to avoid eye contact when we are discussing topics that make us uncomfortable, when we lack interest in the topic or person, or when we are embarrassed, ashamed, or trying to hide something.

Because of its importance in public speaking, we will talk more about eye contact in Chapter 16, "Practicing the Presentation of Your Speech."

Facial Expression

facial expression–*the arrangement of facial muscles to communicate emotional states or reactions to messages.*

Facial expression is the arrangement of facial muscles to communicate emotional states or reactions to messages. Our facial expressions are especially important in conveying the six basic emotions of happiness, sadness, surprise, fear, anger, and disgust that are recognized across cultures (Ekman & Friesen, 1975, pp. 137–138).

Gesture

gestures–*movements of hands, arms, and fingers that we use to describe or to emphasize.*

Gestures are the movements of hands, arms, and fingers that we use to describe or to emphasize. Thus, when a person says, "about this high" or "nearly this round," we expect to see a gesture accompany the verbal description. Likewise, when a person says, "Put that down" or "Listen to me," a pointing finger, pounding fist, or some other gesture often reinforces the point. People do vary, however, in the amount of gesturing that accompanies their speech. Some people "talk with their hands" far more than others.

Posture

posture–*the position and movement of the body.*

Posture is the position and movement of the body. Changes in posture can also communicate. For instance, suddenly sitting upright and leaning forward show increased attention, whereas standing up may signal "I'm done now," and turning one's back to the other conveys a redirection of attention away from the other person.

Christy Gavit/Nonstock

Although the V for victory sign is recognized by people in most cultures, other gestures, such as OK, have different meanings in other cultures.

How Body Motions Are Used

Body motions in general and gestures in particular help us considerably in conveying meaning (Ekman & Friesen, 1969, pp. 49–98).

1. **Body motions may be used to take the place of a word or phrase.** We could make a considerable list of nonverbal symbols that take the place of words or phrases that we use frequently. For instance, thumbs up means "everything is go"; first and second fingers held in a V shape means "peace" or "victory"; shaking the head from side to side means "no" and up and down means "yes"; shrugging the shoulders means "maybe," "I don't care," or "I don't know."

   In many contexts, emblems are used as a complete language. **Sign language** refers to systems of body motions used to communicate, which include sign languages of the deaf and alternate sign languages used by Trappist monks in Europe and the women of Australia (Leathers, 1997, p. 70).

sign language—*systems of body motions used to communicate.*

2. **Body motions may be used to illustrate what a speaker is saying.** We use gestures to illustrate in at least five ways:

   ■ To *emphasize* speech: A man may pound the table in front of him as he says, "Don't bug me."

■ To show the *path* or *direction* of thought: A professor may move her hands on an imaginary continuum when she says, "The papers ranged from very good to very bad."

■ To show *position:* A waiter may point when he says, "Take that table."

■ To *describe:* People may use their hands to indicate size as they say, "The ball is about three inches in diameter."

■ To *mimic:* People may nod their heads as they say, "Did you see the way he nodded?"

3. **Body motions can display the nonverbal expression of feelings.** These emotional displays will take place automatically and are likely to be quite noticeable. For instance, if you stub your toe on a chair as you drag yourself out of bed in the morning, you are likely to grimace in pain. Occasionally we are fooled by these displays when people purposely deintensify or overreact. For example, a baseball player may remain stonefaced when he is hit by a wild pitch and refuse to rub the spot where he has been struck; likewise, a youngster may howl "in pain" when her older sister bumps her by accident.

4. **Body motions may be used to control or regulate the flow of a conversation or other communication transaction.** We use shifts in eye contact, slight head movements, shifts in posture, raised eyebrows, and nodding head to tell a person when to continue, to repeat, to elaborate, to hurry up, or to finish. Effective communicators learn to adjust what they are saying and how they are saying it on the basis of such cues.

5. **Body motions may be used to relieve tension.** As we listen to people and watch them while they speak, they may scratch their head, tap their foot, or wring their hands.

Cultural Variations

Several cultural differences in body motions are well documented.

Eye contact   A majority of people in the United States and in other Western cultures expect those with whom they are communicating to "look them in the eye," but in many societies avoiding eye contact communicates respect and deference (Martin & Nakayama, 1997, p. 149). For instance, in Japan people direct their gaze to a position around the Adam's apple and avoid direct eye contact. Chinese, Indonesians, and rural Mexicans lower their eyes as a sign of deference—to them too much direct eye contact is a sign of bad manners. Arabs, in contrast, look intently into the eyes of the person with whom they are talking—to them direct eye contact demonstrates keen interest. Likewise, there are also differences in use of eye contact in the subcultures of the United States. For instance, African Americans use more continuous eye contact than whites when they are speaking but less when they are listening (Samovar, Porter, & Stefani, 1998, p. 159).

THINKING ABOUT . . .

Body Motions

Describe the five body motions you most frequently use when you speak. Are these used as emblems, illustrators, affect displays, regulators, or tension relievers? Are these effective in helping you convey your message? Are they habits that distract from your message?

Gestures, movements, and facial expression People of other cultures also show considerable differences in their use of gestures, movements, and facial expressions. Gestures in particular can assume completely different meanings. For instance, forming a circle with the thumb and forefinger—the OK sign in the United States—means zero or worthless in France and is a vulgar gesture in Germany, Brazil, and Australia (Axtell, 1999, pp. 44, 143, 212). Displays of emotion also vary. For instance, in some Eastern cultures, people have been socialized to deintensify emotional behavior cues, whereas members of other cultures have been socialized to amplify their displays of emotion. The cultural differences that are related to emotional displays are often reflected in the interpretation that can be given to facial expressions (Samovar, Porter, & Stefani, 1998, p. 157).

Gender Variations

Men and women also show differences in their use of nonverbal communication behavior (Canary & Hause, 1993, p. 141).

Eye contact In the United States, women tend to have more frequent eye contact during conversations than men do (Cegala & Sillars, 1989). For instance, women tend to hold eye contact more than men regardless of the sex of the person they are interacting with (Wood 1997, p. 198).

Facial expression and gesture Women tend to smile more than men do, but their smiles are harder to interpret. Men's smiles generally mean positive feelings, whereas women's smiles tend to be suggestions of responding to affiliation and friendliness (Hall, 1998, p. 169). Gender differences in the use of gestures are so profound that people have been found to attribute masculinity or femininity on the basis of gesture style alone (Pearson, West, & Turner, 1995, p. 126). For instance, women are more likely to keep their arms close to their body, are less likely to lean forward with their body, play more often with their hair or clothing, and tap their hands more often than men do.

Not only do men and women use nonverbal behaviors in different ways, but men and women differ in how they interpret the nonverbal communication behaviors of others. Major difficulties in male–female relationships are often created by inaccurately encoding and decoding nonverbal messages. A number of studies have shown that women are better than men at decoding nonverbal, vocal, and facial cues (Stewart, Cooper, Stewart, & Friedley, 1998, p. 74).

> **THINKING ABOUT...**
>
> **Cultural Variations in Nonverbal Behavior**
>
> What is your cultural heritage? What are the nonverbal behaviors typically associated with that heritage? Which of these behaviors do you display most frequently? How might knowing the cultural heritage of the person with whom you are interacting help you understand what the other is trying to communicate?

Paralanguage

Paralanguage is the nonverbal "sound" of what we hear—*how* something is said. We begin by describing the four vocal characteristics that comprise paralanguage. Then we discuss how vocal interference can disrupt message flow.

paralanguage—*the nonverbal "sound" of what we hear; how something is said.*

Gender Variations in Body Motions

Find a place in the cafeteria or another public spot where you can observe the conversation of others. You are to observe the nonverbal behaviors of three dyads for at least five minutes each. First, observe the interaction of two men, then the interaction of two women, and finally the interaction of a man and a woman. Using the Observation Tally Sheet provided here, record each participant's behavior and any other behavioral cues you note. Using these observation notes, review the material on male and female use of body motions. Did your observations confirm these trends? If they did not, develop an explanation about why they didn't, using Journal Activity 4.1 in your Student Workbook.

Nonverbal Behavior Observation Form: Body Motions

Behavior (frequency)	Participant 1 (sex:__)			Participant 2 (sex:__)		
Eye contact	High	Med	Low	High	Med	Low
Smiling	High	Med	Low	High	Med	Low
Forward lean of body	High	Med	Low	High	Med	Low
Touches or plays with hair	High	Med	Low	High	Med	Low
Touches or plays with clothes	High	Med	Low	High	Med	Low
Taps hand or fingers on surface	High	Med	Low	High	Med	Low
Arm position relative to body	High	Med	Low	High	Med	Low

Vocal Characteristics

By controlling the pitch, volume, rate, and quality of our voice—the four major vocal characteristics—we can complement, supplement, or contradict the meaning conveyed by the language of our message.

pitch–*the highness or lowness of tone.*

Pitch is the highness or lowness of tone. People tend to raise and lower vocal pitch to accompany changes in volume. They may also raise the pitch when they are nervous or lower the pitch when they are trying to be forceful.

volume–*the loudness or softness of tone.*

Volume is loudness or softness of tone. Some people have booming voices that carry long distances, and others are normally soft spoken. Regardless of their normal volume level, people vary their volume depending on the situation and the topic of discussion.

rate–*the speed at which a person speaks.*

Rate is the speed at which a person speaks. People tend to talk more rapidly when they are happy, frightened, nervous, or excited and more slowly when they are problem solving out loud or are trying to emphasize a point.

Quality is the sound of the voice. Each human voice has a distinct tone. Some voices are raspy, some smoky, some have bell-like qualities, and others are throaty. Moreover, each of us uses a slightly different quality of voice to communicate a particular state of mind. We may associate complaints with a whiny, nasal quality; seductive invitation with a soft, breathy quality; and anger with a strident, harsh quality.

Some of us have developed vocal habits that lead others to consistently misinterpret what we say. For instance, some people have cultivated a tone of voice that causes others to believe they are being sarcastic when they are not. If you have concerns about your vocal characteristics, talk them over with your professor. Your professor can observe you and make recommendations for additional help should you need it.

Vocal Interferences

Although most of us are occasionally guilty of using some **vocal interferences** (extraneous sounds or words that interrupt fluent speech), these interferences become a problem when they are perceived by others as excessive and when they begin to call attention to themselves and so prevent listeners from concentrating on meaning. The most common interferences that creep into our speech include the "uh's," "er's," "well's," and "OK's"—and those nearly universal interrupters of Americans' conversation, "you know" and "like."

Vocal interferences may initially be used as "place markers," filling momentary gaps in speech that would otherwise be silence. In this way, we indicate that we have not finished speaking and that it is still our "turn." We may use an "um" when we need to momentarily pause to search for the right word or idea. Although the chance of being interrupted may be real (some people will seek to interrupt at any pause), the intrusion of an excessive number of fillers can lead to the impression that you are unsure of yourself or confused in what you are attempting to say.

Equally prevalent, and perhaps even more disruptive, is the overuse of "you know" and "like." The "you know" habit may begin as a genuine way to find out whether what is being said is already known by others. Similarly, the use of "like" may start from making comparisons such as "Tom is hot, he looks like Denzel Washington." Soon the comparisons become shortcuts as in "He's like really hot!" Finally, the use of "like" becomes pure filler: "Like, he's really cool, like I can't really explain it, but I'll tell you he's like wow!"

Curiously, no matter how irritating the use of "you know" or "like" may be to listeners, they are unlikely to verbalize their irritation. Yet their habitual use can prove to be a handicap in many settings. For example, excessive use of vocal interferences during job interviews, at work, or in class can adversely affect the impression you make.

---

quality–*the sound of the voice.*

THINKING ABOUT . . .

Vocal Characteristics

What happens to your voice in stressful situations? When does your pitch go up? Down? When do you talk loudly? Softly? Fast? Slowly? How aware of these changes are you?

vocal interferences–*sounds that interrupt or intrude into fluent speech flow.*

COMMUNICATE!
Using Technology

Watch a videotape of a movie or a television program. Select a segment where two people are talking. The first time you watch, turn off the sound. Based on nonverbal behaviors alone, determine the climate of the conversation (Are the people flirting? In conflict? Discussing an issue?). What nonverbal behaviors led to your conclusion? Watch the video a second time, observing nonverbals but also listening to variations in volume, pitch, and rate of speed. Do any of these vocal cues add information? Then watch a third time, focusing on what the characters are saying. Now analyze the segment. What percentage of meaning came from nonverbal elements? What did you learn from this exercise?

Go to "Exploring Nonverbal Communication" online to expand your research: http://www.eskimo.com/~slander/nvc

poise—*assurance of manner.*

Self-Presentation

People learn a great deal about us based on how we choose to present ourselves through our choices in clothing and personal grooming, our use of touching, and the way we treat time.

Clothing and Personal Grooming

Choice of clothing and personal grooming will communicate a message. Determine what message you want to send, and then dress and groom yourself accordingly. Lawyers and business managers understand the power of dress and grooming quite well. For instance, an attorney knows that a person charged with drug peddling would be foolish to show up in the courtroom wearing the local gang starter jacket, heavy gold chains, oversized pants, and a backward facing baseball cap. Similarly, business managers periodically adjust their dress codes to make sure they are reflective of the image they want their business to project. For instance, many have been rethinking their decisions about "casual dress days." As Georgie Geyer (1999) pointed out in an editorial, "Korn-Ferry International, the nation's largest executive search firm, experimented all summer with 'five-day-a-week' casual. Finally, it declared the experiment a failure, because 'We found that casual dress fostered a casual attitude'" (p. A12).

Many young people consciously choose clothing styles and personal grooming behaviors that stretch Western norms of "acceptability." From "retro" fashions to hip-hop styles, from blue hair and nail colors to dreadlocks and mohawks, from tattooing to body piercing, more and more people are choosing to use their clothing and appearance to differentiate themselves from some groups and to identify closely with others.

Each of us has the right to express our individuality and to communicate our political feelings in our dress and personal grooming, but we must recognize that doing so sends messages that can create barriers as well as bonds. Part of being a skilled communicator is realizing that the meaning of clothing and grooming depends as much on receivers' perceptions as on our own intentions.

Poise

Poise refers to assurance of manner. As much as 20 percent of the population experience a high degree of nervousness when encountering strangers, speaking in groups, and in public-speaking settings (Richmond & McCroskey, 1995, p. 35). For most people, nervousness decreases as they gain confidence in their ability to function well in the particular setting. Mastery of the skills discussed in the next three parts of this text should help you cope with the nervousness you might face in differing communication situations.

Touch

Through **touch** (the use of hands, arms, and other body parts to pat, hug, slap, kiss, pinch, stroke, hold, embrace, and tickle) we communicate a variety of meanings. In Western culture, we shake hands to be sociable and polite, we pat a person on the back for encouragement, we hug a person to show love, and we clasp raised hands to demonstrate solidarity. Our touching can be gentle or firm, perfunctory or passionate, brief or lingering. And how we touch can communicate our power, our empathy, or our understanding.

People differ in their touching behavior and in their reactions to unsolicited touch from others. Some people like to touch and be touched; other people do not. Women tend to touch others less than men do, but women value touching more than men do. Women view touch as an expressive behavior that demonstrates warmth and affiliation. Men view touch as instrumental behavior; for example, touching females is considered a prelude to sexual activity (Pearson, West, & Turner, 1995, p. 142).

Although U.S. culture is relatively noncontact-oriented, the kinds and amounts of touching behavior within our society vary widely. Touching behavior that seems innocuous to one person may be perceived to be overly intimate or threatening to another. Touch that is perceived to be OK in private may embarrass a person when done in public or with a large group of people. What you communicate by touching may be perceived positively or negatively. Thus, if you want to be perceived as sensitive and caring, it is a good idea to ask the other before touching.

touch–*putting a hand or other body part in contact with another.*

THINKING ABOUT . . .

Touch Orientation

Are you a "touchy-feely" type of person? Where does your touch orientation come from? Are others in your family similar in their reaction to touch? What kinds of touching behavior do you associate with power plays? With expressions of concern? With love? How often do you use touching behavior? How do you respond to the touching behaviors of others? What do you do when someone is using more touch behavior than you are comfortable with?

Kim Robbie/The Stock Market

What is this boy expressing through his touching behavior?

Time

A less obvious aspect of our self-presentation is how we manage and react to others' use and management of what Edward T. Hall (1959) calls *informal time*, including duration, activity, and punctuality (p. 135).

duration–*the amount of time that we regard as appropriate for certain events or activities.*

Duration is the amount of time that we regard as appropriate for certain events or activities. For instance, we may think a sermon should last twenty minutes and a typical class fifty minutes. When the duration of that event or activity differs significantly from our expectations, we begin to attribute meaning to that difference. For example, if we are told that our job interview will take one hour and it is over in twenty minutes, we may conclude that we didn't get the job. Similarly, if the interview stretches to two hours, we may believe we are in strong contention for the job. Because our use of time creates its own meanings, we need to be sensitive to polite conventions about the "appropriate duration" of events and activities.

activity–*what people perceive should be done in a given period.*

Activity refers to what people perceive should be done in a given time period. Many of us work during the day, sleep at night, eat a light meal around midday, and so on. When someone engages in behavior at a time that we deem inappropriate, we are likely to react negatively. For instance, Susan, who prides herself on being available to her employees, may well be put off when Sung Lei calls her at home during the dinner hour to discuss a presentation that is to be delivered at the end of the month. Sung Lei may think she is presenting herself as organized and interested in her work, but Susan may view this interruption as rude and insensitive.

punctuality–*the extent to which one adheres strictly to the appointed or regular time.*

Punctuality is the extent to which one strictly adheres to the appointed or regular time. In many respects, it may be the dimension of time that is most closely related to self-presentation. If you make an appointment to meet your professor in her office at 10 a.m., her opinion of you may differ depending on whether you arrive at 9:50, at 10:00, at 10:10, or at 10:30. Similarly, your opinion of her will differ depending on whether she is there or not at the appointed time. In the United States, strict punctuality is a dominant cultural imperative. When a date is made or an appointment set, one is normally expected to be prompt or risk having early or late arrival interpreted as meaningful.

THINKING ABOUT . . .

Time Orientation

How do you use time? Recall an incident when the duration of an event violated your expectation for appropriate length. How did this violation affect what you thought of the person or what the other person thought of you? How important is it to you that you be punctual? Do you expect others to observe the same punctuality behavior? How does your opinion of others change when they continually deviate from your preferred level of punctuality?

Cultural Variations in Self-Presentation

Just as the meaning of body motions and paralanguage are culturally determined, so too are self-presentation behaviors.

Touch   According to Gudykunst and Kim (1997), differences in touching behavior are highly correlated with culture. In some cultures, lots of contact and touching is normal behavior, whereas in other cultures, individual space is respected and frequent touching is not encouraged. "People in high contact cultures evaluate 'close' as positive and good, and evaluate 'far' as negative and bad. People in low contact cultures evaluate 'close' as negative and bad, and 'far' as positive and good" (p. 235). Latin American and Mediterranean countries are high-contact cultures, northern European cultures are medium to low in contact, and Asian cultures are for the most part low-contact cultures. As you can imagine then, the United States, which is a country of immigrants, is generally perceived to be medium contact, although there are wide differences between individual Americans due to family heritage.

Time A particularly important area of differences concerns perceptions of time. Some cultures, like the dominant culture of the United States, view time *monochronically;* that is, they see time as compartmental, irreversible, and one-dimensional. Time is a scarce resource to be "spent," "saved," and "budgeted." As a result, in the United States, being even a few minutes late may require you to acknowledge your lateness. Being ten to fifteen minutes late usually requires an apology, and being more than thirty minutes late is likely to be perceived as an insult requiring a great deal of explanation to earn the person's forgiveness (p. 161).

People from other cultural backgrounds, such as those from Latin America, Asia, or the Middle East, tend to view time *polychronically,* a view that sees time as continuous and involves engaging in several activities at the same time. To those following a polychronic view of time, the concept of "being late" has no meaning. One arrives when one has completed what came before. In Latin American or Arab cultures, for instance, it is not unusual for either person to be more than thirty minutes late, and neither is likely to expect or offer an apology (p. 160). Although the dominant culture in the United States is monochromatic in the extreme, within some of our Latin American or African American subcultures a polychromatic view of time still influences behavior.

Communication through Management of Your Environment

In addition to the way we use body motions, paralanguage, and self-presentation cues, we communicate nonverbally through the physical environment in which our conversations occur, including the space we occupy, the temperature of the surroundings, the lighting levels, and the colors used in the interior decorations.

Space

As a study, space includes permanent structures, the movable objects within space, and informal space.

Management of permanent structures Permanent structures are the buildings in which we live and work and the parts of those buildings that cannot be moved. Although we may not have much control over their creation, we do exercise control in our selection of them. For instance, when you rent an apartment

COMMUNICATE! Using InfoTrac College Edition

Touching behavior can be perceived as a sign of comforting, affection, or harassment. Using the InfoTrac College Edition subject guide, enter the term "touch." Click on "Periodical References." Then open "Just the Right Touch," Patrick McCormick (June 1999) for a discussion of touch as comforting. Under what circumstances is touch most comforting?

OBSERVE & ANALYZE Journal Activity

Cultural Differences in Self-Presentation

Develop a list of questions related to the self-presentation behaviors discussed here, and record them under Journal Activity 4.4 in your Student Workbook. Using these questions, interview or converse with two international students from different countries. Try to select students whose cultures differ from one another and from the culture with which you are most familiar. Try to understand how people in the international student's country differ from you in their use of nonverbal self-presentation behaviors. Prepare to share what you have learned with your classmates.

or buy a condominium or a home, you consider whether or not it is in tune with
your lifestyle. People who select a fourth-floor loft may view themselves differently from those who select one-room efficiencies. Doctors, lawyers, and other
professionals usually search with care to find homes that fit the image they want
to communicate.

In addition, specific features affect our communication within that environment. For instance, people who live in apartment buildings are likely to become
better acquainted with neighbors who live across the hall and next door than
with those who live on other floors. Similarly, people who share common space
such as laundry facilities or garages are more likely to become acquainted than
those who do not.

Management of movable objects within space Whether the space is a
dormitory room, a living room, a seminar room, or a classroom, we have the
opportunity to arrange and rearrange movable objects to achieve the effect we
want. For example, a manager's office arranged so that the manager sits behind
the desk and the employee chair is on the other side of that desk says, "Let's
talk business—I'm the boss and you're the employee." In contrast, if
the employee chair is at the side of the desk (creating an absence of a formal
barrier), the arrangement says, "Don't be nervous—let's just chat."

Management of informal space Managing *informal space* includes the
space around us at the moment. In the dominant U.S. culture, four distinct distances represent what most people consider appropriate or comfortable in various situations (Hall, 1969):

- *Intimate distance,* up to eighteen inches, is appropriate for private
  conversations between close friends.
- *Personal distance,* from eighteen inches to four feet, is the space in
  which casual conversation occurs.
- *Social distance,* from four to twelve feet, is where impersonal business
  such as job interviews is conducted.
- *Public distance* is anything more than twelve feet.

Of greatest concern to us is the intimate distance, that which we regard as
appropriate for intimate conversation with close friends, parents, and younger
children. If you have become uncomfortable because a person you were talking
with was standing too close to you, you are already aware of how attitudes
toward intimate space influence people's conversation. People usually become
uncomfortable when "outsiders" violate this intimate distance.

Intrusions into our intimate space are acceptable only in certain settings and
then only when all involved follow the unwritten rules. For instance, people will
tolerate being packed into a crowded elevator or subway and even touching others
they do not know provided the others follow such "rules" as standing rigidly,
looking at the floor or the indicator above the door, and not making eye contact
with others. Only occasionally will people who are forced to invade each other's

Robert Azzi/Woodfin Camp & Associates

Differing concepts of informal space: Although you might find it rude for nonintimates to get this close to you in conversation, these men would find it rude if you backed away.

intimate space acknowledge the other as a person. Then they are likely to exchange sheepish smiles or otherwise acknowledge the mutual invasion of intimate distance. In the Spotlight on Scholars, we feature Judee Burgoon, who has focused a great deal of her research on the effects of such intrusions into our intimate space. Her findings develop and test what she calls "expectancy violation theory."

Interpersonal problems occur when one person's use of space violates the behavioral expectations of another. Unfortunately, sometimes one person intentionally violates the space expectations of another. When the violation is between members of the opposite sex, it can be considered sexual harassment. Don may, through violations of informal space, posture, movements, or gestures, appear to "come on" to Donnice. If Donnice does not welcome the attention, she may feel threatened. In this case, Don's nonverbal behavior can be construed as sexual harassment. To avoid perceptions of harassment, people need to be especially sensitive to others' definitions of intimate space.

Our intimate or personal space moves when we move, but we also seek to claim other space whether we currently are occupying it or not. That is, we are likely to look at certain space as our **territory**, as space over which we may claim ownership. If Marcia decides to eat lunch at the company commissary, the space at the table she selects becomes her territory. Suppose that during lunch Marcia leaves her territory to get butter for her roll. The chair she left, the food on the table, and the space around that food are "hers," and she will expect others to stay away. If, when she returns, Marcia finds that someone at the table has moved a glass or a dish into the area that she regards as her territory, she is likely to feel resentful.

OBSERVE & ANALYZE
Journal Activity

Intruding on Personal Space

Find a crowded elevator. Get on it and face the back. Make direct eye contact with the person you are standing in front of. Note his or her reaction. On the return trip, introduce yourself to the person who is standing next to you and begin an animated conversation. Note the reaction of others around you. Get on an empty elevator and stand in the exact center. Do not move when others board. Note their reactions. Record your reactions under Journal Activity 4.5 in your Student Workbook, and be prepared to share what you have observed with your classmates.

territory—*space over which we may claim ownership.*

Judee K. Burgoon, Professor of Communication, University of Arizona, on Nonverbal Expectancy Violations Theory

With seven books and more than 150 articles and book chapters to her credit, Judee K. Burgoon is a leading scholar who has helped shape how we now think about nonverbal com-

munication. Her fascination with nonverbal behavior dates back to a graduate school seminar assignment at the University of West Virginia; she was asked to find out what was known about *proxemics,* the study of space. From that assignment, she says, "I just got hooked. Nonverbal is more elusive and difficult to study, and I've always enjoyed a challenge!"

At the time, scholars believed the road to interpersonal success lay in conforming one's behaviors to social norms about the distances that are appropriate for certain types of interactions and the types of touch that are appropriate for individuals in different kinds of relationships. Thus people would be successful in their interactions as long as they behaved in accord with these norms. Encouraged by one of her professors to "look for the counterintuitive," Burgoon's research uncovered situations where violations of these norms resulted in positive rather than negative consequences. For example, in settings where two people were not well acquainted and one of them began "flirting" by moving closer to the other, thus "violating" that person's space, the other person did not always react by moving away from the violator as expected. In fact, at times the person seemed to welcome the violation and at times may even have moved closer. Similarly, she noticed that touching behavior that violated social norms was sometimes rejected and at other times accepted.

To explain what she saw happening, Burgoon developed and began to test what she named "expectancy violation theory," which is based on the premise that we have strong expectations about how people ought to behave when they interact with us. Whether they meet our expectations affects not only how we interact with them but also such outcomes as how competent, credible, and influential we perceive them to be and what we think of our relationship. She found that how we interpret a violation depends on how we feel about that person. If we like the person, we are likely to read the nonverbal violation as positive ("Gee, she put her arm around me—that means she's really interested in me"). If we don't like the person, we are likely to read the same nonverbal violation as negative ("He better take his arm off of me, this is a clear case of harassment"). And, because we have become sensitized to the situation, the violations will be subject to strong evaluations ("Wow, I really like the feel of her arm around my waist" versus "He's making me feel really uncomfortable"). As Burgoon continued to study violations, she discovered that when a person we really like violates our expectation we are likely to view the interaction as even more positive than we would have if the person had conformed to our expectations. Over the years, Burgoon and her students' numerous research studies have provided strong support for expectancy violation theory.

Burgoon's scholarship has developed like a river. Her first work was a narrow stream with a focus on proxemics, which grew with expectancy violations theory to include all of nonverbal behavior and continues to branch. Presently, in one stream of work she is studying what determines how people adapt their behavior when they experience any type of communication violation. Why and when do people reciprocate the violation (e.g., if someone shouts, you shout back) or compensate for it (e.g., if someone comes too close to you, you step back)? In a second stream, Burgoon is focusing on a specific type of expectancy violation: deception. Here she is trying to sort out the role nonverbal behavior plays in deceitful interactions. Finally, she has begun a stream of work whose purpose is to identify the essential properties of interpersonal communication that are different from the properties of media communication. Whatever branch her research takes, Judee Burgoon brings the same readiness to challenge the current thinking that has been the hallmark of her work. For complete citations of many of her recent publications in these areas, see the references listed at the end of this book.

In addition to teaching a number of courses, Burgoon serves as Director of Graduate Studies, where her role of helping students learn how to conduct research and formulate theory gives her great satisfaction. "Mentoring others is among the major gratifications of doing research. The fun is to teach others what I was taught: always challenge the current assumptions." To learn more about Judee Burgoon's work, log on to her home page at "Judee K Burgoon" http://www.u.arizona.edu/~judee

Many people stake out their territory with markers. For example, Ramon arrives early for the first day of class, finds an empty desk, puts his backpack at the side on the floor, and puts his coat on the seat. He then makes a quick trip to the restroom. If someone comes along while Ramon is gone, moves his backpack and coat and sits down at the desk, that person is violating what Ramon has marked as his territory.

As a student of nonverbal communication, you understand, however, that other people may not look at either the space around you or your territory in quite the same way as you do. Even though the majority of U.S. residents have learned the same basic rules governing the management of space, this does not mean that everyone shares the same respect for the rules or treats the consequences of breaking the rules in the same way.

Temperature, Lighting, and Color

Three other elements of the environment that can be controlled affect communication and "send" messages. These are temperature, lighting, and the colors used in the environment.

Temperature can stimulate or inhibit effective communication by altering people's mood and changing their level of attentiveness. Can you recall the difficulty you have had listening to a teacher in a hot stuffy classroom? Have you found that you become "edgy" when you are cold?

Lighting levels also add meaning to communication messages. In lecture halls and reading rooms, bright light is expected—it encourages good listening and comfortable reading. By contrast, in a chic restaurant, a music listening room, or a television lounge, you expect the lighting to be soft and rather dim, which makes for a cozy atmosphere that invites intimate conversation (Knapp & Hall, 1992, p. 72). We often change the lighting level in a room to change the mood and indicate the type of interaction that is expected. Bright lights encourage activity and boisterous conversations, whereas softer light levels calm and soothe, encouraging quiet and more serious conversations.

Color may stimulate both emotional and physical reactions. For instance, red excites, blue comforts and soothes, and yellow cheers and elevates mood. Professional interior designers who understand how people react to colors may choose blues when they are trying to create a peaceful, serene atmosphere for a living room, whereas they will decorate in reds and yellows in a playroom.

In addition, specific colors also convey information about people and events. For instance, youth gangs often use colors to signal membership. In some communities gang members wear bandannas or other articles of clothing in a specific color.

Cultural Variations in Management of the Environment

As you would expect, the environments in which people feel comfortable depend on their cultural background. In the United States, where we have

---

WHAT WOULD YOU DO?
A QUESTION OF ETHICS

After the intramural mixed-doubles matches on Tuesday evening, most of the players adjourned to the campus grill for a drink and a chat. Marquez and Lisa sat down with Barry and Elana, whom they had lost to that night largely because of Elana's improved play. Although Marquez and Lisa were only tennis friends, Barry and Elana had been going out together for much of the season.

After some general conversation about the tournament, Marquez said, "Elana, your serve today was the best I've seen it this year."

"Yeah, I was really impressed. And as you saw, I had trouble handling it," Lisa added.

"And you're getting to the net a lot better too," Marquez added.

"Thanks, guys," Elana said in a tone of gratitude, "I've really been working on it."

"Well, aren't we getting the compliments today," sneered Barry in a sarcastic tone. Then after a pause, he said, "Oh, Elana, would you get my sweater—I left it on that chair by the other table."

"Come on, Barry, you're closer than I am," Elana replied.

Barry got a cold look on his face, moved slightly closer to Elana, and said emphatically, "Get my sweater for me, Elana—now."

Elana quickly backed away from Barry as she said, "OK Barry—it's cool," and she then quickly got the sweater for him.

"Gee, isn't she sweet," Barry said to Marquez and Lisa as he grabbed the sweater from Elana.

Lisa and Marquez both looked down at the floor. Then Lisa glanced at Marquez and said, "Well, I'm out of here—I've got a lot to do this evening."

"Let me walk you to your car," Marquez said as he stood up.

"See you next week," they both said in unison as they hurried out the door leaving Barry and Elana alone at the table.

1. Analyze Barry's nonverbal behavior. What was he attempting to achieve?

2. How do you interpret Lisa's and Marquez's nonverbal reactions to Barry?

3. Was Barry's behavior ethically acceptable? Explain.

ample land, many people live in individual homes or in large apartments. In other countries, where land is scarce, people live in more confined spaces and can feel "lonely" or isolated in larger spaces. In Asia, most people live in spaces that by our standards would feel quite cramped. Similarly, people from different cultures have different ideas about what constitutes appropriate distances for various interactions. Recall that in the dominant culture of the United States personal or intimate space is eighteen inches or less. In Middle Eastern cultures, however, men move much closer to other men when they are talking (Samovar, Porter, & Stefani, 1998, p. 165). Thus, when an Arab man talks with a man from the United States, one of the two is likely to be uncomfortable. Either the American will feel uncomfortable and invaded or the Arab will feel isolated and too distant for serious conversation. We also differ in the temperature ranges that we find comfortable. People who originate from warmer climates can tolerate heat more easily than people who originate in cooler climates. Even the meanings we assign to colors vary by national culture and religion. In India white not black is the color of mourning, and Hindu brides wear red.

Summary

Nonverbal communication refers to how people communicate through the use of body motions, paralanguage, self-presentation cues, and the physical environment.

Perhaps the most familiar methods of nonverbal communication are what and how a person communicates through body motions and paralanguage. Eye contact, facial expression, gesture, and posture are four major types of body motions. Body motions act as emblems, illustrators, affect displays, regulators, and tension relievers. Likewise, a person's vocal characteristics (volume, rate, pitch, and quality) as well as the vocal interferences ("ahs," "ums," "you knows," and "likes") help us interpret the meaning of the verbal message.

Although verbal and nonverbal communication work together best when they are complementary, nonverbal cues may replace or even contradict verbal symbols. Generally, nonverbal communication is more to be trusted when verbal and nonverbal cues are in conflict.

Through self-presentation cues such as clothing, touching behavior, and use of time, people communicate about themselves and their relationship to others. The physical environment is often overlooked even though we set the tone for conversations and nonverbally communicate through it. The choices people make in their permanent spaces, the way they arrange the objects in those spaces, and the way they control or react to temperature, lighting, and color contribute to the quality and meaning of the communication episodes that occur.

Communicate! Online

Use your Communicate! CD-ROM for quick access to the electronic study resources that accompany this text. Included on your CD-ROM is access to InfoTrac College Edition, the World Wide Web, a demo of WebTutor for Communicate!, and the Communicate! Web site at the Wadsworth Communication Café. The Communicate! Web site offers chapter by chapter activities, quizzes, and a digital glossary.

Review the following key terms and access the activity on identifying facial expressions under Chapter 4 online at

http://communication.wadsworth.com/humancomm/verderber

Key Terms

activity (84)

duration (84)

eye contact or gaze (75)

facial expression (76)

gestures (76)

kinesics or body motions (75)

nonverbal communication
   behaviors (75)

paralanguage (79)

pitch (80)

poise (82)

posture (76)

punctuality (84)

quality (81)

rate (80)

sign language (77)

territory (87)

touch (83)

vocal interferences (81)

volume (80)

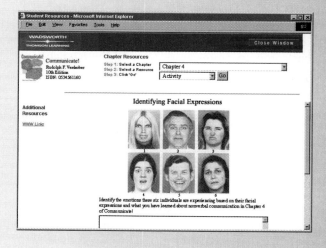

SELF-REVIEW

Establishing a Communication Foundation from Chapters 2 to 4

What kind of a communicator are you? This review looks at ten specifics that are basic to effective communicators. On the line provided for each statement, indicate the response that best captures your behavior: 1, almost always; 2, often; 3, sometimes; 4, rarely; 5, never.

_____ When I speak, I tend to present a positive image of myself. (Ch. 2)

_____ In my behavior toward others, I look for more information to confirm or negate my first impressions. (Ch. 2)

_____ Before I act on perceptions drawn from people's nonverbal cues, I seek verbal verification of their accuracy. (Ch. 2)

_____ My conversation is helped by a large vocabulary. (Ch. 3)

_____ I speak clearly, using words that people readily understand. (Ch. 3)

_____ When I am speaking with people of different cultures or of the opposite sex, I am careful to monitor my word choices. (Ch. 3)

_____ I tend to look at people when I talk with them. (Ch. 4)

_____ Most of my sentences are free from such expressions as "uh," "well," "like," and "you know." (Ch. 4)

_____ I consider the effect of my dress on others. (Ch. 4)

_____ I try to control my environment in ways that help my communication. (Ch. 4)

Based on your responses, select the communication behavior you would most like to change. Write a communication improvement goal statement similar to the sample improvement plan in Chapter 1 (page 25). If you would like verification of your self-analysis before you write a goal, have a friend or fellow worker complete this same analysis for you.

You can complete this Self-Review online under Chapter 4 Activities for Communicate! at the Human Communication Resource Center at the Wadsworth Communication Café:
http://communication.wadsworth.com/humancomm/verderber

Interpersonal communication is informal interaction with others that occurs one-on-one or in small groups. Talking to a friend on campus, chatting on the phone with a classmate about an upcoming test, arguing the merits of a movie with friends, soothing an intimate friend who has been jilted, discussing strategies for accomplishing tasks at work, interviewing for a job, and planning the future with a loved one are all forms of interpersonal communication.

During interpersonal communication, we converse, listen and respond, share feelings, and form relationships. Because interpersonal communication takes place in informal settings, we are often unaware of the importance of interpersonal skills. Too often we think, "I am who I am—how I talk is natural to me—I can't change it." This attitude disregards the fact that we can control how we speak even in the most spontaneous situations. In this section, we look at various aspects of our interpersonal communication to understand the kinds of goals we can achieve and what we can do to meet those goals.

How we communicate affects how others treat and relate to us. Improving our interpersonal communication skills can empower us. People who clearly express their ideas, beliefs, and opinions become influential and exert control over what happens to them and to others whom they care about. When we accurately and precisely encode our thoughts, others gain a better appreciation for our position. This understanding and appreciation increases the likelihood that they will respond in ways that are consistent with our needs.

In this section, we discuss conversation, listening and responding with empathy and understanding, self-disclosure, building and maintaining relationships, and interviewing. With an increased repertoire of interpersonal communication skills, you can select the ones that are most appropriate for the particular communication situation.

two

INTERPERSONAL COMMUNICATION

OBJECTIVES

After you have read this chapter, you should be able to answer these questions:

■ What is a conversation?

■ How does a casual social conversation differ from a pragmatic problem-consideration conversation?

■ What are conversational rules, and what are their distinguishing features?

■ What is the cooperative principle?

■ What are the maxims of the cooperative principle, and how does each apply to conversation?

■ What are the skills associated with effective conversations?

■ What guidelines regulate turn-taking behavior?

■ What is conversational coherence, and how can it be achieved?

■ Why is politeness important in conversation?

■ What additional skills are important for electronically mediated communication?

5

Conversations

As Claude got into the car, he casually asked Phyllis, "How'd things go today?"

"Oh," Phyllis said, as she shrugged her shoulders, "Mindy lost her ball, but Ken found it."

"That was nice of him."

"Well, I guess saying Ken found it isn't quite accurate—actually his foot found it. Luckily the fall didn't hurt him too badly."

"What do you mean, the fall didn't hurt him too badly?" Claude asked, totally confused.

"Well, Dr. Scott says a break like that is often less troublesome than a sprain."

"Ken broke a bone and you say he's not hurt too badly?" Claude replied incredulously.

"In comparison to the picture window," Phyllis said indignantly. "The lamp went through it."

"What does this have to do with Ken falling?"

"Everything! When Ken fell he landed on Buddy who then leaped out of a sound sleep and bumped into the lamp . . ."

"Which fell through the picture window," Claude finished. "Is that all?"

"Yes . . . unless Eleanor decides to sue."

"Our baby sitter? Sue about what?" Claude shouted.

"Calm down, Claude. I just knew you'd get all excited about this. See, when the lamp crashed through the window, Eleanor jumped up to see what had happened and reinjured her back. But I doubt she'll sue. I offered to pay for her operation. But enough about this. Claude—How'd your day go?"

Conversations are the medium of interpersonal communication and the building blocks of good interpersonal relationships. In fact, as Steven Duck, a leading researcher on relationships, pointed out, "If you were to sit and list the things that you do with friends, one of the top items on the list would surely have to be 'talking'" (1998, p. 7). When conversations go well, they are informative, stimulating, and often just good fun. Yet, like Claude and Phyllis's, some conversations can be quite frustrating. By understanding how a conversation works and by taking advantage of its dynamics, we all can become more skillful in the everyday talks we have with others.

In this chapter, we define conversation and discuss its primary characteristics, discuss the types and structure of conversation, consider the rules that conversations follow, look at the cooperative principle that helps to explain how conversation works, and consider the skills of effective conversation. Finally, we offer a competence test of conversation and supply a sample conversation and analysis for your consideration.

Characteristics of Conversation

conversation–*locally managed interactive, informal, extemporaneous, and sequential interchange of thoughts and feelings between two or more people.*

Conversation is a locally managed interactive, informal, extemporaneous, and sequential interchange of thoughts and feelings between two or more people. This definition highlights several key features mentioned by Jan Svennevig (1999) that distinguish conversations from other forms of communication such as public address and debates (p. 8). First, conversations are *locally managed*. This means that only those involved in the conversation determine the topic, who will speak, the order of speaking, and the length each will speak in a turn. Second, conversations are *interactive*; that is, they involve at least two people speaking and listening. Third, conversations are *extemporaneous*, which means the participants have not prepared or memorized what they will be saying. Fourth, conversations are *sequentially organized*; that is, they have openings, middles, and closings. Within each part of the conversation, what one participant says usually relates to what was said by previous speakers, unless the utterance is designed to change the topic on which the participants are conversing.

When people find a conversation satisfying, they tend to seek out the others for additional conversations. If, for instance, Dan meets Carl at a party and both of them found the talk they had about politics stimulating, they are likely to look forward to later conversations.

If results of a conversation are unsatisfactory, people will tend to avoid each other and not invest time or energy in further attempts to develop a relationship.

Types and Structures of Conversation

In this section, we will consider two common kinds of conversational situations that are structured differently: casual social conversation and pragmatic problem-consideration conversation. **Casual social conversations** are marked by discussion of topics that arise spontaneously. The discussion of these topics enables participants to share information, ideas, and opinions and to hear the ideas and opinions of others. Casual social conversations help us to meet our interpersonal needs and to build and maintain our relationships. **Pragmatic problem-consideration conversations** are marked by participants' agreeing to discuss and to resolve specific problems or to plot potential courses of action.

casual social conversations–
discussions of topics that arise spontaneously.

pragmatic problem-consideration conversations–
participants discuss and resolve specific problems or plot potential courses of action.

The Structure of Casual Social Conversations

In a casual social conversation, a topic will be introduced and will be accepted or rejected. If others accept it, it will be discussed until such time as someone introduces another topic that others begin to discuss. A topic is rejected when others choose not to respond and when someone else introduces a different topic that then becomes the focus. This topic change process occurs throughout the conversation.

Suppose Donna and Juanita attend a play together. As they find their seats about fifteen minutes before the play is set to begin, conversation may proceed as follows:

> As they look around, Donna says, "They really did an Art Deco thing with this place, didn't they?"
>
> "Yeah… Hey," Juanita says as she surveys the audience, "it looks as if this is going to be a sellout."
>
> "Certainly does—I see people in the last row of the balcony."
>
> "I thought this would be a popular show. It was a hit when it toured Louisville… and I hear the attendance has been good all week."
>
> Agreeing with Juanita, Donna adds, "Lot's of people I've talked with were trying to get tickets."
>
> "Well it's good for the downtown."
>
> "Yeah," Donna says, as she glances at the notes on the cast. After a few seconds, she exclaims, "I didn't know Gloria VanDell was from Cincinnati!"

Notice what happened. Donna introduced the topic of decorative style. Juanita acknowledges the point, but chooses not to discuss it. Instead, she chooses a different topic. Donna accepts the topic with a parallel comment. Juanita introduces information about what had happened in Louisville. The conversation lasts for two more turns. Then Donna introduces a new topic.

For the remainder of the time before the show starts, Juanita and Donna could converse on one or more topics, sit and read their programs, or engage in some combination of conversing and reading.

The Structure of Pragmatic Problem-Consideration Conversation

In pragmatic problem-consideration conversation, the topic initiated requires the participants to deliberate and reach a conclusion. These conversations may be more orderly than social conversations and may have as many as five parts.

1. **Greeting and small talk.** Problem-consideration conversations usually open with some kind of greeting followed by a very brief conversation on social topics, just to establish rapport.

2. **Topic introduction and statement of need for discussion.** In the second stage, one participant introduces the problem or issue that is the real purpose for the conversation. How this topic is presented or framed affects how the discussion will proceed.

3. **Information exchange and processing.** The conversation then progresses to a series of speaking turns, and participants share information and opinions, generate alternative solutions, discuss the advantages and disadvantages of different options, and so on. Although each of these issues is likely to be addressed, the conversation will probably not be organized like a textbook problem-solving session. The conversationalists may move from subtopic to subtopic and circle back again.

4. **Summarizing decisions and clarifying next steps.** As the conversational partners approach the end of the conversation, they may try to obtain closure on the topic by summarizing their positions and what has been accomplished.

5. **Formal closing.** Once the conversationalists have discussed the issue and clarified the next steps that will be taken, they are ready to end the problem-consideration conversation. Endings enable the conversationalists to either move to a social conversation, begin a new problem consideration, or simply disengage from one another. The formal closing often includes showing appreciation for the conversation.

Although such problem-consideration conversations will vary in length, depending on the nature of the topic and its complexity, the five steps can be seen in this brief dialogue:

April: Hi, Yolanda. How are you doing?

Yolanda: Oh, can't complain too much.

April: I'm glad I ran into you—I need to check something out with you.

COMMUNICATE!
Using Technology

Think of times that you've made a call outside your home using a wireless cellular telephone. How do your conversations differ from those you have made on wired phones? Are they longer? Shorter? More focused on pragmatic problem considerations than on casual social exchanges? Why do you think this is true? What differences do you see in the etiquette of the way you handle such conversations in comparison to the way you would handle them if you were face to face? Read the article "The Ten Commadments of cell phone etiquette" by Dan Briody in the May 26, 2000, online edition of the technology magazine Infoworld. Go to http://www.infoworld.com/articles/op/xml/00/05/26/000526opwireless.xml

Peter L. Chapman

Skills in problem-consideration conversations enable us to resolve difficulties with others while enhancing our relationships.

Yolanda: Can we do this quickly? I've really got to get cracking on the speech I'm doing for class.

April: Oh, this will just take a minute. If I remember right, you said that you'd been to the Dells for dinner with Scot. I'd like to take Rob there to celebrate his birthday, but I wanted to know whether we'd really feel comfortable there.

Yolanda: Sure. It's pretty elegant, but the prices aren't bad and the atmosphere is really nice.

April: So you think we can really do dinner on fifty or sixty dollars?

Yolanda: Oh, yeah. We had a salad, dinner, and a dessert and our bill was under sixty even with the tip.

April: Thanks, Yolanda. I wanted to ask you 'cause I know you like to eat out when you can.

Yolanda: No problem. Gotta run. Talk with you later—and let me know how Rob liked it.

OBSERVE & ANALYZE
Journal Activity

Problem-Consideration Conversations

Identify two recent problem-consideration conversations you have had: one that was satisfying and one that was not. Try to recall exactly what was said. Write the scripts for these conversations under Journal Activity 5.1 in your Student Workbook. Then try to identify each of the five parts of a problem-consideration conversation. Were any parts missing? Retain these scripts for further use later in the chapter.

Rules of Conversation

Although our conversations seems to be random activities with little form or structure, they are actually based on **rules,** "unwritten prescriptions that indicate what behavior is obligated, preferred, or prohibited in certain contexts"

rules—*unwritten prescriptions that indicate what behavior is obligated, preferred, or prohibited in certain contexts.*

Unwritten rules for conversations guide the kind of messages and appropriate behavior for different physical and social contexts.

(Shimanoff, 1980, p. 57). These unwritten rules give us clues as to what kinds of messages and behavior are proper in a given physical or social context or with a particular person or group of people, and they also provide us with a framework in which to interpret the behavior of others.

Characteristics of Rules

Let's begin our discussion by considering what makes a rule a rule and how rules are phrased. As we do this, we will use a common conversation rule as an example: "If one person is talking, another person should not interrupt."

1. **Rules must allow for choice.** This means that rules must give you a choice to follow them or not. When a person is speaking, you can hear the person out, or you can break the rule and interrupt the person—you have a choice.

2. **Rules are prescriptive.** A rule tells you what to do to be successful or effective. If you choose to break the rule, you risk being criticized or punished. If you choose to interrupt, you will be viewed as rude and the speaker might glare at you or verbally upbraid you.

3. **Rules are contextual.** This means that rules apply in some situations but may not apply under different conditions. So most of the time we don't interrupt, but if there is an emergency—like a fire—it is all right to interrupt. When we

communicate with people of a different race, sex, nationality, religion, political affiliation, class, organization, or group, however, effective communication is likely to be more difficult than when we communicate with people from our own culture because their communication rules may well be different from those with which we are familiar.

4. **Rules specify appropriate human behavior.** That means that rules focus on what to do or not do.

Phrasing Rules

Although we phrase rules in many ways, Shimanoff (1980) suggests that we are best able to understand a communication rule if it is stated in an "if-then" format (p. 76). She goes on to state that a rule should begin with *if* to introduce the clause that specifies in what context the rule is operable; the *if* clause should be followed by *then,* which introduces the clause that specifies the nature of the prescription and the behavior that is prescribed. So "*If* X is the situation or context, *then* Y is obligated (preferred or prohibited)."

Here are some conversational rules that are common to Western cultures. Notice that in some cases the word *then* has been omitted, but it is still implied.

If your mouth is full of food, then you must not talk.

If you are spoken to, you must reply.

If another does not hear a question you ask, then you must repeat it.

If you are being spoken to, you should direct your gaze to the speaker.

If more than two people are conversing, you should ensure each has equal time to speak.

If your conversational partners are significantly older than you, then you should refrain from using profanities and obscenities.

If you can't say something nice, then you don't say anything at all.

If you are going to say something that you don't want overheard, then drop the volume of your voice.

THINKING ABOUT . . .

Communication Rules

Identify three communication rules that do not appear in the text list, but that you believe guide your communication behavior. Be sure to phrase each of the three in the "if-then" format.

Effective Conversations Follow the Cooperative Principle

Not only are conversations structured by the rules that participants follow, but they also depend on how well conversational partners cooperate. The **cooperative principle** states that conversations will be satisfying when the contributions made by conversationalists are in line with the purpose of the conversation (Grice, 1975, pp. 44–46). Based on this principle, H. Paul Grice describes the following four conversational **maxims** (requirements):

cooperative principle–*states that conversations will be satisfying when the contributions made by conversationalists are in line with the purpose of the conversation.*

maxims–*conversational requirements.*

quality maxim—*requirement to provide information that is truthful.*

1. The **quality maxim** calls for us to provide information that is truthful. When we purposely lie, distort, or misrepresent, we are not acting cooperatively in the conversation. Being truthful means not only avoiding deliberate lies or distortions but also taking care to avoid any kind of misrepresentation. Thus, if a classmate asks you what the prerequisites for BIO 205 are, you share them if you know them, but you don't speculate or offer your opinion as though it is fact. If you don't know or if you have only a vague recollection, say so.

quantity maxim—*requirement to provide an amount of information that is sufficient or necessary—not too much and not too little.*

2. The **quantity maxim** calls for us to provide an amount of information that is sufficient to satisfy others' information needs and keep the conversation going, but not so lengthy and detailed that we undermine the informal give-and-take that is characteristic of good conversations. Thus, if Sam asks Randy how he liked his visit to St. Louis, Randy's answering "fine" is too brief; his answering with a twenty-minute monologue on all the activities on his trip is likely to be far too long.

relevancy maxim—*requirement to provide information that is related to the topic being discussed.*

3. The **relevancy maxim** calls for us to provide information that is related to the topic being discussed. Comments tangential to the subject, or outright subject changes when other conversational partners are still actively engaged with the current topic, are uncooperative. For example, imagine that Hal, Corey, and Li-sung are chatting about benefits that will accrue for the local homeless shelter from the upcoming 5K walk/run. If Corey asks whether either of them has taken Speech 101, he will be acting uncooperatively. His comments don't relate to the subject.

manner maxim—*requirement to be specific and organized when communicating thoughts.*

4. The **manner maxim** calls for us to be specific and organized when communicating our thoughts. We cooperate by organizing our thoughts and using specific language that clarifies our meanings. When we give information that listeners find obscure, ambiguous, or disorganized, we are not cooperating in sharing meaning. Thus, if a person asked you to explain how to use the new photocopier, you would "walk the person through" the steps of using it rather than rambling on about the machine's features in a confusing order.

Bach and Harnish (1979, p. 64) have proposed two additions to Grice's maxims, the morality maxim and the politeness maxim.

morality maxim—*requirement to speak in ways that meet moral/ethical guidelines.*

5. The **morality maxim** call for us to speak in ways that meet moral/ethical guidelines. For example, in the United States violations of the morality maxim would include repeating information that had been confidentially disclosed or persuading someone else to do something that the speaker knows is wrong or against the other's personal interests.

politeness maxim—*requirement to be courteous to other participants.*

6. The **politeness maxim** calls for us to be courteous to other participants. In our conversations, we should attempt to observe the social norms of politeness in the dominant culture and not purposefully embarrass ourselves or others during the interaction. In the following Diverse Voices feature, Gwendolyn Gong describes how politeness is enacted by her cultural community. In the next section, we will discuss means of practicing politeness.

When Mississippi Chinese Talk

by Gwendolyn Gong, Ph.D.

In her article from which this excerpt is taken, Dr. Gong, an associate professor at Texas A&M, explains how Mississippi Chinese use conversational accommodation and topic shifting to politely reduce conversational discomfort for their conversational partners and themselves. This excerpt focuses on the use of accommodation or deference.

Though my family heritage traces back to an ancestral village in Canton, China, I am a Chinese American, born and reared in the Mississippi Delta. Given that my siblings—in truth, my entire immediate family—served as classic, prolific producers of Southern speech, I find it peculiar that, when I went to graduate school in Indiana, my Hoosier peers and professors saw me as some sort of enigma—an oddity. They would joke, "The picture's fine but adjust the sound." This same type of remark followed me to Texas, where indeed another version of English is spoken. "Adjust the sound." What did that mean? Hadn't these folks ever encountered a Mississippian before? The truth was that they had. But I was different. I was a Mississippi Chinese. Since the 1800s this lush farming area has served as a homeland for approximately 1200 Cantonese Chinese from Southern China who have gradually assimilated into being Southerners of another ilk: Mississippi Chinese (MC). In my experience, one of the most interesting ways by which I have observed how Southern Genteelism and Confucianism reveal themselves is in the talk of the MC.

A major feature that typifies MC speech is deference, the courteous submission or acquiescence to the opinions, wishes, or judgment of another speaker, which may manifest itself in two forms: accommodation (that is, making the non-MC speaker feel comfortable and welcome) and topic shifting (changing the subject of a conversation). Ironically, accommodation that may provide comfort for the non-MC listener may, on occasion, result in discomfort for the MC speaker; conversely, topic shifting oftentimes provides relief

and control for the MC speaker but frustration for the non-MC listener. For non-MC speakers and listeners, understanding of how deference operates among the MC helps to provide a more effective informed exchange between these two groups.

A number of years ago at the institution where I was teaching, I developed a friendship with a colleague. This woman was a master teacher who spoke with authority and often openly revealed to me her earnest but prejudicial concerns about me as a person. Occasionally, we would see each other in passing and chat:

"Hi, Gong. I went to a Thai restaurant on Sunday. I asked for some soy sauce, and the waiter looked at me like I was crazy. What was wrong with asking for some soy sauce? The food was so bad—like bad Chinese food—that I covered it with everything. Why was that guy so mad at me?"

"Asking for soy sauce isn't a crime. I don't know why your waiter was upset," I replied sheepishly. I was not certain why she was broaching me on the topic of Thai food; I'm not expert on it, though I do enjoy that particular cuisine.

"We ought to have lunch. What's your schedule?" my colleague inquired.

"I've already eaten. Plus I've got so much work to finish in my office today. Sorry that I can't join you while you eat." I was uncomfortable, yet truthful.

"What'd ya eat? Betcha had egg rolls, eh? Gong, you're always eating egg rolls—at least you used to. Remember when you first came here years ago? I couldn't believe it—a Chinese, teaching English—with a Southern accent, too. I used to share an office with a fellow named Joe, who'd eat tacos and avocados all the time, and then I'd see you across the hall, eating egg rolls. Right, Gong? Don't ya remember?"

"Well, no I really don't remember, but I suppose it's true," I replied, trying to go along with my colleague. "I do recall Joe and I ate take-out food sometimes. It was a quick way to have lunch," I added, my voice trailing off, diminishing with every syllable. I wished I were anywhere else but here, "talking" with this person. It was embarrassing enough that she made these kinds of remarks to me at all, much less within earshot of other faculty and students. Where could I hide? I thought to myself: "Hang in there; it'll be over soon."

This is only one conversation among many that this professor and I have shared. Out of my deep belief that she did care about me and out of

my respect for her professional accomplishments, I always accommodated this individual's topic selection and conversational moves. I self-consciously defended her, rationalizing that she was just "tone-deaf" and didn't understand her audience very well. She admitted that she had never known an American-born Asian like me before. As a result, I reasoned to myself that I should give her a break, help her avoid "losing face," and prevent her from feeling awkward. Yet I always experienced regret that I voluntarily subjected myself to being bullied, demeaned, and belittled by someone espousing true friendship.

Excerpted from Dr. Gwendolyn Gong, "When Mississippi Chinese Talk," in Our Voices: Essays in Culture, Ethnicity, and Communication, *eds. Alberto Gonzalez, Marsha Houston, and Victoria Chen (Los Angeles, CA: Roxbury Publishing Company, 1994), pp. 110–116.*

OBSERVE & ANALYZE
Journal Activity

Conversational Maxims

Use the two conversation scripts you prepared in the exercise on problem-consideration conversations earlier in the chapter and listed in your Student Workbook under Journal Activity 5.1. Which of the conversational maxims were followed? If there were violations, what were these, and how did they affect the conversation? Can you identify specific conversational rules that were used? Which of these were complied with, which were violated? How does this analysis help you understand your satisfaction with the conversation?

Skills of Effective Face-to-Face Conversationalists

Regardless of how well we think we converse, almost all of us can learn to be more effective. In this section, we discuss several skills that are basic to effective conversationalists.

Have Quality Information to Present

The more you know about a range of subjects, the greater the chance that you will be an interesting conversationalist. Here are some suggestions for building a high-quality information base:

- Read a newspaper every day (not just the comics or the sports).
- Read at least one weekly news or special-interest magazine.
- Watch television documentaries and news specials as well as entertainment and sports programs. (Of course, sports and entertainment are favorite topics of conversation too—but not with everyone.)
- Attend the theater and concerts as well as going to movies.
- Visit museums and historical sites.

Following these suggestions will provide you with a fountain of quality information you can share in social conversations.

As an Initiator, Ask Meaningful Questions

What happens in the first few minutes of a conversation will have a profound effect on how well a social conversation develops. Although asking questions comes easy to some, many people seem at a loss for what to do to get a conversation started. These four question lines will usually help to get a conversation started. Notice that none of them is a yes or no question—each calls for the person to share some specific information.

> *Refer to family:* How is Susan getting along this year at college? How is your dad feeling?
>
> *Refer to the person's work:* What projects have you been working on lately?
>
> *Refer to a sporting activity:* How was the fishing trip you went on last week? What is it about Tiger Woods that enables him to be near his best at major tournaments?
>
> *Refer to a current event:* What do you think is driving people back to more conservative stocks? What do you think we can do to get kids more interested in reading?

Perhaps just looking at these four suggestions will bring other ideas to mind that you can use to start conversations with various acquaintances.

As a Responder, Provide Free Information

Effective conversationalists provide a means of enabling others to continue a conversation by providing free information with their responses. **Free information** is extra information offered during a message that can be used by the responder to continue the conversation.

Many people have difficulty building conversations because of a tendency to reply to questions with one-word responses. If, for instance, Paul asks Jack, "Do you like tennis?" and Jack answers "Yes" and then just looks at Paul, Paul has nowhere to go. To keep the conversation going (or to get it started), Paul has to think of a new line to pursue.

Suppose, however, that after Jack answers "Yes," he goes on to say "I've only been playing for about a year, but I really enjoy it." Now, Paul has a direction to follow. He might turn the conversation to his own experience: "I haven't been playing long myself, but I'm starting to get more confidence, especially with my forehand." Or he might use the information to ask another question: "Are you able to play very often?"

As a respondent, it is important to give free information. As the initiator, it is important to listen for free information. The better the quality of the free information, the more likely it is that the conversation will grow and prove rewarding to both participants.

OBSERVE & ANALYZE
Journal Activity

Conversational Variety

During the next three days, deliberately try to introduce greater variety in your conversations with others. How well are you able to develop and maintain such conversations? Are they more or less satisfying than conversations on weather, sports, and daily happenings? Why? Record your observations in your Student Workbook under Journal Activity 5.2.

free information—*extra information offered during a message that can be used by the responder to continue the conversation.*

crediting sources—*verbally footnoting the specific source from which you have drawn your information and ideas.*

Credit Sources

Crediting sources means verbally footnoting the source from which you have drawn your information and ideas. In a term paper, you give credit to authors you have quoted or paraphrased by footnoting the sources. Similarly, when you use other people's words or ideas in your oral communication, you can credit the source verbally.

By crediting you enable the other participants to evaluate the quality of the information you are sharing. Moreover, by crediting ideas from people who are acquaintances, you make people feel better about themselves and avoid hard feelings. For instance, if a friend presents a creative idea and verbally acknowledges you as the source, you probably feel flattered. If, however, the person acts as though the idea were his own, you are probably hurt or angry. So, when you repeat ideas that you have gotten from others, make sure you give proper credit.

Crediting is easy enough. To give credit where it is due and avoid possible hard feelings, just include the name of the person you got the idea from. For example, in a discussion about course offerings, you might say, "I like the list of courses we have to choose from, but, you know, we should really have a course in attitude change. Laura was the one who put me on to the idea, and I can see why it's a good idea."

Balance Speaking and Listening

Conversations are most satisfying when all participants feel that they have had their fair share of speaking time. We balance speaking and listening in a conversation by practicing turn-taking techniques.

1. **Effective conversationalists take the appropriate number of turns.** In any conversation, the ideal is for all to have approximately the same number of turns. If you discover that you are speaking more than your fair share, try to restrain yourself by mentally checking whether everyone else has had a chance to talk once before you talk a second time. Similarly, if you find yourself being inactive in a conversation, try to increase your participation level. Remember, if you have information to contribute, you are cheating yourself and the group when you do not share it.

2. **Effective conversationalists speak an appropriate length of time on each turn.** People are likely to tune out or become annoyed with those conversational partners who make speeches, filibuster, or perform monologues rather than engaging in the ordinary give-and-take of conversation. Similarly, it is difficult to carry on a conversation with someone who gives one- or two-word replies to questions that are designed to elicit meaningful information. Turns do, of course, vary in length depending on what is being said. If your average statements are much longer or shorter than those of your conversational partners, however, you need to adjust.

3. **Effective conversationalists recognize and heed turn-exchanging cues.** Patterns of vocal tone, such as a decrease of loudness or a lowering of pitch, and use of gestures that seem to show obvious completion of a point are the most obvious turn-taking cues. When you are trying to get into a conversation, look for them.

    By the same token, be careful of giving inadvertent turn-exchanging cues. For instance, if you tend to lower your voice when you are not really done speaking or take long pauses for emphasis when you expect to continue, you are likely to be interrupted because these are cues that others are likely to act on. If you find yourself getting interrupted frequently, you might ask people whether you tend to give false cues. Moreover, if you come to recognize that another person has a habit of giving these kinds of cues inadvertently, try not to interrupt when speaking with that person.

4. **Effective conversationalists use conversation-directing behavior and comply with the conversation-directing behavior of others.** In general, a person who relinquishes his or her turn may define who speaks next. For instance, when Paul concludes his turn by saying, "Susan, did you understand what he meant?" Susan has the right to the floor. Skillful turn takers use conversation-directing behavior to balance turns between those who freely speak and those who may be more reluctant to speak. Similarly, effective turn takers remain silent and listen politely when the conversation is directed to someone else.

    Of course, if the person who has just finished speaking does not verbally or nonverbally direct the conversation to a preferred next speaker, then the turn is up for grabs and goes to the first person to speak.

5. **Effective conversationalists rarely interrupt.** Although interruptions are generally considered inappropriate, interrupting for "clarification" and "agreement" (confirming) are interpersonally acceptable (Kennedy & Camden, 1983, p. 55). For instance, interruptions that are likely to be accepted include relevant questions or paraphrases intended to clarify, such as "What do you mean by 'presumptuous'" or "I get the sense that you think presumptuous behavior is especially bad," and reinforcing statements such as "Good point, Max" or "I see what you mean, Suzie." The interruptions that are likely to be viewed as disruptive or incomplete include those that change the subject or that seem to minimize the contribution of the interrupted person.

Practice Politeness

Politeness, relating to others in ways that meet their need to be appreciated and protected, is universal to all cultures (Brown & Levinson, 1987). Although levels of politeness and ways of being polite vary, according to Brown and Levinson all people have **positive face needs** (the desire to be appreciated and approved, liked

politeness—*relating to others in ways that meet their need to be appreciated and protected.*

positive face needs—*the desire to be appreciated and approved, liked and honored.*

negative face needs–*the desire to be free from imposition or intrusion.*

and honored) and **negative face needs** (the desire to be free from imposition or intrusion).

To meet people's positive face needs, we make statements that show concern, compliment, or use respectful forms of address. For example, it is polite to greet your instructor as "Professor Reynolds" (to use a respectful form of address) or to say "Thanks for the tip on how to work that problem, it really helped" (to compliment).

To meet people's negative face needs, we make statements that recognize that we are imposing or intruding on the time of another. For instance, to recognize that you are imposing, you might say to your professor, "I can see you're busy, but I wonder whether you could take a minute to. . ." or "I know that you don't have time to talk with me now, but I wanted to see whether there was a time that we could meet later today or tomorrow."

face-threatening acts (FTAs)–*engaging in behavior that fails to meet positive or negative face needs.*

Although politeness is always important, it is especially so whenever we say something to a person that might cause the person to "lose face," statements that Brown and Levinson call **face-threatening acts (FTAs)**. We are committing FTAs when our behavior *fails* to meet positive or negative face needs. The goal of politeness theory is not to avoid face threatening—it is normal. Rather, the goal is to lessen or eliminate potential conversational or relationship problems that could result from FTAs.

Suppose your professor returned a set of papers and you believe the grade you received was not reflective of the quality of the paper. You could, of course, say, "I don't think you graded my paper fairly and I want you to reconsider the grade you gave me," a statement that is an FTA without consideration for politeness. Saying something like this that suggests that the professor may have been wrong or may have overlooked something might well cause that professor to lose face. So, what might you say to your professor that would be more appropriate? You have three choices:

COMMUNICATE! Using **InfoTrac College Edition**

Certainly one important aspect of politeness is courtesy. Using InfoTrac College Edition, under the subject "courtesy," click on "Periodical references." Several of the articles listed lament a decline in civility. See, for instance, "Come on, kids, show some respect" by Andrew Steven (1999). Try to get a perspective on such questions as "Does courtesy (politeness) really matter?" and "To what extent?"

1. **You can make the FTA in a way that includes some form of positive politeness.** "I would appreciate it if you could look at my paper again. I've marked the places that I'd like you to consider. My roommate said that you were fair and usually willing to reconsider if there seemed to be a good reason." Although the request still contains a direct imposition on the professor, "I would appreciate it" is much softer than "I want you to." Moreover, the effort to include a positive politeness statement that shows the professor has been kind enough to do favors when there might be a good reason is helpful as well.

2. **You can make the FTA with negative politeness.** "I'm sure you're very busy and don't have time to reread and remark every paper, but I'm hoping you'll be willing to look at my paper again. To minimize the time it might take, I've marked the places that I'd like you to consider. I've also written comments to show why I phrased those sections as I did." Although the request is still a direct imposition, it makes the statement that you recognize

that you are imposing. It also suggests that you wouldn't do it if there weren't at least, potentially, good reasons. Moreover, you've taken time not only to limit how much the professor needs to look at but also to show why you thought the sections were in keeping with the assignment.

3. **You can make the FTA indirectly or off the record.** "Please don't take this the wrong way, but I was surprised by a few of your comments." By saying this in a casual way, you hope your professor might be curious enough to ask what caused you to be surprised. With this opening, you can move to one of the more direct but face-saving approaches.

So, the question is, how do we choose whether to be polite and, if so, which of the three strategies do we use? Brown and Levinson (1987) believe this decision is affected by a combination of three factors:

1. **How well people know each other and their relative status.** The less familiar we are with someone and the higher that person's social status, the more effort we will put into being polite.

2. **The power the hearer has over the speaker.** Most of us will work harder to be polite to those who are powerful than to those who are powerless.

3. **The risk of hurting the other person.** Most of us do not like to intentionally hurt others.

To show how you might apply this theory, let's consider two examples. First, suppose you want to impose on your roommate to take a look at your paper before you turn it in to your professor. Your roommate is your friend, and you get along quite well. The imposition is relatively minor and only mildly threatening—in the past, *both* of you have looked at work the other has done. Moreover, your roommate has no special *power* over you. In light of these considerations, you might not put much effort into trying to be polite. You might make this request without much regard to your roommate's face needs and say, "Danny, take a look at this paper. I need to hand it in tomorrow."

Second, suppose you wish to ask your professor to preread this paper before you submit it for a grade. Because your professor is not your friend (you are socially more distant) and because your professor has considerable power over you (he controls your grade), you will probably want to approach your professor more politely than you did your friend. As a result, you are likely to make a statement that includes a form of positive politeness or a statement that includes a form of negative politeness.

As you come to better understand face needs, you will become better able to accurately diagnose situations in which you should take particular care to engage in polite behavior. In addition, each of us can make the world a bit more humane by working at being polite regardless of situational imperatives.

SKILL BUILDERS Politeness

Skill	Use	Procedure	Example
Relating to others in ways that meet their need to be appreciated and protected.	To determine the degree of politeness necessary to achieve your objective.	1. Recognize when what you are planning to say is likely to be recognized as a face-threatening act. 2. Consider how well you know each other, whether one person holds power over the other, and the risk of hurting the other person. 3. Construct the wording of a positive politeness or a negative politeness statement based on the issues of relationship, power, and risk.	Chris thinks her boss did not consider all that he should have in determining her year's bonus. She might construct the following negative politeness statement: "Mr. Seward, I know you put considerable time into your bonus decisions, but you have been willing to talk about your decisions in the past. I was hoping you'd be willing to take a few minutes to discuss your decision with me."

OBSERVE & ANALYZE
Journal Activity

Using Politeness

Think about a time you committed a face-threatening act (FTA). What did you say? Try to recall as specifically as possible the exact words you used.

Analyze your FTA in terms of familiarity and status, power, and risk. Did you have greater or lesser status? Did you have greater or lesser social power? Was the risk of hurting the person large or small? Write three different ways that you could have made your request. Try one that uses positive face statements; try one that uses negative face statements; try one that combines positive and negative statements. Record your observations and analysis under Journal Activity 5.3 in your Student Workbook.

Skills of Effective Electronically Mediated Conversationalists

Although all of what we have discussed in this chapter is relevant to electronically mediated (EM) communication, communicating online calls for some additional considerations. Whether you are conversing via email, in newsgroups, or in chat rooms, you will want to consider these issues.

Conversing via Email

Recall that **email** is electronic correspondence conducted between two or more users on a network. Although email would seem to be more like letter writing than conversation, email messages can be responded to shortly after they are sent so they start to approach a kind of conversation. Let's consider ways that you can improve your email conversations.

1. **Take advantage of delayed feedback.** Many people treat email as conversation. As a result, we have a tendency to respond with the first thought that comes to mind and to pay little attention to how we are phrasing that thought. So a first step in improving your email use is to remember that you

can and should edit what you write. Never send an email before you have reread what you have written and analyzed it in terms of both what you've said and how you've said it. Don't just correct typos.

email–*electronic correspondence conducted between one or more users on a network.*

2. **Include the wording that you are responding to in your email.** Even though email exchanges may occur on the same day and even within minutes of each other, the originator may not remember exactly what he or she wrote to you originally. When you respond to specific points people made in their messages, it is to your advantage to repeat or paraphrase what they said before you respond.

3. **Take into account the absence of nonverbal cues to meaning.** Whether you are writing a message or responding to a message, keep in mind that the person cannot hear the sound of your voice or see the look on your face or your use of gestures. Nonverbal communication may provide as much 66 percent of the social meaning of a message, so you must determine what you can do in writing that will "fill in the gaps" of meaning.

    Most specialists advise that you choose your words carefully and add more adjectives when appropriate. This advice will often fill in for the absence of nonverbals. For instance, instead of writing, "What you said really bugged me," you might write, "What you said had some merit; I was rather curt with my comments, but the way you said it really hurt my feelings." Now the reader will have a much better idea of your feelings about the response.

Barbara Alper/Stock, Boston

In the hustle and bustle of responding to email, people tend to go with the first thought that comes to mind.

Icons that are used in email to express emotions are called the *emoticons*. For a listing of the various ways you can express nonverbal emotions online, consult the detailed list available at http://www.chatlist.com/faces.html.

4. **Use common abbreviations sparingly, if at all.** Commonly used abbreviations may make your messages shorter, but they do not necessarily make them more meaningful. Although some frequent email users can easily decode these cryptic notations, many who receive these shorthand citations are at a loss to make sense of them. Some common email abbreviations include BTW (by the way), FWIW (for what it's worth), and IMHO (in my humble opinion). We don't sprinkle our conversation with such abbreviations, so why should we sprinkle our email messages with them? Moreover, some receivers might be offended because you are not willing to really say what you mean but instead drop abbreviations.

    An especially dangerous shortcut is the use of capital letters to show emphasis. Rather than making a statement sound important, too often all capital letter messages are perceived as threatening. All capitals in email messages are the equivalent of shouting in face-to-face conversation.

5. **Keep in mind that email messages are not secure.** Because email is so easy to use, we may write email messages that include very confidential material— information that we would ordinarily guard carefully. Keep in mind that a message you write is copied and stored (at least temporarily) on many computers between yours and the recipient's. "In some ways, email messages are like postcards. Anyone 'carrying' the message can read it, even if most would never do so" (Crumlish, 1997, p. 132). If you have something to say that is confidential, could be used against you in some way, or could be totally misinterpreted, it is better to convey that message in a written letter or a private phone call.

    For additional guidelines on the effective use of email, consult this site and its posting on email etiquette: http://www.iwillfollow.com/email.htm.

Conversing via Newsgroups and Internet Chat

newsgroup—*an electronic gathering place for people with similar interests.*

Internet chat—*online interactive message exchange between two or more people.*

Recall that a **newsgroup** is an electronic gathering place for people with similar interests and that **Internet chat** is online interactive message exchange between two or more people. In newsgroups you post articles and people post responses, and in a chat room typed responses appear instantly on participants' computer screens. Thus Internet chat approximates face-to-face conversation in that feedback is relatively instantaneous.

Several of the recommendations for email conversations are equally important in newsgroups and chat rooms. Still, both newsgroups and chat rooms are significantly different from email. For instance, once you have subscribed to a newsgroup, you can spend your time "listening," posting articles, and responding to articles.

Listening, called **lurking**, gives you a kind of pseudointeraction with others. For instance, suppose you join a sports newsgroup that is formed to discuss golfing. You will find that various people will have posted newsgroup articles on issues related to golf. These may range from articles discussing a favorite golfer (such as Tiger Woods, Robert Duvall, Julie Inkster, or Sri Pak) to those talking about ways to improve their game (driving, putting, chipping), to those about golf issues (etiquette, rules), and so forth. Then you can "lurk" by reading an article and the various responses generated by the article but not respond yourself. In this way, you get to learn a little about the personalities of posters and repliers.

Posting gives you a chance to see whether people want to reply to your particular thoughts. You may post an article and generate little if any response. But what you say may touch a nerve, and you may receive many replies, some of which may take the form of **flaming**, a hostile or negative response to what you have written. Some of these are for the specific purpose of getting you engaged in a "flame war." Although you may enjoy such anonymous "face-to-face" verbal combat, more often than not you are wise to avoid taking the bait. In other words, you can just ignore any flaming message that you see.

Most important, posting leaves the door open for responses that are designed to get you engaged in interaction. That is, if a number of people respond, you may respond to a responder and thus begin a kind of "relationship."

This leads us to the third way to spend time, and that is to respond. As mentioned, a thoughtful, favorable response may well motivate the poster to respond to your response.

In addition, in newsgroups (as well as in some chat rooms) you may well be asked to observe newsgroup etiquette because of the number of people involved. "Not observing etiquette in a Newsgroup will result in almost instant criticism and reprimand, usually by more than one participant"(Banks, 1997, p. 106).

Many newsgroups post **FAQs** (frequently asked questions) that list the rules followed by participants in that particular newsgroup. In addition to **netiquette** (Internet etiquette), newsgroups FAQs may include other information such as the history of the group and the kind of jargon that is acceptable. To find a newsgroup's FAQ, look for postings with "FAQ" in the header, or post a polite note asking the location of the FAQ.

In addition to the advice given for newsgroups, for chat rooms you will want to consider these two items as well. In most chat rooms, the conversation is focused on subject areas. Look for a chat room that is discussing the kinds of things you want to discuss (Snell, 1998, p. 258). Moreover, in a chat room everything that is typed appears on the screen. Most people try to preserve their anonymity by using nicknames rather than their real names. You can be whoever you want—so can everyone else. As a result, you really have no idea whether a person you are talking with is male or female, young or old, rich or poor.

lurking–*Internet listening, a kind of pseudointeraction with others.*

flaming–*a hostile or negative response to what you have written.*

FAQs–*frequently asked questions; a list of rules followed by participants in a particular newsgroup.*

netiquette–*Internet etiquette.*

THINKING ABOUT . . .

Internet Conversation

Have you had experience with electronically mediated conversation? Compared to face-to-face conversation, what is the greatest shortcoming of EM conversation? What can you do to compensate for that shortcoming?

How might culture or gender differences affect the conversation between these two people?

Cultural Variations in Effective Conversation

Throughout this chapter, we have been considering behaviors that improve conversation for people in the United States, a low-context culture. Just as various verbal and nonverbal rules vary in low- and high-context cultures, so do they differ in guidelines for conversation. Gudykunst and Masumoto (1996, pp. 30–32) explain differences in conversational patterns between people of low-context and high-context cultures.

First, in low-context culture conversations, we are likely to see differences in word choice, including greater use of such categorical words as *certainly, absolutely,* and *positively.* In high-context culture conversations, we are likely to see greater use of qualifiers such as *maybe, perhaps,* and *probably.*

Second, low-context cultures strictly adhere to the relevancy maxim by valuing relevant comments that are perceived by listeners to be directly to the point. In high-context cultures, individuals' responses are likely to be more indirect, ambiguous, and apparently less relevant because listeners rely more on nonverbal cues to help them understand the speaker's intentions and meaning.

Conversation

Working with another student, prepare to hold either a social or a problem-consideration conversation before the entire class. Limit your conversation to five minutes.) To prepare for the in-class conversation, meet with the other person to select a topic and to practice holding the conversation to get ideas in mind.

    Criteria for evaluation will include how well you followed conversational rules and maxims and other skills of effective face-to-face conversation.

Third, in low-context cultures, the quality maxim is operationalized in truth telling. People are expected to verbally communicate their actual feelings about things regardless of how this affects others. Conversationalists in high-context cultures operationalize the quality maxim differently. They define quality as maintaining harmony, and conversationalists may send messages that verbally mask their true feelings.

Finally, in low-context cultures, periods of silence are considered uncomfortable because when no one is speaking little information is being shared. In high-context cultures, silence in conversation is often meaningful. When three or four people sit together and no one talks, the silence may indicate truthfulness, disapproval, embarrassment, or disagreement, depending on context.

Conversation and Analysis

Use your Communicate! CD-ROM to access a video scenario of the following conversation. Click on Communicate!'s "In Action" feature, and then click on "Susan and Sheila." As you watch Susan and Sheila talking about dating exclusively with others who share their religious faith, notice what each woman says and how they create this conversation together.

We have provided a transcript of Susan and Sheila's conversation as well as our analysis based on the following questions.

1. What type of conversation is this?
2. Identify the conversational maxims that you observe each woman following.
3. Where do you see each woman using the specific skills for effective conversations?

Watch, listen to, and critique the conversation by completing the conversation analysis online. You can compare your analysis to ours by clicking on the "Submit" button at the end of the Communicate! In Action analysis form.

Conversation

Susan and Sheila are in their early twenties. They meet somewhere and have a talk.

Susan: So, how are you and Bill getting along these days?

Sheila: Oh, not too well, Suze. I think the relationship is over. The feelings just aren't there anymore, and, besides, there are so many other problems that have been building up.

Susan: Yeah, you know, I could kinda tell. Is there one specific problem?

Sheila: Well, there's a lot. But I guess the one that's, um, really made a difference is that we're from different religions. 'Cause I'm Jewish and he isn't. I didn't think it would matter at first, but, you know, it does.

Susan: Yeah, you know, I think I was kind of lucky, well, in the long run. When I was in high school my parents wouldn't let me go out with anybody who wasn't Jewish. Man, I resented that at first, but, you know, now I'm kind of glad since I'm starting to think about the future now. And my parents said, you never know what's gonna come out of a high-school relationship.

Sheila: Yeah, I remember that. You *hated* it. You know, it's amazing to realize your parents can actually be right about something.

Analysis

Susan initiates the conversation with a meaningful question.

Shelia answers the question and gives "free information" about her lack of feelings and the presence of multiple problems.

Susan poses a question to probe Sheila for more information.

Sheila follows the quality maxim, sharing specific information that becomes the topical focus of the rest of the conversation.

Susan shifts the topic a bit by speaking about her experiences. This seems to violate the relevancy maxim, but in so doing, she lays the groundwork for later exchanges.

Conversation

Susan: Yes, and now that I look around, I'm not in the predicament that you are of having to get out of a relationship for something that's not what you want.

Sheila: Yeah, but I'm, you know, glad that they didn't restrict me because I think that if they had I would just feel a lot of pressure... You know, I wouldn't have been able to pick whom I wanted to go out with, and I definitely, you know, wouldn't be very independent. You know, I need to make *my own* choices. I think if I know what I want, I feel it's all right.

Susan: That was my problem— having to pick and choose. I mean, my parents would say, "Oh, is he Jewish?" "I don't know, should I ask him?" I mean, they wanted me to say, "Are you Jewish? Oh, you're not? Well, you can't go out with me, then."

Sheila: Yeah, it's frustrating. It's a tough situation. It's frustrating 'cause, I mean, I want to date people that are Jewish, but I can't go around picking on them saying, oh, this one is and this one isn't. You know, I have to be interested in *somebody*.

Susan: So, are you saying then that you're kind of glad that your parents didn't restrict you in that manner, or are you saying that you're glad that they didn't but wish they had?

Sheila: I guess I'm saying that I'm glad they didn't, but sometimes I think it would be better if they had, because I would be more conscious about it.

Analysis

Susan uses the indirect method to deliver the FTA (face threatening ace) of reminding Sheila of her predicament.

Sheila acknowledges Susan's comment and follows it by sharing her feelings in order to keep the conversation going on the subject.

Notice how the use of "you know" as filler both breaks the continuity of what Sheila is saying and detracts from the quality of her message.

Susan extends the conversation by honestly describing her dilemma.

Sheila confirms Susan's feelings and shows that she too is frustrated.

Susan asks questions to clarify what Sheila means.

Sheila and Susan continue to take turns providing relevant information.

Conversation	Analysis
Susan: Yeah, I think it's best to kind of start out early to get an idea in your mind of what you really want to do. I mean, I never thought a relationship in high school would go anywhere, but David and I've been together for four years already. I mean, that's a long time.	
Sheila: I know, I saw you guys together the other day; you looked really nice. I wish I could meet somebody that...	Sheila recognizes Susan's good fortune and then returns to her own situation.
Susan: Yeah, you know, I saw you start shrugging Bill off and just ignoring him.	Susan violates turn taking by interrupting.
Sheila: Well, it depresses me to think about it. I really didn't think that religion would get in the way of our relationship, but it really means a lot to me.	Because they are friends Sheila can continue the conversation by sharing her position.
Susan: So, what are you gonna tell him?	Susan refocuses this problem-solving discussion on what actions Susan is considering.
Sheila: I guess I'll just have to tell him that it's not going to work out, but that depresses me, too.	Sheila answers the question and then adds her feelings, which is sharing free information.
Susan: Don't let it get you too upset. I mean, it's what you want, right?	Susan's remark may have been meant to help Susan feel better, but the abruptness isn't in keeping with the cooperativeness of the majority of the conversation.
Sheila: Yeah, I guess. I mean, I'm just gonna have to do the best that I can.	This dialogue follows most of the guidelines discussed in the chapter.

WHAT WOULD YOU DO?
A QUESTION OF ETHICS

Sarah, John, Louisa, Naima, and Richard all met at a party that the university sponsored during First Year Orientation. During a break, they began sharing where they were from, where they were working, what classes they were taking, and their potential majors. John was having fun talking with Louisa—he thought she was cute, and he wanted to impress her. When she mentioned that she had been involved in theater during high school and was considering majoring in drama, he began to share his own theater experiences. Everyone was politely listening, and interested at first, but he kept talking and talking. Finally, Naima interrupted John and changed the subject, for which the rest of the group was quite grateful.

Throughout their twenty-minute conversation, whenever someone would bring up a new subject, John would immediately take center stage and expound on some wild story that remotely applied. Not only was he long-winded, but his stories seemed to be fabricated. He was the hero in every one—

either through his intellect or his strength. Besides all this, as he talked he included completely inappropriate side comments that were turnoffs to all of the listeners. One by one, each person found a reason to excuse him- or herself. Soon John was standing alone. Several minutes later, John heard the other four around the corner talking. Before he could round the corner and come into their sight, he heard one of them say, "Do you guys want to go down to the coffee house so we can talk in peace? That John was really too much—but I think we can avoid seeing him if we zip out the side door. That way the rest of us can have a chance to talk."

1. Have you ever talked with someone like John? Where did John go wrong in his conversational skills? What should he have done differently?

2. What are the ethical implications of Louisa and the rest of the group's sneaking out the side door without saying anything to John? Defend your position.

Summary

Conversations are informal interchanges of thoughts and feelings that usually occur in face-to-face settings. There are two types of conversations, social conversations and problem-consideration conversations, each of which has a general structure.

Conversations are guided by unwritten prescriptions that indicate what behavior is obligated, preferred, or prohibited. Four characteristics of conversational rules shape the behavior of the participants: rules allow for choice, are prescriptive, are contextual, and specify appropriate behavior.

Effective conversations are governed by the cooperative principle, which suggests that conversations "work" when participants join together to accomplish conversational goals and make the conversation pleasant for each participant. The cooperative principle is characterized by six maxims: quality, quantity, relevancy, manner, morality, and politeness.

Effective conversationalists demonstrate skills in honestly presenting information (including crediting their sources), balancing speaking and listening (through effective turn-taking behavior), maintaining conversational coherence, practicing politeness (through engaging in positive and negative face-saving strategies), and engaging in ethical dialogue.

Communicate! Online

Use your Communicate! CD-ROM for quick access to the electronic study resources that accompany this text. Included on your CD-ROM is access to InfoTrac College Edition, the World Wide Web, a demo of WebTutor for Communicate!, and the Communicate! Web site at the Wadsworth Communication Café. The Communicate! Web site offers chapter by chapter activities, quizzes, a digital glossary, and all the Web links included in this chapter.

Review the following key terms at
http://communication.wadsworth.com/humancomm/verderber

Key Terms

casual social conversations (99)
conversation (98)
cooperative principle (103)
crediting sources (108)
email (113)
face-threatening acts (FTAs) (110)
FAQs (115)
flaming (115)
free information (107)
Internet chat (114)
lurking (115)
manner maxim (104)
maxims (103)

morality maxim (104)
negative face needs (110)
netiquette (115)
newsgroup (114)
politeness (109)
politeness maxim (104)
positive face needs (110)
pragmatic problem-consideration
   conversations (99)
quality maxim (104)
quantity maxim (104)
relevancy maxim (104)
rules (101)

Your Communicate! CD-ROM also includes a video of the conversation between Susan and Sheila featured on pages 118–120. Click on the Communicate! In Action icon on your CD-ROM, then click on "Susan and Sheila." You can watch, listen to, and analyze their conversation. Improve your own conversation skills by learning from this model.

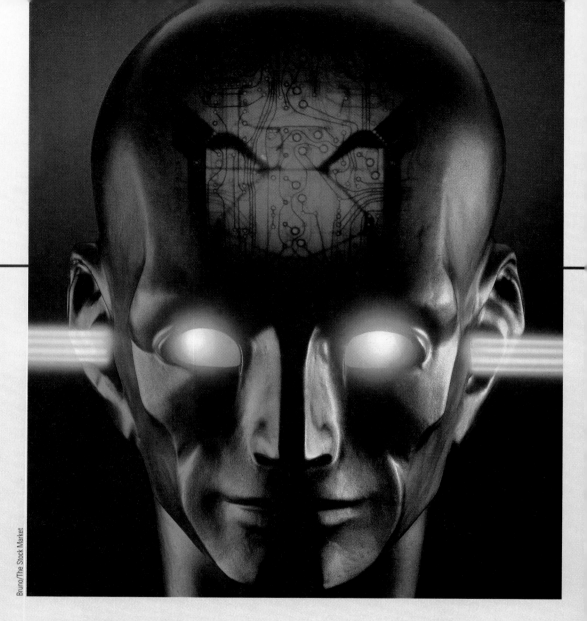

OBJECTIVES

After you have read this chapter, you should be able to answer these questions:

■ What are the five concepts involved in listening?

■ How can you focus your attention?

■ What is empathy?

■ How can you ask questions to increase understanding?

■ How can you paraphrase both the content and the intent of another's message?

■ What are three devices for remembering information?

■ How can you evaluate inferences?

■ How can you make appropriate supporting statements?

■ How can you give reasonable alternative interpretations of events?

6

Listening

"Garson, do you have an extra key to the document cabinet? I misplaced mine, and I have to get into it right away."

"No, I don't have a key, but it doesn't matter because . . ."

"I can't believe it. When I left home this morning, I was sure I had it."

"Bart, it's OK . . ."

"I pulled out my keys—but of course I just had my car key and main door key. I always carry two sets of keys."

"Bart, I've been trying to tell you, just try the . . ."

"It's just like me. I think I've got everything, but just before I check the last time Sue will say something to me and I get sidetracked. Then I just take off."

"Bart, calm down. The door's . . ."

"Calm down?! If I can't get those documents to the meeting, there's going to be hell to pay. We've got six people coming from all over the city just to look at the documents. What am I supposed to say to them?"

"Bart, you don't have to say anything. I've been trying to . . ."

"Oh, sure—I just go in there and say, 'By the way, the documents are locked up in the cabinet and I left my key at home.' Come on, Garson—who's got the other key?"

"Bart, listen!!! I've been trying to tell you—Miller was in the cabinet and, knowing you'd be along in a minute, he left the door open."

"Well, why didn't you tell me?"

listening–*the process of receiving, attending to, and assigning meaning to aural and visual stimuli.*

Are you a good listener—even when you are under pressure like Bart? Or do you sometimes find that your mind wanders when others are talking to you? Listening, "the process of receiving, attending to, and assigning meaning to aural and visual stimuli" (Wolvin & Coakley, 1996, p. 69), is a fundamental skill that affects the quality of our conversations in social and business settings. Despite the importance of listening, many of us do not listen as well as we need to. In this chapter, we will consider the concepts of attending, understanding, remembering, evaluating, and responding.

Attending

attending–*the perceptual process of selecting and focusing on specific stimuli from the countless stimuli reaching the senses.*

Attending is the perceptual process of selecting and focusing on specific stimuli from the countless stimuli reaching the senses. Recall from Chapter 2 that we attend to information that interests us and meets physical and psychological needs. But to be a good listener, we have to train ourselves to attend to what people are saying regardless of our interest or needs.

Let's consider three techniques for consciously focusing attention.

COMMUNICATE! Using InfoTrac College Edition

Why is listening perceived to be important in so many professions? Using InfoTrac College Edition, under the subject of "listening," click on "Periodical references." To answer the question, open articles such as Sandra Hagevik, "Just Listening" (1999) and Sheila C. Bentley "Listening Better: A Guide to Improving What Might Be the Ultimate Staff Skill" (1998). Which specific listening skills seem to be agreed upon as most important?

1. **Get physically and mentally ready to listen.** Physically, good listeners adopt a listening posture. For instance, when good listeners have been told that the next bit of information will be on the test, they are likely to sit upright in their chairs, lean slightly forward, cease any extraneous physical movement, and look directly at the professor. Likewise, mentally they will focus their attention by blocking out miscellaneous thoughts that pass through their minds. Although what you are thinking about may be more pleasant to attend to than what someone is saying to you, you must compel yourself to focus on what is being said.

   Of course, sometimes you can afford to listen without much intensity. People often speak of "vegging out in front of the tube," which usually means "listening" to comedy or light drama as a means of passing time pleasurably. Unfortunately, many people approach all situations as if they were listening to pass time.

2. **Make the shift from speaker to listener a complete one.** Unlike the classroom, where you are supposed to listen continuously for long stretches, in conversation you are called on to switch back and forth from speaker to listener so frequently that you may find it difficult at times to make these shifts completely. If, instead of listening, you spend your time rehearsing what you are going to say as soon as you have a chance, your listening effectiveness will take a nosedive. Especially when you are in a heated conversation, take a second to check yourself—are you preparing speeches

One Big Happy by Rick Detorie. By permission of Rick Detorie and Creators Syndicate.

instead of listening? Shifting from the role of speaker to that of listener requires constant and continuous effort.

3. **Hear a person out before you react.** Far too often we stop listening before the person has finished speaking because we "know" what a person is going to say, yet our "knowing" is really only a guess. Accordingly, cultivate the habit of always letting a person complete his or her thought before you stop listening or try to respond.

    In addition to prematurely ceasing to listen, we often let a person's mannerisms and words "turn us off." For instance, we may become annoyed when a speaker mutters, stammers, or talks in a monotone. Likewise, we may let a speaker's language or ideas turn us off. Are there any words or ideas that create bursts of semantic noise for you, causing you to stop listening attentively? For instance, do you have a tendency to react negatively or tune out when people speak of *gay rights, skinheads, welfare frauds, political correctness,* or *rednecks*? To counteract this effect, try to let a warning light go on when a speaker trips the switch to your emotional reaction. Instead of tuning out or getting ready to fight, be aware of this "noise" and work that much harder to listen objectively. If you can do it, you will be more likely to receive the whole message accurately before you respond.

OBSERVE & ANALYZE
Journal Activity

Attending

Select an information-oriented program on your public television station (such as *NOVA, News Hour with Jim Lehrer,* or *Wall Street Week*). Watch at least fifteen minutes of the show while lounging in a comfortable chair or while stretched out on the floor with music playing on a radio in the background. Then, for the next fifteen minutes, listen as you make a conscious effort to use the guidelines for increasing attentiveness. Under Journal Activity 6.1 in your Student Workbook, contrast your listening behavior while lounging with your listening behavior while attending. What differences did you note between the second segment and the first? What were the results of those differences?

Understanding

Understanding is decoding a message accurately by assigning appropriate meaning to it. Sometimes we do not understand because people use words that are outside our vocabulary or are used in a way that we do not recognize. Fully understanding what a person means requires *active listening,* using specific techniques to ensure your understanding, including empathizing, asking questions, and paraphrasing.

understanding–*decoding a message accurately by assigning appropriate meaning to it.*

Empathy

Empathy is intellectually identifying with or vicariously experiencing the feelings, thoughts, or attitudes of another. When we empathize, we are attempting to understand or experience what another understands or experiences. To do this, generally, we try to put aside our own feelings, thoughts, and attitudes and to "try on" the feelings, thoughts, and attitudes of another and responding appropriately. Three approaches people use when empathizing are empathic responsiveness, perspective taking, and sympathetic responsiveness (Weaver & Kirtley, 1995, p. 131).

Empathic responsiveness occurs when you experience an emotional response parallel to, and as a result of observing, another person's actual or anticipated display of emotion (Stiff et al., 1988, p. 199). For instance, when Monique tells Heather that Brad broke off their engagement, Heather will have used empathic responsiveness if she senses the sadness that Monique is feeling and experiences a similar sense of loss.

Perspective taking—imagining yourself in the place of another—is the most common form of empathizing (Zillman, 1991). For example, if Heather personalizes the message by picturing herself being told that her engagement is off, anticipates and experiences her own emotions were this to occur, and then assumes that Monique must be feeling the same way, Heather is exemplifying perspective taking.

Sympathetic responsiveness is your feeling concern, compassion, or sorrow for another because of the other's situation or plight. The sympathetic responsiveness approach differs from the other two approaches in that you do not attempt to experience the feelings of the other. Rather, you translate your intellectual understanding of what the speaker has experienced into your own feelings of concern, compassion, or sorrow for that person. For instance, imagine that Heather understands that Monique is sad and disappointed, but instead of trying to feel Monique's emotions or experience how she herself would feel in a similar situation Heather feels concern and compassion for her friend. This is a sympathetic response. Because of this difference in perspective, many scholars differentiate sympathy from empathy.

Although people vary in their ability to empathize, most of us should learn to increase our empathy and then decide to practice it. Those of us who are overly "I"-oriented find it especially difficult to see the world from another's point of view. As a result, our ability to empathize is often underdeveloped. Under these circumstances, we may need to exert extra effort to develop our empathizing skills if we are to increase our interpersonal effectiveness.

Though it may seem trite, the first step in improving our empathizing is to take the time and make the effort to respect the person who is speaking. This does not mean that we need to have a deep, personal relationship with others to empathize with them. **Respect** means that we pay serious attention to what others are saying and what they feel about what they are saying. It begins by treating a person as a person with value and not as an object. Respecting others focuses our time and energy on the other, not on the self.

---

empathy–*intellectually identifying with or vicariously experiencing the feelings, thoughts, or attitudes of another and responding appropriately.*

empathic responsiveness–*experiencing an emotional response parallel to another person's actual or anticipated display of emotion.*

perspective taking–*imagining yourself in the place of another.*

sympathetic responsiveness–*feeling concern, compassion, or sorrow for another because of the other's situation or plight.*

THINKING ABOUT . . .

Empathy Approaches

Which of the three approaches to empathy do you rely on most? Under what circumstances would it be difficult for you to use each of these three approaches to empathy?

respect–*paying serious attention to what others are saying and what they feel about what they are saying.*

How well you empathize also depends on how observant you are of others' behavior and how clearly you "read" the nonverbal messages they are sending. To improve your observational skills, try the following. When another person begins a conversation with you, develop the habit of silently posing two questions to yourself: (1) What emotions do I believe the person is experiencing right now? and (2) What are the cues the person is giving that I am using to draw this conclusion? Consciously asking these questions helps you focus your attention on the nonverbal aspects of messages; this is where most of the information on the person's emotional state is conveyed.

To further increase the accuracy of reading emotions, you can use the skill of perception checking—especially when the other person's culture is different from your own. Remember, cultures vary in how and how much emotion is expressed nonverbally. Once you have understood the emotions the other person is feeling, you can then choose the type of empathic response you wish to use.

To become more effective at empathizing with another, (1) adopt an attitude of respect toward the person, (2) concentrate on understanding the nonverbal as well as the verbal messages, (3) use behavioral cues to ascertain his or her emotional state, (4) try to feel with the person, (or) try to recall or imagine

OBSERVE & ANALYZE
Journal Activity

Empathizing Effectively

Describe a time you effectively empathized with another person. Write an analysis of the effort under Journal Activity 6.2 in your Student Workbook. What was the person's emotional state? How did you recognize it? What were the nonverbal cues? Verbal cues? What type of relationship do you have with this person? How similar is this person to you? Have you ever had a real or vicarious experience similar to the one the person was reporting?

SKILL BUILDERS   Empathy

Skill	Use	Procedure	Example
Intellectually identifying with or vicariously experiencing the feelings, thoughts, or attitudes of another.	To create or to promote a supportive climate.	1. Adopt an attitude of respect by actively attending to what the person says. 2. Concentrate on understanding both verbal and nonverbal messages. 3. Use the person's behavioral cues to ascertain his or her emotional state. 4. Try to feel with the person, or try to recall or imagine how you would feel in similar circumstances, or allow yourself to experience your own feelings of concern, compassion, or sorrow for the person. 5. Respond in a way that reflects those feelings.	When Jerry says, "I really feel embarrassed about wearing braces in college," Mary smiles ruefully and replies, "Yeah, it makes you feel like a little kid, doesn't it? I remember the things I had to put up with when I wore braces."

how you would feel in similar circumstances, (or) try to understand what the person is feeling to help yourself experience your own feelings of concern, compassion, or sorrow for that person. Finally, (5) respond in a way that reflects those feelings.

For additional information on empathy and listening, log on to www.psychological-hug.com/indexBP.htm, an empathy and listening skills home page by Lawrence Bookbinder, Ph.D., and Fellow of the American Psychological Association.

Questioning

questioning–*a response designed to get further information or to clarify information already received.*

Active listeners are willing to question to help them get the information they need to understand. A **question** is, of course, a response designed to get further information or to clarify information already received. Although you may have asked questions for as long as you can remember, you may notice that at times your questions either don't get the information you want or irritate, fluster, or cause defensiveness. We can increase the chances that our questions will get us the information we want and reduce negative reactions if we observe these guidelines:

1. **Note the kind of information you need to increase your understanding.** Suppose Maria says to you, "I am totally frustrated. Would you stop at the store on the way home and buy me some more paper?" At this point, you may be a bit confused and need more information to understand what Maria is asking you. Yet if you respond "What do you mean?" you are likely to add to the confusion. Maria, who is already uptight, will probably not know precisely what it is you do not understand. To increase your understanding, you might ask Maria one of these three types of questions:

   - *Questions to get more information on important details.* "What kind of paper would you like me to get, and how much will you need?"
   - *Questions to clarify the use of a term.* "Could you tell me what you mean by 'frustrated'?"
   - *Questions to clarify the cause of the feelings the person is expressing.* "What's frustrating you?"

   Determine whether the information you need is more detail, clarification of a word or idea, or information on the cause of feelings or events; then phrase your question accordingly.

2. **Phrase questions as complete sentences.** Under pressure our tendency is to use one- or two-word questions that may be perceived as curt or abrupt. For instance, when Miles says "Molly just told me that I always behave in ways that are totally insensitive to her needs," instead of asking "How?" you might ask, "Did she give you specific behaviors or describe specific

Bob Daemmrich/Stock, Boston

Increasing empathy includes reading nonverbal messages and asking questions to clarify.

incidents when this happened?" Curt, abrupt questions often seem to challenge the speaker instead of focusing on the kind of information the respondent needs to understand the statement. By phrasing more complete questions, the questioner shows the respondent that he or she has been heard.

3. **Monitor your nonverbal cues so that they convey genuine interest and concern.** Ask questions with a tone of voice that is sincere—not a tone that could be interpreted as bored, sarcastic, cutting, superior, dogmatic, or evaluative. We need to constantly remind ourselves that the way we speak may be even more important than the words we use.

4. **Put the "burden of ignorance" on your own shoulders.** To minimize defensive reactions, especially when people are under stress, phrase your questions to put the burden of ignorance on your own shoulders by prefacing your question with a short statement that suggests that any problem of misunderstanding may be the result of *your* listening skills. For instance, when Drew says, "I've really had it with Malone screwing up all the time," you might say, "Drew, I'm sorry, I'm missing some details that would help me understand your feelings better—what kinds of things has Malone been doing?"

Here are two more examples that contrast inappropriate with more appropriate questioning responses.

Tamara: "They turned down my proposal again!"

Art: [Inappropriate] "Well, did you explain it the way you should have?" *(This question is a veiled attack on Tamara in question form.)*

[Appropriate] "Did they tell you why?" *(This question is a sincere request for additional information.)*

Renee: "With all those executives at the party last night, I really felt strange."

Javier: [Inappropriate] "Why?" *(With this abrupt question, Javier is making no effort to be sensitive to Renee's feelings or to understand them.)*

[Appropriate] "Gee, what is it about your bosses' presence that makes you feel strange?" *(Here the question is phrased to elicit information that will help Javier understand, and it may help Renee understand as well.)*

In summary, to increase your effectiveness at asking questions, (1) note the kind of information you need to increase your understanding of the message, (2) phrase specific, complete sentence questions that focus on getting that information, (3) deliver them in a sincere tone of voice, and (4) in stressful situations put the burden of ignorance on your own shoulders.

Paraphrasing

paraphrasing–*putting your understanding of the message into words.*

In addition to being skilled questioners, active listeners are also adept at **paraphrasing**, putting their understanding of the message into words. For example, during a meeting with his professor to discuss his performance on the first exam, Charley says, "Well, it looks like I really blew this first test—I had a lot of things on my mind." If Professor Jensen responds by saying, "If I understand you correctly, there were things happening to you that took your mind away from studying," she would be paraphrasing.

content paraphrase–*a response that focuses on the denotative meaning of the verbal message.*

feelings paraphrase–*a response that focuses on the emotions attached to the content of the message.*

Paraphrases may focus on content, on feelings underlying the content, or on both. In the previous example, the professor's paraphrase "If I understand you correctly, there were things happening to you that took your mind away from studying" is a **content paraphrase.** It focuses on the denotative meaning of the message. As Charley began to speak, if Professor Jensen noticed that he dropped his eyes, sighed, and slowly shook his head, and she said, "So you were pretty upset with your grade on the last test," her response would be a **feelings paraphrase**—that is, a response that captures the emotions attached to the content of the message.

In real-life settings, we often don't distinguish clearly between content and feelings paraphrases, and our responses might well be a combination of both. All three types of paraphrases for the same statement are shown in this example:

Statement: "Five weeks ago I gave the revised manuscript of my independent study to my project adviser. I felt really good about it because I thought the changes I had made really improved my explanations. Well, yesterday I stopped by and got the manuscript back, and my adviser said he couldn't really see that this draft was much different from the first."

Content paraphrase: "Let me see if I'm understanding this right. Your adviser thought that you hadn't really done much to rework your paper, but you put a lot of effort into it and think this draft was a lot different and much improved."

Feelings paraphrase: "I sense that you are really frustrated that your adviser didn't recognize the changes you had made."

Combination: "If I have this right, you're saying that your adviser could see no real differences, yet you think your draft was not only different but much improved. I also get the feeling that your adviser's comments really irk you."

In addition to paraphrasing when you need a better understanding of a message, you will also want to consider paraphrasing when the message is long and contains several complex ideas, when it seems to have been said under emotional strain, or when you are talking with people for whom English is not their native language.

In summary, to paraphrase effectively, (1) listen carefully to the message, (2) notice what images and feelings you have experienced from the message, (3) determine what the message means to you, and (4) create a message that conveys these images or feelings.

SKILL BUILDERS   Paraphrasing

Skill	Use	Procedure	Example
A response that conveys your understanding of another person's message.	To increase listening efficiency; to avoid message confusion; to discover the speaker's motivation.	1. Listen carefully to the message. 2. Notice what images and feelings you have experienced from this message. 3. Determine what the message means to you. 4. Create a message that conveys these images or feelings.	Grace says, "At two minutes to five, the boss gave me three letters that had to be in the mail that evening!" Bonita replies, "If I understand, you were really resentful that your boss dumped important work on you right before quitting time when she knows you have to pick up the baby at day care."

TEST YOUR COMPETENCE

Writing Questions and Paraphrases

Provide an appropriate question and paraphrase for each of these statements. To get you started, the first conversation has been completed for you.

1. **Luis:** "It's Dionne's birthday, and I've planned a *big* evening. Sometimes I think Dionne believes I take her for granted—well, after tonight she'll know I think she's something special!"
   Question: "What specific things do you have planned?"
   Content paraphrase: "If I'm understanding you, you've planned a night that's going to be a lot more elaborate than what Dionne expects on her birthday."
   Feelings paraphrase: "From the way you're talking, I get the feeling you've really proud of yourself for making plans like these."

2. **Angie:** "Brother! Another nothing class. I keep thinking one of these days he'll get excited about something. Professor Romero is a real bore!"
   Question:
   Content paraphrase:
   Feelings paraphrase:

3. **Guy:** "Everyone seems to be talking about that movie on Channel 5 last night, but I didn't see it. You know, I don't watch much that's on the 'idiot box.'"
   Question:
   Content paraphrase:
   Feelings paraphrase:

4. **Kaelin:** "I don't know if it's something to do with me or with Mom, but lately she and I just aren't getting along."
   Question:
   Content paraphrase:
   Feelings paraphrase:

5. **Aileen:** "I've got a report due at work and a paper due in management class. On top of that, it's my sister's birthday, and so far I haven't even had time to get her anything. Tomorrow's going to be a disaster."
   Question:
   Content paraphrase:
   Feelings paraphrase:

Remembering: Retaining Information

remembering–*being able to retain information and recall it when needed.*

Remembering is being able to retain information and recall it when needed. Too often we forget almost immediately what we have heard. For instance, you can probably think of many times when you were unable to recall the name of a person to whom you were introduced just moments earlier. Three techniques that are likely to work for you in improving your ability to remember information are repeating, constructing mnemonics, and taking notes.

Repeat Information

Repetition—saying something two, three, or even four times—helps listeners store information in long-term memory by providing necessary reinforcement (Estes, 1989, p. 7). If information is not reinforced, it will be held in short-term memory for as little as twenty seconds and then forgotten. So, when you are introduced to a stranger named Jack McNeil, if you mentally say "Jack McNeil, Jack McNeil, Jack McNeil, Jack McNeil," you increase the chances that you will remember his name. Likewise, when a person gives you the directions, "Go two blocks east, turn left, turn right at the next light, and it's in the next block," you should immediately repeat to yourself, "two blocks east, turn left, turn right at light, next block—that's two blocks east, turn left, turn right at light, next block."

Construct Mnemonics

Constructing mnemonics helps listeners put information in forms that are more easily recalled. A **mnemonic device** is any artificial technique used as a memory aid. One of the most common ways of forming a mnemonic is to take the first letters of a list of items you are trying to remember and form a word. For example, an easy mnemonic for remembering the five Great Lakes is HOMES (Huron, Ontario, Michigan, Erie, Superior).

When you want to remember items in a sequence, try to form a sentence with the words themselves or assign words using the first letters of the words in sequence and form an easy-to-remember statement. For example, when you studied music the first time, you may have learned the lines of the treble clef (EGBDF) with the saying "*every good boy does fine.*" (And for the spaces of the treble clef (FACE), you may have remembered the word *face.*)

Take Notes

Although note taking would be inappropriate in most casual interpersonal encounters, it represents a powerful tool for increasing our recall of information when we are involved in telephone conversations, briefing sessions, interviews, business meetings, and listening to speeches. Note taking provides us with a written record we can go back to, and it also enables us to take a more active role in the listening process (Wolvin & Coakley, 1996, p. 239). In short, when you are listening to complex information, take notes.

What constitutes good notes will vary depending on the situation. Useful notes may consist of a brief list of main points or key ideas plus a few of the most significant details. Or they may be a short summary of the entire concept (a type of paraphrase) after the message is completed. For lengthy and rather detailed information, however, good notes likely will consist of a brief outline of what the speaker has said, including the overall idea, the main points of the message, and key developmental material. Good notes are not necessarily very long. In fact, many classroom lectures can be reduced to a short outline of notes (see Figure 6.1).

COMMUNICATE!
Using Technology

Speaker phones, wireless phones, and cellular phones have brought a new level of convenience to communication. These days you can work on your computer, drive, or even cook dinner while you are on the phone. But what effects have these devices had on your listening effectiveness? Next time you are using one of these devices, be conscious of your listening. How well are you doing at attending, understanding, and remembering? Which of the guidelines provided in this chapter should you apply to improve your listening under these conditions?

mnemonic device—*any artificial technique used as a memory aid.*

OBSERVE & ANALYZE
Journal Activity

Creating Mnemonics

Mnemonics are useful memory aids. Under Journal Activity 6.3 in your Student Workbook, construct a mnemonic for the five phases of the listening process identified in this chapter: attending, understanding, remembering, evaluating, and responding. Write down your mnemonic.

Tomorrow, while you are getting dressed, see whether you can recall the mnemonic you created. Then see whether you can recall the phases of the listening process from the cues in your mnemonic. How well did you do? Be prepared to share what you wrote with your classmates.

TEST YOUR COMPETENCE

Listening Test

Have a friend assume the role of a fellow worker on your first day in an office job and read the following information to you once, at a normal rate of speech. As the friend reads the instructions, take notes. Then test yourself by answering the numbered questions without referring to your notes. Then repeat the quiz using your notes this time. How much did your score improve? Although the temptation is great to read this item to yourself, try not to. You will miss both the enjoyment and the value of the exercise if you do.

Since you are new to the job, I'd like to fill you in on a few details. The boss probably told you that typing and distribution of mail were your most important duties. Well, they may be, but let me tell you, answering the phone is going to take most of your time. Now about the typing. Goodwin will give the most, but much of what he gives you may have nothing to do with the department—I'd be careful about spending all my time doing his private work. Mason doesn't give much, but you'd better get it right—she's really a stickler. I've always asked to have tests at least two days in advance. Paulson is always dropping stuff on the desk at the last minute.

The mail situation sounds tricky, but you'll get used to it. Mail comes twice a day—at 10 a.m. and at 2 p.m. You've got to take the mail that's been left on the desk to Charles Hall for pickup. If you really have some rush stuff, take it right to the campus post office in Harper Hall. It's a little longer walk, but for really rush stuff, it's better. When you pick up at McDaniel Hall, sort it. You'll have to make sure that only mail for the people up here gets delivered here. If there is any that doesn't belong here, bundle it back up and mark it for return to the campus post office.

Now, about your breaks. You get ten minutes in the morning, forty minutes at noon, and fifteen minutes in the afternoon. If you're smart, you'll leave before the 10:30 classes let out. That's usually a pretty crush time. Three of the teachers are supposed to have office hours then, and if they don't keep them, the students will be on your back. If you take your lunch at 11:45, you'll be back before the main crew goes.

Oh, one more thing. You are supposed to call Jeno at 8:15 every morning to wake him. If you forget, he gets very upset. Well, good luck.

Without Notes	With Notes	
_____	_____	1. Where are you to take the mail that does not belong here?
_____	_____	2. How often does mail come?
_____	_____	3. When should you be back from lunch?
_____	_____	4. What is Paulson's problem with requests for work?
_____	_____	5. Who gives the most work?
_____	_____	6. What's the problem with Goodwin's request to do work?
_____	_____	7. What are your main jobs, according to the boss?
_____	_____	8. Where are you to take outgoing mail?
_____	_____	9. Where is the post office?
_____	_____	10. How many minutes do you get for your morning break?
_____	_____	11. What is the preferred time to take your lunch?
_____	_____	12. Who are you supposed to give a wake-up call?

Answers:
1. Campus post office (or Harper Hall) 2. Twice a day 3. 12:25 4. Last minute 5. Goodwin 6. Not work-related 7. Typing/distributing mail 8. Charles Hall 9. Harper Hall 10. 10 11. 11:45 12. Jeno

---

OUTLINE

Duties

Typing, distribution of mail important

Answering phone takes most time

Typing

Goodwin gives most—question doing private work

Mason, not give much, but get it right—she's a stickler.

Ask for tests 2 days in advance (watch out for Paulson's last minute)

Mail

10 and 2

Take to Charles Hall

Rush stuff goes to campus PO in Harper

Sort mail from McDaniel Hall—bundle what

doesn't belong and mark for return to the campus PO

Breaks

10 min. morning—take before 10:30

40 min. lunch—take at 11:45

Extra

Call Jeno 8:15   (93 words)

Figure 6.1
Outline.

Critical Analysis

Critical analysis is the process of determining how truthful, authentic, or believable you judge information to be. For instance, when a person tries to convince you to vote for a particular candidate for office or to support efforts to implement legalization of RU 486 (the so-called abortion pill), you will want to listen critically to these messages to determine how much you agree with the speaker and how you wish to respond. If you fail to listen critically to the messages you receive, you risk inadvertently concurring in ideas or plans that may violate your own values, be counterproductive to achieving your goals, or be misleading to others (including the speakers) who value your judgment.

Critical analysis requires that you evaluate the quality of inferences. **Inferences** are claims or assertions based on observation or fact, but they are not necessarily true. Critical listeners evaluate inferences by examining the context in which they occur. An inference is usually presented as part of an argument; that is, a person makes a claim (an inference) and then presents other statements in support of the claim. Here is an example of a simple argument. Joyce says, "Next year is going to be a lot easier than the past year. I got a $200-a-month raise, and my husband's been relieved of some of the extra work he's had to do while they were looking for a replacement for Ed." The statements "I got a $200-a-month raise," and "my husband's been relieved of some of the extra work he's had to do while they were

critical analysis–*the process of determining the truthfulness, authenticity, or believability of the information provided.*

inferences–*claims or assertions based on observations of fact but which may or may not be true.*

looking for a replacement for Ed" are both factual statements that can be documented. Her claim "Next year is going to be a lot easier than the past year" is an inference—a statement that requires support to validate it. Notice that Joyce's inference suggests that she believes there is a relationship between her claim and the facts she presents. Her argument is based on the assumption that more money per month and less work for her husband will make the year easier.

The critical listener asks at least three questions when evaluating any inference:

1. **Is there factual information to support the inference?** Perhaps there is no supporting information; perhaps there is not enough; or perhaps the supporting information is inaccurate. Joyce does have factual statements for support: She received a raise, and her husband has less work to do.

2. **Is the factual support relevant to the inference?** Perhaps the actual or implied statement of relevance is logically weak. In the example, "increased income" is one kind of information that is relevant to "having an easier time." At this stage, it would appear that Joyce does have the makings of a sound argument; however, we need to ask a third question.

3. **Is there known information that would prevent the inference from logically following the factual statements?** Perhaps there is information that is not accounted for that affects the likelihood of the inference. If we learn that getting the $200-a-month raise involves extra duties for Joyce, then we still might question whether the year is likely to be "easier" than the last one.

For many of us, the most difficult of the three questions to answer is the second one: "Is the factual support relevant to the inference?" This question is difficult to answer primarily because the listener must be able to verbalize a statement that shows the relevance. The listener must create the statement because in most informal reasoning the link is only implied by the person presenting the argument. Recall that Joyce never said anything like "A raise and a reduction of work are two criteria for predicting that next year will be a lot easier." Because the relevance is more often implied than stated, we must learn to phrase it.

The key to phrasing the relationship between support and inference to judge its relevance is to ask yourself, "What can I say that would make sense for this inference to follow from these facts?" For instance, suppose Hal says "I see frost on the grass—I think our flowers are goners." What can we say that establishes the relevance of the supporting fact "frost on the grass" to the claim "our flowers are goners"? If I were Hal, I would likely be thinking, "The presence of frost means that the temperature is low enough to freeze the moisture on the grass. If it's cold enough to freeze the moisture on the grass, it's cold enough to kill my flowers." This seems to make sense because we can demonstrate a relationship between frost and the death of unprotected flowers.

Let's try another one. Gina says, "I studied all night and only got a D on the first test—I'm not going to do any better on this one." This statement suggests that Gina sees relevance between the amount of study time before a test and the

Evaluating Inferences

For each of these statements, ask and answer three questions: (1) Is the inference supported with meaningful factual statements? (2) Does the stated or implied relevance between the support and the inference make sense? (3) Is there any other known information that lessens the quality of the inference? Remember, to do this properly you must phrase a reasoning link to tie the supporting information to the inference.

1. "The chess club held a raffle, and they made a lot of money. I think we should hold a raffle too."

2. "Chad is aggressive, personable, and highly motivated—he ought to make a good salesman."

3. "Three of my students last year got A's on this test, five the year before, and three the year before that. There certainly will be some A's this year."

4. "I saw Kali in a maternity outfit—she must be pregnant."

5. "Listen, I like the way Darren thinks, Solomon is an excellent mathematician, and Marco and Ethan are two of my best students. All four are Alpha Alphas. As far as I'm concerned, the Alphas are the group on campus with academic strength."

6. "If Greg hadn't come barging in, I never would have spilled my iced tea."

7. "Maybe that's the way you see it, but to me, when high city officials are caught with their hands in the till and when police close their eyes to the actions of people with money, that's corruption."

8. "Krista wears her hair that way and guys fall all over her—I'm getting myself a hairdo like that."

grade. We could phrase the implied relevance by saying, "Because the time of study before the test, which determines the grade, can be no greater, Gina can't improve her grade."

In this case, the relevance seems questionable. Her reasoning suggests that the only factor in determining a grade is the amount of study time before the test. Experience would suggest that many other factors, such as previous time studying and frame of mind, are of equal if not greater importance.

In short, you are listening critically when (1) you question whether the inference is supported with meaningful factual statements, (2) you question whether the stated or implied relevance between the support and the inference makes sense, and (3) you question whether there is any other known information that lessens the quality of the inference.

Responding Empathically to Give Comfort

Once we have clarified the speaker's message so that we understand it, we may need to provide further emotional comfort to the speaker. To **comfort** means to help people feel better about themselves and their behavior. Comforting occurs when one feels respected, understood, and confirmed.

comforting–*helping people feel better about themselves and their behavior.*

Research on comforting messages shows that people who use a relatively high percentage of sophisticated comforting strategies are perceived as more sensitive, concerned, and involved (Samter, Burleson, & Murphy, 1987; Burleson & Samter, 1990; Kunkel & Burleson, 1999). Obviously, we cannot comfort unless we have first empathized. Over the years, much of the most significant research on comforting has been conducted by Brant Burleson and colleagues, and we feature Burleson in this Spotlight on Scholars.

In the section on Understanding, we discussed two important empathic responses: questioning and paraphrasing. In this section, we consider supporting and interpreting.

SPOTLIGHT ON SCHOLARS

Brant Burleson, Professor of Communication at Purdue University, on Comforting

The seeds for Brant Burleson's interest in comforting behavior were sown during his undergraduate days at the University of Colorado at Boulder where he was taught that all communication was persuasion. This proposition did not square with Burleson's own experiences. As a child of the fifties who came of age during the emotion-filled sixties, Burleson had witnessed lots of hurt and conflict, but he had also seen people engaging in altruism and acts of comforting. These comforting acts, he reasoned, were not aimed at changing anyone's opinion or behavior. They were simply done to help the other person. When Burleson entered graduate school at the University of Illinois, he began to study formally how individuals comfort others. He wanted to establish scientifically whether comforting messages were important and whether they made a difference. Since graduate school, Burleson's work has done much to accomplish this goal.

In his research, Burleson has carefully defined comforting strategies as messages that have the goal of relieving or lessening the emotional distress of others. He has limited his work to looking at how we comfort others who are experiencing mild or moderate sadness or disappointment that happens as a result of everyday events. He has chosen not to study comforting in situations where there is extreme depression or grief because of extraordinary events. He has also chosen to limit his work to the verbal strategies that we use when we comfort. Burleson's care in defining the "domain" of his work is important. By carefully stating the type of emotional distress he is concerned with, and by clearly identifying the limits of his work, Burleson enables those who read his work to understand the types of situations to which his findings apply.

Early on, Burleson worked with James L. Applegate, who had developed a way of judging the sophistication of particular comforting messages. Sophisticated messages were seen as those that acknowledged, elaborated, and legitimized the feelings of another person. Sophisticated comforting strategies are also more listener-centered (aimed at discovering how the distressed person feels), less evaluative, more feeling-centered, more likely to accept the point of view of the other person, and more likely to offer explanations for the feelings being express by the other person.

More recently Burleson and others who study comforting have turned their attention to understanding the results of comforting. Previous research has judged comforting messages only on the extent to which they reduce the immediate distress a person is feeling. Burleson believes the effects of comforting extend beyond this simple instrumental effect. He theorizes that effective comforting should also help the other person be able to cope better in the future. Skilled comforting should also benefit the comforter. When we effectively comfort others, Burleson believes we increase our own self-esteem, and we become better liked by the person we comfort and by those who see us effectively comfort others. Finally, Burleson believes those who are effective at comforting others are likely to have better long-term relationships. A growing list of research studies, some conducted by Burleson and his colleagues, provide support for his theory. For complete citations of many of his and his colleagues publications, see the reference list at the end of this book.

To better understand just why comforting messages help people feel better while other messages don't do anything—or even make people feel worse—Burleson has recently studied theories and research on emotion and factors that lead to emotional distress. This study of emotion dynamics has led to a new understanding of comforting as a conversational process that, at its best, helps distressed others make sense of what has happened to them, work through their feelings, and reappraise the upsetting situation. This view of the comforting process emphasizes the role of empathic listening and the importance of getting upset people to talk about their feelings and experiences in detail. People seem to make sense of their distressing experiences by expressing their thoughts and feelings in narratives or stories. Burleson and his graduate students are currently conducting several studies on sense-making narratives and how these narratives contribute to the reduction of emotional distress. For more information on Burleson's research, go to http://www.sla.purdue.edu/academic/comm/Staff/Faculty.html#Burleson

Supporting

Supporting responses are comforting statements whose goal is to show approval, bolster, encourage, soothe, console, or cheer up. They show that we care about people and what happens to them and demonstrate that we empathize with people's feelings whatever their direction or intensity (Burleson, 1994, p. 5).

supporting responses—
comforting statements whose goal is to show approval, bolster, encourage, soothe, console, or cheer up.

Supporting (approving) positive feelings We all like to treasure our good feelings. When we share them, we don't want them dashed by a listener's inappropriate or insensitive responses. Supporting positive feelings is generally easy, but still requires some care. Consider this example:

Kendra (hangs up the telephone, does a little dance step, and turns to Selena): That was my boss. He said that he'd put my name in for promotion. I didn't believe he would really choose me!

Brian Bailey/Stone

We all like to treasure our good feelings; when we share them, we don't want them dashed by a listener's inappropriate or insensitive responses.

Kendra's statement requires an appropriate verbal response. To do so, Selena must appreciate the feeling people get when they receive good news, or she must envision how she would feel under the same circumstances.

> **Selena:** Kendra, way to go, girl! That's terrific! I am so happy for you. You really seem excited.

Selena's response gives her approval for Kendra to be excited. Her response also shows that she is happy because Kendra seems happy.

Supporting responses like Selena's are much needed. Think of times when you have experienced an event that made you feel happy, proud, pleased, soothed, or amused and needed to express those feelings. Didn't it further your good feelings when others recognized your feelings and affirmed your right to have them?

Supporting (giving comfort) when a person experience's negative feelings When a person has had an unfortunate experience and is in the midst of or is recalling unpleasant emotional reactions, an effective supporting statement provides much-needed comfort. By acknowledging these feelings and supporting the person's right to the feelings, you can help the person further his or her progress at working through the feelings.

For some people, making appropriate responses to painful or angry feelings is very awkward and difficult. But when people are in pain or when they are feeling justifiably angry, they need to be comforted by appropriate supporting statements. Because it can be difficult to provide comfort when we are ill at ease, we need to practice and develop skill at making appropriate supporting statements.

THINKING ABOUT . . .

Sharing Good Feelings

Recall an occasion when you were feeling especially happy, proud, or pleased and chose to share your feelings with someone else. Who did you choose? Why did you choose this person? How did the person react? What effect did that person's reaction have on your immediate feelings? On you relationship with the person? If you had a similar situation, would you again choose to tell this person?

An appropriate comforting statement shows empathy, sensitivity, and may show a willingness to be actively involved if need be. Consider this example:

Bill: My sister called today to tell me that Mom's biopsy came back positive. She's got cancer and it's untreatable.

Dwight: Bill, you must be in shock. I'm so sorry that this is happening. Do you want to talk about it? Is there anything I can do to help you right now?

Notice how Dwight begins by empathizing: "Bill, you must be in shock." He continues with statements that show his sensitivity to the seriousness of the situation: "I'm so sorry that this is happening." Finally, he shows he really cares—he is willing to take time to talk about it, and he asks whether he can do anything for Bill.

We have stressed that comforting responses may reassure, bolster, encourage, soothe, console, or cheer up. It is likely that each situation will call for a slightly different approach—and on some occasions you may want to use more than one approach. For instance, instead of just recognizing that the person is feeling pain ("That must have been a particularly painful experience for you"), you may also want to extend your willingness to help ("Is there anything I can do for you") or provide an optimistic note ("Dawn felt really down when . . . but she was able to get the kind of help that allowed her to get through the ordeal"). In fact, combination approaches are often perceived as most comforting (Clark et al., 1998, p. 237).

Let's contrast this example with another one that seems to be supportive but is really inappropriate:

Jim (comes out of his boss's office clutching the report he had been so sure he would receive praise for): Jacobs tore my report apart. I worked my tail off, tried to do everything he asked, and he just threw it back in my face and told me to redo it.

Aaron (who has not read the report): Jim, I can see why you're angry. You deserved praise for what you did!

Such a response certainly has supporting qualities, and Jim might feel soothed. But supporting that "takes a person's side" can have unintended side effects, especially as in this case because Aaron is in no position to judge whether the report did in fact deserve praise. Instead, Aaron would do better by focusing his supporting response on how hard Jim worked and, therefore, why Jim may be feeling overly angered.

Aaron: He rejected it? After you worked all that overtime, I can see why you're so upset.

Giving empathic support is not the same as making statements that are not true or only telling people what they want to hear. When supportive statements are out of touch with the facts, they can encourage behavior that is actually destructive. When offering comfort through supporting statements, be sure that you don't inadvertently set the person up.

Making an appropriate supporting response is most difficult in situations of high emotion and stress. Sometimes the best supporting response is a nonverbal one. Imagine this scenario: In the final few seconds of a basketball game, with her team trailing by one point, Jory misses an uncontested lay-up. Jory walks off the floor, looks at the coach, and shouts, "I blew it! I lost us the game!"

How should the coach react? A first reaction might be to say, "Don't feel bad, Jory." But Jory obviously does feel bad, and she has a right to those feelings. Another response might be, "Hey, Jory, you didn't lose us the game," but in fact Jory's miss did affect the outcome. Jory is unlikely to find this response helpful because it is inaccurate. Perhaps the best thing the coach can do at that moment is to put an arm around Jory and give a comforting squeeze that says, "It's OK, I understand." Later coach might say, "Jory, I know you feel bad, but without your steal, we wouldn't even have had a chance to win." Still, for the moment, Jory is going to be difficult to console.

Some people think comforting supportive statements come easier to females or even that they are more of a female skill. In fact, some people go so far as to say that men and women are totally different in their views of comfort. But in their detailed analysis of views on comforting, Kunkel and Burleson (1999) found that "Men and women tend to use, if not identical, at least very similar rulers in evaluating the sensitivity and effectiveness of emotional support" (p. 334). So it isn't that men and women see comforting differently; rather, men and women perform differently. Men focus more on behaviors, and women focus more on feelings. In their laboratory study, Derlega, Barbee, and Winstead (1994) found that males were perceived to be somewhat better than females in providing achievement-related support (such as for being passed over for a promotion).

If men recognize the importance of more personal, feelings-oriented types of comforting statements, why don't they do better? Kunkel and Burleson (1999) conclude that "men lack the competence to perform comforting behaviors as sensitively and effectively as women" (p. 335). In short, perhaps men need more practice than women in applying the information presented in this section. Whether you are male or female, you can learn to give effective supportive responses.

In summary, to make effective supporting statements, (1) listen closely to what the person is saying, (2) try to empathize with the dominant feelings, (3) phrase a reply that is in harmony with the feeling you have identified, (4) supplement your verbal response with appropriate nonverbal responses, and (5) if it seems appropriate, indicate your willingness to help.

Interpreting

interpreting responses— *statements that offer a reasonable alternative explanation for an event or circumstance with the goal of helping another to understand the situation from a different perspective.*

Interpreting responses are those that offer a reasonable alternative explanation for an event or circumstance with the goal of helping another to understand the situation from a different perspective. Especially when people's emotions are running high, they are likely to see only one of a number of possible explanations. Consider this following situation.

Travis returns from his first date with Natasha, a woman he has been interested in for some time. He plops down on the couch, shakes his head, and says, "Well that was certainly a disaster! We had a great dinner and saw a really good show, and when I get to her door, she gives me a quick little kiss on the cheek, says, 'Thanks a lot,' and rushes into the house. We didn't even have much time to talk about the play. I guess I can chalk that one up. It's clear she's really not interested in me."

Travis is interpreting Natasha's behavior negatively; he sees her actions as a rejection of him. Martin, Travis's roommate, has been listening to him. Although he does not know what Natasha thinks, he perceives that Travis is only seeing one explanation for these events and that he might be comforted by seeing other possible explanations. So Martin says, "You're right, her behavior was a bit abrupt, but maybe she's had bad experiences with other guys. You know, ones who tried to go too far too fast, so she wasn't really trying to reject you, she was just trying to protect herself."

Whose interpretation is correct? It remains to be seen. Remember, you are not a mind reader—you cannot know for sure why something was done or said. Your primary goal when interpreting is to help a person look at an event from a different point of view. As with supporting statements, it is important to offer interpretation only when it seems plausible and worth considering. The point is not merely to soothe the person's feelings but to help the person see a possibility he or she has overlooked. Most events can be interpreted in more than one way, and we can be supportive by helping people see alternative explanations for things that happen to them. When we do this, we both comfort them and help them more accurately understand what has happened.

THINKING ABOUT . . .

Comforting Responses

Think of the last time you told someone about an event or circumstance in which you felt scared, hurt, disappointed, or angry. Did the person try to comfort you? If so, report what was said. Did the person try to offer alternative interpretations for what had happened? Did this help you? If so, how? If not, why not? What can you learn from this experience that will help you improve your response skills?

Michael Newman/PhotoEdit, Inc.

People often misinterpret feedback. We can support one another by offering alternatives to negative interpretations.

Let's consider two additional examples of appropriate interpreting responses:

Karla: I just don't understand Deon. I say we've got to start saving money, and he just gets angry with me.

Shelley: I can understand why his behavior would concern you (a supportive statement prefacing an interpretation). Perhaps he feels guilty about not being able to save money or feels resentful that you seem to be putting all the blame on him.

Micah: I just don't believe Bradford. He says my work is top-notch, but I haven't got a pay raise in over a year.

Khalif: I can see why you'd be frustrated, but maybe it has nothing to do with the quality of your work. Maybe the company just doesn't have the money.

Both of these examples follow the guidelines for providing appropriate interpreting responses: (1) Listen carefully to what that person is saying. (2) Think of other reasonable explanations for the event or circumstance and decide which alternative seems to best fit the situation as you understand it. (3) Phrase an alternative to the person's own interpretation—one that is intended to help the person see that other interpretations are available. (4) When appropriate, try to preface the interpretive statement with a supporting response.

Figure 6.2 summarizes how good listeners and poor listeners deal with the five aspects of listening: attending, understanding, remembering, evaluating, and responding empathetically.

TEST YOUR COMPETENCE

Supporting and Interpreting

For each of these situations, supply one supporting and one interpreting response.

1. **Statement:** "The milk is all gone! I know there was at least half a carton last night. I'll bet Jeff guzzled it all before he left for work. What did he expect me to put on my corn flakes, root beer? All my brother ever thinks about is himself!"
   Supporting response:
   Interpreting response:

2. **Statement:** "My manager must be trying to fire me or get me to quit. He told me that my error rate was higher than average, and he wants me to go downtown to headquarters and take another ten hours of training on my own time."
   Supporting response:
   Interpreting response:

3. **Statement:** "I just got a call from my folks. My sister was in a car accident and ended up in the hospital. They say she's OK, but the car was totaled. I don't know whether she's really all right or whether they just don't want me to worry."
   Supporting response:
   Interpreting response:

	Good Listeners	**Bad Listeners**
ATTENDING	Attend to important information	May not hear what a person is saying
	Ready themselves physically and mentally	Fidget in their chairs, look out the window, and let their minds wander
	Listen objectively regardless of emotional involvement	Visibly react to emotional language
	Listen differently depending on situations	Listen the same way regardless of the type of material
UNDERSTANDING	Assign appropriate meaning to what is said	Hear what is said but are either unable to understand or assign different meaning to the words
	Seek out apparent purpose, main points, and supporting information	Ignore the way information is organized
	Ask mental questions to anticipate information	Fail to anticipate coming information
	Silently paraphrase to solidify understanding	Seldom or never mentally review information
	Seek out subtle meanings based on nonverbal cues	Ignore nonverbal cues
REMEMBERING	Retain information	Interpret message accurately but forget it
	Repeat key information	Assume they will remember
	Mentally create mnemonics for lists of words and ideas	Seldom single out any information as especially important
	Take notes	Rely on memory alone
EVALUATING	Listen critically	Hear and understand but are unable to weigh and consider it
	Separate facts from inferences	Don't differentiate between facts and inferences
	Evaluate inferences	Accept information at face value
RESPONDING EMPATHICALLY	Provide supportive comforting statements	Pass off joy or hurt; change the subject
	Give alternative interpretations	Pass off hurt; change the subject

Figure 6.2
A summary of the five aspects of listening.

WHAT WOULD YOU DO?
A QUESTION OF ETHICS

Janeen always disliked talking on the telephone—she thought it was an impersonal form of communication. Thus college was a wonderful respite. When friends would call her, instead of staying on the phone she could quickly run over to their dorm or meet them at a coffeehouse.

One day during reading period before exams, Janeen received a phone call from Barbara, an out-of-town friend. Before she was able to dismiss the call with her stock excuses, she found herself bombarded with information about old high school friends and their whereabouts. Not wanting to disappoint Barbara, who seemed eager to talk, Janeen tucked her phone under her chin and began straightening her room, answering Barbara with the occasional "uh-huh," "hmm," or "wow, that's cool!" As the "conversation" progressed, Janeen began reading through her mail and then her notes from class. After a few minutes, she realized there was silence on the other end of the line. Suddenly very ashamed, she said, "I'm sorry, what did you say? The phone . . . uh there was just a lot of static."

Barbara replied with obvious hurt in her voice, "I'm sorry I bothered you, you must be terribly busy."

Embarrassed, Janeen muttered, "I'm just really stressed, you know, with exams coming up and everything. I guess I wasn't listening very well, you didn't seem to be saying anything really important. I'm sorry. What were you saying?"

"Nothing 'important,'" Barbara answered. "I was just trying to figure out a way to tell you. I know that you were friends with my brother Billy, and you see, we just found out yesterday that he's terminal with a rare form of leukemia. But you're right, it obviously isn't really important." With that, she hung up.

1. How ethical was Janeen's means of dealing with her dilemma of not wanting to talk on the phone but not wanting to hurt Barbara's feelings?
2. Identify ways in which both Janeen and Barbara could have used better and perhaps more ethical interpersonal communication skills. Rewrite the scenario incorporating these changes.

Conversation and Analysis

Use your Communicate! CD-ROM to access a video scenario of the following conversation. Click on the "Communicate! In Action" feature, and then click on "Damien and Chris." As you watch Damien and Chris discuss Chris's recent problem at work, focus on Damien's use of listening skills.

1. What does he do that shows he is attending?
2. What does he do that demonstrates his understanding?
3. Does he use critical listening to separate facts from inferences?
4. How does he show empathy?

We have provided a transcript of Damien and Chris's conversation. After you have viewed the conversation on your CD-ROM, read the transcript. In the right-hand column there is space for you to record your analysis. You can also complete your analysis electronically using the Conversation Analysis feature included in Communicate! In Action. From the Conversation Menu on your CD-ROM, click "Analysis" for Damien and Chris. Type your answers to the questions above in the forms provided. When you are finished, click "Submit" to compare your response to the analysis provided by the authors.

Damien and Chris work in a small shop selling shirts and gifts. Usually they get along well, but lately Chris has seemed standoffish. Damien decides to talk with Chris to see if anything is wrong. Damien approaches Chris in the break room.

Conversation

Damien: Chris, you've been kind of quiet lately, man. What's been going on?

Chris: Nothing.

Damien: Come on, man. What's going on?

Chris: Just life. (shrugs) I'm just kind of down right now.

Damien: Well, what am I here for? I thought we were friends.

Chris thinks about it and decides to talk about it.

Chris: Well, Carl's been on my case the last few weeks.

Damien: Why? Did you do something?

Chris: Oh, he says that I'm sloppy when I restock and I'm not always "polite" to our customers. You know, just 'cuz I don't smile all the time. I mean, what does he want—little Mary Sunshine?

Damien: So you're angry with the boss.

Analysis

Conversation

Chris: Yeah, I guess . . . no, no, not so angry, I'm just frustrated. I come in to work every day and I try to do my job and I don't complain. You know, I'm sick and tired of getting stuck back there in the stock room reorganizing everything. It's not like they're paying us big bucks here. And Carl shouldn't expect us to be charming with everybody who walks through that door. I mean, half of the people who walk through that door are, well, they're totally rude and act like jerks.

Damien: Yeah, I feel you on that. Some of those people shouldn't be allowed out in public. What is Carl saying about how you're dealing with the customers?

Chris: Oh, he just says that I've changed and that I'm not being "nice." I mean, he used to call me his top guy.

Damien: I mean, you know how Carl is. He's a fanatic about customer service. You know how, when we first started, he drilled us about being polite and smiling and being courteous at all times. So maybe when he says "you're not being nice," he just means that you're not doing it all the way you used to. I mean, I've noticed a change. I mean, you're just not yourself lately. Is anything going on outside of work?

Chris: You could say that. Sarah and I just bought a house, so money's been a bit tight. Now, she wants to quit her job and start a family, and I'm not sure we can afford it. On top of it all, my kid sister shows up a few weeks ago on our doorstep, pregnant, and now she's living with us, so yeah, it is a bit overwhelming. And I'm a bit worried that Carl's going to fire me!

Analysis

Conversation

Analysis

Damien: Wow, that is a lot of stuff! I can understand why you're down, but did Carl really threaten to fire you?

Chris: No, no, but I'm not perfect and he could use my "attitude" as an excuse to fire me.

Damien: Well, did you think about telling him what's been going on? And maybe, you know, he'll understand and cut you some slack.

Chris: Or he could see that I really have changed and he'd can me.

Damien: Ok, well, just tell me this. Do you like working here?

Chris: Yeah, of course I do.

Damien: OK, well, then, you've just got to tough it out. I mean, you've just got to use the game face on these people. You used to be the best at doing that. So you're just gonna have to get back to being a salesman, and leave everything else behind.

Chris: I guess I never realized how much my problems were affecting my work. I thought Carl was just out to get me, but now you're noticing something too, then maybe I have changed. Thanks, thanks for talking this out.

Summary

Listening is an active process that involves attending, understanding, remembering, evaluating, and responding. Effective listening is essential to competent communication.

Attending is the process of selecting the sound waves we consciously process. We can increase the effectiveness of our attention by (1) getting ready to listen, (2) making the shift from speaker to listener a complete one, (3) hearing a person out before reacting, and (4) adjusting our attention to the listening goals of the situation.

Understanding is the process of decoding a message by assigning meaning to it. Understanding requires empathy, intellectually identifying with or vicariously experiencing the feelings, thoughts, or attitudes of another. We can increase our ability to empathize through caring and concentrating. A key to understanding is to practice active listening: Look for or create an organization for the information, ask questions, and paraphrase.

Remembering is the process of storing the meanings that have been received so they may be recalled later. Remembering is increased by rehearsing information, looking for and storing information by an organizational pattern, grouping information to make it easier to remember, and, when feasible, taking notes.

Evaluating, or critical listening, is the process of separating fact from inference and judging the validity of the inferences made. A fact is a verifiable statement; an inference is a conclusion drawn from facts. You are listening critically when (1) you question whether the inference is supported with meaningful factual statements, (2) you question whether the reasoning statement that shows the relationship between the support and the inference makes sense, and (3) you question whether there is any other known information that lessens the quality of the inference.

Responding empathically gives comfort. Comforting responses give people information about themselves or their behavior. Comforting can be accomplished through supporting and interpreting responses. When we are supportive, we soothe, approve, reduce tension, or pacify the other by acknowledging that we understand what the other is feeling and we support that person's right to be feeling as they are. When we use interpreting responses, we offer a reasonable or alternative explanation for an event or circumstance with the goal of helping another to understand the situation from a different perspective.

Communicate! Online

Use your Communicate! CD-ROM for quick access to the electronic study resources that accompany this text. Included on your CD-ROM is access to InfoTrac College Edition, the World Wide Web, a demo of WebTutor for Communicate!, and the Communicate! Web site at the Wadsworth Communication Café. The Communicate! Web site offers chapter-by-chapter activities, quizzes, and a digital glossary.

Review the following key terms at
http://communication.wadsworth.com/humancomm/verderber

Key Terms

attending (126)
comforting (139)
content paraphrase (132)
critical analysis (137)
empathic responsiveness (128)
empathy (128)
feelings paraphrase (132)
inferences (137)
interpreting responses (144)
listening (126)

mnemonic device (135)
paraphrasing (132)
perspective taking (128)
questioning (130)
remembering (134)
respect (128)
supporting responses (141)
sympathetic responsiveness (128)
understanding (127)

Your Communicate! CD-ROM also includes a video of the conversation between Damien and Chris featured on pages 149–151. Click on the Communicate! In Action icon on your CD-ROM, then click on "Damien and Chris." You can watch, listen to, and analyze their conversation. Improve your own conversation skills by learning from this model.

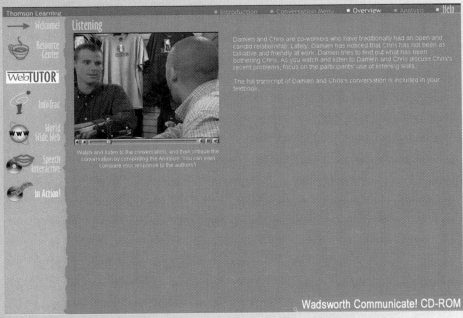

Jeffry W. Myers

OBJECTIVES

After you have read this chapter, you should be able to answer these questions:

■ What do we mean by self-disclosure?

■ What are guidelines for disclosing?

■ When and how does one describe feelings?

■ What are the differences between displaying feelings and describing feelings?

■ What are the differences between passive, aggressive, and assertive responses?

■ How can you assert yourself appropriately?

■ What can you do to improve giving praise and constructive criticism?

Self-Disclosure and Feedback

"**C**huck, when that interviewer at the grocery store asked you whether you'd rather have stuffing than potatoes, you said 'Yes'! We've been married more than twenty years, and I'm just now learning that you like stuffing more than potatoes."

"Well, I'm sorry, Susan," Chuck said sheepishly.

"Chuck," Susan asks, "are there other things that you like or don't like that you haven't told me about during these more than twenty years?"

"Well, probably."

"Chuck, why aren't you telling me about these things?"

"Well, I don't know, Susan. I guess I didn't think they were all that important."

"Not important? Chuck, almost every night that I cook we have potatoes. And frankly, I hate potatoes. I wouldn't care if I never saw a potato again. Now I find out you like stuffing better!"

"Sue, why didn't you ever tell me that you don't like potatoes?"

"Well I, uh-uh . . ."

Poor Chuck—poor Susan—all those years! But is their experience all that unusual? Do we take the time to tell others what we are really thinking and feeling? For a lot of people, the answer is a resounding *no*.

Because the self-disclosure and feedback processes are fundamental to interpersonal communication, in this chapter we will take a closer look at these concepts and will elaborate on the skills associated with each. We discuss self-disclosure, disclosing feelings, owning feelings, and assertiveness.

Self-Disclosure

self-disclosure—*sharing biographical data, personal ideas, and feelings.*

Almost all effective interpersonal communication requires some degree of self-disclosure. The very process of making friends involves learning more about each other. In the broadest sense, **self-disclosure** means sharing biographical data, personal ideas, and feelings. Statements such as "I was 5' 6" in seventh grade" reveal biographical information—facts about you as an individual. Statements such as "I don't think prisons ever really rehabilitate criminals" disclose personal ideas and reveal what and how you think. Statements such as "I get scared whenever I have to make a speech" disclose feelings. Biographical disclosures are the easiest to make, for they are, in a manner of speaking, a matter of public record. It is statements about personal ideas and feelings that most people think of as self-disclosure (Rosenfeld, 2000, p. 6).

Guidelines for Appropriate Self-Disclosure

We know that self-disclosure is important, yet as Affifi and Guerrero (2000) point out, we also know that "individuals often choose to avoid disclosure rather than risk the perceived personal or relational consequences" (p. 179). Disclosure is important—but risky. We can minimize the risk by following guidelines that help us determine appropriate levels of self-disclosure for different interpersonal encounters.

1. **Self-disclose the kind of information you want others to disclose to you.** When people are getting to know others, they begin by sharing information that is usually shared freely among people with that type of relationship in that culture. At early stages in the relationship, this might include information about hobbies, sports, school, and views of current events. One way to determine what information is appropriate to disclose is to ask yourself whether you would feel comfortable having the person disclose that kind of information to you.

2. **Move self-disclosure to deeper levels gradually.** Because receiving self-disclosure can be as threatening as giving it, most people become uncomfortable when the level of disclosure exceeds their expectations. As a relationship

develops, the depth of disclosure increases as well. Thus we are wise to disclose biographical and demographic information early in a relationship and more personal information in a more developed relationship (Dindia, Fitzpatrick, & Kenny, 1997, p. 408).

3. **Continue intimate self-disclosure only if it is reciprocated.** Based on the research, it appears that people expect a kind of equity in self-disclosure (Derlega, Metts, Petronio, & Margulis 1993, p. 33). When it is apparent that self-disclosure will not be returned, you should seriously consider limiting the amount of disclosure you make. Lack of reciprocation generally suggests that the person does not feel the relationship is one in which extensive self-disclosure is truly appropriate. When the response to your self-disclosure tells you that the disclosure was inappropriate, ask yourself what led to this effect. You can learn from a mistake and avoid making the same kind of mistake in the future.

4. **Self-disclose more intimate information only when you believe the disclosure represents an acceptable risk.** There is always some risk involved in disclosing, but as you gain trust in another person, you perceive that the disclosure of more revealing information is less likely to have negative consequences. Incidentally, this guideline explains why people sometimes engage in intimate self-disclosure with bartenders or with people they meet in travel. They perceive the disclosures as safe (representing reasonable risk) because the person either does not know them or is in no position to use the information against them. Unfortunately, some people apparently lack the kinds of relationships with family and friends that would enable them to make these kinds of disclosures to them.

5. **Reserve intimate or very personal self-disclosure for ongoing relationships.** Disclosures about fears, loves, and other deep or intimate matters are most appropriate in close, well-established relationships. When people disclose deep secrets to acquaintances, they are engaging in potentially threatening behavior. Making such disclosures before a bond of trust is established risks alienating the other person. Moreover, people are often embarrassed by and hostile toward others who try to saddle them with personal information in an effort to establish a relationship where none exists.

In the accompanying Diverse Voices selection, "Black and White," Linda Howard describes what she has experienced as a person who is multiethnic and biracial. As you read this except from an interview with Ms. Howard, first try to empathize with her frustration at being stereotyped and, second, consider her courage in disclosing information about herself and her feelings.

Cultural and Gender Differences

As we might expect, levels of self-disclosure and appropriateness of disclosure differ from culture to culture. The United States is considered to be an informal

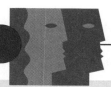

DIVERSE VOICES

Black and White

by Linda Howard

Today we tend to label people as black, white, Asian, Hispanic, and so forth. But what if you are half one and half another? Linda Howard is a recent high school graduate who has been awarded a four-year scholarship to a prominent university in New England. Listen to a transcript of an interview with her.

My parents are Black and White American. I come from a long heritage. I am of French, English, Irish, Dutch, Scottish, Canadian, and African descent.

I don't really use race. I always say, "My father's Black, my mother's White, I'm mixed." But I'm American; I'm human. That's my race; I'm part of the human race.

It's hard when you go out in the streets and you've got a bunch of White friends and you're the darkest person there. No matter how light you are to the rest of your family, you're the darkest person there and they say you're Black. Then you go out with a bunch of Black people and you're the lightest there and they say, "Yeah, my best friend's White." But I'm not. I'm both.

I don't always fit in—unless I'm in a mixed group. That's how it's different. Because if I'm in a group of people who are all one race, then they seem to look at me as being the *other* race . . . whereas if I'm in a group full of [racially mixed] people, my race doesn't seem to matter to everybody else. . . . Then I don't feel like I'm standing out. But if I'm in a group of totally one race, then I sort of stand out, and that's something that's hard to get used to.

It's hard. I look at history and I feel really bad for what some of my ancestors did to some of my other ancestors. Unless you're mixed, you don't know what it's like to be mixed.

I've had people tell me, "Well, you're Black." I'm not Black; I'm Black and White. I'm Black and White American. "Well, you're Black!" No, I'm not! I'm both. It's insulting, when they try and . . . bring it right back to the old standards, that if you have anybody in your family who's Black, you're

Black. . . . I mean, I'm not ashamed of being Black, but I'm not ashamed of being White either; and if I'm both, I want to be part of both. And I think teachers need to be sensitive to that.

See, the thing is, I mix it at home so much that it's not really a problem for me to mix it outside.

I don't think [interracial identity] is that big of a problem It's not killing anybody, at least as far as I know, it's not. It's not destroying families and lives and stuff. It's a minor thing. If you learn how to deal with it at a young age, as I did, it really doesn't bother you the rest of your life, like drugs. . . .

I think we're all racist in a sense. We all have some type of person that we don't like, whether it's from a different race, or from a different background, or they have different habits.

But to me a *serious racist* is a person who believes that people of different ethnic backgrounds don't belong or should be in *their* space and shouldn't invade *our* space: "Don't come and invade *my* space, you Chinese person. You belong over in China or you belong over in Chinatown."

Racists come out and tell you that they don't like who you are. Prejudiced people [on the other hand] will say it in like those little hints, you know, like, "Oh, yes, some of my best friends are Black." Or they say little ethnic remarks that they know will insult you but they won't come out and tell you. "You're Black. I don't want anything to do with you." Racists, to me, would come out and do that.

Both racists and prejudiced people make judgments, and most of the time they're wrong judgments, but the racist will carry his one step further. . . . A racist is a person that will carry out their prejudices.

I had a fight with a woman at work. She's White, and at the time I was the only Black person in my department. Or I was the only person who was *at all* Black in my department. And she just kept on laying on the racist jokes. At one point, I said, "You know, Nellie, you're a racist pig!" And she got offended by that. And I was just joking, just like she'd been joking for two days straight— all the racist jokes that she could think of.

I've got a foot on both sides of the fence, and there's only so much I can take. I'm straddling the fence, and it's hard to laugh and joke with you when you're talking about the foot that's on the other side.

She couldn't understand it. We didn't talk for weeks. And then one day, I had to work with her.

We didn't say anything for the first like two hours of work. And then I just said, "Smile, Nellie, you're driving me nuts!" and she smiled and laughed. And we've been good friends ever since. She just knows you don't say ethnic things around me; you don't joke around with me like that because I won't stand for it from you anymore. We can be friends; we can talk about anything else—except race.

Excerpted from "Case Study: Linda Howard, 'Unless you're mixed, you don't know what it's like to be mixed,'" in Sonia Nieto, Affirming Diversity: The Sociopolitical Context of Multicultural Education, *3rd ed. (New York: Longman, 2000), pp. 50–60. Reprinted by permission of Longman (An imprint of Addison Wesley Longman).*

---

culture (Samovar, Porter, & Stefani, 1998, p. 82). As a result, Americans tend to disclose more about themselves than do people from other cultures. Levels of formality can be inferred by how formally people dress, how formally they address each other, and how much they self-disclose. Germany, for instance, a country that seems like the United States in many ways, has a much higher degree of formality. Germans are likely to dress well even if just visiting friends or going to school. They also use formal titles in their interactions with others and have fewer close friends. Germans are also more private and disclose less than do Americans in similar relationships.

Particularly in the beginning stages of a friendship, such cultural differences can easily lead to misperceptions and discomfort if the people involved are unaware of them. For instance, a person from the United States may perceive an acquaintance from a more formal culture as reserved or less interested in pursuing a "genuine" friendship, whereas the acquaintance may see the person from the United States as discourteously assertive or embarrassingly expressive about personal feelings and other private matters.

Given the differences in culture, can we assume that disclosure always deepens relationships? Gudykunst and Kim (1997) have discovered that, across cultures, when relationships become more intimate self-disclosure increases. In addition, they found that the more partners self-disclosed to each other the more they were attracted to each other and the more uncertainty about each other was reduced (p. 325).

COMMUNICATE!
Using Technology

Sign on to an Internet chat room. Spend at least five minutes just "lurking" (listening). Then begin to participate in the chat. Considering both your comments and those with whom you are "chatting," how do the levels of self-disclosure differ from in-person conversations? Is there really very much self-disclosure occurring? If so, how does it compare to self-disclosure in face-to-face encounters? How can you tell if the disclosures are truthful? If you need an introduction to chat rooms and how to get started, go to http://www.yahoo.com and click on "chat" in the "Connect" section under the Search bar. You can set up a Yahoo! ID to participate in chat.

Zigy Kaluzny/Stone

In general, men tend to
disclose their feelings
less than women, but this
varies by individual and
cultural tradition.

report-talk–*a way to share
information, display
knowledge, negotiate, and
preserve independence.*

rapport-talk–*a way to share
experiences and establish bonds
with others.*

Women tend to disclose more than men, are disclosed to more than men, and are more aware than men of cues that affect their self-disclosure (Dindia, 2000, p. 24; Reis, 1998, p. 213). Of course, this generalization is not true in all cases. Deborah Tannen (1990) argues that one way to capture the differences between men's and women's verbal styles is by paying attention to "report-talk" and "rapport-talk" (p. 77). Her point is that men in our society are more likely to view conversation as **report-talk**—a way to share information, display knowledge, negotiate, and preserve independence. In contrast, women are more likely to use **rapport-talk**—a way to share experiences and establish bonds with others. When men and women fail to recognize these differences in the way they have learned to use conversation, the stage is set for misunderstandings about whether or not they are being truly open and intimate with one another. "Learning about style differences won't make them go away," Tannen remarks, "but it can banish mutual mystification and blame" (pp. 47–48).

Disclosing Feelings

At the heart of intimate self-disclosure is sharing your feelings with someone else, and sharing feelings is a risky business. Why is this so? When we share our feelings about something important, we are generally giving someone else potent knowledge about us that they might use to harm us. Yet all of us experience feelings and have to decide whether and how we disclose them. Obviously, one option we have is to withhold or mask our feelings. If we decide to disclose our feelings, we can display them or we can describe them.

Withholding or Masking Feelings

In our culture, **withholding feelings**—that is, denying them by keeping them inside and not giving any verbal or nonverbal cues to their existence—is considered unhealthy and generally regarded as an inappropriate means of dealing with feelings. Withholding feelings is best exemplified by the good poker player who develops a "poker face," a neutral look that is impossible to decipher. The look is the same whether the player's cards are good or bad. Unfortunately, many people use poker faces in their relationships so that no one knows whether they are hurt, excited, or saddened.

Psychologists believe habitually withholding feelings can lead to physical problems such as ulcers and heart disease as well as to psychological problems such as stress and depression. Moreover, people who withhold feelings are often perceived as cold, undemonstrative, and not much fun to be around.

Is withholding ever appropriate? When a situation is inconsequential, you may well choose to withhold your feelings. For instance, a stranger's inconsiderate behavior at a party may bother you, but there is often little to be gained by disclosing your feelings about it. You don't have an ongoing relationship with the person, and you can deal with the situation simply by moving to another part of the room.

Displaying Feelings

Displaying feelings is expressing feelings through facial reactions, body responses, and emotional verbal reactions. Although displays of feelings are always expressed by nonverbal behavior, they may be accompanied by verbal messages as well. Cheering over a great play at a sporting event, howling when you bang your head against the car doorjamb, and patting a coworker on the back for doing something well are all displays of feelings.

Displays are usually appropriate when the feelings you are experiencing are positive. For instance, when your friend Gloria does something nice for you, and you experience a feeling of joy, giving her a big hug is appropriate. When your supervisor gives you an assignment you have wanted, a big smile and a "Thank you" is an appropriate display of your feeling of appreciation. In fact,

withholding feelings–*denying feelings by keeping them inside and not giving any verbal or nonverbal cues to their existence.*

displaying feelings–*expressing feelings through facial reactions, body responses, and emotional verbal reactions.*

many people need to be more demonstrative of good feelings than they typically are. The bumper sticker "Have you hugged your kid today?" reinforces the point that people we care about need open displays of love and affection.

Displays become detrimental to communication when the feelings you are experiencing are negative—especially when the display of a negative feeling appears to be an overreaction. Although displays of negative feelings may make you feel better temporarily, they are likely to be bad for you interpersonally.

Displays of feeling often serve as an escape valve for very strong emotions. In this way, they may be a more healthy approach than withholding feelings because we "get them out of our system." Unfortunately, especially with negative emotions, these displays can often damage our relationships or cause stress in our relational partners. In many families, children learn to "stay out of dad's way if he's in a 'bad mood.'" Children do this when they have experienced the power of dad's emotional displays. Rather than just display our emotions, we can use the self-disclosure skill of describing feelings to help us share our feelings with others in a manner that does not damage our relationships or cause stress.

Describing Feelings

describing feelings—*naming emotions you are feeling without judging them.*

Describing feelings is naming the emotion you are feeling without judging it. Describing feelings increases the chances of positive interaction and decreases the chances of short-circuiting lines of communication. Moreover, describing feelings teaches others how to treat us by explaining the effect of their behavior. This knowledge gives them the information they need to determine the appropriateness of that behavior. Thus, if you tell Paul that you feel flattered when he visits you, your description of how you feel should encourage him to visit you again. Likewise, when you tell Tony that you feel very angry when he borrows your jacket without asking, he is more likely to ask the next time. Describing your feelings enables you to exercise a measure of control over others' behavior simply by making them aware of the effects their actions have on you.

Many times people think they are describing when in fact they are displaying feelings or evaluating the other person's behavior. The Test Your Competence exercise at the end of this section focuses on your awareness of the difference between describing feelings and either displaying feelings or expressing evaluations.

If describing feelings is so important to effective communication, why don't more people do it regularly? There seem to be at least five reasons many people don't describe feelings.

1. **Many people don't have a very good vocabulary for describing the various feelings they experience.** People can sense that they are angry; however, they may not be able to distinguish between feeling annoyed, betrayed, cheated, crushed, disturbed, envious, furious, infuriated, outraged, or shocked. Each of these words describes a slightly different aspect of what

THINKING ABOUT...

Communicating Your Feelings

Think back over the events of the day. At any time during the day did you feel particularly happy, angry, disappointed, excited, or sad? How did you communicate your feelings to others? Under what circumstances, if any, did you describe your feelings? What appear to be your most common ways of displaying (expressing) your feelings? Think of ways you might make sharing your feelings more interpersonally effective.

W. Hill, Jr./The Image Works

**Describing and sharing
feelings can be difficult
for many people.**

many people lump together as anger. A surprising number of shades of meaning can be used to describe feelings, as shown in Figure 7.1. To become more effective in describing your feelings, you may first need to work to develop a better "vocabulary of emotions."

2. **Many people believe describing their true feelings will make them too vulnerable.** If you tell people what hurts you, it is true that you risk their using the information against you when they want to hurt you on purpose. So it is safer to act angry than to be honest and describe the hurt you feel; it is safer to appear indifferent than to share your happiness and risk being made fun of. Nevertheless, as the old saying goes, "Nothing ventured, nothing gained." If you don't take reasonable risks in your relationships, you are unlikely to form lasting and satisfying relationships. For instance, if Pete calls you by a derogatory nickname that you don't like, you can tell Pete that calling you by that nickname embarrasses you. Pete does have the option of calling you by that name when he wants to embarrass you, but if Pete is ethical and cares about you, he is more likely to stop calling you by that name. If you don't describe your feelings to Pete, however, he will probably continue calling you by that name simply because he doesn't realize that you don't like it. By saying nothing, you reinforce his behavior. The

**THINKING
ABOUT . . .**

**The Vocabulary of
Emotions**

Look at each word in Figure 7.1, say "I feel . . . ," and try to identify the feeling this word would describe. Which of these words are meaningful enough to you that you could use them to help you communicate your feelings?

Words Related to *Angry*

agitated	annoyed	bitter	cranky
enraged	exasperated	furious	hostile
incensed	indignant	infuriated	irked
irritated	mad	offended	outraged
peeved	resentful	riled	steamed

Words Related to *Helpful*

agreeable	amiable	beneficial	caring
collegial	compassionate	constructive	cooperative
cordial	gentle	kindly	neighborly
obliging	supportive	useful	warm

Words Related to *Loving*

adoring	affectionate	amorous	aroused
caring	charming	fervent	gentle
heavenly	passionate	sensitive	tender

Words Related to *Embarrassed*

abashed	anxious	chagrined	confused
conspicuous	disconcerted	disgraced	distressed
flustered	humbled	humiliated	jittery
overwhelmed	rattled	ridiculous	shamefaced
sheepish	silly	troubled	uncomfortable

Words Related to *Surprised*

astonished	astounded	baffled	bewildered
confused	distracted	flustered	jarred
jolted	mystified	perplexed	puzzled
rattled	shocked	startled	stunned

Words Related to *Fearful*

afraid	agitated	alarmed	anxious
apprehensive	bullied	cornered	frightened
horrified	jittery	jumpy	nervous
petrified	scared	shaken	terrified
threatened	troubled	uneasy	worried

Words Related to *Disgusted*

afflicted	annoyed	nauseated	outraged
repelled	repulsed	revolted	sickened

level of risk varies with each situation, but if you have healthy relationships, you will more often improve a relationship by describing feelings than hurt it by doing so.

3. **If they describe their feelings, many people believe others will make them feel guilty about having such feelings.** At a tender age, we all learned about

Words Related to *Hurt*

abused	awful	cheated	deprived
deserted	desperate	dismal	dreadful
forsaken	hassled	ignored	isolated
mistreated	offended	oppressed	pained
piqued	rejected	resentful	rotten
scorned	slighted	snubbed	wounded

Words Related to *Belittled*

betrayed	defeated	deflated	demeaned
diminished	disparaged	downgraded	foolish
helpless	inadequate	incapable	inferior
insulted	persecuted	powerless	underestimated
undervalued	unfit	unworthy	useless

Words Related to *Happy*

blissful	charmed	cheerful	contented
delighted	ecstatic	elated	exultant
fantastic	giddy	glad	gratified
high	joyous	jubilant	merry
pleased	satisfied	thrilled	tickled

Words Related to *Lonely*

abandoned	alone	bored	deserted
desolate	discarded	empty	excluded
forlorn	forsaken	ignored	isolated
jilted	lonesome	lost	rejected
renounced	scorned	slighted	snubbed

Words Related to *Sad*

blue	crestfallen	dejected	depressed
dismal	dour	downcast	gloomy
heavyhearted	joyless	low	melancholy
mirthless	miserable	moody	morose
pained	sorrowful	troubled	weary

Words Related to *Energetic*

animated	bold	brisk	dynamic
eager	forceful	frisky	hardy
inspired	kinetic	lively	peppy
potent	robust	spirited	sprightly
spry	vibrant	vigorous	vivacious

Figure 7.1

A list of more than 200 words that can describe feelings.

"tactful" behavior. Under the premise that "the truth sometimes hurts," we learn to avoid the truth by not saying anything or by telling "little" lies. When you were young, perhaps your mother said, "Don't forget to give grandma a great big kiss." At that time, you may have blurted out, "Ugh— it makes me feel yucky to kiss grandma. She's got a mustache." If your mother then responded, "That's terrible—your grandma loves you. Now you give her a kiss and never let me hear you talk like that again!" you probably felt guilty for having this "wrong" feeling. Yet the thought of kissing your grandmother did make you feel "yucky" whether it should have or not. In this case, the issue was not your having the feelings but the way you talked about them.

4. **Many people believe describing feelings causes harm to others or to a relationship.** If it really bothers Fyodor when his girlfriend, Lana, bites her fingernails, Fyodor may believe describing his feelings may hurt her feelings so much that it will drive a wedge into their relationship. So it is better if Fyodor says nothing, right? Wrong! If Fyodor says nothing, he is still going to be irritated by Lana's behavior. In fact, as time goes on, Fyodor's irritation probably will cause him to lash out at Lana for other things because he can't bring himself to talk about the behavior that really bothers him. Lana will be hurt by Fyodor's behavior, but she won't understand why. By not describing his true feelings, Fyodor may well drive a wedge into their relationship anyway. But if Fyodor describes his feelings to Lana in a nonjudgmental way, she might try to quit biting her nails. They might get into a discussion in which he finds out she doesn't want to bite her nails but that she just can't seem to stop. Perhaps he can help her in her efforts to stop. Or Fyodor might come to see that it really is a small thing, and it may not continue to bother him as much. In short, describing feelings yields a better chance of a successful outcome than does not describing them.

5. **Some people belong to cultural groups in which masking or withholding feelings is culturally appropriate behavior.** In some cultures, for example, harmony among the group or in the relationship is felt to be more important than individuals' personal feelings. People from such cultures may not describe their feelings out of concern for the health of the group.

To describe your feelings, (1) indicate what has triggered the feeling. The feeling results from some behavior, so identify the behavior. (2) Mentally identify what you are feeling—be specific. This sounds easier than it sometimes is. When people experience a feeling, they will sometimes display it without thinking about it. To describe a feeling, you must be aware of exactly what you are feeling. The vocabulary of emotions provided in Figure 7.1 can help you develop your ability to select specific words to describe your feelings. (3) Verbally own the feeling. Begin your statement with "I feel . . ." (4) Verbally state the specific feeling (happy, sad, irritated, vibrant).

Here are two examples of describing feelings: (1) "Thank you for your compliment [trigger]; I [the person having the feeling] feel gratified [the specific feeling] that you noticed the effort I made." (2) "When you criticize my cooking on days I've worked as many hours as you have [trigger], I [the person having the feeling] feel very resentful" [the specific feeling].

To begin with, you may find it easier to describe positive feelings: "You know, your taking me to that movie really cheered me up" or "When you offered

SKILL BUILDERS   Describing Feelings

Skill	Use	Procedure	Example
Putting an emotional state into words.	For self-disclosure; to teach people how to treat you.	1. Indicate what has triggered the feeling.	"As a result of not getting the job, I feel depressed and discouraged" or "Because of the way you stood up for me when I was being put down by Leah, I'm feeling very warm and loving toward you."
		2. Mentally identify what you are feeling. Think specifically. Am I feeling hate? Anger? Joy?	
		3. Verbally own the feeling. Begin your statement with "I feel. . . ."	
		4. Verbally state the specific feeling.	

to help me with the housework, I really felt delighted." As you gain success with positive descriptions, you can try describing negative feelings attributable to environmental factors: "It's so cloudy; I feel gloomy" or "When the wind howls through the crack, I really get jumpy." Finally, you can move to negative descriptions resulting from what people have said or done: "When you step in front of me like that, I really get annoyed" or "When you use that negative tone while you are saying that what I did pleased you, I really feel confused."

Owning Feelings and Opinions

Owning feelings or opinions, or crediting yourself, means making "I" statements to identify yourself as the source of a particular idea or feeling. An "I" statement can be any statement that has a first-person pronoun such as *I, my, me,* or *mine.* "I" statements help the listener understand fully and accurately the nature of the message. For example, instead of saying "Advertising is the weakest department in the corporation" (an unsupported assertion), say *"I believe* advertising is the weakest department in the corporation." Likewise, instead of saying "Everybody thinks Collins is unfair in his criticism," say *"It seems to me* that Collins is unfair in his criticism." Both of these examples contrast a generalized or impersonal account with an "I" statement.

Why do people use vague referents to others rather than owning their ideas and feelings? There are two basic reasons.

owning feelings or opinions– *crediting yourself by making "I" statements to identify yourself as the source of a particular idea or feeling.*

TEST YOUR COMPETENCE

Statements that Describe Feelings

In each set of statements, place a D next to the statement or statements that describe feelings:

1. a. That was a great movie!
   b. I was really cheered up by the story.
   c. I feel this is worth an Oscar.
   d. Terrific!
2. a. I feel you're a good writer.
   b. Your writing brings me to tears.
   c. [You pat the writer on the back] Good job.
   d. Everyone likes your work.
3. a. Yuck!
   b. If things don't get better, I'm going to move.
   c. Did you ever see such a hole?
   d. I feel depressed by the dark halls.
4. a. I'm not adequate as a leader of this group.
   b. Damn—I goofed!
   c. I feel inadequate in my efforts to lead the group.
   d. I'm depressed by the effects of my leadership.
5. a. I'm a winner.
   b. I feel I won because I'm most qualified.
   c. I did it! I won!
   d. I'm ecstatic about winning that award.

Answers

1. b. (a) is evaluative; (c) is an evaluation dressed in descriptive clothing—just because the word *feel* is in a statement does not mean the person is truly describing feelings; (d) is a display.
2. b. (a) is evaluative (there's that word *feel* again); (c) is a display; (d) is evaluative.
3. d. (a) is a display; (b) is the result of feelings but not a description of feelings; (c) is an evaluation in question form.
4. c and d. (a) is evaluative; (b) is evaluative.
5. d. (a) is evaluative; (b) is evaluative; (c) is a display.

1. **To strengthen the power of their statements.** If listeners doubt the statement that "Everybody thinks Collins is unfair in his criticism," they are bucking the collective evaluation of countless people. Of course, not everybody knows and agrees that Collins is unfair. In this instance, the statement really means that one person holds the belief. But people often think that their feelings or beliefs will not carry much power, so they feel the need to cite unknown or universal sources for those feelings or beliefs.

2. **To escape responsibility.** Similarly, people use collective statements such as "everybody agrees" and "anyone with any sense" to escape responsibility

for their own feelings and thoughts. It seems far more difficult for a person to say "I don't like Herb" than it is to say "No one likes Herb."

The problem with such generalized statements is that at best they are exaggerations and at worst they are deceitful and unethical. Being both accurate and honest with others requires taking responsibility for our own feelings and opinions. We all have a right to our reactions. If what you are saying is truly your opinion or an expression of how you really feel, let others know and be willing to take responsibility for it. Otherwise, you may alienate people who would have respected your opinions or feelings even if they didn't agree with them.

THINKING ABOUT . . .

Owning Ideas and Feelings

Under what circumstances are you likely to take credit for your own ideas and feelings? When are you likely to attribute them to some generalized "other"?

Giving Personal Feedback

There are times in our interactions and relationships with others when it is appropriate to comment on how the other person's message or behavior is affecting us. Responses that do this are generally referred to as "giving personal feedback." When we highlight positive behavior and accomplishments, we give positive feedback through praise. When we identify negative harmful behavior and actions, we provide negative feedback through constructive criticism.

Praising

Praising is describing the specific positive behaviors or accomplishments of another. Too often we fail to acknowledge the positive things people say and do. Yet, as you will recall from our earlier discussion of self-concept, our view of who we are—our identity, as well as our behavior—is shaped by how others respond to us. Praise can be used to reinforce positive behavior and to help another develop a positive self-concept.

Praise is not the same as flattery. When we flatter someone, we use excessive compliments that are insincere in order to ingratiate ourselves to that person. When we praise, our compliments are in line with the behavior or accomplishment. We express only admiration that we genuinely feel.

For praise to achieve its goal and not be perceived merely as flattery, we need to focus the praise on the specific action and make sure that the message is worded so that it is in keeping with the significance or value of the accomplishment or behavior. If a friend who tends to be forgetful remembers to return a pair of pliers he borrowed that same day, that is a behavior that should be praised so that it is reinforced. But saying "You're so wonderful, you're on top of everything" reinforces nothing because it is an overly general statement that does not identify a particular behavior or accomplishment. Overly general statements can be perceived as flattery. Gushing "Oh, you remembered to return the pliers! I'm so grateful. That was just unbelievably thoughtful of you"

praising—*describing the specific positive behaviors or accomplishments of another.*

is overkill that will be perceived as insincere. Simply saying something like "Thanks for returning the pliers today; I really appreciate it" would be appropriate. A response like this acknowledges the accomplishment by describing the specific behavior and the positive feeling of gratitude that the behavior has caused. Here are two more examples of appropriate praising.

> **Behavior:** Sonya takes responsibility for selecting and buying a group wedding present for a friend. The gift is a big hit.
>
> **Praise:** "Sonya, the present you chose for Stevie was really thoughtful. Not only did it fit our price range, but Stevie really liked it."

> **Accomplishment:** Cole has just received a letter inviting him to a reception at which he is to receive a scholarship award given for academic accomplishments and community service work.
>
> **Praise:** "Congratulations, Cole. I'm proud of you. It's really great to see that the effort you put into studying as well as the time and energy you have devoted to the Second Harvest Food Program and Big Brothers is being recognized and valued."

Praising responses don't "cost" much, but they are valuable and generally appreciated. Not only does praising provide information and acknowledge the worth of another person, but it can also deepen our relationship with that person because with it increases the openness of the relationship. To increase your effectiveness at praising, try to follow these steps: (1) Make note of the specific behavior or accomplishment that you want to reinforce. (2) Describe the specific behavior or accomplishment. (3) Describe the positive feelings or outcomes that you or others experienced as a result of the behavior or accomplishment. (4) Phrase the response so that the level of praise appropriately reflects the significance of the behavior or accomplishment.

Giving Constructive Criticism

Research on reinforcement theory has found that people learn faster and better through positive rewards such as praise. Nevertheless, there are still times when personal feedback needs to address negative behaviors or actions. **Constructive criticism** is describing the specific negative behaviors or actions of another and the effects that these behaviors have on others. You will be more effective in giving constructive criticism if you proceed in the following ways:

constructive criticism—
describing the specific negative behaviors or actions of another and the effects that these behaviors have on others.

1. **Ask the person's permission before giving criticism.** Obviously, it is best to give this type of feedback when a person specifically asks for it. Even when people don't ask, however, we sometimes need to provide another with constructive criticism. A person who has agreed to hear constructive criticism is likely to be more receptive to it than is someone who is not accorded respect by being asked.

2. **Describe the behavior by accurately recounting precisely what was said or done without labeling the behavior good or bad, right or wrong.** By describing behavior, you lay an informative base for the feedback and increase the chances that the person will listen receptively. Feedback that is preceded with detailed description is less likely to be met defensively. Your description shows that you are criticizing the behavior rather than attacking the person, and it points the way to a solution. For example, if DeShawn asks, "What did you think of the visuals I used when I delivered my report?" instead of saying "They weren't very effective," it would be better to say something like "Well, the type on the first two was rather small, which made the words hard to read." This criticism does not attack DeShawn's self-concept, and it tells him what he needs to do to be more effective.

3. **Preface a negative statement with a positive one whenever possible.** When you are planning to criticize, it is a good idea to start with some praise. Of course, common sense suggests that superficial praise followed by crushing feedback will be seen for what it is. In our example, one could say, "First, the charts and graphs were useful, and the color really helped us to see the problems. Second, the type size on the first two overheads made them hard to read." Here the praise is relevant and significant. If you cannot preface feedback with significant praise, don't try. Prefacing feedback with empty praise will not help the person accept your feedback.

    When you link constructive criticism with praise, try to avoid using the word "but." For some reason, it is easy for a person to miss the praise and interpret only the criticism when "but" is used. In the previous example, notice that by labeling the praise "first" and the criticism "second" the statements gain equal emphasis.

4. **Be as specific as possible.** The more specifically you describe the behavior or the actions, the easier it will be for the person to understand what needs to be changed. In the situation just discussed, it would not have been helpful to say "Some of the slides were kind of hard to read." This comment is so general that DeShawn would have little idea of what to change. Moreover, he may infer that every overhead needs to be redone.

5. **When appropriate, suggest how the person can change the behavior.** Because the focus of constructive criticism is helping, it is appropriate to provide the person with your suggestions that might lead to positive change. In responding DeShawn's request for feedback, one might also add, "When I make overheads, I generally try to use 18-point type or larger. You might want to give that a try." By including a positive suggestion, you not only help the person by providing honest information, you also show that your intentions are positive.

OBSERVE & ANALYZE
Journal Activity

Expressing Criticism

Think about the last time you criticized someone's behavior. Under Journal Activity 7.1 in your Student Workbook, answer the following questions: Which, if any, of the guidelines for constructive feedback did you follow or violate? If you were to do it again, what would you say differently?

Assertiveness

assertiveness–*standing up for ourselves in interpersonally effective ways that exercise our personal rights while respecting the rights of others.*

Assertiveness means standing up for ourselves in interpersonally effective ways that exercise our personal rights while respecting the rights of others. Failure to be assertive may keep you from achieving your goals and may lower your self-esteem. We can understand the specific qualities of assertive communication best if we contrast it with other ways of interacting when we believe our rights, feeling, or needs are in danger of being violated or ignored.

Contrasting Methods of Expressing Our Needs and Rights

When we believe our rights, feelings, or needs are being ignored or violated by others, we can choose to behave in one of three ways: passively, aggressively, or assertively.

passive behavior–*being reluctant to state opinions, share feelings, or assume responsibility for actions.*

Passive behavior People behave **passively** when they do not state their opinions, share feelings, or assume responsibility for their actions. They may behave passively because they fear reprisal, are insecure about their knowledge, or for some other reason. Whatever their motivation, instead of attempting to influence others' behavior, they submit to other people's demands, even when doing so is inconvenient, against their best interests, or violates their rights. For example, when Bill was uncrating the new color television set he purchased at a local department store, he noticed a scratch on the left side of the cabinet. If Bill is upset about the scratch but keeps the set without trying to get the store to replace it, he is behaving passively.

aggressive behavior–*lashing out at the source of discontent with little regard for the situation or for the feelings, needs, or rights of those being attacked.*

Aggressive behavior People behave **aggressively** when they forcefully lash out to achieve their goals with little regard for the situation or for the feelings, needs, or rights of others. Aggressiveness must not be confused with assertiveness. Unlike assertive behavior, aggressive behavior is unethical. Aggressors attempt to achieve their goals without any regard for the needs, rights, or feelings of others. As a result, the people who receive aggressive messages are likely to feel hurt by them regardless of their relationship (Martin, Anderson, & Horvath, 1996, p. 24).

Suppose, after discovering the scratch on the cabinet of his new television set, Bill stormed back to the store, grabbed the first clerk he found, and loudly demanded his money back while accusing the clerk of being a racist for intentionally selling him damaged merchandise. Such aggressive behavior might or might not be successful in getting the damaged set replaced, but it would certainly not be ethical.

Assertive behavior As we have noted, behaving assertively means standing up for yourself in an interpersonally effective way. The difference between assertive behavior and passive or aggressive behavior is not the original feeling

Bruce Ayers/Stone

We often have to assert ourselves. The key is not to fall into aggressive behavior. He seems to be crowding her (aggressive), but she's setting limits (assertive).

behind the response but the way in which we choose to react as a result of what has happened. If Bill chose an assertive response, he would still be angry about bringing home a damaged set. But instead of either doing nothing or verbally assaulting the clerk, Bill might call the store and ask to speak to the clerk from whom he had purchased the set. When the clerk answered, Bill would describe the condition of the TV set and his feelings on discovering a large scratch on the cabinet when he uncrated the set. He would then go on to say that he was calling to find out what to do to return the damaged set and get a new one. Aggressive behavior might also achieve Bill's purpose of getting a new television set, but assertive behavior would achieve the same result at lower emotional cost to everyone involved.

Paulette Dale (1999), a consultant on assertive behavior, contrasts these behaviors as follows: Whereas a submissive or passive response conveys the message *"I'm* not important, *you're* important," and an aggressive response conveys the message *"I'm* important, *you're* nothing," an assertive response conveys the message *"I'm* important, *you're* important, we're *both* important" (pp. 5–6).

OBSERVE & ANALYZE
Journal Activity

Passive, Aggressive, and Assertive Behavior

For the next day or two, observe people and their behavior. Take note of situations where you believe people behaved in passive, aggressive, and assertive ways. Then, under Journal Activity 7.2 in your Student Workbook, answer the following questions: Which of the ways seemed to help the people achieve what they wanted? Which of the ways seemed to maintain or even improve their interpersonal relationship with the other person or other people?

Distinguishing among Passive, Aggressive, and Assertive Responses

Because our interpersonal exchanges will often involve the need to assert ourselves, it is important to learn to distinguish among passive, aggressive, and assertive responses. To highlight the contrasts among the three response styles, let's examine two situations in which the issue is the quality of interpersonal relations.

At work Tanisha works in an office that employs both men and women. Whenever the boss has an especially interesting and challenging job to be done, he assigns it to a male coworker whose desk is next to Tanisha's. The boss has never said anything to Tanisha or to the male employee that would indicate he thinks less of Tanisha or her ability. Nevertheless, Tanisha is hurt by the boss's behavior.

> **Passive:** Tanisha says nothing to the boss. She is very hurt by what she feels is a slight but swallows her pride.
>
> **Aggressive:** Tanisha marches into her boss's office and says, "Why the hell do you always give Tom the plums and leave me the garbage? I'm every bit as good a worker, and I'd like a little recognition!"
>
> **Assertive:** Tanisha arranges a meeting with her boss. At the meeting, she says, "I don't know whether you are aware of it, but during the last three weeks, every time you had a really interesting job to be done, you gave the job to Tom. To the best of my knowledge, you believe Tom and I are equally competent—you've never given me any evidence to suggest that you thought less of my work. But when you 'reward' Tom with jobs that I perceive as plums and continue to offer me routine jobs, it hurts my feelings. Do you understand my feelings about this?" In this statement, she has both described her perception of the boss's behavior and her feelings about that behavior.

If you were Tanisha's boss, which of her responses would be most likely to achieve her goal of getting better assignments? Probably the assertive behavior. Which of her responses would be most likely to get her fired? Probably the aggressive behavior. And which of her responses would be least likely to "rock the boat"? Undoubtedly the passive behavior—but then she would continue to get the boring job assignments.

With a friend Dan is a doctor doing his residency at City Hospital. He lives with two other residents in an apartment they have rented. Carl, one of the other residents, is the social butterfly of the group. Whenever Carl has time off, it seems that he has a date. Like the others, Carl is a bit short of cash, but doesn't feel a bit bashful about borrowing clothes or money from his roommates. One evening, Carl asks Dan if he can borrow his watch, a new, expensive watch Dan received as a present from his father only a few days before. Dan is aware that

Carl does not always take the best care of what he borrows, and he is very concerned about the possibility of Carl's damaging or losing the watch. Which of these responses might Dan make?

Passive: "Sure."

Aggressive: "Forget it! You've got a lot of nerve asking to borrow a brand-new watch. You know I'd be damned lucky to get it back in one piece."

Assertive: "Carl, I know I've lent you several items without much ado, but this watch is special. I've had it only a few days, and I just don't feel comfortable lending it. I hope you can understand how I feel."

What are likely to be the consequences of each of these behaviors? If he behaves passively, Dan is likely to worry the entire evening and harbor some resentment of Carl even if he gets the watch back undamaged. Moreover, Carl will continue to think that his roommates feel comfortable in lending him anything he wants. If Dan behaves aggressively, Carl is likely to be completely taken aback by his explosive behavior. No one has ever said anything to Carl before, so he has no reason to believe that he can't borrow whatever he'd like. Moreover, the relationship between Dan and Carl might become strained. But if Dan behaves assertively, he puts the focus on his own feelings and on this particular object—the watch. His response isn't a denial of Carl's right to borrow items, nor is it an attack on Carl. It is an explanation of why Dan does not want to lend this item at this time.

For a review of the characteristics of assertive behavior, see Figure 7.2.

COMMUNICATE! Using InfoTrac College Edition

As we have seen, assertiveness is sometimes perceived as aggressiveness. Using the InfoTrac College Edition subject guide, enter the term "Assertiveness." Click on "Assertiveness (Psychological)." Look for articles that offer guidelines for being assertive, such as "How to Assert Yourself," Kathiann Kowalski (1998), an article that considers the importance of behaving assertively without becoming aggressive.

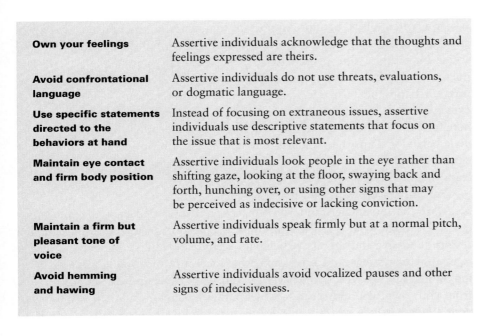

Own your feelings	Assertive individuals acknowledge that the thoughts and feelings expressed are theirs.
Avoid confrontational language	Assertive individuals do not use threats, evaluations, or dogmatic language.
Use specific statements directed to the behaviors at hand	Instead of focusing on extraneous issues, assertive individuals use descriptive statements that focus on the issue that is most relevant.
Maintain eye contact and firm body position	Assertive individuals look people in the eye rather than shifting gaze, looking at the floor, swaying back and forth, hunching over, or using other signs that may be perceived as indecisive or lacking conviction.
Maintain a firm but pleasant tone of voice	Assertive individuals speak firmly but at a normal pitch, volume, and rate.
Avoid hemming and hawing	Assertive individuals avoid vocalized pauses and other signs of indecisiveness.

Figure 7.2
Characteristics of assertive behavior.

It is important to recognize that being assertive will not always achieve your goals. The skills discussed in this book are designed to increase the *probability* of achieving interpersonal effectiveness. Just as with self-disclosure and describing feelings, however, there are risks involved in being assertive. For instance, some people will label any assertive behavior as "aggressive." People who have difficulty asserting themselves often do not appreciate the fact that the potential benefits far outweigh the risks. Remember, our behavior teaches people how to treat us. When we are passive—when we have taught people that they can ignore our feelings—they will. When we are aggressive, we teach people to respond in kind. By contrast, when we are assertive, we can influence others to treat us as we would prefer to be treated.

Here are some useful guidelines for practicing assertive behavior: (1) identify what you are thinking or feeling; (2) analyze the cause of these feelings; (3) choose the appropriate skills to communicate these feelings, as well as the outcome you desire, if any; and (4) communicate these feelings to the appropriate person. If you are having trouble taking the first step to being more assertive, begin with situations in which you are likely to have a high potential for success (Alberti & Emmons, 1995). In addition, try to incorporate the characteristics of assertive behavior outlined in Figure 7.2.

Cultural Variations

Although assertiveness can be thought of as a basic human need, assertive behavior is primarily practiced in Western cultures. In Asian cultures, how one is seen is often felt to be more important than asserting one's beliefs or rights, and a premium is often placed on maintaining a formally correct standard of social interaction. For people from these cultures, maintaining "face" and politeness may be more important than achieving personal satisfaction. In contrast, in Latin and Hispanic societies, men especially are frequently taught to exercise a form of self-expression that goes far beyond the guidelines presented here for assertive behavior. In these societies, the concept of "machismo" guides male behavior. Thus the standard of assertiveness appropriate in our dominant culture can seem inappropriate to people whose cultural frame of reference leads them to perceive it as either aggressive or weak.

For this reason, with assertiveness—just as with any other skill—we need to be aware that no single standard of behavior ensures that we will achieve our goals. Although what is labeled appropriate behavior varies across cultures, the results of passive and aggressive behavior seem to be universal: Passive behavior can cause resentment, and aggressive behavior leads to fear and misunderstanding. When talking with people whose culture, background, or lifestyle differs from your own, you may need to observe their behavior and their responses to your statements before you can be sure of the kinds of behavior that are likely to communicate your intentions effectively.

OBSERVE & ANALYZE
Journal Activity

Learning to Respond Assertively

Identify five situations in the past where you were nonassertive or aggressive. Under Journal Activity 7.3 in your Student Workbook, write the dialogue for each situation. Then substitute an assertive response for the nonassertive or aggressive reactions you expressed in each case.

Developing Assertive Responses

For each of these situations, write a passive or aggressive response, and then contrast it with a more appropriate assertive response.

You come back to your dorm, apartment, or house to type a paper that is due tomorrow, only to find that someone else is using your typewriter.
Passive or aggressive response:
Assertive response:

You are working at a store part-time. Just as your hours are up and you are ready to leave (you want to rush home because you have a nice dinner planned with someone special), your boss says to you, "I'd like you to work overtime, if you would. Martin's supposed to replace you, but he just called and can't get here for at least an hour."
Passive or aggressive response:
Assertive response:

During a phone call to your parents, who live in another state, your mother says, "We're expecting you to go with us when we visit your uncle on Saturday." You were planning to spend Saturday working on your résumé for an interview next week.
Passive or aggressive response:
Assertive response:

You and your friend made a date to go dancing, an activity you really enjoy. When you meet, your friend says, "If it's all the same to you, I thought we'd go to a movie instead."
Passive or aggressive response:
Assertive response:

SKILL BUILDERS Assertiveness

Skill	Use	Procedure	Example
Standing up for yourself and doing so in interpersonally effective ways that describe your feelings honestly and exercise your personal rights while respecting the rights of others.	To show clearly what you think or feel.	1. Identify what you are thinking or feeling. 2. Analyze the cause of these feelings. 3. Choose the appropriate skills necessary to communicate these feelings, as well as any outcome you desire, if any. 4. Communicate these feelings to the appropriate person. Remember to own your feelings.	When Gavin believes he is being unjustly charged, he says, "I have never been charged for a refill on iced tea before—has there been a change in policy?"

Maria Sanchos, a Mexican American graduate of Yale Law School, was excited to be assigned to the Local Employee Fraud Team (LEFT), whose job it was to design a system to uncover theft on the job for the Comptel Corporation. Maria found the company of her other five associates pleasant, except for Theresa Waterson, the leader of the group, whose social skills were as bad as the stereotypical queen bee. Maria wondered why she, of all people, had been appointed to head the project. Maria found herself increasingly angered by Theresa's views on issues of affirmative action and abortion. Several times she wanted to confront Theresa on these issues, but Maria felt that the harmonious relationship of the group was at stake, and she didn't want to risk losing the group's cohesiveness.

Although Maria was able to control herself in most settings, she began to be critical of Theresa's views during group meetings, forcefully pointing out what she considered to be illogical thinking and openly upbraiding Theresa for her mistakes. When one of the men on the task force confronted her privately, she considered trusting him with her problem, yet she unconsciously feared that self-disclosure would make her seem weak, particularly to a white male. Several days later, when the two other women in the group confronted her about her behavior toward Theresa, Maria broke down and told them her problem.

1. What are the ethical issues in this case?
2. Did Maria behave ethically in this situation?
3. If you were one of the women advising Maria, what would you recommend that she do?

Conversation and Analysis

Use your Communicate! CD-ROM to access a video scenario of the following conversation. Click on the "Communicate! In Action" feature and then click on "Trevor and Meg." As you watch Trevor and Meg discuss the future of their relationship, focus on how effectively they are communicating.

1. How do Trevor and Meg disclose their feelings?

2. Note how effective each is at owning feelings and opinions.

3. How well do Trevor and Meg use praise and constructive criticism?

4. Notice how each demonstrates the characteristics of assertive behavior.

5. What is really Meg's fear?

We have provided a transcript of Trevor and Meg's conversation. After you have viewed the conversation on your CD-ROM, read the transcript. In the right-hand column there is space for you to record your analysis. You can also complete your analysis electronically using the Conversational Analysis feature included in Communicate! In Action. From the Conversation Menu on your CD-ROM, click "Analysis" for Trevor and Meg. Type your answers to the questions above in the forms provided. When you are finished, click "Submit" to compare your response to the analysis provided by the authors.

Trevor and Meg have been going together for the last several months of their senior year at college. Now that graduation is approaching, they are trying to figure out what to do about their relationship. They sit and talk.

Conversation

Analysis

Trevor: Meg, I think it's time we talk about making plans for the future. After all, we'll be graduating next month.

Meg: Trevor, you know how uncomfortable I feel about making any long-range plans at this time. We still need to know a lot more about each other before we even think about getting engaged.

Trevor: Why? We've both said we love each other, haven't we?

Meg nods.

Trevor: So why, why's this too soon? What else do we need to know?

Meg: For starters, I'll be going to law school this fall, and this year is going to be difficult. And, you haven't gotten a job yet.

Trevor: Come on, Meg. You're going to law school in the city, so I'll take a job there. I'll have a degree in business, so I can probably get a job most anywhere.

Meg: But Trevor, that's just my point. I know I'll be starting law school; I've always wanted to be a lawyer. And you don't really have any idea what you want to do. And that bothers me. I can't be worrying about you and your career when I'm going to need to focus on my clas ses.

Trevor: But I told you, I can get a job anywhere.

Conversation

Analysis

Meg: Yes, Trevor, but you need more than a job. You need to figure out what kind of job really turns you on. Or else, you risk waking up one day and regretting your life. And, I don't want to be there when that happens. I watched my dad go through a midlife crisis, and he ended up walking out on us.

Trevor: I'm not your dad, Meg. I won't leave you. And don't worry about me, I'll find a job.

Meg: Really? You've known I was going to law school in the city for over a month, but you still haven't even begun a job search. Trevor, right now is the time when people are hiring and you haven't even done your résumé. The longer you wait, the more difficult your search is going to be.

Trevor: Come on Meg, you've already said I'm irresistible. What company wouldn't want me?

Meg: I'm serious, Trevor. Look, I've got a scholarship to pay law school, but it's only going to pay half of my expenses. I'll be taking a loan to get enough money to pay the rest and to have money to live on. I won't have the money or the time to be very supportive of you if you haven't found work. I need the security of knowing that you've got a job and that you are saving money.

Trevor: Well, they say that "two can live as cheaply as one." I was thinking that once you got settled, I'd move in and that will save us a lot of money.

Meg: Whoa, Trevor. You know how I feel about that. I do love you, and I hope that we have a future together. But living together this year is not an option. I think we need at least a year of living on our own to get ourselves settled and make sure that we really are compatible. After all, we come from totally different backgrounds.

Conversation

Analysis

I practically raised myself, and I've paid my own bills since I was 18, while you've been lucky enough to have parents who footed your bills. There have been several times when we've talked about important issues and the differences between us have been obvious, and they worry me.

Trevor: You mean when I was joking around about our different tastes in cars?

Meg: No, Trevor, not cars, that's minor. But we also have greatly different feelings about money and family. You've told me that once you get married you want to start a family immediately. As I see it, I've got a three-year commitment to law school, then seven to ten years of hard work in order to make partner at a good firm. So I'm not sure when I want to start a family. But I know it won't be at least for six years.

Trevor: So, what are you saying, Meg? Is it over? "Thanks for the good time, Trevor, but you're not in my plans?"

Meg: Please don't be sarcastic. I'm not trying to hurt you. It makes me happy to think that we'll spend the rest of our lives together. But I'm worried about several things, so I'm just not ready to commit to that now. Let's just take a year, get settled, and see what happens. I'll love it if you do get a job near where I'm in school. That way we can have time to sort through some of the issues between us.

Trevor: You mean if you can fit me into your schedule? Meg, if we love each other now, aren't we still going to love each other next year? If we wait until we have everything settled we might never get married; there'll always be something. After all, we are two different people. We're never going to agree on everything!

Conversation	Analysis

Meg: Are you saying that with as unsettled that our lives are right now that we can shoulder the additional stress of planning for a marriage?

Trevor: No, what I'm saying is that we live together this year, see how it goes, then if it isn't working we don't have to get married.

Summary

Self-disclosure statements reveal information about ourselves that is unknown to others. Several guidelines can help us decide when self-disclosure is appropriate.

Three ways to disclose our feelings are to withhold them, display them, or skillfully describe them.

Instead of owning our own feelings and ideas, we often avoid disclosure by making generalized statements. The skill of making "I" statements can help us to more honestly assume ownership of our ideas and feelings.

Assertiveness is the skill of stating our ideas and feelings openly in interpersonally effective ways. Passive people are often unhappy as a result of not stating what they think and feel; aggressive people get their ideas and feelings heard but may create more problems for themselves because of their aggressiveness. And, as we might expect, appropriateness of assertiveness varies across cultures.

Some of the characteristics of behaving assertively are owning feelings, avoiding confrontational language, using specific statements directed to the behaviors at hand, maintaining eye contact and firm body position, maintaining a firm but pleasant tone of voice, and avoiding hemming and hawing.

Communicate! Online

Use your Communicate! CD-ROM for quick access to the electronic study resources that accompany this text. Included on your CD-ROM is access to InfoTrac College Edition, the World Wide Web, a demo of WebTutor for Communicate!, and the Communicate! Web site at the Wadsworth Communication

Café. The Communicate! Web site offers chapter-by-chapter activities, quizzes, and a digital glossary.

Review the following key terms at
http://communication.wadsworth.com/humancomm/verderber

Key Terms

aggressive behavior (172)
assertiveness (172)
constructive criticism (170)
describing feelings (162)
displaying feelings (161)
owning feelings or opinions (167)

passive behavior (172)
praising (169)
rapport-talk (160)
report-talk (160)
self-disclosure (156)
withholding feelings (161)

Your Communicate! CD-ROM also includes a video of the conversation between Trevor and Meg featured on pages 179–182. Click on the Communicate! In Action icon on your CD-ROM, then click on "Trevor and Meg." You can watch, listen to, and analyze their conversation. Improve your own conversation skills by learning from this model.

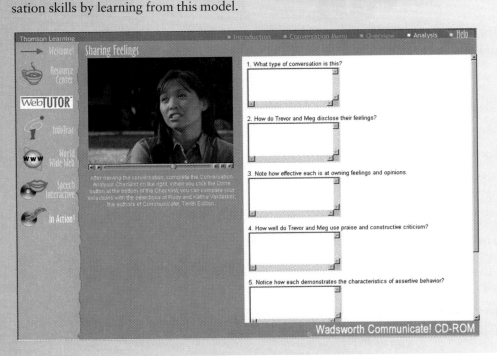

OBJECTIVES

After you have read this chapter, you should be able to answer these questions:

- What are the major types of relationships?

- What are effective ways of starting a relationship?

- How are relationships built on the Internet?

- How are the skills of descriptiveness, openness, tentativeness, and equality used in maintaining relationships?

- What does interpersonal needs theory tell us about relationships?

- What does exchange theory tell us about relationships?

- What is conflict, and why does it occur in relationships?

- What are the five conflict styles, and when is each style appropriate?

- What skills are used to initiate conflict effectively?

- What skills are used in responding to a conflict initiated by another?

Communicating in Relationships

"Janeen, you're spending a lot of time with Angie. What is Liam going to think about that?"

"Come on, Mom, I know you're just teasing me. Yeah, Liam's my boyfriend, and we get along really well, but there are things I just can't talk about with him."

"And you can with Angie?"

"Right. I can tell her what's going on with my writing, for example, and she really understands. And I do the same for her. We enjoy a lot of the same activities, so Angie is good company for me."

good relationship—*one comprised of mutually satisfying interactions with another person.*

Janeen is lucky because she has two close relationships. Interpersonal skills are instrumental in starting, building, and maintaining relationships, and in this chapter we discuss relationships and their dynamics. A **good relationship** is comprised of mutually satisfying interactions with another person.

In this chapter, we begin by identifying three types of relationships, explain the stages or cycle that typical relationships flow through, look at online relationships, and examine two theories of why relationships develop. Then we examine conflict and explain how to use the conflict process to strengthen relationships.

Types of Relationships

We behave differently depending on whether our relationships are personal or impersonal (LaFollette, 1996, p. 4). Moving on a continuum from impersonal to personal, we generally classify the people with whom we have relationships as acquaintances, friends, and close friends or intimates.

Acquaintances

acquaintances—*people we know by name and talk with when the opportunity arises but with whom our interactions are largely impersonal.*

Acquaintances are people we know by name and talk with when the opportunity arises but with whom our interactions are largely impersonal. We become acquainted with those who live near us, are part of our religious community, or perform services for us. Many acquaintance relationships grow out of a particular context. Thus Jim, an accountant, has been preparing Sung Lee's taxes for three years, but they never meet outside of his office and only exchange polite pleasantries or talk about Sung Lee's taxes.

Friends

friends—*people with whom we have negotiated more personal relationships voluntarily.*

Friends are people with whom we have negotiated more personal relationships voluntarily (Patterson, Bettini, & Nussbaum, 1993, p. 145). In the early stages of friendships, people move toward interactions that are less role-bound. That is, Jim and Sung Lee may decide to get together for lunch. If they find that they enjoy each other's company, they may eventually become friends.

What we look for in our friends   As we seek out people as friends, we are drawn toward people we find attractive, who have good social skills, who are responsive to us, and who have similar interests, attitudes, values, and personalities (Fehr, 1996, pp. 52–68).

Relationships may also develop when there are dissimilarities in personality. The saying "opposites attract" is as accurate as "birds of a feather flock together." Stated theoretically, relationships depend on mutual need fulfillment, so people can be attracted to those who are different from them but who fulfill their needs. Thus, opposites attract when the differences between the people are seen as complementary (Winstead, Derlega, & Rose, 1997, p. 26).

What we expect from our friends   Although people may be drawn to each other for many reasons, a variety of research shows that maintaining a real friendship is marked by a high degree of positiveness, assurance, openness, networking, and task sharing (Dindia, 2000, p. 291; Guerrero & Andersen, 2000, p. 178; Stafford & Canary, 1991).

■ *Positiveness.* Friends spend time with each other because they reap positive benefits in doing so. They enjoy each other's company, they enjoy talking with each other, and they enjoy sharing experiences.

■ *Assurance.* Friends **trust** each other. They risk putting their well-being in the hands of another because they trust the other not to intentionally harm their interests.

trust–*to risk putting your well-being in the hands of another.*

■ *Openness.* Friends share personal feelings with each other.

■ *Networking.* Friends show a high level of commitment not only to each other but to each other's friends and family. They are likely to sacrifice

W. Hill, Jr./The Image Works

Friendships are marked by positiveness, assurance, openness, networking, and task sharing.

their time and energy to engage in activities with family and friends of friends.

■ *Task sharing.* Friends help each other with work.

Close Friends or Intimates

close friends or **intimates**–
those with whom we share our deepest feelings.

Close friends or **intimates** are those with whom we share our deepest feelings. People may have countless acquaintants and many friends, but they are likely to have only a few truly intimate friends.

Close friends or intimates differ from "regular" friends mostly in degree of commitment, trust, disclosure, and enjoyment in their relationship. For instance, although friends engage in some self-disclosure, they are not likely to share the secrets of their lives; intimate friends often gain knowledge of the innermost being of their partner.

COMMUNICATE!
Using Technology

Communicate! Using Technology

Record a portion of a movie or TV program in which friends are having a conversation. Analyze it on the basis of expectations of friendships, including positiveness (enjoyment of talking with each other), assurance, openness, networking, and task sharing. Which of these factors seem evident in the conversation? What other elements were shown in the conversation? Did these seem to contribute to or detract from the relationships? In what ways is this conversation typical or atypical of those you have had with your friends? Explain.

passive strategy–*getting information about another through observation.*

active strategy–*getting information about another by asking other people about the person you are interested in.*

interactive strategy–*getting information about another by conversing with the person directly.*

Communication in the Stages of Relationships

Even though no two relationships develop in exactly the same manner, most relationships move through identifiable stages following a "life cycle" that includes starting or building, stability, and deterioration (Duck, 1987; Taylor & Altman, 1987). Whether a relationship moves to the next stage depends on how partners interact.

Starting or Building Relationships

Fundamental to starting or building a relationship is uncertainty reduction, the need for information (Berger & Brada, 1982; Littlejohn, 1999, p. 260). We get information about others **passively** by observing their behavior, **actively** by asking others for information, and **interactively** by conversing with them directly.

The three communication activities we engage in to start and build relationships are striking up conversation, keeping conversation going, and moving toward intimacy.

Striking up a Conversation What happens in the first few minutes of a conversation will have a profound effect on the nature of the relationship that develops. As the old saying goes, you seldom get a second chance to create a first impression. Although thinking up "getting to know you" lines is easy for some, many people become nearly tongue-tied when they want to meet someone and, as a result, make a bad first impression. There are several approaches to starting conversations. Most involve asking questions. A cheerful answer to your question suggests interest in continuing. Refusal to answer or a curt reply may mean that the person is not really interested in talking with you at this time.

1. **Formally or informally introduce yourself.** "Hi, my name is Gordon. What's yours?"

2. **Refer to the physical context.** "This is awful weather for a game, isn't it?" "I wonder how they are able to keep such a beautiful garden in this climate?"

3. **Refer to your thoughts or feelings.** "I really like parties, don't you?" "I live on this floor too—do these steps bother you as much as they do me?" and "Doesn't it seem stuffy in here?"

4. **Refer to the other person.** "Marge seems to be an excellent hostess—have you known her long?" "I don't believe I've had the pleasure of seeing you before—do you work in marketing?"

Keeping the conversation going   Once two people have begun an interaction, they are likely to engage in "small talk" such as information exchange and gossip, conversation that meets social needs with relatively low amounts of risk.

In **idea-exchange communication,** people share information that contains facts, opinions, and beliefs that occasionally reflect values. At the office, Dan may ask Walt about last night's sports scores. Or, on a more serious level, Bonita may talk with Ken about the upcoming election. Although the discussions of elections are "deeper" than conversations about sports, both sets of conversations represent idea-exchanges. This type of communication is important in the early stages of a relationship because through it you learn what the other person is thinking, reassess your attraction level, and decide whether or not you want the relationship to grow.

idea-exchange communication—*sharing information that contains facts, opinions, and beliefs.*

Gossip, relating information whose accuracy may be unknown about people you both know, is one of the most common forms of interpersonal communication. Eggins and Slade (1997) observe, "Every day a considerable amount of time for millions of people is consumed by gossip and as such it is a powerful socializing force" (p. 270).

gossip—*relating information whose accuracy may be unknown about people you both know.*

On one hand, gossip provides an easy way to talk with people without sharing much information about yourself. Statements such as "Do you know Bill? I hear he has a really great job" and "Would you believe that Mary Simmons and Tom Johnson are going together? They never seemed to hit it off too well in the past" are examples of gossip. Most gossip is largely benign because it is virtually public knowledge. People do break up, lose their jobs, get in accidents, win prizes, and so forth. In these circumstances, there is nothing secret, and if the person were there, he or she would likely tell you about what happened.

This kind of small talk occurs during all phases of a relationship but is most common in the early phase because it is considered safe. You can gossip for a long time with another person without really saying anything about yourself or learning anything about the other person. Gossip may be a pleasant way to pass

Friends and Acquaintances

Using Journal Activity 8.1 in your Student Workbook:

1. Identify five people you consider to be your friends. In what kind of context did you first meet? What attracted you to them? What aspects of attraction have proved to be most important as the relationships developed?

2. Identify five people you consider to be acquaintances. List the ways in which communication with your acquaintances differs from communication with your friends.

3. What would need to happen in order for those people you listed as acquaintances to become friends?

self-disclosure–*sharing biographical data, personal ideas, and feelings that are unknown to the other person.*
feedback–*verbal and physical responses to people and their messages.*
Johari window–*a tool for examining the relationship between disclosure and feedback.*

time with people you know but with whom you have no desire or need for a deeper relationship. It also provides a safe way to explore the potential for the relationship to grow because it enables each person to see whether the other reacts similarly to the views expressed about the object of the gossip. This is why conversations at parties are comprised largely of gossip.

On the other hand, gossip can be unethical and malicious. If the information exchanged is found to be inaccurate, the gossip may damage both the relationship in which it was exchanged and other relationships as well. Perhaps the most malicious kind of gossip is that engaged in for the purpose of hurting or embarrassing the person who is not present. For instance, saying "Lonnie had an automobile accident—he ran into another car" is a form of gossip, but it is factual. But if a person goes on to say, "And you know it's probably because of what he had to drink—you know that Lonnie's really been bingeing lately," this goes far beyond reporting what happened. Gossip quickly turns into rumor, and rumors can destroy a person's life.

Moving to deep friendship and intimacy levels In addition to engaging in small talk, people who seek more intimate levels will also begin to talk about more serious ideas and to share their feelings about important matters. By sharing feelings and through the process of self-disclosure individuals really come to know and to understand each other. When people find that they get satisfaction out of being together and that they are able to share ideas and feelings, their friendship grows.

Particularly important to the development of more intimate relationships is using affectionate communication (Floyd & Morman, 1998, p. 157). Affectionate communication includes such nonverbal behaviors as holding hands, putting an arm around a shoulder, sitting close to each other, looking into each other's eyes, hugging each other, and kissing. It also includes verbal behaviors such as saying things like "This relationship is really important to me," "I like you," or "You're a real friend."

Examining Disclosure and Feedback Ratios in Relationships

A healthy interpersonal relationship, especially one on a friendship or intimate level, is marked by a balance of **self-disclosure** (sharing biographical data, personal ideas, and feelings that are unknown to another person) and **feedback** (the verbal and physical responses to people and their messages) within the relationship.

How can you tell whether you and another are sharing enough to keep the relationship growing? The best method is to discuss it. As the basis for a worthwhile discussion, we suggest the use of a **Johari window**, named after its two originators, Joe Luft (1970) and Harry Ingham.

The window is divided into four sections or panes, as shown in Figure 8.1. The first quadrant is called the "open" pane of the window because it represents the information about you that both you and your partner know. It includes information that you have disclosed and the observations about you that your partner has shared with you. If you were preparing a Johari window that represented your side of your relationship with another person, you would include in the open pane all the items of information about yourself that you would feel free to share with that other person.

The second quadrant is called the "secret" pane. It contains all those things that you know about yourself but that your partner does not know about you. This information may run the gamut from where you keep your pencils or why you don't eat meat to deep secrets whose revelation threatens you. If you were preparing a Johari window that represented your side of a relationship with another person, you would include in the secret pane all the items of information that you have not shared with that other person. When you choose to disclose the information with your partner, the information moves into the open pane of the window. If, for example, you had been engaged to be married but on the day of the wedding your fiancee had backed out, this information might be in the secret pane of your window. But when you disclose this fact to your friend, it would move into the open part of your Johari window with this person. Through disclosure, the secret pane of a window becomes smaller and the open pane is enlarged.

The third quadrant is called the "blind" pane. This is the place for information that the other person knows about you but about which you are unaware. Most people have blind spots—aspects of their behavior about which they are unaware. For example, Charley may not know that he snores when he sleeps or that he frowns when he is concentrating. Both of these behaviors would be known by someone who has slept in the same room with him or been with him when he attends class lectures. Information moves from the blind area of the window to the open area through feedback from others. If no one has ever told

THINKING ABOUT . . .

Personal Guidelines for Self-Disclosure

Think of one secret about yourself. How many people know it? How do you decide whom to tell? What consequences (good and bad) have resulted from sharing that secret? Determine a set of guidelines that is appropriate for you in sharing such secrets.

	Known to self	Not known to self
Known to others	Open	Blind
Not known to others	Secret	Unknown

Figure 8.1
The Johari window.

Charley about these behaviors, or if he has refused to believe it when he has been told about them, this information will be in the blind part of his Johari window. When someone tells Charley about them and he accepts the feedback, then the information will move into the open pane of Charley's Johari window with this person. Thus, like disclosure, feedback enlarges the open pane of the Johari window, but in this case it is the blind pane that becomes smaller.

The fourth quadrant is called the "unknown" pane. It contains information about you that you do not know and neither does your partner. Obviously, you cannot develop a list of this information. So how do we know that it exists? Well, periodically we "discover" it. If, for instance, you have never tried hang gliding, then neither you nor anyone else can really know whether you would chicken out or follow through, do it well or crash, love every minute of it or be paralyzed by fear.

As you can see, when you disclose and receive feedback in a relationship, the sizes of the various window panes change (Figure 8.2). As a relationship becomes more intimate, the open pane of both partners' windows become larger, and the secret and hidden parts become smaller.

Figure 8.2a shows a relationship in which little disclosure or feedback is occurring. This person has not shared much information with the other and has received little feedback from this partner as well. We would expect to see this pattern in new relationships or in ones between casual acquaintances.

Figure 8.2b shows a relationship in which a person is disclosing to a partner but the partner is providing little feedback. As you can see, the secret pane is smaller, but the hidden pane is unchanged. A window like this indicates that the individual is able to disclose information but the partner is unable or unwilling to give feedback (or perhaps the individual refuses to accept the feedback that is being given). Part of the way that we learn about who we are comes from the feedback we receive from others, and relationships in which one partner does not provide feedback can become very unsatisfying to the other individual.

Figure 8.2c shows a relationship in which one partner is good at providing feedback but the other is not disclosing. Most of us disclose only when we trust our partners, so this pattern may be an indication that the individual does not have confidence in the relational partner.

Figure 8.2d shows a relationship in which the individual has disclosed information and received feedback, and the open pane of the window has enlarged as a result of both processes. Windows that look like this indicate that

Figure 8.2
Sample Johari windows:
(a) low disclosure, low feedback;
(b) high disclosure, low feedback;
(c) low disclosure, high feedback;
(d) high disclosure, high feedback.

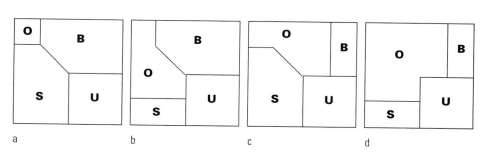

there is sufficient trust and interest in the relationship that both partners are willing to risk by disclosing and giving feedback.

Obviously, to get a complete "picture" of a relationship, each partner's Johari window would need to be examined. As stated at the beginning of this discussion, the window is a useful tool for helping partners examine and discuss the levels of intimacy and trust in their relationship.

Stabilizing Relationships

When two people have a satisfactory relationship, whether as acquaintances, as friends, or as intimates, they look for **stabilization,** a means of maintaining the relationship at that level for some time. Stabilization occurs when two people agree on what they want from each other and are satisfied that they are achieving it.

Unfortunately, as time goes by, people sometimes fall into communication habits that can hurt the stability of the relationship. To maintain stability in the relationship, work consciously to make sure that conversation between partners continues to be descriptive rather than evaluative, open rather than closed, tentative rather than dogmatic, and equal rather than superior.

Speak descriptively Speaking **descriptively** simply means stating what you see or hear in objective language. In earlier chapters, we spoke of describing feelings and describing behavior, both of which are necessities in maintaining a stable relationship.

Speak openly Speaking **openly** means continuing to share true thoughts and feelings without resorting to manipulation. In a good relationship, one person should never be afraid to share a thought with the other. If you find yourself being unwilling to share openly, ask yourself why? What is happening in the relationship that is keeping you from sharing your thoughts and feelings? If you discover something (my partner doesn't listen to me anymore; my partner constantly changes the subject), then you need to discuss that "openly" with your partner.

Speak tentatively Speaking **tentatively** means stating information in a way that suggests the possibility for inaccuracy. Again, as time goes by we may find ourselves saying everything as if we are the supreme authority. Consider the wording and the "sound" of the following pairs:

> "If I remember correctly, Dalton was the sales leader last month."
> "I'm telling you, Dalton had the most sales last month."

> "I think you should consider talking with Glenna before doing anything on your own."
> "You'd be an idiot not to talk with Glenna before doing anything on this."

In each case, the first sentence of each pair is more likely to "go over better" with the other person not only because the tentativeness of the phrasings is likely to be less antagonizing than the dogmatic statement, but also because the

THINKING ABOUT . . .

Johari Windows

Draw a Johari window to depict your relationship with one of your parents. Has the window changed much over time? If so, why?

stabilization–*a means of maintaining the relationship at that level for some time.*

speaking descriptively–*stating what you see or hear in objective language.*

speaking openly–*sharing true thoughts and feelings without resorting to manipulation and hidden agendas.*

speaking tentatively–*stating information in a way that suggests the possibility for inaccuracy.*

tentative statement acknowledges that the words come from the speaker—who may have it wrong. "I'm telling you" leaves no room for possible error; "If I remember correctly" not only leaves room for error but also shows that it is the speaker's recollection and not a statement of universal certainty.

Speak to others as equals   The tendency to sound superior goes along with the tendency to sound certain. Just as tentativeness leads to more convivial conversation, so does speaking to the other as an equal. **Speaking equally** in communication is usually shown by the exclusion of any words or nonverbal signs that might indicate superiority. You may know more on a subject than your partner, but you can still state your views in ways that don't "rub it in." Even a boss at work knows that treating subordinates as inferior will hurt their relationship. Treating a partner as inferior is asking for trouble.

In addition to choosing language carefully, we must also be conscious of the effects of our tone of voice and facial expressions. As we learned earlier, our nonverbal communication can totally negate the meaning of the words we use.

Many times the things we say that hurt our relationships happen because we are just not thinking. It is a good idea to follow the old advice of "engaging your brain before putting your mouth in action." Take a second to remind yourself that a single thoughtless sentence can take minutes, hours, or days to repair—if it is repairable.

Relationship Disintegration

Regardless of how much one party would like a relationship to remain stable or become more intense, there are times when a relationship is destined to disinte-

speaking equally–*excluding any words or nonverbal signs that might indicate superiority.*

Mutual respect and equality create a solid foundation for enduring relationships.

Douglas Kirkland/Sygma

grate. We may discover that we just do not have enough in common to make a go of it. Sometimes when a relationship ends, we are sad—at other times, it is a relief. Regardless of our feelings, it is helpful to end a relationship in an interpersonally competent manner. Even the effects of a wrenching breakup can be somewhat improved with the conscious effort to use good interpersonal communication skills.

Unfortunately, when people decide to end a relationship, they sometimes purposely use strategies that are hurtful. Even when relationships have fallen apart, people should still try to use the constructive skills of describing feelings, owning feelings, and disclosing to make parting as amicable as possible.

Role of Electronic Communication in Building Relationships

New communication technologies are changing the way we build and maintain relationships. Ten years ago people became acquainted mostly with those with whom they had personal physical contact. At the same time, dating services advertised that they could get people in the same community acquainted with each other within a week. Today, people are able to make acquaintances with people around the world within seconds.

Development of Electronically Mediated Relationships

Thanks to technological innovation, people are introduced to others they have never seen through newsgroups, Internet chat rooms, and Internet dating services. Moreover, some people are likely to develop these encounters into personal relationships. Parks and Floyd (1996) found that developing personal relationships is quite common (p. 93). For example, Andrea and Matt "meet" each other as they communicate in a newsgroup dedicated to the subject of "environmental concerns." They already believe they have at least one thing in common—an interest in environmental issues. As the postings continue, they notice that they are the only ones who hold a particular specific view on this issue. Moreover, they begin to see that they hold other ideas in common as well. At this point, they decide to "meet" in a private chat room where they "talk" with each other. Now they are able to begin to explore whether they have other common interests. Before long, they have exchanged email addresses and directly corresponded. If their interest in each other continues to grow, they may arrange to chat on the telephone. If this proves to be satisfactory, they may arrange to meet in person. At some point during this process, they have begun to have a personal relationship: maybe a friendship, maybe an intimate relationship.

Of course, many people in electronically mediated (EM) relationships are perfectly content with just having acquaintances and the opportunity to talk with each other. Parks and Floyd's study shows that nearly a quarter (23.7%) of the people in their newsgroup study reported that they communicated with their partners at least three or four times a week, and over half (55.4%) communicated with their partners on a weekly basis (p. 85). EM relationships are attractive to some busy people largely because they do not have time to "do the bar scene." Other people who begin relationships in face-to-face settings use EM communication to sustain these relationships when work or school requires them to live at a distance. Email, which was developed to be a tool for conducting business, is now widely used by families, friends, and lovers.

Can EM relationships endure? EM communicators seem to lack many of the things emphasized in traditional discussion of relationship development: physical proximity, information about physical appearance, cues about group membership, and information about the broader social context. However, people in EM settings can overcome these shortcomings by emailing, by exchanging photographs either electronically or by mail, by talking on the telephone, and ultimately, by arranging meetings. Think about it. What are some of the benefits and drawbacks to relationships that exist at a distance?

Some critics of EM relationships argue that face-to-face interaction has more social presence than the Internet; the possibility of immediate feedback with face-to-face interaction conveys greater personal closeness (Flaherty, Pearce, & Rubin, 1998, p. 264). In addition, in most EM forms, some of the nonverbal message is lost.

More and more people are turning to EM communication to develop and maintain relationships. EM relationships are attractive to those who have for one reason or another found difficulty making strong interpersonal relationships in person. Because EM communication is planned, people are able to show verbal skillfulness and humor in their writing, and they do not have to deal with physical attraction.

In fact, some individuals report their EM relationships are even better than face-to-face relationships. For instance, a person who had been active in a computer network for church workers said, "I know some of these people better than some of my oldest and best friends" (Parks & Floyd, 1996, pp. 82–83). And a variety of studies report instances of EM relationships blossoming into romance and marriage (Markham, 1998).

But there are important differences between in-person and EM communication that can create difficulties for relational development. J. D. Bigelow (1999), of Boise State University, focuses on three such problems (pp. 636–637):

1. **EM communication is less rich than face-to-face, primarily because text messages are primarily verbal.** As a result of not being able to see or hear the way people present their messages, we may misinterpret the messages. Only with videoconferencing is the full range of nonverbal messages available.

THINKING ABOUT . . .

Maintenance of Internet Relationships

Have you developed either a same-sex or an opposite-sex relationship online? If so, is the relationship continuing? If not, how long did it last? What were some of the elements that made this relationship "satisfying"? If the relationship has ended, were the reasons for its ending any different from reasons for ending face-to-face relationships?

Bruce Ayers/Stone

Of course, many people in electronically mediated (EM) relationships are perfectly content with just having acquaintances and with the opportunity to talk with each other.

2. **EM communication, conducted via keyboard entries, is slower paced than face-to-face conversation.** Although this slower rate may provide a person more time for thought, this slower transmission reduces the spontaneity that is an important characteristic of face-to-face interaction.

3. **EM communicators are invisible.** EM communicators often preserve their privacy by using online identities and perhaps by representing themselves differently.

From Internet to In-Person Relationships

In face-to-face relationships, trust is built over time. We meet a person and then begin interacting. As a result of the behavior we encounter, we then make decisions about trust. For instance, we loan a book and consider when and if it is returned; we make a date and consider whether and how often the person is on time; we tell the person something that is personal and consider whether that person keeps the information to him- or herself or communicates it to others. Through such experiences, we determine whether or not we can trust the person and thus whether or not we want to move toward a more intimate relationship (Goldberg, 1999, p. 113).

In EM relationships, making a trust evaluation is more difficult. Some of the media through which relationships are developed are very "opaque." That is, we lose most of the spontaneity and most of the information normally available through nonverbal channels. As a result, our capacity to judge the accuracy of the trustworthiness of the behavior of another is limited.

The Dark Side of Electronically Mediated Relationships

Despite its appeal, using EM communication to form relationships has led to several unethical practices.

Abuse of anonymity   One unethical practice for Internet-based relationships is the common practice of assuming a fictitious online persona. A serious question for Internet relationships is, "What kind of a relationship can be forged when users are not honest about who they are?" This practice removes both accountability and responsibility. Without these, sound relationships are not possible. Kramer and Kramarae (1997) assert that women have the most to lose from fictitious identity usage (p. 236).

Dishonesty   A second unethical practice is the ease with which one can deceive. People lie about their sex, physical attributes, and also create fictitious careers, homes, and so forth. Because we do not "know" our EM partner in person, we are severely limited in our abilities to independently confirm what we are told. Those in EM relationships need to proceed with caution. It is wise to be skeptical of what people tell you about themselves—especially at the beginning of such a relationship. As Jenny Preece points out, "Online romances of any sort may fail when real-life meetings result in dashed fantasies. For example, online no one is overweight, but in reality a person's extra 25 pounds can make a difference. And dishonesty works only as long as the relationship remains online only" (2000, p. 156).

In the early stages of the relationship, it is also wise to limit the personal information you divulge. Remember, in any communication situation, self-disclosure should occur only if it is reciprocated. Even then, begin slowly and with less personal issues before moving to more sensitive information.

Abuse of anonymity and dishonesty are of special concern for EM relationships formed by children. In 1998, seventeen million children ages two to eighteen were online. That number is expected to grow in five years to more than forty-two million children (Okrent, 1999, p. 41). It is especially important for parents to monitor children's EM relationships. Interestingly enough, some parents decline to monitor their kids' online chatting, likening it to violating their privacy by eavesdropping on their phone calls. But as Okrent cautions, "There's a difference: when your child's on the phone, she knows for certain who's on the other end of the line" (p. 41). Parents need to learn how to monitor their children's Internet usage and to use software capable of blocking access to objectionable sites.

technological addictions—
nonchemical (behavioral) addictions that involve human–machine interaction.

Addiction   A third potential problem for children and adults alike is **technological addictions,** defined as nonchemical (behavioral) addictions that involve human–machine interaction (Griffiths, 1998, p. 62). The seductiveness of communicating electronically can result in the disruption of ongoing interpersonal relationships. One extreme example was reported in a recent *Cincinnati Enquirer* article ("Angry Wife," 1999). It appears that a wife became angry because her husband was on the Internet at 2:05 a.m. He had been online until 4 a.m. the previous day "chatting" with women. In an act of desperation, anger, jealousy, and frustration, this wife tried to cut the power cords on the computer before attacking it with the meat cleaver. She pleaded no contest to domestic violence and resisting arrest and was fined two hundred dollars.

Theoretical Perspectives on Relationships

What determines whether or not we will try to build a relationship with another person? Why do some relationships never move beyond a certain level or begin to deteriorate? Two theories—interpersonal needs theory and exchange theory—provide answers to these questions.

Interpersonal Needs Theory

Interpersonal needs theory proposes that whether or not a relationship is started, built, or maintained depends on how well the people involved meet each other's interpersonal needs for affection, inclusion, and control (Schutz, 1966, pp. 18–20).

The need for **affection** reflects a desire to express and to receive love. The people you know probably run the gamut of showing and expressing affection both verbally and nonverbally. At one end of the spectrum are those who avoid close ties, seldom show strong feelings toward others, and shy away from people who show or want to show affection. At the other end of the spectrum are those who thrive on establishing "close" relationships with everyone. They think of all others as intimates, immediately confide in persons they have met, and want everyone to consider them close friends. Somewhere in between these two extremes are "personal" people, those who can express and receive affection easily and who derive pleasure from many kinds of relationships with others.

The need for **inclusion** reflects a desire to be in the company of other people, and everyone has some need to be social. At one end of the continuum are those who prefer to be left alone. Occasionally, they seek company or enjoy being included with others, but they do not require a great deal of social interaction to feel satisfied. At the other end of the continuum are those who need constant companionship and feel tense when they must be alone. Their doors are always open—everyone is welcome, and they expect others to welcome them. Of course, most of us do not belong to either of these extreme types. Rather, we are sometimes comfortable being alone and at other times need and enjoy interacting with others.

interpersonal needs theory–*proposes that whether or not a relationship is started, built, or maintained depends on how well each person meets the interpersonal needs of the other.*

affection need–*a desire to express and to receive love.*

inclusion need–*a desire to be in the company of other people.*

control need–*a desire to influence the events and people around us.*

The need for **control** reflects a desire to influence the events and people around us. As with the other two interpersonal needs, people vary in how much control they require. At one extreme are persons who seem to shun responsibility and do not want to be in charge of anything. At the other extreme are persons who need to dominate others at all times and become anxious if they cannot. Again, most people fall somewhere between these two extremes, needing to lead at certain times but content to follow the lead of others at other times.

How can this analysis help us understand communication in relationships? Relationships develop and deteriorate in part because of the compatibility or incompatibility of individuals' interpersonal needs. As you interact with others, you can detect whether their needs for affection, inclusion, and control seem compatible with yours. Suppose that Emily and Dan have been seeing each other regularly and both see their relationship as close. If, in response to Dan's attempt to put his arm around Emily while they were watching television, Emily slightly stiffens, it might suggest that Emily does not have quite the same need for affection as Dan. It should be emphasized that people's needs do differ; moreover, people's needs change over time. When other people's needs at any given time differ significantly from ours and we fail to understand that, we can misunderstand what is going wrong in our communication.

Schutz's theory of interpersonal needs is useful because it helps explain a great deal of interpersonal behavior (Trenholm, 1991, p. 191). In addition, research on this model has been generally supportive of its major themes (Shaw, 1981, pp. 228–231). Interpersonal needs theory does not, however, explain *how* people adjust to one another in their ongoing relationships. The next theory we discuss will help us develop this understanding.

Exchange Theory

exchange theory–*proposes that relationships can be understood in terms of the exchange of rewards and costs that take place during individuals' interactions.*

rewards–*outcomes that are valued by a person.*

costs–*outcomes that a person does not wish to incur.*

Another way of understanding our relationships is on the basis of **exchange theory**. John W. Thibaut and Harold H. Kelley (1986) developed this theory. They believe relationships can be understood in terms of the exchange of rewards and costs that take place during individuals' interactions (pp. 9–30). **Rewards** are positively valued outcomes such as good feelings, prestige, useful information, and fulfillment of emotional needs that are valued by a person. **Costs** are negatively valued outcomes such as time, energy, anxiety, and emotional pain that the person does not wish to experience. For instance, Sharon may wish to talk with Jan if she anticipates learning how to solve a tough problem, but she may be reluctant to spend that time with Jan if she expects to be annoyed by Jan's air of superiority during the interaction.

According to Thibaut and Kelley, people seek interaction situations in which their reward/cost ratio is best. So whether Sharon asks Jan to explain the calculus problem to her depends on (1) whether Sharon believes the positive value she receives from the information is greater than the cost to her self-esteem from Jan's snide comments and (2) whether getting this information from Jan will result in a better reward/cost ratio than if Sharon gets the information elsewhere, perhaps from a paid tutor.

This analysis can be extended from single interactions to relationships. If the ratio of rewards of a relationship compared to the costs of the relationship are higher than other alternative relationships, then the person will experience the relationship as pleasant and satisfying. But if, over an extended period, the net rewards (reward minus cost) in a relationship fall below what is available elsewhere, the person will come to view the relationship as unsatisfactory or unpleasant.

If people have a number of relationships they perceive as giving them a good reward/cost ratio, they will set a high satisfaction level and will probably not be satisfied with low-outcome relationships. By contrast, people who have few positive interactions will be satisfied with relationships and interactions that people who enjoy high-outcome relationships would find unattractive. For instance, Devon may continue to go with Erica even if she treats him very poorly because, compared to other relationships he has had, the net rewards he gets from the relationship are on par. In fact, some people will stay in a relationship that others view as abusive because they do not see themselves as having better alternatives. Joan may stay with Charley even though he periodically beats her because she believes he is a good provider who is loving when he is sober, and besides, "Who else would marry a forty-five-year-old woman with three children?"

Thibaut and Kelley's exchange theory is based on the assumption that people consciously and deliberately weigh the rewards and costs associated with any relationship or interaction and make comparisons to alternative choices. That is, people seek out relationships that benefit them and avoid those that are costly (Trenholm, 1991, p. 72). It can be useful to examine your relationships from a reward/cost perspective, especially if your relationship is stagnating. You may recognize areas where costs are greater than rewards either for you or for the other person. If so, you may be able to change some aspects of the relationship before it deteriorates completely.

> **THINKING ABOUT . . .**
>
> **Needs Theory and Exchange Theory**
>
> Think of one specific intimate relationship you have. Explain the development and maintenance of this relationship. How can needs theory or exchange theory be used to explain why this relationship developed as it did?

Conflict

When two people have an honest relationship, it is inevitable that there will be times when one person's attempt to satisfy his or her own needs will conflict with the other person's desires. When this happens, the partners experience conflict. **Interpersonal conflict** is the result of a situation wherein the needs or ideas of one person are at odds or in opposition to the needs or ideas of another. In these conflict situations, participants have choices about how they act and how they communicate with each other.

interpersonal conflict—*the result of a situation wherein the needs or ideas of one person are at odds or in opposition to the needs or ideas of another.*

Estate of Cybil Shelton/Peter Arnold, Inc.

Withdrawal during conflict usually just postpones—and worsens—the confrontation.

Although many people view conflict as bad (and, to be sure, conflict situations are likely to make us anxious and uneasy), conflict is often useful in confronting and resolving honest differences. In this section, we will look at five styles of managing conflict and then suggest specific communication strategies that can be used to initiate and respond to conflict effectively.

Styles of Managing Conflict

When faced with conflict, people can withdraw, accommodate, force, compromise, or collaborate (Cahn, 1990; Cupach & Canary, 1997; Filley, 1975).

withdrawal–*a form of conflict management in which people physically or psychologically remove themselves from the conflict.*

Withdrawing When people **withdraw**, they physically or psychologically remove themselves from the conflict. People may physically withdraw by leaving the site. For instance, when Justina says, "Eduardo, I thought we agreed that you'd pay my folks back the $60 you owe them this week," Eduardo may withdraw physically by walking downstairs. Eduardo would be withdrawing psychologically if he ignores Justina and continues to read the paper.

Considered from an individual satisfaction standpoint, withdrawal creates a lose-lose situation because neither party to the conflict really accomplishes what he or she wants. Although Eduardo temporarily escapes from the conflict, he knows it will come up again.

mulling–*thinking about or stewing over an actual or perceived problem until the conflict is perceived as more severe and results in blaming behavior.*

Considered from a relational satisfaction standpoint, both kinds of withdrawal usually have negative consequences. When used repeatedly, withdrawal leads to relationship decline. Why? Because neither party eliminates nor attempts to manage the nature of the conflict. Moreover, withdrawal results in what Cloven and Roloff (1991) call "mulling behavior" (p. 136). By **mulling**, they mean thinking about or stewing over an actual or perceived problem until the conflict is perceived as being more severe and results in blaming behavior.

Withdrawal may be effective as a temporary effort to create time to think. For instance, Eduardo might say, "Hold it a minute; let me think about this while I get a cup of coffee, and then we'll talk about this some more." A few minutes later, having calmed down, Eduardo may return, ready to approach and deal with the conflict.

In certain circumstances, withdrawal may actually be a appropriate. When neither the relationship nor the issue is really important, withdrawing is a good strategy. For example, at a party at which Josh and Mario have just met, the subject turns to gun control. Josh may politely excuse himself to go talk with other people when he realizes that he strongly disagrees with the position Mario is advocating. In this case, Josh judges that it simply is not that important to resolve the disagreement with Mario—his relationship with Mario just is not that important.

Accommodating Accommodating is giving in to the other's needs while ignoring your own. For instance, Juan would like to spend his vacation alone with Mariana, but when she says, "I think it would be fun to have Sarah and Paul come with us, don't you?" Juan replies, "OK, whatever you want."

Considered from an individual satisfaction standpoint, accommodation is a win-lose situation. The person who accommodates loses and allows the other person to win.

From a relational satisfaction standpoint, habitual accommodation has two problems. First, conflicts resolved through accommodation may lead to poor decision making because important facts, arguments, and positions are not voiced. Second, from an exchange theory perspective, habitual accommodation results in the accommodater's consistently receiving less. Eventually this can result in the accommodater's seeking more balanced exchange relationships.

Habitually accommodating is a problem, but when the issue really isn't that important but the relationship is, it is appropriate and effective to accommodate. For instance, whether to have chicken or fish for dinner may be unimportant to you, but if your in-laws prefer fish, you may accommodate them.

Moreover, it should be noted that accommodating is a preferred style of dealing with conflict in some cultures. In Japanese culture, for instance, it is thought to be more humble and face-saving to accommodate than to risk losing respect through conflict (Lulofs & Cahn, 2000, p. 114).

Forcing Forcing is demanding through physical threats, verbal attacks, coercion, or manipulation that your needs be satisfied or your ideas be accepted. The phrase "might makes right" captures the forcing style.

Considered from an individual satisfaction standpoint, forcing is win-lose. Forcers demand their way with little regard to the cost borne by others.

From a relational satisfaction standpoint, forcing rarely improves and usually hurts a relationship. Because of this, forcing is only appropriate when the issue is very important and the relationship is not and in emergencies when quick and decisive action must be taken to ensure safety or minimize harm.

accommodating–*a form of conflict management in which people attempt to satisfy others' needs while ignoring their own.*

forcing–*demanding through physical threats, verbal attacks, coercion, or manipulation that your needs be satisfied or your ideas be accepted.*

compromising—*both parties make sacrifices to find common ground.*

collaborating—*problem solving by addressing the needs and issues of each party to arrive at a solution that is mutually satisfying.*

Compromising   **Compromising** occurs when both people make sacrifices to find common ground, attempting to resolve the conflict by providing at least some satisfaction for both parties. Under this approach, both people give up some part of what they really want or believe, or they trade one thing they want to get something else.

From a personal satisfaction standpoint, compromising creates a lose-lose situation because both parties in one sense "lose" even as they "win." Although compromising is a popular style, there are significant problems associated with it. One of special concern is that the quality of a decision is affected if one of the parties "trades away a better solution" to effect the compromise. Compromising is appropriate when the relationship is important, the issues have no simple solution, and both people have a strong interest in some parts of the issue.

From a relational satisfaction standpoint, compromise does not damage long-term relationships because both parties gain some satisfaction.

Collaborating   **Collaborating** is problem solving by addressing the needs and issues of each party to arrive at a solution that is mutually satisfying. During collaboration, people discuss the issues and their feelings about the issues and identify the characteristics that are important for them to find in a solution.

Thus from an individual satisfaction standpoint, collaboration is win-win because the conflict is resolved to the satisfaction of all.

From a relational satisfaction standpoint, collaboration is positive because both sides feel that they have been heard. They get to share ideas and weigh and consider information. Whatever the solution, it is a truly collaborative effort. In effect, collaboration proves to be the most appropriate and the most effective means of managing conflict. In the Spotlight on Scholars that follows, we can see how the research of Daniel Canary has validated the importance of both appropriateness and effectiveness in conflict management.

Resolving conflict through collaborative discussion requires a problem-solving approach. Let's go back to Justina and Eduardo's conflict over the sixty dollars Eduardo was supposed to pay back to Justina's folks. Eduardo is angry with Justina for her failure to recognize his problems. So, how do they collaborate?

In general, the collaborative approach includes five parts: (1) defining the problem, (2) analyzing the problem (what are its causes and symptoms), (3) developing mutually acceptable criteria for judging solutions (what goals do we want to achieve), (4) suggesting possible solutions (what could we do), and (5) selecting the best solution. Sometimes not all the steps are needed.

For instance, after Justina points out her parents' need for the money, Eduardo quietly explains that he also owes some money on his credit card bill so he can't pay her folks immediately. As they discuss this, Justina sees that because the credit card interest is so high Eduardo needs to pay off the credit card debt as quickly as possible so that he has money to pay her folks. After more discussion, Eduardo suggests that while he is paying the credit card debt he could come up with some money each month for her folks. Justina suggests ten dollars a month until the debt is paid. Eduardo agrees that he could handle that.

COMMUNICATE! Using InfoTrac College Edition

How do college students deal with conflict? Using the InfoTrac College Edition subject guide, enter the term "interpersonal conflict." Check the periodical references under Interpersonal Conflict. You'll find articles that look at conflict in a variety of settings such as marriage, family structure, children's adjustment, and so on. See Marianne Bell and David Forde's article, "A factorial survey of interpersonal conflict resolution" in the *Journal of Social Psychology*. Does the behavior described in this article fit you? Do any of the research findings surprise you? Why?

SPOTLIGHT ON SCHOLARS

Daniel J. Canary, Professor of Communication, Hugh Downs School of Human Communication, Arizona State University, on Conflict Management

Dan Canary, citing the personal benefit in studying conflict, stated, "I learned how to control my own behavior and become more effective in my personal relationships." Canary's initial curiosity about effective conflict management behaviors was piqued when he was in graduate school at the University of Southern California.

At the time, he was a classmate of Brian Spitzberg, who formulated the theory that relational competence is a product of behaviors that are both appropriate and effective, and Bill Cupach, who was studying conflict in relationships. Although Canary saw the connection between their work, it was several years later—after he experienced successful and unsuccessful resolutions of significant conflict episodes in his personal life—that he began in earnest to study how the way people behave during conflict episodes affects their relationships.

Scholars can become well-known by developing a new theory that more clearly describes what really happens when we interact, by carrying out a series of research studies that test and elaborate on the theories developed by others, or by organizing, integrating, and synthesizing the theories and research work that has been done in an area so that people who are not specialists in the particular area can better understand what is known. Dan Canary's reputation has been made in both of the latter types of scholarship.

Canary's research studies are helping to identify the behaviors that lead to perceiving a person as a competent conflict manager. Although people will view some of the communication behaviors to manage conflict as appropriate and some behaviors as effective, Canary agrues that both are necessary to be perceived as competent. Drawing on Spitzberg's competence theory, Canary's research studies are designed to identify conflict behaviors that accomplish both of the goals of appropriateness and effectiveness. The results of his studies consistently show that integrative conflict strategies—problem-solving, collaborating, and compromising approaches that display a desire to work with the other person—are perceived to be both appropriate and effective (i.e., competent). Furthermore, his studies have shown that when one partner in a relationship is thought to be a competent conflict manager, the other one trusts him more, is more satisfied with the relationship, and perceives the relationship to be more intimate.

His research studies identify specific conflict management behaviors that are viewed as appropriate or effective. Canary has found that when a person acknowledges the arguments of others (e.g., "Uh huh, I can see how you would think that") and when a person agrees with the arguments that others make to support their points (e.g., "Gee that's a good point that I hadn't really thought about") the person was viewed as having appropriately handled the conflict. To be viewed as effective, however, required a different set of behaviors. According to Canary's findings, conflict handling behaviors that are viewed to be effective included stating complete arguments, elaborating and justifying one's point of view, and clearly developing one's ideas. In a conflict situation, Canary noticed that what was viewed as appropriate alone had the potential to be ineffective because appropriate behaviors seemed to involve some sort of agreement with the other person.

Canary reasoned that there must be ways to be both appropriate and effective in conflict situations.

This led him to consider methods of sequencing, or ordering, messages in a conflict episode. His preliminary results have revealed that competent communicators (those perceived to be both appropriate and effective) will begin by acknowledging the other's viewpoint or agreeing with part of the other's argument, *before* explaining, justifying, and arguing for their own viewpoint. In using this sequence, Canary believes competent communicators help "frame" the interaction as one of cooperative problem solving rather than as one of competing interests wherein only one party can "win."

Many of Canary's major contributions to the study of conflict in personal relationships are included in two books: *Relationship Conflict* (coauthored with William Cupach and Susan Messman) is a synthesis of the diverse conflict literature that was written for graduate students and other scholars; *Competence in Interpersonal Conflict* (coauthored with Cupach) focuses on how readers can increase their competence at managing interpersonal conflict in a variety of settings. For complete citations of these and other Canary publications, see the references list at the end of this book.

Canary teaches courses in interpersonal communication, conflict management, and research methods. His research involves a quickly applied conflict rating system that people can use to observe conflict in an efficient yet valid way.

In the next section, we will look at the collaborative approach from both an initiating and a responding framework.

The five different styles of conflict management, with their characteristics, outcomes, and appropriate usage, are summarized in Figure 8.3 on pages 208 and 209. Much of the remainder of this chapter focuses on guidelines for accomplishing good collaborative discussion.

THINKING ABOUT ...

Conflict Style

What is your preferred conflict style? Which style is most difficult for you to use?

Communication Skills for Resolving Conflicts through Collaboration

One person usually initiates a conflict, and the other person responds to it. Whether you initiate or respond to conflict, you can practice collaboration by using specific communication skills and verbal strategies. In this section, we will consider how to initiate conflict and how to respond to conflicts initiated by others.

Initiating Conflict Appropriately

Many people avoid conflict because they do not know how to initiate a conflict conversation effectively. The following guidelines (as well as those for responding to conflict in the next section) are based on work from several fields of study (Adler 1977; Gordon 1970; Whetten & Cameron, 1998) and will help you initiate conflict in a way that reduces defensiveness and invites collaboration.

1. **State ownership of the apparent problem.** If you are trying to study for a test in your most difficult course and the person next door is playing her stereo so

loud that your walls are shaking and you can't concentrate, it is important to acknowledge that *you* are the one who is angry, hurt, or frustrated. Thus to resolve *your* problem, you decide to confront your neighbor. You show ownership if you say something like, "Hi, I'm having a problem that I need your help with. I'm trying to study for a midterm in my most difficult class . . ."

2. **Describe the potential conflict in terms of the behavior you observe, the consequences, and your feelings about it.** The behavior, consequences, and feelings framework means that when a behavior happens, consequences result, and you feel a certain way (Gordon 1971). It is important to include all three of these steps for the other person to fully understand the issue. This framework requires you to *describe* for the other person what you see or hear, what happens to you as a result, and what feeling you experience. This "b-c-f" approach uses the skills of owning feelings, describing behavior, and describing feelings—all skills that we discussed earlier.

In the example of the loud stereo, you might follow up on the opening by saying: (B) "When I hear your stereo, (C) I get distracted and can't concentrate, which makes it even harder for me to study, (F) and then I get frustrated and annoyed."

Let's review this. *The loudness of the stereo* is the behavior (B) you observe that has consequences. *I get distracted and can't concentrate, which makes it even harder for me to study* are the consequences (C) that result from this behavior. *I get frustrated and annoyed* are the feelings (F) that you experience.

3. **Avoid letting the other person change the subject.** When you approached your neighbor about the stereo, suppose she said, "Oh come on, everyone plays their stereos loudly in this neighborhood." Don't let yourself get into talking about "everybody." Get back to the point by saying, "Yes, I understand it's a noisy neighborhood and loud music normally doesn't bother me. But I'm still having a problem right now, and I was hoping you could help me." Notice how this gets the focus back on the problem that you are having.

4. **Phrase your solution in a way that focuses on common ground.** Once you have been understood, suggest your solution. Your solution is more likely to be accepted if you can tie it to a shared value, common interest, or shared constraint. In our example, you might say, "I think we both have had times when even little things get in the way of our being able to study. So even though I realize I'm asking you for a special favor, I hope you can help me out by turning down your stereo while I'm grinding through this material." In short, the better you are at initiating conflict appropriately, the more likely you will get a beneficial outcome.

5. **Think through what you will say before you confront the other person, so that your request will be brief and precise.** Perhaps the greatest problem most of us have with initiating conflict is that we have good intentions of keeping on track but our emotions get the best of us and either we say things we shouldn't or we go on and on and annoy the other person.

OBSERVE & ANALYZE
Journal Activity

Conflict Episodes

In your Student Workbook under Journal Activity 8.3, describe a conflict episode you have recently experienced. How did you and the other person behave? What was the outcome of the conflict? How did you feel about it then? Now? Could the conflict have been handled in a different way that would have resulted in a better outcome?

Approach	Characteristics	Goal	Outlook
Withdrawal	Uncooperative, unassertive	To keep from dealing with conflict	I don't want to talk about it.
Accommodation	Cooperative, unassertive	To keep from upsetting the other person	Getting my way isn't as important as keeping the peace.
Force	Uncooperative, assertive	To get my way	I'll get my way regardless of what I have to do.
Compromise	Partially cooperative, partially assertive	To get partial satisfaction	I'll get partial satisfaction by letting the other person get partial satisfaction as well.
Collaboration	Cooperative, assertive	To solve the problem together	Let's talk this out and find the best solution possible for both of us.

Before you go charging over to your neighbor's room, think to yourself, "What am I going to say?" Take a minute to practice. Say to yourself, "I need to own the problem and then follow the b-c-f formula." Then practice a few statements until you think you can do it when your neighbor comes to the door.

Responding to Conflict Effectively

It is more difficult to respond effectively to a potential conflict than to initiate one because it is easy to become defensive if the person does not initiate the conflict effectively. If the initiator phrases the problem appropriately, "I'm having a problem that I need your help with," most likely you would say something like, "I'm sorry, I know what you mean. I didn't even think that my stereo might be bother anyone. Here, I'll turn it down." With this response, the conflict is immediately resolved.

But not all initiators will understand the problem, behavior, consequences, feelings approach to initiating conflict, and you may well face a situation that will require great skill.

Individual Satisfaction	Relational Satisfaction	Relational Effects	When Appropriate
Lose/lose: neither party gets satisfaction	Negative: no resolution	Drives wedge into relationship: results in mulling and blaming	Either as temporary disengagement or when issue is unimportant
Lose/win: the other party gets satisfaction	Negative: neither party feels good about the process	Hurts relationship because one person takes advantage	To build social credits or when the issue is unimportant
Win/lose: one party, the forcer, gets satisfaction	Negative: physical and psychological pain for the loser	Hurts relationship because one person feels intimidated	In emergencies; when it is critical to one's or others' welfare; if someone is taking advantage of you
Lose/lose or win/win: neither party is fully satisfied	Neutral to positive: at least partial satisfaction for both	May help or hurt because satisfaction is compromised	When issue is moderately important, when time is short, or when other attempts don't work
Win/win: both parties feel satisfied with the process	Positive: relationship strengthened because mutual benefits	Helps the relationship because both sides are heard	Anytime

Figure 8.3
Styles of conflict management.

1. **Disengage.** Put your emotional "shields" up. When the *Enterprise* is about to be attacked or has just been fired upon, *Star Trek* buffs know that the Captain shouts, "Shields up!" With its shields in place, the ship is somewhat protected from enemy fire, and the Captain and crew are able to problem solve effectively.

   We also need to learn to mentally put our shields up when someone becomes overly aggressive in initiating a conflict. Placing an emotional barrier between us gives us time to disengage emotionally so we can retain our problem-solving ability. So, put those shields up, and while you are "counting to ten," think of how to turn this into a problem-solving session.

2. **Listen to nonverbal cues as well as to the verbal message.** Just as in every other kind of interpersonal communication, listening is fundamental to resolving conflict. As Allan Barsky (2000, p. 77) points out, "you must not only listen, but ensure that the other parties know that you are listening and understanding them." But your listening must involve awareness of nonverbal cues as well as verbal messages, for as Berger argued (1994), failure to account for the nonverbal communication is to "doom oneself to study the tip of a very large iceberg" (p. 493).

SKILL BUILDERS   Describing Behavior, Consequences, and Feelings

Skill	Use	Procedure	Example
Describing the basis of a conflict in terms of behavior, consequences, and feelings (b-c-f).	To help the other person understand the problem completely.	1. Own the message. 2. Describe the behavior that you see or hear. 3. Describe the consequences that result. 4. Describe your feelings.	Jason says, "I have a problem that I need your help with. When I tell you what I'm thinking and you don't respond (b), I start to think you don't care about me or what I think (c), and this causes me to get very angry with you (f)."

Infante, Rancer, and Jordan (1996) found that the people they studied recognized that behaviors such as smiling, pleasant facial expression, relaxed body posture, and a warm and sincere voice are more likely to keep conflict from occurring or from escalating than a tense/frowning face, grinding teeth, stern/staring eyes, clenched fists, and a loud voice (p. 322).

Let's say, however, that you are faced with the conflict initiator who says to you, "Turn down that damn radio. Even an idiot would realize that playing it at top volume is likely to tee off someone who is trying to study." In addition to the harsh words, you are also likely to see and hear several unaffirming nonverbal behaviors.

3. **Respond empathically with genuine interest and concern.** When someone initiates a potential conflict inappropriately, that person is still watching you closely to see how *you* react. Even if you disagree with the complaint, you should demonstrate empathy for the person's feelings. Sometimes you can do this by allowing the initiator to vent his or her emotions while you listen. Only when he or she has calmed down can you begin to problem solve. In this case, however, you might well start by saying, "I'm sorry, I can see that you are angry with me."

4. **Paraphrase your understanding of the problem and ask questions to clarify issues.** Most people are unaware of the b-c-f framework, so you may need to paraphrase to make sure that you are understanding. For instance, let's suppose the person says, "What in the world are you thinking?" If information is missing (as with this initiating statement), you can ask questions that reflect the b-c-f framework: "Is it the volume of the music or the type of music that is distracting?" "So, you were studying all right before I turned on my music?" "Are you angry with me or frustrated by your inability to concentrate—or is something else going on?"

Sometimes people will initiate a conflict episode on minor issues when what really needs to be considered has not been mentioned.

©1995 Baby Blues Partnership. Distributed by King Features Syndicate. Reprinted with special permission of King Features Syndicate, Inc.

5. **Seek common ground by finding some aspect of the complaint to agree with.** This does not mean giving in to the other person. Nor does it mean that you should feign agreement on a point that you do not agree with. However, using your skills of supportiveness, you can look for points with which you can agree (Adler, 1977).

Let's take our ongoing example: "Turn down that damn radio. Even an idiot would realize that playing it at top volume is likely to tee off someone who is trying to study." In response, you could agree in part: "I understand how frustrating it can be when I can't concentrate." You could agree in principle: "Yes, I agree it's best to study in a quiet place." You could agree with the initiator's perception: "I can see that you are finding it difficult to study with music in the background." Or you could agree with the person's feelings: "It's obvious that you're frustrated and annoyed."

You do not need to agree with the initiator's conclusions or evaluations. You need not accommodate. But by agreeing to some aspect of the complaint, you create a common ground on which a problem-solving discussion can take place.

6. **Ask the person to suggest alternatives.** As soon as you are sure you have agreed on a definition of the problem, ask the person what he or she thinks will best solve the problem. The initiator has probably spent time thinking about what needs to be done, and asking for suggested solutions signals your willingness to listen and cooperate. You may be surprised to find that what is suggested seems reasonable to you. If not, you may be able to craft an alternative that builds on one of the ideas presented. In either case, by asking for suggestions you communicate your trust in the other person, thus strengthening the problem-solving climate.

Learning from Conflict-Management Failures

Ideally, you want to resolve conflicts as they occur. Nevertheless, there will be times when no matter how hard both persons try, they will not be able to resolve the conflict.

Especially when the relationship is important to you, take time to analyze your inability to resolve the conflict. Ask yourself these questions: "Where did

OBSERVE & ANALYZE
Journal Activity

Conflict Failures

Think of a recent conflict you experienced in which the conflict was not successfully resolved. Analyze what happened using the concepts from this chapter. In your Student Workbook under Journal Activity 8.4, answer the following questions. What type of conflict was this? What style did you adopt? What was the other person's style? How did styles contribute to what happened? How well did your behavior match the guidelines recommended for initiating and responding to the conflict? How might you change what you did if you could "redo" this conflict episode?

things go wrong?" "Did one or more of us become evaluative?" "Did I use a style that was inappropriate to the situation?" "Did we fail to implement the problem-solving method adequately?" "Were the vested interests in the outcome too great?" "Am I failing to use such basic communication skills as paraphrasing, describing feelings, and perception checking?" "Did I fall back on what Turk and Monahan (1999, p. 232) label 'repetitive non-optimal behaviors'—verbal abuse, dishonest replies, or sarcasm—automatically when I became angry?"

By taking time to analyze your behavior, you put yourself in a better position to act more successfully in the next conflict episode you experience. Conflict is inevitable; you can count on having opportunities to use this knowledge again.

WHAT WOULD YOU DO?
A QUESTION OF ETHICS

Sally and Ed had been seeing each other for more than three years when Ed moved 150 miles away to attend college. When he left, they promised to continue to see each other and agreed that should either of them want to start seeing someone else they would tell the other person before doing so.

During the first five months that Ed was away, Sally became friendly with Jamie, a coworker at the childcare center on the campus of the local junior college. Jamie had a great sense of humor, and during working hours he and Sally would often tease each other to the point that other coworkers accused them of flirting. On several occasions, they had dinner together before their night class, usually on Jamie's request, and on a couple of the weekends that Ed hadn't come home, they had seen a movie together. As time went on, it became apparent to Sally that Jamie's interest in her was going beyond the point of just being friends. Because she didn't want to risk losing his companionship, Sally had never mentioned Ed.

On Friday of that week, just as Sally and Jamie were about to leave the childcare center and head for a movie, the door swung open and in walked Ed. Sally hadn't been expecting him, but she took one look at him, broke into a big smile and ran over and gave him a warm embrace. Too absorbed with her own excitement, Sally didn't even notice

Jamie's shock and disappointment. She quickly introduced Ed to Jamie and then casually said to Jamie, "See you Monday!" and left with Ed.

That weekend, Ed confessed that he wanted to end their relationship. He had gone out with a woman who lived down the hall from him in his dorm a couple of times and saw the relationship blossoming. Sally was outraged. She accused Ed of acting dishonestly by violating their agreement about seeing other people and told him that he had used her until he was secure at college. Their conversation continued to go downhill, and eventually Ed left.

On Monday, when Sally saw Jamie at work, he was very aloof and curt. She asked him if he wanted to get a bite to eat before class and was genuinely surprised when he answered with an abrupt "No." As she ate alone, she pondered her behavior and wondered if and how she could ever rectify her relationship with Jamie.

1. Sort out the ethical issues in this case. Under which ethical guidelines would Sally's, Ed's, and Jamie's actions be considered ethical or unethical?

2. Using guidelines from this chapter, role-play different key moments in this scenario, changing them to improve the communication ethics and outcome of the situation.

Conversation and Analysis

Use your Communicate! CD-ROM to access a video scenario of the following conversation. Click on the "Communicate! In Action" feature, and then click on "Jan and Ken." As you watch Jan and Ken's conversation, focus on how the nature of their relationship influences their interaction.

1. What does each person do to help maintain the relationship?

2. How does each person handle this conflict?

3. How well does each person listen to the other?

4. Are Jan and Ken appropriately assertive?

5. Notice how well each provides feedback and describes feelings.

We have provided a transcript of Jan and Ken's conversation. After you have viewed the conversation on your CD-ROM, read the transcript. In the right-hand column there is space for you to record your analysis. You can also complete your analysis electronically using the Conversational Analysis feature included in Communicate! In Action. From the Conversation Menu on your CD-ROM, click "Analysis" for Jan and Ken. Type your answers to the questions above in the forms provided. When you are finished, click "Submit" to compare your response to the analysis provided by the authors.

Jan and Ken are in their early to middle twenties. They meet at Jan's apartment. Jan and Ken have been good friends for most of their lives. But because of what she said last week, Ken believes Jan has betrayed their friendship.

Conversation

Analysis

Ken: Jan, we need to talk. Why'd you tell Shannon about what happened between Katie and me? Now Shannon doesn't want to talk to me.

Jan: *(silence for a moment as she realizes he knows)* Ken, I'm sorry, I didn't mean to tell her. It just kind of slipped out when we were talking.

Ken: Sorry? Sorry is not enough. I told you that in private and you promised that you'd keep it just between you and me.

Conversation

Analysis

Jan: Ken, I told her that long before the two of you started dating. You know, Shannon and I, we've been friends for a long time. We were just talking about guys and cheating and stuff. It wasn't about you specifically.

Ken: It wasn't about me? It was totally about me. You had no right to tell *anyone* that, under any circumstances. Now Shannon doesn't trust me. She thinks I'm a lowlife that sleeps around.

Jan: Well, I'm sorry, but the two of you weren't even dating, yet.

Ken: Oh, that's irrelevant. You know, it would be irrelevant even if Shannon and I weren't dating. But you know, the point is I thought I could trust you and tell you anything and that it would go no further.

Jan: Yeah, like the time I told you I was thinking about dropping out of school for a semester and you just happened to tell my dad?

Ken: Ah, that's not the same thing.

Jan: You know what, it's *exactly* the same. I trusted you and you squealed. My dad lit into me big-time. He should have never known I was thinking about that. I trusted you, and you betrayed me!

Ken: Well look, I was just trying to look out for you. I knew you were making a big mistake and I was just trying to stop you. And besides, you know I was right! *(gets discouraged)* Don't change the subject, here. Are you saying that you telling Shannon is some sort of payback for me telling your dad?

Jan: No, I'm just trying to point out that you've got no right to throw stones!

Conversation

Analysis

Ken: You know what? Then maybe neither of us can trust the other. Maybe we just shouldn't tell each other anything that we don't want broadcast to the world, huh?

Jan: Don't be such a jerk. I'm sorry, OK?

Ken: Well, that's not good enough. You ruined any chance I had with her.

Jan: Are you saying that something I said about what you did a long time ago is ruining your chances?

Ken: Yeah, it might.

Jan: Ken, if she truly valued your friendship, something that you did a long time ago shouldn't matter.

Ken: Well, maybe you're right.

Jan: Look, I said I'm sorry and I meant it. I'm also sorry about, you know, throwing in what you told my dad. I know that wasn't fair, but you know, you really hurt my feelings when you blew up at me like that.

Ken: Listen, listen, I shouldn't have, I shouldn't have told your dad. I should have probably encouraged you to talk to him. We still friends?

Summary

Interpersonal communication helps develop and maintain relationships. A good relationship is any mutually satisfying interaction with another person.

We have three types of relationships. Acquaintances are people we know by name and talk with, but with whom our interactions are limited in quality and quantity. Friendships are marked by degrees of warmth and affection, trust, self-disclosure, commitment, and expectation that the relationship will endure. Close or intimate friends are those with whom we share our deepest feelings, spend a lot of time, or mark the relationship in some special way.

The life cycle of a relationship includes starting or building, stabilizing, and ending. In the starting or building stage, people strike up a conversation, keep conversations going, and move to more intimate levels. People nurture relationships through the skills of describing, openness, tentativeness, and equality. Many relationships end. We may terminate them in interpersonally sound ways or in ways that destroy our chances to continue the relationship on any meaningful level. The Johari window is a tool for examining the ratio of openness to closedness in a relationship.

Many people develop relationships on the Internet through chatrooms and email. Electronically mediated relationships may be subject to anonymity and dishonesty. Addiction to the Internet can disrupt relationships.

Two theories are especially useful for explaining the dynamics of relationships. Schutz sees relationships in terms of the ability to meet the interpersonal needs of affection, inclusion, and control. Thibaut and Kelley see relationships as exchanges: People evaluate relationships through a reward/cost analysis, weighing energy, time, and money invested against satisfaction gained.

A primary factor leading to termination of a relationship is failure to manage conflict successfully. We cope with conflicts in a variety of ways: withdrawing, accommodating, forcing, compromising, and collaborating. When we are concerned about the long-term relationship, collaboration is often most appropriate.

When you have a problem with a person, initiate the conflict using basic communication skills. Own the problem; describe the basis of the conflict in terms of behavior, consequences, and feelings; plan what you will say ahead of time; avoid evaluating the other person's motives; and phrase your request so that it focuses on common ground.

When responding to another person's problem, watch for nonverbal cues, put your shields up, respond empathically with genuine interest and concern, paraphrase your understanding of the problem, seek common ground, and ask the person to suggest alternatives.

Finally, learn from conflict-management failures.

Communicate! Online

Use your Communicate! CD-ROM for quick access to the electronic study resources that accompany this text. Included on your CD-ROM is access to Info-Trac College Edition, the World Wide Web, a demo of WebTutor for Communicate!, and the Communicate! Web site at the Wadsworth Communication Café. The Communicate! Web site offers chapter-by-chapter activities, quizzes, and a digital glossary.

Review the following key terms at
http://communication.wadsworth.com/humancomm/verderber

Key Terms

accommodating (203)
acquaintances (186)
active strategy (188)
affection need (199)
close friends or **intimates** (188)
collaborating (204)
compromising (204)
control need (200)
costs (200)
exchange theory (200)
feedback (190)
forcing (203)
friends (186)
good relationship (186)
gossip (189)
idea-exchange communication (189)

inclusion need (199)
interactive strategy (188)
interpersonal conflict (201)
interpersonal needs theory (199)
Johari window (190)
mulling (202)
passive strategy (188)
rewards (200)
self-disclosure (190)
speaking descriptively (193)
speaking equally (194)
speaking openly (193)
speaking tentatively (193)
stabilization (193)
technological addictions (198)
trust (187)
withdrawal (202)

Your Communicate! CD-ROM includes a video of the conversation between Jan and Ken featured on pages 213–215. Click on the Communicate! In Action icon on your CD-ROM, then click on "Jan and Ken." You can watch, listen to, and analyze their conversation, and improve your own conflict management skills.

OBJECTIVES

After you have read this chapter, you should be able to answer these questions:

- What should you do to prepare for a job interview?

- What are the important elements of a written résumé?

- How do you prepare cover letters and résumés electronically?

- What are the characteristics of open and closed, primary and secondary, and neutral and leading questions?

- How do you conduct a job interview?

- Can you identify typical questions used by job interviewers?

Interviewing

At 3:30 p.m. sharp, Chet arrived at the door of the personnel director of Grover Industries for his interview. The secretary led him into the office and introduced him to Miles Beddington.

"Sit down," Beddington said, "and we'll get started. Well, I've looked over your résumé, and now I have just a few questions. How did you get interested in Grover Industries?"

"Our Student Placement Office said you were hiring."

"And for what kind of a position do you think you would be most suited?"

"One where I could use my skills."

"What skills do you have to offer our company that would make you a good hire for us?"

"Well, I'm a hard worker."

"Are you familiar with our major products?"

"Not really. I haven't had time yet to look you up."

"I see. Well, how do you know that you could be helpful to us?"

"Well, because I work really hard."

"What kinds of experience have you had in business?"

"Um, let's see, well, I sold magazines for my high school. And my sister-in-law owns her own business, and I hear her talking about it a lot."

"OK, what do you see as some of your major skills?"

"I told you, I can work really hard!"

"Well, Chet, companies are impressed by hard workers. We're talking to other applicants, of course. So, I'll be in touch."

When Chet got home, Tanya asked, "How did the interview go?"

"Great," Chet replied, "Mr. Beddington was impressed by the fact that I'm a hard worker."

What do you think Chet's chances are for the job?

Although interviewing for a job is often a traumatic experience, especially for those who are going through it for the first time, applicants for nearly every position in nearly any field will go through at least one interview, and possibly several. At its worst, an interview can be a waste of time for everyone; at its best, an interview can reveal vital information about an applicant as well as enable the applicant to judge the suitability of the position, the company, and the tasks to be performed.

A skillfully conducted interview can help interviewers determine the applicant's specific abilities, ambitions, energy, ability to communicate, knowledge and intelligence, and integrity. Moreover, it can help the interviewee show his or her strengths in these same areas.

The job interview is a special type of interpersonal situation with specific demands. Let's consider some of the procedures and methods an interviewee can use in taking part in an interview as well as those used by an interviewer in conducting an interview.

Responsibilities of the Job Applicant

Interviews are an important part of the process of seeking employment. Even for part-time and temporary jobs, you will benefit if you approach the interviewing process seriously and systematically. There is no point in applying for positions that are obviously outside your area of expertise. It may seem a good idea to get interviewing experience, but you are wasting your time and the interviewer's if you apply for a position you have no intention of taking or for which you are not qualified.

When you are granted an employment interview, remember that all you have to sell is yourself and your qualifications. Recall from our discussion of self-presentation in Chapter 4 how much your nonverbal behavior contributes to the impression you make. You want to show yourself in the best possible light. Take care with your appearance; if you want a particular job, dress in a way that is acceptable to the person or organization that may—or may not—hire you.

Preparing for the Interview

Of course you will want to be fully prepared for the interview. Two important tasks you must complete before the interview itself are writing a cover letter and preparing a résumé. The goal of the résumé (and cover letter) is to "sell yourself and get an interview" (Schmidt & Conaway, 1999, p. 92).

cover letter—*a short, well-written letter expressing your interest in a particular position.*

Write a cover letter The **cover letter** is a short, well-written letter expressing your interest in a particular position. Always address the letter to the person with the authority to hire you (and not, for example, to the personnel department). If you do not already have the appropriate person's name, you can probably get it by telephoning the company. Because you are trying to stimulate the reader's interest in *you*, make sure that your cover letter does not read like a form letter. The cover letter should include the following elements: where and how you found out about the position, your reason for being interested in this company, your main skills and accomplishments (summary of a few key points), how you fit the requirements for the job, items of special interest about you that would relate to your potential for the job, and a request for an interview. The letter should be one page or less. You should always include a résumé with the letter.

Include a résumé The **résumé**, a summary of your skills and accomplishments, is your "silent sales representative" (Stewart & Cash, 2000, p. 274). Although there is no universal format for résumé writing, there is some agreement on what should be included and excluded. In writing your résumé, include the following information cast in a form that increases the likelihood of your being asked to an interview:

1. **Contact information:** Your name, address, and telephone numbers at which you can be reached. (Always)
2. **Job objective:** A one-sentence objective focusing on your specific area(s) of expertise. (Important for full-time career positions)

résumé—*a summary of your skills and accomplishments.*

Patti & Milt Putnam/The Stock Market

OBSERVE & ANALYZE
Journal Activity

**Real versus
Ideal Résumés**

In your Student Workbook under Journal Activity 9.1, prepare a draft of your résumé based on the skills and accomplishments you have today. Next, draft the ideal résumé you wish to have at graduation or five years from now. Then, record your answers to the following questions: How are the résumés diffferent? What specific actions must you take now to ensure that your future résumé looks like your ideal one? During this exercise, focus on the content, not the format, of your résumé.

Once you have spotted some good job opportunities, refine your résumé and cover letter to address each job.

3. **Employment history:** Paid and nonpaid experiences beginning with the most recent. Be sure to give employment dates and briefly list important duties and accomplishments.

4. **Education:** Schools attended, degree completed or expected, date of completion, with focus on courses that are most directly related to the job.

5. **Military experience:** Include rank and service and achievements, skills, abilities, and discharge status.

6. **Relevant professional certifications and affiliations:** Memberships, offices held.

7. **Community activities:** Community service organizations, clubs, and so forth, including offices and dates.

8. **Special skills:** Fluency in foreign languages, computer expertise.

9. **Interests and activities:** Only those that are related to your objective.

10. **References:** People who know your work, your capabilities, and your character who will vouch for you. Include only a statement that references are available on request.

Notice that the list does not include such personal information as height, weight, age, sex, marital status, health, race, religion, or political affiliation, nor does it include any reference to salary. Although you need not include references, you should already have the permission of people whom you will use as references.

In addition, you should consider what format your résumé will follow: how wide your margins will be, how elements will be spaced and indented, and so on. The résumé should be no more than three pages. For traditional college students, one or two pages should be your goal. Moreover, the résumé should be neat, carefully proofread to be error free, and reproduced on good quality paper. Try to look at your résumé from the employer's point of view. What do you have to present that can help the employer solve problems? Think in terms of what the company needs, and present only your skills and accomplishments that show you can do the job. Most important, be tactful but truthful in what you present. You should emphasize your strengths, but avoid exaggerating facts, a procedure that is both deceptive and unethical. Figure 9.1 shows a sample cover letter, and Figure 9.2 shows a sample résumé of a person who has just graduated from college.

Electronic Cover Letters and Résumés Electronic cover letters and résumés are those that are sent online. Electronic résumés have become quite popular with employers and job seekers. For example, from 1995 to 1999 the percentage of the résumés that were received electronically by Microsoft increased from 5% to 50% (Criscito, 2000, p. 2). Employers like electronic résumés because they then can sift through large numbers looking only for particular qualifications or characteristics. Candidates like electronic résumés because they can send essentially the same materials online, saving time and money.

Although electronic cover letters and résumés contain the same content, they may differ is several ways (Schmidt & Conaway, 1999, pp. 98–99). Many of the

---

COMMUNICATE! Using InfoTrac College Edition

Under the subject "cover letter," see "The intelligent standout résumé and cover letter," Linda Bates Parker (Oct. 1998) and "Great letters and why they work," Dean Rieck (June 1998). Compare their recommendations. Note at least two recommendations on preparing résumés and cover letters that you would want to follow.

2326 Tower Place
Cincinnati, OH 45220
April 8, 2001

Mr. Kyle Jones
Acme Marketing Research Associates
P.O. Box 482
Cincinnati, OH 45201

Dear Mr. Jones:

I am applying for the position of first-year associate at Acme
Marketing Research Associates, which I learned about through the
Office of Career Counseling at the University of Cincinnati. I am
a senior mathematics major at the University of Cincinnati who is
interested in pursuing a career in marketing research. I am highly
motivated, eager to learn, and I enjoy working with all types of
people. I am excited by the prospect of working for a firm like
Acme Marketing Research Associates where I can apply my leadership
and problem-solving skills in a professional setting.

As a mathematics major, I have developed the analytical
proficiency that is necessary for working through complex
problems. My courses in statistics have especially prepared me for
data analysis, and my more theoretical courses have taught me how
to construct an effective argument. My leadership training and
opportunities have given me the ability to work effectively in
groups and have taught me the benefits of both individual and
group problem solving. My work on the Strategic Planning Committee
has given me an introduction to market analysis by teaching me
skills associated with strategic planning. Finally, from my
theatrical experience, I have gained the poise to make
presentations in front of small and large groups alike. I believe
these experiences and others have shaped who I am and have helped
me to develop many of the skills necessary to be successful. I am
interested in learning more and continuing to grow.

I look forward to having the opportunity to interview with you in
the future. I have enclosed my résumé with my school address and
phone number. Thank you for your consideration. I hope to hear
from you soon.

Sincerely,

Elisa C. Vardin

Figure 9.1
Sample cover letter.

Elisa C. Vardin   2326 Tower Avenue
                                                         Cincinnati, Ohio 45220
                                                         Phone: (513) 861-2497
                                                         Email: Elisa Vardin@UC.edu

Professional Objective

To use my intellectual abilities, quantitative knowledge, communication skills, and proven
leadership ability creatively to further the organizational mission of a high-integrity marketing
research organization.

EDUCATIONAL BACKGROUND

UNIVERSITY OF CINCINNATI, Cincinnati, OH. B.A. in Mathematics, June 2001. GPA 3.36. Dean's List.

NATIONAL THEATER INSTITUTE at the Eugene O'Neill Theater Center, Waterford, CT. Fall 1998.
       Acting, Voice, Movement, Directing, and Playwriting.

WORK AND OTHER BUSINESS-RELATED EXPERIENCE

REYNOLDS & DeWITT, SENA WELLER ROHS WILLIAMS, Cincinnati, OH. Summer 2000.
       Intern at Brokerage/Investment Management Firm. Provided administrative support. Created
       new databases, performance comparisons, and fact sheets in Excel and Word files.

MUMMERS GUILD, University of Cincinnati, Spring 1998–Spring 2000.
       As treasurer, responsible for all financial/accounting functions for this undergraduate theater
       community.

SUMMERBRIDGE CINCINNATI, Cincinnati Country Day School, Cincinnati, OH. Summer 1999.
       Full-time teacher in a program dedicated to helping "at-risk" junior high students develop an
       interest in learning. Taught two courses in 7th grade mathematics, 6th and 7th grade speech
       communication class, sign language course; Academic adviser; Club leader. Organized five-
       hour diversity workshop and three-hour tension-reduction workshop for staff.

STRATEGIC PLANNING COMMITTEE, Summit Country Day School, Cincinnati, OH. Fall 1996–1997.
       Worked with the Board of Directors (one of two students) to develop the first Strategic Plan
       for this 1000-student independent school (Pre-K through 12).

AYF INTERNATIONAL LEADERSHIP CONFERENCE, Camp Miniwanca, Shelby, MI. Summers 1996–1998.
       Leadership conference sponsored by American Youth Foundation bringing campers from 50
       states and 26 countries. Skills learned: visioning, vision-based goal setting, forming action
       steps, and revisioning.

PERSONAL

UNIVERSITY OF CINCINNATI: Musical Theater: Lifetime involvement, including leads and
       choreography for several shows. A cappella singing group: 1998–2001, Director 2000–2001.
       Swing Club: 1998–2000, President and Teacher of student-run dance club. Junior High
       Youth Group Leader: 1999. Math Tutor: 2000. Aerobics Instructor: 1999–2000. University
       of Cincinnati Choral Society: 1999–2000. American Sign Language Instructor: Winter 1999,
       2000. Six years voice lessons. 12 years off and on training in ballet, tap, jazz, modern, and
       acrobatics. Macintosh and IBM proficient.

REFERENCES

       On request.

Figure 9.2
Sample résumé.

differences take into account the fact that they will be scanned electronically. Thus, it is wise to avoid such things as boldface, italics, and bullet points because they will "only confuse computerized word searches or interfere with the scanning process" (p. 98). The most important thing to remember for a scannable or email résumé is to keep the format simple. For instance, the sample résumé in Figure 9.2 is more likely to work electronically if the material in the right column (address, phone, email) were moved to a position under the name and flush left. Likewise, indented material can be moved to flush left, perhaps with a space after each title.

There are three kinds of electronic résumés: the paper résumé that becomes an electronic version when it is scanned into a computer; an ASCII text email-able version (a generic computer file that you create especially to send through cyberspace); and a multimedia résumé that is given a home page at a fixed location on the Internet for anyone to visit (Criscito, 2000, p. 2).

A scanned résumé can be attached to an email and sent directly to a company's recruiters over the Internet. If you already have a paper résumé, scanning allows you to send the résumé without retyping it. A résumé that has been prepared, saved, and sent as a generic ASCII text file has the advantage of being able to be read by anyone regardless of the word processing software he or she is using (Criscito, 2000, p. 3). Such a document can be sent as a file to company recruiters or posted to the home page of a company, a job bank, or a newsgroup. Finally, when you post your résumé on a home page, you have dramatically increased the likelihood that someone who is seeking employees with your qualifications will see your résumé and inquire about your interest in their company.

For more detailed information on electronic résumés and job applications, see any of the numerous new books on résumés—for example, Steven Graber (2000), *The Everything Résumé Book: Great Résumés for Everybody from Student to Executive.*

The Interview

Interviews are used by the company to decide whom to hire. During the interview, the interviewer assesses candidates to determine whether they have the skills and abilities needed for the job. More important, during the interview, judgments about the candidate's personality and motivation are made. Here are some guidelines to help you prepare for the interview.

1. **Do your homework.** Learn about the company's services, products, ownership, and financial health. Knowing about a company shows your interest in that company and will usually impress the interviewer. Moreover, you will be in a better position to discuss how you can contribute to the company's mission.

2. **Rehearse the interview.** For most of us, job interviews are at least somewhat stressful. To help prepare yourself so that you can perform at your best, it is a good idea to practice interviewing. First, try to anticipate some of the questions you will be asked and craft thoughtful answers. You might even try

COMMUNICATE!
Using Technology

Today many companies post job listings on the Internet and allow candidates to complete part of the job search process electronically. On the Internet go to http://www.Monster.com. Look to see whether there are jobs listed in your field. Pay special attention to the application directions.

School:
How did you select the school you attended?
How did you determine your major?
What extracurricular activities did you engage in at school?
In what ways does your transcript reflect your ability?
How were you able to help with your college expenses?

Personal:
What are your hobbies? How did you become interested in them?
Give an example of how you work under pressure.
At what age did you begin supporting yourself?
What causes you to lose your temper?
What are your major strengths? Weaknesses?
Give an example of when you were a leader and what happened.
What do you do to stay in good physical condition?
What was the last non-school-assigned book that you read? Tell me about it.
Who has had the greatest influence on your life?
What have you done that shows your creativity?

Position:
What kind of position are you looking for?
What do you know about the company?
Under what conditions would you be willing to relocate?
Why do you think you would like to work for us?
What do you hope to accomplish?
What qualifications do you have that make you feel you would be beneficial to us?
How do you feel about traveling?
What part of the country would you like to settle in?
With what kind of people do you enjoy interacting?
What do you regard as an equitable salary for a person with your
    qualifications?
What new skills would you like to learn?
What are your career goals?
How would you proceed if you were in charge of hiring?
What are your most important criteria for determining whether you will
    accept a position?

Figure 9.3
Frequently asked interview questions.

writing out or saying answers aloud. Give careful thought to such subjects as your salary expectations, your possible contributions to the company, and your special skills. Figure 9.3 presents some questions frequently asked in interviews.

3. **Dress appropriately.** You want to make a good impression, so it is important that you look neat, clean, and appropriate. Men should wear a collared shirt, dress slacks, and a tie and jacket. Women should wear a conservative dress or a suit. According to a survey of 153 companies conducted by Northwestern University, the factor that is first in leading to rejection is poor personal appearance (Schmidt & Conaway, 1999, p. 110).

Michael Newman/PhotoEdit, Inc.

Listen carefully and give yourself time to think before answering an important question.

4. Be prompt at arriving. The interview is the company's first exposure to your work behavior. If you are late for such an important event, the interviewer will conclude that you are likely to be late for work. Give yourself extra time in travel to cover any possible traffic problems. Plan to arrive fifteen or twenty minutes before your appointment.

5. Be alert, look at the interviewer, and listen actively. Remember that your non-verbal communication tells a lot about you. Company representatives are likely to consider eye contact and posture as clues to your self-confidence.

6. Give yourself time to think before answering a question. If the interviewer asks you a question that you had not anticipated, give yourself time to think before you answer. It is better to pause and appear thoughtful than to give a hasty answer that may cost you the job. If you do not understand the question, paraphrase it before you attempt to answer.

7. Ask questions about the type of work you will be doing. The interview is your chance to find out if you would enjoy working for this company. You might ask the interviewer to describe a typical workday for the person who will get the job. If the interview is conducted at the company offices, you might ask to see where you would be working. In this way, you prepare yourself to know how you will respond to a job offer.

8. Show enthusiasm for the job. If you are not enthusiastic during an interview, the interviewer is likely to reason that you may not be the person for the job. Employers look for and expect applicants to look and sound interested.

9. **Do not engage in long discussions on salary.** The time to discuss salary is when the job is offered. If the company representative tries to pin you down, ask, "What do you normally pay someone with my experience and education for this level position?" Such a question enables you to get an idea of what the salary will be without committing yourself to a figure first.

10. **Do not harp on benefits.** Again, detailed discussions about benefits are more appropriate after the company has made you an offer.

Interpersonal Skills in Interviewing Others

In your work relationships you will experience interviewing from both sides of the desk—you will need experience at both interviewing and being interviewed. Once on the job, you may be called on to interview customers about complaints, interview coworkers to get information relevant to your work, interview prospective employees, and so forth. So you need to know how to plan and conduct interviews.

As an interviewer, you represent the link between a job applicant and the company. Much of the applicant's impression of the company will depend on his or her impression of you, so you will want to be able to provide answers to questions the applicant may have about your company. In addition to the obvious desire for salary information, an applicant may seek information about opportunities for advancement, influences of personal ideas on company policy, company attitudes toward personal life and lifestyle, working conditions, and so forth. Moreover, you are primarily responsible for determining whether this person will be considered for the position available or for possible future employment with the company.

Determining the Procedure

The most satisfactory employment interview is probably a highly to moderately structured one. In the unstructured interview, the interviewer tends to talk more

DILBERT reprinted by permission of United Features Syndicate, Inc.

What Interviewers Look For

Call a large local company and make an appointment to interview a person in the human resources department whose job it is to interview candidates for employment. Develop a set of interview questions and follow-ups. Focus your interview on obtaining information about the person's experiences that will help you. For example, you might ask, "What are the characteristics you like to see an interviewee demonstrate?" or "How do you decide whom to interview?" In your Student Workbook under Journal Activity 9.2, write the questions you plan to ask, leaving space between each question. During the interview sketch the answers to each of the questions and any follow-up questions you may have used. After you have conducted the interview, be prepared to discuss your findings in class.

and to make decisions based less on valid data than in the structured interview (Stewart & Cash, 2000, p. 238). Especially if you are screening a large number of applicants, you want to make sure that all have been asked the same questions and that the questions cover subjects that will be most revealing of the kind of information you will need to make a reasonable decision.

Before the time scheduled for the interview, become familiar with all the available data about the applicant: application form, résumé, letters of recommendation, and test scores, if available. These written data will help determine some of the questions you will want to ask.

Conducting an Interview

An **interview** is a structured conversation with the goal of exchanging information that is needed for decision making. A well-planned interview comprises a list of questions designed to get the needed information. Interviews, like speeches and essays, have an appropriate opening, body, and conclusion.

Opening the interview   Open the interview by stating its purpose and introducing yourself if you have not previously met.

Sometimes interviewers begin with "warm-up" or easy questions to help establish rapport. A good interviewer senses the nature of the situation and tries to use a method that is most likely to encourage the other person to talk and provide adequate answers. Although warm-up questions may be helpful, most participants are ready to get down to business immediately, in which case warm-up questions may be counterproductive (Cogger, 1982).

Questions used in the body of the interview   The body of the interview consists of the primary questions to which you need answers. Because the quality of information depends on how the questions are phrased, let's consider the characteristics of three types of questions you will ask: open or closed, neutral or leading, primary or secondary (Stewart & Cash, 2000, p. 80).

Open questions are broad-based questions that ask the interviewee to respond with whatever information he or she wishes. Open questions range from those with virtually no restrictions, such as "What can you tell me about yourself?" or "What seems to be the problem?" to those that give some direction, such as "What is your one accomplishment that has best prepared you for

interview–*a structured conversation with the goal of exchanging information that is needed for decision making.*

open questions–*broad-based questions that ask the interviewee to respond with whatever information he or she wishes.*

closed questions–*narrowly focused questions that require very brief answers.*

neutral questions–*questions that allow a person to give an answer without direction from the interviewer.*

leading questions–*questions phrased in a way that suggests the interviewer has a preferred answer.*

primary questions–*open or closed questions that the interviewer plans ahead of time.*

secondary or **follow-up questions**–*planned or spontaneous questions that are designed to pursue the answers given to primary questions.*

this job?" or "Can you tell me the steps you took in using the product?" Interviewers ask open questions to encourage the person to talk, providing the interviewer with an opportunity to listen and to observe. Keep in mind, however, that open questions take time to answer and give respondents more control, which means that interviewers can lose sight of their original purpose if they are not careful (Tengler & Jablin, 1983).

By contrast, **closed questions** are narrowly focused questions that require very brief answers. Closed questions range from those that can be answered with yes or no, such as "Have you had a course in marketing?" to those that require only a short answer, such as "How many restaurants have you worked in?" By asking closed questions, interviewers can both control the interview and obtain large amounts of information in a short time. Closed questions seldom enable the interviewer to know why a person gave a certain response, nor are they likely to yield much voluntary information; therefore, both open and closed questions are used in employment interviews.

Open and closed questions may be either neutral or leading. **Neutral questions** allow a person to give an answer without direction from the interviewer, such as "How do you like your new job?" The neutral question avoids giving the respondent any indication of what the interviewer thinks about the issue or how the question should be answered. By contrast, **leading questions** are phrased in a way that suggests the interviewer has a preferred answer, such as "You don't like the new job, do you?" In most employment interviews, neutral questions are preferred.

Primary questions are those open or closed questions that the interviewer plans ahead of time. They serve as the main points for the interview outline. **Secondary** or **follow-up questions** may be planned or spontaneous, but they are designed to pursue the answers given to primary questions. Some follow-up questions encourage the person to continue ("And then?" "Is there more?"); some probe into what the person has said ("What does 'frequently' mean?" "What were you thinking at the time?"); and some probe the feelings of the person ("How did it feel to get the prize?" "Were you worried when you didn't find her?"). The major purpose of follow-up questions is to motivate a person to enlarge on an answer because interviewees' answers may be incomplete or vague, interviewees may not really understand how much detail you are looking for, and occasionally interviewees may be purposely evasive. See Figure 9.3 for a sample of the kinds of questions you may want to ask.

Closing the interview   Toward the end of the interview, you should always explain to the interviewee what will happen next and how the information you gathered will be used. Explain the procedures for making decisions based on the information. Also, let the interviewee know whether and how he or she will receive feedback on the decision. Then close the interview in a courteous, neutral manner, thanking the interviewee for his or her time and interest.

Throughout the interview, be careful of your own presentation, try not to waste time, and give the applicant time to ask questions.

After three years of working at Everyday Products as a clerk, Mark had decided to look for another job. As he thought about preparing a résumé, he was struck by how little experience he had for the kind of job he wanted.

When he talked with Ken about this, Ken said, "Exactly what have you been doing at Everyday?"

"Well, for the most part I've been helping others look for information—I've also done some editing of reports."

"Hm," Ken thought for a while. "Why not retitle your job as Editorial Assistant—it's more descriptive."

"But my official title is Clerk."

"Sure, but it doesn't really describe what you do. This way you show major editorial experience. Don't worry, everybody makes these kinds of changes—you're not really lying."

"Yeah, I see what you mean. Good idea!"

1. Is it interpersonally ethical for Mark to follow Ken's advice? Why?
2. How should we deal with statements like "Everybody does it"?

Summary

At work we use our interpersonal skills to get a job, to interview job candidates, to relate to colleagues and clients, and to exercise leadership.

Before you interview for a job, you need to take the time to learn about the company and prepare an appropriate cover letter and résumé that are designed to motivate an employer to interview you. If you choose to send your cover letter or résumé electronically, make sure you edit it appropriately. For the interview itself, you should be prompt, be alert and look directly at the interviewer, give yourself time to think before answering difficult questions, ask intelligent questions about the company and the job, and show enthusiasm for the position.

To interview well, you need to learn to ask primary and secondary, open and closed neutrally worded questions effectively. When you are interviewing prospective applicants for a job, structure your interview carefully to elicit maximal information about these candidates. Before the interview starts, become familiar with the data contained in the interviewee's application form, résumé, letters of recommendation, and test scores, if available. Be careful how you present yourself: do not waste time, avoid loaded questions, do not ask questions that violate fair employment practice legislation, and give the applicant an opportunity to ask questions. At the end of the interview, explain to the applicant what will happen next in the process.

Communicate! Online

Use your Communicate! CD-ROM for quick access to the electronic study resources that accompany this text. Included on your CD-ROM is access to InfoTrac College Edition, the World Wide Web, a demo of WebTutor for Communicate!, and the Communicate! Web site at the Wadsworth Communication Café. The Communicate! Web site offers chapter-by-chapter activities, quizzes, and a digital glossary.

Review the following key terms and complete the Self-Review for Interpersonal Communication featured on the next page at

http://communication.wadsworth.com/humancomm/verderber

Key Terms

closed questions (230)

cover letter (220)

interview (229)

leading questions (230)

neutral questions (230)

open questions (229)

primary questions (230)

résumé (221)

secondary or **follow-up questions** (230)

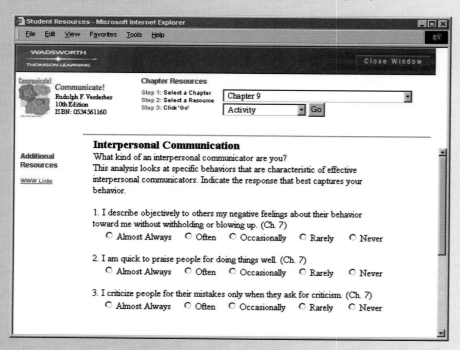

SELF-REVIEW

Interpersonal Communication from Chapters 5 to 9

What kind of an interpersonal communicator are you? This analysis looks at specific behaviors that are characteristic of effective interpersonal communicators. On the line provided for each statement, indicate the response that best captures your behavior: 1, almost always; 2, often; 3, occasionally; 4, rarely; 5, never.

_____ In conversation, I am able to make relevant contributions without interrupting others. (Ch. 5)

_____ When I talk I try to provide information that satisfies others' needs and keeps the conversation going. (Ch. 5)

_____ When I'm not sure whether I understand, I seek clarification. (Ch. 6)

_____ When a person describes an unfortunate experience, I am able to provide appropriate comfort. (Ch. 6)

_____ I listen attentively, regardless of my interest in the person or the ideas. (Ch. 6)

_____ I describe objectively to others my negative feelings about their behavior toward me without withholding or blowing up. (Ch. 7)

_____ I am quick to praise people for doing things well. (Ch. 7)

_____ I criticize people for their mistakes only when they ask for criticism. (Ch. 7)

_____ I am able to maintain a positive communication climate by speaking in ways that others perceive as descriptive, nondogmatic, and nonmanipulative. (Ch. 8)

_____ When I find myself in conflict with another person, I am able to discuss the issue openly without withdrawing or appearing competitive or aggressive. (Ch. 8)

_____ I have an up-to-date résumé ready for immediate use. (Ch. 9)

_____ I present myself well when I am being interviewed. (Ch. 9)

Based on your responses, select the interpersonal communication behavior that you would most like to change. Write a communication improvement plan similar to the sample goal statement in Chapter 1 (page 25). If you would like verification of your self-review before you write a contract, have a friend or a coworker complete this same analysis for you.

You can complete this Self-Review online under Chapter 9: Activities on the Communicate! Web site at the Wadsworth Communication Café

http://communication.wadsworth.com/humancomm/verderber

Communicate! Web Site

three

We live in a society that increasingly relies on committees, task forces, and teams: small groups of people working together to reach decisions. From our families to our workplaces, we rely on group processes and the decisions and actions that result from group process in nearly every facet of our lives. But when we begin to converse with others in a small group for the purposes of creating or problem solving, the communication process becomes more complex. Our communication in groups can enhance or detract from our ability to develop and maintain our relationships while we arrive at decisions and solutions that meet personal and group goals. In this two-chapter unit, we begin by discussing the characteristics of group settings that add to the complexity of the communication process and must be skillfully managed for groups to work effectively. We conclude with discussion of how roles and leadership can be used to manage the communication processes in groups.

GROUP COMMUNICATION

Jim Krantz/Stone

OBJECTIVES

After you have read this chapter, you should be able to answer these questions:

- What characterizes effective groups?
- How can group discussion lead to improving group goal statements?
- What is the optimum size for a group?
- What factors affect cohesiveness in groups?
- How can a group improve its cohesiveness?
- How do groups form, maintain, and change their norms?
- How does the physical setting affect group interaction?
- What are the stages of group development?
- What are the steps of the problem-solving method?
- What constraints result in groups being ineffective at problem solving, and how can they be managed?

10

Participating in Group Communication

Members of the Alpha Production Team at Meyer Foods were gathered to review their hiring policies. At the beginning of the meeting, Kareem, the team facilitator, began, "You know why I called you together. Each production team has been asked to review its hiring practices. So, let's get started." After a few seconds of silence, Kareem said, "Drew, what have you been thinking?"

"Well, I don't know," Drew replied, "I haven't really given it much thought." (There were nods of agreement all around the table.)

"Well," Jeremy said, "I'm not sure that I even remember what our current policies are."

"But when I sent you the email notice of this meeting, I attached a preliminary analysis of our practices and some questions I hoped each of us would think about before this meeting," Kareem replied.

"Oh, is that what that was?" Byron said. "I read the part about the meeting, but I guess I didn't get back to look at the attachment."

"Look," answered Kareem, "I think the CEO is looking for some specific recommendations from the team."

"Kareem, anything you think would be appropriate would be OK with me," Dawn added.

"Well, how about if we each try to come up with some ideas for next time," Kareem suggested. "Meeting adjourned."

As the group dispersed, Kareem overheard Drew whisper to Dawn, "These meetings sure are a waste of time, aren't they?"

Perhaps you have been part of a work group at school, at work, or at your church. If so, the opening dialogue probably sounds familiar. When group meetings are ineffective, it is easy to point the finger at the leader, but often, as is the case with this group, the responsibility for the "waste of time" or other ineffectiveness lies not with one person but with the complex nature of communication in group settings. Because most of us spend some of our time interacting in group settings, we need to learn how group process works and how to participate in ways that maximize group effectiveness.

In this chapter, we examine how people working in groups solve problems and make decisions through the interactions that they have. We begin by examining characteristics of groups that affect how members communicate to solve problems effectively and make decisions. Next, we discuss how groups develop and the kinds of communication that occur during each stage of group development. Then we consider strategies effective groups use to solve problems and make decisions. Finally, we describe three constraints that limit the effectiveness of groups and suggest communication tactics for overcoming each constraint.

Characteristics of Effective Work Groups

work group–*a collection of three or more people who must interact and influence one another to accomplish a common purpose.*

A **work group** is a collection of three or more people who must interact and influence one another to accomplish a common purpose. A group is more than an aggregation of individuals. Six people riding in an elevator are not a work group. Should the elevator stop and become stuck between floors, and the people begin to talk with each other to solve the problem of how to get the elevator moving, they would become a work group.

Effective work groups have clearly defined goals to which members are committed; have an optimum number of members who represent diverse personalities, knowledge bases, skills, and viewpoints; develop appropriate levels of cohesiveness; conform to rules and norms that facilitate the open exchange of information, ideas, and opinions; and conduct their work in a physical setting that encourages interaction.

Clearly Defined Goals

group goal–*a future state of affairs desired by enough members of the group to motivate the group to work toward its achievement.*

A **group goal** is a future state of affairs desired by enough members of the group to motivate the group to work toward its achievement (Johnson & Johnson, 2000, p. 78). Goals become clearer to members, and members become more committed to goals, when they are discussed. Through these discussions, members are able to make sure goal statements are specific, consistent, challenging, and acceptable.

First, goal statements must be specific. A **specific goal** is precisely stated, measurable, and behavioral. For example, the crew at a local fast food restaurant that began with the goal of "increasing profitability of the store" made the goal more specific and meaningful by revising the goal statement to read: "During the next quarter, the second shift night crew will increase the profitability of the store by reducing food costs on their shift by 1 percent through reducing the amount of food thrown away due to precooking."

Second, goal statements must be consistent. **Consistent goals** are complementary; that is, achieving one goal does not prevent the achievement of another. To meet the consistency test, the team will have to believe that reducing the amount of precooking will not interfere with maintaining their current level of service. If they do not believe that these two goals can be accomplished simultaneously, they will need to reformulate the goals so that they are compatible.

Third, goal statements must be challenging. **Challenging goals** require hard work and team effort; they motivate group members to do things beyond what they might normally accomplish. The crew determined that a goal of 1 percent was a significant challenge.

Fourth, goal statements must be acceptable. **Acceptable goals** are seen as meaningful by team members and are goals to which members feel personally committed. Because people tend to support things that they help to create, group members who participate in setting their own goals are likely to exert high effort to see that the goals are achieved. Likewise, a group member who does not believe a goal is reasonable or just is likely to be unmotivated or to resist working toward accomplishing the goal. Because the members of the crew helped to formulate the profitability goal, they are more likely to work to achieve it.

specific goal–*a goal that is precisely stated, measurable, and behavioral.*

consistent goals–*goals that are complementary; that is, achieving one goal does not prevent the achievement of another.*

challenging goals–*goals that are difficult to achieve and that require hard work and team effort.*

acceptable goals–*goals seen as meaningful by team members and to which they feel personally committed.*

THINKING ABOUT . . .

Group Goals

Have you ever participated in a study group? Did the group discuss its goals? What effect did discussing or not discussing group goals have on the outcome?

DILBERT reprinted by permission of United Features Syndicate, Inc.

Board Member Skills

Visit the Web site of a large company, such as General Motors, General Electric, or Coca Cola. Search the site and find the names and brief background sketches of the members of the Board of Directors. Analyze the ways in which the members are similar or different. In your Student Workbook under Journal Activity 10.1, write answers to the following questions: What relevant knowledge and skills might each bring to the group's decision process? What viewpoints are not represented by the board members? How might an absence of these viewpoints affect their discussions?

homogeneous group–*group in which members have a great deal in common.*

heterogeneous group–*group in which various ages, levels of knowledge, attitudes, and interests are represented.*

cohesiveness–*the degree of attraction members have to one another and to the group's goal.*

Optimum Number of Diverse Members

Effective groups are composed of enough members to ensure good interaction but not so many members that discussion is stifled. In general, as the size of a group grows, so does the complexity it must manage. For example, Bostrom (1970) reminds us that the addition of one member to a group has a geometric effect on the number of relationships. When only Jeff and Sue are in a group, there is only one relationship to manage. But when a third person, Bryan, joins them the group now has four relationships to manage (Jeff-Sue, Bryan-Jeff, Bryan-Sue, Bryan-Sue-Jeff). As groups grow in size and complexity, the opportunities for each member to participate drop, leading to member dissatisfaction (Gentry, 1980). When many people cannot or will not contribute, the resulting decision is seldom a product of the group's collective thought (Beebe et al., 1994, p. 125).

So what is the "right" size for a group? It depends. In general, research shows that the best size for a group is the smallest number of people capable of effectively achieving the goal (Sundstrom, 1990); for many situations, this might mean as few as three to five people. As the size of the group increases, the time spent discussing and deciding increases as well. This argues for very small groups because they will be able to make decisions more quickly. However, as the goals, problems, and issues become complex, it is unlikely that very small groups will have the diversity of information, knowledge, and skill needed to make high-quality decisions. For many situations, then, a group of five to seven or more might be desirable.

More important than having a certain number of people in a group is having the right combination of people in the group. Notice the heading of this section was "optimum number of *diverse* members." To meet this test, it is usually better to have a heterogeneous group rather than a homogeneous group. A **homogeneous group** is one in which members have a great deal in common. By contrast, a **heterogeneous group** is one in which various demographics, levels of knowledge, attitudes, and interests are represented. For example, a group composed of seven women accounting students would be considered a homogeneous group; a group composed of male and female students from three different colleges would be considered a heterogeneous group.

Effective groups are likely to be composed of people who bring different but relevant knowledge and skills into the group discussion (Valacich et al., 1994). In homogeneous groups, members are likely to know the same things, come at the problem from the same perspective, and, consequently, be likely to overlook some important information or take shortcuts in the problem-solving process. In contrast, heterogeneous groups are likely to have different information, perspectives, and values, and consequently, discuss issues more thoroughly before reaching a decision.

Cohesiveness

Cohesiveness is the degree of attraction members have to one another and to the group's goal. In a highly cohesive group, members genuinely like and respect each other, work cooperatively to reach the group's goals, and generally perform better than noncohesive groups (Evans & Dion, 1991). In contrast, in a group that is not cohesive, members may be indifferent toward or dislike each other, have little interest in what the group is trying to accomplish, and may even work in ways that prevent the group from being successful.

Research (Balgopal, Ephross, & Vassil, 1986; Widmer & Williams, 1991) has shown that several factors lead to developing cohesiveness in groups: attractiveness of the group's purpose, voluntary membership, feeling of freedom to share opinions, and celebration of accomplishments.

1. **Attractiveness of the group's purpose.** Social or fraternal groups, for example, build cohesiveness out of devotion to service or brotherhood. In a decision-making group, attractiveness is likely to be related to how important the task is to members. If Daniel is part of a group of students who must develop a computer program using the language they are learning in class, the cohesiveness of the group will depend in part on how interested the group is in developing such a program.

Nita Winter Photography

As groups become more diverse, achieving cohesiveness becomes more difficult.

team building activities—
activities designed to help the group work better together.

2. **Voluntary membership.** When we are forming groups, we should give people some control over joining. So important is this for fostering cohesiveness that each recruit in the all voluntary military of the United States is allowed to choose his or her specialty. Likewise, Daniel's group is likely to develop cohesiveness more easily if they are able to volunteer to work on the task of developing a computer program.

    If group members are appointed, or if group members are having a little difficulty really getting comfortable with working together, a group may benefit from **team building activities** designed to help the group work better together (Clark, 1994). Often this means having the group meet someplace outside of its normal setting where they can engage in activities designed to help them recognize each other's strengths, share in group successes, and develop rituals. As they learn to be more comfortable with each other socially, they are likely to become more comfortable in the group setting as well.

3. **Feeling of freedom to share opinions.** Feeling comfortable in disagreeing with the ideas and positions of others is an important aspect of group cohesion. If Daniel's computer science group is comfortable sharing contrasting ideas without fear of being chastised, they are likely to develop more cohesiveness.

    Moreover, group members should feel free to converse about their goals very soon after the group is formed. During this discussion, individual members should be encouraged to express their ideas about the goals of the group and to hear the ideas of others. Through this discussion process, the group can clarify goals and build group commitment.

4. **Celebration of accomplishments.** Groups should be encouraged to set subgoals that can be achieved early. Groups that feel good about the work they are accomplishing develop a sense of unity. Once early subgoals are accomplished, the group can celebrate these achievements. Celebrations of early achievements cause members to more closely identify with the group and to see it as a "winner" (Renz & Greg, 2000, p. 54).

Keep in mind that the more heterogeneous the group the more difficult it is to build cohesiveness. We know that heterogeneous groups generally arrive at better decisions, so we need to structure group conversations that can develop cohesiveness in all types groups. This is why team building activities, development of freedom to express controversial ideas, and celebration of achievements are so important with heterogeneous groups.

In addition, members should be taught to communicate in ways that foster supportive patterns of cooperative interaction. Groups become cohesive when individual members feel valued and respected. By using the skills of active listening, empathizing, describing, and collaborative conflict management, you can help heterogeneous groups become cohesive.

THINKING ABOUT . . .

Cohesiveness

Can a high level of cohesiveness in a group actually become counterproductive? Have you ever been part of such a group? If so, consider how high cohesiveness hurt the group's decision-making ability.

Moreover, groups should set aside specific times during which the group stops working on its task and instead focuses on team relationships, enabling members to discuss and resolve personal differences before these hurt team cohesiveness and team performance.

Norms

Norms are expectations for the way group members will behave while in the group. Effective groups develop norms that support goal achievement (Shimanoff, 1992) and cohesiveness (Shaw, 1981). Norms begin to be developed early in the life of the group. Norms grow, change, and solidify as people get to know one another better. Group members usually comply with norms and are sanctioned by the group when they do not.

Norms can be developed through formal discussions or informal group processes (Johnson & Johnson, 2000, p. 28). Some groups choose to formulate explicit **ground rules,** prescribed behaviors designed to help the group meet its goals and conduct its conversations. These may include sticking to the agenda, refraining from interrupting others, actively listening to others, requiring full participation, focusing argument on issues rather than personalities, and sharing decision making.

In most groups, however, norms evolve informally. When we become part of a new group, we try to act in ways that would have been considered appropriate in other groups in which we have participated. If the other members of our new group behave in ways that are consistent with our interpretation of the rules for behavior, an informal norm is established. For example, suppose Daniel and two other group members show up late for a meeting. If the group has already begun discussion and the latecomers are greeted with cold looks, showing that other members of this group do not abide by being late, then this group will develop an on-time norm. A group may never discuss informal norms that develop, but all veteran group members understand what they are and behave in line with the expectations of these informally established norms.

When group members violate a group norm, they are usually sanctioned. The severity of the sanction depends on the importance of the norm that was violated, the extent of the violation, and the status of the person who violated the norm. Violating a norm that is central to a group's performance or cohesiveness will generally receive a harsher sanction than will violating a norm that is less central. Minor violations of norms, or violation of a norm by a newcomer, or violations of norms that are frequently violated will generally receive more lenient sanctions. Group members who have achieved higher status in the group (for example, those that have unique skills and abilities needed by the group) receive more lenient sanctions or escape sanctioning.

norms–*expectations for the way group members will behave while in the group.*

ground rules–*prescribed behaviors designed to help the group meet its goals and conduct its conversations.*

Some norms turn out to be counterproductive. For example, suppose that at the beginning of the first meeting of a work group a few folks start cutting up, telling jokes and stories, and generally ignore attempts by others to begin more serious discussion. If the group seems to encourage or does not effectively sanction this behavior, then this dallying behavior will become a group norm. As a result, the group may become so involved in these behaviors that work toward the group's goals gets delayed, set aside, or perhaps even forgotten. If counterproductive behavior such as this continues for several meetings and becomes a norm, it will be very difficult to change.

What can a group member do to try to change a norm? Renz and Greg (2000) suggest that you can help your group change a counterproductive norm by (1) observing the norm and its outcome, (2) describing the results of the norm to the group, and (3) soliciting opinions of other members of the group (p. 52). For instance, you might observe whether every meeting begins late, note how long dallying tends to continue, determine whether discussion is productive, and judge whether extra meetings are necessary. Then you could start the next meeting by reporting the results of your observations and asking for reaction from group members.

The Physical Setting

working environment—*the physical setting in which a group works.*

A good **working environment** is important for group effectiveness. The physical setting in which a group works should be located conveniently for most members. It should be at a comfortable temperature, and the space should be of appropriate size for the size and work of the group. The space should be comfortably furnished and contain all the resources the group needs to perform its tasks. Seating should be arranged to facilitate group interaction.

When a group meets on an ongoing basis, it will want to choose a location that is convenient for its members. By choosing a location that is easily accessible, the group makes it easier for all members to attend. When locations are chosen that are inconvenient for members, a norm of lateness or absence may develop.

The temperature of the room in which a group meets affects the way in which the group interacts. People in rooms they perceive to be too warm are not only uncomfortable but may feel crowded, which results in negative behaviors. Similarly, when the temperature of a room or meeting place is too cold, group members tend to become distracted.

The space in which a group meets should be appropriate for the size and composition of the group and the nature of what they are trying to accomplish during their time together. When the space is too big for the group, members will feel overwhelmed and distant from each other. In some cases, they may have trouble hearing one another. When the space is too small, the group will experience feelings of crowding. We have all found ourselves in situations in which room size contributed to negative experiences. Men and women seem to differ on their space preferences. Women generally find smaller rooms more comfortable than do men, who prefer larger spaces (Freedman, Klevansky, & Ehrich, 1971).

The physical setting can affect both group interaction and decision making (Figure 10.1). Seating can be too formal. When seating approximates a board of directors seating style, as illustrated in Figure 10.1a, where people sit indicates their status. In this style, a dominant-submissive pattern emerges that can inhibit group interaction. People who sit at the head of the table are likely to be

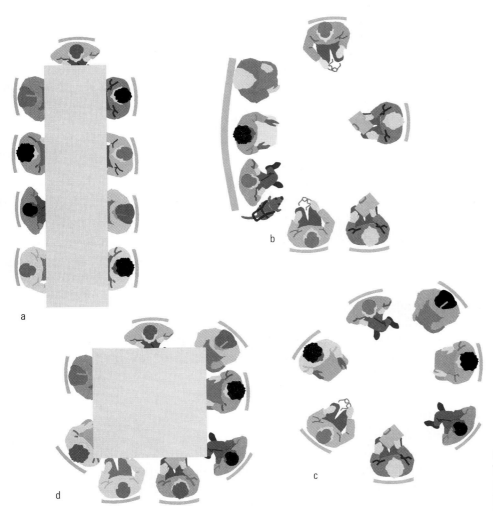

Figure 10.I
Which group members do you think will be able to arrive at a decision easily? Why or why not?

OBSERVE & ANALYZE
Journal Activity

Physical Settings

During the next week, keep a record of all the group settings you participate in. Note the physical setting (location, temperature, size of space, seating configuration), the interaction patterns (who talks, who listens, who agrees, who disagrees), and your satisfaction with the group discussion (high to low). At the end of the week, using Journal Activity 10.2 in your Student Workbook, analyze the data to see how the physical settings might have influenced group interaction and your satisfaction with the process. What conclusions can you draw from this analysis?

looked to for leadership and are seen as having more influence than those members who sit on the side. People who sit across the table from one another interact with one another more frequently but also find themselves disagreeing with one another more often than they disagree with others at the table.

Seating that is excessively informal can also inhibit interaction. For instance, in Figure 10.1b, the three people sitting on the couch form their own little group; the two people seated next to each other form another group; and two members have placed themselves out of the main flow. In arrangements such as these, people are more likely to communicate with the people adjacent to them than with others. In such settings, it is more difficult to make eye contact with every group member. Johnson and Johnson (2000) maintain that "easy eye contact among members enhances the frequency of interaction, friendliness, cooperation, and liking for the group" (p. 174).

The circle, generally considered the ideal arrangement for group discussions and problem solving, is depicted in Figure 10.1c. Circle configurations increase participant motivation to speak because sight lines are better for everyone and everyone appears to have equal status. When the location of the group meeting does not have a round table, the group may be better off without a table or with an arrangement of tables that makes a square, which approximates the circle arrangement, as shown in Figure 10.1d.

Stages of Group Development

Once assembled, groups tend to move through stages of development. Although numerous models have been proposed to describe the stages of group development, Tuckman's (1965) model has been widely accepted because it identifies the central issues facing a group at each stage in its development. He named these stages forming, storming, norming, performing, and adjourning. Research by Wheelen and Hochberger (1996) has confirmed that groups can be observed moving through each of these stages. In this section, we describe each of the stages of group development and discuss the nature of communication during each phase.

Forming

forming—*the initial stage of group development during which people come to feel valued and accepted so that they identify with the group.*

Forming is the initial stage of group development during which people come to feel valued and accepted so that they identify with the group. At the beginning of any group, individual members will experience feelings of discomfort caused by the uncertainty they are facing in this new social situation. Politeness and tentativeness on the part of members may characterize group interactions as members try to become acquainted with others, understand how the group will work, and find their place in the group. During forming, any real disagreements between people remain unacknowledged as members strive to be seen as flexible. During this stage, if the group has formally appointed group leaders, group members depend on them for clues as to how they should behave. Members work to fit in and to be seen as likable.

Anderson (1988) suggests that during forming we should express positive attitudes and feelings while refraining from abrasive or disagreeable comments, we should make appropriately benign self-disclosures and wait to see if they are reciprocated, and we should try to be friendly, open, and interested in others. This means using active listening and empathizing skills to become better acquainted with other members of the group, and smiling, nodding, and maintaining good eye contact to make conversations a bit more relaxed.

Storming

Storming is the stage of group development during which the group clarifies its goals and determines the roles each member will have in the group power structure. The stress and strain that arise when groups begin to make decisions are a natural result of the conflicting ideas, opinions, and personalities that begin to emerge during decision making. In the forming stage, members are concerned about fitting in, whereas in the storming stage, members are concerned about expressing their ideas and opinions and finding their place. One or more members may begin to question or challenge the formal leader's position on issues. In groups that do not have formally appointed leaders, two or more members may vie for informal leadership of the group. During this phase, the overpoliteness exhibited during forming may be replaced by snide comments, sarcastic remarks, or pointedly aggressive exchanges between some members. While storming, members may take sides, forming cliques and coalitions.

Storming, if controlled, is an important stage in a group's development. During periods of storming, the group is confronted with alternative ideas, opinions, and ways of viewing issues. Athough storming will occur in all groups, some will manage it better than others will. When storming in a group is severe, it can threaten the group's survival. When a group does not storm, it may experience **groupthink**, a deterioration of mental efficiency, reality testing, and moral judgment that results from in-group pressure (Janis, 1982, p. 9). To avoid groupthink, we should encourage constructive disagreement, we should self-monitor what we say to avoid name-calling and using inflammatory language, and we should use the active listening skills we studied earlier with emphasis on paraphrasing and honest questioning (Anderson, 1988).

storming–*the stage of group development during which the group clarifies its goals and determines the roles each member will have in the group power structure.*

groupthink–*when group members discourage the open expression of real conflict during decision making.*

COMMUNICATE!
Using Technology

Groupthink

For a complete discussion of groupthink, see Shannon's Groupthink Application at http://oak.cats.ohiou.edu/~sk260695/skthink.html. What are the causes of groupthink? What can members of a group do to avoid groupthink in their decision-making process?

Norming

Norming is the stage of group development during which the group solidifies its rules for behavior, especially those that relate to how conflict will be managed. As the group successfully completes a storming phase, it moves into a phase where members begin to apply more pressure on each other to conform. During this phase, the norms or standards of the group become clear. Members for the most part comply with norms, although those who have achieved higher status or power may continue to occasionally deviate from them. Members who do not comply with norms are sanctioned.

During norming, competent communicators pay attention to the norms that are developing. Then, they adapt their communication styles to the norms of the group. When communicators who are monitoring norm development determines that a norm is too rigid, too elastic, or in other ways counterproductive, they initiate a group discussion about their observations. As you would expect, these conversations are best received when the person initiating them uses the skills of describing behavior using specific and concrete language.

Performing

Performing is the stage of group development when the skills, knowledge, and abilities of all members are combined to overcome obstacles and meet goals successfully. Through each of the stages, groups are working to accomplish their goals. Once members have formed social bonds, settled power issues, and developed their norms, however, they "get in the groove," becoming more effective at creative problem solving and task performance. During this stage, conversations are focused on problem solving and sharing task-related information, with little energy directed to relationship building. Members who spend the group's time in chitchat not only detract from the effectiveness of the group but risk being perceived as unprepared or lazy. Performing is the most important stage of group development. This is the stage in which members freely share information, solicit ideas from others, and work to solve problems.

Adjourning

Adjourning is the stage of group development in which members assign meaning to what they have done and determine how to end or maintain interpersonal relations they have developed. Some groups are brought together for a finite time period, whereas for other groups work is continuous. Regardless of whether a group is short term or ongoing, all groups experience endings. A short-term project team will face adjourning when it has completed its work within the time period specified for its existence. Ongoing groups also experience endings. When the team has reached a particular goal, finished a specific project, or lost members to reassignments or resignations, it will confront the same developmental challenges faced by short-term groups in this phase.

Keyton's (1993) study of the adjourning phase of group development points to two challenges that groups face during this phase. First, groups need to construct meaning from their shared experience by evaluating and reflecting on the experience. They may discuss what led to their successes or failures, recall events and share memories of stressful times, and celebrate accomplishments. Second, members will need to find ways to sever or maintain interpersonal relationships that have developed during the group's life together. During this phase, people in the group may explore ways to maintain contact with those they have particularly enjoyed working with. They may continue the relationship on a purely social level or plan to undertake additional work together.

Keyton thinks that it is especially important for groups to have a termination ritual which can range from an informal debriefing session to formalized celebrations with group members and their friends, family, and colleagues. Whatever form the ritual takes, Keyton believes such a ritual "affects how they [members] will interpret what they have experienced and what expectations they will take with them to similar situations" (p. 98).

The phases of group development explain the work that groups must do to aid the socioemotional development of the group. How the group develops through these phases is important to how effectively it works. But achieving group goals is also the result of how well the group uses the problem-solving process. We now turn our attention to understanding the problem-solving process and the communication skills that provide the focus for the performing stage of group development.

Problem Solving in Groups

Research shows that groups follow many different approaches to problem solving. Some groups move linearly through a series of steps to reach consensus, and some move in a spiral pattern in which they refine, accept, reject, modify, and combine ideas as they go along. Whether groups move in something approximating an orderly pattern or go in fits and starts, those groups that arrive at high-quality decisions are likely to accomplish certain tasks during their deliberations. These tasks include identifying a specific problem, analyzing the problem, arriving at criteria that an effective solution must meet, identifying possible alternative solutions to the problem, comparing the alternatives to the criteria, and determining the best solution or combination of solutions.

Defining the Problem

Much wheel-spinning takes place during the early stages of group discussion as a result of members' not understanding their specific goal. It is the duty of the person, agency, or parent group that forms a particular work group to give the group a charge, such as "work out a new way of selecting people for merit pay increases." However, rarely will the charge be stated in such a way that the group does not need to do some clarification of its own. Even when the charge seems clear, effective groups will want to make sure they are focusing on the real problem and not just symptoms of the problem. Let's look again at the charge "work out a new way of selecting people for merit pay increases." What is wrong with this as a problem definition? "Work out a new way of selecting" is too general to be meaningful. A clearer question would be "What are the most important criteria for selecting people for merit pay increases?"

Even when a group is given a well-defined charge, it will need to gather information before it can accurately define the specific problem. Accurately defining the problem requires the group to understand the background, history, and status of the problem. This means collecting and understanding a variety of information.

As early as possible, the group should formally state the problem in writing. Unless the group can agree on a formal definition of the problem, there is little likelihood of the group's being able to work together toward a solution.

Effective problem definitions have these four characteristics.

1. **They are stated as questions.** Problem-solving groups begin from the assumption that solutions are not yet known, so problems should be stated as questions to be answered. For example, the merit pay committee might define the problem it will solve as follows: What are the most important criteria for determining merit pay increases? Phrasing the group's problem as a question furthers the spirit of inquiry.

2. **They contain only one central idea.** If the charge includes two questions— "Should the college abolish its foreign language and social studies requirements?"—the group should break it down into two separate questions: Should the college abolish its foreign language requirement? Should the college abolish its social studies requirement?

3. **They use specific and precise language to describe the problem.** For instance, the problem definition "What should the department do about courses that aren't getting the job done?" may be well intentioned, and participants may have at least some idea about their goal, but such vague wording as "getting the job done" can lead to problems later. Notice how this revision makes the intent much clearer: "What should the department do about courses that receive low scores on student evaluations?"

4. **They can be identified as a question of fact, value, or policy.** How we organize our problem-solving discussion will depend on the kind of question we are addressing: a question of fact, value, or policy.

Questions of fact are concerned with discovering what is true or to what extent something is true. Implied in such questions is the possibility of determining truth through the process of examining facts by way of directly observed, spoken, or recorded evidence. For instance, "Did Smith steal equipment from the warehouse?" "Did Mary's report follow the written guidelines for the assignment?" and "Do the data from our experiment support our hypothesis?" are all questions of fact. The group will discuss the validity of the evidence it has to determine what is true.

Questions of value concern subjective judgments of what is right, moral, good, or just. Questions of value can be recognized because they often contain evaluative words such as *good, reliable, effective,* or *worthy*. For instance, the program development team for a TV sitcom aimed at young teens may discuss, "Is the level of violence in the scripts we have developed appropriate for programs designed to appeal to children?" or "Is the proposed series of ads too sexually provocative?" Although we can establish criteria for "too sexually provocative" and "effectively" and measure material against those criteria, the criteria we choose and the evidence we accept depend on our judgment. A different group of people using different values might come to a different decision.

Questions of policy concern what courses of action should be taken or what rules should be adopted to solve a problem. "Should the university support international workers rights?" and "Where should the new landfill be built?" are both questions of policy. The inclusion of the word *should* in questions of policy makes them the easiest to recognize and the easiest to phrase of all problem statements.

questions of fact—*questions concerned with discovering what is true or to what extent something is true.*

questions of value—*questions that concern subjective judgments of what is right, moral, good, or just.*

questions of policy—*questions that concern what courses of action should be taken or what rules should be adopted to solve a problem.*

TEST YOUR COMPETENCE

Stating Problems

Indicate whether each of the following is a question of fact (F), a question of value (V), or a question of policy (P).

_____ 1. What should we do to increase the quality of finished parts?

_____ 2. Are African American drivers stopped by police more frequently than other drivers?

_____ 3. Should television news organizations use exit polls to call elections?

_____ 4. Is John guilty of involuntary manslaughter?

_____ 5. Is seniority the best method of handling employee layoffs?

_____ 6. What is the best vacation plan for our family?

Answers: 1. P 2. F 3. P 4. F 5. V 6. V

Analyzing the Problem

Analysis of a problem entails finding out as much as possible about the problem and determining the criteria that must be met to find an acceptable solution. Three types of information can be helpful in analyzing problems. Most groups begin by sharing the information individual members have acquired through their experience. This is a good starting place, but groups that limit their information gathering to the existing knowledge of members often make decisions based on incomplete or faulty information.

A second source of information that should be examined includes published materials available through libraries, electronic databases, and the Internet. From these sources, a group can access information about the problem that has been collected, analyzed, and interpreted by others. Just because information is published, however, does not mean that it is accurate or valid. Accuracy and validity are especially an issue when the information comes from an Internet source, and the group will also have to evaluate the relevance and usefulness of the information.

A third source of information about a problem can be gleaned from other people. At times, the group may want to consult experts for their ideas about a problem or conduct a survey to gather information from a particular target group. Both of these processes are discussed in detail in Chapter 13, "Doing Research."

Once group members have gathered information, it must be shared with other members. It is important for group members to share new information to fulfill the ethical responsibility that comes with group discussion. A study by Dennis (1996) shows that groups tend to spend more time discussing information common to group members if those with information don't work to get the information heard. The tendency to discuss common information while ignoring unique information leads to less effective decisions. To overcome this tendency, groups need to ask each member to discuss the information he or she has uncovered that seems to contradict his or her personal beliefs about the issue. When addressing a complex issue, separate information sharing from decision making by holding separate meetings spaced far enough apart to enable members to think through their information.

Determining Solution Criteria

Once a group understands the nature of the problem, it is in a position to determine what tests a solution must pass in order to solve the problem. The criteria become the decisive factors in determining whether a particular solution will solve the problem. The criteria that are selected should be ones that the information gathered has suggested are critical to successfully solving the problem.

The criteria that the group decides on will be used to screen alternative solutions. Solutions that do not meet the test of all criteria are eliminated from further consideration. For example, a local citizens' committee is charged with selecting a site for a new county jail. The group arrives at the following phrasing for the problem: "Where should the new jail be located?" After the group agrees on this wording, they can then ask the question, "What are the criteria for a good site for a new jail?"

In that discussion, suppose members contribute information related to the county's budget, the need for inmates to maintain family contact, concerns about proximity to schools and parks, and space needs. After considering this kind of information, the group might then select the following criteria for selecting a site:

- Maximum cost of $500,000 for purchasing the land.
- A location no more than three blocks from public transportation.
- A location that is one mile or more from any school, daycare center, playground, or youth center.
- A lot size of at least ten acres.

When groups discuss and decide on criteria before they think about specific solutions, Kathryn Young and her colleagues (2000) suggest that groups increase the likelihood that they will be able to avoid becoming polarized and will be more likely to come to a decision that all members can accept.

Identifying Possible Solutions

For most policy questions, many possible solutions are possible. The trick is to tap the creative thinking of group members so that many ideas are generated. At this stage of discussion, the goal is not to worry about whether a particular solution fits all the criteria but to come up with a large list of ideas.

One way to identify potential solutions is to brainstorm for ideas. **Brainstorming** is a free-association procedure generating as many ideas as possible by being creative, suspending judgment, and combining or adapting the ideas of others. It involves verbalizing your ideas as they come to mind without stopping to evaluate their merits. Members are encouraged, however, to build on the ideas presented by others. In a ten- or fifteen-minute brainstorming session, a group may come up with twenty or more possible solutions depending on the nature of the problem. For instance, the group working on the jail site question might mention ten or more in just a few minutes of brainstorming, such as sites that individual members have thought of or that they have heard others mention.

brainstorming–*a free-association technique for generating as many ideas as possible by being creative, suspending judgment, and combining or adapting the ideas of others.*

John Coletti/The Picture Cube

Brainstorming can be an effective method of problem solving in a group. Each person is encouraged to state ideas as they come to mind.

SKILL BUILDERS Brainstorming

Skill

An uncritical, nonevaluative process of generating associated ideas.

Use

To generate a list of potential solutions to a problem.

Procedure

1. Verbalize ideas as they come to mind.

2. Refrain from evaluating the merits of ideas.

3. Encourage outrageous and unique ideas.

4. Build on or modify the ideas of others.

5. Use extended effort to generate more ideas.

6. Record the ideas.

Example

Problem: "What should we do to raise money to help a child who needs a liver transplant?" Ideas: sell cookies, sell candy, sell wrapping paper, wrap packages at mall for donations, find corporate sponsors, have a corporate golf outing, a youth golf outing, a tennis tournament, a bowling tournament, a paint-ball tournament, auction donated paintings, do odd jobs for money.

Evaluating Solutions

Once the group has a list of possible solutions, it needs to compare each solution alternative to the criteria that it developed. During this phase, the group must determine whether each criterion is equally important or whether certain criteria should be given more weight in evaluating alternative solutions. Whether a group weighs certain criteria more heavily or not, it should use a process that ensures that each alternative solution is thoroughly assessed against all of the criteria.

Research by Randy Hirokawa (1987) confirmed that high-quality decisions are made by groups that are "careful, thoughtful, and systematic" in evaluating their options (p. 10). In another study, Hirokawa (1988) noted that it is common for groups to begin by eliminating solutions that clearly do not meet important criteria and then to compare the positive features of solutions that remain.

Deciding

A group brought together for problem solving may or may not be responsible for making the actual decision, but it is responsible for presenting its recommendation. **Decision making** is the process of choosing among alternatives. The following five methods differ in the extent to which they require that all members agree with the decision and the amount of time it takes to reach a decision.

1. **The expert opinion method.** Once the group has eliminated those alternatives that do not meet the criteria, the group asks the member who has the most expertise to select the final choice. This method is quick, and it is useful when one member is much more knowledgeable about the issues or has a greater stake in implementation of the decision.

COMMUNICATE! Using InfoTrac College Edition

Under the subject "problem solving discussion," click on "Periodical references." Scroll to "group problem solving." Since "teamwork" is a "hot topic," see "Teamworking in its contexts: Antecedents, nature and dimensions." Look for information on different designs for teams.

decision making–*the process of choosing among alternatives.*

SKILL BUILDERS   Problem-Solving Fact/Value Questions

Skill	Use	Procedure	Example
Arriving at a conclusion about a fact or value question.	A guide for groups to follow in arriving at conclusions to fact or value questions.	1. Clarify the specific fact or value question. 2. Analyze the problem by determining the criteria that must be met to establish the fact or value. 3. Examine the facts to determine whether the subject meets those criteria.	The question is whether Branson is an effective leader. The key criteria for determining effective leadership are having a vision and being able to motivate employees. Evidence shows that Branson is successful in meeting both criteria.

SKILL BUILDERS   Problem-Solving Policy Questions

Skill	Use	Procedure	Example
Arriving at a solution to a policy question by following six steps.	A guide for groups to follow in finding solutions to policy questions.	1. Clarify the specific policy problem question. 2. Analyze the problem. 3. Determine the solution criteria that must be met to find an acceptable solution. 4. Brainstorm potential solutions. 5. Evaluate the solutions to determine which best meet the criteria. 6. Decide which is best.	Question: "What should we do to increase alumni donations to the Department Scholarship Fund?" The group begins by discussing "Why are alumni not donating to the fund?" and asking "What criteria must be met to find an acceptable solution?" After brainstorming potential solutions, the group evaluates each and selects the one or ones that best meet the criteria.

OBSERVE & ANALYZE
Journal Activity

Decision Methods

Remember an instance when a group you were part of made a poor decision using a majority rule method. In your Student Workbook under Journal Activity 10.3, analyze why the decision was a poor one. Then answer the following questions: Would a different decision method have helped? If so, what method might have been more effective? Why?

2. **The average group opinion method.** When using this approach, each member of the group ranks the alternatives that meet all the criteria. These rankings are then averaged, and the alternative receiving the highest average ranking becomes the choice. This method is useful for routine decisions or when a decision needs to be made quickly. It can also be used as an intermediate straw poll to enable the group to eliminate low-scoring alternatives before moving to a different process for making the final decision.

3. **The majority rule method.** When using this method, the group votes on each alternative, and the one that receives the majority of votes (50 percent + 1) is selected. Although this method is considered democratic, it can create problems for implementation. If the majority voting for an alternative is slight, then there may be nearly as many members who do not support the choice as there are those that do. If these minority members object strongly to the choice, they may sabotage implementation of the solution either through active or passive means.

4. **The unanimous decision method.** In this method, the group must continue deliberation until every member of the group believes the same solution is the best. As you would expect, it is very difficult to arrive at truly unanimous decisions, and to do so takes a lot of time. When a group reaches unanimity, however, it can expect that each member of the group will be fully committed to selling the decision to others and to helping implement the decision.

5. **The consensus method.** This method is an alternative to the unanimous decision method. In consensus, the group continues deliberation until all members of the group find an acceptable variation, one they can support and are committed to helping implement. Members of a consensus group may believe there is a better solution than the one that has been chosen, but they feel they can support and help implement the one they have agreed to. Although easier to achieve than reaching unanimity, arriving at a consensus is still difficult. Although the majority rule method is widely used, selecting the consensus method is a wise investment if the group needs everyone's support to implement the decision successfully.

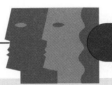

DIVERSE VOICES

The Group: A Japanese Context

by Delores Cathcart and Robert Cathcart

One of Japan's most prominent national characteristics is the individual's sense of the group. Loyalty to the group and a willingness to submit to its demands are key virtues in Japanese society.

This dependency and the interdependency of all members of a group is reinforced by the concept of *on*. A Japanese is expected to feel an indebtedness to those others in the group who provide security, care, and support. This indebtedness creates obligation and when combined with dependency is called *on*. *On* functions as a means of linking all persons in the group in an unending chain because obligation is never satisfied, but continues throughout life. *On* is fostered by a system known as the *oyabun-kobun* relationship. Traditionally the *oyabun* is a father, boss, or patron who protects and provides for a son, employee, or student in return for his or her service and loyalty. This is not a one-way dependency. Each boss or group leader recognizes his own dependency on those below. Without their undivided loyalty he or she could not function. Oyabun are also acutely aware of this double dimension because of having had to serve a long period of *kobun* on the way up the hierarchy to the position at the top. All had oyabun who protected and assisted them, much like a father, and now each must do the same for their kobun.

Oyabun have one or more kobun whom they look after much as if they were children. The more loyal and devoted the "children" the more successful the "father."

This relationship is useful in modern life where large companies assume the role of superfamily and become involved in every aspect of their workers' lives. Bosses are oyabun and employees are kobun. . . .

This uniquely Japanese way of viewing relationships creates a distinctive style of decision making known as *consensus decision*. The Japanese devotion to consensus building seems difficult for most Westerners to grasp but loses some of its mystery when looked at as a solution to representing every member of the group. In a system that operates on oyabun-kobun relationships nothing is decided without concern for how the outcome will affect all. Ideas and plans are circulated up and down the company hierarchy until everyone has had a chance to react. This reactive process is not to exert pressure but to make certain that all matters affecting the particular groups and the company are taken into consideration. Much time is spent assessing the mood of everyone involved and only after all the ramifications of how the decision will affect each group can there be a quiet assent. A group within the company may approve a decision that is not directly in its interest (or even causes it difficulties) because its members know they are not ignored, their feelings have been expressed and they can be assured that what is good for the company will ultimately be good for them. For this reason consensus decisions cannot be hurried along without chancing a slight or oversight that will cause future problems.

The process of consensus building in order to make decisions is a time-consuming one, not only because everyone must be considered, but also because the Japanese avoid verbalizing objections or doubts in order to preserve group harmony. The advice, often found in American group literature, that group communication should be charac-terized by open and candid statements expressing individual personal feelings, wishes, and dislikes, is the antithesis of the Japanese consensus process. No opposing speeches are made to argue alternate ideas; no conferences are held to debate issues. Instead, the process of assessing the feelings and mood of each work group proceeds slowly until there exists a climate of agreement. This process is possible because of the tight relationships that allow bosses and workers to know each other intimately and to know the group so well that needs and desires are easy to assess.

Excerpted from Delores Cathcart and Robert Cathcart, "The Group: A Japanese Context." From Intercultural Communication: A Reader, *8th ed., eds. Larry A Samovar and Richard E. Porter (Belmont, CA Wadsworth, 1997), pp. 329–339. Reprinted by permission of the author.*

Constraints on Effective Decision Making

Following a structured problem-solving process should help groups be more effective, but groups may still face cognitive, affiliative, and social constraints that can interfere with constructive decision making (Gouran & Hirokawa, 1996; Janis, 1989)

cognitive constraints–

constraints that occur when a group feels under pressure as a result of a difficult task, shortage of information, or limited time.

affiliative constraints–

constraints that occur when some or all members of the group are more concerned about maintaining harmonious relationships with others than they are about making high-quality decisions.

Cognitive constraints occur when a group feels under pressure as a result of a difficult task, a shortage of information, or limited time. Signs of cognitive constraints are comments like "How do they expect us to get this done in a week?" or "We've got a ton of material to sift through." Overcoming these constraints requires a group to assure itself that the task is important enough to give the necessary time and compensate for the difficulty. For instance, over-hauling the method of producing a product will take more time than most would like to spend, but if the overhaul is a necessity to keep a company above water, then the time is well spent.

Affiliative constraints occur when some or all members of the group are more concerned about maintaining harmonious relationships with others than they are about making high-quality decisions. Signs of affiliative constraints are reluctance of some members to talk, backing down for no apparent reason, and reluctance to show any disagreement. Working through these constraints is often a matter of practicing the interpersonal skills we covered in the early part of this book. Dealing with this might also require assigning someone to serve as a **devil's advocate,** taking the opposite side of the argument just to test the apparent consensus. Once a group sees that constructive argument is healthy when it is good-natured, the group is more likely to be honest with its opinions.

Egocentric constraints occur when members of the group have high needs for control or are driven by other personal needs. These people see issues in terms of a "win-lose." They feel that by getting the group to accept their position they "win." If the group chooses another alternative, they have suffered a personal loss. What drives egocentric individuals is not necessarily a strong preference for one alternative but the need to be "right." Statements like "Well, I know that most of you are new to the commission and have lots of ideas, but I have served in this capacity for the past five years, and so I know what won't work" are sure signs of egocentrism. Egocentric constraints are difficult to overcome, but egocentric individuals are not incapable of rational thinking. Inviting them to verbalize the information upon which they are basing their conclusions can sometimes help them to modify their position and move into problem solving.

devil's advocate–*a person who is assigned the task of taking the opposite side of the argument from the one the group appears to be supporting.*

egocentric constraints–*constraints that occur when members of the group have high needs for control or are driven by other personal needs.*

WHAT WOULD YOU DO?
A QUESTION OF ETHICS

The Community Service and Outreach committee of Students in Communication was meeting to determine what cause should benefit from the annual fund-raising Talent Contest that SIC held each year.

"So," said Mark, "does anyone have any ideas about whose cause we should sponsor?"

"Well," replied Glenna, "I think we should give it to a group that's doing literacy work."

"Sounds good to me," replied Mark.

"My aunt works at the Boardman Center as the literacy coodinator, so why don't we just adopt them?" asked Glenna.

"Gee, I don't know much about the group," said Reed.

"Come on, you know, they help people learn how to read," replied Glenna sarcastically.

"Well, I was kind of hoping we'd take a look at sponsoring the local Teen Runaway Center," offered Angelo.

"Listen, if your aunt works at the Boardman Center," commented Laticia, "let's go with it."

"Right," said Pablo, "that's good enough for me."

"Yeah," replied Heather, "let's do it and get out of here."

"I hear what you're saying, Heather," Mark responded, "I've got plenty of other stuff to do."

"No disrespect meant to Glenna, but wasn't the Boardman Center in the news because of questionable use of funds?" countered Angelo. "Do we really know enough about them?"

"OK," said Mark, "enough discussion. I've got to get to class. All in favor of the literacy program at the Boardman Center indicate by saying 'aye.' I think we've got a majority. Sorry, Angelo, you can't win them all."

"I wish all meetings went this smoothly," Heather said to Glenna as they left the room. "I mean, that was really a good meeting."

1. What did the group really know about the Boardman Center? Is it good group discussion practice to rely on a passing comment of one member?

2. Regardless of whether the meeting went smoothly, is there any ethical problem with this process? Explain.

Summary

Effective groups meet several criteria: They develop clearly defined goals, have an optimum number of diverse members, work to develop cohesiveness, establish norms, and establish a good working environment.

Once groups have assembled, they tend to move through five stages of development: forming, getting people come to feel valued and accepted so that they identify with the group; storming, clarifying goals while determining the roles each member will have in the group power structure; norming, solidifying rules for behavior; performing, overcoming obstacles and meeting goals successfully; and adjourning, assigning meaning to what they have done, and determining how to end or maintain interpersonal relations they have developed.

Once the group has reached the performing stage, they begin to move through a series of steps of problem solving, including defining the problem as a question of fact, value, or policy; analyzing the problem; determining solution criteria; identifying possible solutions; evaluating solutions; and deciding.

Throughout the problem-solving process, members need to deal with the cognitive, affiliative, and egocentric constraints that groups encounter.

Communicate! Online

Use your Communicate! CD-ROM for quick access to the electronic study resources that accompany this text. Included on your CD-ROM is access to InfoTrac College Edition, the World Wide Web, a demo of WebTutor for Communicate!, and the Communicate! Web site at the Wadsworth Communication Café. The Communicate! Web site offers chapter-by-chapter activities, quizzes, and a digital glossary.

Review the following key terms at
http://communication.wadsworth.com/humancomm/verderber

Key Terms

acceptable goals (239)	**groupthink** (247)
adjourning (248)	**heterogeneous group** (240)
affiliative constraints (258)	**homogeneous group** (240)
brainstorming (253)	**norming** (248)
challenging goals (239)	**norms** (243)
cognitive constraints (258)	**performing** (248)
cohesiveness (240)	**questions of fact** (251)
consistent goals (239)	**questions of policy** (251)
decision making (255)	**questions of value** (251)
devil's advocate (259)	**specific goal** (239)
egocentric constraints (259)	**storming** (247)
forming (246)	**team building activities** (242)
ground rules (243)	**work group** (238)
group goal (238)	**working environment** (244)

Your Communicate! Web site at the Wadsworth Communication Café maintains a chapter-by-chapter listing of the URLs included in this text and many additional sites that expand text content. For example, for Chapter 10, you can access a Web site developed and maintained by Brian A. Connery and John L. Vohs from the University of California at Davis that provides supplemental information on Tuckman's four phases of group development, which were discussed on page 246.

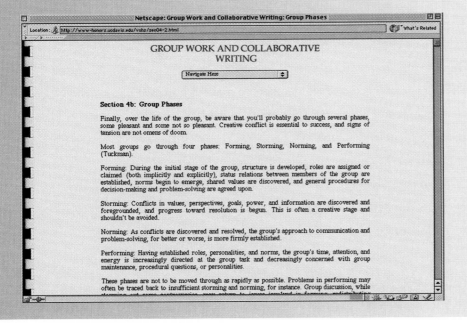

OBJECTIVES

After you have read this chapter, you should be able to answer these questions:

- What are roles, and why are they important in groups?
- How do members choose their roles?
- What types of roles do members of groups enact?
- What behaviors are expected of all members to make group meetings effective?
- What is leadership, and why is it important to a group?
- What are the tasks of leadership?
- What characterizes the communication behavior of leaders?
- How does leadership develop in a group?
- What behaviors can help an individual become a leader?
- What should the leader of a meeting do to make the meeting successful?

11

Member Roles and Leadership in Groups

"**W**ell, since we're all here, let's get started. The agenda calls for us to begin by reviewing the three bids we received for landscaping services. Dontonio, will you be the recorder again?"

"Sure, Ray, no problem."

"OK. Sarella, we know we can depend on you to have studied the bids. So why don't you start us out by summarizing what you found?"

"Well, only three of the six companies submitted detailed bids in line with our request. After reviewing each, I concluded that they all will provide the same basic services and on similar schedules. Two of the bids came in at about the same amount, but the other one is much higher. The two lower bids were from Wildflowers and from J&M."

"Well, I've never heard of Wildflowers, but my brother-in-law used J&M for a while and dropped them because they ran over his flower beds with their big riding movers. I don't think we want that here."

"Hey, Jose, be careful, my boyfriend works for J&M and I don't think his crews are that irresponsible."

"Judith, I don't think Jose meant his comment as a personal attack on your boyfriend. I think he was just trying to share something he had heard."

"Yeah, you're right, Shawn, thanks. Sorry, Jose. It's a good thing we have Shawn to keep us from popping off at each other."

Our beginning conversation is typical of interactions in groups. If you listened closely, you could hear that the members of this group were not only discussing the topic but were each acting in the ways expected of them by others in the group.

Our goal in this chapter is to explain how members of groups take on specific roles that help or detract from the effectiveness of the group. A **role** is a specific pattern of behavior that one group member performs based on the expectations of other members. We will learn about the types of roles members assume and how these roles are developed. Then we will look more closely at leadership roles. Most groups can identify one person who serves as its leader, and we will examine those characteristics that distinguish leaders from other group members. We will also discuss several types of leaders and how groups develop leaders. Toward the end of the chapter, we will present behavioral guidelines that will increase your chances of becoming a leader in your group. Finally, we will discuss what leaders must do to facilitate group meetings.

role–*a specific pattern of behavior that one group member performs based on the expectations of other members.*

Member Roles

The roles group members play depend on their personalities and what is required or needed by the group. Four common types of roles are task-related, maintenance, procedural, and self-centered roles.

Task-Related Roles

task-related role–*specific pattern of behavior that directly helps the group accomplish its goals.*

Task-related roles require specific patterns of behavior that directly help the group accomplish its goals. Members who play task roles are likely to be information or opinion givers, information or opinion seekers, or analyzers.

information or opinion giver–*individual who provides content for the discussion.*

Information or opinion givers provide content for the discussion. People who perform these roles are expected to have developed expertise or to be well informed on the content of the task and to share what they know with the group. The more material you have studied, the more valuable your contributions will be. "Well, the articles I read seem to agree that . . ." and "Based on the years I've been in the community and given what the recent citizens' poll revealed, I think we should . . ." are statements typical of information and opinion givers.

information or opinion seeker–*individual who probes others for their ideas and opinions on issues before the group.*

Information or opinion seekers are expected to probe others for their ideas and opinions on issues before the group. Typical comments by those performing these roles include, "Before going further, what information do we have about how raising fees is likely to affect membership?" or "How do other members of the group feel about this idea?"

analyzer–*individual who probes the content and the reasoning of members during discussion.*

Analyzers are expected to probe the content and the reasoning of members during discussion. In so doing, their role is to question what is being said and to help members understand the hidden assumptions in their statements. Analyzers make statements such as "Enrique, you're generalizing from only one instance. Can you give us some others?"

Maintenance Roles

Maintenance roles require specific patterns of behavior that help the group develop and maintain good member relationships, group cohesiveness, and effective levels of conflict. Members who play maintenance roles are likely to be supporters, tension relievers, harmonizers, or interpreters.

Supporters are expected to encourage others in the group. When another member contributes to the group, supporters show appreciation through their nonverbal or verbal behavior. Nonverbally, supporters may smile, nod, or vigorously shake their heads. Verbally, they demonstrate support through statements like "Good point, Ming," "I really like that idea, Nikki," or "It's obvious you've really done your homework, Janelle."

Tension relievers are expected to recognize when group members are stressed or tiring and to intervene in some way that relieves the stress or reenergizes the group. People who are effective in this role are able to tell jokes, kid around, and tell light-hearted stories so that the group is refreshed when it returns to the task. In some situations, a single well-placed one-liner will get a laugh, break the tension or the monotony, and jolt the group out of its lethargy. Although the tension reliever momentarily distracts the group from its task, this helps the group remain cohesive.

Harmonizers are expected to intervene in group discussions when conflict is threatening to harm group cohesiveness or the relationships between specific group members. Tension relievers distract group members, whereas harmonizers mediate and reconcile differences between group members. Harmonizers are likely to make statements such as "Tom, Jack, hold it a second. I know you're on opposite sides of this, but let's see where you might have some agreement," "Cool it, everybody, we're really coming up with some good stuff; let's not lose our momentum by getting into name-calling."

Interpreters are expected to be familiar with the differences in the social, cultural, and gender orientations of members of the group and to use this knowledge to help group members understand each other. Interpreters are especially important in groups whose members are culturally diverse (Jensen & Chilberg, 1991). For example, an interpreter might say, "Paul, Lin Chou is Chinese, so when she says that she will think about your plan she probably means that she does not support your ideas, but she doesn't want to embarrass you in front of the others." Or an interpreter might say, "Jim, most of us are Latino, and in our culture it is considered impolite to begin business before we socialize and catch up with one another."

maintenance role–*specific pattern of behavior that helps the group develop and maintain good member relationships, group cohesiveness, and effective levels of conflict.*

supporter–*individual who encourages others in the group.*

tension reliever–*individual who recognizes when group members are stressed or tiring and intervenes in some way that relieves the stress or reenergizes the group.*

harmonizer–*individual who intervenes in group discussions when conflict is threatening to harm group cohesiveness or the relationships between specific group members.*

interpreter–*individual who is familiar with the differences in the social, cultural, and gender orientations of members of the group and uses this knowledge to help group members understand each other.*

Procedural Roles

Procedural roles require specific patterns of behavior that help the group manage its problem-solving process. Members who play procedural roles are likely to be expediters, recorders, or gatekeepers.

Expediters are expected to keep track of what the group is trying to accomplish and to help move the group through the agenda. When the group has strayed, expediters will make statements like "I'm enjoying this, but I can't quite see what it has to do with resolving the issue" or "Let's see, aren't we still trying to find out whether these are the only criteria that we should be considering?"

Recorders are expected to take careful notes of the what the group has decided and the evidence upon which the decisions are based. Recorders usually distribute edited copies of their notes to group members prior to the next meeting. Sometimes these notes are published as **minutes,** which become a public record of the group's activities.

Gatekeepers are expected to manage the flow of conversation so that all members have an equal opportunity to participate. If one or two members begin to dominate the conversation, the gatekeeper is expected to acknowledge

procedural role–*specific pattern of behavior that helps the group to manage its problem-solving process.*

expediter–*individual who keeps track of what the group is trying to accomplish and helps to move the group through the agenda.*

recorder–*individual who takes careful notes of what the group has decided and the evidence upon which the decisions are based.*

minutes–*a public record of a group's activities.*

gatekeeper–*individual who manages the flow of conversation so that all members have an equal opportunity to participate.*

> ### THINKING ABOUT . . .
>
> #### Roles
>
> Which of the roles discussed in this section on member roles do you perform most frequently when you are in a group? Which role is easiest for you to perform? Which role is most difficult for you? Why?

Nita Winter Photography

Some members help the group by performing procedural roles such as expediter or recorder.

this and to invite other members of the group to participate. Gatekeepers also notice nonverbal signals that indicate that a member wishes to speak. The gatekeeper is the one who sees that Juanita is on the edge of her chair, eager to comment, and says, "Let me interrupt you, Doug. We haven't heard from Juanita, and she seems to have something she wants to say."

Self-Centered Roles

Self-centered roles reflect specific patterns of behavior that focus attention on individuals' needs and goals at the expense of the group. Task-related, maintenance, and procedural roles must be played for groups to be effective, but self-centered roles detract from group effectiveness. Members who play self-centered roles are likely to be aggressors, jokers, withdrawers, or monopolizers.

Aggressors seek to enhance their own status by criticizing almost everything or blaming others when things get rough and by deflating the ego or status of others. Aggressors should be confronted and helped to assume a more positive role. They should be asked whether they are aware of what they are doing and of the effect their behavior is having on the group.

Jokers attempt to draw attention to themselves by clowning, mimicking, or generally making a joke of everything. Unlike tension relievers, the joker is not focused on helping the group to relieve stress or tension. Rather, a joker disrupts work when the group is trying to focus on the task. Jokers should also be confronted and encouraged to use their abilities when the group needs a break but to refrain from disrupting the group when it is being productive.

Withdrawers can be expected to meet their own goals at the expense of group goals by not participating in the discussion or the work of the group. Sometimes withdrawers do so by physically missing meetings. At other times, withdrawers are physically present but remain silent in discussion or refuse to take responsibility for doing work. When a person has assumed this role, the group needs to find out why the person is choosing not to participate. When possible, the goals of the withdrawer need to be aligned with the goals of the group. For example, members of a group noticed Marianne came late to meetings and didn't seem to be prepared. The group finally confronted her and learned that she was late arriving because of her job. She also indicated that she did not contribute because she usually missed so much of the discussion. This group was able to change meeting dates, and Marianne became a fully participating member.

Monopolizers can be expected to talk all the time, giving the impression that they are well read, knowledgeable, and of value to the group. They should be encouraged when their comments are helpful and reined in when they are talking too much or when their comments are not helpful.

Normal Distribution of Roles

What proportion of time in a "normal" group should be devoted to the various roles described in this section? According to Robert Bales (1971), one of the

self-centered role–*specific pattern of behavior that focuses attention on individuals' needs and goals at the expense of the group.*

aggressor–*individual who tries to enhance his or her own status by criticizing almost everything or blaming others when things get rough and by deflating the ego or status of others.*

joker–*individual who attempts to draw the group's attention by clowning, mimicking, or generally making a joke of everything.*

withdrawer–*individual who meets his or her own goals at the expense of group goals by not participating in the discussion or the work of the group or by physically missing meetings.*

monopolizer–*individual who talks all the time to give the impression that he or she is well read, knowledgeable, and of value to the group.*

leading researchers in group interaction processes, 40 to 60 percent of discussion time is spent giving and asking for information and opinion; 8 to 15 percent of discussion time is spent on disagreement, tension, or unfriendliness; and 16 to 26 percent of discussion time is characterized by agreement or friendliness (positive maintenance functions). We can apply two norms as guidelines for effective group functioning: (1) approximately half of all discussion time should be devoted to information sharing, and (2) group agreement time should far outweigh group disagreement time.

Member Responsibilities in Group Meetings

Although members specialize in particular roles during group discussions and problem solving, members of effective groups also assume common responsibilities for making their meetings successful. Here are some guidelines prepared by a class of university students to help group members prepare, behave, and follow up in a manner that will increase the effectiveness of the meeting ("Guidelines," 1998).

Preparing

As the chapter opening vignette illustrated, too often people think of group meetings as a happening that requires attendance but no particular preparation. Countless times we have observed people who bring packets of material about a meeting with them but have spent little, if any, time studying the material. The reality is that meetings should not be treated as impromptu events but as activities that pool information from well-prepared individuals. Here are some important steps to take prior to attending a meeting.

1. **Study the agenda.** Determine the purpose of the meeting and what you need to do to be prepared. Consider the agenda as an outline for preparation.

2. **Study the minutes.** If this is one of a series of meetings, study the minutes and your own notes from the previous meeting. Each meeting is not a separate event. What happened at one meeting should provide the basis for preparation for the next meeting.

3. **Prepare for your contributions.** Read handouts and do the necessary research to become better informed about items on the agenda. If no handouts are given, it is up to you to think of the kinds of information you will

need to be a productive member of the group. Bring any materials that you have uncovered that will help the group accomplish the agenda. If appropriate, discuss the agenda with others who will not be attending the meeting and solicit their ideas concerning issues to be discussed in the meeting.

4. **Prepare to play a major role.** Consider which roles you are assigned or which you are interested in playing. What do you need to do to play those roles to the best of your ability?

5. **List questions.** Make a list of questions related to agenda items that you would like to have answered during the meeting.

Participating

Go into the meeting with the expectation that you will be a full participant. If there are five people in the group, all five should be participating.

1. **Listen attentively.** Concentrate on what others are saying so that you can use your material to complement, supplement, or counter what has been presented.

Rob Lewine/The Stock Market

Effective meetings occur when well-prepared participants choose to communicate in effective ways.

2. **Stay focused.** In a group setting, it is easy to get the discussion going in non-productive directions. Keep your comments focused on the specific agenda item under discussion. If others have gotten off the subject, do what you can to get people back on track.

3. **Ask questions.** "Honest" questions whose answers you do not already know help to stimulate discussion and build ideas.

4. **Take notes.** Even if someone else is responsible for providing the official minutes, you will need notes that help you follow the line of development. Also, these notes will help you remember what has been said.

5. **Play devil's advocate.** When you think an idea has not been fully discussed or tested, be willing to voice disagreement or encourage further discussion.

6. **Monitor your contributions.** Especially when people are well prepared, they have a tendency to dominate discussion. Make sure that you are neither dominating the discussion nor abdicating your responsibility to share insights and opinions.

Following Up

When meetings end, too often people leave and forget about what took place until the next meeting. But what happens in one meeting provides a basis for what happens in the next; be prepared to move forward at the next meeting.

1. **Review and summarize your notes.** Try to do this shortly after you have left the meeting while ideas are still fresh in your mind. Make notes of what needs to be discussed next time.

2. **Evaluate your effectiveness.** How effective were you in helping the group move toward achieving its goals? Where were you strong? Where were you weak? What should you do next time that you did not do in this meeting?

3. **Review decisions.** Make note of what your role was in making decisions. Did you do all that you could have done?

4. **Communicate progress.** Inform others who need to know about information conveyed and decisions that were made in the meeting.

5. **Follow up.** Make sure you complete all assignments you received in the meeting.

6. **Review minutes.** Compare the official minutes of the meeting to your own notes, and report any significant discrepancies that you find.

THINKING ABOUT ...

Member Responsibilities

Consider your own behavior when you are a member of a group. Which of the preparation, participation, and follow-up guidelines do you need to work on to become a more valuable member of a problem-solving group? Why?

Leadership

Although performance of all task, maintenance, and procedural roles aid groups in accomplishing their goals, good leadership is also necessary to accomplish group goals. A great number of definitions of leadership have been offered by scholars, but common to most definitions is the notion that **leadership** is a process of influencing members to accomplish group goals (Shaw, 1981, p. 317). As you will recall, influence is a communication process that brings about changes in the beliefs and actions of others, but leadership is more than influence. It is the use of influence to aid the group in reaching its goals. Leadership involves motivating other members to continue working toward common objectives. Let's look at how leadership serves a group.

leadership–*the process of influencing members to accomplish group goals.*

The Function of Leadership

In their book on small-group communication, Fisher and Ellis (1990) argue that leadership is involved in performing "vital functions" in the group. These functions include influencing the group's procedures and task accomplishment and maintaining satisfactory relationships between members.

Because various roles in the group are specifically designed to fulfill each of these functions, leadership can be shared by all group members. However, in most groups, some of the roles that are necessary for effective group functioning are not assumed by members. Current thinking is that the leader's role is to step in and assume whatever roles are needed in the group at a particular time that are not being assumed by other group members (Rothwell, 1998, p. 168).

B. Aubrey Fisher (1985), a noted communication scholar, believes that those filling the leadership role must be versatile and able to adapt their behavior to the situation. Leaders are adept at listening to the group and becoming attuned to what the group needs at a particular time. Based on what they have heard, leaders adapt their behavior to the situation and influence the group to behave in ways that will lead to goal accomplishment.

COMMUNICATE! Using InfoTrac College Edition

Under the subject "leadership," click on "Periodical references." Scroll to "Principles of Leadership," by Edward Moyers, July 15, 2000. Look for the heading "II. Leadership is not a popularity contest," and find the statement "Respect is what a true leader strives for—not to be just liked by all the people you are involved with." Of the eight ways of earning respect, which one or two do you believe it is most important to put into practice? Why?

Types of Leaders

A group will often have more than one leader. Many groups have a designated **formal leader,** an assigned leader who is given legitimate power to influence others. The formal leader may be appointed by some entity outside the group. For example, the dean of the college might appoint a student to chair a committee of students and faculty who are reviewing the college's policy on class attendance. In some settings, the group itself elects a formal leader. Instead of appointing someone to lead the committee, the dean may have requested that the committee elect its own chair. In both cases, the person who assumes formal

formal leader–*an assigned leader who is given legitimate power to influence others.*

leadership of the group will have gained legitimate power on which to base influence attempts. In one case, the authority comes from outside the group; in the other case, it comes from inside the group.

During its work life, a group may have only one formal leader, but several people may play leadership roles. **Informal leaders** are members of the group whose authority to influence stems from the power they gain through their interactions in the group. Informal leaders do not have legitimate power; rather, their influence attempts are usually based on expert or referent power.

How Members Gain and Maintain Informal Leadership

According to research by Ernest Bormann (1990), members who become informal leaders of a group are not really selected. Rather, they are the members who emerge through a two-step elimination process. During the first step of the process, members form crude impressions about one another based on early interactions. During this phase, members who do not demonstrate the commitment or skillfulness necessary to fulfill leadership roles are eliminated. Among those who are less likely to emerge as leaders are those who do not participate (either due to shyness or indifference); those who are overly strong and bossy in their opinions and positions; those who are perceived to be uninformed, less intelligent, or unskilled; and those with irritating interpersonal styles.

During the second phase, those who are still acceptable to the group may vie for power. Sometimes one contender will become an informal leader because the group faces a crisis that this member recognizes and is better able to help the group remedy than others are. At other times, a contender may become an informal leader because one or more members of the group have come to trust this person and openly support influence attempts made by that contender.

In some groups, one of the contenders will eventually be recognized by most members of the group as the informal leader. In other groups, two or more contenders may comfortably share informal leadership by specializing and engaging in complementary behavior. For example, one leader might be particularly attuned to group relationships and may use influence to keep conflict at healthy levels. The other leader may be skilled at keeping the group on track and moving through the agenda during meetings. In general, however, the members of the group will be more susceptible to the informal leadership of those contenders who provide appropriate combinations of procedural, task, and relationship maintaining influences.

Students are often interested in how they can exert leadership in a group. Because leadership is demonstrated through communication behaviors, following these recommendations can help you gain influence.

1. **Actively participate in discussions.** When members do not participate, others may view them as disinterested or uninformed. Indicate your interest and commitment to the group by participating in group discussions.

---

informal leaders–*members of the group whose authority to influence stems from the power they gain through their interactions in the group.*

OBSERVE & ANALYZE
Journal Activity

Emerging Roles and Leadership

Identify a recently formed group of at least five members to which you belong where informal leaders have emerged. In your Student Workbook under Journal Activity 11.2, identify the roles that each member of the group seems to play. Remember, a member may perform more than one role. Then answer the following questions: Is there a formal leader? Who are the informal leaders? How did they emerge? What is it that each does that leads you to believe that person is fulfilling leadership functions? Why were each of the other members of the group eliminated from informal leadership? Suppose the goal of your group was changed. In what way might this affect the leadership of your group?

2. **Come to group meetings prepared.** Uninformed members rarely achieve leadership, whereas those who demonstrate expertise gain the power to influence us.

3. **Actively listen to the ideas and opinions of others.** Because leadership requires analyzing what a group needs, the leader must understand the ideas and needs of members. When you actively listen, you also demonstrate your willingness to consider a point of view different from your own. We are more likely to accept influence attempts when we believe the person really understands us.

4. **Avoid stating overly strong opinions.** When other members of the group perceive that someone is inflexible, they are less likely to accept that person as a leader.

5. **Actively manage meaning.** During problem solving, members can become unclear about what is happening. As a result, they experience uncertainty. If you have a mental map or framework that can help the group clarify and understand issues it is facing, you can use it to influence the group. Gail T. Fairhurst has explored how leaders manage meaning in groups; she calls this process **framing**. You can read about her work in the Spotlight on Scholars.

framing–*managing meaning in a group.*

SPOTLIGHT ON SCHOLARS

Gail T. Fairhurst, Professor of Communication, University of Cincinnati, on Leadership in Work Organizations

According to Gail T. Fairhurst, who has been studying organizational communication throughout her career, leadership is not a trait possessed by only some people, nor is it a simple set of behaviors that can be learned and then used in any situation. Rather, Fairhurst's research has convinced her that leadership is the process of creating social reality by managing the meanings that are assigned to certain behaviors, activities, programs, and events.

Further, she believes leadership is best understood as a relational process.

Fairhurst's current work is focused on how organizational leaders frame issues for their members. Framing is the process of managing meaning by selecting and highlighting some aspects of a subject while excluding others. When we communicate our frames to others, we manage meaning because we are asserting that our interpretation of the subject should be taken as "real" over other possible interpretations. How leaders choose to verbally frame events at work is one way that leaders influence workers' and others' perceptions.

Framing is especially important when the organization experiences change, such as downsizing. To reduce uncertainty during times of change, members of the organization seek to understand what the change means to them personally and to the way they work in the organization. Leaders are expected to help members understand what is happening and what it means. By framing the change, leaders select and highlight some features of the change while downplaying others, providing a lens through which organizational members can understand what the change means.

In *The Art of Framing* (with Robert A. Sarr), Fairhurst says that leaders use five language forms or devices to frame information: metaphors, jargon or catch phrases, contrast, spin, and stories. Metaphors show how the change is similar to something that is already familiar. For instance, leaders may frame downsizing with weight and prizefighting metaphors, suggesting that the organization is "flabby and needs to get down to a better fighting weight so it can compete effectively." Jargon or catch phrases are similar to metaphors because they help us understand the change in language with which we are already familiar. Leaders may use jargon and catch phrases with words such as "lean and mean." Contrast frames help us understand what the change is by first seeing what it is not. Leaders may use contrast frames by suggesting that the downsizing "is not an attempt to undermine the union, it is simply an attempt to remain competitive." Spin frames cast the change in either a positive or negative light. Leaders may use a positive spin frame by pointing out that the company will not use forced layoffs but will instead use early retirements and natural attrition to reduce the size of the workforce. Story frames make the change seem more real by serving as an example, such as recounting the success of another well-known company that used the same strategy.

Fairhurst has also studied how the meaning of a change is continually reframed as members of the organization work out the specifics of how to implement the change. She analyzed the transcripts of tape-recorded conversations between managers and their subordinates during times when a company was undergoing a significant change in the way it worked. Her analysis has revealed that employees' reactions to change are often framed as "predicaments" or "problems," showing that they are confused or unclear about the change. Sometimes employees feel that what they are being asked to do is in conflict with the goals of the change. In response, the leader might counter the employee predicament by using one of several reframes—for example, "personalization." Using personalization, a leader might point out the specific behaviors the member needs to adopt to be in line with the change. Fairhurst suggests that such reframing techniques help members understand what to do next to bring about the change.

Fairhurst's experience in analyzing the real conversations of managers and subordinates indicates that many of those in organizational leadership roles are not very good at framing and, as a result, may need to be trained to develop mental models that they can draw on to be more effective during their day-to-day interactions with workers. For complete citations of many of Fairhurst's publications, see the references list at the end of this book.

Fairhurst has served a five-year term as Head of the Department of Communication Arts at the University of Cincinnati. Since then, she has resumed her role as an active member of the faculty. In addition to teaching courses in organizational communication at both the graduate and undergraduate levels, Fairhurst works with the Center for Environmental Communication Studies, a research and consulting organization she helped found.

Gender Differences in Emerging Leaders

A question that has generated considerable research is whether the gender of a leader has any effect on a group's acceptance of leadership. Some research suggests that gender does affect group acceptance, but not because women lack the necessary skills. A persistent research finding is that messages are evaluated differently depending on the source of the message (Aries, 1998, p. 65). Thus, the same behavior may be perceived differently depending on whether it is performed by a woman or a man. For example, a group member says, "I think we are belaboring the point and should move on." If the speaker is a woman, the comment may well be perceived as bossy, dominating, and critical. If a man makes the same comment, he is more likely to be perceived as being insightful and task-oriented. One problem women face is that their efforts to show leadership may be differently interpreted.

Moreover, gender-role stereotypes can lead to devaluing cooperative and supportive behaviors that many women use quite skillfully. Yet, as Sally Helgesen (1990) points out, many female leaders are successful because they respond to people and their problems with flexibility and because they are able to break down barriers between people at all levels of the organization.

Fortunately, changes in perception are occurring as the notion of "effective" leadership changes. Patricia Andrews (1992) supports this conclusion, noting that it is more important to consider the unique character of a group and the skills of the person serving as leader than the gender of the leader (p. 90). She goes on to show that a complex interplay of factors (including how much power the leader has) influences effectiveness more than gender does. As Jurma and Wright (1990) have pointed out, research studies have shown that men and women are equally capable of leading task-oriented groups (p. 110).

Moreover, by the mid-1990s, studies were showing that task-relevant communication was the only significant predictor of who would emerge as leaders, regardless of gender. Katherine Hawkins's (1995) study noted no significant gender differences in the production of task-relevant communication. Such communication, it seems, is the key to emergent leadership in task-oriented group interaction—for either gender.

Leading Group Meetings

How many times have you complained that a meeting you attended was a waste of time? Good group meetings do not just happen. Rather, they are intentionally planned, facilitated, and followed up. One of the principal duties that both formal and informal leaders perform is to plan and run effective group meetings. Here are some guidelines that can help leaders make meetings productive.

Before the Meeting

1. **Prepare the agenda.** An agenda is an organized outline of the items that need to be covered during a meeting. Items for the agenda come from reviewing the minutes of the last meeting to determine what the group

agreed to take as next steps and from new issues that have arisen since the last meeting. Effective leaders make sure the agenda is appropriate for the length of the meeting. Figure 11.1 shows an agenda for a group meeting to decide which one of three courses to offer over the Internet next semester.

2. **Decide who should attend the meeting.** In most cases, all members of a group will attend meetings. Occasionally, one or more members of the group may not need to attend a particular meeting but may only need to be informed of the outcomes of the meeting.

March 1, 2001

To: Campus computer discussion group
From: Janelle Smith
Re: Agenda for discussion group meeting

Date: March 8, 2001
Place: Student Union, Conference Room A
Time: 3:00 p.m. to 4:30 p.m. (Please be prompt.)

Meeting Objectives:

We will familiarize ourselves with each of three courses that have been proposed for Internet-based delivery next semester.

We will evaluate each course against the criteria we developed last month.

We will use a consensus decision process to determine which of the three courses to offer.

Agenda for Group Discussion:

Review of Philosophy 141
    Report by Justin on Philosophy 141 proposal
    Committee questions
    Comparison of PHIL 141 to criteria

Review of Art History 336
    Report by Marique on Art History 336 proposal
    Committee questions
    Comparison of ARTH 336 to criteria

Review of Communication 235
    Report by Kathryn on Communication 235
    Committee questions
    Comparison of COMM 235 to criteria

Consensus building discussion and decision.
    Which proposals fit the criteria?
    Are there non-criteria-related factors to consider?
    Which proposal is more acceptable to all members?

Discussion of next steps and task assignments.

Set date of next meeting.

Figure 11.1
Agenda for Internet course committee.

3. **Arrange an appropriate location and meeting time.** Be sure that the location has all the equipment and supplies the group will need to work effectively. This may include arranging for audiovisual equipment, computers, and other specialized equipment. Groups become less effective in long meetings, and ideally a meeting should last no longer than ninety minutes. If a meeting must be planned for a longer period of time, schedule hourly breaks to avoid fatigue.

4. **Distribute the agenda.** The agenda should be in the hands of attendees several days before the meeting. Unless group members get an agenda ahead of time, they will not be able to prepare for the meeting.

5. **Speak with each participant prior to the meeting.** It is important to understand members' positions and personal goals. Spending time preworking issues helps the leader anticipate conflicts that are likely to emerge and plan how to manage them so that the group makes effective decisions and maintains cohesiveness.

During the Meeting

1. **Review and modify the agenda.** Begin the meeting by reviewing the agenda and modifying it based on members' suggestions. Because things can change between the time an agenda is distributed and when the meeting is held, reviewing the agenda ensures that the group is working on items that are still important and relevant. Reviewing the agenda also gives members a chance to control what is to be discussed.

2. **Monitor roles members assume and consciously play needed roles that are unfilled by others.** The role of the leader during a discussion is to provide the task or procedural direction and relationship management that the group lacks. Leaders need to maintain awareness of what specific roles are needed by the group at a specific time. When other group members are assuming the necessary roles, the leader need do nothing. But when there is need for a particular role and members are not assuming that role, the leader should perform the necessary behaviors. For example, if the leader notices that some people are talking more than their fair share and that no one else is trying to draw out quieter members, the leader should assume the gatekeeper role and ask reluctant members to comment on the discussion.

3. **Monitor the time so that the group stays on schedule.** It is easy for a group to get bogged down in a discussion. Although another group member may serve as expediter, it is the leader's responsibility to make sure the group stays on schedule.

4. **Monitor conflicts and intervene as needed.** A healthy level of conflict should be encouraged in the group so that issues are fully examined. But if the conflict level becomes dysfunctional, the leader may need to mediate so that relationships are not unduly strained.

5. **Periodically check to see if the group is ready to make a decision.** The leader of the group should listen for agreement and move the group into its formal decision process when the leader senses that discussion is no longer adding insight.

6. **Implement the group's decision rules.** The leader is responsible for overseeing that the decision-making rule the group has agreed to is used. If the group is deciding by consensus, the leader must make sure that all members feel that the chosen alternative is one that they can support. If the group is deciding by majority rule, the leader calls for the vote and tallies the results.

7. **Before ending the meeting, summarize decisions.** To bring closure to the meeting and to make sure that each member leaving the meeting is clear about what has been accomplished, the leader should summarize what has happened in the meeting, reiterate task responsibilities assigned to members, and review the next steps that have been planned.

8. **Ask the group to decide if and when another meeting is needed.** Ongoing groups should be careful not to meet just for the sake of meeting. Leaders should clarify with members when, and if, future meetings are necessary. The overall purposes of future meetings will dictate the agenda that will need to be prepared.

Leaders need to maintain awareness of the specific roles that are needed by the group at a specific time.

Michael Newman/PhotoEdit, Inc.

Meeting Follow-up

1. **Review the meeting outcomes and process.** A good leader learns how to be more effective by reflecting on and analyzing how well the previous meeting went. Leaders need to think about whether the meeting accomplished its goals and whether group cohesion was improved or damaged in the process.

2. **Prepare and distribute a summary of meeting outcomes.** Although some groups have a member who serves at the recorder and who distributes minutes, many groups rely on their leaders. A written record of what was agreed to, accomplished, and next steps serve to remind group members of the work they have to do. If the group has a recorder, the leader should check to make sure that minutes are distributed in a timely manner.

3. **Repair damaged relationships through informal conversations.** If the debate during the meeting has been heated, it is likely that some people have damaged their relationships with others or left the meeting angry or hurt. Leaders can help repair relationships by seeking out these participants and talking with them. Through empathetic listening, leaders can soothe hurt feelings and spark a recommitment to the group.

4. **Follow up with members to see how they are progressing on items assigned to them.** When participants have been assigned specific task responsibilities, the leader should check with them to see if they have encountered any problems in completing those tasks.

Evaluating Group Effectiveness

There is an old saying that goes, "A camel is a horse built by a committee." Although this saying is humorous, for some groups it is also true. If we are to avoid ending up with camels when we want horses, we need to understand how to assess a group's effectiveness and how to improve group processes based on those evaluations. Groups can be evaluated on the quality of the decision, the quality of role taking, and the quality of leadership.

The Decision

The questionnaire in Figure 11.2 provides one method for evaluating the quality of a group's decision based on three major aspects of groups: group characteristics, member relationships, and problem-solving ability.

That a group meets to discuss an issue does not necessarily mean that it will arrive at a decision. As foolish as it may seem, some groups thrash away for hours only to adjourn without having reached a conclusion. Of course, some groups discuss such serious problems that a decision cannot be made without

Rate the group as a whole on each of the following questions using this scale:
1 = always, 2 = often, 3 = sometimes, 4 = rarely, 5 = never.

Group Characteristics

_____ 1. Did the group have a clearly defined goal to which most members were committed?

_____ 2. Did the group's size fit the tasks required to meet its goals?

_____ 3. Was group member diversity sufficient to ensure that important viewpoints were expressed?

_____ 4. Did group cohesiveness aid in task accomplishment?

_____ 5. Did group norms help accomplish goals and maintain relationships?

_____ 6. Was the physical setting conducive to accomplishing the work?

Member Relationships

_____ 1. Did members feel valued and respected by others?

_____ 2. Were members comfortable interacting with others?

_____ 3. Did members balance speaking time so that all members participated?

_____ 4. Were conflicts seen as positive experiences?

_____ 5. Did members like and enjoy each other?

Group Problem Solving

_____ 1. Did the group take time to define its problem?

_____ 2. Was high-quality information presented to help the group understand the problem?

_____ 3. Did the group develop criteria before suggesting solutions?

_____ 4. Were the criteria discussed sufficiently and based on all of the information available?

_____ 5. Did the group use effective brainstorming techniques to develop a comprehensive list of creative solution alternatives?

_____ 6. Did the group fairly and thoroughly compare each alternative to all solution criteria?

_____ 7. Did the group follow its decision rules in choosing among alternatives that met the criteria?

_____ 8. Did the group arrive at a decision that members agreed to support?

Figure 11.2
Form for evaluating group decisions.

several meetings. In such cases, it is important that the group adjourn with a clear understanding of what the next step will be. When a group "finishes" its work without arriving at some decision, however, the result is likely to be frustration and disillusionment.

Individual Participation and Role Behavior

Although a group will struggle without good leadership, it may not be able to function at all without members who are willing and able to meet the task, maintenance, and procedural functions of the group. The assessment form in Figure 11.3 provides a simple checklist that can be used for evaluating each group member.

Name of Participant: _____

For the participant named above, on each of the following rate the participant on a scale of 1 to 5: 1 = excellent, 2 = good, 3 = average, 4 = fair, 5 = poor.

Meeting Behavior

_____ 1. Prepared and knowledgeable

_____ 2. Contributed ideas and opinions

_____ 3. Actively listened to the ideas of others

_____ 4. Politely voiced disagreement

_____ 5. Completed between-meeting assigned tasks

Performance of Task-Oriented Roles

_____ 1. Acted as information or opinion giver

_____ 2. Acted as information seeker

_____ 3. Acted as analyzer

Performance of Procedural Roles

_____ 1. Acted as expediter

_____ 2. Acted as recorder

_____ 3. Acted as gatekeeper

Performance of Maintenance Roles

_____ 1. Acted as supporter

_____ 2. Acted as tension reliever

_____ 3. Acted as harmonizer

_____ 4. Acted as interpreter

Avoidance of Self-Centered Roles

_____ 1. Avoided acting as aggressor

_____ 2. Avoided acting as joker

_____ 3. Avoided acting as withdrawer

_____ 4. Avoided acting as monopolizer

Qualitative Analysis

Based on the quantitative analysis above, write a two- to five-paragraph analysis of the person's participation. Be sure to give specific examples of the person's behavior to back up your conclusions.

Figure 11.3

Form for evaluating individual participation.

Leadership

Some group discussions are leaderless, although no discussion should be without leadership. If there is an appointed leader—and most groups have one—evaluation can focus on that individual. If the group is truly leaderless, the evaluation should consider attempts at leadership by various members or focus on the apparent leader who emerges from the group. Figure 11.4 contains a simple checklist for evaluating group leadership.

TEST YOUR COMPETENCE

Analyzing Participation

Divide into groups of about four to six. Each group should be given or should select a problem to solve that requires research. After researching the issue, each group then has approximately thirty to forty minutes of class time to hold a problem-solving discussion. While group A is discussing, members of group B should observe and, after the discussion, analyze the proceedings. To practice using the three assessment forms, one-third of the observers should do a decision analysis (Figure 11.2); one-third should do an individual member analysis (Figure 11.3); and one-third should do a leadership analysis (Figure 11.4). After the discussions, the observers should share their observations with the group. In the next class period, group B discusses and group A observes and analyzes.

   Problems may relate to campus issues such as "What should be done to improve parking (advising, registration) on campus?" or community concerns such as "How can citizens be encouraged to recycle (vote in local elections, avoid littering)?"

Was there a formal group leader? Yes No
If yes, name this person: _____
Who were the informal leaders of the group?
   a. _____
   b. _____
   c. _____
Which of these leaders was most influential in helping the group meet its goals?
Rate this leader on each of the following questions using a scale of 1 to 5:
1 = always, 2 = often, 3 = sometimes, 4 = rarely, 5 = never.
_____   1. Demonstrated commitment to the group and its goals.
_____   2. Actively listened to ideas and opinions of others.
_____   3. Adapted his or her behavior to the immediate needs of the group.
_____   4. Avoided stating overly strong opinions.
_____   5. Managed meaning for the group by framing issues and ideas.
_____   6. Was prepared for all meetings.
_____   7. Kept the group on task and on schedule.
_____   8. Made sure that conflicts were handled effectively.
_____   9. Implemented the group's decision rules effectively.
_____   10. Worked to repair damaged relationships.
_____   11. Followed up after meetings to see how members were progressing
                 on assignments.

Figure 11.4
Form for evaluating leadership.

Y ou know, Sue, we're going to be in deep trouble if the group doesn't support McGowan's resolution about dues reform."

"Well, we'll just have to see to it that all the arguments in favor of that resolution are heard, but in the end it's the group's decision."

"That's very democratic of you, Sue, but you know that if it doesn't pass you're likely to be out on your tail."

"That may be, Heather, but I don't see what I can do about it."

"You don't want to see. First, right now the group respects you. If you would just apply a little pressure on a couple of the members, you'd get what you want."

"What do you mean?"

"Look, this is a good cause. You've got something on just about every member of the group. Take a couple of members aside and let them know that this is payoff time. I think you'll see that some key folks will see it your way."

Heather may well have a point about how Sue can control the outcome. Should Sue follow Heather's advice? Why or why not?

Summary

When individuals interact in groups, they assume roles. A role is a specific pattern of behavior that a member of the group performs based on the expectations of others.

There are four types of roles: task-oriented roles, maintenance roles, procedural roles, and self-centered roles. Members select the roles they will play based on how roles fit with their personality, what is required of them by virtue of a position they hold, and what roles the group needs to have assumed that are not being played by other members. One role that is of particular importance to effective group functioning is the leadership role.

Leadership is the process of influencing members to accomplish goals. As such, leadership is a general role that includes providing whatever is needed by the group but missing in other members' behavior. Groups may have a single leader, but more commonly leadership is shared among group members. Groups may have both formal and informal leaders. Formal leaders have formal authority given to them either by some entity outside of the group or by the group members themselves. Informal leaders emerge during a two-stage process. Individuals who want to become recognized as informal leaders in a group should come to group meetings prepared, actively participate in discussions, actively listen to others, avoid appearing bossy or stating overly strong opinions, and manage the meaning for other participants by framing.

Both members and leaders can improve the effectiveness of the meetings they attend by premeeting preparations, during-meeting behaviors, and postmeeting activities.

Communicate! Online

Use your Communicate! CD-ROM for quick access to the electronic study resources that accompany this text. Included on your CD-ROM is access to InfoTrac College Edition, the World Wide Web, a demo of WebTutor for Communicate!, and the Communicate! Web site at the Wadsworth Communication Café. The Communicate! Web site offers chapter-by-chapter activities, quizzes, and a digital glossary.

Review the following key terms and complete the Self-Review for Group Communication featured on the next page at

http://communication.wadsworth.com/humancomm/verderber

Key Terms

aggressor (267)
analyzer (264)
expediter (266)
formal leader (271)
framing (273)
gatekeeper (266)
harmonizer (265)
informal leaders (272)

information or opinion giver (264)
information or opinion seeker (264)
interpreter (265)
joker (267)
leadership (271)
maintenance role (265)
minutes (266)
monopolizer (267)

procedural role (266)
recorder (266)
role (264)
self-centered role (267)
supporter (265)
task-related role (264)
tension reliever (265)
withdrawer (267)

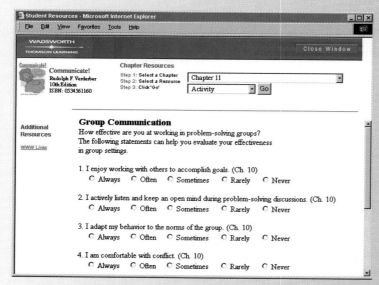

SELF-REVIEW

Group Communication from Chapters 10 and 11

How effective are you at working in problem-solving groups? The following statements can help you evaluate your effectiveness in group settings. Use this scale to assess the frequency with which you perform each behavior: 1 = always, 2 = often, 3 = sometimes, 4 = rarely, 5 = never.

_____ I enjoy working with others to accomplish goals. (Ch. 10)

_____ I actively listen and keep an open mind during problem-solving discussions. (Ch. 10)

_____ I adapt my behavior to the norms of the group. (Ch. 10)

_____ I am comfortable with conflict. (Ch. 10)

_____ I avoid performing self-centered roles in the group. (Ch. 11)

_____ I am equally adept at performing task-oriented, procedural, and maintenance roles in the group. (Ch. 11)

_____ I come to group meetings prepared. (Ch. 11)

_____ During group meetings, my active participation makes positive contributions to goal accomplishment and maintaining good relationships. (Ch. 11)

_____ After meetings, I complete tasks I have been assigned and review meeting notes and minutes. (Ch. 11)

To verify this self-analysis, have a friend or fellow group member complete this review for you. Based on what you have learned, select the group communication behavior you would most like to improve. Write a communication improvement plan similar to the sample goal statement in Chapter 1 (page 25).

You can complete this Self-Review online under Chapter 11: Activities on the Communicate! Web site at the Wadsworth Communication Café

http://communication.wadsworth.com/humancomm/verderber

Developing skill at public speaking is important to you. Why? Skill at public speaking is a form of empowerment. In the public arena, effective speakers are able to communicate information to people in ways that stimulate their interest and help them understand and remember. Good public speakers are also able to communicate information in ways that influence people's attitudes and behavior.

Moreover, in the work environment, effective speaking is necessary to move up the organizational ladder. From presenting oral reports and proposals to responding to questions or training coworkers, we all spend important time in speaking activities.

Still, many of us think that effective speakers are born not made—nothing could be further from the truth. Even Demosthenes—the great Athenian orator often cited as the prototype of brilliant speaking—was highly criticized as a speaker when he first entered public life. In fact, the time and effort he spent improving his speaking stands as a testament to the importance and value of hard work. The lesson to be learned? Effective public speaking is a learned activity.

To have the greatest chance of speaking effectively in any situation, you need to have a plan or strategy for achieving your goal. An effective speech plan is a product of five action steps that are explained in Chapters 12 through 16: (1) determine a specific speech goal that is adapted to your audience and occasion (Chapter 12); (2) gather and evaluate material for use in the speech (Chapter 13); (3) organize and develop material in a way that is best suited to your particular audience (Chapter 14); (4) develop a strategy for adapting material to your specific speech audience (Chapter 15); and (5) practice the speech (Chapter 16).

In the final two chapters, we consider additional skills related specifically to speeches intended to inform and to persuade.

IV

PUBLIC SPEAKING

OBJECTIVES

After you have read this chapter, you should be able to answer these questions:

- How do you brainstorm for topics?

- How do you compile audience data?

- How do you predict level of audience interest in, knowledge of, and attitude toward a topic?

- What are the key physical and psychological conditions affecting the speech?

- How do you test your speech goal?

12

Donna Montez is a marine biologist. She knows that her audience wants to hear her talk about marine biology, but she doesn't know what aspect of the topic would most interest her audience.

Ben Petrocelli is running for office, and he is going to give a speech to people living in the West End. His goal is to say something that will motivate these constituents to vote for him.

Dan Wong has been invited to speak to an assembly at his old inner-city high school. He thinks he may have a lot to say to these students coming up behind him, but most of all he wants them to understand the qualities a person needs to do well in college.

Ayanna Cartland is taking a public speaking class, and her first speech is scheduled for two weeks from tomorrow. As of today, she doesn't have the foggiest idea of what she is going to talk about.

Do any of these situations seem familiar? Donna has a general subject, but it is too broad for a single speech. Ben has identified his goal, but he doesn't know what topic will help him achieve it. Dan has isolated his most important message, but he must now figure out how best to present it to this audience. Then there is Ayanna. All she is sure of is that she must give a speech—soon!

Having an effective speech plan will help you solve all of these problems. An effective speech plan is a product of five action steps. In this chapter, we consider the first step: **Determine a specific speech goal that is adapted to your audience and occasion.** This involves selecting a topic from a subject area that is important to you and that you know something about, analyzing your audience and the speech setting, and finally, articulating your goal by determining the response you want from your audience. Although each task in the process is discussed separately, they do overlap and are sometimes accomplished in a different order.

Selecting a Topic from a Subject Area

In real-life settings, people are invited to give speeches because of their expertise on a particular subject, but selecting the best topic is often left in the hands of the speaker. What is the difference between a subject and a topic? A **subject** is a broad area of knowledge, such as the stock market, cognitive psychology, baseball, or the Middle East. A **topic** is some specific aspect of a subject. Thus, an authority on the subject of the stock market might be prepared to speak on such diverse topics as the nature of the New York Stock Exchange, the NASDAQ, investment strategies, or bull versus bear markets.

The goal of this section is to help you identify a suitable subject area and then select potential specific topics from that subject area.

Identifying Subjects

When you are asked (or required) to give a speech, use the same criteria for identifying subjects as those used by professional speakers. Start by identifying subject areas (1) that are important to you and (2) that you know something about. Then select suitable topics within those areas.

Subjects that meet these criteria probably include such things as your vocation (major, prospective profession, or current job), your hobbies or leisure activities, and special interests (social, economic, educational, or political concerns). Thus, if retailing is your actual or prospective vocation, tennis is your favorite activity, and problems of illiteracy, substance abuse, and toxic and non-toxic waste are your special concerns, then these are subject areas from which you could draw topics.

subject—*a broad area of knowledge, such as the stock market, cognitive psychology, baseball, or the Middle East.*

topic—*some specific aspect of a subject.*

Rob Lewine/The Stock Market

You will be a more effective speaker if you plan your speech carefully so that your goal is clear to your audience.

It is tempting to think, "Why not just talk about something I know an audience wants to hear about?" The reason for avoiding this temptation is that an audience chooses to listen to a speaker *because* of perceived expertise or insight on a particular subject. Even professional speakers can get in "over their heads" when they speak on subjects they know little about.

As an inexperienced speaker, it is especially important to choose topics in those subject areas in which you already have spent months or years developing expertise and insight.

Figure 12.1 contains subjects that students from just two classes listed for their major or vocation, hobby or interest, and issue or concern.

Brainstorming for Topics

Once you have identified your subject area, a few good topics may come to mind. But most of us need to list potential choices to draw from. To stimulate your thinking, try using a form of **brainstorming**. As we discussed in Chapter 10, this is a free-association procedure that generates as many ideas as possible.

To brainstorm for topics, divide a sheet of paper into three columns. Using the column headings in Figure 12.1 as your guide, write one subject area at the

brainstorming–*a free-association procedure that generates as many ideas as possible.*

Figure 12.1
Student subject lists.

Major or Vocational interest	Hobby or Activity	Issue or Concern
communication	soccer	crime
disc jockey	weight lifting	governmental ethics
marketing	music	environment
public relations	travel	media impact on society
elementary teaching	photography	censorship
sales	mountain biking	same-sex marriage
reporting	hiking	taxes
hotel management	volleyball	presidential politics
motherhood	advertising	cloning
fashion design	genealogy	global warming
law	backpacking	child abuse
human resources	horseback riding	road rage
computer programming	sailing	illiteracy
nurse	swimming	effects of smoking
doctor	magic	women's rights
politics	gambling	abortion

Brainstorming for Topics

In your Student Workbook under Activity 12.1, divide the page into three columns. Label column one with your major or vocation, such as "Art History"; label column two with a hobby or an activity, such as "Chess"; and label column three with a concern or an issue, such as "Water pollution." Working on one column at a time, brainstorm a list of at least twenty related topics for each column (see Figure 12.2).

Check one topic in each column that has special meaning to you or that seems particularly appropriate for your classroom audience. Then select one topic from these three for your first speech.

top of each column. Work for at least a few minutes on each column, brainstorming topics for each subject area. Although you may not finish all the columns in one sitting, try to list at least twenty items in each column before you begin evaluating them. When the list under each column is complete, read the entries and check the topics that strike you as particularly important or that might be of special interest to your audience. For instance, a person who listed the subject area of "magic" as his or her hobby might list the topics shown in Figure 12.2.

Why does brainstorming help? Brainstorming enables you to take advantage of a basic commonsense principle. It is easier to select a correct answer to a multiple-choice question than to think of the answer to the same question without the choices. So too, it is easier to select a topic from a list than to come up with a topic out of the blue. Instead of asking "What should I talk about?" ask yourself "What is the topic under each subject heading that is most compelling to me?" When you start with a subject area of expertise and interest, you often can list twenty, thirty, fifty, or even more related topics.

Hobby: Magic

tricks	Houdini	secrets	card tricks
paraphernalia	Copperfield	vanishing	animals
staging	training	trap doors	dexterity
sleight-of-hand	Magic Castle	rigging	
displacement	vocabulary	costs	
magicians	dangers	staging	

Figure 12.2
Brainstorming.

Analyzing the Audience

Because speeches are given for a particular audience, early in your preparation process you need to conduct an analysis of your prospective audience. **Audience analysis** is the study of the specific audience for your speech. It includes (1) gathering essential audience demographic data to determine in what ways a majority of audience members are alike and (2) making predictions of audience level of interest in, knowledge of, and attitudes toward you and your topic. The results of this analysis can guide you in selecting supporting material and in organizing and presenting your speech in ways that adapt to that audience.

audience analysis—*the study of the specific audience for a speech.*

Kinds of Audience Data Needed

The first step is to gather essential audience demographic data to determine in what ways a majority of audience members are alike. The specific categories in which you need accurate data are age, education, gender, occupation, income, culture, geographic uniqueness, and group affiliation.

Age Data needed are the average age and the age range of your audience.

Education Data needed are whether audience members have high school, college, or postcollege education or whether their education levels are mixed.

Gender Data needed are whether your audience will be primarily male, primarily female, or fairly well balanced.

Jeff Greenberg/PhotoEdit

What challenges would this audience pose for a speaker running for city council?

Occupation Data needed are whether the majority of your audience have a single occupation, such as nursing, banking, drill-press operating, teaching, or sales.

Income Data needed are whether the average income level of the audience is high, low, or average.

Culture Data needed are whether your audience is alike ethnically, including race, religion, and nationality.

Geographic uniqueness Data needed are whether audience members are from the same state, city, or neighborhood.

Group affiliation Data needed are whether the majority of audience members belong to the same social or fraternal group.

Ways of Gathering Data

Now that we have considered the kinds of audience data you need, let's consider three ways you can gather that information.

1. **You can gather data through observation.** If you are at all familiar with members of your audience (as you are likely to be with members of your classroom audience), you can get much of the significant data about them from personal observation. For instance, from being in class for even a couple of sessions, you will have a good idea of class members' approximate age, the ratio of men to women, and their racial makeup. As you listen to them talk, you will learn more about their interest in, knowledge of, and attitudes about many issues.

2. **You can gather data by questioning the person who scheduled your speech.** When you are invited to speak, ask your contact person to supply as much audience data as possible. Even if the information is not as specific as you would like, it will still be useful. Be especially sure to ask for the kind of data that will be likely to be most important for your topic. For instance, you may be speaking on a topic for which audience education level is especially important.

3. **You can make intelligent guesses about audience demographics.** If you cannot get information in any other way, you will have to make informed guesses based on such indirect information as the general makeup of the people who live in a specific community or the kinds of people who are likely to attend a speech on your topic.

Using Data to Predict Audience Reactions

The next step in audience analysis is to use the data you have collected to predict the audience's potential interest in, knowledge of, and attitudes toward you and your topic. These predictions form a basis for the development of your speech strategy, which we will consider in greater detail in Chapter 15, "Adapting Verbally and Visually."

COMMUNICATE!
Using Technology

**Attitude Toward
Your Topic**

There are many organizations that poll public opinion on topics. If you have no idea about how your specific audience might react to your topic, you may be able to find some idea of general attitudes by accessing public opinion polls. The following Web sites are good places to look for opinion polls:

http://www.Washingtonpost.com (Click "OnPolitics," then "Polls")
http://www.pollingreport.com
http://www.gallup.com

Audience interest Your first goal is to predict how interested the audience is likely to be in learning about your topic. For instance, suppose you are planning to give a speech on cholesterol to your classroom audience. You can predict that you will have to build audience interest. Why? For most college-age students, the cholesterol–heart attack connection is not meaningful.

Audience understanding Your second goal is to predict whether the audience has sufficient background to understand your information. For instance, for a speech on big band music or folk music, an older audience is likely to have better background knowledge than a younger audience. However, for a speech on rap music, a younger audience is likely to have better background knowledge than an older audience.

Audience attitude toward you as speaker Your third goal is to predict your audience's attitude toward you. Your success in informing or persuading an audience is likely to depend on whether it perceives you to be a credible source of information. **Credibility** is based on whether a person seems to be knowledgeable (having the necessary information to give this speech), trustworthy (being honest, dependable, and ethical), and personable (showing enthusiasm, warmth, friendliness, and concern for members of the audience).

credibility—whether the audience perceives a speaker to be knowledgeable, trustworthy, and personable.

Checklist: Audience Analysis

Data

1. The audience education level is ____ high school ____ college ____ post-college.

2. The age range is from ____ to ____ . The average age is about ____ .

3. The audience is approximately ____ percent male and ____ percent female.

4. My estimate of the income level of the audience is ____ below average ____ average ____ above average.

5. The audience is basically ____ the same race ____ a mixture of races.

6. The audience is basically ____ the same religion ____ a mixture of religions.

7. The audience is basically ____ the same nationality ____ a mixture of nationalities.

8. The audience is basically from ____ the same state ____ the same city ____ the same neighborhood ____ different areas.

Predictions

1. Audience interest in this topic is likely to be ____ high ____ moderate ____ low, because _____ .

2. Audience understanding of the topic will be ____ great ____ moderate ____ little, because _____ .

3. Audience attitude toward me as speaker is likely to be ____ positive ____ neutral ____ negative, because _____ .

4. Audience attitude toward my topic will be ____ positive ____ neutral ____ negative, because _____ .

OBSERVE & ANALYZE
Journal Activity

Analyzing Your Audience

In your Student Workbook under Activity 12.2, complete the audience analysis checklist shown in Figure 12.3.

1. Next to the second heading, Predictions, write the topic you plan to use for your first speech.

2. Fill in the checklist, including both data about your classroom audience and predictions about their reactions to your topic.

3. Save the results. You will use the data from this checklist to help you determine a strategy for adapting to your audience.

Figure 12.3
Audience analysis checklist.

Audience attitude toward your topic Your final goal is to predict your audience's attitude toward your topic. This assessment is especially important if your goal is to attempt to change a belief or move the audience to action. Audience attitudes are usually expressed by opinions. Except for polling the audience, there is no way to be sure about your assessment, but you can make reasonably accurate estimates based on demographic knowledge. For instance, a meeting of the local Right-to-Life chapter will look at abortion differently than will a meeting of NOW (National Organization for Women). The more data you have about your audience and the more experience you have in analyzing audiences, the better are your chances of accurately judging audience attitudes.

Considering the Setting

setting—the location for a speech.

The location for your speech, or the **setting,** provides you with guidelines for both meeting audience expectations and determining the tone of the speech. Because your class meets regularly at the same time under the same conditions, your consideration of setting is not much of a challenge. For speeches under other conditions, however, you will need to spend time considering the setting. Let's review the questions about the setting that are most important to answer.

1. **How large will the audience be?** If you are anticipating a small audience (perhaps up to fifty people or so), you will be close enough to all of them to talk in a normal voice and feel free to move about. In contrast, if you anticipate a large audience, you will probably need a microphone, and you will be less likely to be able to move about.

2. **When will the speech be given?** A speech given early in the morning requires a different approach from one given right after lunch or in the evening. If a speech is scheduled after a meal, for instance, the audience may be lethargic, mellow, or even on the verge of sleep. As a result, you may want to insert more "attention getters" (examples, illustrations, and stories) to counter potential lapses of attention.

3. **Where in the program does the speech occur?** If you are the only speaker or the featured speaker, you have an obvious advantage—you are the focal point of audience attention. In the classroom, however, and in other settings where there are many speeches, your place on the schedule may affect how you are received. For example, if you go first, you may need to "warm up" the listeners and be prepared to meet the distraction of a few audience members strolling in late. If you speak last, you must counter the tendency of the audience to be weary from listening to several speeches.

4. **What is the time limit for the speech?** The time limit for classroom speeches is usually quite short, so you will want to make sure that you are not packing too much information into your speech. "Three Major Causes of Envi-

A. Ramey/Stock, Boston, PictureQuest

In planning your speech, use the setting and the occasion to guide you in selecting your content and tone.

ronmental Degradation" can be presented in five minutes, but "A History of the Human Impact on the Environment" cannot. Problems with time limits are not peculiar to classroom speeches. Any speech setting includes actual or implied time limits. For example, a Sunday sermon may be limited to twenty to thirty minutes.

5. **Are there special expectations for the speech?** Every occasion provides some special expectations. At an Episcopalian Sunday service, for example, the congregation expects the minister's sermon to have a religious theme. For classroom speeches, one of the major expectations is meeting the assignment. Whether the speech assignment is defined by purpose (to inform or to persuade), by type (expository or descriptive), or by subject (book analysis or current event), your goal should reflect the nature of that assignment.

6. **Where will the speech be given?** Because classrooms vary in size, lighting, seating arrangements, and the like, consider the factors that may affect your presentation. In a long, narrow room, you may need to speak louder than usual to reach the back row. In a darkened room, make sure the lights are on and that the blinds or shades are open to bring in as much light as possible.

   Venues outside of school settings offer even greater variations in conditions. Ask for specific information about seating capacity, shape, number of rows, nature of lighting, existence of a speaking stage or platform, distance between speaker and first row, and so on, before you speak.

7. **What equipment is necessary to give the speech?** For some speeches, you may need a microphone, a chalkboard, or an overhead or slide projector

> **Checklist: Occasion and Setting**
>
> 1. Where will the speech be given? _____
> 2. How large will the audience be? _____
> 3. When will the speech be given? _____
> 4. Where in the program does the speech occur? _____
> 5. What is the time limit for the speech? _____
> 6. What are the expectations for the speech? _____
> 7. What equipment is necessary to give the speech? _____

Figure 12.4
Setting checklist.

OBSERVE & ANALYZE
Journal Activity

Analyzing the Occasion and Setting

In your Student Workbook under Activity 12.3, complete the occasion and setting checklist shown in Figure 12.4.

1. Answer the questions about the occasion and setting for your first speech.

2. Save the results. You will use the data from this checklist to help you determine strategies for adapting to your audience.

general goal–*the intent of the speech (to entertain, to inform, or to persuade).*

and screen. In most instances, speakers have some kind of speaking stand, but it is wise not to count on it. If the person who has contacted you to speak has any control over the setting, be sure to explain what you need—but always have alternative plans in case what you have asked for is unavailable. It is frustrating to plan a slide presentation, for example, and then discover that there is no place to plug in the projector!

Writing the Speech Goal

Once you have chosen your topic and analyzed the audience and setting for your speech, you continue the preparation process by identifying the general goal you are hoping to achieve and then writing a specific speech goal.

General Goal

The **general goal** is the intent of your speech. Most speeches can be classified as those that are meant to entertain, inform, or persuade. Because speech is a complex act that may affect an audience in different ways, these headings are useful only to show that in any public speaking act one overriding general goal is likely to predominate. Consider the following examples.

Jay Leno's opening monologue on *The Tonight Show* is intended to entertain, even though it may include material that is perceived as informative or persuasive. Likewise, a political candidate's speech is intended to persuade listeners to vote for him or her even though it may include some material that is perceived as amusing or informative.

Although some public speakers give speeches solely for the purpose of entertaining, in this text we focus attention on informative and persuasive speeches, the kinds of speeches most of us give in our daily lives.

Specific Goal

The **specific goal,** or specific purpose, is a single statement that specifies the exact response the speaker wants from the audience. For a speech on the topic "Evaluating Diamonds," the goal could be stated as "I would like the audience to understand the four major criteria for evaluating a diamond." For a speech on "Supporting the United Way," the goal could be stated as "I would like the audience to donate money to the United Way." In the first example, the goal is informative: The speaker wants the audience to understand the criteria. In the second example, the goal is persuasive: The speaker wants the audience to donate money. Figure 12.5 gives further examples of specific goals that clearly state how each speaker wants the audience to react to a particular topic.

Now let us consider a step-by-step procedure for completing the specific speech goal.

specific goal—a single statement that specifies the exact response the speaker wants from the audience.

1. **Write a first draft of your speech goal that includes the infinitive phrase that articulates the response you want from your audience.** Suppose Julia begins her first draft on the topic of Illiteracy by writing, "I want my audience to understand illiteracy." With this goal statement, Julia recognizes that her goal is to have the *audience* understand something. Julia now has the start of an informative speech goal. Suppose instead, she had started, "I want to explain illiteracy." Although it appears to be a reasonable goal, this statement puts the emphasis on the *speaker* rather than on audience response. Make sure that the specific goal begins with an expression of desired audience response.

Entertainment Goals

I would like my audience to be amused by my portrayal of an over-the-hill football player.

I would like my audience to laugh at my experience as a waiter.

Informative Goals

I would like my audience to understand the characteristics of the five common types of coastlines.

I would like my audience to understand the three basic forms of mystery stories.

Persuasive Goals

I would like my audience to believe that drug testing by business and industry should be prohibited.

I would like my audience to join Amnesty International.

Figure 12.5
Specific speech goals.

2. **Revise your first draft until you have written a complete sentence that specifies the nature of the audience response.** The draft, "I want my audience to understand illiteracy," is a good start, but "understand illiteracy" is not clear. Exactly "what" about illiteracy is it that Julia wants her audience to understand? As Julia works with the wording, she amends it to read, "I would like the audience to understand three aspects of the problem of illiteracy." This draft is a complete sentence statement of her speech goal. Notice that it includes the desired audience response, "to understand three aspects of illiteracy."

   Now the question becomes, does the phrase "understand three aspects of illiteracy" fully capture what she will be talking about? Is Julia concerned with illiteracy in general? Or illiteracy in a specific situation? As Julia thinks about it, she sees that what she really wants to focus on is how illiteracy hurts people who are trying to function well at work. With this in mind, she revises the goal by writing, "I would like the audience to understand three aspects of the problem of illiteracy *in the workplace.*" Now she has the goal limited not only in number but also in situation.

3. **Make sure that the goal contains only one idea.** Suppose Julia had written, "I would like the audience to understand three aspects of the problem of illiteracy in the workplace and to prove how it is detrimental to both industry and the individual." This draft includes two distinct ideas; either one can be used but not both. Together they blur the focus of the speech. Julia must make a decision: (1) Does she want to focus her talk on aspects of the problem? If so, her goal statement would be, "I would like the audience to understand three major aspects of illiteracy in the workplace." (2) Does she want to focus on how harmful it is? If so, her goal statement would be, "I would like to prove that illiteracy in the workplace is detrimental to the individual and to industry."

4. **Revise the infinitive or infinitive phrase until it indicates the specific audience reaction desired.** If you regard your ideas as useful but noncontroversial, then your intent is primarily informative, and the infinitive that expresses your desired audience reaction should take the form "to understand" or "to appreciate." If, however, the main idea of your speech is controversial, a statement of belief, or a call to action, then your intent is persuasive and will be reflected in such infinitives as "to believe" or "to change."

5. **Write at least three different versions of the goal.** The clearer your specific goal, the more purposeful and effective your speech is likely to be. Even if Julia likes her first sentence, she should write at least one additional version. The second version may prove to be an even clearer statement. For instance, on a second try, she might write, "I would like the audience to understand three major effects of the problem of illiteracy in the workplace." Changing "three aspects" to "three major effects" gives the goal a different emphasis. She may decide she likes that emphasis better.

COMMUNICATE! Using InfoTrac College Edition

Access InfoTrac College Edition and click on PowerTrac. From the search index, choose Journal Name (jn). Enter "Vital Speeches" in Search box. Highlight Vital Speeches in View box and click View. Find a speech on a topic that interests you. Then read that speech and identify the speaker's goal. Was the goal clearly stated in the introduction? Was it implied but clear? Was it unclear? Note how this analysis can help you clarify your own speech goal.

Relationship among Subjects, Topics, Goals, and Thesis Statements

The specific goal is a statement of how you want your audience to respond. The **thesis statement** is a sentence that outlines the specific elements of the speech supporting the goal statement. For example, for a speech on evaluating diamonds, Sandy wrote:

Specific goal: I would like the audience to understand the major criteria for evaluating a diamond.

Thesis statement: Diamonds are evaluated on the basis of carat (weight), color, clarity, and cutting.

Notice that the specific goal clearly states what Sandy wanted the audience to do (understand the major criteria), but it does not *identify* the criteria for actually evaluating. Because Sandy had worked in a jewelry store, she already knew the information about criteria; she was able write a thesis statement showing the criteria of carat, color, clarity, and cutting before doing any research.

We mention the thesis statement in this chapter to give you an idea of the relationship among subject, topic, general goal, specific goal, and thesis statement. (See Figure 12.6.) If you think you have enough understanding of your specific goal to sketch a thesis statement, then go ahead. By specifying the focus of the speech, you give yourself even more direction when beginning research. The thesis statement is discussed further in Chapter 14.

OBSERVE & ANALYZE
Journal Activity

Writing Speech Goals

In your Student Workbook under Activity 12.4, following the five-step procedure outlined in the text, write a speech goal for the topic you have selected for your first speech.

thesis statement—*a sentence that outlines the specific elements of the speech supporting the goal statement.*

SKILL BUILDERS   Writing Speech Goals

Skill	Use	Procedure	Example
A single statement that specifies the exact response the speaker wants from the audience.	To give direction to the speech.	1. Write a first draft. 2. Revise the draft until you have a complete sentence that states the specific response or behavior you want from your audience. 3. Make sure the goal statement contains only one idea. 4. Revise the infinitive or infinitive phrase until it indicates the specific audience reaction desired. 5. Write at least three different versions of the goal statement.	Ken first writes, "I want my audience to know what to look for in buying a canine companion." As he revises, he arrives at the wording "I want my audience to understand four considerations in purchasing the perfect canine companion." Once Ken assures himself that the goal has a single focus and that the infinitive "to understand" indicates the preferred audience reaction desired, he then writes two differently worded goals to make sure his first one is the best.

Subject area: Career counseling

Topic: Networking

General speech goal: To inform

Specific goal: I want the audience to understand the procedure for networking in career development.

Thesis statement: You can use networking most effectively if you make networking a high priority, position yourself in places of opportunity, advertise yourself, and follow up on your contacts.

Subject area: Finance

Topic: Debt

General speech goal: To inform

Specific goal: I would like the audience to understand two major factors that are increasing the problem of personal debt in the United States.

Thesis statement: Personal debt is facilitated by easy access to credit and need for instant gratification.

Subject area: National Collegiate Athletic Association (NCAA)

Topic: Sanctions

General speech goal: To persuade

Specific goal: I would like the audience to believe that sanctions are an ineffective means of punishing colleges that violate NCAA rules.

Thesis statement: NCAA sanctions do not deter colleges from violating rules, they do not make it difficult for schools to field winning teams, and they do not prevent sanctioned colleges from receiving financial support.

Figure 12.6
Relationship among subject, topic, general goal, specific goal, and thesis statement.

Summary

The first step of effective speech preparation is to determine your speech goal. You begin by selecting a subject that you know something about and are interested in, such as a job, a hobby, or a contemporary issue of concern to you. To arrive at a specific topic, brainstorm a list of related words under each subject heading. When you have brainstormed at least twenty topics, you can check the specific topic under each heading that is most meaningful to you.

The next step is to analyze the audience and occasion to decide how to shape and direct your speech. Audience analysis is the study of your audience's knowledge, interests, and attitudes. Gather specific data about your audience to determine how its members are alike and how they differ. Use this information

Although Glen and Adam were taking the same speech course, they were in different sections. One evening when Adam was talking with Glen about his trouble finding a topic, Glen mentioned that he was planning to speak about affirmative action. Because the number of different speech goals from this topic seemed unlimited, Glen didn't see any harm in showing Adam his bibliography, so he brought it up on his computer screen.

As Adam was looking at it, Glen went down the hall to get a book he had lent to a friend earlier that morning. While Glen was away, Adam thought he would take a look at what else Glen had in the file. He was soon excited to see that Glen had a complete outline on the goal "I want the class to understand the steps in designing a home page." Figuring he could save himself some time, Adam printed the outline; he justified his action on the basis that it represented a good start that would give him ideas. As time ran short, Adam decided just to use Glen's outline for his own speech.

Later in the week, Glen's instructor happened to be talking to Adam's instructor about speeches she had heard that week. When she mentioned that Glen had given a really interesting speech on home pages, Adam's teacher said, "That's interesting, I heard a good one just this morning. Now what did you say the goal of the speech you heard was?" When the goals turned out to be the same, Glen's instructor went back to her office to get the outline that she would be returning the next day. As the two instructors went over the outlines, they saw that the two speeches were exactly the same. They left messages for both Adam and Glen to meet with them and the department head the next day.

1. What is the ethical issue at stake?
2. Was there anything about Glen's behavior that was unethical? Anything about Adam's?
3. What should be the penalty, if any, for Glen? For Adam?

to predict audience interest in your topic, level of understanding of your topic, and attitude toward you and your topic. Also, consider how the occasion of the speech and its physical setting will affect your overall speech plan.

Once you have a speech topic and have accounted for your audience and setting, you can determine your speech goal and write a thesis statement. The general goal of a speech is to entertain, to inform, or to persuade. The specific goal is a complete sentence that specifies the exact response the speaker wants from the audience. Writing a specific speech goal involves the following five-step procedure: (1) Write a first draft of your speech goal. (2) Revise your first draft until you have written a complete sentence that states the specific response or behavior you want from your audience. (3) Make sure that the goal contains only one idea. (4) Revise the infinitive or infinitive phrase until it indicates the specific audience reaction desired. (5) Write out at least three different versions of the goal before deciding on one.

Communicate! Online

Use your Communicate! CD-ROM for quick access to the electronic study resources that accompany this text. Included on your CD-ROM is access to InfoTrac College Edition, the World Wide Web, a demo of WebTutor for Communicate!, and the Communicate! Web site at the Wadsworth Communication Café. The Communicate! Web site offers chapter-by-chapter activities, quizzes, and a digital glossary.

Review the following key terms at

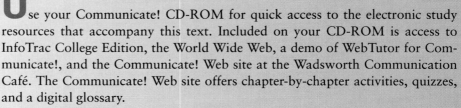

http://communication.wadsworth.com/humancomm/verderber

Key Terms

audience analysis (293)
brainstorming (291)
credibility (296)
general goal (298)
setting (296)

specific goal (299)
subject (290)
thesis statement (301)
topic (290)

InfoTrac College Edition is an excellent tool to help narrow your speech topic. Use the password that accompanied a new copy of this text and your Communicate! CD-ROM to access this database.

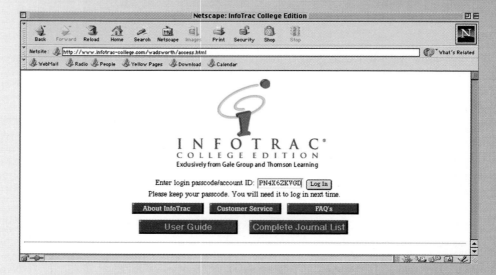

Once you have logged on, enter your search term in the InfoTrac College Edition entry box as shown below. Be sure the button for "Subject guide" is selected. Click on "Search."

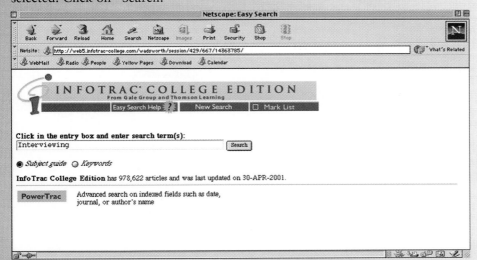

A list of subjects containing your search term appears with links to periodical references, subdivisions, and related subjects. Review the listing or click on "View Periodical references." Are you able to narrow your speech topic?

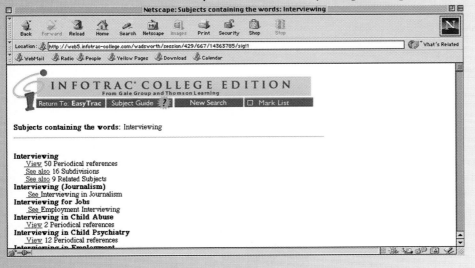

Bruce Ayers/Stone

OBJECTIVES

After you have read this chapter, you should be able to answer these questions:

- What are the key sources of information for speeches?
- What is the difference between factual and opinion statements?
- How can you determine whether a source will be useful?
- What should be included on note cards?
- What is the best way to cite sources in a speech?

13

Doing Research

Jeremy was concerned. He was scheduled for his first speech in a week, but he hadn't begun to find information. When he was in high school, he remembered discussing the subject of media violence in a class, and he was really taken with the subject. Just a couple of months ago he had read an article in a magazine at the doctor's office, but he couldn't remember the issue of the magazine the article was in. He decided he'd better get to the library, but he wasn't sure how he should proceed to find information.

Jeremy's experience is not unlike that of many of us. We believe our views on subjects are worth being heard, but we just do not know how to go about explaining or supporting what we want to say.

You will recall that an effective speech plan is a product of five action steps. In this chapter, we consider the second of the five action steps for preparing a speech: **Gather and evaluate material for use in the speech.** Your search is for high-quality information that will meet two functions: (1) support the specific speech goal, and (2) adapt to the audience. Research involves knowing where to look, knowing what to look for, and citing what you find.

Where to Look: Traditional and Electronic Sources of Information

Whatever your speech topic, you will want to look at all available sources of information. Effective speakers develop a research strategy that starts by considering their own knowledge and experiences, moves on to potential information from books, relevant periodicals, and other specialized sources accessed manually and through electronic databases—like InfoTrac College Edition—and considers the possibility of information that can be gained through interviews and surveys.

Personal Knowledge, Experience, and Observation

If you have chosen to speak on a topic you know something about, you are likely to have material that you can use as examples and personal experiences in your speech. For instance, musicians have special knowledge about music and instruments, entrepreneurs about starting up their own businesses, and marine biologists about marine reserves. Thus Erin, who is a member of the varsity volleyball team, can draw material from her own experience and experiences of her teammates for her first speech on "How to Spike a Volleyball."

For many topics, your personal knowledge from experience can be supplemented with careful observation. If, for instance, you are planning to talk about how a small claims court works or how churches help the homeless find shelter and job training, you can learn about each of these by attending small claims sessions or visiting a church's outreach center. By focusing attention on specific behaviors and taking notes of your observations, you will have a record of specifics that you can use in your speech.

Library Manual and Electronic Research

Much of your best speech material is likely to come from research found in books, relevant periodicals, and other specialized sources. These sources can be

F. Pedrick/The Image Works

Most online catalogs now also include search capabilities that enable you to enter "keywords" that you are likely to find most useful for your topic searches.

accessed manually or via **electronic databases,** which enable information retrieval from computer terminals.

Whereas in the past libraries had a card catalog listing all books and indexes held by the library and periodical catalogs listing magazines and journals in various categories, today books and periodicals are likely to be posted electronically. As a result, in this section we'll mention hard copy sources, but assume that you will have access to electronic databases.

Since library methods and procedures change frequently due to increased usage of electronic means of research, please heed the following advice when you're confused: Ask a librarian for help. Within a short period of time, he or she can help you learn about your library's resources. A librarian can also refer you to one of the many workshops and learning programs that are sponsored by college and university libraries.

Books Most libraries have transferred records of their book holdings to a computer online catalog system. But whether you are looking in a card catalog or on a computer, books are listed by title, author, and subject. Although you may occasionally know the title or author of a book you want, more often you will be looking for books using a subject label, such as "violence in the mass media."

electronic database—
information stored so that it can be retrieved from a computer terminal.

In addition to being able to search for author, title, and subject, most online catalogs now also include search capabilities that enable you to enter keywords that you are likely to find most useful for your topic searches. Even with this user-friendly system, you may find that you need to exercise some creativity in discovering the best "keywords" to use in the search.

For instance, if Jeremy looks for books on the subject "violence in the mass media," within a few minutes of creative thinking he could come up with several keyword designations that would bring a variety of *hits*—that is, books available. Notice the differences in hits Jeremy found using each of the following keywords:

media violence 95

violence in mass media 57

violence television 88

Under "media violence," one book listed was *Mayhem: Violence as Public Entertainment*. Information about this book is shown on the library card in Figure 13.1. Although some of the information on the card may seem to be irrelevant, you certainly would want to note the *location* (for instance, the University of Cincinnati has several college libraries and one all university library on campus), the *call number*, and the *book's availability*. The other bit of useful information is under "Note," which tells you that the book includes bibliographical references and an index.

In addition to providing a great deal of useful information, finding a book on your topic often leads you to additional sources. For instance, the library card for Sissela Bok's book *Mayhem* shows a bibliography of references including twenty-two pages of sources. Jeremy might find several excellent additional sources from the *Mayhem* bibliography alone.

Although using electronic access is a quick way to find appropriate books, it is not the only way. For instance, if you have the call number for a book, you

Author:	Bok, Sissela
Title:	Mayhem: Violence as public entertainment
Pub Info:	Reading, Mass: Addison-Wesley, c 1998
Description:	x, 194p.; 24 cm
Note:	"A Merloyd Lawrence" book
	Includes bibliographical references (p. 159–181) and Index
Subject:	Violence in Mass Media
OCLC#:	38218736
ISBN:	0201489791
LCCN	97048620

Location	Call No.	Status
1) Langsam stacks	P96 V5 B65 1998	Available

Figure 13.1
Library card.

can go to the section of the library in which books using that general call number are housed (in this case P96 V5 B65) and find other books on that subject in the same place. You can then thumb through them quickly to check their relevance.

Periodicals Magazines and journals that appear at fixed periods are called **periodicals.** Material from weekly, biweekly, and monthly magazines is more current than that which you find in books, so a periodical is likely to be your best source when your topic is "in the news," when the topic is so limited in scope that it is unlikely to provide enough material for a book, or when you are looking for a very specific aspect of a particular topic.

periodicals–magazines and journals that appear at fixed periods.

Most libraries no longer keep hard copy volumes of periodical indexes; look for the electronic indexes that your college or university subscribes to. Here are some sources for popular journals such as *Time* and *Newsweek* as well as academic journals such as *Communication Quarterly* and *Journal of Psychology.*

InfoTrac College Edition, the electronic index available to you by virtue of buying this textbook, gives you access to articles in more than seven hundred popular magazines and academic journals. Moreover, you can use InfoTrac College Edition from home or from your college dormitory if you have Internet access.

InfoTrac University Library is a more complete version of *InfoTrac College Edition.* It is available online at most college and university libraries and provides access to several hundred additional popular magazines and academic journals.

Periodical Abstract, available online in most college and university libraries, provides access to articles in more than one thousand popular magazines and academic journals. Offerings of these online catalogs is likely to vary from place to place, so it is wise to check with a librarian to see which of these and other catalogs you have access to at your university library.

If you are accessing the indexes electronically, you begin by typing in the subject heading you are researching. The computer will search the index's database and bring up citations that are related to your subject. You can then choose to access the individual articles and read or print them off the computer or use the list of citations to locate the original articles in your library's periodical section. For instance, Rhonda has identified Ecstasy as a topic under the heading of "designer drugs" on her brainstorming list. Rhonda had written her tentative speech goal as, "I want my audience to understand the dangers of the drug Ecstasy." Working from her computer at home, Rhonda opens up InfoTrac College Edition and types in "ecstasy" and finds fifty-two citations including:

The Lure of Ecstasy: The elixer best known for powering raves is an 80-year-old illegal drug. *Time* June 5, 2000 v155 I23 p62+

The fight against ecstasy. *Maclean's* May 1, 2000 p. 31

Ecstasy is becoming a drug of choice. *Alcoholism & Drug Abuse Weekly* March 13, 2000 v12 I11 p8

All three of these are available for downloading. At the University of Cincinnati college library, Rhonda could open the extended InfoTrac University Library index or Periodical Abstracts and find lists that include some of these and some different articles. Become familiar with the online indexes available at your library.

Some articles listed in indexes cannot be downloaded. For these, you will then go to your library's journal and magazine index to see whether the library has hard copies of the journal articles you want. Then you can manually access those journals.

Now let's turn to other resources your library is likely to have on its reference shelves.

Encyclopedias   Most libraries have a recent edition of *Encyclopedia Britannica, Encyclopedia Americana,* or *World Book Encyclopedia.* An encyclopedia can be a good starting point for research. Encyclopedias give an excellent overview of many subjects, but you certainly should never limit your research to encyclopedias. Your library is likely to have a wide variety of specialized encyclopedias to choose from in areas such as religion, philosophy, and science. For instance, your library is likely to have the *African American Encyclopedia, Latino Encyclopedia, Asian American Encyclopedia, Encyclopedia of Computer Science, Encyclopedia of Women,* and *Encyclopedia of Women in American Politics,* as well as many more.

Many libraries now have *Encyclopedia Britannica* online. If so, you will be able to access it just as you did the periodical sources.

Statistical sources   Statistical sources present numerical information on a wide variety of subjects. When you need facts about demography, continents, heads of state, weather, or similar subjects, refer to one of the many single-volume sources that report such data. Two of the most popular sources in this category are *The Statistical Abstract of the United States* (now available online), which provides reference material for numerical information and various aspects of American life, and *The World Almanac and Book of Facts.* You will find many other almanacs in the same reference material section where these two sources are housed.

Biographical sources   When you need accounts of a person's life, from thumbnail sketches to reasonably complete essays, you can turn to one of the many biographical sources available. In addition to full-length books and encyclopedia entries, consult such books as *Who's Who in America* and *International Who's Who.* Your library is also likely to carry *Contemporary Black Biography, Dictionary of Hispanic Biography, Native American Women, Who's Who of American Women, Who's Who Among Asian Americans,* and many more.

Books of quotations   A good quotation can be especially provocative as well as informative. You are most likely to be familiar with *Bartlett's Familiar Quotations,* which has quotations from historical as well as contemporary figures.

But your library is also likely to have *The International Thesaurus of Quotations, Harper Book of American Quotations, My Soul Looks Back, 'Less I Forget: A Collection of Quotations by People of Color, The New Quotable Woman,* and *The Oxford Dictionary of Quotations.*

Newspapers Newspaper articles are excellent sources of facts about and interpretations of both contemporary and historical issues. At a minimum, your library probably holds both an index of your nearest major daily newspaper and the *New York Times Index.*

Three electronic newspaper indexes that are most useful if they are available to you are (1) *National Newspaper Index,* which indexes five major newspapers: the *New York Times,* the *Wall Street Journal, Christian Science Monitor, Washington Post,* and *Los Angeles Times;* (2) *Newsbank,* which provides not only the indexes but also the text of articles from more than 450 U.S. and Canadian newspapers; and (3) InfoTrac College Edition's *National Newspaper Index.*

United States government publications Some government publications are especially useful for locating primary sources. The *Federal Register* publishes daily regulations and legal notices issued by the executive branch and all federal agencies. It is divided into sections such as rules and regulations and Sunshine Act meetings. Of special interest are announcements of hearings and investigations, committee meetings, and agency decisions and rulings. The *Monthly Catalog of United States Government Publications* covers publications of all branches of the federal government. It has semiannual and annual cumulative indexes by title, author/agency, and subject.

The Internet

Whatever your topic, you will want to begin with library sources. More than likely, you will find that plenty of material is available at your library, manually or through electronic indexes and other online databases.

In addition, you may want to access the **Internet,** an international electronic collection of thousands of smaller networks. The World Wide Web (WWW) is such a network and is used widely in searching for information on a broad range of topics. Today, most students with access to a university library or computer labs or terminals at various locations on campus have access to this vast supply of information. Public libraries also often provide Internet access. This access connects you to databases and bulletin boards, scholarly and professional electronic discussion groups, library holdings at colleges and universities across the United States and abroad, and even enables you to take online courses.

If your school or public library does not have access to the Internet and you have your own personal computer (Mac or PC) and a modem, you can purchase access by subscribing to a commercial server such as America Online

> **COMMUNICATE! Using InfoTrac College Edition**
>
> Use InfoTrac College Edition to find information on the subject you have selected for your speech. Click on "Periodical references." Look for articles that include information that seems relevant to your speech. Whether you download the article or make note cards, make sure that you have the necessary data to cite the source of information if you use it in your speech.

Internet—*an international electronic network of networks.*

(AOL), CompuServe, or Prodigy. For a fee, they will give you the modem software you need to connect to the Internet. Additionally, you will be charged a monthly access fee. With this subscription, you get features such as an email address, customer support services, up-to-date news and stock prices, access to countless computer games, and the ability to shop for almost anything you can think of online. Some databases have an additional connection charge or are available only to those who subscribe to their particular service.

Tips for Researching

Have a strategy and organize your search. Go first to library resources. Then, if you do not have all that you want or need, conduct research on the Web.

When you type in a keyword for your search, find out which computer symbols help limit and focus your search. For example, if Jeremy is using AltaVista and puts quotation marks around the words "media violence," he will only get hits in which these two words appear together. If he does not use quotations, he will get hits in which either word appears, which gives him a lot of information that is not useful to his speech.

If you wait until the last minute to finish researching your speech topic and you plan to use the Internet for source material, you may have to wait to get online. Modems connect via telephone lines, and many people may be "dialing in" at the same time you are. Rather than hits, you may only get a busy signal. Start early on your research!

Be especially suspicious of online sources that cite information that seems far out of line with what you have gotten elsewhere. There is no research librarian either organizing Internet information or ensuring that it is up to date—or even correct. The Internet contains information that is self-published, and it is up to you to evaluate the information and authorship of the material. Make sure that a source is given and that the material is dated (Courtright & Perse, 1998, p. 261). If a source is not given and the material is not dated, don't use the material.

Skimming to Determine Source Value

Because you are likely to uncover far more articles and books than you can use, you will want to skim sources to determine whether or not to read them in full. **Skimming** is a method of rapidly going through a work to determine what is covered and how.

If you are evaluating a magazine article, spend a minute or two finding out whether it really presents information on the exact area of the topic you are exploring and whether it contains any documented statistics, examples, or quotable opinions. (We will examine the kind of information to look for in the next section.) If you are evaluating a book, read the table of contents carefully, look at the index, and skim pertinent chapters, asking the same questions as you would for a magazine article.

skimming–*a method of rapidly going through a work to determine what is covered and how.*

Skimming helps you decide which sources should be read in full, which should be read in part, and which should be abandoned. Minutes spent in such evaluation will save hours of reading.

If you are compiling a periodical bibliography on the computer, you will discover that the services your library subscribes to are likely to include short abstracts for each article that comes up on the computer screen. A look at these abstracts will help you determine which sources you want to read in their entirety. Once you have the sources in hand, however, you still need to follow a skimming procedure.

Interviewing

Like media reporters, you may get some excellent information from **interviewing**, skillfully asking and answering questions. To be effective, select the best person to interview and have a list of good questions to ask.

interviewing–skillfully asking and answering questions.

Selecting the best person Somewhere on campus or in the larger community there are people who have information you can use in your speech. Usually a few telephone calls will lead you to the person who would be best to talk with about your topic. Rhonda, who is speaking on "designer drugs," may well call the college/university health service and make an appointment with a doctor or nurse to get specific campus-related information on such drugs. When you have decided whom you should interview, make an appointment— you cannot walk into an office and expect the prospective interviewee to drop

E. Crews/The Image Works

Interviews are a good source for personal narratives that can be used to support key ideas.

everything just to talk to you. Be forthright in your reasons for scheduling the interview. Whether your interview is for a class speech or for a different audience, say so.

Before going to the interview, make sure you have done some research on the topic. Interviewees are more likely to talk with you if you appear informed; moreover, familiarity with the subject will enable you to ask better questions.

Writing good questions The heart of an effective interviewing plan is a list of good questions that are likely to be a mix of open and closed primary or follow-up questions that are phrased to be neutral rather than leading.

Recall from our discussion of questions in Chapter 9, **open questions** are broad-based questions that ask the interviewee to provide whatever information he or she wishes to answer the questions. **Closed questions** are narrowly focus questions that require very brief answers. **Neutral questions** are those that enable a person to give an answer without direction from the interviewer. **Leading questions** are phrased in a way that suggests the interviewer has a preferred answer. **Follow-up questions** can be planned or be spontaneous but are designed to pursue the answers given to primary questions.

The content of your questions will depend on what information you want to get. Try to formulate a list that stays on the subject so that you can get the information you need without taking up too much time.

How many questions you plan to ask depends on how much time you have for the interview. Keep in mind that you never know how a person will respond. Some people are so talkative and informative that in response to your first question they answer every question you were planning to ask in great detail; other people will answer each question with just a few words.

Early in the interview, plan to ask some questions that can be answered easily and that will show your respect for the person you are interviewing. In an interview with a professor, you might start with background questions such as "How did you get interested in doing research on the effects of media violence?" The goal is to get the interviewee to feel at ease and to talk freely.

The body of the interview includes the major questions you have prepared. You may not ask all the questions you have prepared, but you should continue the interview until you have the important information you intended to get. Be sure your questions are designed to get the information necessary to achieve your goal.

Figure 13.2 shows some of the questions you might ask to get information on the effects of television violence on viewers.

Conducting the interview By applying the interpersonal skills we have discussed in this book, you will find that you can turn your careful planning into an excellent interview.

---

open questions–*broad-based questions that ask the interviewee to provide whatever information he or she wishes.*

closed questions–*narrowly focused questions that require brief answers.*

leading questions–*questions phrased in a way that suggests the interviewer has a preferred answer.*

neutral questions–*questions phrased without direction from the interviewer.*

follow-up questions– *questions designed to pursue the answers given to primary questions.*

Background information
How did you get interested in doing research on the effects of television violence?

Findings
Does your research show negative effects of television violence on viewers?
Are heavy viewers more likely to show negative effects than light viewers?
Have you found evidence that shows major effects on aggressiveness?
Desensitization?
Have you found evidence that shows effects on civility?

Action
Are the effects great enough to warrant limiting viewing of violent programming for children?
Do you have any recommendations that you would offer the viewing public?

Figure 13.2
Sample questions.

1. **Be courteous during the interview.** Start by thanking the person for taking the time to talk to you, and throughout the interview respect what the person says regardless of what you may think of the answers.

2. **Listen carefully.** Incorporate the skills relating to attending, understanding, and remembering, with special emphasis on asking questions, paying attention to nonverbal cues, and paraphrasing.

3. **Keep the interview moving.** Although some people will get so involved that they will not be concerned with the amount of time spent, most people have other important business to attend to.

4. **Make sure your nonverbal reactions are in keeping with the tone you want to communicate.** Monitor your facial expressions and gestures. Maintain good eye contact with the person. Nod to show understanding. And smile occasionally to maintain the friendliness of the interview.

Processing the interview   As soon as possible after the interview, sit down with your answers to the questions and make note cards of the key points you want to use in the speech. It is likely that your notes were taken in an outline or shorthand form, so be sure you can make sense out of them. If at any point you are not sure whether you have accurately transcribed what the person said, take a minute to telephone the interviewee to make sure.

Surveys

A **survey,** often in the form of a questionnaire, is a means of gathering information directly from people. Surveys may be conducted orally or in writing. For speeches on such diverse topics as student reaction to dormitory food or the local volleyball team's chances in an upcoming match, you can obtain useful

survey–*a means of gathering information directly from people through the use of a questionnaire.*

information through a survey. The four kinds of questions most likely to be used in a survey are called two-sided, multiple-choice, scaled, and open-ended.

1. **Two-sided questions get a yes–no or true–false response.** These questions are used most frequently to get easily sorted answers. For a survey on television violence, you might consider a two-sided phrasing such as this:

     Do you believe prime time television programming contains too much violence?
     _____Yes   _____No

     Although two-sided questions do not offer people the opportunity to express their degree of agreement or disagreement, you do get a quick count of opinion. Also, these surveys are easy to conduct orally.

2. **Multiple-choice questions give respondents alternatives.** For a survey of student television viewing, you might use the following question:

     For the following question, check the choice that is most accurate.

     I watch television
     _____   0 to 5 hours a week
     _____   5 to 10 hours a week
     _____   10 to 15 hours a week
     _____   15 to 20 hours a week
     _____   more than 20 hours a week

3. **Scaled questions allow a range of responses to a statement.** Scaled responses are particularly good for measuring the strength of a person's attitude toward a subject. For a question about television violence, you might want to give each person a range of choices. Here is an example that measures a range of audience attitudes.

     For the following statement, circle the answer that best represents your opinion:

     I believe programming on prime time television contains too much violence.

     Strongly agree | Agree somewhat | Don't know | Disagree somewhat | Strongly disagree

You could, of course, include more than one question.

4. **Open-ended questions encourage a statement of opinion.** These questions produce the greatest amount of depth, but because of the likelihood of a wide variety of responses, they are the most difficult to process. For your survey on television violence, you might ask this open-ended question:

     If you were to write a letter to the FCC about whether there was too much violence on prime time television, what would you recommend?

After you give the survey you need to process the results. If the survey indicates a clear-cut trend, then use the results of the poll to help make a point in your speech. If the poll is inconclusive, then it is wise to avoid making too much of the results.

OBSERVE & ANALYZE
Journal Activity

Listing Sources

For the topic you selected for your first speech, fill in the following information in your Student Workbook under Activity 13.1.

1. Working with manual or computerized versions of your library's card catalog or periodical indexes (including InfoTrac College Edition), list a total of six specific books and/or magazine articles that appear to provide information for your topic.

2. Name a person you could interview for additional information for this topic.

3. Write survey questions—if a survey is appropriate.

What Information to Look For

Whatever the source, you will be looking for factual statements and expert opinions.

Factual Statements

Factual statements are those that can be verified. "A recent study confirmed that preschoolers watch an average of 28 hours of television a week," "The Gateway Solo laptop comes with a CD-ROM drive," and "Johannes Gutenberg invented printing from movable type in the 1400s" are all statements of fact that can be verified. One way to verify information that appears to be factual is to check it against material from another source on the same subject.

Be especially skeptical of "facts" that are asserted on the Internet. Because anyone can say virtually anything online, you need to especially vigilant. Never use any information that is not carefully documented unless you have corroborating sources.

factual statements–*statements that can be verified.*

Expert Opinions

Expert opinions are interpretations and judgments made by authorities in a particular subject area. "Watching 28 hours of television a week is far too much for young children," "Having a CD-ROM drive in your computer is a necessity," and "The invention of printing from movable type was for all intents and purposes the start of mass communication" are all *opinions* based on the factual statements made previously. Whether they are *expert opinions* or not depends on who made the statements.

How do you tell an expert from a "quack"? First, the expert is recognized by others in his or her field. Second, the expert must be knowledgeable about the matter at hand. For instance, a history professor may qualify as an expert in his or her field of study of Ancient Greece but not qualify as an expert in Incan history.

If you plan to use expert opinions in your speech, identify them as opinions and indicate to your audience the level of confidence that should be attached to the statement. For instance, an informative speaker may say, "The temperatures throughout the 1990s were much higher than average. Paul Jorgenson, a space biologist, believes these higher than average temperatures represent the first stages of the greenhouse effect, but the significance of these temperatures is not completely accepted as fact."

Although opinions cannot entirely take the place of documented facts, expert opinions can be used to interpret and give weight to the facts you have discovered.

expert opinions– *interpretations and judgments made by authorities in a particular subject area.*

Drawing Information from Multiple Cultural Perspectives

How facts are perceived and what opinions are held often are influenced by a person's cultural background. Therefore, it is important to draw your information from culturally diverse perspectives by seeking sources that have differing cultural orientations and by interviewing experts with diverse cultural backgrounds. For example, when Carrie was preparing for her speech on proficiency testing in grade schools, she purposefully searched for articles written by noted Hispanic, Asian, and African American, as well as European American, authors. In addition, she interviewed two local school superintendents—one from an urban district and one from a suburban district. Because she consciously worked to develop diverse sources of information, Carrie felt more confident that her speech would more accurately reflect all sides of the debate on proficiency testing.

Dr. Molefi Kete Asante, an internationally renowned scholar, believes that limiting our research by only considering the viewpoints of those who are like us promotes racism that is then transmitted as we speak. The accompanying Spotlight on Scholars features his work.

SPOTLIGHT ON SCHOLARS

Molefi Kete Asante, Professor of Africology, Temple University, on the Language of Prejudice and Racism

Molefi Kete Asante is an activist scholar who believes it is not enough to know, one must act to humanize the world. Over his career Asante has sought not only to understand what he studied, but also to use that knowledge to help people discover how to exert their power.

In 1968, at the age of 26, Asante completed his Ph.D. in Speech Communication from UCLA. As a graduate student, Asante studied language and the rhetoric of agitation, and in his dissertation, he analyzed the speeches of one of the most zealous agitators during the American Revolution, Samuel Adams. During the late 1960s, however, Asante focused his attention on another revolution occurring in the United States that he found more compelling. Demonstrating his insatiable appetite for intellectual work, at the same time that he was working on his dissertation he also wrote *The Rhetoric of Black Revolution*, published in 1969.

As a scholar grounded in communication and the rhetoric of agitation, Asante began to notice how racism and communication were intertwined. As his thinking evolved, he began to formulate the theory that racism in our culture is embedded in our language system.

According to Asante, racism stems from a thought system that values a particular race over another. As a phenomenon of language, racism is demonstrated by what people say about others and how they justify their personal attitudes and beliefs. What Asante discovered is that our language reflects the "knowledge system" we are taught. In the United States and much of the world, this knowledge system reflected a European rather than a multicultural view of human events and achievements.

For instance, in most schools, the study of the arts or philosophy or science focuses only on the contributions made by Europeans or European Americans. As a result of the focus of these studies, we "learn" that nothing substantial or important originated from anywhere else. Thus we come to value the music, literature, rituals, and values of Europeans over those of other cultural groups. Since racism comes from valuing a particular race above another, Asante reasons, it was inevitable that mono-ethnic Eurocentric approaches to education would result in our developing racist thoughts and a racist language structure that reifies those thoughts.

To combat racism and racist language, Asante believes that we must first enlarge our knowledge base to accurately reflect the contributions that have been made by other racial and cultural groups. For example, the history that is taught needs to reflect the substantial contributions that Africa, China, and other non-European groups have made to the development of humankind. Likewise, the literature and art that is studied needs to reflect and be drawn from a body that includes the work of various racial and ethnic groups. When people learn that all racial and cultural groups have made significant contributions to the development of humankind, they will be less prone to view themselves as superior or inferior to others.

As a contribution to providing the kinds of information that we all need to learn, in 1987 Asante wrote *Afrocentricity,* a book that seeks to discover, understand, and reclaim the contributions that many cultures, especially African cultures, have made to our common intellectual heritage. Since that time, Asante has focused his own learning and his scholarship on discovering, reclaiming, and sharing the contributions of African culture and philosophy.

Asante's influence has been widespread. He served as the first Director of Afro-American Studies at UCLA, Department Head of Speech Communication at SUNY Buffalo, and Chair of the Department of African American Studies at Temple University, where he established the first Ph.D. program in African American Studies. He is internationally known for his work on Afrocentricity and African culture. He has published over 30 books, edited 9 others, and authored over 80 book chapters and journal articles. In the process, he has led an intellectual revolution among scholars working in numerous disciplines. Although he is noted for his scholarship, Asante says, "Working with students is the centerpiece of what I do." He currently teaches undergraduate courses on the African American Church and 20th Century Mass Media in Black Communities and graduate courses in Ancient Egyptian Language and Culture and Egyptian Origins of Rhetoric. For a list of some of Asante's major publications, see the References at the end of the book.

His interest in his personal African heritage has caused him to trace his family ancestry back to Ghana. Recently, in Ghana, he was "enstooled," a ceremony that formally acknowledges a person as a member of Ghanaian royalty. At that ceremony he was given the name "Nano Okru Asante Peasah, Kyidomhene of Tafo."

Verbal Forms of Information

Factual information and expert opinions come in or may be presented as examples and illustrations, statistics, anecdotes and narratives, comparisons and contrasts, or quotable explanations and opinions.

examples–*specific instances that illustrate or explain a general factual statement.*

Examples   **Examples** are specific instances that illustrate or explain a general factual statement. One or two short examples like the following are often enough to help make a generalization meaningful.

> **One way a company increases its power is to buy out another company. Recently Kroger bought out Fred Meyer Inc. to make it the largest grocery firm in the country.**

> **Professional billiard players practice many long hours every day. Jennifer Lee practices as much as ten hours a day when she is not in a tournament.**

Examples are useful because they provide concrete detail that makes a general statement more meaningful to the audience.

Although most of the examples you find will be real, you may find hypothetical examples you can use. **Hypothetical examples** are those drawn from reflections about future events. They develop the idea "What if . . . ?" In the following excerpt, John A. Ahladas (1989) presents some hypothetical examples of what it will be like in the year 2039 if global warming continues:

hypothetical examples– *examples drawn from reflections about future events.*

> **In New York, workers are building levees to hold back the rising tidal waters of the Hudson River, now lined with palm trees. In Louisiana, 100,000 acres of wetland are steadily being claimed by the sea. In Kansas, farmers learn to live with drought as a way of life and struggle to eke out an existence in the increasingly dry and dusty heartland. . . . And reports arrive from Siberia of bumper crops of corn and wheat from a longer and warmer growing season. (p. 382)**

Now let us consider guidelines for selecting and using examples. First, the examples should be clear and specific enough to create a clear picture for the audience. Consider the following generalization and support:

Generalization: Electronics is one of the few areas in which products are significantly cheaper today than they were in the 1980s.

Supporting example: In the mid-1980s, Motorola sold cellular phones for $5,000 each; now a person can buy a Motorola cellular phone for under $150.

With this single example, the listener has a vivid picture of tremendous difference in about a fifteen-year period.

Second, the examples you use should not be misleading. If cellular phones were the *only* electronics product for which prices were so much less over that same period, this vivid example would be misleading and unethical. Any misuse of data is unethical, especially if the user knows better.

Good examples can give a clear, vivid picture in relatively few words. It is a good idea to follow this rule of thumb in preparing your speeches: Never let a generalization stand without at least one example.

statistics–*numerical facts.*

Statistics   **Statistics** are numerical facts. Statistical statements, such as "Only six out of every ten local citizens voted in the last election" or "The cost of living rose 0.6 percent in January of 2000," enable you to pack a great deal of

C. Orrico/SuperStock, Inc.

Use statistics from only the most reliable sources and double-check any startling statistics with another source.

information into a small package. Statistics can provide impressive support for a point, but when they are poorly used in the speech, they may be boring and, in some instances, downright deceiving. Here are some guidelines for using statistics effectively.

1. **Record only statistics whose reliability you can verify.** Taking statistics from only the most reliable sources and double-checking any startling statistics with another source will guard against the use of faulty statistics.

2. **Record only recent statistics so that your audience will not be misled.** For example, if you find the statistic that only 9 of 100 members of the Senate, or 9 percent, are women (true in 1999), you would be misleading your audience if you used that statistic in a speech. If you want to make a point about the number of women in the Senate, find the most recent statistics. Check for both the year and the range of years to which the statistics apply.

3. **Look for statistics that are used comparatively.** By themselves, statistics are hard to interpret. When used comparatively, they have much greater impact.

In a speech on chemical waste, Donald Baeder (1980) points out that chemicals are measured in parts per billion or even parts per trillion. Notice how he goes on to use comparisons to put the meaning of the statistics in perspective:

One part per billion is the equivalent of one drop—one drop!—of vermouth in two 36,000 gallon tanks of gin and that would be a very dry martini even by San Francisco standards! One part per trillion is the equivalent of one drop in two thousand tank cars. (p. 497)

4. **Do not overuse statistics.** Although statistics may be an excellent way to present a great deal of material quickly, be careful not to overuse them. A few pertinent numbers are far more effective than a battery of statistics. When you believe you must use many statistics, try preparing a visual aid, perhaps a chart, to help your audience visualize them.

Anecdotes and narratives Anecdotes are brief, often amusing stories; **narratives** are tales, accounts, personal experiences, or lengthier stories. Because holding audience interest is so important in a speech and because audience attention is likely to be captured by a story, anecdotes and narratives are worth looking for, creating, and using. For a five-minute speech, you have little time to tell a detailed story, so one or two anecdotes or a very short narrative would be preferable.

The key to using stories is to make sure that the point of the story states or reinforces the point you make in your speech. In his speech John Howard made a point about failure to follow guidelines (2000, p. 618).

> **The knight was returning to the castle after a long, hard day. His face was bruised and badly swollen. His armor was dented. The plume on his helmet was broken, and his steed was limping. He was a sad sight.**
>
> **The lord of the castle ran out and asked, "What hath befallen you, Sir Timothy?"**
>
> **"Oh, Sire," he said, "I have been laboring all day in your service, bloodying and pillaging your enemies to the West."**
>
> **"You've been doing what?" gasped the astonished nobleman. "I haven't any enemies to the West!"**
>
> **"Oh!" said Timothy. "Well, I think you do now."**
>
> **There is a moral to this little story. Enthusiasm is not enough. You need to have a sense of direction.**

Good stories and narratives are often humorous, but sentimental, suspenseful, and dramatic ones will work as well.

Comparisons and contrasts One of the best ways to give meaning to new ideas is through comparison and contrast. **Comparisons** illuminate a point by showing similarities. Although you can easily create comparisons using information you have found, you should still keep your eye open for creative comparisons developed by the authors of the books and articles you have found.

anecdotes–*brief, often amusing stories.*

narratives–*tales, accounts, personal experiences, or lengthier stories.*

comparisons–*illuminate a point by showing similarities.*

Comparisons may be literal or figurative. Literal comparisons show similarities of real things:

The walk from the lighthouse back up the hill to the parking lot is equal to walking up the stairs of a thirty-story building.

Figurative comparisons express one thing in terms normally denoting another:

I always envisioned myself as a four-door sedan. I didn't know she was looking for a sports car!

Comparisons make ideas not only clearer but also more vivid. Notice how Stephen Joel Trachtenberg (1986) used figurative comparison to demonstrate the importance of the willingness to take risks, even in the face of danger, in his speech to the Newington High School Scholars' Breakfast:

The eagle flying high always risks being shot at by some hare-brained human with a rifle. But eagles and young eagles like you still prefer the view from that risky height to what is available flying with the turkeys far, far below. (p. 653)

Whereas comparisons show similarities, **contrasts** show differences. Notice how this humorous contrast dramatizes the difference between "participation" and "commitment":

contrasts–*showing differences.*

If this morning you had bacon and eggs for breakfast, I think it illustrates the difference. The eggs represented "participation" on the part of the chicken. The bacon represented "total commitment" on the part of the pig! (Durst, 1989, pp. 309–310)

Quotations When you find an explanation, an opinion, or a brief anecdote that seems to be exactly what you are looking for, you may quote it directly in your speech. Because audiences want to listen to your ideas and arguments, however, they do not want to hear a long string of quotations. Nevertheless, a well-selected quotation might be perfect in one or two key places.

Quotations can both explain and vivify. Look for quotations that make a point in a particularly clear or vivid way. For example, in his speech on "Enduring Values for a Secular Age," Hans Becherer (2000, p. 732), Executive Officer at Deere & Company, used this Henry Ford quote to show the importance of enthusiasm to progress:

Enthusiasm is at the heart of all progress. With it, there is accomplishment. Without it, there are only alibis.

Frequently, historical or literary quotations can reinforce a point vividly. Cynthia Opheim (2000, p. 60), Chair of the Department of Political Science at Southwest Texas State University, in her speech "Making Democracy Work" quoted Mark Twain on the frustration of witnessing legislative decision making when she said:

There are two things you should never watch being made: sausage and legislation.

To take advantage of such opportunities, you need access to one or more of the many available books of quotations that we mentioned earlier in this chapter. Most books of quotations are organized by topic, which helps in finding a particularly appropriate quote to use in your speech.

plagiarism–*using material without crediting the source.*

Keep in mind that when you use a direct quotation it is necessary to credit the person who formulated it. Using any quotation or close paraphrase without crediting its source is **plagiarism,** an unethical act.

Recording Information and Citing Written and Electronic Sources

Whether the research materials you find are factual statements or opinions, you need to record the information accurately and keep a careful account of your sources so that they can be cited appropriately.

Recording Information

How should you record information you plan to use? Because you can never be sure of the final order in which it is used, it is best to record information on note cards.

In the note card method, each factual statement or expert opinion, along with bibliographical documentation, is recorded on a separate four-by-six-inch or larger index card. Although it may seem easier to record all material from one source on a single sheet of paper (or to photocopy source material), sorting and arranging material is much easier when each item is recorded separately. On each card, indicate the topic of the recorded information, the information, and the publication data. Any part of the information that is quoted directly should be enclosed with quotation marks.

Publication data differ depending on whether the information is from a book, a periodical or newspaper, or a Web site. For a book, include names of authors, title of the book, the place of publication and the publisher, the date of publication, and the page or pages from which the information is taken. For a periodical or newspaper, include the name of the author (if given), the title of the article, the name of the publication, the date, and the page number from which the information is taken. For online sources, include the URL for the Web site, the heading under which you found the information, and the date that you accessed the site. Specifics and samples for preparing source citations (including interviews) for inclusion in the complete outline are shown in Chapter 14. In all cases, list source information in enough detail so that the information can be found later if needed. Figure 13.3 illustrates a useful note card sample.

Topic: Ebola
Heading: Resurfacing of the disease

   "After lying dormant for three years, the Ebola virus has resurfaced—this time in Uganda, where 31 people have died from the deadly disease."

   Henry Wasswa, "Ebola outbreak in northern Uganda claims 31 lives in past two weeks," <u>Naples Daily News</u>, October 16, 2000, p. 11A.

Figure 13.3

Example of a note card recording information.

As your stack of information grows, sort the material, placing each item under a heading to which it is related. For instance, for a speech on Ebola, the deadly disease that has broken out in Africa, you might have note cards related to causes, symptoms, and means of transmission. The card in Figure 13.3 would be indexed under the heading Resurfacing of the disease.

The number of sources that you should use depends in part on the type of speech. For a narrative of a personal experience, you will be the main, if not the only, source. For reports and persuasive speeches, however, speakers ordinarily use several sources. For a speech on Ebola in which you plan to talk about causes, symptoms, and means of transmission, you should probably have two or more note cards under each heading. Moreover, the note cards should come from at least three different sources. One-source speeches often lead to plagiarism; furthermore, a one- or two-source speech simply does not give sufficient breadth of material. By selecting and using the information from several sources, you will accumulate enough information to enable you to develop an original approach to your topic.

Citing Sources in Speeches

In your speeches, as in any communication in which you use ideas that are not your own, you should credit your sources. Including sources not only helps the audience to evaluate the content but also adds to your credibility. In addition, citing sources will give concrete evidence of the depth of your research. Failure to cite sources, especially when you are presenting information that is meant to substantiate a controversial point, is unethical.

In a written report, ideas taken from other sources are designated by footnotes; in a speech these notations must be included within the context of your statement of the material. Your citation need not be a complete representation of all the bibliographical information. Figure 13.4 gives examples of several ways to cite sources in a speech.

Although you do not want to clutter your speech with bibliographical citations, make sure to mention the sources of your most important information.

"According to an article about Japanese workers in last week's <u>Time</u> magazine . . . "

"In the latest Gallup poll cited in the February 10 issue of <u>Newsweek</u> . . . "

"But to get a complete picture we have to look at the statistics. According to the 2000 Statistical Abstract, the level of production for the European Economic Community rose from . . . "

"In a speech on business ethics delivered to the Public Relations Society of America last November, Preston Townly, CEO of the Conference Board, said . . . "

Figure 13.4
Appropriate speech source citations.

SKILL BUILDERS   Recording Data

Skill	Use	Procedure	Example
Having a written record of information drawn from a source with complete documentation.	To provide information and its source in a speech or to report the documentation to anyone who might question the accuracy of the information.	1. Indicate the topic in the upper-left-hand corner. 2. Record each factual statement or expert opinion on a separate four-by-six-inch or larger index card. Any part of the information that is quoted directly should be enclosed with quotation marks. 3. For a book, write the name of the author, the title, the publisher, the date, and the page number from which the information was taken. 4. For a periodical or newspaper, write the name of the author, if one is given, the title of the article, the name of the periodical or newspaper, the date, and the page number from which the information was taken. 5. For online sources, include the URL for the Web site, the author and title if one is given, the heading under which you found the information, and the date that you accessed the site.	While gathering material for a speech on U.S. Postal Service monetary problems, Tamika found an article with relevant information. In the upper-left-hand corner of one four-by-six-inch card, she wrote U.S. Postal Service Debt. Then she wrote the data she had discovered: After five years of operating at a surplus, the U.S. Postal Service "has plunged as much as $3 billion in the red, its greatest deficit in modern history." Marianne Lavelle, "Why the Postman Can't Deliver Profits: Full Service Costs the Postal Service Dearly," *U.S. News & World Report,* April 9, 2001, p. 46.

Preparing Note Cards

Using information from the books, magazines, newspapers, or online sources that you listed in the Observe and Analyze Journal Activity 13.1, prepare six note cards citing information such as examples, statistics, anecdotes and narratives, comparisons and contrasts, or quotations, that you can consider using for your first speech.

On your note cards, be sure to include the publication data listed in this section of the text for the books, magazines, newspapers, or online sources you used.

"**D**an, I was wondering whether you'd listen to the speech I'm giving in class tomorrow. It will only take about five minutes."

"Sure."

Tom and Dan found an empty classroom and Tom went through his speech.

"What did you think?"

"Sounded pretty good to me. I could follow the speech—I knew what you wanted to do. But I was wondering about that section where you had the statistics. You didn't give any source."

"Well, the fact is I can't remember the source."

"You remember the statistics that specifically but you don't remember the source?"

"Well, I don't remember the statistics all that well, but I think I've got them about right."

"Well, you can check then, can't you?"

"Check it? Where? That would take me hours. And after all, I told you I think I have them about right."

"But Tom, the accuracy of the statistics seem pretty important to what you said."

"Listen, trust me on this—no one is going to say anything about it. You've already said that my goal was clear, my main points were clear, and I sounded as if I know what I'm talking about. I really think that's all Goodwin is interested in."

"Well, whatever you say, Tom. I just thought I'd ask."

"No problem, thanks for listening. I thought I had it in pretty good shape, but I wanted someone to hear my last practice."

"Well, good luck!"

1. What do you think of Tom's assessment of his use of statistics that "No one is going to say anything about it"?

2. Does Tom have any further ethical obligation? If so, what is it?

Summary

Effective speaking requires high-quality information. You need to know where to look for information, what kind of information to look for, how to record it, and how to cite sources in your speeches.

To find material, begin by exploring your own knowledge, experience, and observations. Then work outward through library and electronic sources, interviewing, and surveying. Look for material in books, periodicals, encyclopedias, statistical sources, biographical sources, newspapers, government publications, microfilm indexes, computer databases, and the Internet. By skimming material you can quickly evaluate sources to determine whether or not to read them in full.

Two major types of supporting material for speeches are factual statements and expert opinions. Factual statements report verifiable occurrences. Expert opinions are interpretations of facts made by qualified authorities. Although you will use some of your material as you find it, you may want to present the information in a different form. Depending on your topic and speech goal, you may use facts and opinions orally as examples, anecdotes, narratives, statistics, quotations, comparisons, and contrasts.

A good method for recording material that you may want to use in your speech is to record each bit of data along with necessary bibliographical documentation on a separate note card. As your stack of information grows, sort the material under common headings. During the speech, cite the sources for the information.

Communicate! Online

Use your Communicate! CD-ROM for quick access to the electronic study resources that accompany this text. Included on your CD-ROM is access to InfoTrac College Edition, the World Wide Web, a demo of WebTutor for Communicate!, and the Communicate! Web site at the Wadsworth Communication Café. The Communicate! Web site offers chapter-by-chapter activities, quizzes, and a digital glossary.

Review the following key terms at
http://communication.wadsworth.com/humancomm/verderber

Key Terms

anecdotes (324)

closed questions (316)

comparisons (324)

contrasts (325)

electronic database (309)

examples (332)

expert opinions (319)

factual statements (319)

follow-up questions (316)

hypothetical examples (322)

Internet (313)

interviewing (315)

leading questions (316)

narratives (324)

neutral questions (316)

open questions (316)

periodicals (311)

plagiarism (326)

skimming (314)

statistics (322)

survey (317)

The InfoTrac College Edition database contains hundreds of articles from reliable periodicals and journals. You can use this database to research your speech topic. Use the password that accompanied a new copy of this text and your Communicate! CD-ROM to log onto InfoTrac College Edition.

Enter your speech topic in the InfoTrac College Edition entry box as shown below. Be sure the button for "Keywords" is selected. Click on "Search."

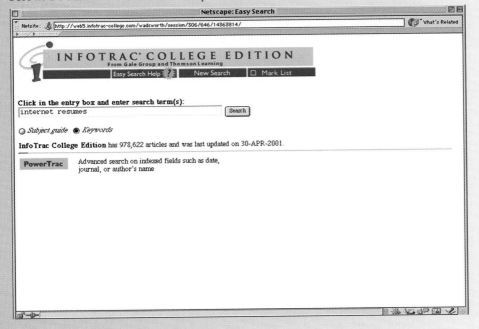

A list of citations containing your keyword search appears with the option to view the text and retrieval choices. Click on this link to view your article.

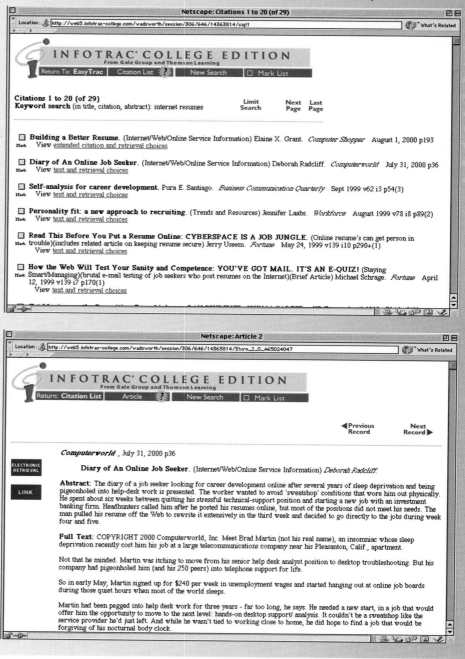

By clicking on "Electronic Retrieval" to the left of the article, you have the option to view, print, or email the article you selected.

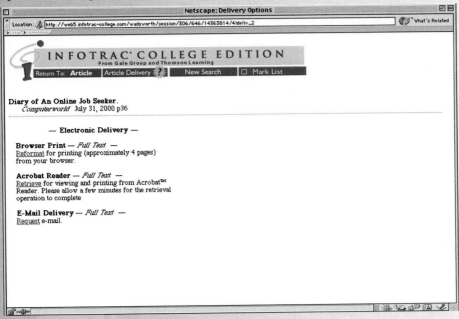

Christie's Images/SuperStock, Inc.

OBJECTIVES

After you have read this chapter, you should be able to answer these questions:

- How do you construct a thesis statement?

- How do you determine the main points for your speech?

- How do you determine the best order for your speech?

- What is the goal of transitions?

- What are the goals of an effective speech introduction?

- What are the most common types of speech introductions?

- What are the essentials of an effective speech conclusion?

- What are the major elements of a well-written speech outline?

14

Organizing

"Troy, that was a terrific speech. I haven't heard so many good stories in a long time."

"You're right, Brett, the stories were interesting, but, you know, I had a hard time following it."

"Well, he was talking about ways that we can help save the environment—but, you're right, I can't seem to remember anything but that one point about recycling. Let's see, what were the other key points?"

Troy and Brett's experience is not that unusual; even well-known speakers sometimes give speeches that are not as clearly organized as they could be. Yet a speech that is well organized is far more likely to achieve its goal than one that is not. In this chapter, we consider the third of the five action steps: **Organize and develop material in a way that is best suited to your particular audience.** This action step involves (1) outlining the body of the speech, (2) preparing the introduction, (3) preparing the conclusion, (4) listing sources, and (5) completing the outline. Think of an outline not as an entire speech written in outline form but as a road map for the audience to follow. As you consider ways to present the speech, use your outline to test the logic, development, and overall strength of the structure of your speech before you prepare the wording or begin practicing its delivery.

Outlining the Body of the Speech

Because the introduction is the first part of the speech to be heard by the audience, many speakers assume that they should begin outlining with the introduction. When you think about it, however, you will realize that it is difficult to work on an introduction before you have considered the material to be introduced. It is best to prepare the body of your speech first: Write a thesis statement, select and state the main points, and determine the best order. Once you have outlined the body of your speech, you can select and develop the examples, quotations, and other elements that explain or support your main points. This supporting material is discussed later in the chapter.

Writing a Thesis Statement

thesis statement—*a sentence that outlines the elements of the specific goal statement.*

Once you have a tentative speech goal and have drawn together information for your speech, begin framing the structure of the speech by writing a **thesis statement,** a sentence that outlines the elements of the specific goal statement. The clearer your thesis statement is at this stage of preparation, the easier it is to select, state, and begin to build your main points. Because Erin is a member of the women's varsity volleyball team, she already knows her subject matter well enough to write her thesis statement as "The three steps for executing an effective volleyball spike are to have a good approach, a powerful swing, and a good follow-through."

Often, however, you will have collected a variety of information related to your specific speech goal. Then you have to make a decision about what information is the most important for achieving your goal. Let's consider an example to illustrate how you might proceed to select the points you want to talk about now that you have found most of the information you will use in your speech.

When Emming wrote the specific goal "I would like the audience to under-stand the major criteria for finding a suitable credit card," he already had a few ideas about what he might focus on in the speech. But it wasn't until he completed most of his research that he really had enough information to write down seven specific ideas of what might be the key criteria for finding a suitable credit card:

- interest rate
- convenience
- discounts
- annual fee
- rebates
- institutional reputation
- frequent flyer points

If you are able to list several potential topics for your main points, then you can begin to evaluate them and select the most relevant ones for your thesis statement. For instance, Emming noticed that several of his sources talked about the importance of both interest rate and annual fee. Moreover, nearly every source mentioned at least one inducement, such as rebates. Emming crossed out those criteria (topics) that did not have as much support and combined individual inducements under a single heading. At this stage, his list looked like this:

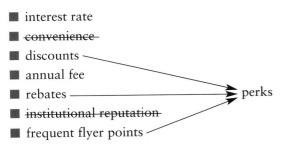

- interest rate
- ~~convenience~~
- discounts
- annual fee
- rebates ────────────────► perks
- ~~institutional reputation~~
- frequent flyer points

Now Emming was able to write his tentative thesis statement using this structure: "Three criteria that will enable the audience to find the most suitable credit card are level of real interest rate, annual fee, and advertised perks (inducements)."

Outlining Main Points

Once you have determined a thesis statement, you can begin outlining the main points that will make up the body of your speech. **Main points** are complete sentence representations of the ideas that you have used in your thesis statement. Think of your main points as the key building blocks of a speech—the ideas you want your audience to remember if they remember nothing else.

main points—*complete sentence representations of the ideas that you have used in your thesis statement.*

SKILL BUILDERS   Thesis Statement

Skill	Use	Procedure	Example
A sentence that outlines the specific elements of the speech supporting the goal statement.	To identify items of information that will become the subject of the main points of the speech.	1. List the elements of your speech goal that might become the main points of your speech. 2. After selecting the specific elements that best reflect your speech goal, combine them into a complete sentence that is your thesis statement.	For her speech goal, good novels are the product of several important qualities, Vanessa listed "creativity," "vividness," "plot," "character," "background," "setting," and "dialogue." As she weighed and evaluated her information, she elected to write the thesis statement, "Good writing is the product of creative plot, character, and setting."

Write main points as complete sentences It is important to write main points as complete sentences because only sentences can fully express the relationships associated with the key elements of the thesis statement. For instance, if Emming said "My three main points are real interest rate, annual fee, and advertised inducements," you would have some idea of what he was talking about, but you would not understand the points as criteria. To make the relationships clear, further refinement is needed. Using Roman numerals to represent main point designations, Emming might write a first draft of the main points of his speech like this:

I. Examining the interest rate is one criterion that you can use to find a credit card that is suitable for where you are in life.

II. Another criterion that you can use to make sure that you find a credit card that is suitable for where you are in life is to examine the annual fee.

III. Finding a credit card can also depend on weighing the advertised perks, which is the third criterion that you will want to use to be sure that it is suitable for where you are in life.

Notice that we emphasized that this is a first draft. Sometimes our first draft contains the wording we want to use. More often, however, we find that our first attempt needs revision.

Revise main points To revise your main points, ask these questions:

- Are the main points clear?
- Are the main points parallel in structure?
- Are the main points meaningful?
- Are the main points limited to five or fewer in number?

For practice, let's consider Emming's main points more carefully. Emming has made a pretty good start: The three main points are complete sentences that capture the essence of the thesis statement. Now let's see how Emming might work with these statements to assure himself that he has the *best* wording for his points.

1. **Are the main points clear?** Main points are **clear** when their wording is likely to call up the same images in the minds of all audience members. For his speech, Emming has written the third main point as follows:

> III. Finding a suitable credit card can also depend on weighing the advertised perks, which is the third criterion that you will want to use to be sure that it is suitable for where you are in life.

As he reviews the wording of the main point, he notices that it is repetitive ("suitable . . . suitable"), too general ("where you are in life"), and wordy ("which is the third criterion that you will want to use to be sure that it is suitable").

Emming sees that he could improve the clarity of the main point by cutting all the words before "weighing the advertised perks," cutting "which," and changing the rest of the sentence to "is the third criterion for finding a suitable credit card." After these changes, Emming would then have a main point written as follows:

> III. Weighing the advertised perks is the third criterion for finding a suitable credit card.

Now let's consider the second question.

2. **Are the main points parallel in structure?** Main points are **parallel** when their wording follows the same structural pattern, often using the same introductory words. Parallel structure helps the audience recognize main points by recalling a pattern in the wording. For example, Emming notices that each of his main points begins with different wording. He might decide to create a parallel structure by focusing on each main point as a "criterion." Then his draft of the main points, echoing the wording of his thesis statement, would be as follows:

> I. One criterion for finding a suitable credit card is to examine the interest rate.
> II. A second criterion for finding a suitable credit card is to examine the annual fee.
> III. A third criterion for finding a suitable credit card is to weigh the perks.

Parallelism may be achieved in many other ways. A second common way is to start each sentence with an active verb. Let's suppose that Kenneth is writing a speech on how to antique a table. In his first draft of the main points, Kenneth might identify these main points:

clarity of main points– *wording of points is likely to call up the same images in the minds of all audience members.*

parallel structure of main points–*wording of points follows the same structural pattern, often using the same introductory words.*

I. Clean the table thoroughly.
II. The base coat can be painted over the old surface.
III. A stiff brush, sponge, or piece of textured material can be used to apply the antique finish.
IV. Then you will want to apply two coats of shellac to harden the finish.

With careful revision, Kenneth might construct a final draft where the main points are made parallel by beginning each point with an active verb (italicized):

I. *Clean* the table thoroughly.
I. *Paint* the base coat over the old surface.
III. *Apply* the antique finish with a stiff brush.
IV. *Harden* the surface with two coats of shellac.

Notice how this small change clarifies and strengthens his message so that his audience can immediately identify the key steps in the process.

Now that we have considered the first two questions, let's consider the third.

meaningful main points– *content of points is informative.*

3. **Are the main points meaningful?** Main points are **meaningful** when they are truly informative. If the main points are not really meaningful, the audience gets no significant information and has no motivation for remembering them. Let's go back to Emming's first main point. Suppose he had written it as follows:

I. Thinking about the interest is one important thing.

What would his audience learn from this statement? Not much. Contrast that wording with this:

I. One criterion for finding a suitable credit card is to examine the interest rate.

Now the audience has the opportunity to connect the idea of interest rates to a meaningful task—choosing a suitable credit card.

Now let's consider the final question.

limited number of main points–*points limited to five or fewer.*

4. **Are the main points limited in number?** Main points are **limited in number** when the total is five or fewer. As you begin to phrase prospective main points, if your thesis statement is still too broad (or if you stray from it), you may find your list growing to five, seven, or even ten points that seem to be main ideas. A list that long is usually a clue that some points are really "subpoints" or repeat other points. If you have more than five points, group similar points under a single heading, or determine whether some points are subpoints that can be included under main points. Then you can revise your thesis statement accordingly.

Suppose you were giving a speech on shooting an effective foul shot. You might start with this list of points:

I. Face the basket before shooting.
II. Hold your shoulders parallel to the foul line.

  III. Spread your feet comfortably with your knees bent.
  IV. Put your foot that is opposite to your shooting arm slightly forward.
   V. Hold the ball in your shooting hand with your elbow bent.
  VI. Concentrate on a spot just over the rim.
 VII. Straighten your knees as you shoot the ball.
VIII. Follow through after the ball is released.

Now notice how you can make the steps even more meaningful by grouping them under three headings:

   I. First, square yourself to the basket.
    A. Face the basket before shooting.
    B. Hold your shoulders parallel to the foul line.
  II. Second, have proper balance.
    A. Spread your feet comfortably with your knees bent.
    B. Put your foot that is opposite to your shooting arm slightly forward.
 III. Third, deliver the ball smoothly.
    A. Hold the ball in your shooting hand with your elbow bent.
    B. Concentrate on a spot just over the rim.
    C. Straighten your knees as you shoot the ball.
    D. Follow through after the ball is released.

Notice that this organization actually results in more items (eleven versus eight), but it is easier to remember two to four items under each of three main headings than it is to remember eight separate items.

Determining the Best Order

A speech can be organized in many different ways. Your objective is to find or *create* the structure that will help the audience make the most sense of the material. Although "real speeches" come with many types of organization, three basic orders are useful for the beginning speaker to master: topic, time, and logical reasons.

    Topic order organizes the main points of the speech by categories or divisions of a subject. This is an extremely common way of ordering main points because nearly any subject may be subdivided or categorized in many different ways. The order of the topics may go from general to specific, least important to most important, or in some other logical sequence.

    In this example, the topics are presented in the order that the speaker believes is most suitable for the audience and speech goal, with the most important point at the end:

    Specific goal: I want the audience to understand three proven elements for ridding our bodies of harmful toxins.

    Thesis statement: Three proven elements involved in ridding our bodies of harmful toxins are reducing animal foods, hydrating, and eating natural whole foods.

topic order—*organizing the main points of the speech by categories or divisions of a subject.*

Main points:
  I. One proven element involved in ridding our bodies of harmful toxins is reducing our intake of animal products.
 II. A second proven element involved in ridding our bodies of harmful toxins is eating more natural whole foods.
III. A third proven element involved in ridding our bodies of harmful toxins is keeping well hydrated.

Emming's speech on the three criteria that will enable the audience to find the credit card that is most suitable is another example of a speech using topic order.

time or **chronological order**—
organizing the main points of the speech by a sequence of ideas or events, focusing on what comes first, second, third, and so on.

    Time or **chronological order** follows a sequence of ideas or events; it focuses on what comes first, second, third, and so on. When you select a chronological arrangement of main points, the audience understands that there is a particular importance to both the sequence and the content of those main points. Time order is most appropriate when you are explaining how to do something, how to make something, how something works, or how something happened. Kenneth's speech on steps in antiquing a table is one example of time order.

    In the following example, notice how the order of main points is as important to the logic of the speech as the wording:

Specific goal: I want the audience to understand the four steps involved in preparing an effective résumé.

Thesis statement: The steps of preparing a résumé include gathering relevant information, deciding on an appropriate format, planning the layout, and polishing the statements of information.

Main points:
  I. First, gather relevant information.
 II. Second, decide on an appropriate format.
III. Third, plan the layout.
IV. Fourth, polish the statements of information.

Although the designations first, second, and so forth are not necessary to the pattern, their inclusion helps the audience to understand that the sequence is important.

logical reasons order—
organizing the main points of the speech with statements that indicate why the audience should believe something or behave in a particular way.

    Logical reasons order emphasizes *why* the audience should *believe* something or *behave* in a particular way. Unlike the other two arrangements of main points, the logical reasons order is most appropriate for a persuasive speech.

Specific goal: I want the audience to donate money to the United Way.

Thesis statement: Donating to the United Way is appropriate because your one donation covers many charities, you can stipulate which specific charities you wish to support, and a high percentage of your donation goes to charities.

Main points:

I. You should donate to the United Way because one donation covers many charities.

II. You should donate to the United Way because you can stipulate which charities you wish to support.

III. You should donate to the United Way because a high percentage of your donation goes directly to the charities.

As we mentioned earlier, these three organizational patterns are the most common ones. As you develop your public-speaking skill, you may find that you will need to revise an existing pattern or create a totally different one to meet the needs of your particular subject matter or audience.

In summary, to organize the body of your speech, (1) turn your speech goal into a thesis statement that forecasts the main points, (2) state the main points in complete sentences that are clear, parallel, meaningful, and limited to five in number, and (3) organize the main points in the pattern best suited to your material and the needs of your specific audience.

Selecting and Outlining Supporting Material

The main points outline the structure of your speech. Whether your audience understands, believes, or appreciates what you have to say usually depends on how well those main points are explained and supported.

As we saw in Chapter 13, factual statements and expert opinions are the principal types of research information used in speeches. Once the main points are in place, you can select the most relevant of those materials and decide how to build each main point.

List Supporting Material

First, write down a main point. Then, under that main point list all the information you have found that you believe is related to that main point. Don't worry if ideas are out of order or don't seem to relate to each other. Your goal in this section is to see what you have to work with. For example, Figure 14.1 shows Emming's full list of supporting material as well as how Emming edited this list for his first main point.

Organize Supporting Material

Once you have listed the items of information that make the point, look for relationships between and among ideas. As you analyze, draw lines connecting information that fits together logically, and cross out information that seems

Peter L. Chapman

Select material from your research that you believe is related to each main point.

irrelevant or doesn't really fit. You may also combine similar ideas that are stated in different words.

Similar items that you have linked can often be grouped under broader headings. For instance, Figure 14.1 shows how Emming identified four statements related to specific percentages and two statements related to types of interest rate. You are also likely to find information that you decide not to include in the outline. (See the two items that Emming crossed out.)

Now read this outline of Emming's first main point in which he creates two headings with subheadings for each and omits the two items that he crossed out. Also notice that the outline follows a consistent form: Main points are

I. One criterion for finding a suitable credit card is to examine the interest rate.
   Most credit cards carry an average of 18 percent.
   Some cards carry an average of as much as 21 percent.
   ~~Some cards offer a grace period.~~
   ~~Department store rates are often higher than bank rates.~~
   Average rates are much higher than ordinary interest rates.
   Variable rate means that the rate will change from month to month.
   Fixed rate means that the rate will stay the same.
   Many companies quote very low rates (6 percent to 8 percent) for specific periods.

Figure 14.1
Emming's supporting materials list and how he edited it.

designated with Roman numerals; major subpoints are designated with capital letters; and supporting points are designated with Arabic numbers.

   I. One criterion for finding a suitable credit card is to examine the interest rate.

      A. Interest rates are the percentages that a company charges you to carry a balance on your card past the due date.

         1. Most credit cards carry an average of 18 percent, which is much higher than ordinary interest rates.

         2. Some cards carry an average of as much as 21 percent.

         3. Many companies quote very low rates (6 percent to 8 percent) for specific periods.

      B. Interest rates can be variable or fixed.

         1. A variable rate means that the rate will change from month to month.

         2. A fixed rate means that the rate will stay the same.

The outline lists supporting material; it does not include all of the development. For instance, in this speech, Emming might build points by using personal experiences, examples, illustrations, anecdotes, statistics, quotations, and other forms of supporting material. The outline only needs to include enough supporting information to ensure that you can explain and clarify the point you are making. Later, if you believe some of the other supporting material needs to be included in the outline, you can add it.

Outlining Section Transitions

Transitions are words, phrases, or sentences that show a relationship between other words, phrases, or sentences. In this chapter, we focus on what we call section transitions. We will consider other types of transitions in Chapter 15, "Adapting Verbally and Visually."

Section transitions are complete sentences that link major sections of a speech. They may summarize what has gone before and show movement to the next main idea. These transitions act like a tour guide leading the audience through the speech and are helpful when you do not want to take a chance that the audience might miss something.

Section transitions work best at breaks from one part of the speech to another or from one main point to another. For example, suppose Kenneth has just finished the introduction of his speech on antiquing tables and is now ready to launch into his main points. Before stating his first main point he might say: "Antiquing a table is a process that has four steps—now let's consider the first of those four steps." When his listeners hear this transition, they are mentally prepared to listen to the wording of the first main point.

transitions—*words, phrases, or sentences that show a relationship between other words, phrases, or sentences.*
section transitions—*complete sentences that link major sections of a speech.*

Michael Newman/PhotoEdit, Inc.

Section transitions mentally prepare the audience to move to the next main idea.

COMMUNICATE! Using InfoTrac College Edition

Using InfoTrac College Edition, click on PowerTrac. Press on Key Word and drag down to Journal Name. Enter "Vital Speeches." View Vital Speeches and find Johnson, Geneva B. "Service: Life beyond self."

1. What is her speech goal?
2. Outline her main points. Were they clearly stated? If not, how might she have increased their clarity? If so, what led to their clarity?
3. Identify any transitions between main points. Which transition(s) seemed particularly informative or useful? Why?
4. How does she conclude her speech? What goals does her conclusion meet?

When he finishes talking about the first main point, he might use another section transition: "Now that we see what is involved in cleaning the table, let's move on to the second step." You might be thinking, "This sounds repetitive to me" or "If I used all these transitions my audience will think I'm treating them like four-year-olds!" Nothing could be further from the truth.

Section transitions are important for two reasons. First, they help the audience follow the flow of the speech. If every member of the audience were able to pay one hundred percent attention to every word, perhaps section transitions would not be needed. But as people's attention rises and falls during a speech, they often find themselves wondering where they are. Section transitions give us a mental jolt and say, "Pay attention."

Second, section transitions are important in helping us retain information. We may well remember something that was said once in a speech, but our retention is likely to increase markedly if we hear something more than once. Good transitions are important in writing, but they are even more important in speaking. If listeners get lost or think they have missed something, they cannot check back as they can with writing. By using good transitions, speakers help listeners stay with them and remember more of the information.

In a speech, if we forecast main points, then state each main point, and have transitions between each point, audiences are more likely to follow and to remember the organization.

On your speech outline, section transitions are written in parentheses at the junctures of the speech.

Preparing the Introduction

At this stage of preparation, you are well enough prepared to consider the introduction that you will use.

Because the introduction is critical in establishing your relationship with your audience, it is worth investing the time to compare different openings. Try working on two or three different introductions; then pick the one you believe will work best for your specific audience and speech goal.

How long should the introduction be? Most introductions range from 5 to 10 percent of the speech. Thus, for a five-minute speech (approximately 750 words), an introduction of 35 to 75 words is appropriate; for a thirty-minute speech, an introduction of two to four minutes is appropriate. Your introduction should be long enough to put listeners in a frame of mind that will encourage them to hear you out without being so long that it leaves too little time to develop the substance of the speech. Of course, the shorter the speech, the shorter the introduction.

Goals of the Introduction

For any speech, a good introduction will get attention and lead into the content of the speech. A good introduction may also establish credibility, set the tone for the speech, and create a bond of goodwill between speaker and audience. Let's look at each of these goals in more detail.

Getting attention An audience's physical presence does not guarantee that they will listen to your speech. Therefore, your first goal is always to create an opening that will win the listeners' attention. You can arouse their interest by providing them with a reason they need to know the information you will be presenting. In the next section, we discuss several types of attention-getting devices you may use.

Leading into content Audiences want to know what the speech is going to be about, so it is also important to forecast your organization in the introduction. For instance, in a speech on campaigning, after your attention-getter, you may say, "In this speech, I'll explain the four stages of a political campaign." A clear forecast of the main points is appropriate unless you have some special reason for not revealing the organization.

Establishing your credibility Regardless of your topic or goal, your audience may wonder why they should pay attention to what *you* have to say. Although credibility is built and maintained throughout the speech, if you have any thought that your audience may not recognize your credentials for speaking on this topic, it is a good idea to say something about your earning the right to talk on this topic. For instance, when Erin starts her speech on the volleyball spike, her audience is likely to feel more comfortable with her as an authority if she mentions that she is a member of the women's varsity volleyball team.

OBSERVE & ANALYZE
Journal Activity

Outlining the Speech Body

In your Student Workbook under Journal Activity 14.2, outline the body of your first speech.

1. Write your speech goal at the top of the page.
2. Write your thesis statement next.
3. Select the headings from your thesis statement.
   Write the prospective main points in outline form.
   Revise the wording of the main points so that each is written in a complete sentence that is clear, parallel, and meaningful.
   Based on the nature of the material and your audience, determine the best order for the main points: topic order, time order, or logical reasons order. If need be, rewrite the main points in this order.
4. List the factual statements, expert opinions, and other information you have found to develop each main point.
   Group the points of information that relate to each other.
   Subordinate material so that each subpoint contains only one idea.
5. Write section transition statements in the body of the outline that summarize the previous main point or forecast the next main point.

Setting a tone A humorous opening will signal a lighthearted tone; a serious opening signals a more thoughtful or somber tone. A speaker who starts with a rib-tickling ribald story is putting the audience in a lighthearted, devil-may-care mood. If that speaker then says, "Now let's turn to the subject of abortion (or nuclear war or drug abuse)," the audience will be confused and the speech may be doomed.

Creating a bond of goodwill In the first few words, you often establish how an audience will feel about you as a person. If you are enthusiastic, warm, and friendly and give a sense that what you are going to talk about is in the audience's best interest, the audience will feel more comfortable spending time listening to you.

Types of Introductions

Ways to begin a speech are limited only by your imagination. In very short speeches—the kind you will be giving this term—you will want to focus on getting attention and leading into the content of the speech. You can get your audience's attention with a startling statement, a question, a story, a personal reference, a quotation, or a suspense opening. Any of these devices can be adapted to both short and longer speeches.

Startling statement One excellent way to grab your listeners' attention and focus on the topic quickly is to open with a startling statement that will override the various competing thoughts in your listeners' minds. This example illustrates the attention-getting effect of a startling statement:

> **If I pointed a pistol at you, you would be justifiably scared. But at least you would know the danger to your life. Yet every day we let people fire away at us with messages that are dangerous to our pocketbooks and our minds, and we seldom say a word. I'm talking about television advertisers.**
>
> **Today I want to look at our choices in how we can go about letting our feelings about advertising be heard.**

In just seventy-six words—about thirty seconds—this introduction grabs attention and leads into the speech.

rhetorical question–

a question seeking a mental rather than a vocal response.

Rhetorical question Asking a **rhetorical question**, a question seeking a mental rather than a vocal response, is another appropriate opening for a short speech. Here a student begins her speech on counterfeiting with three short questions:

> **What would you do with this twenty-dollar bill if I gave it to you? Take your friend to a movie? Treat yourself to a pizza and drinks? Well, if you did either of these things, you could get in big trouble—this bill is counterfeit!**
>
> **Today I want to share with you the extent of counterfeiting of American money worldwide and what our government is doing to curb it.**

Again, a short opening (seventy words, less than thirty seconds) gets attention and leads into the speech.

Story If you have a good story that gets an audience's attention and is really related to the goal of the speech, you probably have an unbeatable opening. Because many good stories are rather long, they are often more appropriate for speeches with time limits of ten minutes or more. However, you will occasionally find or think of a story that you can abbreviate that is just right for your speech (Ettinger, 2000, p. 727).

> Last summer, Buffalo Bills quarterback Doug Flutie was watching the final game of the Women's World Cup soccer match on TV with his 12-year-old soccer-playing daughter, Alexa. During the match, the hugely successful advertisement for Gatorade featuring superstar Michael Jordan and U.S. Team star Mia Ham came on, at which time Alexa asked, "Dad, who's the guy with Mia?"
>
> My optimistic belief is that perceptions are in the eye of the beholder and role models like Mia are setting the stage for a new world view.

Although Ettinger's opening was well over 150 words, this 89-word revision would work well for a five- to seven-minute classroom speech.

Personal reference Although any good opening should engage the audience, the personal reference is directed solely to that end. In addition to getting attention, a personal reference can be especially effective at engaging listeners as active participants in a speech. A personal reference opening like this one on exercise may be suitable for a speech of any length:

> Say, were you panting when you got to the top of those four flights of stairs this morning? I'll bet there were a few of you who vowed you're never going to take a class on the top floor of this building again. But did you ever stop to think that maybe the problem isn't that this class is on the top floor? It just might be that you are not getting enough exercise.
>
> Today I want to talk with you about how you can build an exercise program that will get you and keep you in shape, yet will only cost you three hours a week, and not one red cent.

Quotation A particularly vivid or thought-provoking quotation makes an excellent introduction to a speech of any length. You will need to use your imagination to relate the quotation to your topic so that it yields maximum benefits. For instance, in the beginning of her introduction, notice how Suzanne Morse, Director of the Pew Partnership for Civic Change (2001), uses a quotation to get the attention of her audience:

> A few years ago, one of America's foremost philosophers, Yogi Berra, remarked to his wife on a trip to the Baseball Hall of Fame in Cooperstown, New York, "We are completely lost but we are making good time." I am afraid Yogi's observation may be true for more than just his navigational skills. For Americans, our direction on the important social issues of the day finds us lost but still driving.
>
> As we think about strategies for change needed for America's third century, we must go in new directions. (p. 186)

Suspense If you can start your speech in a way that gets the audience to ask, "What is she leading up to?" you may well get them hooked for the entire speech. The suspense opening is especially valuable when the topic is one that the audience ordinarily might not be willing to listen to if the speech were opened less dramatically. Consider the attention-getting value of this introduction:

> **It costs the United States more than $116 billion per year. It has cost the loss of more jobs than a recession. It accounts for nearly 100,000 deaths a year. I'm not talking about cocaine abuse—the problem is alcoholism. Today I want to show you how we can avoid this inhumane killer by abstaining from it.**

Notice that by putting the problem, "alcoholism," at the end, the speaker encourages the audience to try to anticipate the answer. And because the audience may well be thinking "narcotics," the revelation that the answer is alcoholism is likely to be that much more effective.

Outlining the Conclusion

Shakespeare said, "All's well that ends well," and nothing could be truer of a good speech. A conclusion has two major goals: (1) to wrap up the speech so that it reminds the audience of what you have said and (2) to hit home so that the audience will remember your words or consider your appeal. Even though the conclusion will be a relatively small part of the speech—seldom more than 5 percent (thirty-five to forty words of a five-minute speech)—it is worth the time and effort to make it effective.

Speakers select the type of conclusion for their speeches on the basis of the speech goal and the likely appeal to the audience. To determine how you will conclude your speech, try out two or three conclusions, then choose the one that you believe will best reinforce your speech goal with your audience. You will want to master four basic types of conclusions: summary, story, appeal to action, and emotional impact conclusions.

Summary Conclusions

By far the easiest way to end a speech is to summarize the main points. Thus, the shortest appropriate ending for a speech on the warning signs of cancer would be, "So remember, if you experience a sudden weight loss, lack of energy, or blood in your urine or bowels, you should see a doctor immediately." Such an ending restates the key ideas the speaker wants the audience to remember. Summaries are appropriate for either informative or persuasive speeches.

Effective speakers often summarize to achieve the first speech goal—wrapping up the speech so that it reminds the audience of what they have said. But effective speakers are likely to supplement their summaries with material designed to achieve the second goal—hitting home so that the audience will remember their

An effective conclusion will wrap up your speech and hit home in a way that will help the audience remember your message.

words or consider their appeal. The other types of conclusions presented here can be used to supplement or replace the summary.

Story Conclusions

Storylike, or anecdotal, material that reinforces the message of the speech works just as well for the conclusion as for the introduction. In his speech on banking, Edward Crutchfield (1980) ends with a personal experience, showing that bankers must be ready to meet competition coming from any direction:

> I played a little football once for Davidson—a small college about 20 miles north of Charlotte. One particularly memorable game for me was one in which I was blindsided on an off-tackle trap. Even though that was 17 years ago, I can still recall the sound of cracking bones ringing in my ears. Well, 17 years and 3 operations later my back is fine. But, I learned something important about competition that day. Don't always assume that your competition is straight in front of you. It's easy enough to be blindsided by a competitor who comes at you from a very different direction. (p. 537)

Storylike conclusions will work for either informative or persuasive speeches.

Appeal to Action Conclusions

The appeal to action is a common way to end a persuasive speech. The **appeal** describes the behavior that you want your listeners to follow after they have heard the arguments. Notice how Heather Ettinger concludes her speech on Shattering the Glass Floor (2000) with a strong appeal to action:

appeal–*describes the behavior that you want your listeners to follow after they have heard the arguments.*

We have to stop thinking someone else will change the world. We've got to get it that we're the ones.

As you drive home tonight, remember to lift while you climb and outstretch that hand to help another woman, another girl. Let's shatter the glass floor. Let's be women donors who are leaders of fundamental change. (p. 730)

By their nature, appeals are most relevant for persuasive speeches, especially when the goal is to motivate an audience to act.

Emotional Impact Conclusions

No conclusion is more impressive than one that drives home the most important points with real emotional impact. Consider the way Richard Lamm (1998), of the Center of Public Policy and Contemporary Issues, ends his speech on unexamined assumptions with a powerful emotional appeal for unity:

Diverse people must unify or they have conflicts. Melting pots that don't melt become pressure cookers. A country is not a rooming house where we just live while we make our living. What is the social glue that holds diverse people together? Beware of "pyrrhic victories." Listen to John Gardner: "If a community is lucky, and fewer and fewer are, it will have a shared history and tradition. It will have its 'story,' its legends and heroes and will re-tell those stories often. It will have symbols of group identity—a name, a flag, a location, songs and stories in common—which it will use to heighten its merciless sense of belonging. To maintain the sense of belonging and the dedication and commitment so essential to community life, members need inspiring reminders of shared goals and values." (p. 714)

Like the appeal, the emotional conclusion is likely to be used for a persuasive speech where the goal is to reinforce belief, change belief, or motivate an audience to act.

Listing Sources

Regardless of the type of speech or how long or how short it will be, list your sources on the outline alphabetically by last name of author or by category with items listed alphabetically in each category: books, magazines, newspapers, electronic databases, experience, observation, and interviews.

1. **Books.** For a book, write the name of the author (last name first), the title of the book, the chapter or the article if the book is a collection of chapters and articles written by different people, the place of publication and the publisher, and the publication date. For example:

OBSERVE & ANALYZE
Journal Activity

Writing Speech Conclusions

In your Student Workbook under Journal Activity 14.4, prepare three separate conclusions that you believe would be appropriate for the body of the speech you outlined in Journal Activity 14.2, and present each aloud.

Then write answers to the following questions: Which one works best? Why?

Tobin, David L. *Coping Strategies Therapy for Bulimia Nervosa.* Washington, DC: American Psychological Association, 2000.

Janzen, Rod, "Five Paradigms of Ethnic Relations," pp. 63–72, in Larry Samovar and Richard Porter, Eds., *Intercultural Communication,* 8th ed., Belmont, CA: Wadsworth Publishing, 1997.

2.   **Magazines, Academic Journals, and Newspapers.** For such periodicals, write the name of the author (last name first) if one is given, the title of the article, the name of the magazine, journal, or newspaper, the date, and the page number from which the information was taken. Here are some examples:

Magazine:

Quinn, Jane Bryant, "Should You Be Worried?" *Newsweek,* August 17, 1998, 40–42.

Academic Journal:

Flanigan, Andrew J., & Metzger, Miriam J. "Internet Use in the Contemporary Media Environment." *Human Communication Research,* (Jan. 2001), 153–181.

Newspaper:

DiFilippo, Dana, "Year-round Schools Gaining Popularity," *The Cincinnati Enquirer,* August 1, 1998, B5, B7.

3.   **Electronic Databases.** When you take material from the Web or some other electronic source, try to include as much documentation as possible so that a person could find what you have cited. Here is an example:

http://www.biopsychiatry.comm/mdmadip.htm. MDMA (Ecstasy): The Effects of E on Mood and Cognition. Listed in April 2001.

4.   **Experience and Observation.** If you are drawing from your own experience or observation, list the nature of that experience or observation. Here are two examples:

Work experience: Fegel's Jewelry, senior year of high school, 1999–2000.
Observation: Visited Schoenling Brewery, April 22, 2000. Spent an hour on the floor observing the use of various machines in the total process and employees' responsibilities at each stage.

5.   **Interviews.** If you have conducted an interview, list the name of the person, the person's position, and the date of that interview:

Interview with Bruno Mueller, diamond cutter at Fegel's Jewelry, March 19, 2001.

Completing the Outline

Now that you have all the parts, it is time to put everything together in complete outline form. Use this checklist to be sure you have an outline that will be most useful to you as you move into adaptation and rehearsal.

1. **Have I used a standard set of symbols to indicate structure?** Main points usually are indicated by Roman numerals, major subdivisions by capital letters, minor subheadings by Arabic numerals, and further subdivisions by lowercase letters.

2. **Have I written main points and major subdivisions as complete sentences?** Complete sentences help you to see (1) whether each main point actually develops your speech goal and (2) whether the wording makes your intended point. Unless the key ideas are written out in full, it will be difficult to follow the next guidelines.

3. **Do main points and major subdivisions contain a single idea?** This guideline ensures that the development of each part of the speech will be relevant to the point. Thus, rather than

    I. The park is beautiful and easy to get to.

    divide the sentence so that both parts are separate:

    I. The park is beautiful.
    II. The park is easy to get to.

    The two-point example sorts out distinct ideas so that the speaker can line up supporting material with confidence that the audience will see and understand its relationship to the main points.

4. **Does each major subdivision relate to or support its major point.** This principle is called *subordination*. Consider the following example:

    I. Proper equipment is necessary for successful play.
        A. Good gym shoes are needed for maneuverability.

B. Padded gloves will help protect your hands.

C. A lively ball provides sufficient bounce.

D. And a good attitude doesn't hurt.

Notice that the main point deals with equipment; A, B, and C (shoes, gloves, and ball) relate to the main point. But D, attitude, is not equipment and should appear somewhere else, if at all.

5. **Are the total words in the outline limited to no more than one-third the total number of words anticipated in the speech?** An outline is only a skeleton of the speech, not a manuscript with letters and numbers. The outline should be short enough to allow you to experiment with methods of development during practice periods and to adapt to audience needs during the speech itself. An easy way to judge whether your outline is about the right length is to be sure that it contains no more than one-third the number of words in the actual speech. Because approximate figures are all you need, to compute the approximate maximum words for your outline, start by assuming a speaking rate of 160 words per minute. (Last term, the speaking rate for the majority of speakers in my class was 140 to 180 words per minute.) Thus, using the average of 160 words per minute, a three- to five-minute speech would contain roughly 480 to 800 words, and the outline should be 160 to 300 words. An eight- to ten-minute speech, roughly 1,280 to 1,600 words, should have an outline of approximately 426 to 533 words.

Now that we have considered the various parts of an outline, let us put them together for a final look. The outline in Figure 14.2 illustrates the principles in practice. The commentary in the right-hand column focuses on each guideline we have considered.

OBSERVE & ANALYZE
Journal Activity

Completing the Speech Outline

In your Student Workbook under Journal Activity 14.5, using information from the four previous journal activities, complete the sentence outline for your first speech. Include your sources at the end of the outline.

Compare what you have written to the sample outline (Figure 14.2) to make sure that it conforms to the guidelines discussed in this chapter. Make sure you have included your speech goal, a thesis statement, an introduction, clearly written main points, transitions between main points, a conclusion, and a list of sources.

Summary

A speech is organized with an introduction, a body, and a conclusion.

First, organize the body of the speech. Begin by writing a thesis sentence based on the speech goal. When you have the potential main points, select the ones you will use. Main points are written as complete sentences that are specific, vivid, and written in parallel language.

A speech can be organized in many different ways depending on the type of speech and the nature of the material. Some of the most common organizational patterns are time, topic, and logical reasons.

Main points are embellished with supporting material. A useful process is to begin by listing the potential material, then subordinating the material in a way that clarifies the relationship between and among subpoints and main points.

ANALYSIS

Write your specific goal at the top of the page. Refer to the goal to test whether everything in the outline is relevant.

The heading *Introduction* sets the section apart as a separate unit. Whether or not every goal of the outline is shown in the wording of the main points, the introduction attempts to (1) get attention, (2) set a tone, (3) gain goodwill, (4) establish credibility, and (5) lead into the body.

The thesis statement states the elements that are suggested in the specific goal. In the speech, the thesis statement serves as a forecast of the main points.

The heading *Body* sets this section apart as a separate unit. In this example, main point I begins a topical pattern of main points. It is stated as a complete, meaningful sentence.

The two major subdivisions designated by A and B indicate the equal weight of these points.

The second level subdivisions designated by 1, 2, and 3 for the major subpoint A and 1 and 2 for the major subpoint B give the necessary information for understanding the subpoints. The number of major and second level subpoints is at the discretion of the speaker. After the first two stages of subordination, words and phrases may be used in place of complete sentences in further subdivisions.

This transition reminds listeners of the first main point and forecasts the second.

Main point II, continuing the topical pattern, is a complete, meaningful statement paralleling the wording of main point I. Furthermore, notice that each main point considers only one major idea.

OUTLINE

Specific Speech Goal: I would like the audience to understand the major criteria for finding a suitable credit card.

Introduction
I. How many of you have been hounded by credit card vendors outside the Student Union?
II. They make a credit card sound like the answer to all of your dreams, don't they?
III. Today I want to share with you three criteria you need to consider carefully before deciding on a particular credit card.

Thesis Statement: Three criteria that will enable the audience to find the credit card that is most suitable for them are level of real interest rate, annual fee, and advertised perks.

Body
I. One criterion for finding a suitable credit card is to examine the interest rate.
  A. Interest rates are the percentages that a company charges you to carry a balance on your card past the due date.
    1. Most credit cards carry an average of 18 percent.
    2. Some cards carry an average of as much as 21 percent.
    3. Many companies quote very low rates (6 to 8 percent) for specific periods.
  B. Interest rates can be variable or fixed.
    1. Variable rates mean that the rate will change from month to month
    2. Fixed rates mean that the rate will stay the same.

(Now that we have considered rates, let's look at the next criterion.)

II. A second criterion for finding a suitable credit card is to examine the annual fee.
  A. The annual fee is the cost the company charges you for extending you credit.
  B. The charges vary widely.
    1. Some cards advertise no annual fee.
    2. Most companies charge fees that average around twenty-five dollars.

OUTLINE

(After you have considered interest and fees, you can weigh the benefits that the company promises you.)

III. A third criterion for finding a suitable credit card is to weigh the perks.
- A. Perks are extras that you get for using a particular card.
  1. Some companies promise rebates.
  2. Come companies promise frequent flier miles.
  3. Some companies promise discounts on "a wide variety of items."
- B. Perks don't outweigh other criteria.

Conclusion

I. So, getting the credit card that's right for you may be the answer to your dreams.
II. But only if you exercise care in examining interest rates, annual fee, and perks.

Sources

Bankrate Monitor, October 2000, http://www.Bankrate.com
Lee, Jinkook, & Hogarth, Jeanne M., Relationships among information search activities when shopping for a credit card. *Journal of Consumer Affairs, 34,* Winter 2000, p. 330 (Downloaded from InfoTrac College Edition).
Lloyd, Nancy, "Charge Card Smarts," *Family Circle,* Feb. 1998, pp. 32–33.
Orman, Suze, "Minding Your Money," *Self,* Feb. 1998, p. 98.
Rose, Sarah, "Prepping for College Credit," *Money,* Sept. 1998, pp. 156–157.
Royal, Leslie E., Smart credit card use. *Black Enterprise, 31,* Nov. 2000, p. 193 (Downloaded from InfoTrac College Edition).

ANALYSIS

This transition summarizes the first two criteria and forecasts the third.

Main point III, continuing the topical pattern, is a complete, meaningful statement paralleling the wording of main points I and II.

Throughout the outline, notice that main points and subpoints are factual statements. The speaker adds examples, experiences, and other developmental material during practice sessions.

The heading *Conclusion* sets this section apart as a separate unit. The content of the conclusion is intended to summarize the main ideas and leave the speech on a high note.

A list of sources should always be a part of the speech outline. The sources should show where the factual material of the speech came from. The list of sources is not a total of all available sources, only those that were used directly or indirectly. Each of the sources is shown in proper form.

Figure 14.2
Sample speech outline with annotation.

Prepare transitions to be used between points. Transitions are complete sentences that link major sections of a speech.

Second, outline the introduction to gain attention, set the tone for the speech, create goodwill, and lead into the body of the speech. Typical speech introductions include startling statements, questions, stories, personal references, quotations, or suspense.

Third, outline the conclusion. A well-designed speech conclusion ties the speech together and ends it on a high note. Typical conclusions include summaries, stories, appeals to action, and emotional impact statements.

Fourth, list the sources.

Finally, to refine the outline, use a standard set of symbols, use complete sentences for main points and major subdivisions, limit each point to a single idea, relate minor points to major points, use no more than five main points, and make sure the outline length is no more than one-third the number of words of the final speech.

WHAT WOULD YOU DO?
A QUESTION OF ETHICS

As Marna and Gloria were eating lunch together, Marna happened to ask Gloria, "How are you doing in Woodward's speech class?"

"Not bad," Gloria replied. "I'm working on this speech about product development. I think it will be really informative, but I'm having a little trouble with the opening. I just can't seem to get a good idea for getting started."

"Why not start with a story—that always worked for me in class."

"Thanks, Marna, I'll think on it."

The next day when Marna ran into Gloria again, she asked, "How's that introduction going?"

"Great. I've prepared a great story about Mary Kay—you know, the cosmetics woman? I'm going to tell about how she was terrible in school and no one thought she'd amount to anything. But she loved dabbling with cosmetics so much that she decided to start her own business—and the rest is history."

"That's a great story. I really like that part about being terrible in school. Was she really that bad?"

"I really don't know—the material I read didn't really focus on that part of her life. But I thought that angle would get people listening right away. And after all, I did it that way because you suggested starting with a story."

"Yes, but . . ."

"Listen, she did start the business. So what if the story isn't quite right? It makes the point I want to make—if people are creative and have a strong work ethic, they can make it big."

1. What are the ethical issues here?

2. Is anyone really hurt by Marna's opening the speech with this story?

3. What are the speaker's ethical responsibilities?

Communicate! Online

Use your Communicate! CD-ROM for quick access to the electronic study resources that accompany this text. Included on your CD-ROM is access to InfoTrac College Edition, the World Wide Web, a demo of WebTutor for Communicate!, and the Communicate! Web site at the Wadsworth Communication Café. The Communicate! Web site offers chapter-by-chapter activities, quizzes, and a digital glossary.

Review the following key terms and complete the Speech Outlining exercises available under Activities for Chapter 14 at

http://communication.wadsworth.com/humancomm/verderber

Key Terms

appeal (351)
clarity of main points (339)
limited number of main points (340)
logical reasons order (342)
main points (337)
meaningful main points (340)

parallel structure of main points (339)
rhetorical question (348)
section transitions (345)
thesis statement (336)
time or **chronological order** (342)
topic order (341)
transitions (345)

Student Resources - Microsoft Internet Explorer

File   Edit   View   Favorites   Tools   Help

WADSWORTH
THOMSON LEARNING

Close Window

Communicate!
Rudolph F. Verderber
10th Edition
ISBN: 0534561160

Chapter Resources
Step 1: Select a Chapter
Step 2: Select a Resource
Step 3: Click 'Go'

Chapter 14

Activity   Go

Additional
Resources

WWW Links

Outlining Your Speech

You can email the results of this activity - your completed speech outline - to your instructor. To do so, provide the following information.

1. What is your speech title?
For example; Emming's Speech referenced on page 337 of your text was "Credit Cards."

Speech Title

2. What is your speech goal?
For example, Emming's goal was "I want the audience to be able to find the credit card that is most suitable for them."

OBJECTIVES

After you have read this chapter, you should be able to answer these questions:

- What can you do to develop common ground?

- What can you do to create or build audience interest?

- What can you do to adapt to your audience's level of understanding?

- What can you do to build the audience's perception of you as a speaker?

- What can you do to reinforce or change an audience's attitude toward your topic?

- What criteria do you use to select and construct visual aids?

- What do you include in an audience adaptation strategy?

15

Adapting Verbally and Visually

Jeremy asked his friend Gloria to listen to one of his speech rehearsals. As he finished the final sentence of the speech, "So, violence does affect people in several ways—it not only desensitizes them to violence, it also contributes to making them behave more aggressively," he asked Gloria, "So, what do you think?"

"You're giving the speech to your classmates, right?"

"Yeah."

"Well, you had a lot of good material, but I didn't hear anything that showed that you had members of the class in mind—you could have been giving the speech to any audience!"

Jeremy had forgotten something that has been recognized as long as speeches have been given: that a speech is intended for a specific audience.

audience adaptation–*the active process of verbally and visually relating material directly to the specific audience.*

Audience adaptation is the active process of verbally and visually relating material directly to the specific audience. You will recall that an effective speech plan is a product of five action steps. In this chapter, we consider the fourth step: **Develop a strategy for adapting material to your specific speech audience.** This involves (1) developing common ground, (2) building and maintaining audience interest, (3) relating to the audience's level of understanding, (4) reinforcing or changing audience attitudes toward you or your topic, and (5) relating information visually. In Chapter 16, we continue to emphasize these means of adapting through speech presentation.

Developing Common Ground

common ground–*awareness that the speaker and the audience share the same or similar information, feelings, and experiences.*

The first and in many ways the most important way speakers show awareness of their audience's presence is to use specific means of developing **common ground,** the awareness that the speaker and the audience share the same or similar information, feelings, and experiences.

Use Personal Pronouns

personal pronouns–*pronouns referring directly to the one speaking, spoken to, or spoken about.*

One way of developing common ground is to use **personal pronouns,** pronouns referring directly to the one speaking, spoken to, or spoken about. Merely by

When you develop common ground with your audience, they will relate better to what you are saying.

Bob Daemmrich/Stock, Boston

using the terms "you," "us," "we," and "our," you give listeners verbal signs that you are talking with them.

In his speech on effects of television violence, instead of saying, "When *people* think about violence on TV, *they* often wonder how it affects viewers," Jeremy could say, "When *you* think about violence on TV, *you* may wonder how it affects viewers." The use of just these two personal pronouns in the sentence may not seem like much, but it can mean the difference between audience attention and audience indifference to you and your speech.

Ask Rhetorical Questions

A second way of developing common ground is to ask **rhetorical questions,** questions phrased to stimulate a mental response rather than an actual spoken response on the part of the audience. For instance, in the television violence example, making one more change in the sample sentence would increase the sense of audience participation in the speech:

> **When you watch a particularly violent TV program, have you ever asked yourself, "I wonder whether watching such violent programs has any negative effects on viewers?"**

Rhetorical questions generate audience participation; once the audience participates, it becomes more involved in the content. Rhetorical questions must be sincere to be effective, so practice them until you can ask these questions naturally and sincerely.

Share Common Experiences

A third way of developing common ground is to share common experiences by selecting and presenting personal experiences, examples, and illustrations that *show* what you and the audience have in common. For instance, in his speech about effects of television violence, Jeremy might say something like, "Remember how sometimes at a key moment when you're watching a really scary movie you may close your eyes." In this case, Jeremy calls on the audience to provide their own personal moment of fear. That can be just as powerful as if he had taken the time to present the details of one particular incident.

Personalize Information

A fourth way of creating common ground is to **personalize** information by relating to specific audience references. Suppose you are giving a speech in California on the effects of the Japanese economy on U.S. markets, and you want to help listeners understand geographic data about Japan. You could cite the following statistics from the 2001 *World Almanac:*

> **Japan is small and densely populated. The nation's 126 million people live in a land area of 146,000 square miles that gives them a population density of 867 persons per square mile. (p. 803)**

rhetorical questions–*questions phrased to stimulate a mental response rather than a spoken response.*

COMMUNICATE! Using InfoTrac College Edition

Click on PowerTrac. Press on Key Word and drag down to Journal Name. Enter "Vital Speeches." View Vital Speeches and find a speech on or related to your topic, and read that speech. Look for ways the speaker attempted to create common ground. Did the speaker use personal pronouns or rhetorical questions? Share common experiences? Personalize information? If you find many examples, how did they help make the speech better? If you found few examples, how would their use have made the speech better?

personalize–*relating information to specific audience references.*

Although this passage relates the information, it is not at all related to the specific audience. You could state the same information in a way that would be both more interesting and more meaningful to your California audience:

> **Japan is a small, densely populated nation. Her population is 126 million—only about half that of the United States. Yet the Japanese are crowded into a land area of only 146,000 square miles—roughly the same size as the state of California. Just think of the implications of having one-half the population of the United States living in California, where 30 million now live. In addition, Japan packs 867 persons into every square mile of land, whereas in the United States we average about 74 persons per square mile. Japan, then, is about 12 times as crowded as the United States.**

This revision includes an invented comparison of the unknown, Japan, with the familiar, the United States and home state of California. Even though most Americans do not have the total land area of the United States on the tip of the tongue, they know that the United States covers a great deal of territory. Likewise, a California audience would have a mental picture of the size of their home state compared to the rest of the nation. If you were speaking to an audience from another part of the country, you could make your comparison to a different state, such as Texas, New York, or Florida. Such detailed comparisons enable the audience to visualize just how small and crowded Japan is.

Reworking information so that it creates common ground will take time, but the effort pays big dividends. Your listeners are always going to be asking, "What does this have to do with me?" Unless the way you present your information answers that question, your speeches are not going to be as effective as they should be. Examples, stories, illustrations, and quotations that relate to your audience answer that question.

Joan Gorham, the subject of the Spotlight on Scholars, has conducted many research projects that show the effect of adaptation, or what she calls "immediacy," on building attention and ensuring audience retention of information.

Creating and Maintaining Audience Interest

Listeners' interest depends on whether they believe the information has personal impact: "What does this have to do with me?" Let's consider four principles you can use to build and maintain audience interest: timeliness, proximity, seriousness, and vividness.

Timeliness

timely–*providing information that can be used now.*

Listeners are more likely to be interested in information they perceive as **timely**—they want to know how they can use the information *now*. Suppose for

Joan Gorham, Professor of Communication Studies and Associate Dean of Academic Affairs, Eberly College of Arts and Sciences, West Virginia University, on Immediacy

Joan Gorham began her professional career as a high school teacher, so it is not surprising that her substantial body of research has focused on "immediacy," the use of communicative behaviors to enhance the physical and psychological closeness between a teacher and student that ultimately affects student learning. Her first major work on the role of implicit communication in teaching was her dissertation at Northern Illinois University in which she contrasted how a teacher's "silent messages," those sent through nonverbal channels, affected both adult and child learners.

When Gorham accepted a position at West Virginia University, she began building on research by Jan Andersen, James McCroskey, Virginia Richmond, and others on the specific subject of immediacy. Although at that time she had not really intended to focus her lifetime research on immediacy, Gorham explained, "The research just grew out of itself. As I reported the data from one study, I found myself with many unanswered questions that motivated me to initiate new studies on different facets of the subject."

Taken together, Gorham's studies are helping teachers to understand how their communication behavior affects their relationship with their students and how it is associated significantly with student learning outcomes. Some of the early research on immediacy suggested that the learning outcome was just a perception. That is, students reported that they learned more from more immediate teachers, but these studies had not documented actual learning gains. As Gorham refined her research methods, she began to see results that supported the hypothesis that immediacy is directly correlated with learning.

Because the learning process consists of arousal, attention, and recall, Gorham believes teachers who demonstrate appropriate immediacy not only are more likely to stimulate their students to pay attention but also are more likely to increase the students' interest and motivation. As a result, students more easily understand and ultimately remember the information being presented.

From a practical sense, then, what specific behaviors must teachers use to increase their immediacy? From Gorham's studies, we learn that teachers gain immediacy in part through such nonverbal behaviors as using gestures, looking directly at students, smiling, moving around the classroom, and using variety in their vocal expressions. Moreover, Gorham's studies have shown that teachers gain immediacy through such verbal behaviors as using personal examples, relating personal experiences, using humor, using personal pronouns, addressing students by name, conversing with students outside of class, praising students' work, and soliciting students' perceptions about assignments.

Gorham's studies show that teachers can engage in behaviors that increase student motivation and ultimately student learning. Gorham has also probed the other side of the question. Are there behaviors related to immediacy that teachers exhibit that are "demotivating"—that is, behaviors that cause students to decrease attention and interest? Although students identify teacher behaviors as a factor in motivating them to do their best in college courses, Gorham found that negative teacher behaviors are perceived by students as more central to their "demotivation" than positive factors are to their motivation. Some of the most demotivating teacher behaviors noted by students are lacking a sense of humor, lacking in dynamic behavior, lacking empathy for students' perspectives, not being available for individual help, using nonimmediate nonverbal behaviors, and using too many stories or examples—engaging in overkill.

Can teachers learn to increase their immediacy and reduce nonimmediate behaviors? Gorham's research has shown that teachers can accurately monitor their own use of specific immediacy behaviors. Thus, as teachers are made aware of the critical role that immediacy plays in student motivation and learning, Gorham believes teachers can modify their own behavior and work toward incorporating the methods that lead to appropriate levels of immediacy. High-immediacy teachers are rated by students as higher in extroversion, composure, competence, and character than are low-immediacy teachers. They are rated as more similar to their students in attitude, but more expert than nonimmediate teachers. Students report being significantly more likely to engage in behaviors recommended by teachers who use immediacy behaviors. Thus learning the appropriate degree of immediacy between teachers and students becomes an important goal in the teaching–learning process.

In addition to her work as Associate Dean of Academic Affairs, Gorham also teaches courses in media effects, media literacy, and nonverbal and intercultural communication. In the future, Gorham plans to continue with replication and extension of her studies, but she is also interested in engaging in longitudinal studies of motivation and immediacy. For titles of several of her research publications, see the reference list at the end of this book. For more information about Gorham and her work, go to http://www.as.wvu.edu/~jgorham/jghp.html

your speech on "The criteria for evaluating the quality of diamonds," you determine that the topic is not likely to kindle much immediate audience interest. Here is an introduction that may help motivate your audience to see knowledge of diamonds as timely:

> **In thinking about a gift for your spouse or significant other to celebrate a special occasion, you may have though briefly about purchasing a diamond ring, earrings, or necklace. But, if you're like me, you might be shying away from that thought because you really don't know much about diamonds and you think you couldn't afford it. Well, today I'd like to help you out some by talking about criteria for evaluating the quality of diamonds.**

Proximity

proximity–*information with a relationship to personal space.*

Listeners are more likely to be interested in information that has **proximity**, a relationship to their personal space. Psychologically we pay more attention to information that affects our "territory" than to information that we perceive as remote. You have probably heard speakers say something like this: "Let me bring this closer to home by showing you...." Statements like this work because information becomes important to people when they perceive it as affecting "their own backyard." If, for instance, you are giving a report on the difficulties the EPA is having with its environmental cleanup campaigns, you would want to focus on examples in the audience's community. If you do not have that kind of information, take time to find it. For instance, for the EPA topic, a well-placed telephone call to the local or regional EPA office, or even to your local newspaper, will get the information you need to make the connection.

Seriousness

Listeners are more likely to be interested in information that is **serious,** that has a physical, economic, or psychological impact on them. To build or maintain interest during a speech on toxic waste, you could show serious *physical* impact by saying "Toxic waste affects the health of all of us"; you could show serious *economic* impact by saying "Toxic waste cleanup and disposal are expensive—they raise our taxes"; or you could show serious *psychological* impact by saying "Toxic waste erodes the quality of our life and the lives of our children."

Think of how your classroom attention picks up tremendously when the professor reveals that a particular piece of information is going to "be on the test." The potential serious economic impact (not paying attention can cost you a lowered grade) is often enough to jolt you into attention. Most of us just don't put our attention into high gear unless we see the seriousness of information.

serious–*information having physical, economic, or psychological impact.*

Vividness

Listeners are more likely to be interested in anecdotes, examples, and other information that are **vivid**—that arouse our senses. For instance, in the middle of a speech on toxic waste, you may see attention flagging as you present technical information. Instead of waiting until you have lost the audience, you might choose this time to say, "Let me share with you a story that illustrates the gravity of toxic waste."

Just because you have a great number of attention-getting stories, examples, and illustrations does not mean that you have to use all of them. The effective speaker is sensitive to audience reaction at all times. When the audience is really with you, there is no need to break the rhythm. But when you sense the audience is not following your ideas, that is the time to lighten up with material that will pique attention. Keep in mind, however, that such information must pertain directly to the point you are making or it will be counterproductive.

Also remember that there is almost no way to keep audience members on the edge of their seats throughout the entire speech. Some sections of a speech may demand more from an audience. Any speech, regardless of quality, has highs and lows. The difference between an excellent speech and a mediocre one is that the highs are much higher and the lows are at the level of the mediocre speech's highs.

vivid–*information that arouses our senses.*

COMMUNICATE!
Using Technology

Go to History and Politics Outloud at www.hpol.org. This audio archive includes "Historical Voices" and is funded by the National Endowment for the Humanities in partnership with Michigan State University. You can search for a particular speaker or browse by speech date. Read the description provided with each clip to assess how well the speaker adapted to the audience.

Adapting to the Audience's Level of Understanding

If you predict that your listeners do not have the necessary background to understand the information you will present in your speech, you will need to orient them. If, however, you predict that your audience has sufficient background, you will need to present the information in a way that will ensure continuous understanding.

Orienting Listeners

Because your listeners are likely to stop paying attention if they are lost at the start of your speech, a good rule of thumb is to err on the side of expecting little knowledge rather than expecting too much. So, if there is any reason to believe some people may not have necessary background knowledge, take time to review basic facts. For instance, for a speech about changes in political and economic conditions in Eastern Europe, you can be reasonably sure that everyone in your audience is aware of the breakup of the Soviet Union and Yugoslavia. However, they may not remember all of the specific countries that have been created. Before launching into changing conditions, remind your listeners of the names of the nations that you are going to be talking about.

Because some of your listeners may be well oriented, a good way to present that information without insulting their intelligence is to give the impression that you are reviewing information the audience remembers. By saying "As you will remember," "As we have come to find out," "As we all learned in our high school courses," your orientation will be accepted as review statements and not put-downs. For instance, for the speech on changes in political and economic conditions in Eastern Europe, you might say, "As you will recall, the former Soviet Union now consists of the following separate states." If listeners already know the information, they will see your statements as reminders. If they do not know it, they are getting the information in a way that does not call attention to their information gaps—they can act as if they do in fact remember.

How much orientation you give depends on how much time is available. When you do not have enough time to give a complete background, determine where a lack of information will impinge on your ability to get through to your audience and fill in the crucial information that closes those gaps.

Presenting New Information

Even when we predict that our audience has the necessary background information, we still need to work on ways of presenting new information that ensures continued understanding. Speakers can use devices such as defining, describing, exemplifying, and comparing to help clarify information that may be confusing or difficult for some audience members. A speaker must keep in mind that an audience is made up of individuals, and thus an effective speaker anticipates the different comprehension styles of those individuals. As you plan your speech, ask the following questions:

1. **Have you defined all key terms carefully?** For instance, if your speech goal is, "I want my audience to understand four major problems faced by those who are functionally illiterate," in the opening of your speech you might present this definition:

   By "functionally illiterate," I mean people who have trouble accomplishing transactions entailing reading and writing in which an individual wishes to engage.

2. **Have you supported every generalization with at least one specific example?** For instance, suppose that you made the statement,

   Large numbers of Americans who are functionally illiterate cannot read well enough to understand simple directions.

   You could then use the example,

   For instance, a person who is functionally illiterate might not be able to read or understand a label that says "take three times a day after eating."

3. **Have you compared or contrasted new information to information your audience already understands?** For instance, if you wanted the audience to sense what it feels like to be functionally illiterate, you might compare the problems of functional illiterates to problems many have experienced, such as dealing with a foreign language:

   Many of us have taken a foreign language in school. But as we enter a "foreign" territory, we often discover that even road signs are a little difficult to comprehend when we're under even a little pressure. For instance, when I was fortunate enough to get to Montreal last summer, I saw a sign that said that what I was looking for was "à droit." I thought I could handle simple directions, yet for just a minute I was puzzling whether "à droit" was "to the right" or "to the left." Just imagine what it must be like if for so many "simple" ideas or directions you had to puzzle for a while and run the risk that you were making a major mistake.

   In short, at any point in a speech where there appears to be any difficulty in understanding an idea or a concept, be prepared to define, exemplify, and compare or contrast.

4. **Have you used more than one means of development for significant points you want the audience to remember?** This final bit of advice is based on a sound psychological principle: The more different kinds of explanations a speaker gives, the more listeners will understand. Let's go back to a significant statement we made earlier:

   Large numbers of Americans who are functionally illiterate cannot read well enough to understand simple directions.

To this statement we added an example:

For instance, a person who is functionally illiterate might not be able to read or understand a label that says "take three times a day after eating."

The example makes the statement more meaningful.

Now let's see how we can build that statement even further:

A significant number of Americans are functionally illiterate. That is, large numbers of Americans, about 20 percent of the adult population, or around 35 million people, have serious difficulties with common reading tasks. They cannot read well enough to understand simple cooking instructions, directions on how to work an appliance, or rules on how to play a game. For instance, a person who is functionally illiterate might not be able to read or understand a label that says "take three times a day after eating."

The first statement, "A significant number of Americans are functionally illiterate," consists of eight words that are likely to be uttered in slightly less than five seconds! A listener who coughs, drops her pencil, or happens to remember an appointment she has during those five seconds will miss the entire sentence. The first example adds twenty-five words. Now it is likely that more people will get the point. The expanded example contains eighty-five words. Now, even in the face of some distractions, it is likely that most listeners will have heard and registered the information.

In short speeches you cannot fully develop every bit of information. You can, however, identify two or three of your highest priority bits of information and build them fully using two or three different kinds of development.

Building a Positive Attitude toward You as the Speaker

If you predict that the audience will have a positive attitude toward you as a speaker, then you need only try to maintain that attitude. If, however, you predict that the audience has no opinion or for some reason has a negative attitude toward you, then you will want to build your **credibility,** the level of trust an audience has or will have in you. There are several ways to do this.

credibility–*the level of trust an audience has or will have in the speaker.*

Building Audience Perception of Your Knowledge and Expertise

The first step in building a perception of knowledge and expertise is to go into the speaking situation fully prepared. Audiences have an almost instinctive knowledge of when a speaker is "winging it," and most audiences lose respect for a speaker who has not thought enough of them or the situation to have a well-prepared message.

Reuters Newsmedia Inc./CORBIS

Your audience will expect you to have a wealth of high-quality examples, illustrations, and personal experiences in your speech.

The next step is to show your audience that you have a wealth of high-quality examples, illustrations, and personal experiences. Recall how much more favorably you perceive your professors who have an inexhaustible supply of supporting information as opposed to those professors who present, and seem to have, only the barest minimum of facts.

The third step is to show any direct involvement you have had with the topic area. In addition to increasing the audience's perception of your depth of knowledge, your personal involvement increases the audience's perception of your practical understanding of the issues and your personal concern for the subject. For example, if you are speaking on toxic waste, your credibility will increase manifold by sharing with the audience your personal experiences in petitioning for local environmental controls.

Building Audience Perception of Your Trustworthiness

The more your listeners see you as one of them, the easier it will be for you to establish your **trustworthiness**, your character, and your apparent motives for speaking. The more your listeners see you as different, the more difficult it will be. Part of building credibility depends on your ability to bridge gaps between you and members of your audience.

First, listeners will make value judgments of your character based on their assessment of your moral and ethical traits. As you plan your speech, ask yourself what you can do in the speech to demonstrate that you are honest, industrious, dependable, and a morally strong person.

trustworthiness–*speaker's character and apparent motives for speaking.*

In addition, listeners will consider your apparent motives. Early in your speech, it is important to show why listeners need to know your information. Then, throughout the speech, you can emphasize your sincere interest in their well-being. For a speech on toxic waste, for example, you could explain *how* a local dumpsite adversely affects the community.

Building Audience Perception of Your Personality

Audience perceptions of your personality are likely to be based on their first impressions of you. Try to dress appropriately, groom yourself carefully, and carry yourself in an attractive manner. The old compliment "He/she cleans up real good" is one to remember.

In addition, audiences react favorably to a speaker who acts friendly. A smile and a pleasant tone of voice go a long way in showing a warmth that will increase listeners' comfort with you and your ideas.

We will discuss three additional features of personality (enthusiasm, eye contact, and vocal expressiveness) in Chapter 16 on speech presentation.

Adapting to the Audience's Attitude toward Your Speech Goal

Adapting to listeners' attitudes toward your speech goal is especially important for persuasive speeches, but it can be important for informative speeches as well. An audience **attitude** is a predisposition for or against people, places, or things that is usually expressed as an opinion.

attitude–*a predisposition for or against people, places, or things that is usually expressed as an opinion.*

At the outset, try to predict whether listeners will view your topic positively, negatively, or have no opinion. If, for instance, you think your listeners would view the topic of refinishing furniture positively or neutrally, then you can move forward with your speech. If, however, you think your listeners really view refinishing furniture as too hard or unimportant, then you will need to take time early in the speech to change their opinion. In Chapter 18 on persuasive speaking, we will consider strategies for dealing with listeners' attitudes in more detail.

Special Problems of Speakers from Different Cultures

This chapter has been written with the assumption that you have been raised in the United States. But even in the United States you may have to adapt to cultural differences of your listeners. For instance, Mexican Americans, Japanese Americans, and African Americans raised in the United States may maintain a strong sense of their Mexican, Japanese, or African heritage and as a result may see things differently from each other. In the Diverse Voices box, Shirley Weber's experience gives you a sense of one of the kinds of differences that you may have to adapt to.

The Need to Be: The Socio-Cultural Significance of Black Language

by Shirley N. Weber

One of the major differences in adapting to different groups is understanding their expectations and their reactions to your words. In this excerpt, Shirley Weber describes the black perspective on the audience's role in speaking.

To fully understand and appreciate black language and its function in the black community, it is essential to understand that while philosophies that govern the different groups in Africa vary, some general concepts are found throughout African cultures. One of the primary principles is the belief that everything has a reason for being. Nothing simply exists without purpose or consequences. This is the basis of John's explanation of the four basic elements of life, which are Muntu, mankind; Kintu, things; Hantu, place and time; and Kuntu, modality. These four elements do not exist as static objects but as forces that have consequences and influence. For instance in Hantu, the West is not merely a place defined by geographic location, but a force that influences the East, North, and South. Thus, the term "Western world" connotes a way of life that either complements or challenges other ways of life. The Western world is seen as a force and not a place. (This is applicable to the other three elements also.) Muntu, or man, is distinguished from the other three elements by his possession of Nommo, the magical power of the word. Without Nommo, nothing exists. Consequently, mankind, the possessor of Nommo, becomes the master of all things. . . .

Nommo is so powerful and respected in the black community that only those who are skillful users of the word become leaders. One of the main qualifications of leaders of black people is that they must be able to articulate the needs of the people in a most eloquent manner. And because Muntu is a force who controls Nommo, which has power and consequences, the speaker

must generate and create movement and power within his listeners. One of the ways this is done is through the use of imaginative and vivid language. Of the five canons of speech, it is said that Inventio or invention is the most utilized in black American. Molefi Asante called it the "coming to be of the novel," or the making of the new. So that while the message might be the same, the analogies, stories, images, and so forth must be fresh, new, and alive.

Because nothing exists without Nommo, it too is the force that creates a sense of community among communicators, so much so that the speaker and audience become one as senders and receivers of the message. Thus, an audience listening and responding to a message is just as important as the speaker, because without their "amens" and "right-ons" the speaker may not be successful. This interplay between speaker and listeners is called "call and response" and is a part of the African world view, which holds that all elements and forces are interrelated and indistinguishable because they work together to accomplish a common goal and to create a sense of community between the speaker and the listeners.

This difference between blacks and whites was evident, recently, in a class where I lectured on Afro-American history. During the lecture, one of my more vocal black students began to respond to the message with some encouraging remarks like "all right," "make it plain," "that all right," and "teach." She was soon joined by a few more black students who gave similar comments. I noticed that this surprised and confused some of the white students. When questioned later about this, their response was that they were not used to having more than one person talk at a time, and they really could not talk and listen at the same time. They found the comments annoying and disruptive. As the lecturer, I found the comments refreshing and inspiring. The black student who initiated the responses had no difficulty understanding what I was saying while she was reacting to it, and did not consider herself "rude."

In addition to the speaker's verbal creativity and the dynamic quality of the communication environment, black speech is very rhythmic. It flows like African languages in a consonant-vowel-consonant-vowel pattern. To achieve this rhythmic effect, some syllables are held longer and are accented stronger and differently from standard English, such as DE-troit. This rhythmic pattern is learned early by young blacks and is reinforced by the various styles it complements.

Excerpted from Shirley N. Weber, "The Need to Be: The Socio-Cultural Significance of Black Language." From Intercultural Communication: A Reader, *7th ed., eds. Larry A. Samovar and Richard E. Porter (Belmont, CA: Wadsworth, 1994), pp. 220–225. Reprinted by permission of the author.*

In addition, the chances of students in this course coming from foreign cultures has increased dramatically. Suppose, for a minute, that you are a person who has recently immigrated to the United States or has moved here for your higher education. Being less familiar with the general United States culture, you may have a more difficult time adapting to your classroom audiences than do other students in the class.

Two of the problems with adaptation for people from foreign backgrounds are difficulty with the English language and lack of a common set of experiences to draw from. Difficulty with the language includes both difficulty with pronunciation and difficulty with vocabulary and idiomatic speech. Both of these could make you feel self-conscious. But the lack of a common set of experiences to draw from may be even more significant. So much of our information is gained through comparison and examples that the lack of common experiences may make drawing comparisons and using appropriate examples much more difficult.

What can you do to help you through the public-speaking experience? Difficulty with pronunciation might require you to speak more slowly and to articulate as clearly as possible. Also, make sure that you are comfortable with your topic. You might want to consider talking about aspects of your homeland. Because you would be providing new information, your classmates would likely look forward to hearing you speak. It would be useful for you to practice at least once with a person raised in the United States. Ask that person to help you make sure you are using language and examples and comparisons that the audience will be able to relate to.

Most U.S. students are much more tolerant of mistakes made by people who are speaking in what is for them their second or even third language than they are of mistakes made by their fellow American-born students. This will work in your favor. Also, keep in mind that the more practice you get speaking to people from this culture, the more comfortable you will become with the language and with your ability to relate to the people you meet here.

Adapting to Audiences Visually

At this point in preparation, you are ready to consider how to adapt to audiences through **visual aids,** a form of speech development that enables the audience to see as well as to hear information. Visual aids help to clarify and dramatize verbal information, and using them will pay off for you. How? First, people are likely to learn considerably more when ideas appeal to both eye and ear than when they appeal to the ear alone (Tversky, 1997, p. 258). Second, people are likely to remember information shown on visual aids even over long periods (Patterson, Danscreau, & Newbern, 1992, pp. 453–461). Let's consider visual aids you can carry and visual aids you can make. Then we will consider media for visual aids, designing them, and making choices.

visual aid–*a form of speech development that enables the audience to see as well as to hear information.*

Visual Aids You Can Carry

Many times your speech can be helped by using a visual aid you can carry to class.

Yourself On occasion, *you* can be your own best visual aid. For instance, through descriptive gestures you can show the height of a tennis net; through your posture and movement you can show the motions involved in the butterfly swimming stroke; and through your own attire you can illustrate the native dress of a foreign country.

Objects A cell phone, a basketball, or a braided rug are the kinds of objects you can bring to class that can be seen by the audience. Objects make good visual aids if (1) they are large enough to be seen (consider how far away people will be sitting) and (2) small enough to carry around with you. For instance, Erin used a volleyball throughout much of her speech to show the audience how to spike.

Models When an object is too large to bring to the speech site or too small to be seen, a three-dimensional model may prove a worthwhile substitute. If you were to talk about a turbine engine, a suspension bridge, an Egyptian pyramid, or the structure of an atom, a model might well be the best visual aid. Working models can be especially eye-catching.

Photographs Photos are useful visual aids when you need an exact reproduction. To be effective, they need to be large enough to be seen from the back of the room and simple enough to make your point at a glance.

David Shopper/Stock, Boston

**Slides and overhead trans-
parencies get and hold
attention and can be seen
by the entire audience.**

Films Although films can be brought to class, they are seldom appropriate for speeches—mostly because films so dominate that the speaker loses control. Occasionally during a longer speech you may want to use short clips of a minute or two each. Still, because projecting film requires darkening the room for that portion of time, using film in a speech is often disruptive. Moreover, to use films you must bring a projector to class with you.

Slides The advantage of slides over film is that you can control when each image will be shown. The remote-control device enables you to pace your slides and to talk about each one as long as necessary. As with films, slides require darkening the room while they are projected, and novice speakers may lose control of their audience. And as with films, you must bring a projector to class with you.

Visual Aids You Can Create

The next group of visual aids require more work for you because you have to create them.

Drawings Simple drawings are easy to prepare. If you can use a compass, a straightedge, and a measure, you can draw well enough for most speech purposes. For instance, if you are making the point that water skiers must hold their arms straight, with the back straight and knees bent slightly, a stick figure

Figure 15.1
Sample drawing.

such as the one in Figure 15.1 will illustrate the point. Stick figures may not be as aesthetically pleasing as professional drawings, but they work just as well. In fact, elaborate, detailed drawings are not worth the time and effort and actually may obscure the point you wish to make.

Maps   Like drawings, maps are relatively easy to prepare. Simple maps enable you to focus on landmarks (mountains, rivers, and lakes), states, cities, land routes, or weather systems. Figure 15.2 is a good example of a map that focuses on weather systems.

Charts   A **chart** is a graphic representation that distills a lot of information and presents it to an audience in an easily interpreted format. Word charts and organizational charts are the most common.

Word charts are often used to preview material that will be covered in a speech, to summarize material, and to remind an audience of speech content. For his speech on credit cards, Emming might make a word chart that lists key

chart–*a graphic representation that presents information in an easily interpreted format.*

word chart–*a summary, list, or outline.*

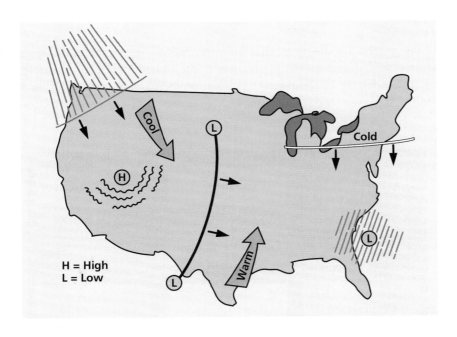

Figure 15.2
Sample map.

CRITERIA FOR EVALUATING CREDIT CARDS

1. Interest Rate

2. Annual Fee

3. Perks

Figure 15.3
Sample word chart.

topics such as those shown in Figure 15.3. Typically an outline can be considered a word chart.

Organizational charts use symbols and connecting lines to diagram step-by-step progressions through a complicated procedure or system. The chart in Figure 15.4 illustrates the organization of a student union board.

Word charts or organizational charts can be drawn on large pads of paper and mounted on an easel. Then, as you are talking, you can flip the pages to move from one chart to another.

organizational chart–*diagram of a complicated system or procedure using symbols and connecting lines.*

Graphs A **graph** is a diagram that compares information. Bar graphs, line graphs, and pie graphs are the most common.

Bar graphs, diagrams that compare information with vertical or horizontal bars, can show relationships between two or more variables at the same time or at various times on one or more dimensions. For instance, for a speech on fluctuations in the economy, the bar graph in Figure 15.5 shows a sharp drop in the GDP (gross domestic product) between the end of the fourth quarter in 1999 and the fourth quarter in 2000.

Line graphs are diagrams that indicate changes in one or more variables over time. In a speech on the population of the United States, for example, the line graph in Figure 15.6 shows the population increase, in millions, from 1810 to 2000.

graph–*a diagram that compares information.*

bar graph–*a diagram that compares information with vertical or horizontal bars to show relationships between two or more variables at the same time or at various times on one or more dimensions.*

line graph–*a diagram that indicates changes in one or more variables over time.*

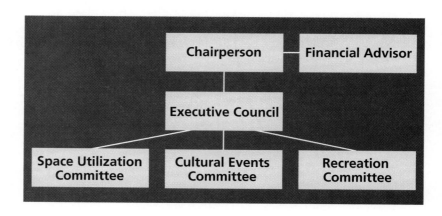

Figure 15.4
Sample organizational chart.

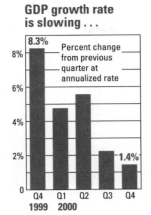

Figure 15.5
Sample bar graph.
U.S. News & World Report, February 12,
2001, p. 22.

Pie graphs are diagrams that show relationships among parts of a single unit. In a speech on the effect of tax cuts, a pie graph such as the one in Figure 15.7 could be used to show public opinion.

pie graph–*a diagram that shows relationships among parts of a single unit.*

Media for Showing Visual Aids

You can use several media to show your visual aids.

Handouts On the plus side, you can prepare handouts (material printed or drawn on sheets of paper) quickly, and all the people in the audience can have their own professional-quality material to refer to and take with them from the speech. On the minus side is the distraction of distributing handouts and the potential for losing the audience's attention when you want it to be on you. Before you decide on handouts, consider each of the following means of showing visual aids. If you do decide on handouts, it is a good idea to distribute them at the end of the speech.

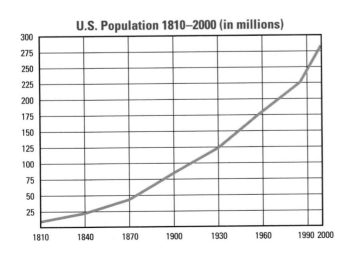

Figure 15.6
Sample line graph.

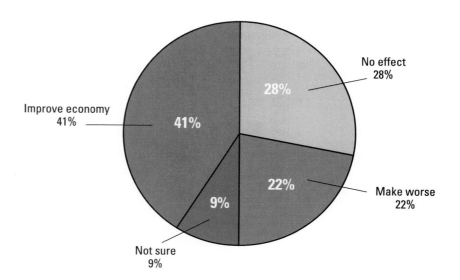

Figure 15.7
Sample pie graph.
Time, February 19, 2001, p. 30.

Chalkboard As a means of displaying simple information, the chalkboard, a staple in every college classroom, is unbeatable. Unfortunately, the chalkboard is also easy to misuse and to overuse. Moreover, it is unlikely that the chalkboard would be your first choice for any major analysis of a process or procedure because of its limitations in displaying complex material. Nevertheless, effective use of the chalkboard should be a part of any professional speaker's repertoire.

One common error in using the chalkboard is to write too much material while you are talking, an error that often results in displays that are either illegible or partly obscured by your body as you write. A second common error is to spend too much time talking to the board instead of to the audience.

The chalkboard is best used for short items of information that can be written in a few seconds. If you plan to draw or write while talking, practice doing it. If you are right-handed, stand to the right of what you are drawing. Try to face at least part of the audience while you work. Although it may seem awkward at first, your effort will enable you to maintain contact with your audience and will enable the audience to see what you are doing while you are doing it.

Overhead transparencies Perhaps the easiest and most common way to display visual aids is to project them onto a screen via an overhead projector. Overheads can be made by hand (traced or hand-lettered), by machine (copy machine, thermographic, color lift), or by computer. A major advantage of overheads is that you can make them rather easily and inexpensively if you have access to a computer, a copy machine, and overhead (acetate) sheets. If you own a computer, you are likely to have the software (Microsoft Word, PowerPoint, or PageMaker) that you need. If you do not own a computer, your college computer lab is likely to have the necessary equipment and software to help you. Once you have made the visual aid, and if you have access to an ink-jet or laser printer, you can print it on acetate sheets and display it via the overhead projector. If you have access to a dot matrix printer, you will have to print it on regular paper and take it to a copy service to be converted to a transparency.

Overheads work well in nearly any setting, and unlike other kinds of projections, they do not require dimming the lights in the room. Moreover, overheads can be useful for showing how formulas work, for illustrating various computations, or for analyzing data because it is possible to write, trace, or draw on the transparency while you are talking. This is best left to experienced presenters, however. In the beginning, stick to overheads that are complete, so you can concentrate on your speech and not on adding data during your speech.

Computer-mediated visual aids Today, in professional presentations, many of the graphics that are used are rendered by computer. Whereas overheads require only an overhead projector (standard in many college classrooms), computer-mediated visual aids require much more complicated equipment. Still, those who are "with it" are adept at creating computer graphics. Moreover, the availability of software designed especially for producing "presentation graphics" is rapidly changing how many speakers prepare their visual materials. With the right equipment, graphics can be displayed directly onto a screen or TV monitor as a computer "slide show," printed out and enlarged, photographed to make slides, or used to create overhead transparencies or handouts.

Except for complex multimedia presentations, computer graphics are not so much a new type of visual aid as a new way of producing visual aids. They do have the ability to add a very polished look to your speech, and because computer graphics presentations are becoming commonplace in many business environments, it is important to be familiar with this method. Computers are so easily accessible today and so advanced in capabilities that any professional speaker should experiment with one of the many computer graphics systems (such as Microsoft PowerPoint, Adobe Persuasion, or Lotus Freelance) to prepare visual material for speeches.

Today, many colleges and universities have dedicated classrooms that house or are user-ready for advanced electronic equipment. If your school is one of these, then you are likely to be able to sign up for workshops where you can learn how to use this equipment. If you have not tried a presentation graphics package or if you are unsure of which one to try and what its capabilities might be, investigate computer magazines for reviews of graphics software. With a few keystrokes or with the click of a "mouse," you can change lines of facts and figures into a variety of graphic displays using these kinds of software.

Additionally, access to the Internet enables you to download and store your own "library" of images. Depending on the presentation graphics software you have, you can insert virtually any image from your library into your presentation.

If you have access to a scanner, you can also transfer a photograph from a book or magazine directly to your computer library. Preparing good presentations using computer graphics does take time and practice, however. It is best to start simple, importing images only as you become more comfortable with the software capabilities.

Designing Drawings, Overheads, and Computer Projections

The visual aids that people are most likely to use in their presentations are drawings, overheads, or computer projections. Let's examine a few of the principles that you will want to consider to maximize their value.

1. **Use printing or a type size that can be seen easily by your entire audience.** Whether you are planning to use a drawing or an overhead, check your lettering for size by moving as far away from the visual aid you have created as the farthest person in your audience will be sitting. If you can read the lettering and see the details from that distance, then both are large enough. If not, draw another sample and check it for size. Because projection will increase the size of your lettering, try 36 points for major headings, 24 points for subheadings, and 18 points for text. Figure 15.8 illustrates how these look on paper. Type printed at a size of 36 points will project to two-and-a-half to three inches on the screen, 24-point type will project to one to two inches, and 18-point type will project to one-half to one inch.

2. **Use a typeface that is pleasing to the eye.** Modern software packages (like Microsoft Word) come with a variety of typefaces. Figure 15.9 shows Helvetica and Times, two standard typefaces in regular and bold-face 18 point size. If neither of these is pleasing to you, you are likely to

Points   Use

36	MajorHeadings
24	Subheads
18	Text material

Figure 15.8
Visual aid print sizes.

Helvetica

Selecting Typefaces
Selecting Typefaces

Times

Selecting Typefaces
Selecting Typefaces

Figure 15.9

Typefaces in 18 point regular and boldface.

have other choices to draw from. Be sure the typeface you choose is easy to read. Many typefaces that look especially pretty or dramatic are difficult to read.

3. **Use upper- and lowercase type.** The combination of upper- and lowercase is easier to read. Some people think that printing in all capital letters emphasizes. This may be true in some instances, but ideas printed in all capital letters are more difficult to read—even when the ideas are written in short phrases.

4. **Try to limit the lines of type to no more than six phrases.** You don't want the audience to have to spend a long time reading your visual aid—you want them to listen to you. Limit the number of lines to six or fewer and write points as phrases rather than complete sentences.

5. **Focus on information that you will emphasize in the speech.** We often get ideas for visual aids from other sources, and the tendency is to include all the material that was in the original. But for speech purposes, keep the aid as simple as possible. Focus on the key information and eliminate anything that distracts or takes emphasis away from the point you want to make.

    Because the tendency to clutter is likely to present a special problem on graphs, let's consider two graphs that show college enrollment by age of students (Figure 15.10). The graph on the left shows all eleven categories mentioned; the graph on the right simplifies this information by combining age ranges with small percentages. The graph on the right is not only easier to read but also emphasizes the highest percentage classifications.

6. **Make sure information is laid out in a way that is aesthetically pleasing.** Layout involves ensuring white space around the whole message, indenting subordinate ideas, and using different sized type as well as different treatments, such as bolding and underlining.

7. **Add clip art where appropriate.** If you are working with computer graphics, you may consider adding clip art. Most computer graphics packages have a

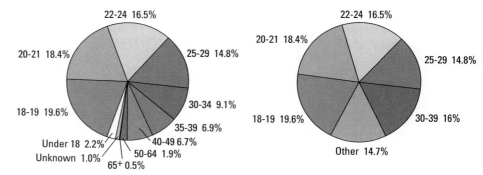

Figure 15.10
Comparative graphs.
Chronicle of Higher Education, Almanac
Issue, August 28, 1998, p. 18.

wide variety of clip art that you can import to your document. You can also buy relatively inexpensive software packages that contain thousands of clip art images. A relevant piece of clip art can make the image look both more professional and more dramatic. Be careful, because clip art can be overdone. Don't let your message be overpowered by unnecessary pictures.

Now let's see if we can put all of this advice to work. Figure 15.11 contains a lot of important information that the speaker has presented, but notice how unpleasant this is to the eye. As you can see, this visual aid ignores all the rules for effective presentation. However, with some thoughtful simplification, this speaker could produce the visual aid shown in Figure 15.12, which sharpens the focus by emphasizing the key words (reduce, reuse, recycle), highlighting the major details, and adding clip art for a professional touch.

I WANT YOU TO REMEMBER THE THREE R'S OF RECYCLING

Reduce the amount of waste people produce like over-packing or using material that won't recycle.

Reuse by relying on cloth towels rather than paper towels, earthenware dishes rather than paper or plastic plates, and glass bottles rather than aluminum cans.

Recycle by collecting recyclable products, sorting them appropriately, and getting them to the appropriate recycling agency.

Figure 15.11
A cluttered and cumbersome visual aid.

Remember the three R's of recycling

Reduce waste

Reuse
cloth towels
dishes
glass bottles

Recycle
collect
sort
deliver

Figure 15.12
A simple but effective visual aid.

Making Choices

Here are some of the key questions you will want to answer to make the best choices of visual aids.

1. **What are the most important ideas in helping me achieve my speech goal?** Visual aids and the material on them are likely to be remembered. Try to use them only with the most important ideas of the speech.

2. **How large is the audience?** The kind of visual aids that will work for a group of twenty or less is far different from the kind that will work for an audience of one hundred or more. For instance, for an audience of twenty or less, like most of your classroom speeches, you can choose to show relatively small objects and small models—everyone will be able to see them. For very large audiences, you will need projections that can be seen from one hundred to two hundred feet away with ease.

3. **Is necessary equipment readily available?** There will be times when you will be speaking in an environment that is not equipped for electronic displays. At the University of Cincinnati, for example, most rooms are equipped only with

Selecting Visual Aids

1. Carefully study the verbal information you are planning to use in the speech. In your Student Workbook under Journal Activity 15.1, indicate where you believe visual aids would be effective in creating audience interest, facilitating understanding, or increasing retention. Limit your choices to four or five spots at most, since your time limits for a first speech are likely to be four to six minutes.

2. Then indicate which kinds of visual aids would be most effective in each of the places you have identified: Yourself? Objects? Models? Charts? Pictorial representations? Projections? Chalkboard? Handouts? Computer graphics?

3. Finally, indicate specifics for the visual aids themselves. For instance, if you have elected to use a chart for one place, what are you likely to put on it?

speech plan—*a written strategy for establishing common ground, developing and maintaining interest, ensuring understanding, and coping with potential negative reactions to you as a speaker or to your topic or goal.*

a chalkboard, an overhead projector, and electrical outlets. If you want to use most anything else, you have to bring it yourself or schedule through a university office if the item is available. Be prepared! In any situation in which you have scheduled equipment from an outside source, prepare yourself for the possibility that the equipment may not arrive on time or that the equipment will not work the way you thought it would. Call ahead, get to your speaking location early, and have an alternative visual aid to use, just in case.

4. **Is the time involved in making or getting the visual aid or equipment cost effective?** Visual aids are supplements. You use them to accent what you are doing verbally. If you believe a particular visual aid will help you better achieve your goal, then the time spent is well worth it. But large amounts of time spent preparing visual aids to illustrate minor points is seldom cost effective.

5. **How many visual aids should I consider?** Unless you are doing a slide show in which the total focus of the speech is on visual images, the number of visual aids to use is likely to be relatively few. For the most part, you want the focus of the audience on you, the speaker. Use visual aids when their use will hold attention, exemplify an idea, or help the audience remember. With each of these goals, the more visual aids used, the less value will occur. For a five-minute speech, three visual aids used at crucial times will get attention, exemplify, and stimulate recall far better than using six or eight throughout your speech.

A Plan of Adaptation

Now that we have considered how to adapt speech information to a given audience verbally and visually, it is time to focus on writing a **speech plan,** a written strategy for establishing common ground, maintaining interest, ensuring understanding, and coping with potential negative reactions to you as a speaker or to your topic or goal. Even though your classroom audience may be similar to you in age, race, religion, academic background, and so forth, you must still think through your strategy carefully.

Formulating a plan begins with looking over the Audience Analysis Checklist you prepared for your speech in Chapter 12 (page 295), with special emphasis on the predictions you made. Using this information, write a draft of your speech plan by answering these questions.

1. **What will I do to establish and maintain common ground?** Begin by considering how you might use personal pronouns and rhetorical questions, common experiences, hypothetical situations, and personalized information to maintain common ground.

Jim Pickerell/Stock Connection/PictureQuest

**Once you have analyzed your
audience, you need to develop
a plan of adaptation to address
that audience.**

2. **What will I do to build and maintain interest?** Write down what you will do to show timeliness, proximity, and seriousness of impact. Also indicate what attention-getting techniques you plan to use during the speech to rebuild or heighten interest. Indicate where you can use visual aids to gain or heighten interest.

3. **How will you ensure that the audience has enough background information?** Show what you will do to orient your listeners *if* they have insufficient background to understand your speech.

4. **What will you do to build and maintain your credibility?** Write how you will attempt to show your knowledge or expertise, trustworthiness, and appealing personality.

5. **What will you do to build and maintain a positive attitude toward your topic?** Write about how you will show the importance of understanding the information you will present. If your speech topic is controversial, show why the audience needs to listen even if they oppose your beliefs.

For practice, let us look at how Emming might proceed. Recall that Emming is speaking to inform his class about the criteria for evaluating credit cards. The complete outline for his speech is contained in Figure 14.2 (pages 356–357). Figure 15.13 is Emming's audience analysis.

Figure 15.13
Audience analysis for credit card criteria speech.

Audience Analysis

My audience will be about twenty college students, twelve women and eight men; three of the twenty are African American, one is Asian American; they are of different religions, and eighteen of them range in age from eighteen to twenty, with two about twenty-three to twenty-five.

Predictions

Audience interest: Audience interest is likely to be high because my classmates are at an age where credit cards are starting to become important to them. Still, there may be some who believe that because they already have a credit card they don't need to pay much attention.

Audience understanding: Because of their general familiarity with the use of credit cards for paying bills, I don't anticipate spending time talking about what a credit card is.

Attitude toward speaker: My audience's attitude toward me may be generally positive, but members may not be ready to accept my expertise on credit cards.

Attitude toward topic: Although audience attitude about getting credit cards now may vary, they still are likely to be open to hearing about criteria because they are likely to be interested in investigating getting a card in the near future. Even those who already have credit cards may find my speech useful as a means of determining whether they should switch to a different card.

As a result of these predictions, Emming might write the speech plan shown in Figure 15.14.

Speech Plan

Common ground: Throughout the speech I will use personal pronouns and ask appropriate rhetorical questions. I will personalize information related to the three criteria I present.

Interest: I will start with an attention-getter. To maintain interest throughout the speech, I will present specific examples for each main point.

Understanding: Because members of the audience are familiar with the idea of credit cards, I won't have to define them. However, most will not be familiar with how people can get caught up in credit card debt, so I will use specific examples

(continued)

OBSERVE & ANALYZE
Journal Activity

A Speech Plan for Adapting to the Audience

In your Student Workbook in Journal Activity 12.2, you wrote an audience analysis for your first speech that looked like Emming's, shown in Figure 15.13. Now, under Journal Activity 15.2, write a speech plan and an audience adaptation strategy, in which you include specifics about how you will adapt to your audience using information that you included in Activity 12.2. Emming's plan, shown in Figure 15.14, may be used as a model. Incorporate the following headings: (1) common ground, (2) audience interest, (3) audience level of understanding, (4) audience attitude toward you, the speaker, and (5) audience attitude toward your speech goal. Where appropriate, include discussion of your use of visual aids.

to show what can happen if users are not careful. I will also use overhead projections to summarize the criteria and to show statistics.

Attitude toward speaker: Audience attitude toward me may be skeptical. Because I am Asian American, I may be seen as different from the majority of the class. But I am used to associating with people of all races and ethnic backgrounds without difficulty, so I am not concerned with any problems of adapting to the class. Still, they are likely to question my expertise with the use of credit cards, so I will have to be especially careful to present information accurately and to give personal examples showing my understanding of the information.

Attitude toward topic or speech goal: Although their attitude toward the topic of credit cards is likely to be favorable, I will still attempt to feature good information to keep their attitude toward the subject positive.

Figure 15.14

Speech plan for credit card criteria speech.

WHAT WOULD YOU DO?
A QUESTION OF ETHICS

"Kendra, I heard you telling Jim about the speech you're giving tomorrow. You think it's a winner, huh?"

"You got that right, Omar. I'm going to have Bardston eating out of the palm of my hand."

"You sound confident."

"This time I have reason to be. See, Professor Bardston's been talking about the importance of audience adaptation. These last two weeks that's all we've heard—adaptation, adaptation."

"What does she mean?"

"Talking about something in a way that really relates to people personally."

"OK—so how you going to do that?"

"Well, you see, I'm giving this speech on abortion. Now here's the kick. Bardston let it slip that she's a supporter of Right to Life. So what I'm going to do is give this informative speech on the Right to Life movement. But I'm going to discuss the major beliefs of the movement in a way that'll get her to think that I'm a supporter. I'm going to mention aspects of the movement that I know she'll like."

"But I've heard you talk about how you're pro-choice."

"I am—all the way. But by keeping the information positive, she'll think I'm a supporter. It isn't as if I'm going to be telling any lies or anything."

1. In a speech, is it ethical to adapt in a way that resonates with your audience but isn't in keeping with what you really believe?
2. Could Kendra have achieved her goal using a different method? How?

Summary

Speakers adapt to their audiences by speaking directly to them and by planning strategies that create or build audience interest, adapt to audience levels of understanding, and adapt to the audience's attitude toward the speaker and toward the speech goal.

Direct audience adaptation includes using personal pronouns, rhetorical questions, common experiences, and personalizing information.

Strategies for maintaining or increasing interest include stressing the timeliness of the information, the impact on the audience's personal space, and the seriousness of the personal impact. Strategies for adapting to the audience's understanding of the information depend on the audience's existing knowledge level. If the audience lacks specific topic knowledge, then fill in necessary background information. Strategies for building your credibility include going into the speech fully prepared and showing a sincere interest in the audience's well-being. To adapt to audience attitudes toward the speech goal, focus on showing why the audience needs to know about the topic.

Visual aids include the speaker, objects, charts, pictorial representations, projections, chalkboard, handouts, and computer graphics. Visual aids have the greatest impact if they are used in ways that best reinforce the points of the speech.

Take time to design visual aids that are large enough and that are pleasing to the eye. Focus on items of information that you will emphasize in the speech.

For your first few speeches, it may help to write out a speech plan that specifies how you will adapt your speech to the specific audience.

Communicate! Online

Use your Communicate! CD-ROM for quick access to the electronic study resources that accompany this text. Included on your CD-ROM is access to InfoTrac College Edition, the World Wide Web, a demo of WebTutor for Communicate!, and the Communicate! Web site at the Wadsworth Communication Café. The Communicate! Web site offers chapter-by-chapter activities, quizzes, and a digital glossary.

Review the following key terms and complete the Plan for Audience Adaptation under Forms for Chapter 15 at

http://communication.wadsworth.com/humancomm/verderber

Key Terms

attitude (372)	**pie graph** (379)
audience adaptation (362)	**proximity** (366)
bar graphs (378)	**rhetorical questions** (363)
chart (377)	**serious** (367)
common ground (362)	**speech plan** (386)
credibility (370)	**timely** (364)
graph (378)	**trustworthiness** (371)
line graphs (378)	**visual aid** (375)
organizational charts (378)	**vivid** (367)
personal pronouns (362)	**word charts** (377)
personalize (363)	

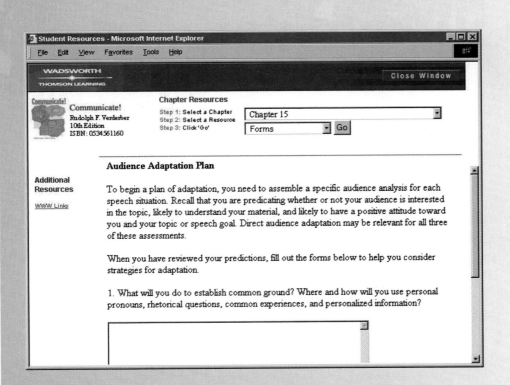

© Lee Kline

OBJECTIVES

After you have read this chapter, you should be able to answer these questions:

■ What is extemporaneous speaking?

■ What elements of language are most relevant to public speaking?

■ What characteristics result in conversational quality?

■ What are the characteristics of effective speech practice?

■ What are comforting ideas about speaker nervousness?

■ What are specific behaviors for limiting nervousness?

■ By what criteria is an effective speech measured?

16

Practicing the Presentation of Your Speech

As Nadia sat down, everyone in the audience burst into spontaneous applause.

"I don't understand it, Marv. I thought my speech was every bit as good as Nadia's, but when I got done all I got was the ordinary polite applause that everyone gets regardless of what they've done. Of course, I'm not as pretty as Nadia."

"Come on, Syl, she's good looking, but that's not why she got such a reception. Your speech was good. You had a good topic, lots of good information, and solid organization. But, I'll tell you, buddy, you didn't deliver your speech anywhere near as well as she did."

Marv recognized what has been well documented throughout the ages—good delivery is a necessity of effective speaking. Why? Delivery is the source of the audience's contact with the speaker's mind, and although delivery cannot improve the ideas of a speech, it can help to make the most of those ideas. Even if you are not by nature a gifted speaker, you can improve your delivery immensely if you are willing to practice.

You will recall that an effective speech plan is a product of five action steps. In this chapter, we consider the fifth step: **Practice the presentation of your speech.** The wording of your speech should be clear, vivid, and emphatic, and your delivery should be in a conversational style that shows enthusiasm, vocal expressiveness, spontaneity, fluency, and eye contact.

Although speeches may be presented impromptu (on the spur of the moment without prior preparation), by manuscript (completely written out and then read aloud), or by memory (completely written out and then memorized), the material you have been reading will help you in all situations. It is designed to help you present your speeches extemporaneously. An **extemporaneous speech** is carefully prepared and practiced, but the exact wording is determined at the time of utterance.

extemporaneous speech– *carefully prepared and practiced speech but with the exact wording determined at the time of utterance.*

In this chapter, we will consider verbal components of presentation, nonverbal components of presentation, characteristics of conversational style, guidelines for effective practice, coping with nervousness, and criteria for evaluating a speech. Then we will look at a sample speech.

Components to Practice in Your Speech

As you practice, you will be analyzing the verbal and nonverbal components of your presentation. Let's consider these elements in more detail.

Verbal Components

Listeners cannot "reread" what you have said. To be an effective speaker, it is important to use specific, concrete, and precise words (as discussed in Chapter 3), but you will also want to work to make your wording vivid and emphatic.

Vivid words are descriptive, full of life, vigorous, bright, and intense. For example, a baseball announcer might say, "Jackson made a great catch," but a more vivid account would be, "Jackson leaped and made a one-hand catch just as he crashed into the center field wall." The words *leaped, one-handed catch,* and *crashed* paint an intense verbal picture of the action. Vivid speech begins with vivid thought. You are much more likely to *express* yourself vividly if you can *sense* the meanings you are trying to convey.

Vividness is often expressed in similes and metaphors. A **simile** is a direct comparison of dissimilar things and is usually expressed with the words *like* or *as*. Clichés such as "She walks like a duck" and "She sings like a nightingale" are both similes. A more vivid simile would be like the one expressed by an elementary school teacher who said that being back at school after a long absence "was like trying to hold 35 corks under water at the same time" (Hensley, 1995, p. 703). This is a fresh, imaginative simile for the nature of the public school teacher's task.

A **metaphor** is a comparison that establishes a figurative identity between objects being compared. Instead of saying that one thing is like another, a metaphor says that one thing is another. Thus, problem cars are "lemons" and a team's porous infield is a "sieve." A more original metaphor in a reply to the statement that TV is just a toaster with pictures might be "This particular toaster is not just browning bread. It is cooking our country's goose" (Hundt, 1995, p. 675).

Although similes and metaphors can add vividness to a speech, it is wise to stay away from trite clichés. Try to develop original metaphors for your speech.

Emphasis gives force or intensity to words or ideas. In your speeches, try to emphasize through proportion, repetition, and use of transitions.

Emphasizing by proportion means spending more time on one idea than on another, resulting in your listeners' *perceiving* that point as more important.

Emphasizing by repeating means saying important words or ideas more than once. You can either repeat the exact words, "A ring-shaped coral island almost or completely surrounding a lagoon is called an atoll—the word is atoll," or you can restate the idea in different language, "The test will comprise about four essay questions; that is, all the questions on the test will be the kind that require you to discuss material in some detail."

Emphasizing through transitions means using words that show and emphasize idea relationships. In Chapter 14, we talked about section transitions that summarize, clarify, and forecast. Word transitions can be used to serve some additional functions:

- To add material: also, and, likewise, again, in addition, moreover, similarly, further.
- To add up consequences, summarize, or show results: therefore, and so, so, finally, all in all, on the whole, in short, thus, as a result.
- To indicate changes in direction or contrasts: but, however, yet, on the other hand, still, although, while, no doubt.
- To indicate reasons: because, for.
- To show causal or time relationships: then, since, as.
- To explain, exemplify, or limit: in other words, in fact, for example, that is to say, more specifically.

Finally, whether you are trying to be specific, precise, vivid, or emphatic, make sure that you use words that are understood by all your listeners. Sometimes speakers believe they will be more impressive if they use a large vocabulary. But

simile—*a direct comparison of dissimilar things.*

metaphor—*a comparison that establishes a figurative identity between objects.*

emphasis—*giving force or intensity to your words or ideas.*

emphasis by proportion—*spending more time on ideas that you want to be perceived as more important.*

emphasis by repeating—*saying important ideas several times, not just once.*

emphasis by transitions—*using words that show relationships between ideas.*

OBSERVE & ANALYZE
Journal Activity

Similes and Metaphors

As you read newspaper and magazine articles and listen to people talk over the next few days, make note of both trite and original similes and metaphors. In your Student Workbook under Journal Activity 16.1, write at least three that you thought were particularly well used. Then briefly indicate how and why they impressed you.

using "big" words often seems pompous, affected, or stilted. When you have a choice, select the simplest, most familiar word that expresses your precise meaning.

Nonverbal Components

You will recall from our earlier discussion that nonverbal components of speech presentation are voice, articulation, and bodily action.

voice—*the pitch, volume, rate of speed, and sound quality of your speech.*

Voice includes pitch (highness and lowness on a scale), volume (loudness), rate (speed of speech), and quality (tone, timbre, or sound of voice). Make sure your listeners perceive your voice as pleasant: neither too high, nor too low; neither too loud, nor too soft; neither too fast, nor too slow.

"LADIES AND GENTLEMEN... IS *THAT* MY VOICE?.. I NEVER HEARD IT AMPLIFIED BEFORE. IT SOUNDS SO WEIRD. HELLO. HELLO. I CAN'T BELIEVE IT'S ME. WHAT A STRANGE SENSATION. ONE, TWO, THREE... HELLO. WOW..."

Articulation is shaping speech sounds into recognizable oral symbols that combine to produce a word. Articulation is often confused with **pronunciation,** the form and accent of various syllables of a word. In the word *statistics,* for instance, articulation refers to shaping the ten sounds (s-t-a-t-i-s-t-i-k-s); pronunciation refers to grouping and accenting the sounds (sta-tis´-tiks). If you are unsure of how to pronounce a word in a speech, consult a dictionary for the proper pronunciation.

Consider whether you add a sound where none appears (ath*a*lete for athlete), leave out a sound where one occurs (libary for lib*r*ary), transpose sounds (re*va*lent for re*lev*ant), or distort sounds (tru*f* for tru*th*). Although some of us have consistent articulation problems that require speech therapy (such as substituting *th* for *s* consistently in speech), most of us are guilty of carelessness that can be corrected.

Check to make sure that you are not guilty of two of the most common articulation faults: slurring sounds (running sounds and words together) or leaving off word endings. Spoken English always will contain some running together of sounds. For instance, most people are likely to say "tha-table" for "that table"—it is simply too difficult to make two "t" sounds in a row. But many of us slur sounds and drop word endings to excess. "Who ya gonna see?" for "Who are you going to see?" illustrates both of these errors. If you have a mild case of "sluritis" caused by not taking the time to form sounds clearly, you can make considerable improvement by taking ten to fifteen minutes three days a week to read passages aloud, trying to overaccentuate each sound. Some teachers advocate "chewing" your words—that is, making sure that lips, jaw, and tongue move carefully for each sound you make. As with most other problems of delivery, speakers must work conscientiously several days a week for months to improve significantly.

Figure 16.1 lists many common problem words that people are likely to mispronounce or misarticulate.

A major concern of speakers from different cultures and different parts of the country is their *accent:* the inflection, tone, and speech habits typical of the natives of a country, region, or even a state or city. When should you work to lessen or eliminate any accent you may have? If your accent is so "heavy" or different from people's expectations that you have difficulty communicating effectively, or if you expect to go into teaching, broadcasting, or another profession where an accent may have an adverse effect on your performance, you should make an effort to lessen or eliminate your accent.

Bodily action includes your facial expression, gestures, posture, and movement. We discussed bodily actions in Chapter 4, and in this section, we want to focus on aspects of those nonverbal behaviors that you will want to consider for public speaking.

Make sure that your **facial expressions** (your eye and mouth movements) are appropriate to what you are saying. Audiences respond negatively to deadpan expressions or perpetual grins or scowls. Audiences respond positively to honest and sincere expressions that reflect your thoughts and feelings. Think actively about what you are saying, and your face will respond accordingly.

Your **gestures** are the movements of your hands, arms, and fingers that describe and emphasize. If gesturing does not come easily to you, it is probably

---

articulation–*shaping speech sounds into recognizable oral symbols that combine to produce a word.*

pronunciation–*the form and accent of various syllables of a word.*

THINKING ABOUT . . .

Voice and Articulation Problems

Indicate what you regard as your major problem of voice and articulation (such as speaking in a monotone or slurring words). Mentally outline a plan for working on the problem.

bodily action–*facial expression, gestures, posture, and movement.*

facial expressions–*eye and mouth movement.*

gestures–*movements of hands, arms, and fingers.*

Word	Correct	Incorrect
arctic	arc'-tic	ar'-tic
athlete	ath'lete	ath'a-lete
family	fam'-a-ly	fam'-ly
February	Feb'-ru-ary	Feb'-yu-ary
get	get	git
larynx	ler'-inks	lar'-nix
library	ly'brer-y	ly'-ber-y
particular	par-tik'-yu-ler	par-tik'-ler
picture	pic'-ture	pitch'-er
recognize	rek'-ig-nize	rek'-a-nize
relevant	rel'-e-vant	rev'-e-lant
theater	thee'-a-ter	thee-ay'-ter
truth	truth	truf
with	with	wit or wid

Figure 16.1
Problem words.

best not to force yourself to gesture in a speech. To encourage gestures, leave your hands free at all times to help you "do what comes naturally." If you clasp your hands behind you, grip the sides of the speaker's stand, or put your hands into your pockets, you will not be able to gesture naturally even if you want to.

posture—*the position or bearing of the body.*

Your **posture** is the position or bearing of your body. In speeches, an upright stance and squared shoulders communicate a sense of poise to an audience. Speakers who slouch may give an unfavorable impression of themselves, including the impression of limited self-confidence and an uncaring attitude. If you find yourself in some peculiar posture during the speech, return to the upright position with your weight equally distributed on both feet.

movement—*motion of the entire body.*

Your **movement** refers to the motion of your entire body. Ideally, movement should help focus on transitions, emphasize ideas, or call attention to a particular aspect of the speech. Avoid such unmotivated movement as bobbing and weaving, shifting from foot to foot, or pacing from one side of the room to the other. At the beginning of your speech, stand up straight on both feet.

poise—*assurance of manner.*

Poise refers to assurance of manner. A poised speaker is able to avoid mannerisms that distract the audience such as taking off or putting on glasses, smacking the tongue, licking the lips, or scratching the nose, hand, or arm. As a general rule, anything that calls attention to itself is negative, and anything that helps reinforce an important idea is positive. Likewise, a poised speaker is able to control speech nervousness, a topic we will discuss later in this chapter.

In this section, we have looked at several elements of delivery that may seem especially difficult to achieve for people with handicaps. The Diverse Voices box shows that regardless of apparent handicaps people can build confidence and succeed in speaking.

You're Short, Besides!

by Dr. Sucheng Chan

Although nearly everyone shows nervousness at the thought of speaking in public, some people face more difficult situations than others. In this excerpt, Dr. Chan tells us about problems that to many would seem nearly impossible to surmount. She not only overcame apparent problems but used them as motivation to succeed.

I was stricken simultaneously with pneumonia and polio at the age of four. Uncertain whether I had polio of the lungs, seven of the eight doctors who attended me—all practitioners of Western medicine—told my parents they should not feel optimistic about my survival. A Chinese fortune teller my mother consulted also gave a grim prognosis. All these pessimistic predictions notwithstanding, I hung onto life, if only by a thread. Being confined to bed was thus a mental agony as great as my physical pain. But I was determined to walk.

We left China as the Communist forces swept across the country in victory. We found an apartment in Hong Kong. After a year and a half in Hong Kong, we moved to Malaysia. The years in Malaysia were the happiest of my childhood even though I was consistently fending off children who ran after me calling, *"Baikah! Baikah!"* ("Cripple! Cripple!" in the Hokkien dialect commonly spoken in Malaysia). The taunts of children mattered little because I was a star pupil. I won one award after another for general scholarship as well as for art and public speaking. Whenever the school had important visitors, my teacher always called on me to recite in front of the class.

A significant event that marked me indelibly occurred when I was twelve. That year my school held a music recital and I was one of the students chosen to play the piano. I managed to get up the steps to the stage without any problem, but as I walked across the stage, I fell. Out of the audience, a voice said loudly and clearly, "Ayah! a *baikah* shouldn't be allowed to perform in public." I got up before anyone could get on stage to help me and, with tears streaming uncontrollably down my face, I rushed to the piano and began to play. That I managed to do so made me feel really strong. I never again feared ridicule.

Regardless of racial or cultural background, most handicapped people have to learn to find a balance between the desire to attain physical independence and the need to take care of ourselves by not overtaxing our bodies.

I've often wondered if I would have been a different person had I not been physically handicapped. I really don't know, though there is no question that being handicapped has marked me. But at the same time I usually do not *feel* handicapped—and consequently, I do not *act* handicapped. People are therefore less likely to treat me as a handicapped person. There is no doubt, however, that the lives of my parents, sister, husband, other family members, and some close friends have been affected by my physical condition. They have had to learn not to hide me away at home, not to feel embarrassed by how I look or react to people who say silly things to me, and not to resent me for the extra demands my condition makes on them. Perhaps the hardest thing for those who live with handicapped people is to know when and how to offer help.

So, has being physically handicapped been a handicap? It all depends on one's attitude. Some years ago, I told a friend that I had once said to an affirmative action compliance officer (somewhat sardonically since I do not believe in the head count approach to affirmative action) that the institution which employs me is triply lucky because it can count me as nonwhite, female, and handicapped. He responded, "Why don't you tell them to count you four times?. . . Remember, you're short, besides!"

Excerpted from Making Waves *by Asian Women United. © 1989 by Asian Women United. Reprinted by permission of the author.*

Achieving a Conversational Quality

conversational quality–*a style of presentation that sounds like conversation to listeners.*

In your speech practice, as well as in the speech itself, the final measure of your presentation is how well you use your vocal and nonverbal components to develop a **conversational quality,** a style of presentation that *sounds* like conversation to your listeners. Five components of conversational quality are enthusiasm, vocal expressiveness, fluency, directness (eye contact), and spontaneity.

Enthusiasm

enthusiasm–*excitement or passion about the topic.*

Enthusiasm is excitement or passion about the topic. If sounding enthusiastic does not come naturally to you, make sure you have a topic that really excites you. Even normally enthusiastic people can have trouble sounding enthusiastic when they choose an uninspiring topic. Then, focus on how your listeners will benefit from what you have to say. If you are convinced that you have something worthwhile to communicate, you are likely to feel and show more enthusiasm.

To validate the importance of enthusiasm, think of how your attitude toward a class differs depending on whether the professor's presentation says

TEST YOUR COMPETENCE

Monitoring Voice and Bodily Action

Use one of these methods to monitor your nonverbal behavior.

1. Practice a portion of your speech in front of a mirror to see how you look to others when you speak. (Although some speakers swear by this method, others find it a traumatic experience.)
2. Videotape your speech, and replay it for analysis.
3. Have a friend listen to a practice. Give your friend some directions, such as "Raise your hand every time I begin to rock back and forth." By getting specific feedback when the behavior occurs, you can learn to become aware of it and make immediate adjustments.

SKILL BUILDERS Enthusiasm

Skill	Use	Procedure	Example
Using your voice and bodily action to show the audience that you are excited about the topic and your opportunity to talk with the audience about it.	To ensure audience perception of the importance and relevance of the information to them.	1. Make sure you are truly excited about your topic. 2. As you speak, re-create your original feelings of excitement. 3. Focus on sharing that feeling of excitement with the audience.	As Trisha was practicing her speech on Alberta, Canada, she refocused on her feelings of awe as she first saw mountain peak after mountain peak. She also reminded herself of how much she wanted her audience to actually "see" what she had experienced.

"I'm really excited to be talking with you about geology (or history or English literature)" as opposed to "I'd rather be anywhere than talking to you about this subject." A speaker who looks and sounds enthusiastic will be listened to, and that speaker's ideas will be remembered (Williams & Ware, 1976, p. 50).

Vocal Expressiveness

The greatest sign of enthusiasm is **vocal expressiveness,** the vocal contrasts in pitch, volume, rate, and quality that affect the meaning audiences get from the sentences you present. A total lack of vocal expressiveness produces a **monotone,** a voice in which the pitch, volume, and rate remain constant, with no word, idea, or sentence differing significantly from any other. Although few people speak in a true monotone, many severely limit themselves by using only two or three pitch levels and relatively unchanging volume and rate. An actual or near monotone not only lulls an audience to sleep, but more important, diminishes chances of audience understanding.

For instance, if the sentence "We need to prosecute abusers" is presented in a monotone, listeners would be uncertain of the message the speaker wanted to communicate. To illustrate how vocal expressiveness affects meaning, read this sentence aloud four times. The first time emphasize *We,* the second time emphasize *need,* the third time emphasize *prosecute,* and the fourth time emphasize *abusers* (Figure 16.2).

vocal expressiveness—vocal contrasts in pitch, volume, rate, and quality that affect the meaning audiences get from the sentences you present.

monotone—a voice in which the pitch, volume, and rate remain constant, with no word, idea, or sentence differing significantly from any other.

We need to prosecute abusers.
We *need* to prosecute abusers.
We need to *prosecute* abusers.
We need to prosecute *abusers.*

Figure 16.2
Vocal expressiveness.

SKILL BUILDERS   Vocal Expressiveness

Skill	Use	Procedure	Example
Using contrasts in pitch, volume, rate, and quality.	To express the meanings you want audiences to get from the sentences you present.	1. Identify the words you want to stress to best express your intended meaning. 2. Raise your pitch or increase your volume on key words.	As Marquez thought about what he wanted to emphasize, he said, "You need to put your *left hand* at the *bottom* of the bat."

When you emphasize *We*, it answers the question "Who will do it?" When you emphasize *need*, it answers the question "How important is it?" When you emphasize *prosecute*, it answers the question "What are we going to do?" When you emphasize *abusers*, it answers the question "Who will be prosecuted?" To ensure audience understanding, your voice must be expressive enough to delineate shades of meaning.

Spontaneity

spontaneity–*being so responsive to your ideas that the speech seems as fresh as a lively conversation, even though it has been well practiced.*

Speakers who are enthusiastic and vocally expressive are also likely to present their speeches so that they sound spontaneous. **Spontaneity** means being so responsive to your ideas that the speech seems as fresh as a lively conversation, even though it has been well practiced.

How can you make your outlined and practiced speech sound spontaneous? Learn the *ideas* of the speech—don't *memorize words*. Suppose someone asks you about the route you take on your drive to work. Because you are familiar with the route, you need not write it out or memorize it—you can present it spontaneously because you "know it." You develop spontaneity in your speeches by getting to know the ideas in your speech as well as you know the route you take to work.

Fluency

fluency–*devoid of hesitations and such vocal interferences as "uh," "er," "well," "okay," "you know," and "like."*

Effective presentation is also **fluent,** devoid of hesitations and such vocal interferences as "uh," "er," "well," "okay," "you know," and "like" (see Chapter 4). Fluency can be developed through awareness and practice. Train yourself to hear your interferences by getting a friend to listen to practice sessions and call attention to them. As you learn to hear them, you will find that you can start to eliminate them from your speech practices and eventually from the speech itself.

SKILL BUILDERS   Spontaneity

Skill	Use	Procedure	Example
Being responsive to the ideas of your speech.	To ensure that your audience perceives your speech as a lively and fresh interaction even though it has been well practiced.	1. Learn the ideas of your speech. 2. In each practice, express the idea and its development in slightly different language.	As Connie was talking about day care, she allowed herself to report a personal experience that she had not planned on using in the speech.

Eye Contact

In public speaking, **eye contact** involves looking at various groups of people in *all parts* of an audience throughout a speech. As long as you are looking at people and not at your notes or the ceiling, floor, or window, everyone in the audience will perceive you as having good eye contact.

One way of ensuring eye contact is to think of your audience as a collection of groups sitting in various places around the room. Then, at random, talk for four to six seconds with each group. Perhaps start with a Z pattern. Talk with the group in the back left for a few seconds, then glance at people in the far right for a few seconds, and then move to a group in the middle, a group in the front left, and then a group in the front right. Then perhaps reverse the order, starting in the back right. Eventually you will find yourself going in a random pattern in which you look at all groups over a period of a few minutes. Such a pattern ensures that you do not spend a disproportionate amount of your time talking with those in front of you or in the center of the room.

Maintaining eye contact helps your speech in several ways.

1. Maintaining eye contact helps the audience concentrate on the speech. If speakers do not look at us while they talk, we are unlikely to maintain eye contact with them. This break in mutual eye contact often decreases concentration on the speaker's message.

2. Maintaining eye contact increases the audience's confidence in you, the speaker. Just as you are likely to be skeptical of people who do not look you in the eye as they converse, so too audiences will be skeptical of speakers who do not look at them. Eye contact is perceived as a sign of sincerity. Speakers who fail to maintain eye contact with audiences are perceived almost always as ill at ease and often as insincere or dishonest (Burgoon, Coker, & Coker, 1986).

eye contact—*looking at various groups of people in all parts of an audience throughout a speech.*

SKILL BUILDERS   Eye Contact

Skill	Use	Procedure	Example
Looking directly at members of the audience while you are talking with them.	To strengthen the sense of interaction.	1. Consciously look at the faces of groups of people in your audience while you are talking. 2. If your eyes drift away, try to bring them back.	As Bill was talking about how people can sign up for tutoring other students, he was talking to people near the back of the room. When he looked down at his notes to make sure he had included all he wanted, he found himself continuing to look at his note card rather than at the audience. As he moved to the next point of his speech, he forced himself to look at people sitting in the front right of the room.

3. **Maintaining eye contact helps you gain insight into the audience's reaction to the speech.** Audiences that pay attention are likely to look at you with varying amounts of intensity. Listeners who do not pay attention are likely to yawn, look out the window, and slouch in their chairs. By monitoring your audience's behavior, you can determine what adjustments, additions, and deletions you should make in your plans. As speakers gain greater skill, they can make more and better use of the information they get about listeners through eye contact with them.

Rehearsal

rehearsing–practicing the presentation of your speech aloud.

At this stage of preparation you are ready to begin **rehearsing,** practicing the presentation of your speech aloud. In this section, we consider a timetable for preparation and practice, use of notes, use of visual aids, and guidelines for effective rehearsals.

Timetable for Preparation and Practice

Inexperienced speakers often believe they are ready to present the speech once they have finished their outline. But a speech that is not practiced is likely to be far less effective than it would have been had you given yourself sufficient practice time. In general, if you are not an experienced speaker, try to complete the

Dave Shaefer/Jeroboam

When practicing your speech, try to make the practice session as similar to the speech situation as possible.

outline at least two days before the speech is due so that you have sufficient practice time to revise, evaluate, and mull over all aspects of the speech. Figure 16.3 provides a useful timetable for preparing a classroom speech.

Is there really a relationship between practice time and speech effectiveness? A study by Menzel and Carrel (1994) offers tentative confirmation for the general hypothesis that more preparation time leads to better speech performance. They concluded that "the significance of rehearsing out loud probably reflects the fact that verbalization clarifies thought. As a result, oral rehearsal helps lead to success in the actual delivery of a speech" (p. 23).

7 days (or more) before	Select topic; begin research.
6 days before	Continue research.
5 days before	Outline body of speech.
4 days before	Work on introduction and conclusion.
3 days before	Finish outline; find additional material if needed; have all visual aids completed.
2 days before	First rehearsal session.
1 day before	Second rehearsal session.
Due date	Give speech.

Figure 16.3
Timetable for preparing a speech.

Using Notes in Your Speech

speech notes—*outline of speech plus quotations and statistics to be used.*

Speech notes consist of a word or phrase outline of the speech, plus hard-to-remember information such as quotations and statistics. Appropriate notes are composed of key words or phrases that help trigger your memory. Notes will be most useful to you when they consist of the fewest words possible written in lettering large enough to be seen instantly at a distance. Many speakers condense their written preparatory outline into a brief word or phrase outline.

For a speech in the three- to five-minute category, one or two three-by-five note cards are all you will need. For a speech in the five- to ten-minute category, two to four three-by-five-inch note cards should be enough: one card for goal and introduction, one or two cards for the body, and one card for the conclusion. When your speech contains a particularly good quotation or a complicated set of statistics, you may want to write them in detail on separate three-by-five cards. Two typical sets of notes made from the body of the preparatory outline illustrated in Chapter 14 are shown in Figure 16.4.

Phrase Note Cards	Brief Word Note Cards
How many hounded by vendors?	**Hounded?**
Three criteria: IR, Fee, Perk	3C's
1st C: examine IR's	IR's
IR's are % charged	percents
• average of 18%	18 ave
• as much as 21%	21 high
• start low 6 to 8% but restrictions	6–8
IR's variable or fixed	variable fixed
• variable change	change
• fixed stay same	stay same
T considered IR's: next C	T
2d C: examine annual fee	Ann Fee
AF cost company charges	charges
vary	vary
• some no annual	from no
• most average $25	ave $25
T IR's, fees, weigh bens	T
3d C: weigh perks—extras	Perks—extras
• rebates	rebates
• freq flier miles	freq flier
• discounts	discounts
P's not outweigh factors	not outweigh
So, 3 C's IR, Fee, Perk	So, 3 C's

Figure 16.4
Two examples of note cards for credit card criteria speech.

During practice sessions, use the notes as you would in the speech. Either set the notes on the speaker's stand or hold them in one hand and refer to them only when needed. Speakers often find that the act of making a note card is so effective in helping cement ideas in the mind that during practice, or later during the speech itself, they do not need to use the notes at all.

Using Visual Aids in Your Speech

Many speakers think that once they have prepared good visual aids they will have no trouble using them in the speech. However, many speeches with good visual aids have become shambles because of the lack of careful practice with them. Here are several guidelines for preparing to use visual aids effectively in your speech.

1. **Carefully plan when to use visual aids.** Indicate on your outline (or on your speech notes) exactly when you will use the visual aid and when you will remove it. Work on statements for introducing the visual aids, and practice different ways of showing the visual aids until you are satisfied that everyone in the audience will be able to see them.

Pedrick/The Image Works

Visual aids can add dramatic interest to your speech.

2. **Consider audience needs carefully.** If a visual aid you are planning to use does not contribute directly to the audience's attention to, understanding of, or retention of information on your topic, then consider dropping it.

3. **Show visual aids only when talking about them.** Because visual aids will draw audience attention, show them only when you are talking about them, and remove visual aids from sight when they are no longer the focus of attention.

   Often a single visual aid contains several bits of information. To keep audience attention where you want it, prepare the visual aid with cover ups. Then, as you move from one portion of the visual aid to another, you can remove covers to expose the portion of the visual aid that you are then discussing.

4. **Talk about the visual aid while showing it.** You know what you want your audience to see in the visual aid. Tell your audience what to look for, explain the various parts, and interpret figures, symbols, and percentages.

5. **Display visual aids so that everyone in the audience can see them.** If you hold the visual aid, position it away from your body and point it toward the various parts of the audience. If you place your visual aid on a chalkboard or easel or mount it in some way, stand to one side and point with the arm nearest the visual aid. If it is necessary to roll or fold the visual aid, bring some transparent tape to mount it to the chalkboard or wall so that it does not roll or wrinkle.

6. **Talk to your audience, not to the visual aid.** You may need to look at the visual aid occasionally, but it is important to maintain eye contact with your listeners as much as possible, in part so that you can gauge how they are reacting to your visual material. When speakers become too engrossed in their visual aids, they tend to lose contact with the audience entirely.

7. **Pass objects around the audience with caution.** People look at, read, handle, and think about whatever they hold in their hands. While they are so occupied, they may not be listening to you. Keep control of people's attention by telling them what they should be looking at and when they should be listening to you.

Guidelines for Effective Rehearsal

A good rehearsal period involves practicing the speech, analyzing it, and practicing it again.

First practice

1. Audiotape your practice session. If you do not own a recorder, try to borrow one. You may also want to have a friend sit in on your practice.

2. Read through the outline once or twice to refresh ideas in your mind. Then put the outline out of sight. Use the note cards you are planning to use in your speech.

3. Make the practice as similar to the speech situation as possible, including using any visual aids you have prepared. Stand up and face your imaginary audience. Pretend that the chairs, lamps, books, and other objects in your practice room are people.

4. Write down the time that you begin.

5. Begin speaking. Keep going until you have presented your entire speech.

6. Write down the time you finish. Compute the length of the speech for this first practice.

Analysis Replay the tape. Look at your outline again. Did you leave out any key ideas? Did you talk too long on any one point and not long enough on another? Did you clarify each of your points? Did you try to adapt to your anticipated audience? (If you had a friend or relative listen to your practices, have them help with your analysis.) Were your note cards effective? Make any necessary changes before your second practice.

Second practice Go through the six steps outlined for the first practice. By practicing a second time right after your analysis, you are more likely to make the kind of adjustments that begin to improve the speech.

After you have completed one full rehearsal consisting of two sessions of practices and analysis, put the speech away until that night or the next day. Although you may need to go through the speech one or several more times, there is no value in cramming all the practices into one long rehearsal time. You may find that an individual practice right before you go to bed will be very helpful; while you are sleeping, your subconscious will continue to work on the speech. As a result, you are likely to find significant improvement in your mastery of the speech when you practice again the next day.

How many times you practice depends on many variables, including your experience, your familiarity with the subject, and the length of your speech.

Ensuring spontaneity When practicing, try to learn the speech, not memorize it. Recall that memorizing the speech involves saying the speech the same way each time until you can give it word for word without notes. **Learning the speech** involves understanding the ideas of the speech but having the freedom to word the ideas differently during each practice. To illustrate the method of learning a speech, let's use a short portion of the speech outline for the credit card criteria speech as the basis for the practice. That portion of the outline reads as follows:

A. Interest rates are the percentages that a company charges you to carry a balance on your card past the due date.
1. Most credit cards carry an average of 18 percent.

Now let us consider three practices that focus on this small portion of the outline.

First practice: "Interest rates are the percentages that a company charges you to carry a balance on your card past the due date. Most credit cards carry an average of 18 percent. Did you hear that?—18 percent."

learning the speech–
understanding the ideas but being able to present them using different words in each practice session.

Rehearsal Log

In your Student Workbook under Journal Activity 16.2, keep a separate log for each time you practiced your speech aloud and standing up as if facing your audience.

For your first practice, indicate how long you spoke. Then write two or three sentences focusing on what went well and what you need to improve.

For each additional speech practice, indicate where in the speech you made changes to build interest, clarify points, and build a positive attitude toward you and your topic. Also, indicate where you made changes to improve language, delivery, and use of visual aids.

Finally, answer the following questions: How many times did you practice aloud for this speech? When did you feel you had mastery of the ideas of the speech?

nervousness—*fear or anxiety about public speaking.*

Second practice: "Interest rates are the percentages that a company charges you when you don't pay the balance in full and thus still owe the company money. Most credit cards carry an average of 18 percent—think of that, 18 percent. So, if you leave a balance, every month before you know it, you're going to be paying a lot more money than you thought you would."

Third practice: "Interest rates are the percentages that a company charges you when you don't pay the balance in full—you can rack up a lot of debt by not paying on time. Most credit cards carry an average of 18 percent. Did you hear that? A whopping 18 percent at a time when you can get about any kind of a loan for less than 10 percent."

Notice that point A and subpoint 1 of the outline are in all three versions. As this illustrates, the essence of the outline will be a part of all your practices. Because you have made slight variations each time, when you finally give the speech there will be that sense of spontaneity. In your speech, you probably will use wording that is most meaningful to you, and yet you will be assured that you are likely to get the key point across.

Coping with Nervousness

By far the most asked question about speaking is, "What can I do about nervousness?" It is important to realize that nearly everyone reports nervousness about speaking, and we can all learn to cope with that nervousness.

Let's begin by identifying what nervousness is all about. Whether we call it **nervousness,** stage fright, speech fright, shyness, reticence, speech apprehension, or some other term, the meaning of that feeling is essentially the same: a fear or anxiety about public speaking interaction.

Much of what we know about the fear of speaking comes from research conducted by James McCroskey, who has developed the most valid instrument for measuring what he calls communication apprehension. The Spotlight on Scholars provides insight into his research program.

Although we may feel some degree of nervousness in any situation, the majority of us notice it most in public speaking. Some of this nervousness is cognitive—that is, we think about how nervous we are likely to be. Much of the nervousness is behavioral—that is, we physically display characteristics. For instance, we may experience stomach cramps, sweaty palms, dry mouth, and the use of such filler expressions as "ums," "likes," and "you knows." At times, the behavior is avoiding speaking in public or speaking for the shortest period of time possible when required to speak.

To help cope with this nervousness, keep in mind that fear is not an either-or matter; it is a *matter of degree.* Most of us are somewhere between the two

James McCroskey, Professor and Former Chair of the Department of Communication at West Virginia University, on Communication Apprehension

Jim McCroskey's academic interest had been in public speaking and debate, so it was somewhat by chance that he became involved in the study of what was to become a focus of his life-long scholarship. One day McCroskey got a call from a therapist at the university's Psychology Center who was concerned about a student who was suicidal and kept repeating "I just can't face giving my speech." The thought that some people's fear of speaking in public was so profound that they considered suicide preferable to speaking was so compelling to McCroskey that he began an in-depth study of what he eventually called "communication apprehension."

Although a lot had been written about what was then called "stage fright," McCroskey found that there was no agreement about its causes and no way to go about measuring it. Since that time, McCroskey has made a significant contribution to our understanding of communication apprehension and ways of measuring it. When instruments for measuring a variable are developed, they must be both valid and reliable—*valid* in that the instrument must be proved to measure apprehension and not other related things, and *reliable* so that people with similar amounts of apprehension will score the same and that people who are measured more than once will receive a similar score. McCroskey and his colleagues' work culminated in what is considered the primary measure of communication apprehension, the Personal Report of Communication Apprehension (PRCA).

McCroskey first published this self-report instrument in 1970. Since then, there have been several versions.

Although apprehension can be measured by observation (examining the behaviors exhibited during communication) and physiological response (outfitting people with measuring devices to record physiological information during speech), McCroskey found that the self-report instrument (having people fill out a questionnaire detailing their feelings and opinions) was the most valid and reliable. In laypersons' terms, he explains, "Many times the people we observe may be terrified, but show no outward signs. Likewise, many times people register tremendous physiological reaction to the thought of public speaking, but when questioned, some of these people don't recognize their reactions as fear. Rather, they report excitement or other feelings that aren't at all debilitating. On the other hand, when people report, 'I'm scared stiff,' you can pretty well believe that they are."

From the research that uses the PRCA, we have learned that fifteen to twenty percent of the U.S. population experiences high levels of "trait" communication apprehension. "Trait apprehension" means that some people seem to be predisposed to be apprehensive and will show high levels of nervousness in all forms of speech including public speaking, interpersonal communication, and group communication. Likewise, we have learned that nearly everyone experiences times of high "state" communication apprehension. "State apprehension" means that under some circumstances people will show high levels of nervousness in a single communication context such as public speaking.

McCroskey's research has made it possible to identify high communication apprehension students and provide appropriate intervention programs. Through these programs, people with high communication apprehension do not eliminate their fears but rather learn to reduce their tension so that they can function competently.

Later, McCroskey's interest in communication apprehension led him to related studies in talking frequency (verbal activity, talkativeness, compulsive communicators) and preference to approach or avoid communication (reticence, unwillingness to communicate, and willingness to communicate). During the last twenty years, he has validated scales for measuring both willingness to communicate and talkativeness.

What is next for McCroskey? Recently, he has begun to study genetic causes of apprehension. Although we can now identify those who suffer from communication apprehension and help them reduce their fears, there seem to be limits to how much reduction can take place for particular individuals. He believes genetic study is the wave of the future and may ultimately provide answers to dealing completely with communication apprehension.

Over the last forty years, McCroskey has published more than 175 articles, 40 books, 40 book chapters, and presented more than 250 convention papers. Currently he teaches courses in communication in instruction, organizational communication, interpersonal communication, nonverbal communication, and a graduate seminar.

As we might expect, McCroskey has received many awards for his scholarship, including the prestigious Robert J. Kibler Memorial Award of the National Communication Association and the Distinguished Research Award from the National Association of Teacher Educators. For a partial list of McCroskey's publications in communication apprehension, see the references at the end of this book.

McCroskey's scholarship—from identifying those with communication apprehension to finding ways to help people reduce their apprehension—has helped tremendous numbers of people become more competent communicators. For more information about McCroskey and his work, see

http://www.as.wvu.edu/~jmccrosk/jcmhp.html **www**

---

extremes of no nervousness at all and total fear. The point is, nervousness about speaking in public is *normal*.

Many of us believe we would be better off if we could be totally free from nervousness. But Gerald Phillips (1977), a speech scholar who studied public-speaking nervousness for more than twenty years, says that is not true. Phillips noted that "learning proceeds best when the organism is in a state of tension" (p. 37). In fact, it helps to be a little nervous to do your best. If you are lackadaisical about giving a speech, you probably will not do a good job.

Because at least some tension is constructive, our goal is to learn how to cope with our nervousness. Phillips cites results of studies that showed that nearly all students with nervousness still experienced tension, but almost all of them had learned to cope with the nervousness. Phillips goes on to say that "apparently they had learned to manage the tension; they no longer saw it as an impairment, and they went ahead with what they had to do" (p. 37).

Now let's look at some reassuring information about nervousness.

1. **Despite nervousness, you can make it through your speech.** Very few people are so bothered that they are unable to function. You may not enjoy the "flutters" you experience, but you can still deliver an effective speech.

2. **Listeners are not as likely to recognize your fear as you might think.** The thought that audiences will notice an inexperienced speaker's fear often increases that fear. Thoughts that an audience will be quick to laugh at a speaker who is hesitant or that it is just waiting to see how shaky a person appears can have devastating effects. But the fact is that members of an audience, even speech instructors, greatly underrate the amount of stage fright they believe a person has (Clevenger, 1959, p. 136).

3. **The better prepared you are, the better you will cope with nervousness.** Many people show extreme nervousness because either they are not well prepared or they think they are not well prepared. As Gerald Phillips has said, a positive approach to coping with nervousness is "(1) learn how to try, (2) try, and (3) have some success" (Phillips, 1991, p. 6). As you learn to recognize when you are truly prepared, you will find yourself paying less attention to your nervousness. A study by Kathleen Ellis (1995) reinforces previous research "that indicates that students' self-perceived public speaking competency is indeed an important predictor of their public speaking anxiety" (p. 73).

4. **The more experience you get in speaking, the better you can cope with nervousness.** Beginners experience some fear because they do not have experience speaking in public. As you give speeches—and see improvement in those speeches—you will gain confidence and worry less about any nervousness you might experience. As a recent study of the impact of basic courses on communication apprehension indicated, experience in a public-speaking course was able to reduce students' communication apprehension scores (Rose, Rancer, & Crannell, 1993, p. 58).

5. **In addition, experienced speakers learn to channel their nervousness.** The nervousness you feel is, in controlled amounts, good for you. It takes a certain amount of nervousness to do your best. What you want is for your nervousness to dissipate once you begin your speech. Just as soccer players are likely to report that the nervousness disappears once they engage in play, so too should speakers find nervousness disappearing once they get a reaction to the first few sentences of an introduction.

Specific Behaviors

Now let's consider specific behaviors that are likely to help you control your nervousness.

1. **Pick a topic you are comfortable with.** Whereas an unsatisfactory topic lays the groundwork for a psychological mind-set that almost guarantees nervousness at the time of the speech, having a topic you know about and that is important to you lays the groundwork for a satisfying speech experience.

> **THINKING ABOUT...**
>
> **Nervousness**
>
> Are you nervous at the thought of giving a speech? What thoughts and behaviors show your nervousness?

2. **Take time to prepare fully.** If you back yourself into a corner and must find material, organize it, write an outline, and practice the speech all in an hour or two, you almost guarantee failure and destroy your confidence. However, if you do a little work each day for a week before the assignment, you will experience considerably less pressure and increased confidence.

Keep in mind that giving yourself enough time to prepare fully includes sufficient time for rehearsal. In this regard, speechmaking is much like athletics. If you assure yourself that you have carefully prepared and practiced, you will do the kind of job of which you can be proud.

3. **Try to schedule your speech at a time that is psychologically best for you.** When speeches are being scheduled, you may be able to choose the time. Are you better off "getting it over with"? If so, volunteer to go first. Will listening to others make you feel better? If so, try to schedule your speech near the end of the class period.

4. **Control your food and beverages.** Do not eat a big meal right before speaking—you may get a stomachache or feel overly loggy. Avoid stimulants like caffeine and sugar—they can get you too revved up. Also, avoid drinking milk—milk and milk products can produce a mucus that can affect your voice negatively. The best thing to drink before a speech is water. If you experience dry mouth, try sucking on a mint shortly before you speak.

5. **Visualize successful speaking experiences. Visualization** is a technique for nervousness that involves developing a mental strategy and picturing yourself implementing that strategy successfully. How many times have you said to yourself, "Well, if I had been in that situation I would have . . ."? Such statements are a form of visualization. Joe Ayres and Theodore S. Hopf (1990), two scholars who have conducted extensive research on visualization, have found that, if people can visualize themselves going through an entire process, they have a much better chance of succeeding when they are in the situation (p. 77).

Visualization has been used as a major means of improving sports skills. One example is a study of players trying to improve their foul shooting percentages. Players were divided into three groups. One group never practiced, one group practiced, and one group visualized practicing. As any of us would expect, those who practiced improved far more than those who did not. What seems amazing is that those who only visualized practicing improved almost as much as those who actually practiced (Scott, 1997, p. 99). Imagine what happens when you visualize and practice as well!

By visualizing speechmaking, people seem not only to be able to lower general apprehension but also report fewer negative thoughts when they actually speak (Ayres, Hopf, & Ayres, 1994, p. 256). Successful visualiza-

---

visualization–*picturing yourself doing something successfully.*

COMMUNICATE! Using InfoTrac College Edition

Visualization

Visualization has been recognized as a means of improving performance in many areas, most specifically in athletics. Open PowerTrac and type the keyword "visualization." You will find many recent sources covering many different areas. Look for "Do Try This at Home," in *Women's Sports and Fitness,* May 1997, and "The Mind of a Champion," *Natural Health,* Jan.–Feb. 1997. Look specifically for suggested procedures for using visualization.

Bob Daemmrich/Stock, Boston

Speakers can use the secrets of winning athletes: Realize that your initial nervousness can prime you for the speech ahead and will decline once you start speaking, and visualize success before you start.

tion begins during practice periods: See yourself as calm and smiling as you approach the podium. Remind yourself that you have good ideas, that you are well prepared, and that your audience wants to hear what you have to say. See the audience nodding approvingly as you speak. See them applauding as you finish.

6. **Give yourself positive affirmations before you approach the stand.** For instance, you might say to yourself, "I'm excited about having the opportunity to share this information with the class," "I've done my best to get ready and now I'm ready to speak." Such statements help put you in a positive frame of mind. Although these statements are not magic, they get us thinking on the right track.

    If you find yourself doing negative self-talk instead, confront your negative statements with positive ones. For instance, if you find yourself saying, "I'm scared," intervene and say, "No, I'm excited."

    If you find yourself saying, "Oh, I'm going to forget," say "I've got note cards. If I do forget, I'll pause, look at my notes, and go on."

    If you find yourself saying, "I'm a lousy speaker, what am I doing here?" say "I'm doing the best I can do for today—and that's okay."

systematic desensitization–
repeatedly being exposed to a feared stimulus and associating it with something pleasurable.

cognitive restructuring–
identifying illogical beliefs and formulating more appropriate beliefs.

7. **Pause for a few seconds before you begin.** When you reach the stand, stop a few seconds before you start to speak. Take a deep breath while you make eye contact with the audience; that may help get your breathing in order. Try to move about a little during the first few sentences; sometimes a few gestures or a step one way or another is enough to break some of the tension.

Persistent Nervousness

When is speaker nervousness a real problem? When it becomes debilitating—when the fear is so great that a person is unable to go through giving a speech. Unfortunately many of those students respond by dropping the course. But that is not an answer to speech anxiety. In all areas of life, people have to give speeches—they have to get up before peers, people from other organizations, customers, and others to explain their ideas. Although it is never too late to get help, a college speech course is the best time to start working on coping with speech nervousness. Even if your fears prove to be more perception than reality, it is important to take the time to get help.

To start, see your professor outside of class and talk with him or her about what you are experiencing. Your professor should be able to offer suggestions for people you can see or programs you can attend. You may be able to find a program in **systematic desensitization,** which repeatedly exposes people to the stimulus they fear, associating it each time with something pleasant. Another alternative is **cognitive restructuring,** in which people identify the illogical beliefs they hold and formulate more appropriate beliefs, in individualized instruction.

But before you get overly concerned, keep in mind that there are very few speech students who have been so hurt by fear that they cannot deliver a speech. Use your speech course as a resource to help you learn and develop the skills that will enable you to achieve even when you feel extremely anxious.

Criteria for Evaluating Speeches

In addition to learning to prepare and present speeches, you are learning to critically analyze the speeches you hear. From a pedagogical standpoint, critical analysis of speeches not only provides the speaker with both an analysis of where the speech went right and where it went wrong but also gives you, the critic, insight into the methods that you want to incorporate or, perhaps, avoid in presenting your own speeches.

Although speech criticism is context specific (analyzing the effectiveness of an informative demonstration speech differs from analyzing the effectiveness of a persuasive action speech), in this section we look at criteria for evaluating public speaking in general. Classroom speeches are usually evaluated on the basis of how well the speaker has met specific criteria of effective speaking.

In Chapters 12 through 16, you have been learning not only steps of speech preparation but also the criteria by which speeches are measured. The critical assumption is that if a speech has good content, is well organized, and is well presented it is more likely to achieve its goal. Thus, the critical apparatus for evaluating any speech comprises questions that relate to the basics of content, organization, and presentation.

Figure 16.5 is a diagnostic speech checklist. Use this series of questions to analyze your first speech.

Thinking Critically about Speeches

Check all items that were accomplished effectively.

Content
_____ 1. Was the goal of the speech clear?
_____ 2. Did the speaker have high-quality information?
_____ 3. Did the speaker use a variety of kinds of developmental material?
_____ 4. Were visual aids appropriate and well used?
_____ 5. Did the speaker establish common ground and adapt the content to the audience's interests, knowledge, and attitudes?

Organization
_____ 6. Did the introduction gain attention, gain goodwill for the speaker, and lead into the speech?
_____ 7. Were the main points clear, parallel, and in meaningful complete sentences?
_____ 8. Did transitions lead smoothly from one point to another?
_____ 9. Did the conclusion tie the speech together?

Presentation
_____ 10. Was the language clear?
_____ 11. Was the language vivid?
_____ 12. Was the language emphatic?
_____ 13. Did the speaker sound enthusiastic?
_____ 14. Did the speaker show sufficient vocal expressiveness?
_____ 15. Was the presentation spontaneous?
_____ 16. Was the presentation fluent?
_____ 17. Did the speaker look at the audience?
_____ 18. Were the pronunciation and articulation acceptable?
_____ 19. Did the speaker have good posture?
_____ 20. Was speaker movement appropriate?
_____ 21. Did the speaker have sufficient poise?

Based on these criteria, evaluate the speech as (check one):
_____ excellent, _____ good, _____ satisfactory, _____ fair, _____ poor.

Figure 16.5
Speech critique checklist.

Presenting Your First Speech

1. Prepare a three- to five-minute informative or persuasive speech. An outline is required.

2. As an addendum to the outline, you may wish to write a specific plan for adapting the speech that discusses strategies for (1) getting and maintaining attention, (2) facilitating understanding, (3) and building a positive attitude toward you and your speech.

3. Criteria for evaluation include the essentials of topic and purpose, content, organization, and presentation. Use the speech critique checklist to evaluate the speech. As you practice your speech, use the checklist to ensure that you are meeting the basic criteria in your speech. A sample student outline and speech follow.

Sample Speech: Habitat for Humanity, by Miranda Branton[1]

In addition to learning to prepare and present speeches, you are learning to critically analyze the speeches you hear. For this first speech assignment, we consider criteria related to the basics of content, organization, and presentation. The diagnostic checklist in Figure 16.5 shows a series of questions that will be used in the analysis of your first speech based on the Test Your Competence: Presenting Your First Speech.

This section contains a speech outline, a speech plan, and a sample speech with analysis. The outline, approximately 350 words, is an appropriate length when considering that the specific goal, thesis statement, and transitions that are written out in full are included in the count. The speech plan presents the strategy

---

[1] This speech was presented in Speech Class, University of Cincinnati, and is reprinted with permission, as edited, of Miranda Branton.

Critiquing a Speech

Use the speech critique checklist in Figure 16.5 to evaluate a speech you have listened to in or out of class. Using the data on the checklist, write a two- to five-page paper explaining your evaluation.

the speaker will employ. As you read the speech itself, you will notice how Miranda uses additional material to build the speech and to adapt to her audience.

Speech Outline

Specific goal: I want my audience to comprehend the three functions of Habitat for Humanity.

Introduction
 I. Have you ever heard of Habitat for Humanity?
 II. Habitat for Humanity is an organization that provides a chance for low-income families to own their homes.

Thesis statement: The three functions of Habitat for Humanity are to educate people in the community about the works of the group, to raise funds to build homes, and to build and rehabilitate houses.

Body
 I. One function of Habitat for Humanity is to educate people in the community about the works of the group.
   A. Other housing programs work against poor people being able to afford adequate housing.
     1. They pay more than 30 percent of their monthly income for rent and utilities.
     2. Yet they often have no hot water, electricity, or toilets.
   B. Habitat was formed by Millard and Linda Fuller.
     1. They developed the concept of "partnership housing."
     2. Today, Habitat seeks to eliminate homelessness and make decent shelter a matter of conscience and action.
(To help provide housing, there must be funding.)
 II. The second function of Habitat for Humanity is to raise funds.
   A. Donations are the main funding for Habitat.
   B. Habitat sometimes partners with the government who "sets the stage" for construction.
     1. The government may donate land, infrastructure for streets, or assist with utilities.
     2. The government may also donate housing for Habitat to rehabilitate.
(Raising money allows Habitat to build houses.)
 III. A third function of Habitat is to build houses in partnership with local affiliates and home owners.
   A. Families in need of a home apply to Habitat for their approval.
     1. Families are chosen by level of need.
     2. Families must be devoted to becoming partners in the program.

B. Habitat houses are then sold to partners.
   1. Home prices are low.
   2. Families make low monthly payments.

Conclusion

   I. Habitat for Humanity helps people in poverty to own their own homes.
   II. Its successes are known worldwide by achieving the goals of educating people about the works of the group, raising funds to build homes, and building and rehabilitating houses.

Sources

Habitat for Humanity International, http://www.habitat.org

Maudlin, Michael G. God's contractor. *Christianity Today, 43,* June 14, 1999. p. 44 (Downloaded from InfoTrac College Edition).

Starling, Kelly. Habitat for Humanity: Interracial organization builds houses and dreams. *Ebony, 53* (Nov 1997), p. 200 (Downloaded from InfoTrac College Edition).

University of Cincinnati's Habitat for Humanity Campus Chapter, http://www.soa.uc.edu/org/habitat

U.S. Department of Housing and Urban Development, http://www.hud.gov

Plan for Adapting to Audience

1. **Getting and maintaining interest.** I plan to begin the speech with a question to capture audience attention. During the speech, I will ask questions to get and maintain interest.

2. **Facilitating understanding.** I do not believe the information I will present is difficult to understand. I will work to keep technical jargon to a minimum. I believe that my examples, which are relevant to class experience, will help make the information easy to understand. I have organized my speech following a topical pattern. All three of my main points are complete sentences, and I will have transitions between points.

3. **Building a positive attitude.** I plan to build credibility by showing my command of the information and by using documented sources to support my points.

Speech and Analysis

Read the following speech aloud. Then analyze it on the basis of key criteria drawn from the speech critique checklist (see Figure 16.5): clear goal; introduction that gets attention and leads into the speech; clear, parallel, meaningful complete sentence main points; meaningful development; conclusion that ties the speech together and leaves it on a high note.

Speech

Have any of you ever heard about Habitat for Humanity? Well, today I'm going to tell you a little about the organization that provides a chance for low-income families to own their own homes. The three functions of Habitat for Humanity are to educate people in the community about affordable housing issues and the works of the group, to raise funds to build homes, and to build and rehabilitate houses in partnership with local affiliates and home owners.

One function of Habitat for Humanity is to educate people in the community about affordable housing issues and the works of the group. Habitat was formed by Millard and Linda Fuller when they developed "partnership housing" at a small interracial farming community. Partnership housing is when those in need will work side by side with volunteers to build simple, decent houses for themselves. Millard and Linda Fuller did this with everyone in the community. According to their Web site, Habitat for Humanity seeks to eliminate poverty housing and homelessness from the world, and to make decent shelter a matter of conscience and action.

Did you realize that there are many housing problems in the United States? According to the U.S. Affordable Housing Statistics Sheet, nearly 30 million U.S. households face one or more of the following problems: Many people have cost burdens because they are paying over 30 percent of their monthly income for all their rent and utilities. For example, if a household had a combined income of $900, they would be paying over $300 for just the rent and utilities. Another problem is that there is often overcrowding due to more people living in the house than the total number of rooms in the house. Another problem is physical shortcomings due to things like no hot water, no electricity, no toilets, and no bathtub or shower. Could you imagine living in conditions like these? The U. S. Census Bureau's 1993 American Housing Survey states that one poor family in several lives in housing that is severely physically inadequate. In order to help provide housing, there must be funding to build.

Analysis

Miranda uses a question to get audience attention. Then she provides us with a basis for listening to her speech. Finally, she previews main points.

Miranda's first main point is a complete sentence focusing on one function—to educate people.

Here she cites her source for her statement of Habitat's goal.

This question serves to adapt to her audience by asking for their response.

Here she not only provides the answer, but also uses an example to show the cost burden specifically.

Again, she uses a question as a means of audience adaptation and then presents the extent of the problem. She finishes this main point with a transition to the second point.

Speech

The second function of Habitat for Humanity is to raise funds to help build their homes. Donations are the main funding for Habitat. The funds are used as the donor designates. So, if a gift is needed for a certain building project, it will be given to that project. Any other undesignated gifts will be used where they are needed the most. Habitat sometimes partners with the government to "set the stage" for construction, helping to relieve the poverty housing. Setting the stage usually consists of the government donating land, donating infrastructure for streets, or assisting with utilities. The government may also donate housing for Habitat to rehabilitate. Raising money enables Habitat to build the houses for people.

A third function of Habitat is to build and rehabilitate houses in partnership with local affiliates and home owners. Families that are in need of a home have to apply to Habitat for their approval. Families are chosen by level of need through the Habitat affiliation's family selection committee. A second requirement is that the family must be devoted to becoming partners in the program. If they are willing to meet this requirement, they will be a "partner family" with Habitat. The third requirement is the family's ability to repay a no-interest loan.

Did any of you think that the houses were given away by Habitat? I thought that they were. I thought that they just worked for the houses. But Habitat houses are sold to partners—they are not given away. The partner family makes monthly payments on a no-interest loan and these payments are used to build more houses for other people. The home owners also invest "sweat equity," which means that they will spend long, laborious hours in order to build their own home. Now, Habitat doesn't give them houses, but the monthly mortgage prices are very low. A survey on Habitat homeowners by the U.S. Department of Housing and Urban Development says that the average home costs $33,478. The average mortgage payment is $269 per month. These prices are much lower than they would be for comparable homes on the open market—homes that would ordinarily cost

Analysis

Miranda's second main point, also a complete sentence, focuses on raising funds to build houses.

Here she explains what she means by "setting the stage."

Her third complete sentence main point focuses on rehabilitation in partnership with home owners.

Good explanation of requirements.

Another question that draws the audience into the speech.

Good explanation of "sweat equity."

After providing statistics that show the costs, she puts the cost into perspective by comparing it with the cost on the open market. She concludes the point by emphasizing the importance of Habitat.

Speech

$100,000 or more. The homes may not be free, like some of you may have thought and I thought, but Habitat gives a great opportunity for those who are less fortunate to own their homes.

Habitat for Humanity helps people in poverty to own their own homes. Its successes are known worldwide by achieving the three goals: educating people about affordable housing issues and the works of the group, raising funds to build homes, and building and rehabilitating houses in partnership with local affiliates and home owners.

Analysis

Her conclusion is a summary of the three goals. A good first speech, with an introduction that gains attention and gives necessary orientation, three well-supported main points, enough audience adaptation to hold interest, and a good conclusion.

WHAT WOULD YOU DO?
A QUESTION OF ETHICS

Terry Weathers is running for student-body president and has asked her friend Megan to deliver the key speech of support at the All University Candidates' Meeting. Being a good friend, Megan agrees.

Megan works several days developing the speech, and she believes she has prepared a really good one. The problem is that although Megan can prepare excellent speeches she suffers from stage fright. She is scared to death to give this one in front of such a large audience. So, she asks Donnell Gates, a guy in her speech class who wows audiences with his engaging manner, to deliver the speech she wrote at the event.

Donnell thought about her request and left the following message on her voice mail: "Listen, you know I'm not crazy about Terry, so I would never vote for her. But since I don't really care who wins this election, I'll give the speech. Hey, I just enjoy the power I have over an audience!"

1. Now that Megan knows that Donnell doesn't care for Terry, should she let him give the speech?
2. And what about Donnell? Should he give such a speech knowing that he wouldn't support Terry himself?

Summary

Although speeches may be presented impromptu, by manuscript, or by memory, the material you have been reading is designed to help you present your speeches extemporaneously—that is, carefully prepared and practiced but with the exact wording determined at the time of utterance.

The verbal components of effective presentation are clarity, vividness, and emphasis. The nonverbal elements of presentation include voice, articulation, and bodily action.

Effective speaking uses verbal and nonverbal components to achieve a conversational quality that includes enthusiasm, vocal expressiveness, spontaneity, fluency, and eye contact.

To rehearse an extemporaneous speech, complete the outline at least two days in advance. Between the time the outline has been completed and the time the speech is to be given, practice the speech several times, weighing what you did and how you did it after each practice. You may wish to use brief notes, especially for longer speeches, as long as they do not interfere with your delivery.

All speakers feel nervous as they approach their first speech. Some nervousness is cognitive (in the mind) and some is behavioral (physically displayed). Rather than being an either-or matter, nervousness is a matter of degree.

Because at least some tension is constructive, our goal is not to get rid of nervousness but to learn how to cope with it. First, realize that nervousness is normal. Second, you can use several specific behaviors to help control excessive nervousness. And, if you're well prepared, you will be able to achieve a more relaxed presentation.

If nervousness is truly detrimental to your performance, see your professor outside of class and talk with him or her about what you are experiencing. Your professor should be able to offer suggestions for people you can see or programs you can attend.

Speeches are evaluated on how well they meet the guidelines for effective content, organization, language, and delivery.

Communicate! Online

Use your Communicate! CD-ROM for quick access to the electronic study resources that accompany this text. Included on your CD-ROM is access to InfoTrac College Edition, the World Wide Web, a demo of WebTutor for Communicate!, and the Communicate! Web site at the Wadsworth Communication Café. The Communicate! Web site offers chapter-by-chapter activities, quizzes, and a digital glossary.

Review the following key terms at
http://communication.wadsworth.com/humancomm/verderber

Key Terms

articulation (397)

bodily action (397)

cognitive restructuring (416)

conversational quality (400)

emphasis (395)

emphasis by proportion (395)

emphasis by repeating (395)

emphasis by transitions (395)

enthusiasm (400)

extemporaneous speech (394)

eye contact (403)

facial expression (397)

fluency (402)

gestures (397)

learning the speech (409)

metaphor (395)

monotone (401)

movement (398)

nervousness (410)

poise (398)

posture (398)

pronunciation (397)

rehearsing (404)

simile (395)

speech notes (406)

spontaneity (402)

systematic desensitization (416)

visualization (414)

vocal expressiveness (401)

voice (396)

If you videotaped your speech rehearsal as suggested under Communicate! Using Technology on page 409, you can use the Speech Evaluation Checklist included under Checklist for Chapter 16 at the Communicate! Web site to assess your performance.

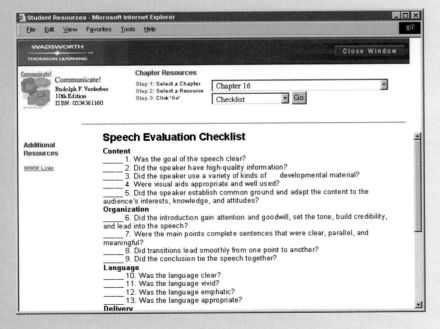

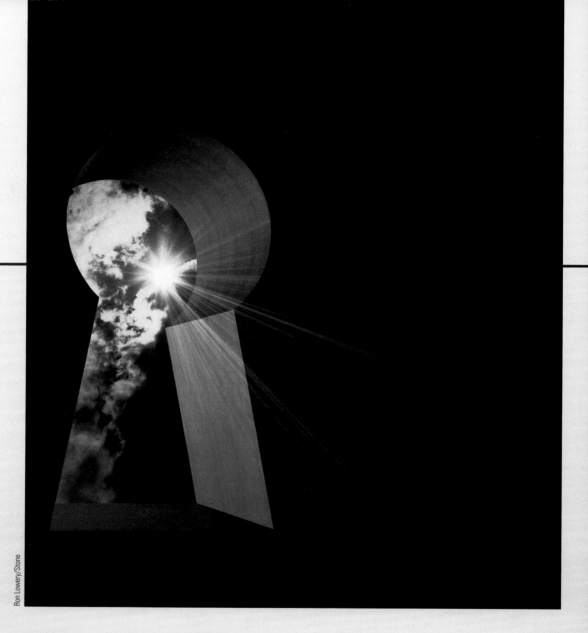

Ron Lowery/Stone

OBJECTIVES

After you have read this chapter, you should be able to answer these questions:

- What are the three goals of informative speaking?
- What are the tests of presenting ideas creatively?
- What can you do to increase your credibility?
- How can you proceed to leave the impression that what you have said is new and relevant?
- What key techniques can you use to emphasize information?
- What are the major methods of informing?
- What are the key criteria for evaluating an informative speech?

17

Informative Speaking

For several months, a major architectural firm had been working on designs for the arts center to be built in the middle of downtown. Members of the city council and guests from various constituencies in the city, as well as a number of concerned citizens, were taking their seats as the long-anticipated presentation was about to begin. As Linda Garner, mayor and presiding officer of the city council, finished her introduction, Donald Harper, the principal architect of the project, walked to the microphone to begin his speech.

COMMUNICATE! Using InfoTrac College Edition

Using InfoTrac College Edition, under the subject of "Learning," click on "Learning, Psychology of." Look for articles that discuss "how people learn" and "how people think" to gain additional information that is relevant to informative speaking. Read one or more articles to help you better understand how to prepare your informative speech.

This is but one of many scenarios played out every day as speakers struggle to help us increase our understanding of complex issues. In this chapter, we build on the action steps of general speech preparation by focusing on informative speaking.

As an informative speaker, your rhetorical goals are to present information in a way that holds interest, facilitates understanding, and increases the likelihood of remembering. We begin by focusing on principles of informing that you can use to consider (1) how to *create interest* so the audience will listen, (2) how to *explain* in a way that will help the audience understand, and (3) how to *discuss* the information in a way that will help the audience remember. Then we consider four methods of informing that effective speakers must master. We conclude the chapter with a sample informative speech that illustrates these principles.

Principles of Informing

You will be a more effective informative speaker if you apply principles of credibility, intellectual stimulation, creativity, relevance, and emphasis.

Credibility

Principle 1: Audiences are more likely to listen to you if they like, trust, and have confidence in you.

Although we have already discussed the bases of *credibility* (knowledge/expertise, trustworthiness, and personality), we emphasize it here because building or maintaining your credibility is essential to your success. If your listeners have faith in you, they will be more willing to learn. The three points mentioned here are reminders of what you must do in your speech to establish credibility.

1. **Demonstrate your expertise.** As an informative speaker, you must talk knowledgeably and fluently, with command of your information and without stumbling and making a variety of misstatements.

2. **Emphasize your interest in the audience's well-being.** Likewise, you must show your listeners that you care about them and what happens to them.

3. **Look and sound enthusiastic.** Finally, you must show enthusiasm for your information.

You probably will see the cumulative effect of credibility during this course. As your class proceeds from speech to speech, some speakers will grow in stature in your mind and others will diminish.

John Elk III/Stock, Boston

Your credibility will be high if what you say and how you look illustrates your expertise on the topic.

Intellectual Stimulation

Principle 2: Audiences are more likely to listen to information they perceive to be intellectually stimulating.

Information will be perceived as **intellectually stimulating** when it is new to audience members and when it meets deep-seated needs to know.

When we say *new,* we mean information either that most of the audience is not familiar with or that presents new insights or twists on a familiar topic. If you really have researched your topic, you are likely to have information that will be new to a majority of your audience. For example, a topic likely to be perceived as new that is a very important one to learn about for college students—especially women—is the drug rohypnol. On one hand, it gives a cheap but dangerous high; on the other hand, it is being used by people to lower the defenses and resistance of others. Even if the audience has heard about the so-called rape drug, they are unlikely to know much of its history, properties, and other dangers.

When you are considering talking about a topic that most of the people in your audience are familiar with, brainstorm for a new angle, new application, or new perspective. For instance, during the basketball season, a speaker who first considers talking about how to shoot a jump shot would be wiser to brainstorm other topics that would help viewers get a much better understanding of the game as they watch it, such as "pick and roll," "matchup zone defenses," "using the press," or "breaking a press."

But just being new is not enough. The information must also meet the audience's deep-seated hunger for knowledge and insight. Part of the informative

intellectually stimulating– *information that is new to audience members and meets deep-seated needs to know.*

speaker's job is to feed that hunger. Every day we are touched by ideas and issues that we do not fully grasp, but we often ignore them, partly out of insufficient motivation to find additional information. For instance, several years ago scientists discovered an "ice man" buried in a glacier of the southern Alps, the well-preserved body of a man who lived between four and five thousand years ago. Newspaper headlines announced the significance of the discovery. Readers were excited by the information, but they probably did not pursue study of the topic. The informative speaker seizes the topic and links the significance of the ice man to an understanding of our own history and development, which may well stimulate our natural intellectual curiosity.

Let's consider a more typical example. Suppose you are planning a speech on new cars. From the April issue of *Consumer Reports* alone—the month in which comparative statistics and ratings are given for all new cars—you could find information that would be intellectually stimulating. For instance, we are aware that over time Japanese-made cars have captured an increasingly large share of the U.S. market at least partly because of perceived quality issues. How are U.S. companies responding to those issues? Are American-made cars achieving higher quality ratings? Are American-made cars "competitive"? Are sales increasing? Equally stimulating speeches could explore information on safety features, mileage data, or styling.

You may work from your brainstorming list to find a topic. But, for an important informative speech, do not be satisfied with a superficial topic. Brainstorm until you have a new angle that you can pursue.

Here are some topics that meet this important criterion.

acupuncture	stock market	global warming	AIDS
hurricanes	sexual harassment	social security	cloning
vegetarianism	Special Olympics	homophobia	poverty
child abuse	media violence	environment	welfare
immigration	sports values	censorship	discrimination

Keep in mind that these topics are just "headings." If one of them strikes a chord with you, work with it until you can arrive at an aspect of the topic that will be intellectually stimulating.

Creativity

Principle 3: Audiences are more likely to listen to, understand, and remember information that is presented creatively.

creativity–*a person's capacity to produce new or original ideas and insights.*

Creativity may be defined as a person's capacity to produce new or original ideas and insights (Eysenck, 1994, p. 200). Although you may be thinking "I'm just not a creative person," all of us can be creative if we are willing to work at it. Let's consider how you can proceed that will result in creative speaking.

1. **Gather enough high-quality information to provide a broad base from which to work.** Contrary to what many of us may think, creativity is more likely a product of perspiration than inspiration. If you have more quality information than you really need for the speech, you have more flexibility and more choices.

2. **Give yourself enough time for the creative process to work.** Many students finish their outline just in time to "go over the speech" once before they present it. Then they wonder why they are not able to "be creative." Your mind needs time to reflect on your outline and information. This is why we recommended completing your outline for a classroom speech *at least* two days before the actual presentation. With that time, you are likely to find that the morning after an uninspiring practice you suddenly have two or three fresh ideas to work with. While you were sleeping, your mind was still going over the material. When you awoke, the product of unconscious or subconscious thought reached your consciousness. You can facilitate creatively simply by giving your mind time to work with your information.

3. **Be prepared to pursue a creative idea when it comes.** Have you ever noticed how ideas seem to come at odd times—while you are cleaning your room, mulching the garden, or waiting at a stoplight? Have you also noticed that when you try to recall those "great" ideas, they are likely to have slipped away? Many speakers, writers, and composers carry pencil and paper with them at all times, and when an idea comes, they make a note of it. Not all of these flights of fancy are flashes of creative genius, but some of them are good or at least worth exploring. If you do not make a note of your ideas, you will never know whether they are good.

4. **Force yourself to practice sections of the speech in different ways.** Too often, when our outline is finished, we act as if it is cast in stone. Then we keep going over it the same way "to learn it." Take the time to practice in different ways rather than being content with the first way of presenting material that comes to mind. If you purposely phrase key ideas in different ways in each of the first few practices, you give yourself choices. Although some of the ways you express a point may be similar, trying new ways will stretch your mind, and chances are good that one or two of the ways will be far superior and much more imaginative than any of the others. Let's focus on one example to see how creativity can help you think about alternative choices.

Creating alternative choices Suppose you are planning to give a speech on climatic variation in the United States and that your research has uncovered the data shown in Figure 17.1. We will use these data to show (1) that one set of data can suggest several lines of development on one topic and (2) that the same point can be made in many different ways.

City	Yearly Temperature (in degrees Fahrenheit)		Precipitation (in inches)	
	High	**Low**	**July**	**Annual**
Chicago	95	–21	3.7	35
Cincinnati	98	–7	3.3	39
Denver	104	–3	1.9	15
Los Angeles	104	40	trace	15
Miami	96	50	5.7	56
Minneapolis	95	–27	3.5	28
New Orleans	95	26	6.1	62
New York	98	–2	4.4	42
Phoenix	117	35	0.8	7
Portland, ME	94	–18	3.1	44
St. Louis	97	–9	3.9	37
San Francisco	94	35	trace	19
Seattle	94	23	0.9	38

Figure 17.1
Temperature and precipitation highs and lows in selected U.S. cities.

Study your information, and ask what is unusual or noteworthy and why. The information in Figure 17.1 includes several unusual or noteworthy points. First, you might notice that yearly *high* temperatures in U.S. cities vary far less than yearly *low* temperatures. The yearly highs in July were about 96 degrees for Miami and 95 for Minneapolis, whereas the yearly lows were 50 degrees in Miami and –27 degrees in Minneapolis—a 77-degree difference! Conventional wisdom would suggest that high temperatures should vary nearly as much as low temperatures, which might lead you to ask, "Why is this not so?"

You might also notice that it hardly ever rains on the west coast in the summer. Two of the three west coast cities, Los Angeles and San Francisco, show only a trace of rain in July and a third, Seattle—a city often considered a rainy city—shows nine-tenths of an inch in July. This is almost three inches less than any eastern city and five inches less than Miami. Why is there so little rain on the west coast in July? Why is there so much more rain in the east?

Finally, in the major cities cited in the east and in the midwest, you might notice that July, a month thought to be hot and dry, produces more than the average one-twelfth of the annual precipitation. Conventional wisdom suggests July as the driest month of the year. Why do we perceive July to be a dry month? Why isn't it?

Thus, as we study the data in this one chart, we can raise questions that suggest at least three different lines of development for a speech on climate: Why are highs so similar but lows so different? Why is there so much more rain in the summer in the midwest and east than in the west? Why is July wetter in most cities than we would expect?

Create different ways of making the same point Using only the information from the climatic data, let's consider two ways of supporting the point that "Yearly high temperatures in U.S. cities vary far less than yearly low temperatures."

1. Of the thirteen cities selected, ten (77 percent) had yearly highs between 90 and 100 degrees. Four (30 percent) had yearly lows above freezing; two (15 percent) had yearly lows between zero and 32 degrees; and seven (54 percent) had low temperatures below zero.

2. Cincinnati, Miami, Minneapolis, New York, and St. Louis—cities at different latitudes—all had yearly high temperatures of 95 to 98 degrees. In contrast, the lowest temperature for Miami was 50 degrees, and the lowest temperatures for Cincinnati, Minneapolis, New York, and St. Louis were –7, –27, –2, and –9 degrees, respectively.

Can you find another way of making the same point?

As we discussed previously, to be creative you must give yourself time to think.

Relevance

Principle 4: Audiences are more likely to listen to and remember information they perceive as relevant.

Rather than acting like sponges that absorb every bit of information, most of us act more like filters: We listen only to that information we perceive to be relevant. **Relevance** is the personal value people find in information when it relates to their needs and interests. Relevance might be measured by the audience's "need to know."

Finding **vital information**—information the audience perceives as a matter of life or death—may be the ultimate in relevance. Police cadets, for instance, will see information explaining what they should do when attacked as vital. Similarly, students may perceive information that is necessary to their passing a test as vital. When speakers show listeners that information is critical to their well-being, they have a compelling reason to listen.

Of course, information does not have to be vital to be perceived as relevant. But always ask yourself in what way the material you plan to present is truly important to the audience, and emphasize that connection in your speech. For example, in a speech on Japan, a topic that may seem distant from the audience's felt needs and concerns, you can increase the perception of relevance by focusing on the importance of Japanese manufacturing to our economy, including local jobs. In a speech on the Egyptian pyramids, you can increase perception of relevance by relating pyramid construction to contemporary building construction. In any speech you give, it is up to you to show how the information relates to the audience's needs and interests.

OBSERVE & ANALYZE
Journal Activity

Different Ways of Presenting Information

Evaluate the two different ways of presenting variable temperature data suggested in the text. In your Student Workbook under Journal Activity 17.1, indicate which way you believe is better and explain why. Create a third way that is somewhat different. Is the way you created even better? If so, explain why. If not, explain why not.

relevance–*the personal value that people find in information when it relates to their needs and interests.*

vital information–*information the audience perceives as a matter of life or death.*

Although determining relevance is important throughout the speech, it is especially important during your introduction when audience members are sure to ask themselves, "Why should I listen to a speech on . . . ?" Notice how this opening for a speech on high-speed rail transportation establishes relevance:

> **Have you been stuck in a traffic jam lately? Have you started what you had hoped would be a pleasant vacation only to be trampled at the airport, or worse, to discover when you got to your destination that your luggage hadn't? We're all aware that every year our highways and our airways are getting more congested. At the same time, we are facing a rapidly decreasing supply of petroleum. Today, I'm going to tell you about one of the most practical means for solving these problems—high-speed rail transportation.**

Emphasis

Principle 5: Audiences are more likely to understand and to remember information that is emphasized.

Audiences will remember only some of the content presented in a speech—the rest is likely to be lost over time. Part of your challenge is to determine what you want the audience to retain and then to give that information proper emphasis. To do so, you must prioritize your information.

Ordinarily, the highest priority information in your speech includes the specific goal, the main points, and key facts that give meaning to the main points. So, if you are giving a speech on choosing a credit card, you would want to make sure the audience remembered these elements:

- **The goal:** to understand the three criteria for evaluating a credit card offer.
- **The main points:** three criteria for evaluating credit cards are know the real interest rates, know the annual fees, and know the unique benefits.
- **Important facts:** interest rates tend to be quite high—up to 18 percent or more; fees range from twenty to thirty dollars on most cards; many offer unique benefits such as frequent flier miles, cash-back rebates, or coupons.

Once you have prioritized your information, plan a strategy for increasing the audience's retention of these items. In previous chapters, we have discussed various methods of emphasizing information. Let's remind ourselves of the importance of visual aids, repetition, transitions, humorous stories, and one additional method, mnemonics.

Use visual aids Recall that visual aids emphasize because we remember more when we can associate pictures with words. Especially for informative speeches, you will want to think very carefully about the kind of visual aid that will work best for you.

Repeat important words and ideas Recall that just because a word is spoken does not necessarily mean that we perceive it. One of the best ways of breaking through is sheer repetition. Also, recall that you might repeat a word or you might restate an idea in a slightly different way. Remember, however, that when repetition is overdone it loses its effectiveness. In your speech, repeating a few important words and ideas will pay dividends—but repeating too many words or ideas will backfire.

Use transitions to guide audience thinking Listeners cannot go back if they get lost, so it is especially important for speakers to do what they can to help audiences see where they have been and where they are going. Thus, in the introduction of the speech, you tell the audience what you will cover: "In this speech, we will look at the three criteria for choosing a credit card." Then, as you proceed through a long main point, you might remind your listeners where you are going by saying, "So we've seen that one criterion for choosing a credit card is the interest rate, now let's consider a second criterion, the annual fee." And before the end of the speech you might review, "So, in this speech we've looked at the three criteria for choosing a credit card: interest rates, annual fees, and unique benefits.

The value of such clarifying structure is tremendous. Because listeners' minds may wander, you must exercise control in how you want the audience to perceive what you say. I have heard listeners swear that a speaker never stated the second main point of the speech when in reality the point was stated, but in a way that had no effect on the audience. Clarifying structure, through transitions, helps your audience recognize where you are in the speech and why your point is significant.

Use humor to stress key points Of all the forms of presenting information, our own experience shows that people are more likely to remember information in humorous story form. For instance, suppose you were giving a speech on the importance of having perspective. Your main point might be that a problem that seems enormous at the moment might turn out to be minor in a few days, so being able to put events into perspective saves a great deal of psychological wear and tear. To cement the concept of *perspective*, you might tell a story like this one:

> **A first-time visitor to the races bet two dollars on the first race on a horse that had the same name as his elementary school. The horse won and the man was ten dollars ahead. In each of the next several races, he bet on horses such as "Apple Pie," his favorite, and "Kathie's Prize," after his wife's name, and he kept winning. By the end of the sixth race he was 700 dollars ahead. He was about to go home when he noticed that in the seventh race, Seventh Veil was scheduled in the number seven position, and was currently going off at odds of seven to one. The man couldn't resist—he bet his entire 700 dollars. And sure enough, the horse came in seventh. When he got home his wife asked, "How did you do?" Very calmly he looked at his wife and said, "Not bad—I lost two dollars." That's perspective.**

Romilly Lockyer/The Image Bank

Audiences are more likely to remember information presented in a humorous story form.

mnemonics–*memory aids.*

Create memory aids for your audience   You can help your listeners retain more of your speech by suggesting memory aids, formally called **mnemonics.** For instance, if you are giving a speech on the criteria for evaluating diamonds, you might want the audience to remember that the criteria for evaluating a diamond are weight, clarity, tint, and shape. But your audience is more likely to remember this information if you list the criteria as "carat, clarity, color, and cutting." Why? With a little bit of creativity, you have created a memory aid— the four criteria all begin with the letter "C."

acronyms–*words formed from initial letters of each of the successive parts of a compound term, common words that comprise the first letters of objects or concepts, or sentences with each word starting with a letter that signals something else.*

Mnemonics may be **acronyms,** words formed from initial letters of each of the successive parts of a compound term (NATO, OPEC), common words that comprise the first letters of objects or concepts (HOMES for the five Great Lakes), or sentences with each word starting with a letter that signals something else ("Every good boy does fine" for the five lines of the musical staff). For instance, in her speech on the healing power of listening, Carol Koehler (1998), a professor of communication and medicine, offered the word CARE to reflect the qualities of the therapeutic communicator: C stands for concentrate, A stands for acknowledge, R stands for response, and E stands for emotional control (pp. 543–544).

association–*the tendency of one thought to stimulate recall of another, similar thought.*

Most memory aids are a form of association. An **association** is the tendency of one thought to stimulate recall of another, similar thought. Suppose you are trying to help the audience remember the value of color in a diamond. Because blue is the most highly prized tint and yellow or brown tints lower a diamond's value, you might associate blue tint with "the blue-ribbon prize" and yellow (or brown) tint with "a lemon." Thus, the best diamond gets the "blue ribbon" and the worst diamond is a "lemon."

Figurative associations like these fall into the two categories of similes and metaphors. Recall that a simile is a comparison using "like": "A computer screen is like a television monitor." A metaphor states an identity: "Laser printers are the Cadillacs of computer printers." I still remember vividly a metaphor I heard in a speech more than twenty years ago. A student explained the functioning of a television tube by saying, "A television picture tube is a gun shooting beams of light." If you make your associations striking enough, your audience will remember your point as well as I remember that point about how a television tube works.

Methods of Informing

In the first part of this chapter, we presented fundamental principles of informative speaking. In this part, we consider the informative skills of narrating, describing, defining, explaining processes or demonstrating, and exposition. Each of these represents both an informative *skill* and a *type* of informative speech. At times, you may use some or all of these skills in a single speech. At other times, you may prepare an informative speech based primarily on one of the skills.

Narrating

Recall from Chapter 13 that a **narrative** is a story, a tale, or an account (often humorous) that has a point or climax. A joke has a punch line; a fable has a moral; other narratives have climactic endings that make the stories interesting. Thus, the primary goal of a narrative is to make a point in such a unique or interesting way that the audience will remember it because of the way it was presented. In a speech about the costs of faulty listening, suppose you exemplified your point with this narrative:

> **Abraham suffered great personal cost by working all day to finish a report for the five o'clock deadline, only to find as he turned it in that he was a day early.**

This one-sentence narrative about Abraham can then be developed to be both more interesting and more memorable. Let's consider three major elements of narration and how they can increase the power of this particular narrative statement.

1. **Narratives are built with supporting details.** Narratives can be long or short depending on the number and degree of development of supporting details used to build the story to maximize its effect. For instance, in the narrative of Abraham's report, you could introduce details such as how Abraham got to work at 6 A.M., more than two hours earlier than usual, to find the time to work on the report and how Abraham had to turn down a lunch invitation from a man he had been trying to see for three weeks about an important issue of company policy.

COMMUNICATE!
Using Technology

Informative speeches become more interesting when the information seems relevant and the speaker credible. One way to enhance your credibility and to acquire information that is specific to your speech is to correspond through email with a respected expert on the subject. In your email message to an expert, ask a specific question that is relevant to your topic and not answered in the existing printed material you have found. Then you can report the answers you receive in your speech as follows: "In an email I recently received from . . . , she told me that . . ."

narrative–*a story, a tale, or an account (often humorous) that has a point or climax.*

2. **Narratives usually maintain suspense.** Part of the power of the narrative can be increased by withholding the punch line until the end. If you can tease the audience, you will hold their attention. The audience will be trying to see whether they can anticipate what you are going to say. Vocally, a slight pause before delivering the punch line will heighten the effect:

Abraham worked all day to finish his report for the five o'clock deadline, only to discover when he turned it in [pause] it was one full day early!

3. **Narratives include dialogue when possible.** A story will be much more enjoyable to an audience if they can hear it unfold through dialogue. For instance, notice how our one-line story improves with this presentation:

As Abraham burst into his boss's office with his report in hand, his boss's secretary stared at him, dumbfounded. When he said breathlessly, "Here's the report, right on the dot!" she exclaimed, "Abraham, the report isn't due until tomorrow!"

Describing

describing—telling what something looks like.

Informative speeches can be made more vivid by **describing,** telling what it looks like. To describe effectively requires you to observe particular descriptive characteristics and to create vivid ways to communicate those observations. Let's consider the characteristics of description and the means of revising creatively.

Characteristics of description Description is based on observation of size, shape, weight, color, composition, age and condition, and the relationship among various parts.

How large is the place or object? If it's an object, how heavy is it? Both size and weight are most descriptive when they are presented comparatively: "The book is the same length and width as your text, but about twice as thick." "The suitcase weighed 70 pounds, about twice the weight of a normally packed suitcase."

What is the object's shape? What color is it? Simple shapes are easily described by words such as round, triangular, oblong, spherical, conical, cylindrical, and rectangular. Complex objects are best described as a series of simple shapes. Color, an obvious component of description, is difficult to describe accurately. Although most people can visualize black and white, the primary colors (red, yellow, and blue), and their complements (green, purple, and orange), very few objects are exactly these colors. Perhaps the best way to describe a color is to couple it with a common referent. For instance, "lemon yellow," "brick red," "green as a grape," or "sky blue" give rather accurate approximations.

What is the object made of? What is its age or condition? A ball of aluminum does not look the same as a ball of yarn. A pile of rocks gives a different impression than a pile of straw. A brick building looks different from a steel, wood, or glass building. Whether an object is new or old can make a difference in its appearance. Because age by itself may not be descriptive, an object is often discussed in terms of condition. Well-read books become tattered, older buildings become dilapidated, land becomes eroded. Age and condition together often prove valuable in developing informative descriptions.

How does an object fit together? If the object you want to describe is complex, its parts must be fitted into their proper relationship before a mental picture emerges. Remember the story of the blind men who described an elephant in terms of what each felt? The one who felt the trunk said the elephant was like a snake; the one who felt a leg said the elephant was like a tree; and the one who felt the body said the elephant was like a wall. When it is relevant to your description, be sure audiences understand how the parts fit together.

Revising descriptions Description is improved with careful revision. For most people, vivid description does not come easily—we are not used to describing vividly in ordinary conversation. In practicing a speech, the speaker has the opportunity to work on the language, revising general and bland statements to make them more specific and vivid. We can work with a single, simple idea to illustrate the revision process. Consider this sentence:

Several pencils were on Jamal's desk.

This statement of fact tells us that pencils (plural) were on a desk, but it gives no real description.

Revising this description begins by asking questions that relate to the essentials of description we discussed. By asking "How many pencils? What color were they?" specific descriptive details come to mind. This revision answers those questions:

Five yellow pencils decorated Jamal's desk.

"Five" is more descriptive than "several" because it is more specific; "yellow" begins a description of how they looked; "decorated" is more descriptive than "on" because it carries a mental picture.

Now ask the questions "What condition were the pencils in? How were they arranged?" In the following two sentences, we get completely different descriptions of the pencils based on the answers to these questions:

Five finely sharpened yellow pencils lined the side of Jamal's desk, side by side in perfect order from longest to shortest.

Five stubby, well-chewed pencils of different colors, all badly in need of sharpening, were scattered about Jamal's desk.

These examples begin to show the different pictures that can be created depending on how you use the observed details.

Continued revision may lead to your trying to memorize the speech. As you practice, try to keep the essentials in mind but use slightly different wordings each time to express your descriptions. By making minor changes each time, you will avoid memorizing the speech.

Defining

Because of its importance in solving problems, learning, and understanding, **defining**—explaining what a word means—is essential for effective communication because it helps audiences understand and relate to key concepts (Weaver, 1970, p. 212). In your informative speeches, you are likely to use both short and extended definitions.

Short definitions Short definitions are used to clarify concepts in as few words as possible. Effective speakers learn to define by synonym and antonym, classification and differentiation, use or function, and etymological reference.

1. **Synonyms and antonyms.** Using a synonym or an antonym is the quickest way to define a word because you are able to indicate an approximate, if not exact, meaning in a single sentence. **Synonyms** are words that have the same or nearly the same meanings; **antonyms** are words that have opposite meanings. Defining by synonym is defining by comparison—for a word that does not bring up an immediate concrete meaning, we provide one that does. Synonyms for *prolix* include *long, wordy,* and *verbose.* Its antonyms are *short* and *concise.* Synonyms are not duplicates for the word being defined, but they do give a good idea of what the word means. Of course, the synonym or antonym must be familiar to the audience or its use defeats its purpose.

2. **Classification and differentiation.** When you define by classification, you give the boundaries of the particular word and focus on the single feature that differentiates that word from words with similar meanings. Most dictionary definitions are of the classification–differentiation variety. For instance, a dog may be defined as a carnivorous, domesticated mammal of the family Canidae. "Carnivorous," "mammal," and "family Canidae" limit the boundaries to dogs, jackals, foxes, and wolves. "Domesticated" differentiates dogs from the other three.

3. **Use or function.** A third short way to define is by explaining the use or function of the object represented by a particular word. Thus, when you say, "A *plane* is a hand-powered tool used to smooth the edges of boards," or "A scythe is a piece of steel shaped in a half circle with a handle attached that is used to cut weeds or high grass," you are defining tools by indicating their use. Because the use or function of an object may be more important than its classification, often this is an excellent method of definition.

4. **Etymology.** **Etymology** is the derivation or history of a particular word. Because meanings of words change over time, origin may reveal very little about modern meaning. In some instances, however, the history of a word lends additional insight that will help the audience not only better remember the meaning but also bring the meaning to life. For instance, a "censor" originally was one of two Roman magistrates appointed to take the census and, later, to supervise public morals. The best source of word derivation is the Oxford English Dictionary.

defining–*explaining what a word means.*

synonyms–*words that have the same or nearly the same meanings.*

antonyms–*words that have opposite meanings.*

etymology–*the derivation or history of a particular word.*

Example and comparison Regardless of which short definition form you use, most statements need to be supplemented with examples, comparisons, or both to make them understandable. That is especially true when you define abstract words. Consider the word "just" in the following sentence: "You are being *just* in your dealings with another when you deal *honorably* and *fairly.*" Although *just* has been defined by synonym, listeners still may be unsure of the meaning. If we add, "If Paul and Mary do the same amount of work and we reward them by giving them an equal amount of money, our dealings will be just; if, on the other hand, we give Paul more money because he's a man, our dealings will be unjust." In this case, the definition is clarified with both an example and a comparison.

For some words, a single example or comparison will be enough. For other words or in communicating with certain audiences, you may need several examples and comparisons.

Extended definitions Often a word is so important to a speech that an extended definition is warranted. An extended definition is one that serves as an entire main point in a speech or, at times, an entire speech. Thus, an entire speech can be built around an extended definition of a term such as *freedom, equality, justice, love,* or *impressionistic painting.*

An extended definition begins with a single-sentence dictionary definition or stipulated definition. For example, *Webster's Third New International Dictionary* defines jazz as "American music characterized by improvisation, syncopated rhythms, contrapuntal ensemble playing, and special melodic features peculiar to the individual interpretation of the player." This definition suggests four topics ("improvisation," "syncopation," "ensemble," and "special melodies") that could be used as a basis for a topical order for a speech.

The key to the effectiveness of the speech would be how well you explain each topic. Your selection and use of examples, illustrations, comparisons, personal experiences, and observations will give the speech its original and distinctive flavor.

Explaining Processes or Demonstrating

Many informative speeches involve **explaining processes**—telling how to do something, how to make something, or how something works. For instance, the boss might explain the process of going through various stages in order to be promoted, an engineer can explain how a turbojet works, an author might explain how to get a book published, or a student in class might explain the process of producing a nightly edition of ESPN's SportsCenter. A demonstration involves going through the complete process that you are explaining, for example, on how to get more power on a forehand table-tennis shot, on how to make fettuccine noodles, or on how to purify water.

Whereas a process explanation tells how to do something, how to make something, or how something works, often with the help of visual aids, a demonstration involves a live, hands-on visual portrayal of the process. For

explaining processes–*telling how to do something, how to make something, or how something works.*

instance, a computer trainer might demonstrate how to use new software, a chef might demonstrate how to bone a chicken, or a golf pro might demonstrate how to hit out of sand traps. Some of these demonstrations are completely hands-on, performing the entire step-by-step procedure; others are partial demonstrations, using various visual aids. To explain or to demonstrate processes effectively, speakers need to delineate clear steps and explanations of those steps.

When the task is relatively simple, such as how to get more power on a forehand table-tennis shot, you may want to try a **complete demonstration,** going through the complete process in front of the audience. If so, practice until you can do it smoothly and easily under the pressure of facing an actual audience. Because the actual demonstration is likely to take longer than in practice (you are likely to have to make some modifications during the speech to enable everyone in the room to see the demonstration), you may want to make sure that the final practice is somewhat shorter than the maximum time limit you will have for the speech.

For a relatively complicated process, you may want to consider the **modified demonstration,** in which you complete various stages of the demonstration at home and do only part of the actual work in front of the audience. Suppose you were going to demonstrate construction of a floral display. Actually performing the construction from scratch is too complex and time-consuming for a speech-length presentation. Instead, you could prepare a complete set of materials to begin the demonstration, a mock-up of the basic floral triangle, and a completed floral display. During the speech, you would describe the materials needed and then begin demonstrating how to make the basic floral triangle. Rather than trying to get everything together perfectly in a few seconds, you could remove, from a bag or some concealed place, a partially com-

complete demonstration–
going through the complete process in front of the audience.

modified demonstration–
completing various stages of the demonstration at home and doing only part of the complete demonstrating in front of the audience.

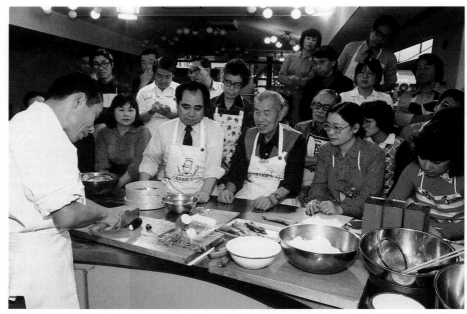

Demonstrations must be carefully prepared and organized if audiences are to retain the information.

J.P. Laffont/Sygma

pleted arrangement illustrating the floral triangle. You would then use this in your demonstration, adding flowers as if you were planning to complete it. Then, from another bag, you could remove the completed arrangement to illustrate one of the effects you were discussing. Conducting a modified demonstration of this type is often easier than trying to complete an entire demonstration in a limited time.

Throughout a demonstration, speak slowly and repeat key ideas often. We learn best by doing, so if you can include audience participation, you may be even more successful. In a speech on origami, or Japanese paper folding, you could explain the principles, then pass out paper and have audience members each make a figure. Actual participation will increase interest and ensure recall. Finally, through other visual aids, you could show how these principles are used in more elaborate projects.

Although your audience may be able to visualize a process through vivid word pictures (in fact, in your impromptu explanations in ordinary conversation, it is the only way you can proceed), you will probably want to make full use of visual aids in a demonstration speech. Perhaps more than with any other kind of informative speech, carefully prepared visual material may be essential to listeners' understanding.

Exposition

Throughout history, people have had an insatiable need to know. Unanswered questions stimulate research; research yields facts; and facts, when properly ordered and developed, yield understanding. Oral communication of the understanding of these questions is made through expository speaking.

Although any speech of explanation is in a sense an expository speech, in this section an **expository speech** is defined as one that places emphasis on understanding an idea and that requires outside source material to give the speech depth. For example, "the causes of teen violence," "the practice of Islamic religion," "the origin and classifications of nursery rhymes" are all examples of topics for expository speaking.

expository speech–*speech that places emphasis on understanding an idea and that requires outside source material to give depth.*

An expository speech embodies all of the principles discussed in the first part of the chapter. Thus, it is an excellent assignment for a major informative speech. The speech beginning on page 445 is a good example of exposition.

Criteria for Evaluating Informative Speeches

In this chapter, we have been looking at the principles of informative speaking. In this section, we will draw together the criteria for evaluating informative speaking and then look at a sample informative speech outline and speech.

Check all items that were accomplished effectively.

Primary Criteria

_____ 1. Was the specific goal designed to increase audience information?
_____ 2. Did the speaker show creativity in idea development?
_____ 3. Was the speaker effective in establishing his or her credibility on this topic?
_____ 4. Was the information intellectually stimulating?
_____ 5. Did the speaker show the relevance of the information?
_____ 6. Did the speaker emphasize the information?
_____ 7. Was the organizational pattern appropriate for the intent and content of the speech?

General Criteria

_____ 1. Was the specific goal clear?
_____ 2. Was the introduction effective?
_____ 3. Were the main points clear?
_____ 4. Was the conclusion effective?
_____ 5. Was the language clear, vivid, and emphatic?
_____ 6. Was the speech delivered enthusiastically, with vocal expressiveness, spontaneously, fluently, and with eye contact?

Evaluate the speech as (check one):
_____ excellent, _____ good, _____ average, _____ fair, _____ poor.

Figure 17.2
Checklist for critiquing an informative speech.

The criteria for evaluating an informative speech differ somewhat from the general criteria for evaluating public speaking presented in Chapter 16, but many of the general criteria still apply. Figure 17.2 provides a checklist for critical evaluation of an informative speech. The primary criteria include specific elements that must be met in an informative speech. The general criteria section highlights elements necessary for any effective speech.

TEST YOUR COMPETENCE

Prepare an Informative Speech

Prepare an informative speech. An outline and a list of sources are required. Criteria for evaluation include means of ensuring audience interest, understanding information, retaining information, and building credibility. Use the checklist in Figure 17.2 to help you evaluate your speech.

As an addendum to the outline, write a plan for adapting the speech to your audience based on the predictions you make by completing an audience analysis (see Figure 15.13 for a sample audience analysis). In the plan, include three short sections discussing strategies for (1) getting and maintaining interest, (2) facilitating audience understanding, and (3) increasing retention. The sample speech at the end of this chapter illustrates one way to make such a plan. Where appropriate, comment on use of visual aids and the role of language and delivery techniques for implementing that plan.

You can watch, listen to, and evaluate the following informative speech by Hillary Carter-Liggett, a member of the Moorpark College Forensics Team, Moorpark, California, under Speech Interactive on your Communicate! CD-ROM.

Sample Speech: Who Was Shakespeare? by Hillary Carter-Liggett[1]

This section contains a sample speech outline, speech plan, and speech that is designed to inform the audience on who wrote Shakespeare's works.

Speech Outline

Specific goal: I want my audience to understand the Stratfordian and Oxfordian claims for the authorship of Shakespeare's works and how they compare.

Introduction
 I. Have you ever experienced writer's block?
 II. So did Shakespeare as portrayed in the Academy Award–winning picture *Shakespeare in Love,* a movie that has rekindled the controversy over who wrote "Shakespeare's" works.

Thesis statement: Two schools of thought on authorship of Shakespearean works are the Stratfordian (Shakespeare, the actor, is the author) and the Oxfordian (Edward de Vere is the author), and their comparison on the basis of the education, life experience, and parallels between lives and literature of the two men.

Body
 I. The Stratfordian's claim is that it is possible that a man of humble origins could be the author.
   A. Although few sources are available to document Shakespeare's early life, they do verify his existence.
      1. He became an actor in 1594.
      2. After he died, the first folio of Shakespeare's work was published.
   B. Evidence exists that he did or could have written the works.
      1. His name was on the plays when they were published.

---

[1] Hillary Carter-Liggett presented this speech as a member of the Moorpark College Forensics Team, Moorpark, CA. She currently attends Bradley University.

    2. Ben Johnson, a contemporary playwright worked with Shakespeare and never mentioned his not being the author.

(Now that we've considered the Stratfordian school, let's consider the Oxfordian.)

II. The Oxfordian's claim is that enough indirect evidence is available to support Edward de Vere as the true author.
    A. First, de Vere's Bible marks 43% of the Biblical references in Shakespeare's writings.
    B. Second, the subject of most of the sonnets is Henry Wriothsley, a man that de Vere was known to have had an affair with.
    C. Third, de Vere was known to have secretly written plays.

(Now let's compare the evidence.)

III. The two claims can be further compared on the basis of three criteria.
    A. The first criterion is education.
        1. Shakespeare is believed to have had the equivalent of a high school education.
        2. De Vere entered Cambridge at age nine, earned a Master's degree from Oxford, and studied law at Gray's Inn.
    B. The second criterion is life experiences.
        1. Shakespeare never traveled abroad, but was an actor who was very familiar with the theatre.
        2. De Vere spent a great deal of time abroad in Italy and France.
    C. The third criterion is parallels between life and literature.
        1. Shakespeare had a son named Hamlet.
        2. De Vere was captured by pirates, provided 3,000 pounds for an excursion of three merchant ships owned by a man named Lock who was shady (called "shy").

Conclusion

I. In either case we have no direct evidence assuring authorship by either person.

II. Until such evidence is found we are left to wonder whether the plays, written by another author, would still "sound as sweet."

Sources

Gibson, Helen, et al. The bard's beard? He's hot again and so is that nagging question: Who really wrote Shakespeare? *Time,* Feb. 15, 1999, pp. 74–75.

Heller, Scott. In centuries' old debate, Shakespeare doubters point to new evidence. *Chronicle of Higher Education,* June 4, 1999, p. A22.

Matus, Irvin. *Shakespeare in Fact.* New York: Continuum, 1994.

Paster, Gail Kern. The sweet swan. *Harper's,* April 1999, pp. 38–41.

Sabran, Joseph. *Alias Shakespeare.* Every word doth almost tell my name. *Harper's,* April 1999, pp. 54–55.

Satchell, Michael. Hunting for good Will. *U.S. News & World Report,* July 24, 2000, p. 71.

Whalen, Richard F. *Shakespeare: Who Was He?: The Oxford Challenge to the Bard of Avon.* New York: Praeger, 1994.

Plan for Adapting to Audience

1. **Getting and maintaining interest.** I plan to begin the speech by referring to *Shakespeare in Love,* a movie that nearly everyone in the audience is likely to have seen. During the speech, I believe that my quotations and examples as well as my clear and vivid language will help maintain interest. Likewise, I believe that the quality of the information itself will hold audience interest.

2. **Facilitating understanding.** First, I believe my listeners will appreciate the clarity of the information that I present. Second, I will present information clearly and concisely and use visual aids in appropriate places.

3. **Increasing retention.** My primary means of increasing attention will be emphasis through repetition and transitions. I will preview the three main points in the introduction, state each clearly as main points, and then repeat them again in the conclusion. I also believe that through the contrasts I make, students will remember them.

Speech and Analysis

Read the following speech aloud at least once. Then analyze it on the basis of the primary criteria in the checklist in Figure 17.2: creative, credible, intellectually stimulating, relevant, and emphatic. Most important, assess the speech for its informative value. This is an edited version of the speech as it was originally given. Listen to the speech as it was originally given and compare it with this revised version by clicking on Speech Interactive for Communicate! on your Communicate! CD-ROM.

Speech

Have you ever experienced writer's block? Maybe even as you were preparing your speech, you prayed for a muse. Such was the premise of the Academy Award–winning Best Picture—*Shakespeare in Love,* a movie Americans spent over 100 million dollars to see, but also one that rekindled the flame of controversy over the question, Who actually wrote Shakespeare's works? Was it the man called Shakespeare? Or someone else? Why should we care? "Shakespeare" is one of the most respected authors in the world. His honeyed words wove a web that continues to move us to laughter and tears today, hundreds of years after his death. As a result, Shakespeare's works are integral to education at almost every level. So for

Analysis

Notice how Hillary begins with a question that we are likely to nod "yes" to. Then she moves into her opening featuring reference to Shakespeare in Love *that is designed both to adapt to audience information and build interest.*

Good series of questions designed to build audience interest.

Speech

all who have enjoyed his works, we like to see what is being argued by the scholars. So, today we'll look first at the traditional, or what has been called the Stratfordian, school of thought, second at the challenger, which has been called the Oxfordian school of thought, and, third, at comparisons of education, life experience, and parallels between lives and the literature.

The Stratfordian's claim is that it is possible that a man of humble origins came into the world a pauper and left it a literary prince. What do we know about Shakespeare's background? Joseph Sabran, author of *Alias Shakespeare,* observes that a handful of wedding and birth announcements are the only written records we have of the first half of Shakespeare's life.

William Shakespeare—A Timeline	
1554	Born
1582	Marries Ann Hathaway
1587	Moves to London
1594	Actor—Chamberlain's Men
	Writes plays
1604	Moves home to Stratford
1616	Dies
1623	First folio of works published

Legal documents indicate that, sometime after he turned twenty, Shakespeare left his family and went to London in order to avoid being prosecuted for a deer-poaching incident. In London, Shakespeare became an actor and in 1594 became involved with the Chamberlain's Men. This is when Shakespeare was supposed to have turned out most of his material. After 1604, he went home to Stratford, where he died in 1616. In 1623, the first folio of Shakespeare's work was published.

Although we have little specific documentation of any aspect of his early life, according to Gail Kern Paster, editor of *The Shakespeare Quarterly,* all that his defenders "need to prove is that such a man from Stratford could have written the plays, not that he did so."

Analysis

She uses her thesis statement as a transition leading into the body of the speech.

Throughout the speech, Hillary cites information from numerous sources and documents each.

Here Hillary outlines what we do know about Shakespeare the man.

This sketch provides information about his life, but offers no proof that he wrote the works under his name.

Here, Hillary displays a timeline visual aid that helps the audience follow her sketch of his life.

After showing that "could have written the plays" is an important bit of support, she goes on to present these two specific bits of information that provide indirect support of Shakespeare's authorship.

Speech	**Analysis**

And in fact Stratfordians are able to present some evidence, since his name was on the plays when they were published. Additionally, contemporary playwright Ben Johnson knew and worked with Shakespeare and never mentioned him not being the real author of the plays.

So, now let's consider the Oxfordian school of thought. The Oxfordians argue that Edward de Vere, the Earl of Oxford, is the rightful author of the works we ascribe to Shakespeare. Why de Vere? Roger Smitmatter in his article in the 1999 *Chronicle of Higher Education* looks to the de Vere Bible for proof. Smitmatter discovered that in the Geneva Bible that de Vere purchased in 1570, a remarkable 43% of Biblical references in Shakespeare's writings are specifically annotated or underlined.

Her second main point announces the claim of the Oxfordian school.

Her question here sets up the key statements that follow.
Notice that this material shows de Vere's familiarity with material in Shakespeare's works.

Second, the sonnets also testify to de Vere as their author. Why? As Sabran explains, the subject of most of the sonnets is the young Earl of Southampton, Henry Wriothsley—a man that de Vere was known to have had a homosexual affair with.

She enumerates the second piece of Oxfordian support and provides information that suggests that de Vere had experience with the material of the sonnets.

Third, in Oxford at the time it was considered undignified to submit one's writing to the public, and it would have been especially scandalous for a nobleman such as de Vere. Moreover, the book *The Art of English Poesi,* published in 1589, lists de Vere as a nobleman who was known to have secretly written plays.

Notice that each of these three points provides information that shows us why de Vere is even considered as the prospective author.

Now let's review the evidence of the two on the basis of their education, life experiences, and parallels between life and literature.

Now she leads into the final part of the speech, a comparison of information on three important criteria that are useful in determining authorship.

At this point Hillary displays a chart showing criteria for comparison that is covered with three cardboard sections. As she speaks about each criterion, she removes the section of cardboard covering that criterion. This process of unveiling helps keep the audience focused on the appropriate section.

Criteria for Comparison	
Shakespeare	De Vere
Education	
Stratford Free School	Cambridge U.—BA
High school equivalent	Oxford U.—MA
	Gray's Inn—Law
Homes	
London	England
Stratford	Italy
	France
Life Experience	
Frequent legal trouble	Member of Court

Speech

First, education. Shakespeare is believed to have had the equivalent of a high school education from the Stratford Free School, but we have no more specific information to show any depth of education. De Vere, on the other hand, entered Cambridge at the age of nine, where he earned a bachelor's degree and then went on to earn a master's degree from Oxford, followed by his study of the law (a common theme in Shakespearean plays) at Gray's Inn.

Second, life experiences. Shakespeare lived most of his life in Stratford and London, and there is no record of his having traveled abroad. However, he was an actor, very familiar with the theater. De Vere spent a great deal of time abroad, particularly in Italy and France, the setting for many of the plays.

Third, the parallels between life and literature. Shakespeare had a son named Hamlet. De Vere, like Hamlet, was captured by pirates. His father-in-law was Lord Burghley—the man his contemporaries believed was the basis for the character Polonius, and his mother, like Hamlet's mother, remarried, shortly after her husband's death, a man of much lower social standing. The play *Merchant of Venice* focuses on money lending, and we know that Shakespeare was often in debt. Shylock lent the sum of 3,000 ducats to Antonio for an excursion made by three merchant ships, but the ships are lost at sea. De Vere provided 3,000 pounds for an excursion of three merchant ships looking for gold ore. The ships came back empty and declared bankruptcy. Ironically, the ships were owned by a man named Lock, while the prefix "shy" means disreputable or shady, and experts can find no precedent for the name "Shylock" anywhere else in history.

Without a doubt, we have only scratched the surface of the arguments on this issue today. Certainly there are some interesting facts in support of the Oxfordian school and de Vere. On the other hand, over the years we have no proof that Shakespeare didn't write the plays. Perhaps, as time goes by, another candidate's name will come up—or perhaps

Analysis

Here she shows why we question "Shakespeare's" preparedness for writing—and exemplifies de Vere's strong educational base.

Here she explore's life experiences—another sound criterion—and gives evidence to support each of the views.

This section shows that scholars have uncovered parallels in the life of de Vere and Shakespearean works. These sound impressive in light of lack of material to support such parallels in Shakespeare's life.

Here she relates a particularly interesting parallel. Again, the information is provocative but doesn't prove authorship.

Hillary finishes her brief analysis of the positions. Her point? No significant proof for either, but enough speculative information to kindle further analysis.

Speech

scholars will uncover solid evidence to prove the case for Shakespeare, de Vere, or someone else. Meanwhile we are left to wonder whether the plays, written by another author, would still "sound as sweet."

Analysis

Overall good sources, information, organization, and idea development. Moreover, the language of the speech is clear, vivid, and engaging.

Summary

Informative speeches are those in which the primary goal is to create understanding. As an informative speaker, your rhetorical challenge is to present information in a way that facilitates attending, understanding, and remembering.

To accomplish these goals, speakers can learn to incorporate several principles. Audiences are more likely to show interest in, understand, and remember information (1) if it is presented creatively, (2) if they like, trust, and have confidence in the speaker, (3) if they perceive it to be new, (4) if they perceive it to be relevant, and (5) if it is emphasized.

Creativity involves using material in an imaginative way. Speakers are perceived to be credible if they are competent, have good intentions, are of good

WHAT WOULD YOU DO?
A QUESTION OF ETHICS

After class, as Gina and Paul were discussing what they intended to talk about for their first speeches, Paul said, "I think I'm going to talk about the Mayan ruins."

"That sounds interesting, Paul, but I didn't know that you were a history buff."

"I'm not. But Gina, the way I see it, Professor Henderson will really be impressed with my speech because my topic will be so academic."

"That may be," Gina replied, "but didn't he stress that for the first speech we should talk about a topic that was important to us and that we knew a lot about?"

"Right," Paul said sarcastically, "he wants to hear me talk about basketball? Not on your life. Trust me on this one—when I get the good grade, you'll know what I mean."

1. Is Paul's proposed behavior unethical? Why?
2. What should Gina say to challenge Paul's last statement?

character, and have a pleasant personality. New information has even greater impact when it is perceived as being novel. Information is perceived as relevant if it is vital or important. Information is likely to be remembered if it is repeated, if it is introduced with external transitions, if it is associated, or if it is presented humorously.

Methods of informing include narrating, describing, demonstrating, and defining. Narrating is telling a story, usually one with a point or climax related to the theme of the speech. Describing means creating a verbal picture through vivid descriptions of size, shape, weight, color, composition, age and condition, and the relationship among parts. Demonstrating involves showing how to do something, how to make something, or how something works. Both full and modified demonstrations often are enhanced by visual aids. Defining is giving the meaning of a word or concept through classification and differentiation, synonym and antonym, use and function, or etymology. Defining can be enhanced with the use of examples and comparisons.

Communicate! Online

Use your Communicate! CD-ROM for quick access to the electronic study resources that accompany this text. Included on your CD-ROM is access to InfoTrac College Edition, the World Wide Web, a demo of WebTutor for Communicate!, and the Communicate! Web site at the Wadsworth Communication Café. The Communicate! Web site offers chapter-by-chapter activities, quizzes, and a digital glossary.

Review the following key terms at
http://communication.wadsworth.com/humancomm/verderber

Key Terms

acronyms (436)   **defining** (440)

antonyms (440)   **describing** (438)

association (436)   **etymology** (440)

complete demonstration (442)   **explaining processes** (441)

creativity (430)   **expository speech** (443)

intellectually stimulating (429)   **relevance** (433)
mnemonics (436)   **synonyms** (440)
modified demonstration (442)   **vital information** (433)
narrative (437)

Speech Interactive helps you prepare for your own speech performance and effectively provide feedback to your peers by critiquing the speeches of other students, such as Hillary. In addition to Hillary's informative speech on Shakespeare, Speech Interactive for Communicate! includes an informative speech on airline black boxes and a persuasive speech on trucks. Click on Speech Interactive on your Communicate! CD-ROM to access the sample speeches.

Fred Sieb Photography

OBJECTIVES

After you have read this chapter, you should be able to answer these questions:

- What is the difference between affecting behavior and moving to action?
- What is the value of assessing audience attitude toward the goal?
- What are good reasons?
- What kinds of material give support to reasons?
- What are some common fallacies?
- What are typical persuasive speaking organizational patterns?
- What does a persuasive speaker do to motivate an audience?
- What are major ethical guidelines?

Persuasive Speaking

As she finished her speech, the entire audience rose as a body and cheered. Over the din, the chair shouted, "All those in favor, say 'aye'" and as one everyone roared "aye" as a testament to her lucid and persuasive argument. As she walked to her seat, people reached to pat her on the back, and those who could not touch her chanted her name: "Sheila . . . Sheila . . . !"

"Sheila! Wake up," Denny said as he shook her shoulder, "you're supposed to be working on your speech."

persuasive speaking–*a*
process in which a speaker
presents a message intended to
affect an audience in a way that
is likely to reinforce a belief,
change a belief, or move an
audience to act.

Perhaps you have imagined yourself giving such a stirring speech that your audience cheered wildly at your persuasive powers. Although everything works well in our fantasies, our real-life attempts to persuade are not always so successful. **Persuasive speaking,** a process in which a speaker presents a message intended to affect an audience in a way that is likely to reinforce a belief, change a belief, or move an audience to act, is perhaps the most demanding speech challenge.

Now let us turn to specific principles that are designed to help you increase the likelihood of achieving your persuasive speech goals. Then we will look at a sample persuasive speech.

Principles of Persuasive Speaking

The following principles focus on what you can do to increase the probability of being an effective persuasive speaker.

Writing a Specific Goal

Principle 1: You are more likely to persuade an audience when you can articulate specifically what you want your audience to believe or do.

Your persuasive speeches are likely to be designed to establish or change beliefs or to move to action.

Although a speech goal that is phrased *to establish or change a belief* may result in having listeners act upon that belief, your primary emphasis is on having them agree with you that the belief you present is reasonable. Here are some goal statements written specifically to seek audience acceptance of a belief:

- I want the audience to believe that the city should build a downtown entertainment center.
- I want the audience to believe that small schools are better for insecure students than are large schools.
- I want the audience to believe that the federal income-tax deduction for house-payment interest should be abolished.
- I want the audience to believe that the speed limit on all interstate highways should be raised to seventy miles per hour.

Notice that in each case you would be advocating what should or ought to be believed—not what audience members should or ought to *do* as a result of that belief.

Speeches designed *to move an audience to action* go beyond gaining agreement on a belief—they state exactly what you want your audience to *do*. Here are some goal statements that seek action:

■ I want my audience to donate money to the food-bank drive.

■ I want the members of my audience to write to their congressional representative to support legislation in favor of gun control.

■ I want my audience members to attend the school's production of *Grease*.

Adapting to Audience Attitude

Principle 2: You are more likely to be able to persuade when you direct your goal and your information to your audience's attitude.

An **attitude** is "a general or enduring positive or negative feeling about some person, object, or issue" (Petty & Cacioppo, 1996, p. 7). People's attitudes are usually expressed verbally as **opinions**. Thus, saying "I think physical fitness is important" is an opinion that reflects a favorable attitude about physical fitness.

Because much of the success of a speech depends on determining how an audience is likely to react to your goal, you must find out where the audience stands. You make such judgments based on demographic information and opinion polls (see Chapter 12). The more data you have about your audience and the more experience you have in analyzing audiences, the better are your chances of judging audience attitudes accurately.

Audience attitudes (expressed by opinions) may be distributed along a continuum from highly favorable to hostile (Figure 18.1). Even though any given audience may have one or a few individuals' opinions at nearly every point along the distribution, audience opinion tends to cluster at a particular point. That cluster point represents the general audience attitude for that topic. Because it would be impossible to direct your speech to all the various shades of attitudes held by the members of your audience, you must classify audience attitude as predominantly "in favor" (already holding a particular belief), "no opinion" (uninformed, neutral, or apathetic), or "opposed" (holding an opposite point of view) so you can develop a strategy that adapts to that attitude.

Now let us consider specific strategies for adapting to audiences. Suppose your goal is written, "I want my audience to believe that they should alter their intake of saturated fats." As you will see, your assessment of audience attitude may affect how you phrase your goal and how you select your information.

In favor   If you believe your listeners are already in favor of your belief, then you may want to change the goal to focus on a specific course of action.

For instance, if members of your audience already favor limiting their intake of saturated fats, it would be a mistake to focus on changing their belief. What is likely to keep people who have a favorable attitude from acting is their lack of motivation. Your job is to provide a specific course of action around which they

attitude—*a general or enduring positive or negative feeling about some person, object, or issue.*

opinion—*verbal expression of a belief or attitude.*

OBSERVE & ANALYZE
Journal Activity

Writing Persuasive Speech Goals

In your Student Workbook under Journal Activity 18.1, write the specific goal you are considering for your persuasive speech assignment, and then rewrite it two or three times with slightly different wordings.

Identify your goal as one of establishing or changing a belief or seeking action. If at this stage you do not know what your audience believes, you may wish to hold off on the final wording of your goal until you finish Journal Activity 18.2.

Hostile	Opposed	Mildly opposed	Neither in favor nor opposed	Mildly in favor	In favor	Highly in favor

Figure 18.1
Opinion continuum.

AP/Wide World Photos

A political candidate speaking to a group of supporters should focus on moving them to action.

can rally. When you believe your listeners are on your side, try to crystallize their attitudes, recommit them to a particular direction, or suggest a specific course of action that will serve as a rallying point. The presentation of a thoughtful and specific solution increases the likelihood of audience action.

Even when audience members are on your side, they may perceive what you want them to do as impractical. If so, they are likely to ignore your appeal regardless of its merits. For instance, if your goal is to have class members increase their exercise, taking the extra time necessary to exercise may seem impractical given their workload. However, if your on-campus facility has a nautilus room, you may be able to show them how they can increase their exercise by using otherwise "wasted" time between classes or before or after lunch, in which case they may see the practicality of your goal.

No opinion If you believe your listeners have no opinion, then you will focus on goals that establish a belief or goals that move the audience to action.

If you believe your audience has no opinion because it is *uninformed*, the strategy should be to give enough information to help your audience understand the subject before you develop persuasive appeals directed toward establishing a belief or moving listeners to action. For instance, if you believe your audience is uninformed about the need to lower saturated fat intake, then early in the speech you need to define "saturated fat," talk about how cholesterol is formed, and share medical evidence about its effects on the human body. Be careful about how much time you spend on this informative part of the speech. If it takes more than half of your allotted time to explain what you are talking about, you may not have enough time to do much persuading.

If you believe your audience has no opinion because it is *neutral,* then you see your audience as being able to reason objectively and accept sound reasoning. In this case, your strategy will involve presenting the best possible arguments and supporting them with the best information you can find. If your assessment is correct, you stand a good chance of success with that strategy.

If you believe your audience members have no opinion because they are *apathetic,* all of your effort may be directed to moving them out of their apathy. Members of your audience may know what saturated fat is, know how cholesterol is formed, and even understand the medical information of negative effects, but they may not seem to care. Instead of emphasizing the information with this audience, you would emphasize motivation. You will need less material that proves the logic of your arguments and more material that is directed to your listeners' personal needs.

Opposed If you believe your listeners are opposed, then your strategy will depend upon whether their attitude is slightly negative or totally hostile.

If you believe your listeners are *slightly opposed* to your proposal, you can approach them rather directly with your argument, hoping that its weight will swing them to your side. If your audience is slightly opposed to lowering their saturated-fat intake, you can present good reasons and evidence supporting the proposal.

Another part of your strategy should concern the presentation of arguments in ways that lessen your listeners' negative attitudes without arousing their hostility. With a negative audience, take care to be objective with your material and make your case clearly enough that those members who are only mildly negative will consider the proposal and those who are very negative will at least understand your position.

If you believe your audience is *hostile* toward your goal, you may want to approach the topic indirectly or to consider a less ambitious goal. To expect a

When speaking to an audience hostile to your viewpoint, adjust your speech to call for a more modest change of attitude.

complete shift in attitude or behavior as a result of one speech is probably unrealistic. If you present a modest proposal that seeks a slight change in attitude, you may be able to get an audience to at least consider the value of your message. Later, when the idea begins to grow, you can ask for a greater change. For instance, the audience may be comprised of people who are "fed up" with appeals to monitor their diets. If you believe your goal is important to them regardless of their negative attitude, then develop a strategy that will be more subtle. This will involve recognizing their hostility and talking about the topic in a way that will not arouse that hostility.

Figure 18.2 summarizes the strategy choices we have reviewed for audiences with different attitudes toward your topic.

Giving Good Reasons and Evidence

Principle 3: You are more likely to persuade an audience when the body of your speech contains good reasons and evidence that support your speech goal.

Human beings take pride in being rational; we seldom do anything without some real or imagined reason. Since the 1980s, persuasive speech theory has focused sharply on persuasion as a cognitive activity; that is, people form cognitive structures to create meaning for experiences (Deaux, Dane, & Wrightsman, 1993, p. 19). To meet this audience need, the main points of a persuasive speech are usually stated as **reasons**—statements that tell why a proposition is justified (Woodward & Denton, 2000, p. 100).

Finding reasons Reasons are statements that answer why you should believe or do something. If you have expertise in the subject matter, you are likely to know some of the reasons. For example, if you are an exercise buff and you "want the audience to walk two miles at least three times a week," you know that three of the reasons for walking are (1) to help us control weight, (2) to help us strengthen our cardiovascular system, and (3) to help us feel better.

For most of your persuasive speeches, however, you will want to do research to verify or discover reasons so that you can choose the best ones for your speech. For example, for a speech goal phrased "I want the audience to believe that the United States should overhaul the welfare system," you might discover these six reasons:

- The welfare system costs too much to maintain.
- The welfare system is inequitable.
- The welfare system does not help those who need help most.
- The welfare system has been grossly abused.
- The welfare system does not encourage recipients to seek work.
- The welfare system does not encourage self-support.

Once you have a list of possible reasons, weigh and evaluate them to select three or four good ones. Here are some criteria for evaluating possible reasons.

AUDIENCE ATTITUDES If audience members are . . .	then they may . . .	STRATEGY CHOICES and you can . . .
Highly in favor	■ be ready to act	■ provide practical suggestions ■ put emphasis on motivation rather than on information and reasoning
In favor	■ already share many of your beliefs	■ crystallize and reinforce existing beliefs and attitudes to lead them to a course of action
Mildly in favor	■ be inclined to accept your view, but with little commitment	■ strengthen positive beliefs by emphasizing supporting reasons
Neither in favor nor opposed	■ be uninformed	■ emphasize information relevant to a belief or move to action
	■ be neutral	■ emphasize reasons relevant to belief or action
	■ be apathetic	■ concentrate on motivating them to see the importance of the proposition or seriousness of the problem
Mildly opposed	■ have doubts about the wisdom of your position	■ give them reasons and evidence that will help them to consider your position
Opposed	■ have beliefs and attitudes contrary to yours	■ emphasize sound arguments ■ concentrate on shifting beliefs rather than on moving to action ■ be objective to avoid arousing hostility
Hostile	■ be totally unreceptive to your position	■ plant the "seeds of persuasion" ■ try to get them to understand your position

Figure 18.2

Adapting persuasive speech strategies to audience attitudes.

1. **Good reasons can be supported.** Some reasons that sound impressive cannot be supported with facts. For example, "The welfare system has been grossly abused" sounds like a good reason, but if you cannot find facts to support so strong a statement, either modify it or do not use it in your speech. You

will be surprised at how many reasons mentioned in various sources have to be dropped from consideration for a speech because they cannot be well supported.

2. **Good reasons are relevant to the proposition.** Sometimes statements look like reasons, but they do not supply much proof. For instance, "The welfare system is supported by socialists" may sound like a reason for overhauling it to people who dislike socialism, but it does not offer any direct proof that the system needs overhauling.

3. **Good reasons will have an impact on the intended audience.** Suppose you have a great deal of factual evidence to back up the statement "The welfare system does not encourage recipients to seek work." Even though it is a well-supported reason, it would be an ineffective reason to use in a speech where the majority of the audience did not see "seeking work" as a primary criterion for evaluating the welfare system. Although you cannot always be sure about the potential impact of a reason, you can estimate its possible impact based on your audience analysis. For instance, on the topic of welfare reform, some audiences would be more concerned with costs, equity, and abuses of the system.

The Spotlight on Scholars features Richard Petty's research on attitude change and behavior.

SPOTLIGHT ON SCHOLARS

Richard Petty, Professor of Psychology, the Ohio State University, on Attitude Change

As an undergraduate political science major, Richard Petty got so interested in how people change their attitudes that he chose to minor in psychology where he could not only take more courses in attitude change but also learn empirical research methods. He then decided to go on to graduate work in psychology at the Ohio State University where he could focus on studying attitude change and persuasion. Like many scholars, the subject of his doctoral dissertation, attitude change induced by persuasive communications, laid the foundation for a career of research.

When Petty began his research, the psychological scholarship of the previous forty years had been unable to demonstrate a relationship between people's attitudes and their behavior. Petty believed this was because some attitudes were consistently related to behavior but other attitudes were not. The key was to understand how attitudes were formed and which processes led to strong rather than weak attitudes. Now, Petty's work is in the forefront of scholars who have demonstrated that attitude change and behavior are in fact related, but in a complex way.

During the last twenty years, Petty has published scores of research articles on his own and with colleagues on various aspects of attitude and persuasion to find out under what circumstances attitudes affect behavior. His work with various collaborators has been so successful that he has gained international acclaim. Not only have many of his works been published worldwide, but the theory of the Elaboration Likelihood Model (ELM) of persuasion that he developed in collaboration with John Cacioppo has become the most cited theoretical approach to attitude and persuasion.

In its most basic form, Petty and Cacioppo's theory says that attitude change is likely to occur from one of just two relatively distinct "routes to persuasion." The first type, the central route, occurs as a result of a person's careful and thoughtful consideration of the true merits of the information presented in support of a claim. The second type, the peripheral route, occurs as a result of simple cues in the persuasion context (such as an attractive source) that induce change without necessitating scrutiny of the central merits of the claim. Following their initial speculation about these two routes to persuasion, Petty and Cacioppo developed, researched, and refined the theory supporting the ELM.

The ELM "is a theory about the processes responsible for attitude change and the strength of the attitudes that result from those processes." The ELM hypothesizes that what is persuasive to a person and how lasting any attitude change is likely to be are dependent on how motivated and able people are to assess the merits of a speaker, an issue, or a position. People who are highly motivated and are able to think are likely to study available information about the claim. As a result, they are more likely to arrive at a reasoned attitude that is well articulated and bolstered by information received via the central route. For people who are less motivated or able to study information related to the claim, attitude change can result from a number of less resource-demanding processes that do not require effortful evaluation of the relevant information. They are affected more by information through the peripheral route, but these attitude changes are likely to be weaker in endurance and prediction of behavior.

So what impact does Petty's research have on speakers who seek to persuade? First, speakers must recognize that attitude change is a result of a combination of choices of the means of persuasion as well as choices made by members of the audience on how deeply they wish to probe into the information. Using the ELM, speakers can better understand and predict the variables that will affect attitudes by what processes in general situations and what the consequences of these attitudes are. Thus sound reasons and supporting evidence adapted to audience needs should account for attitude change when listener thinking is expected to be deep. In contrast, apparent credibility and emotional images should be more likely to account for change when listener thinking is expected to be superficial. Moreover, the attitudes changed by considerable mental effort tend to be stronger than those changed by little thought.

This complexity of attitude change suggests that not only must a speaker have the necessary information to form well-constructed arguments, but the speaker must also have the artistic sense to understand important aspects of the audience (locus of belief, time constraints, interest, and so forth) and have the artistic power to, as Aristotle once said, use available means of persuasion effectively.

Where is Petty going from here? He will certainly continue working on aspects of attitude change for as he says, "I never finish a project without discovering at least two unanswered questions arising from the research." In addition, in a series of studies with Duane Wegener, he is interested in finding out how people behave when they believe their judgments might have been inappropriate or biased.

Currently Petty teaches both graduate and undergraduate courses in attitudes and persuasion, research methods, and theories of social psychology. Petty has written scores of research articles and several books dealing with aspects of attitude, attitude change, and persuasion. For titles of several of his publications, see the references at the end of this book. For more information about Richard Petty and his work go to http://www.psy.ohio-state.edu/petty/

Finding evidence to support your reasons By themselves, reasons are only unsupported statements. Although some reasons are self-explanatory and occasionally have a persuasive effect without further support, most listeners look for factual statements and expert opinion to support the reasons before they will either accept or act on them.

As we learned in Chapter 12, the best support for reasons is verifiable factual statements. Thus, if you give the reason "Alzheimer's disease is a major killer" in a speech designed to motivate people to donate money to Alzheimer's research, the statement "According to statistics presented in an article in a recent *Time* magazine, Alzheimer's disease is the fourth leading cause of death for adults" is factual support.

Statements from people who have good reputations for knowledge on the subject represent expert opinions. An expert opinion to support the reason that "Alzheimer's disease is a major killer" might be the statement, "According to the Surgeon General, 'By 2050 Alzheimer's disease may afflict 14 million people a year.'"

Whether your evidence is a supposed factual statement or an opinion, you will want to ask at least three questions to assure yourself that what you present is "good" evidence.

1. **What is the source of the evidence?** This question involves both the people who offered the opinions or compiled the facts and the book, journal, or source where they were reported. Just as some people's opinions are more reliable than others, so are some printed sources more reliable than others. If evidence comes from a poor source, an unreliable source, or a biased source, seek verification of it in other sources, or drop it from the speech.

2. **Is the evidence recent?** Products, ideas, and statistics are best when they are recent. You must ask when the particular evidence was true. Five-year-old evidence may not be true today. Furthermore, an article in last week's newsmagazine may be using five-year-old evidence in the story.

3. **Is the evidence relevant?** Make sure your evidence directly supports the reason. If it does not, leave it out of the speech.

Testing reasoning So far, we have concentrated on presenting good reasons and supporting them well. To test the validity of your reasoning more completely, however, look at the relationship between the reasons and the evidence given in support. When you do that, you can ask questions to test the logic of the reasoning.

Several kinds of reasoning links can be established between reasons and their evidence or between reasons, evidence, and the speech goal.

1. **Generalization from examples.** You are reasoning by generalization from example when you argue that what is true in some instances/examples (evidence) is true in all instances (conclusion). Generalization links are the basis

COMMUNICATE! Using InfoTrac College Edition

Under the subject "attitude change," click on periodical references. Look for articles that discuss how audiences process information. Make a special effort to find an article or articles by Richard Petty.

reasoning by generalization from example—*arguing that what is true in some instances/examples is true in all instances.*

for polls and predictions. For example, here is a statement of some factual evidence, "Tom, Jack, and Bill studied and got A's," and the conclusion based on it is "Anyone who studies will get an A." The reasoning link can be stated, "What is true in these representative instances will be true in all instances." To test this kind of argument, you should ask, "Were enough instances (examples) cited? Were the instances typical? Are negative instances accounted for? If the answer to any of these questions is "No," the reasoning is not sound.

2. **Causation.** You are reasoning by causation when your conclusion is presented as the effect of a single circumstance or set of circumstances. Causation links are among the most prevalent types of arguments you will discover. Here is an example: "We've had a very dry spring" (evidence); "The wheat crop will be lower than usual" (conclusion). The reasoning link can be stated, "The lack of sufficient rain causes a poor crop." To test this kind of argument, you should ask, "Are the conditions described by the data (evidence) alone important enough to bring about the particular conclusion? If we eliminate these conditions, would we eliminate the effect?" If the answer to one of these questions is "No," the reasoning is not sound. You can also ask, "Do some other conditions that accompany the ones cited in the evidence cause the effect?" If so, the reasoning is not sound.

reasoning by causation— *presenting a conclusion as the effect of a single circumstance or set of circumstances.*

3. **Analogy.** You are reasoning by analogy when your conclusion is the result of a comparison with a similar set of circumstances. Although reasoning by analogy is very popular, it is regarded as the weakest form of reasoning.

reasoning by analogy—*when your conclusion is the result of a comparison with a similar set of circumstances.*

Aaron Haupt/Stock, Boston/PictureQuest

When the government makes manufacturers place warning labels on products, it is trying to influence consumers through reasoning by causation.

OBSERVE & ANALYZE
Journal Activity

Selecting Reasons

In your Student Workbook under
Journal Activity 18.3, write the
specific goal you will use for your
first persuasive speech.

1. Write at least six reasons that
   support your specific goal.

2. Place stars next to the three or
   four reasons you are planning to
   use. Briefly explain why they are
   the best.

reasoning by sign–*when your
conclusion is based on the
presence of observable data that
usually or always accompany
other unobserved variables.*

hasty generalization–
*presenting a generalization that
is either not supported with
evidence or is supported with
only one weak example.*

false cause–*when the alleged
cause fails to be related to, or to
produce, the effect.*

The analogy link is often stated, "What is true or will work in one set of circumstances is true or will work in a comparable set of circumstances." Here is an example: "Off-track betting has proved very effective in New York" (evidence); "off-track betting will prove effective in raising state revenues in Ohio" (conclusion). The reasoning link can be stated, "If something works in New York, it will work in Ohio because Ohio and New York are so similar." To test this kind of argument, you should ask, "Are the subjects really comparable? Are the subjects being compared really similar in all important ways?" If the answer to these questions is "No," the reasoning is not sound. You can also ask, "Are any of the ways that the subjects are dissimilar important to the conclusion?" If so, the reasoning is not sound.

4. **Sign.** You are reasoning by sign when your conclusion is based on the presence of observable data that usually or always accompany other unobserved variables. If, for example, you see longer lines at the downtown soup kitchen, the presence of that condition (longer lines) is usually or always an indicator of something else (the worsening of the recession), and we can predict the existence of this unobserved variable. Signs are often confused with causes, but signs are indications and sometimes effects, not causes. Longer lines at soup kitchens are a sign of the worsening recession. The longer lines may be an effect of a recession, but they do not cause the recession. To test this kind of argument, you should ask, "Do the data cited always or usually indicate the conclusion drawn? Are sufficient signs present?" If not, the reasoning is not sound.

Avoiding fallacies   When you think you have finished constructing reasons, take a minute to make sure that you have not been guilty of any of the four common fallacies.

1. **Hasty generalization.** Because the instances cited should represent most to all possibilities, enough must be cited to satisfy the listeners that the instances are not isolated or hand-picked. Hasty generalization, presenting a generalization (perhaps a reason) that is either not supported with evidence or perhaps is supported with only one weak example, is a very common fallacy of reasoning.

2. **False cause.** False cause occurs when the alleged cause fails to be related to, or to produce, the effect. It is human nature to look for causes for events, but the tendency to identify and label something that happened or existed before the event or at the time of the event as the cause is often a fallacy. Think of the people who blame loss of money, sickness, and problems at work on black cats that ran in front of them or mirrors that broke or ladders they walked under. We recognize these as false cause superstitions.

3. **Appeal to authority.** Attempting to argue from authority can lead to the appeal to authority fallacy wherein the testimony is from a person who is not an authority on the issue. For instance, advertisers are well aware that the public idolizes athletes, movie stars, and television performers. Because of this, people are likely to accept the word of these famous folks on subjects they may know little about. When a celebrity tries to get the viewer to purchase a car based on the celebrity's supposed "expert" knowledge, the argument is a fallacy.

4. **Ad hominem argument.** An ad hominem argument attacks the person making the argument rather than the argument itself. Literally, *ad hominem* means "to the man." For instance, if Bill Bradley, the former U.S. senator as well as former New York Knicks basketball player, presented the argument that athletics are important to the development of the total person, the reply "Great, all we need is some jock justifying his own existence" would be an example of an ad hominem argument.

    Such a personal attack often is made as a smokescreen to cover a lack of good reasons and evidence. Ad hominem name-calling is used to try to encourage the audience to ignore a lack of evidence, and it is often used in political campaigns. Make no mistake, ridicule, name-calling, and other personal attacks are at times highly successful, but they are almost always fallacious.

appeal to authority–*using "expert" testimony from a person who is not an authority on the issue.*

ad hominem argument–*attacking the person making the argument rather than the argument itself.*

> **THINKING ABOUT . . .**
>
> **Fallacies**
>
> For the next day, pay attention to what your friends, relatives, and acquaintances say to support their arguments. Did you hear people using any of these four fallacies? Why do you think people used these fallacies?

Organizing Reasons to Meet Audience Attitudes

Principle 4: You are more likely to persuade an audience when you organize your reasons according to expected audience reaction.

Although speakers may create any organization for their speech, statement of logical reasons, problem–solution, comparative advantages, and motivational are common patterns you are likely to select for your persuasive speech organization. So that you can contrast the patterns and better understand their use, we will use the same proposition (specific goal) and the same (or similar) reasons to illustrate each pattern. Moreover, we will describe each pattern, show the audience attitudes for which it is most applicable, and describe the logic of the order.

Statement-of-logical-reasons pattern The statement of logical reasons is a straightforward organization in which you present the best-supported reasons you can find following an order of second-strongest first, strongest last, and other reason(s) in between. It will work when your listeners have no opinion on the subject, are apathetic, or are perhaps only mildly in favor or opposed.

> **Proposition:** I want my audience to vote in favor of the school tax levy on the November ballot.
>
> I. Income will enable the schools to restore vital programs. (second strongest)

II. Income will enable the schools to give teachers the raises they need to keep up with the cost of living.

III. The actual cost to each member of the community will be very small. (strongest)

In a speech using the statement-of-logical-reasons pattern, the logic of the organization may be stated as follows: When good reasons and evidence are presented supporting a proposal, the proposal should be adopted.

Problem–solution pattern   The problem–solution pattern provides a framework for clarifying the nature of the problem and for illustrating why a given proposal is the best one. The problem–solution pattern often is organized around three general reasons: (1) there is a problem that requires action, (2) the proposal will solve the problem, and (3) the proposal is the best solution to the problem because it will provide positive consequences. This pattern is also a straightforward presentation of reasons, so it is likely to work best for a topic that is relatively unfamiliar to an audience—one in which they are unaware that a problem exists—or for an audience that has no opinion or is mildly pro or con. A problem–solution organization for the school tax levy proposition might look like this:

Proposition: I want my audience to vote in favor of the school tax levy on the November ballot.

I. The shortage of money is resulting in serious problems for public education. (statement of problem)

II. The proposed increase is large enough to solve those problems. (solution)

III. For now, a tax levy is the best method of solving the schools' problems. (consequences)

In a speech using the problem–solution pattern, the logic of the organization showing the relationship between the reasons and the speech goal may be stated as follows: When a problem is presented that is not or cannot be solved with current measures and the proposal can solve the problem practically and beneficially, then the proposal should be adopted.

Comparative-advantages pattern   The comparative-advantages pattern enables the speaker to place all the emphasis on the superiority of the proposed course of action. Rather than presenting the proposition as a solution to a grave problem, it presents the proposition as one that ought to be adopted solely on the basis of the advantages of that proposition over what is currently being done. Although this pattern can work for any audience attitude, it works best when the audience agrees either that there is a problem that must be solved or that the proposition is superior to its competitors when no particular problem is at issue.

For example, when people elect to eat out, they have a variety of choices, so a speech advocating "Le Petit France" would emphasize its advantages over its competition. A comparative-advantages approach to the school tax levy proposition would look like this:

> **Proposition**: I want my audience to vote in favor of the school tax levy on the November ballot.
>
> I. Income from a tax levy will enable schools to raise the standards of their programs. (advantage 1)
>
> II. Income from a tax levy will enable schools to hire better teachers. (advantage 2)
>
> III. Income from a tax levy will enable schools to better the educational environment. (advantage 3)

In a speech using the comparative-advantages pattern, the logic of the organization that shows the relationship between the reasons and the speech goal may be stated as follows: When reasons are presented that show a proposal is a significant improvement over what is being done, then the proposal should be adopted.

Motivational pattern   The motivational pattern, the final pattern we will consider, combines problem solving and motivation. It follows a problem-solution pattern but includes required steps designed to heighten the motivational effect of the organization. Much of the thinking behind motivational patterns is credited to Allan Monroe, a professor at Purdue University. Motivational patterns usually include a five-step, unified sequence that replaces the normal introduction, body, conclusion model: (1) an attention step, (2) a need step that fully explains the nature of the problem, (3) a satisfaction step that explains how the proposal solves the problem in a satisfactory manner, (4) a visualization step that provides a personal application of the proposal, and (5) an action appeal step that emphasizes the specific direction listener action should take. A motivational pattern for the school tax levy proposition would look like this:

> **Proposition**: I want my audience to vote in favor of the school tax levy on the November ballot.
>
> I. Comparisons of worldwide test scores in math and science have refocused our attention on education. (attention)
>
> II. The shortage of money is resulting in cost-saving measures that compromise our ability to teach basic academic subjects well. (need, statement of problem)
>
> III. The proposed increase is large enough to solve those problems in ways that allow for increased emphasis on academic need areas. (satisfaction, how the proposal solves the problem)

motivation–*forces acting on or
within an organism to initiate
and direct behavior.*

incentive–*a goal objective that
motivates.*

IV. Think of the contribution you will be making not only to the education of
your future children but also to efforts to return our educational system
to the world level it once held. (visualization of personal application)

V. Here are "Vote Yes" buttons that you can wear to show you are willing
to support this much-needed tax levy. (action appeal showing specific
direction)

Because motivational patterns are variations of problem–solution patterns,
the logic of the organization is much the same: When the current means are not
solving the problem, a new solution that does solve the problem should be
adopted.

Motivation

Principle 5: You are more likely to persuade an audience when your language
motivates them.

Motivation, "forces acting on or within an organism to initiate and direct
behavior" (Petri, 1996, p. 3), is often a result of incentives and emotional language.

Incentives An **incentive** is simply "a goal objective that motivates" (Petri,
1996, p. 185). Thus, if a speaker says that in addition to helping clean up the
environment by collecting aluminum cans and glass and plastic bottles you can
earn money by turning them in to a recycling center, you might see earning
money for your efforts as an incentive to recycling.

For an incentive to have value, it must be meaningful. *Meaningfulness*
involves an emotional reaction. Eric Klinger (1977) believes people pursue those
objects, events, and experiences that are emotionally important for them. Recycling would be a meaningful goal for someone looking for ways to participate in
cleaning up the environment but not for someone who does not care about the
environment or about earning small amounts of money. An incentive is most
powerful when it is part of a meaningful goal.

1. **Force of incentives.** People are more likely to perceive incentives as meaning-
    ful if the incentives present a favorable cost-reward ratio. As we discussed in
    Chapter 8, social interactions can be explained in terms of rewards received
    and costs incurred by each member of an interaction. Recall that rewards
    are such incentives as economic gain, good feelings, prestige, or any other
    positive outcome; costs are units of expenditure such as time, energy, money,
    or any negative outcome of an interaction.

    Let's apply this idea to a speech setting. Suppose you are asking your
    audience to volunteer an hour a week to help adults learn to read. The time
    you are asking them to give is likely to be perceived as a *cost* rather than as
    an incentive; however, you may be able to describe volunteering in a way
    that it is perceived as a reward, a meaningful incentive. That is, you may be
    able to get members of the audience to feel civic-minded, responsible, or

helpful as a result of volunteering time for such a worthy cause. In the speech, if you can show that those rewards or incentives outweigh the cost, you can increase the likelihood of volunteering.

2. **Using incentives to meet basic needs.** Many theorists who take a humanistic approach to psychology have argued that incentives are most powerful when they meet basic needs. One of the most popular needs theories is that of Abraham Maslow (1954). His theory suggests that people are more likely to act when a speaker's incentive satisfies a strong unmet need in members of the audience.

Maslow devised a hierarchy of needs that is particularly useful in providing a framework for needs analysis. Maslow divided basic human needs into seven categories arranged in a hierarchy that begins with the most fundamental needs. The seven categories are illustrated in Figure 18.3: physiological needs, including food, drink, and life-sustaining temperature; safety and security needs, including long-term survival and stability; belongingness and love needs, including the need to identify with friends, loved ones, and family; esteem needs, including the quest for material goods, recognition, and power or influence; cognitive needs, including the need for knowledge and understanding; aesthetic needs, including the need for order and beauty; and self-actualization needs, including the need to develop one's self to realize one's full potential. By placing these needs in a hierarchy, Maslow suggested that one set of needs must be met or satisfied before the next set of needs emerges. In theory, then, a person will not be motivated to meet an esteem need of gaining recognition until basic physiological, safety, and belongingness and love needs have been met.

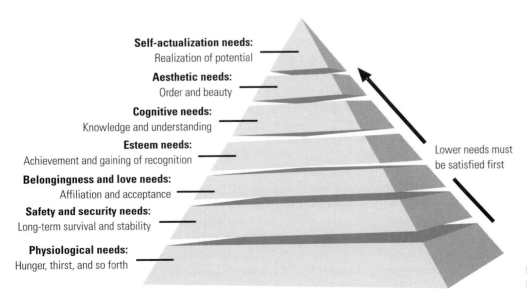

Self-actualization needs:
Realization of potential

Aesthetic needs:
Order and beauty

Cognitive needs:
Knowledge and understanding

Esteem needs:
Achievement and gaining of recognition

Belongingness and love needs:
Affiliation and acceptance

Safety and security needs:
Long-term survival and stability

Physiological needs:
Hunger, thirst, and so forth

Lower needs must
be satisfied first

Figure 18.3
Maslow's hierarchy of needs.

What is the value of this analysis to you as a speaker? First, it suggests the kinds of needs you may appeal to in your speeches. Second, it enables you to understand why a line of development will work on one audience and fail with another. For instance, in hard economic times, people are more concerned with physiological and safety needs and so will be less responsive to appeals to affiliation and altruism. Thus, during economic hard times, fund-raisers for the arts will experience far more resistance to giving than they otherwise would. Third, and perhaps most crucial, when your proposition conflicts with a felt need, you will have to be prepared with a strong alternative in some category or in a more fundamental category. For instance, if your proposal is going to cost people money (say, higher taxes), you will have to show how the proposal satisfies some other comparable need (perhaps by increasing their security).

Arousing emotions through language   Even with good incentives directed to basic needs, to motivate an audience to act, you must appeal to their emotions. **Emotions** (anger, fear, surprise, joy) are subjective conscious experiences triggered by actions or words that are accompanied by bodily arousal and by overt expressions (Weiten, 1998, p. 406). Effective persuasive speech development entails both logical and emotional elements that act interdependently. Therefore, we need to look for good reasons and for support that will, if properly phrased, arouse these emotions.

As you work on your speeches, determine the emotion(s) you want to arouse, the kinds of information necessary to arouse those emotion(s), and how this information can be phrased for maximum effect. Let's consider each of these.

1. **What emotion(s) do you want your audience to experience as you make your point?** The emotion(s) you want to arouse will differ from speech to speech. For instance, in a speech calling for more humane treatment of the elderly, you may decide that you want your listeners to feel sadness, anger, grief, caring, or perhaps, guilt. In contrast, in a speech designed to get the audience to attend your school's production of a musical, you may want your listeners to feel joy, excitement, or enthusiasm.

2. **What information do you have that could be used to stimulate those emotions?** For the speech on the elderly, if you have determined that you want your listeners to feel sadness about their treatment in nursing homes, you might have data from interviews with elderly individuals that show that their only talk of the future is the inevitability of death; or perhaps you have accounts of social workers saying that many older people live totally in the past and are reluctant to talk about or even think about the future; or perhaps you have information showing that many nursing homes do very little to give their clients anything to look forward to.

emotions–*subjective experiences triggered by actions or words that are accompanied by bodily arousal and by overt behavior.*

Herman J. Kokojan/Black Star/PictureQuest

Vividly moving narratives or examples can elicit emotional responses in audience members and move them to action.

3. **How can you phrase your information to elicit those emotions?** How well you motivate is likely to depend on how well you phrase your information, but remember to keep ethical considerations in mind when you try to tap into powerful emotions.

    For the speech on the elderly, you might be considering an introduction like this one:

    Currently, elderly people are alienated from society. A high percentage live in nursing homes, live on small fixed incomes, and exist out of the mainstream of society.

    But with just the addition of a question and language that creates more vivid pictures, you could make this statement much more emotionally powerful:

    Currently, elderly people are alienated from the society that they worked their entire lives to support. What happens to elderly people in America? They become the forgotten segment of society. They are often relegated to "old people's homes" so that they can live out their lives and die without being "a bother" to their sons and daughters. Because they must exist on relatively small fixed incomes, they are confined to a life that for many means separation from the very society they helped to create.

    You are likely to find that some of your best opportunities for using meaningful emotional appeal occur in the introduction and conclusion of your speech. Notice how emotional appeals heighten the power of the following introduction and conclusion in a student speech on euthanasia.[1] She began her speech as follows:

Let's pretend for a moment. Suppose that on the upper right-hand corner of your desk there is a button. You have the power by pushing that button to quickly and painlessly end the life of one you love: your brother or father. This loved one has terminal cancer and will be confined to a hospital for his remaining days. Would you push the button now? His condition worsens. He is in constant pain, and he is hooked up to a life-support machine. He first requests, but as the pain increases he pleads for you to help. Now would you push that button? Each day you watch him deteriorate until he reaches a point where he cannot talk, he cannot see, he cannot hear—he is only alive by that machine. Now would you push that button?

After giving reasons for changing our laws on euthanasia, she concluded her speech as follows:

I ask again, how long could you take walking into that hospital room and looking at your brother or father in a coma, knowing he would rather be allowed to die a natural death than to be kept alive in such a degrading manner? I've crossed that doorstep—I've gone into that hospital room, and let me tell you, it's hell. I think it's time we reconsider our laws concerning euthanasia. Don't you?

Regardless of your beliefs about the subject of euthanasia, you probably will have to agree that you would be inclined to experience sadness as you empathize with her feelings.

Building Credibility

Principle 6: You are more likely to persuade an audience when they view you as a credible source.

As we have seen, maintaining credibility is important to speaker effectiveness in all types of speaking. In previous chapters, we have outlined the nature of credibility and the characteristics that you need to develop to be perceived as credible. In addition to being well prepared, emphasizing your interest in the audience, and looking and sounding enthusiastic, in persuasive speaking you must behave ethically. The following four guidelines are fundamental to ethical persuasive speaking.

1. **Tell the truth.** Of all the guidelines, this may be the most important. An audience that consents to listen to you is extending you its trust and expects that you will be honest with them. Consequently, if people believe you are lying to them or if they later learn that you have lied, they will reject you and your ideas. But telling the truth means more than avoiding deliberate, outright lies. If you are not sure whether information is true, do not use it until you have verified it. Ignorance is seldom accepted as an excuse.

---

[1] By permision of Betsy Burke.

2. **Keep your information in perspective.** Many people get so excited about their information that they exaggerate its importance. Although a little exaggeration might be accepted as a normal product of human nature, when the exaggeration is perceived as distortion, most people will consider it the same as lying. For instance, suppose you discover that capital punishment has lowered the murder rates in a few states but that in many other states the statistics are inconclusive. In your speech, if you assert that statistics show that murder rates are lower in states with capital punishment, you would be distorting the evidence. Because the line between some exaggeration and gross exaggeration or distortion is often difficult to distinguish, most people see any exaggeration as unethical.

3. **Resist personal attacks against those who oppose your ideas.** There seems to be almost universal agreement that name-calling and other irrelevant personal attacks are detrimental to a speaker's trustworthiness. Responsible listeners recognize that such tactics do not contribute to the speaker's argument and represent an abuse of the privileged status the speaker enjoys.

4. **Give the source for all damning information.** Where ideas originate is often as important as the ideas themselves, especially when a statement is damning. If you are going to discuss wrongdoing by individuals or organizations or condemn an idea by relying on the words or ideas of others, provide the sources of your information and arguments. Moreover, because the mention of wrongdoing brings communication to the edge of what is legally defined as slander, speakers should be aware of the legal as well as the ethical pitfalls of making damning statements without proof.

Gender and Cultural Differences

So far in this chapter we have discussed reasoning, appealing to emotions, and building credibility—three forms of proof that Aristotle, who wrote the first comprehensive treatment of persuasive speaking, called *logos, pathos,* and *ethos.* A legitimate question is whether women and people of other cultures use and appreciate the forms that are based on male speaking in a predominantly Eurocentric culture. The answer is that in all cultures male and female public speakers use these same means of persuasion—the differences are in how women and people from other cultures *emphasize* each of these means. Whereas U.S. male culture relies on good reasons supported with factual information and expert opinion, other cultural groups may put more emphasis on the credibility of the speaker or on emotional arousal and expressiveness (Fisher, 1988; Friday, 2000; Lieberman, 1995). The Diverse Voices feature provides some examples of differences between American and Arab cultures when speaking persuasively.

So, how should you proceed? Again, the advice of Aristotle in his *Rhetoric* is useful to any speaker. When he discussed adapting to audiences, he pointed out that if an audience was truly homogeneous a speaker would want to use forms of

DIVERSE VOICES

A Comparison of Arab and American Conceptions of "Effective" Persuasion

by Janice Walker Anderson

People from different cultures are likely to have different views about how to speak and write persuasively. In this excerpt, Janice Walker Anderson describes some differences in the ways Arabs consider persuasiveness.

Although mass media reports on events in the Middle East translate the words used by Arab leaders, the reports seldom explain the different cultural standards in Arab societies for evaluating reasonableness. "We can say that what is 'reasonable,'" intercultural communication scholars Condon and Yousef (1975) explain, "is not fully separable from cultural assumptions." This analysis indicates some of the differences between Arab and American cultural orientations toward what constitutes "effective" persuasion.

Before beginning the analysis, it is first necessary to acquaint American readers with some of the basics of Arab and Muslim orientations toward argumentation. "While only a small percentage (about 10%) of present-day Arabs are Bedouins," Gudykunst and Kim explain in *Communicating with Strangers,* "contemporary Arab culture holds the Bedouin ethos as an ideal to which, in theory at least, it would like to measure up. While values such as materialism, success, activity, progress, and rationality are featured in American culture, Arab societies revolve around the core values of "hospitality, generosity, courage, honor, and self-respect."

As H. Samuel Hamod indicated in "Arab and Moslem Rhetorical Theory and Practice," storytellers performed a vital function for the Bedouin tribes because few people could read or write: "Their tribal storytellers functioned as historians and moralists in recounting battles and instances of outstanding bravery and cunning." These storytellers, or what we today might call poets, performed important political functions by

establishing a means for interpreting and directing action. As A. J. Almaney and A. J. Alwan explained, a poet's poems "might arouse a tribe to action in the same manner as. . .[a politician] in a modern political campaign. . . . He was both a molder and agent of public opinion." Some attributed magical powers to these storytellers because they controlled the power of language which could act upon the human emotions and rouse the people to action. To this day, poets are held in the highest esteem in Arab societies.

In addition, Arab cultures connect inspired language and religion. Arabic plays an important religious role in Islamic societies. All Muslims, regardless of their nationality, must use Arabic in their daily prayers. The language of the Quran is considered a miracle in itself because it was produced by the Prophet Mohammed, who was illiterate. Consequently, Muslims believe that the Quran cannot be faithfully translated into other languages.

The power of words lay not in their ability to reflect human experience, but in their ability to transcend it, to reach toward that which lay beyond human experience—the divine. To this day, the Quran stands as the ultimate book of style and grammar for Arabs. The cultural equivalent in the West would be using the King James Version of the Bible as our style manual.

The Arab's appreciation for the persuasive power of the rhythm and sound of words leads to a style that relies heavily on devices that heighten the emotional impact of a message. Certain words are used in speaking that have no denotative meaning. "These are 'firm' words because the audience knows the purpose behind their use, and the words are taken as a seal of definiteness and sincerity on the part of the speaker." Other forms of assertion, such as repetition and antithesis, are also quite frequent. Emphatic assertions are expected, Almaney and Alwan explain: "If an Arab says exactly what he means without the expected assertion, other Arabs may still think he means the opposite."

Hamod explains the reasoning behind the Arab's emphasis on stylistic concerns. "He who speaks well is well educated; he who is well educated is more qualified to render judgments and it is his advice we should follow. Eloquence and effectiveness were equated." An Arab writer establishes credibility by displaying ability and artistry with the language.

Yet, given the vastly different assumptions about the role of persuasion in society, it is not surprising that misunderstandings occur between Americans and Arabs, even when the same "language" is used. Communicating across a cultural gap requires more than just a knowledge of respective vocabularies. It also requires an understanding of the different cultural rules for what constitutes "reasonable" political debate.

Excerpted from The Howard Journal of Communications, *Vol. 2, No. 1 (Winter 1989–90), pp. 81–114. Reprinted by permission of the publisher. Janice Walker Anderson is in the Communication Department, College at New Paltz, State University of New York.*

proof, references, and examples that would relate to their particular experience. But when an audience is largely heterogeneous, a speaker would find it most useful to speak to what he called "the golden mean"—that is, a composite that covered the majority of that audience.

Presentation

Principle 7: You are more likely to persuade an audience if you develop an effective oral presentation style.

Previous chapters have addressed characteristics of presentation that you must develop to increase your effectiveness, including the importance of practicing your speech until your presentation (language and delivery) enhances it. Although this section is short, you must not forget that it is through your presentation that your listeners "see" your speech.

Criteria for Evaluating Persuasive Speeches

In this chapter, we have been looking at principles of persuasive speaking. Now let's apply those principles to evaluating and presenting a persuasive speech. Figure 18.4 outlines the criteria for evaluating a persuasive speech. Use this checklist to evaluate the sample persuasive speech that follows.

TEST YOUR COMPETENCE

Prepare a Persuasive Speech

1. Prepare a four- to seven-minute speech in which you affect audience belief or move your audience to action. An outline is required.

2. As an addendum to the outline, write a persuasive speech plan for adapting to your specific audience that explores these questions:
    a. How does your goal adapt to whether your prevailing audience attitude is in favor, no opinion, or opposed?
    b. What reasons will you use, and how will the organizational pattern you select fit your topic and audience?
    c. How will you establish your credibility with this audience?
    d. How will you motivate your audience by using incentives or by appealing to their emotions?

Use the information in the checklist (see Figure 18.4) to support your plan.

Check all items that were accomplished effectively.

Primary Criteria
_____ 1. Was the specific goal designed to affect a belief or move an audience to action?
_____ 2. Did the speaker present clearly stated reasons?
_____ 3. Did the speaker use facts and expert opinions to support these reasons?
_____ 4. Was the organizational pattern appropriate for the type of goal and assumed attitude of the audience?
_____ 5. Did the speaker use emotional language to motivate the audience?
_____ 6. Was the speaker effective in establishing his or her credibility on this topic?
_____ 7. Was the speaker ethical in handling material?

General Criteria
_____ 1. Was the specific goal clear?
_____ 2. Was the introduction effective?
_____ 3. Was the organizational pattern appropriate for the intent and content of the speech?
_____ 5. Was the conclusion effective?
_____ 6. Was the language clear, vivid, emphatic, and appropriate?
_____ 7. Was the delivery convincing?

Evaluate the speech as (check one):
_____ excellent _____ good _____ average _____ fair _____ poor

Figure 18.4

Checklist for critiquing a persuasive speech.

You can watch, listen to, and evaluate the following persuasive speech by Charone Frankel, a student at San Francisco State University, under Speech Interactive on your Communicate! CD-ROM.

Sample Speech: Dangerous Trucks, by Charone S. Frankel[2]

This section contains an example of a persuasive speech outline, a speech plan, and a speech.

Speech Outline

Specific goal: I want my audience to believe that we should solve the problem of highway deaths caused by unsafe trucks.

Introduction
  I. On the night Heidi Jorgenson was killed in a truck accident, she had been planning her wedding.
 II. The trucking industry must be held accountable for their increasing number of accidents.

Thesis statement: Unsafe trucking is a growing problem that should be corrected before more people lose their lives needlessly.

Body
  I. Trucking safety is a major problem.
      A. The more than 75 million trucks traveling in the United States are involved in some 250,000 crashes and 6,000 fatalities every year.
      B. While fatality rates for most vehicles have remained constant, truck-related deaths have risen 20 percent since 1992.
(Now that we've seen the extent of the problem, let's look at why it exists.)
 II. The trucking industry has some terrible safety habits.
      A. Worst is the practice of making truckers drive too many hours.
          1. Thirty percent of truck wrecks are caused by driver fatigue.
          2. Truckers drive 66 to 75 hours a week even though they are supposed to be limited to 60 hours.
          3. The American Trucking Association wants changes in laws to allow truckers to stay on the road longer.
      B. Nearly as bad is the fact that the trucking industry is not bothering to use new safety equipment that is available.
          1. Trucking companies are skeptical of the costs.
          2. Moreover, trucking companies refuse to recognize the safety benefits.
(The problem is great, but he cure is relatively easy.)
III. The problem can be greatly reduced in two ways.

---

2 Speech, as edited, by permission of Charone S. Frankel.

    A. First, the government needs to take a more active role.
        1. The government needs to be prodded to enforce laws that are already on the books.
        2. The government needs to pass legislation that would increase fines for safety violations.
        3. The government needs to pass legislation requiring companies to install safety equipment.
    B. Second, we as individuals can help.
        1. We can lobby Congress to act.
        2. We can take a more active role in following safety practices.

Conclusion
    I. We have seen the seriousness of the problem.
    II. We must work to solve the problem if we think our livves are worth more than the paltry $2400 the trucking company was fined for the accident that killed Heidi.

Sources:

Chappell, Lindsay. "Push for Big Rig Safety May Benefit Suppliers." *Automotive News,* September 6, 1999, p. 20.

Lavelle, Marianne. "The Killer Trucks: Lax Safety Rules, Long Hours Wreak Havoc on the Roads." *U. S. News & World Report,* September 13, 1999, pp. 12–18.

"Big Rig Crash." KTVU News, Channel 2, January 24, 2000.

"McCain-Schuster Motor Carrier Bill." *Congressional Daily,* May 27, 1999.

Speech Plan

Audience attitude toward goal: My perception is that my audience is neutral on the subject of truck safety—largely because they are not familiar with the extent of the problem. But since most of us have had occasion to be fearful of the number of trucks and the way they're driven on major highways, I think the audience will be willing to listen to me. I will attempt to build a positive attitude by using information that they can relate to and understand.

Organization: I have organized my speech following a problem–solution order. Since I believe that my audience will be at least neutral at the start, I think this straightforward organization will work.

Credibility: I plan to build credibility by showing my familiarity with material that illustrates the problems in the trucking industry. I have good sources, and I will document key information throughout the speech.

Motivation: I will try to motivate them by beginning with a vivid example that I believe will get their attention and get them emotionally involved. Then, throughout the speech, I will try to relate my information to audience experiences.

Speech and Analysis

Read the following speech aloud. Then, analyze it on the basis of the primary criteria on the checklist in Figure 18.4: goal, reasons, support, organization, motivation, credibility, and ethics. This is an edited version of the speech as it was originally given. Listen to the speech as it was originally given and compare it with this revised version by clicking on Speech Interactive for Communicate! on your Communicate! CD-ROM.

Speech

At 10 P.M. on May 27th of last year, Heidi Jorgenson and her fiancé, Doug, were driving home after a meeting with their priest at which they planned their upcoming wedding. Without warning, a 300-pound steel blade fell off a tractor-trailer coming toward them in the opposite lane and sheared off the top passenger side of Doug and Heidi's car, killing Heidi instantly.

Later it was discovered that the trucker was driving illegally, for his company had failed to obtain an oversized-load permit. The driver and company were fined twenty-four hundred dollars. Twenty-four hundred dollars to taking a human life! Does that sound like justice? Probably not, but according to the *U.S. News and World Report,* September 13, 1999, the trucking industry has been blatantly breaking the law and getting away with it for years. Minimally enforced safety regulations and nearly nonexistent punishment of violators have caused heavy trucks to become by far the most dangerous vehicles on the road.

Unsafe trucking is a growing problem that must be corrected before more people lose their lives. In addressing this issue we will examine the problem, show why it exists, and look at the solutions that must be enacted if we are to solve this problem.

Let's start with the point that trucking safety is a major problem. According to the *U.S. News and World Report,* there are about 75 million trucks traveling more than 160 trillion miles a year throughout the United States. According to the *Journal of Safety and Health,* these trucks are involved in close to 250,000 crashes and 6,000 fatalities every year.

Analysis

Charone begins with an emotional anecdote designed to get attention and to arouse an emotional reaction from her audience.

Notice the repetition to emphasize the injustice.

Here and throughout the speech, she cites her sources for information.

Here Charone states her goal and forecasts her main points.

Good use of documented statistics.

Speech

Let's get a mental picture of what 6,000 fatalities really means. Take the total number of people here at this tournament (500), and multiply that by twelve. And while fatality rates for most types of vehicles have remained constant over the years, truck-related deaths have actually risen 20 percent since 1992, hear that—20 percent, according to the May 27, 1999, issue of *Congress Daily.*

So the question a reasonable person might ask, then, is "Why have trucks become so dangerous?" By taking a close look at the current system, we'll see how the trucking industry practically invites tragedies like Heidi Jorgensen's.

My point? The trucking industry has some terrible safety habits. Worst of all is the widespread practice of making truckers drive . . . and drive . . . and drive until they are barely conscious. Jim Hall, Chairman of the National Transportation Safety Board, says that 30 percent of all truck wrecks are actually caused by driver fatigue. Numerous studies have shown that truckers routinely dust past the federal limit of 60 hours a week on the road. In fact, a study done last year for the Department of Transportation shows that truckers are averaging 66 hours on the road behind the wheel and 75 hours if they don't belong to a union. Can you imagine driving 75 hours a week? And that's apparently still not enough because the American Trucking Association says that its top priority is to change the laws to allow truckers to stay on the road longer!

But in addition to staying on the road too much, most of the trucking industry is simply not bothering to use a multitude of new safety equipment that is available. The reason, according to the September 6th, 1999, *Automotive News,* is that trucking companies are skeptical about the costs and benefits of safety devices. To put it another way, trucking companies don't feel that saving lives of people like you and me is enough of a "benefit" to justify spending money on safety equipment. Clearly it is the attitudes and policies of both our government and the trucking industry that are causing these 6,000 deaths every year.

Analysis

With this comparison Charone hopes to help the audience visualize the number.

Again, through repetition, she emphasizes the percentage of the increase.

Here she moves to her second point—why the problem exists.

Charone does an excellent job of emphasizing the number of hours and dramatizing their inappropriateness.

Notice how she vilifies the industry by showing how they put cost ahead of lives.

Speech

The good news is that solving this problem is a fairly straightforward process. Since we cannot rely on the trucking industry to regulate itself, our government needs to step in and start forcing trucking companies to clean up their acts.

First of all, current legislation needs to be enforced a lot more strictly. No more 75-hour weeks for drivers! We also need to pass new legislation that would increase fines for safety violations and make it mandatory that truckers rest for 10 to 14 hours between hauls. Furthermore, it is imperative that trucking companies be required by law to install safety equipment in their vehicles. According to the *Automotive News,* for about an additional 15 percent of what trucks currently cost, they can have new anti-rollover technology, more powerful disc brakes, a crash avoidance sensor system, and an onboard computerized data recorder that would prevent speedy drivers from falsifying their logbooks.

More importantly, we as individuals need to realize that we have a vested interest in making trucks safer. We all must support truck safety legislation. One thing you can do is lobby in favor of former President Clinton's proposal to increase fines and make 10- to 14-hour rests between hauls mandatory. Another thing you can do that may have a direct impact on how safe the roads are for you is to take an active role in protecting yourself. Make sure to give those big trucks plenty of clearance. Don't follow them too closely, and remember: if you can't see their mirrors, they can't see you. These things will help make the roads safer for all of us.

We have now taken a look at the problem of unsafe trucking. We have seen how both industry carelessness and government apathy have caused close to 6,000 deaths each year, and we have seen that there is a clear solution. Unsafe trucking is a growing problem, and it must be corrected before more people lose their lives. Heidi Jorgensen was supposed to have been married last October. Instead, she is in the ground. The trucking industry has been getting away with murder, and it is going to continue until we decide to put an end to it. I certainly hope you think that your life is worth more than 2,400 dollars.

Analysis

Here she moves on to tell us what needs to be done.

Notice that in light of what she has said previously, none of these recommendations seem to be out of line.

Here she emphasizes that the cost (a 15 percent increase) is not too much when the goal is saving lives.

Charone involves the audience by showing that they can play an important role in solving the problem

She enumerates specific behaviors that we can engage in to help solve the problem.

She begins her conclusion by reviewing the reasons. She then returns to her opening anecdote to add power to her conclusion. Throughout the speech Charone blends logical information and emotional appeal quite well. This is a very good persuasive speech that follows the problem–solution pattern.

WHAT WOULD YOU DO?
A QUESTION OF ETHICS

Alejandro had decided that for his final speech he would motivate members of the class to donate money to the Downtown Food Bank. He was excited about this topic because when he was a senior in high school he had volunteered at the Food Bank, and he had seen firsthand the face of hunger in this community.

He planned to support his speech with three reasons: (1) that an increasing number of people in the community needed food, (2) that government agencies were unable to provide sufficient help, and (3) that a high percentage of every dollar donated to the Food Bank went to buy food.

As he researched these points, however, he discovered that the number of families in need had not really risen in the past two years and that government sponsorship of the Food Bank had increased. Then, when he examined the Food Bank's financial statements, he discovered that only 68 percent of every dollar donated was actu-

ally spent on food. Faced with this evidence, he just didn't think his reasons and evidence were very strong.

Yet, because of his experience he still thought the Food Bank was a cause that deserved financial support, so he decided to focus his entire speech on the heartwarming case of the Hernando family. Ineligible for government assistance, over the years this family of ten had managed to survive because of the aid they received from the Food Bank. Today, several of the children have graduated from college, and one is a physician working in the barrio. By telling this story of one family's struggle to survive, Alejandro thought he would be successful in persuading the class.

Would it be ethical for Alejandro to give his speech in this way? If so, why? If not, what would he need to do to make the speech ethical?

Summary

Persuasive speeches are designed to establish or change a belief or motivate an audience to act. The principles governing persuasive speeches are similar to those presented for informative speeches, as are the steps of speech preparation.

First, write a clear persuasive speech goal stating what you want your audience to believe or do.

Second, analyze your audience's interest and knowledge levels and attitude toward your goal.

Third, build the body of the speech with good reasons, statements that answer why the proposition is justified. Support reasons with facts and expert opinion.

Fourth, create an organization for the speech that suits your goal and your analysis of the audience. Four common organizational patterns for persuasive speeches are statement of logical reasons, problem–solution, comparative advantages, and motivational.

Fifth, motivate your audience by reworking language to appeal to the emotions, especially in your main points, introduction, and conclusion.

Sixth, use your credibility advantageously. Especially in persuasive speaking, one of the most important ways of building credibility is to behave in an ethical manner.

Seventh, deliver the speech convincingly. Good delivery is especially important in persuasive speaking.

Communicate! Online

Use your Communicate! CD-ROM for quick access to the electronic study resources that accompany this text. Included on your CD-ROM is access to InfoTrac College Edition, the World Wide Web, a demo of WebTutor for Communicate!, and the Communicate! Web site at the Wadsworth Communication Café. The Communicate! Web site offers chapter-by-chapter activities, quizzes, and a digital glossary.

Review the following key terms and complete the Self-Review for Public Speaking on page 487 online at

http://communication.wadsworth.com/humancomm/verderber

Further, you can analyze Charone's persuasive speech, on the previous pages, under Speech Interactive on your Communicate! CD-ROM.

Key Terms

ad hominem (467)

appeal to authority (467)

attitude (457)

emotions (472)

false cause (466)

hasty generalization (466)

incentive (470)

motivation (470)

opinion (457)

persuasive speaking (456)

reasoning by analogy (465)

reasoning by causation (465)

reasoning by generalization from example (464)

reasoning by sign (466)

reasons (460)

Speech Interactive helps you prepare for your own speech performance and provide feedback to your peers by critiquing the speeches of other students such as Charone.

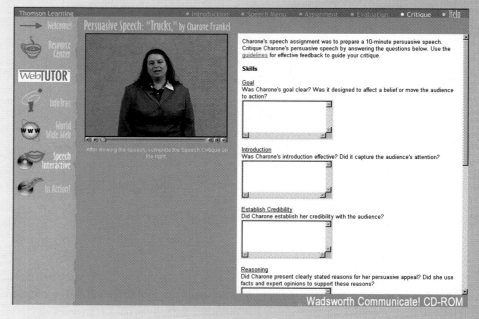

SELF-REVIEW

Public Speaking from Chapters 12 to 18

What kind of a public speaker are you? The following analysis looks at eleven specifics that are basic to a public-speaking profile. On the line provided for each statement, indicate the response that best captures your behavior: 1, almost always; 2, often; 3, occasionally; 4, rarely; 5, never.

_____ When I am asked to speak, I am able to select a topic and determine a speech goal with confidence. (Ch. 12)

_____ When I speak, I use material from a variety of sources. (Ch. 13)

_____ In my preparation, I construct clear main points and organize them to follow some consistent pattern. (Ch. 14)

_____ In my preparation, I am careful to be sure that I have developed ideas to meet audience needs. (Ch. 15)

_____ When I speak, I sense that my audience perceives my language as clear and vivid. (Ch. 16)

_____ I look directly at members of my audience when I speak. (Ch. 16)

_____ My public-speaking voice shows variation in pitch, speed, and loudness. (Ch. 16)

_____ When I speak, my bodily actions help supplement or reinforce my ideas; I feel and look involved. (Ch. 16)

_____ I have confidence in my ability to speak in public. (Ch. 16)

_____ When I give informative speeches, I am careful to use techniques designed to get audience attention, create audience understanding, and increase audience retention. (Ch. 17)

_____ When I give persuasive speeches, I am careful to use techniques designed to build my credibility, prove my reasons, and motivate my audience. (Ch. 18)

Based on your responses, select the public-speaking behavior you would most like to change. Write a communication improvement plan similar to the sample in Chapter 1 (page 25). If you would like verification of your self-analysis before you write a goal statement, have a friend or a coworker complete this same analysis for you.

References

Adamopoulos, J. (1999). The emergence of cultural patterns of interpersonal behavior. In J. Adamopoulos & Y. Kashima (Eds.), *Social psychology and cultural context* (pp. 63–76). Thousand Oaks, CA: Sage.

Adler, R. B. (1977). *Confidence in communication: A guide to assertive and social skills.* New York: Holt, Rinehart & Winston.

Affifi, W. A., & Guerrero, L. K. (2000). Motivations underlying topic avoidance in close relationships. In S. Petronio (Ed.), *Balancing the secrets of private disclosures* (pp. 165–180). Mahwah, NJ: Erlbaum.

Ahladas, J. A. (1989, April 1). Global warming. *Vital Speeches,* 381–384.

Alberti, R. E., & Emmons, M. L. (1995). *Your perfect right: A guide to assertive living* (7th ed.). San Luis Obispo, CA: Impact.

Anderson, J. (1988). Communication competency in the small group. In R. Cathcart & L. Samovar (Eds.), *Small group communication, A reader.* Dubuque, IA: Wm. Brown.

Andrews, P. H. (1992). Sex and gender differences in group communication: Impact on the facilitation process. *Small Group Research, 23,* 90.

Angry wife becomes computer hacker. (1999, June 30). *Cincinnati Enquirer,* p. B2.

Aries, E. (1998). Gender differences in interaction: A reexamination. In D. J. Canary & K. Dindia (Eds.), *Sex differences and similarities in communication: Critical essays and empirical investigations of sex and gender in interaction* (pp. 65–81). Mahwah, NJ: Erlbaum.

Asante, M. K. (1998). *The Afrocentric idea.* Philadelphia, PA: Temple University Press.

Asante, M. K. (1998). Identifying racist language: Linguistic acts and signs. In M. L. Hecht (Ed.) *Communicating prejudice* (pp. 87–98). Thousand Oaks, CA: Sage.

Asante, M. K. (1982). Black male and female communicators in an Afrocentric relationship. In L. Gary (Ed.). *The black male.* Thousand Oaks, CA: Sage.

Asante, M. K., & Gudykunst, W. (Eds.). (1989). *Handbook of intercultural and international communication.* Thousand Oaks, CA: Sage.

Axtell, R. E. (1999). *Gestures: The do's and taboos of body language around the world* (rev. ed). New York: Wiley.

Ayres, J., & Hopf, T. S. (1990, January). The long-term effect of visualization in the classroom: A brief research report. *Communication Education, 39,* 75–78.

Ayres, J., Hopf, T. S., & Ayres, D. M. (1994, July). An examination of whether imaging ability enhances the effectiveness of an intervention designed to reduce speech anxiety. *Communication Education, 43,* 252–258.

Bach, K., & Harnish, R. M. (1979). *Linguistic communication and speech acts.* Cambridge, MA: MIT Press.

Baeder, D. L. (1980, June 1). Chemical wastes. *Vital Speeches,* 496–500.

Bales, R. F. (1971). *Personality and interpersonal behavior.* New York: Holt, Rinehart & Winston.

Balgopal, P. R., Ephross, P. H., & Vassil, T. V. (1986). Self help groups and professional helpers. *Small Group Research, 17,* 123–137.

Banks, M. A. (1997). *Web psychos, stalkers and pranksters.* Scottsdale, AZ: Coriolis Group.

Baron, R. A., & Byrne, D. (2000). *Social psychology* (9th ed.). Boston: Allyn & Bacon.

Barsky, A. E. (2000). *Conflict resolution for the helping professions.* Belmont, CA: Brooks/Cole.

Becherer, H. W. (2000, September 15). Enduring values for a secular age: Faith, hope and love. *Vital Speeches,* 732–734.

Beebe, M. B., Anthony, T., Salas, E., & Driskell, J. E. (1994). Group cohesiveness and quality of decision making. *Small Group Research, 25,* 189–204.

Berger, C. R. (1994). Power, dominance, and social interaction. In M. L. Knapp & G. R. Miller (Eds.), *Handbook of interpersonal communication* (2nd ed., pp. 450–507). Thousand Oaks, CA: Sage.

Berger, C. R., & Brada, J. J. (1982). *Language and social knowledge: Uncertainty in interpersonal relations.* London: Arnold.

Bigelow, J. D. (1999). The Web as an organizational behavior learning medium. *Journal of Management Education, 23,* 635–650.

Bodenhausen, G. V., & Macrae, C. N. (1996). The self-regulation of intergroup perception: Mechanisms and consequences of stereotype suppression. In C. N. Macrae, C. Stangor, & M. Hewstone (Eds.), *Stereotypes and stereotyping* (pp. 227–254). New York: Guilford Press.

Bormann, E. (1990). *Small group communication: Theory and practice.* New York: Harper & Row.

Bostrom, R. (1970). Patterns of communicative interaction in small groups. *Speech Monographs, 37,* 257–263.

Brown, P., & Levinson, S. (1987). *Politeness: Some universals in language usage.* Cambridge, U.K.: Cambridge University Press.

Burgoon, J. K. (1994). Nonverbal signals. In M. L. Knapp & G. R. Miller (Eds.), *Handbook of interpersonal communication* (2nd ed., pp. 229–285). Thousand Oaks, CA: Sage.

Burgoon, J. K., Coker, D. A., & Coker, R. A. (1986). Communicative effects of gaze behavior: A test of two contrasting explanations, *Human Communication Research, 12,* 495–524.

Burgoon, J. K., & Dunbar, N. E. (2000). An interactionist perspective on dominance-submission: Interpersonal dominance as a dynamic, situationally contingent social skill. *Communication Monographs,* Mar., pp. 96–121.

Burgoon, J. K., Johnson, M. L., and Koch, P. T. (1998). The nature of measurement of interpersonal dominance. *Communication Monographs, 65,* 309–335.

Burgoon, J. K., & Poire, B. A. (1999). Nonverbal cues and interpersonal judgments: Participant and observer perceptions of intimacy, dominance, composure, and formality. *Communication Monographs,* June, 105–124.

Burleson, B. R. (1994). Comforting messages: Significance, approaches and effects. In B. R. Burleson, T. L. Albrecht, & I. G. Sarason (Eds.), *Communication of social support: Messages, interactions, relationships, and community* (pp. 3–28). Thousand Oaks, CA: Sage.

Burleson, B., & Jones, S. (first author) (1999). The impact of situational variables on helpers' perceptions of comforting messages: an attibutional analysis. *Communication Research, 24,* 530–555.

Burleson, B., & Kunkel, A. (first author) (1999). Assessing explanations for sex differences in emotional support. *Human Communication Research, 25,* 307–340.

Burleson, B. R., & Samter, W. (1985). Consistencies in theoretical and naive evaluations of comforting messages. *Communication Monographs, 52,* 103–123.

Burleson, B. R., & Samter, W. (1990). Effects of cognitive complexity on the perceived importance of communication skills in friends. *Communication Research, 17,* 165–182.

Cahn, D. D. (1990). Intimates in conflict: A research review. In D. D. Cahn (Ed.), *Intimates in conflict: A communication perspective* (pp. 1–24). Hillsdale, NJ: Erlbaum.

Canary, D. J., Cupach, W. R., & Messman, S. J. (1995). *Relationship conflict: Conflict in parent–child, friendship, and romantic relationships.* Thousand Oaks, CA: Sage.

Canary, D. J., & Hause, K. (1993). Is there any reason to research sex differences in communication? *Communication Quarterly, 41,* 129–144.

Canary, D. J., & Semic, B. A. (first author) (1997). Trait argumentativeness, verbal aggressiveness, and minimally rational argument: An observational analysis of friendship discussions. *Communication Quarterly,* Fall, 355–378.

Canary, D. J., & Stafford, L. (first author) (1991). Maintenance strategies and romantic relationship type, gender, and relational characteristics. *Journal of Social and Personal Relationships, 8,* 217–242.

Carpenter, A. (1996). *Facts about cities* (2nd ed.). New York: H. W. Wilson.

Cegala, D. J., & Sillars, A. L. (1989). Further examination of nonverbal manifestations of interaction involvement. *Communication Reports, 2,* 45.

Chronical of higher education, The, August 27, 1999.

Clark, N. (1994). *Teambuilding: A practical guide for trainers.* New York: McGraw-Hill.

Clark, R. A., Pierce, A. J., Finn, K., Hsu, K., Toosley, A., & Williams, L. (1998). The impact of alternative approaches to comforting, closeness of relationship, and gender on multiple measures of effectiveness. *Communication Studies, 49* (Fall), 224–239.

Clevenger, T., Jr. (1959, April). A synthesis of experimental research in stage fright. *Quarterly Journal of Speech, 45,* 134–145.

Cloven, D. H., & Roloff, M. E. (1991). Sense-making activities and interpersonal conflict: Communicative cures for the mulling blues. *Western Journal of Speech Communication, 55,* 134–158.

Cogger, J. W. (1982). Are you a skilled interviewer? *Personnel Journal, 61,* 842–843.

Cornog, M. W. (1998). *Merriam Webster's vocabulary builder.* Springfield, MA: Merriam Webster.

Courtright, J. A., & Perse, E. M. (1998). *Communicating online: A guide to the Internet.* Mountain View, CA: Mayfield.

Criscito, P. (2000). *Résumés in Cyberspace* (2nd ed.). Hauppauge, NY: Barron's Educational Series, Inc.

Crumlish, C. (1997). *The Internet for busy people* (2nd ed.). Berkeley, CA: Osborne/McGraw-Hill.

Crutchfield, E., Jr. (1980, June 15). Profitable banking in the 1980s. *Vital Speeches,* 535–537.

Cupach, W. R., & Canary, D. J. (1997). *Competence in interpersonal conflict.* New York: McGraw-Hill.

Dale, P. (1999). *"Did you say something, Susan?" How any woman can gain confidence with assertive communication.* Secaucus, NJ: Carol.

Deaux, K., Dane, F. D., & Wrightsman, L. S. (1993). *Social psychology* (6th ed.). Belmont, CA: Wadsworth.

DeKlerk, V. (1991). "Expletives: Men only?" *Communication Monographs, 58,* 156–169.

Demo, D. H. (1987). Family relations and the self-esteem of adolescents and their parents. *Journal of Marriage and the Family, 49,* 705–715.

Dennis, A. R. (1996). Information exchange and use in small group decision making. *Small Group Research, 27,* 532–550.

Derlega, V. J., Barbee, A. P., & Winstead, B. A. (1994). Friendship, gender, and social support: Laboratory studies of supportive interactions. In B. R. Burleson, T. L. Albrecht, & I. G. Sarason (Eds.), *Communicating of social support: Messages, interactions, relationships, and community* (pp. 136–151). Thousand Oaks, CA: Sage.

Derlega, V. J., Metts, S., Petronio, S., & Margulis, S. T. (1993). *Self-disclosure.* Newbury Park, CA: Sage.

Dindia, K. (2000). Relational maintenance. In C. Hendrick & S. S. Hendrick (Eds.), *Close relationships: A sourcebook* (pp. 287–300). Thousand Oaks, CA: Sage.

Dindia, K. (2000). Sex differences in self-disclosure, reciprocity of self-disclosure, and self-disclosure and liking: Three meta-analyses reviewed. In S. Petronio (Ed.), *Balancing the secrets of private disclosures* (pp. 21–36). Mahwah, NJ: Erlbaum.

Dindia, K., Fitzpatrick, M. A., & Kenny, D. A. (1997, March). Self-disclosure in spouse and stranger interaction: A social relations analysis. *Human Communication Research, 23,* 388–412.

Duck, S. (1987). How to lose friends without influencing people. In M. E. Roloff & G. R. Miller (Eds.), *Interpersonal processes: New directions in communication research* (pp. 278–298). Beverly Hills, CA: Sage.

Duck, S. (1998). *Human relationships* (3rd ed.). Thousand Oaks, CA: Sage.

Durst, G. M. (1989, March 1). The manager as a developer. *Vital Speeches,* 309–314.

Eggins, S., & Slade, D. (1997). *Analyzing casual conversation.* Washington, DC: Cassell.

Ekman, P., & Friesen, W. V. (1969). The repertoire of nonverbal behavior: Categories, origins, usage, and coding. *Semiotica, 1,* 49–98.

Ekman, P., & Friesen, W. V. (1975). *Unmasking the face.* Englewood Cliffs, NJ: Prentice-Hall.

Ellis, K. (1995, January). Apprehension, self-perceived competency, and teacher immediacy in the laboratory-supported public speaking course: Trends and relationships. *Communication Education, 44,* 64–78.

Estes, W. K. (1989). Learning theory. In A. Lesgold & R. Glaser (Eds.), *Foundations for a psychology of education* (pp. 1–49). Hillsdale, NJ: Erlbaum.

Ettinger, H. R. (2000, September 15). Shattering the glass floor: Women donors as leaders of fundamental change. *Vital Speeches,* 727–730.

Evans, C., & Dion, K. (1991). Group cohesion and performance: A meta-analysis. *Small Group Research, 22,* 175–186.

Eysenck, H. J. (1994). The measurement of creativity. In M. A. Boden (Ed.), *Dimensions of creativity* (pp. 199–242). Cambridge, MA: MIT Press.

Fairhurst, G. T. (2001). Dualism in leadership. In F. M. Jablin & L. L. Putnam (Eds.). *The New Handbook of Organizational Communication* (pp. 379–439). Thousand Oaks, CA: Sage.

Fairhurst, G. T. (1993). Echoes of the vision: When the rest of the organization talks total quality. *Management Communication Quarterly, 6,* 331–371.

Fairhurst, G. T., & Sarr, R. A. (1996). *The art of framing.* San Francisco: Jossey-Bass.

Fehr, B. (1996). *Friendship processes.* Thousand Oaks, CA: Sage.

Filley, A. C. (1975). *Interpersonal conflict resolution.* Glenview, IL: Scott, Foresman.

Fisher, G. (1988). International negotiation. In L. A. Samovar & R. E. Porter (Eds.), *Intercultural communication: A reader* (5th ed., pp. 192–200). Belmont, CA: Wadsworth.

Flaherty, L. M., Pearce, K. J., & Rubin, R. B. (1998). Internet and face-to-face communication: Not functional alternatives. *Communication Quarterly, 46* (Summer), 250–268.

Floyd, K., & Morman, M. T. (1998). The measurement of affectionate communication. *Communication Quarterly, 46* (Spring), 144–162.

Forgas, J. P. (1991). Affect and person perception. In J. P. Forgas (Ed.), *Emotion and social judgments* (pp. 263–291). New York: Pergamon Press.

Forgas, J. P. (2000). Feeling and thinking: Summary and integration. In J. P. Forgas (Ed.), *Feeling and thinking: The role of affect in social cognition* (pp. 387–406). New York: Cambridge Press.

Freedman, J. L., Klevansky, S., & Ehrich, P. R. (1971). The effect of crowding on human task performance. *Journal of Applied Psychology, 1*(1), 7–25.

Friday, R. A. (2000). Contrasts in discussion behaviors of German and American managers. In L. A. Samovar & R. E. Porter (Eds.), *Intercultural communication: A reader* (7th ed., pp. 224–235). Belmont, CA: Wadsworth.

Gardenswartz, L., & Rowe, A. (1998). *Managing diversity: A complete desk reference and planning guide* (rev. ed.). New York: McGraw-Hill.

Gentry, G. (1980). Group size and attitudes towards the simulation experience. *Simulation and Games, 11,* 451–460.

Geyer, G. A. (1999, September 15). Dressing in the name of respect. *Cincinnati Enquirer,* p. A12.

Gmelch, S. B. (1998). *Gender on campus: Issues for college women.* New Brunswick, NJ: Rutgers University Press.

Goldberg, B. (1999). *Overcoming high-tech anxiety: Thriving in a wired world.* San Francisco, CA: Jossey-Bass.

Goleman, D. (1998). *Working with emotional intelligence.* New York: Bantam Books.

Gordon, T. (1970). *Parent effectiveness training.* New York: Peter H. Wyden.

Gordon, T. (1971). *The basic modules of the instructor outline for effectiveness training courses.* Pasadena, CA: Effectiveness Training Associates.

Gorham, J., & Christophel, D. M. (1995). A test–retest analysis of student motivation, teacher immediacy, and perceived sources of motivation and demotivation in college classes. *Communication Education, 44,* 292–307.

Gorham, J., Cohen, S. H., & Morris, T. L. (1997). Fashion in the classroom II: Instructor immediacy and attire. *Communication Research Reports, 14,* 11–24.

Gorham, J. C., Morris, S. H., & Tracy, L. (1999). Fashion in the classroom III: Effects of instructor attire and immediacy in natural classroom interactions. *Communication Quarterly,* Summer, 281–299.

Gouran, D. S., & Hirokawa, R. Y. (1996). Functional theory and communication in decision-making groups: An expanded view. In R. Y. Hirokawa & M. S. Poole (Eds.), *Communication and group decision making* (2nd ed., pp. 55–80). Thousand Oaks, CA: Sage.

Graber, S. (2000). *The everything résumé book: Great résumés for everybody from student to executive.* Holbrook, MA: Adams Media.

Grice, H. P. (1975). Logic and conversation. In P. Cole and J. L. Morgan (Eds.), *Syntax and semantics. Vol. 3. Speech acts* (pp. 41–58). New York: Academic Press.

Griffiths, M. (1998). Internet addiction: Does it really exist? In J. Gackenbach (Ed.), *Psychology and the Internet: Intrapersonal, interpersonal, and transpersonal implications* (pp. 61–76). San Diego, CA: Academic Press.

Gudykunst, W. B., & Kim, Y. Y. (1997). *Communicating with strangers: An approach to intercultural communication* (3rd ed.). Boston: Allyn & Bacon.

Gudykunst, W. B., & Matsumoto, Y. (1996). Cross-cultural variability of communication in personal relationships. In W. B. Gudykunst, S. Ting-Toomey, & T. Nishida (Eds.), *Communication in personal relationships across cultures* (pp. 19–56). Thousand Oaks, CA: Sage.

Guerrero, L. K., & Andersen, P. A. (2000). Emotion in close relationships. In C. Hendrick & S. S. Hendrick (Eds.), *Close relationships: A sourcebook* (pp. 171–184). Thousand Oaks, CA: Sage.

Guidelines for meeting participants. (1998, Fall). Unpublished manuscript developed by students in BAD 305, Understanding behavior in organizations. Northern Kentucky University.

Hall, E. T. (1959). *The silent language.* Greenwich, CT: Fawcett.

Hall, E. T. (1969). *The hidden dimension.* Garden City, NY: Doubleday.

Hall, J. A. (1998). How big are nonverbal sex differences? The case of smiling and sensitivity to nonverbal cues. In D. J. Canary & K. Dindia (Eds.), *Sex differences and similarities in communication: Critical essays and empirical investigations of sex and gender in interaction* (pp. 155–178). Mahwah, NJ: Erlbaum.

Hattie, J. (1992). *Self-concept.* Hillsdale, NJ: Erlbaum.

Hawkins, K. W. (1995). Effects of gender and communication content on leadership emergence in small, task-oriented groups. *Small Group Research, 26,* 234–249.

Helgesen, S. (1990). *The female advantage: Women's ways of leadership.* New York: Doubleday.

Hensley, C. W. (1995, September 1). Speak with style and watch the impact: Make things happen. *Vital Speeches,* 703.

Hirokawa, R. Y. (1987). Why informed groups make faulty decisions. *Small Group Behavior, 18,* 3–29.

Hirokawa, R. Y. (1988). Group communication and decision-making performance: A continued test of the functional perspective. *Human Communication Research, 14,* 487–515.

Hollman, T. D. (1972). Employment interviewers' errors in processing positive and negative information. *Journal of Psychology, 56,* 130–134.

Horner, E. R. (Ed.). (1998). *Almanac of the 50 states: Data profiles with comparative tables.* Palo Alto, CA: Information Publications.

Howard, J. A. (2000, August 1). Principles in default: Rediscovered and reapplied. *Vital Speeches,* 618–619.

Hundt, R. E. (1995, September 1). Serving kids and the community: Do we want TV to help or hurt children? *Vital Speeches,* 675.

Infante, D. A., Rancer, A. S., & Jordan, F. F. (1996). Affirming and nonaffirming style, dyad sex, and perception of argumentation and verbal aggression in an interpersonal dispute. *Human Communication Research, 22,* 315–334.

Janis, I. L. (1982). *Groupthink: Psychological studies of policy decisions and fiascoes.* Boston: Houghton Mifflin.

Janis, I. L. (1989). *Crucial decisions: Leadership in policy making and crisis management.* New York: Free Press.

Jensen, A. D., & Chilberg, J. C. (1991). *Small group communication: Theory and application.* Belmont, CA: Wadsworth.

Johnson, D., & Johnson, F. (2000). *Joining together: Group theory and group skills* (7th Ed.). Boston: Allyn & Bacon.

Jones, E. E. (1990). *Interpersonal perception.* New York: W. H. Freeman.

Jordan, J. V. (1991). The relational self: A new perspective for understanding women's development. In J. Strauss & G. R. Goethals (Eds.), *The self: Interdisciplinary approaches* (pp. 136–149). New York: Springer-Verlag.

Jurma, W. E., & Wright, B. C. (1990). Follower reactions to male and female leaders who maintain or lose reward power. *Small Group Research, 21,* 110.

Jussim, L. J., McCauley, C. R., & Lee, Y.-T. (1995). Why study stereotype accuracy and inaccuracy? In Y.-T. Lee, L. J. Jussim, & C. R. McCauley, (Eds.). *Stereotype accuracy: Toward appreciating group differences* (pp. 3–28). Washington, DC: American Psychological Association.

Kellerman, K. (1992). Communication: Inherently strategic and primarily automatic. *Communication Monographs, 59,* 288–300.

Kennedy C. W., & Camden, C. T. (1983). A new look at interruptions. *Western Journal of Speech Communication, 47,* 55.

Keyton, J. (1993). Group termination: Completing the study of group development. *Small Group Research, 24,* 84–100.

Klinger, E. (1977). *Meaning and void: Inner experience and the incentives in people's lives.* Minneapolis: University of Minnesota Press.

Knapp, M. L., & Hall, J. A. (1992). *Nonverbal communication in human interaction* (3rd ed.). New York: Holt, Rinehart & Winston.

Koehler, C. (1998, June 15). Mending the body by lending an ear: The healing power of listening. *Vital Speeches,* 543–544.

Kramer, J., & Kramarae, C. (1997). Gendered ethics on the Internet. In J. M. Makau & R. C. Arnett (Eds.), *Communication ethics in the age of diversity* (pp. 226–244). Chicago: University of Illinois Press.

LaFollette, H. (1996). *Personal relationships: Love, identity, and morality.* Cambridge, MA: Blackwell.

Lamm, R. (1998, September 15). Unexamined assumptions: Destiny, political institutions, democracy and population, *Vital Speeches,* 712–714.

Leathers, D. (1997). *Successful nonverbal communication: Principles and applications* (3rd ed.). Boston, Allyn & Bacon.

Lieberman, D. A. (1995). Ethnocognitivism, problem solving, and hemisphericity. In L. A. Samovar & R. E. Porter (Eds.), *Intercultural communication: A reader* (7th ed., pp. 178–193). Belmont, CA: Wadsworth.

Littlejohn, S. W. (1999). *Theories of human communication* (6th ed.). Belmont, CA: Wadsworth.

Luft, J. (1970). *Group processes: An introduction to group dynamics.* Mountain View, CA: Mayfield.

Lulofs, R. S., & Cahn, D. D. (2000). *Conflict: From theory to action* (2nd ed.). Boston: Allyn & Bacon.

Markham, A. N. (1998). *Life online: Researching real experience in virtual space.* Walnut Creek, CA: AltaMira.

Markus, H. R., & Kitayama, S. (1991). Cultural variation in the self-concept. In J. Strauss & G. R. Goethals (Eds.), *The self: Interdisciplinary approaches* (pp. 18–48). New York: Springer-Verlag.

Martin, J. N., & Nakayama, T. K. (1997). *Intercultural communication contexts.* Mountain View, CA: Mayfield.

Martin, M. M., Anderson, C. M., & Horvath, C. L. (1996). Feelings about verbal aggression: Justifications for sending and hurt from receiving verbally aggressive messages. *Communication Research Reports, 13*(1), 19–26.

Maslow, A. H. (1954). *Motivation and personality.* New York: Harper & Row.

McCrae, C. N., Milne, A. B., and Bodenhausen, G. V. (1994). Stereotypes as energy-saving devices: A peek inside the cognitive toolbox. *Journal of Personality and Social Psychology, 66,* 37–47.

McCroskey, J. C. (1978). Validity of the PRCA as an index of oral communication apprehension. *Communication Monographs, 45,* 192–203.

McCroskey, J. C., & Neuliep, J. W. (1997). The development in intercultural and interethnic communication apprehension scales. *Communication Research Reports, 14,* 145–157.

McCroskey, J. C., & Tenin, J. J. (1999). Goodwill: A re-examination of the construct and its measurement. *Communication Monographs, 66,* 90–103.

Menzel, K. E., & Carrell, L. J. (1994). The relationship between preparation and performance in public speaking. *Communication Education, 43,* 17–26.

Michener, H. A., & DeLamater, J. D. (1999). *Social psychology* (4th ed.). Orlando, FL: Harcourt Brace.

Miller, M. (1999). *The Lycos personal Internet guide.* Indianapolis, IN: Que Corporation.

Morse, S. (2001, January 1). The rap of change: A new generation of solutions. *Vital Speeches,* 186–189.

Mruk, C. (1999). *Self-esteem: Research, theory, and practice* (2nd ed.). New York: Springer.

Mulac, A. (1998). The gender-linked language effect: Do language differences really make a difference? In D. J. Canary & K. Dindia (Eds.), *Sex differences and similarities in communication: Critical essays and empirical investigations of sex and gender in interaction* (pp. 127–154). Mahway, NJ: Erlbaum.

Nieto, S. (2000). *Affirming diversity: The sociological context of multicultural education* (3rd ed.). New York: Longman.

Ogden, C. K., & Richards, I. A. (1923). *The meaning of meaning.* London: Kegan, Paul, Trench, Trubner.

Okrent, D. (1999, May 10). Raising kids online: What can parents do? *Time,* 38–43.

Opheim, C. (2000, November 1). Making democracy work: Your responsibility to society. *Vital Speeches,* 60–61.

Parks, M. R., & Floyd, K. (1996). Making friends in cyberspace. *Journal of Communication, 46,* 80–97.

Patterson, B. R., Bettini, L., & Nussbaum, J. F. (1993). The meaning of friendship across the life-span: Two studies. *Communication Quarterly, 41,* 145.

Patterson, M. E., Danscreau, D. F., & Newbern, D. (1992). Effects of communication aids on cooperative teaching. *Journal of Educational Psychology, 84,* 453–461.

Pearson, J. C., West, R. L., & Turner, L. H. (1995). *Gender & communication* (3rd ed.). Dubuque, IA: Brown & Benchmark.

Petri, H. L. (1996). *Motivation: Theory, research, and applications* (4th ed.). Belmont, CA: Wadsworth.

Petty, R. E., & Cacioppo, J. (1996). *Attitudes and persuasion: Classic and contemporary approaches.* Boulder, CO: Westview.

Petty, R. E., DeSteno, D., & Rucker, D. (2001). The role of affect in persuasion and attitude change. In J. Forgas (Ed.), *Handbook of affect and social cognition* (pp. 212–233). Mahwah, NJ: Erlbaum.

Petty, R. E., Wheeler, S. C., & Bizer, G. Y. (2000). Attitude functions and persuasion: An elaboration likelihood approach to matched versus mismatched messages. In G. R. Maio & J. M. Olson (Eds.), *Why we evaluate: Functions of attitudes* (pp. 133–162). Mahwah, NJ: Erlbaum.

Phillips, G. (1977). Rhetoritherapy versus the medical model: Dealing with reticence. *Communication Education, 26,* 34–43.

Phillips, G. (1991). *Communication incompetencies: A theory of training oral performance behavior.* Carbondale, IL: Southern Illinois University Press.

Preece, J. (2000). *Online communities.* New York: Wiley.

Reardon, K. K. (1987). *Interpersonal communication: Where minds meet.* Belmont, CA: Wadsworth.

Reis, H. T. (1998). Gender differences in intimacy and related behaviors: Context and process. In D. J. Canary & K. Dindia (Eds.), *Sex differences and similarities in communication: Critical essays and empirical investigations of sex and gender in interaction* (pp. 203–232). Mahwah, NJ: Erlbaum.

Renz, M. A., & Greg, J. B. (2000). *Effective small group communication in theory and practice.* Boston: Allyn & Bacon.

Richards, I. A. (1965). *The philosophy of rhetoric.* New York: Oxford University Press.

Richmond, V. P., & McCroskey, J. C. (1995). *Communication: Apprehension, avoidance, and effectiveness* (4th ed.). Scottsdale, AZ: Gorsuch Scarisbrick.

Rose, H. M., Rancer, A. S., & Crannell, K. C. (1993). The impact of basic courses in oral interpretation and public speaking on communication apprehension. *Communication Reports, 6* (Winter), 54–60.

Rosenfeld, L. B. (2000). Overview of the ways privacy, secrecy, and disclosure are balanced in today's society. In S. Petronio (Ed.), *Balancing the secrets of private disclosures* (pp. 3–18). Mahwah, NJ: Erlbaum.

Rothwell, J. D. (1998). *In mixed company* (3rd ed.). Fort Worth, TX: Harcourt Brace.

Samovar, L. A., & Porter, R. E. (2000). Understanding intercultural communication: An introduction and overview. In L. A. Samovar and R. E. Porter (Eds.), *Intercultural communication: A reader* (9th ed., pp. 5–16). Belmont, CA: Wadsworth.

Samovar, L. A., Porter, R. E., & Stefani, L. A. (1998). *Communication between cultures* (3rd ed.). Belmont, CA: Wadsworth.

Sampson, E. E. (1999). *Dealing with differences: An introduction to the social psychology of prejudice.* Fort Worth, TX: Harcourt Brace.

Samter, W., Burleson, B. R., & Murphy, L. B. (1987). Comforting conversations: The effects of strategy type evaluations of messages and message producers. *Southern Communication Journal, 52,* 263–284.

Schmidt, W. V., & Conaway, R. N. (1999). *Results-oriented interviewing: Principles, practices, and procedures.* Boston: Allyn & Bacon.

Schutz, W. (1966). *The interpersonal underworld.* Palo Alto, CA: Science & Behavior Books.

Scott, P. (1997, January–February). Mind of a champion. *Natural Health, 27,* 99.

Shaw, M. E. (1981). *Group dynamics: The psychology of small group behavior* (3rd ed.). New York: McGraw-Hill.

Sherman, R. A. (1999). *Mr. Modem's Internet guide for seniors.* San Francisco, CA: Sybex.

Shimanoff, M. (1992). Group interaction and communication rules. In R. Cathcart & L. Samovar (Eds.), *Small group communication: A reader.* Dubuque, IA: Wm. Brown.

Shimanoff, S. B. (1980). *Communication rules: Theory and research.* Beverly Hills, CA: Sage.

Snell, N. (1998). *Teach yourself the Internet in 24 hours* (2nd ed.). Indianapolis: Sams.Net.

Spitzberg, B. H. (1997). Violence in intimate relationships. In W. R. Cupach & D. J. Canary (Eds.), *Competence in interpersonal conflict* (pp. 174–201). New York: McGraw-Hill.

Spitzberg, B. H. (2000). A model of intercultural communication competence. In L. A. Samovar and R. E. Porter (Eds.), *Intercultural communication: A reader* (9th ed., pp. 375–387). Belmont, CA: Wadsworth.

Spitzberg, B. H., & Cupach, W. R. (Eds.). (1998). *The dark side of close relationships.* Hillsdale, NJ: Lawrence Erlbaum Associates.

Spitzberg, B. H., & Duran, R. L. (1995). Toward the development and validation of a measure of cognitive communication competence. *Communication Quarterly, 43,* 259–274.

Stewart, C. J., & Cash, W. B., Jr. (2000). *Interviewing: Principles and practices.* Boston: McGraw-Hill.

Stewart, L. P., Cooper, P. J., Stewart, A. D., & Friedley, S. A. (1998). *Communication and gender* (3rd ed.). Boston, MA: Allyn & Bacon.

Stiff, J. B., Dillard, J. P., Somera, L., Kim, H., & Sleight, C. (1988). Empathy, communication and prosocial behavior. *Communication Monographs, 55,* 198–213.

Sundstrom, E., DeMeuse, K. P., & Futrell, D. (1990, February). Work teams: Applications and effectiveness. *American Psychologist,* 120–133.

Svennevig, J. (1999). *Getting acquainted in conversation: A study of initial interactions.* Philadelphia: John Benjamins.

Tannen, D. (1990). *You just don't understand.* New York: Morrow.

Taylor, D. A., & Altman, I. (1987). Communication in interpersonal relationships: Social penetration theory. In M. E. Roloff & G. R. Miller (Eds.), *Interpersonal processes: New directions in communication research* (pp. 257–277). Beverly Hills, CA: Sage.

Tengler, C. D., & Jablin, F. M. (1983). Effects of question type, orientation, and sequencing in the employment screening interview. *Communication Monographs, 50,* 261.

Terkel, S. N., & Duval, R. S. (Eds.). (1999). *Encyclopedia of ethics.* New York: Facts on File.

Thibaut, J. W., & Kelley, H. H. (1986). *The social psychology of groups* (2nd ed.). New Brunswick, NJ: Transaction Books.

Trachtenberg, S. J. (1986, August 15). Five ways in which thinking is dangerous. *Vital Speeches,* 653.

Trenholm, S. (1991). *Human communication theory* (2nd ed.). Englewood Cliffs, NJ: Prentice-Hall.

Tuckman, B. (1965). Developmental sequence in small groups. *Psychological Bulletin, 63,* 384–399.

Turk, D. R., & Monahan, J. L. (1999). "Here I go again": An examination of repetitive behaviors during interpersonal conflicts. *Southern Communication Journal, 64* (Spring), 232–244.

Tversky, B. (1997). Memory for pictures, maps, environments, and graphs. In D. G. Payne & F. G. Conrad (Eds.), *Intersections in basic and applied memory research* (pp. 257–277). Mahwah, NJ: Erlbaum.

Valacich, J. S., George, J. F., Nonamaker, J. F., Jr., & Vogel, D. R. (1994). Idea generation in computer based groups: A new ending to an old story. *Small Group Reseach, 25,* 83–104.

Watzlawick, P., Beavin, J. H., & Jackson, D. D. (1967). *Pragmatics of human communication.* New York: Norton.

Weaver, J. B., III, & Kirtley, M. B. (1995). Listening styles and empathy. *Southern Communication Journal, 60,* 131–140.

Weaver, R. (1970). Language is sermonic. In R. L. Johanannesen, R. Strickland, & R. T. Eubanks (Eds.), *Language is sermonic* (pp. 201–226). Baton Rouge: Louisiana State University Press.

Weiten, W. (1998). *Psychology: Themes and variations* (4th ed.). Pacific Grove, CA: Brooks/Cole.

Weston, D. (1999). *Psychology: Mind, brain, and culture* (2nd ed.). New York: Wiley & Sons.

Wheelen, S. A., & Hochberger, J. M. (1996). Validation studies of the group development questionnaire. *Small Group Research, 27*(1), 143–170.

Whetten, D. A., & Cameron, K. S. (1998). *Developing management skills* (4th ed.). New York: HarperCollins.

Widmer, W. N., & Williams, J. M. (1991). Predicting cohesion in a coacting sport. *Small Group Research, 22,* 548–570.

Williams, R. G., & Ware, J. E., Jr. (1976). Validity of student ratings of instruction under different incentive conditions: A further study of the Dr. Fox effect. *Journal of Educational Psychology, 68,* February 1976, 48–56.

Winstead, B. A., Derlega, V. J., & Rose, S. (1997). *Gender and close relationships.* Thousand Oaks, CA: Sage.

Wolvin A., & Coakley, C. G. (1996). *Listening* (5th ed.). Dubuque, IA: Brown & Benchmark.

Wood, J. T. (1997). *Gendered lives: Communication, gender, and culture* (2nd ed.). Belmont, CA: Wadsworth.

Wood, J. T., & Dindia, K. (1998). What's the difference? A dialogue about differences and similarities between women and men. In D. J. Canary & K. Dindia (Eds.), *Sex differences and similarities in communication: Critical essays and empirical investigations of sex and gender in interaction* (pp. 19–40). Mahwah, NJ: Erbaum.

Woodward, G. C., & Denton, R. E., Jr. (2000). *Persuasion and influence in American life* (4th ed.). Prospect Heights, IL: Waveland.

The world almanac and book of facts, 2001 (p. 803). Mahwah, NJ: World Almanac Books.

Young, K. S., Wood, J. T., Phillips, G. M., & Pederson, D. J. (2000). *Group discussion: A practical guide to participation and leadership* (3rd ed.). Prospect Heights, IL: Waveland.

Zebrowitz, L. A. (1990). *Social perception.* Pacific Grove, CA: Brooks/Cole.

Zillmann, D. (1991). Empathy: Affect from bearing witness to the emotions of others. In J. Bryant & D. Zillmann (Eds.), *Responding to the screen: Reception and reaction processes* (pp. 135–167). Hillsdale, NJ: Erlbaum.

Index

Photo Credits

This page constitutes an extension of the copyright page. We have made every effort to trace the ownership of all copyrighted material and to secure permission from copyright holders. In the event of any question arising as to the use of any material, we will be pleased to make the necessary corrections in future printings. Thanks are due to the following authors, publishers, and agents for permission to use the material indicated.

Chapter 1. **4:** Geoff Brightling / FPG International **7:** Addison Geary / Stock, Boston **14:** Steve Dunwell / The Image Bank **18:** Michael Keller / The Stock Market **23:** Tony Freeman / PhotoEdit, Inc. **Chapter 2.** **28:** Sam Rappaport **33:** Myrleen Ferguson / PhotoEdit, Inc. **36:** Charles Gupton / Stone **41:** Bob Daemmrich / Stock, Boston **Chapter 3.** **50:** Janet Wooley / The Illustration Works, Inc. **56:** Frank & Ernest reprinted by permission of NEA, Inc. **63:** Suzanne Szasz / Photo Researchers, Inc. **65:** Shoe, by Jeff MacNelly, reprinted by permission: Tribune Media Services **Chapter 4.** **72:** Jose L. Palaez / The Stock Market **74:** © Sidney Harris **77:** Christy Gavitt / Nonstock **83:** Kim Robbie / The Stock Market **87:** Robert Azzi / Woodfin Camp & Assoc. **92:** Photographs of six faces from *Unmasking the Face* (Ekman & Friesen, 1975). By permission of Paul Ekman. **Chapter 5.** **96:** Hulton Getty / Stone **101:** Peter L. Chapman **102:** John Coletti / The Picture Cube **113:** Barbara Alper / Stock, Boston **116:** Ralph A. Reinhold / The Picture Cube **Chapter 6.** **124:** Bruno / The Stock Market **127:** One Big Happy by Rick Detorie. By permission of Rick Detorie and Creators Syndicate. **131:** Bob Daemmrich / Stock, Boston **142:** Brian Bailey / Stone **145:** Michael Newman / PhotoEdit, Inc. **Chapter 7.** **154:** Jeffry W. Myers **160:** Zigy Kaluzny / Stone **163:** W. Hill, Jr. / The Image Works **173:** Bruce Ayers / Stone **Chapter 8.** **184:** Johnny Johnson / Stone **187:** W. Hill, Jr. / The Image Works **194:** Douglas Kirkland / Sygma **197:** Bruce Ayers / Stone **202:** Estate of Cybil Shelton / Peter Arnold, Inc. **211:** © 1995 Baby Blues Partnership. Distributed by King Features Syndicate. Reprinted with special permission of King Features Syndicate, Inc. **Chapter 9.** **218:** Diana Ong / SuperStock **221:** Patti & Milt Putnam / The Stock Market **227:** Michael Newman / PhotoEdit, Inc. **229:** DILBERT reprinted by permission of United Features Syndicate, Inc. **Chapter 10.** **236:** Jim Krantz / Stone **239:** DILBERT reprinted by permission of United Features Syndicate, Inc. **241:** Nita Winter Photography **254:** John Coletti / The Picture Cube **Chapter 11.** **262:** Daryl Torckler / Stone **266:** Nita Winter Photography **269:** Rob Lewine / The Stock Market **278:** Michael Newman / PhotoEdit, Inc. **Chapter 12.** **288:** Michael R. Schneps / The Image Bank **291:** Rob Lewine / The Stock Market **293:** Jeff Greenberg / PhotoEdit, Inc. **297:** A. Ramey / Stock, Boston, PictureQuest **Chapter 13.** **306:** Bruce Ayers / Stone **309:** F. Pedrick / The Image Works **315:** E. Crews / The Image Works **323:** C. Orrico / SuperStock, Inc. **Chapter 14.** **334:** Christie's Images / SuperStock, Inc. **344:** Peter L. Chapman **346:** Michael Newman / PhotoEdit, Inc. **351:** Charles Gupton / The Stock Market **354:** Cathy copyright 1983 Cathy Guisewite. Reprinted with permission of Universal Press Syndicate. All rights reserved. **Chapter 15.** **360:** © 1998 Mark MacLaren **362:** Bob Daemmrich / Stock, Boston **371:** Reuters Newsmedia Inc. / CORBIS **376:** David Shopper / Stock, Boston **387:** Jim Pickerell / Stock Connection / PictureQuest **Chapter 16.** **392:** © Lee Kline **396:** © Sidney Harris **405:** Dave Shaefer / Jeroboam **407:** Pedrick / The Image Works **415:** Bob Daemmrich / Stock, Boston **Chapter 17.** **426:** Ron Lowery / Stone **429:** John Elk III / Stock, Boston **436:** Romilly Lockyer / The Image Bank **442:** J.P. Laffont / Sygma **Chapter 18.** **454:** Fred Sieb Photography **458:** AP / Wide World Photos **459:** Christopher Morris / Black Star Publishing / PictureQuest **465:** Aaron Haupt / Stock, Boston / PictureQuest **473:** Herman J. Kokojan / Black Star / PictureQuest